AF324276

MATHEMATICAL ASPECTS OF NATURAL AND FORMAL LANGUAGES

World Scientific Series in Computer Science – Vol. 43

MATHEMATICAL ASPECTS OF NATURAL AND FORMAL LANGUAGES

Edited by

Gheorghe Păun

Institute of Mathematics
Romanian Academy of Sciences

Published by

World Scientific Publishing Co. Pte. Ltd.

P O Box 128, Farrer Road, Singapore 9128

USA office: Suite 1B, 1060 Main Street, River Edge, NJ 07661

UK office: 73 Lynton Mead, Totteridge, London N20 8DH

Library of Congress Cataloging-in-Publication Data

Mathematical aspects of natural and formal languages / edited by
  Gheorghe Păun.
        p.   cm. -- (Series in computer science ; v. 43)
    ISBN 9810219148
    1. Programming languages (Electronic computers)--Mathematics.
  I. Păun, Gheorghe.   II. Series.
  QA76.7.M376   1994
  511.3--dc20   94–30230
                                                            CIP

Copyright © 1994 by World Scientific Publishing Co. Pte. Ltd.

*All rights reserved. This book, or parts thereof, may not be reproduced in any form
or by any means, electronic or mechanical, including photocopying, recording or any
information storage and retrieval system now known or to be invented, without
written permission from the Publisher.*

For photocopying of material in this volume, please pay a copying fee through
the Copyright Clearance Center, Inc., 27 Congress Street, Salem, MA 01970, USA.

Printed in Singapore.

PREFACE

The present volume contains papers written in honour of Professor Solomon Marcus, on the occasion of his 70th birthday (March 1, 1995), by students, colleagues, collaborators and friends of his throughout the world. Out of the wide mathematical (and non-mathematical) concerns of S. Marcus, this book deals with mathematical linguistics only, without referring, for instance, to mathematical analysis, his first domain of research, to mathematical models in the study of poetry, theatrical works, fairy tales, social and human development, etc.

Although arranged in alphabetic order by first author name, the articles could be clustered in chapters directly or indirectly related to topics where S. Marcus has challenging contributions: contextual grammars (introduced in 1969 with descriptive linguistics motivation, but turning out to be deeply connected with basic issues in formal language theory and combinatorics on words), grammatical inference, grammar systems, two dimensional languages, algebraic approaches to languages, semiotics, natural language modelling, and so on and so forth.

It is worth emphasizing that the bibliography of the papers which follow includes both references to "old titles" (such as *Finite Automata and Grammars*, The Publishing House of the Romanian Academy of Sciences, Bucharest, 1964, one of S. Marcus's first books and one of the earliest monographs in formal language theory — unfortunately still only in Romanian) and to very recent titles (such as the papers about rough sets, to appear in the *Bulletin of the Polish Academy of Sciences*). This is a sign of continuity and of perenniality and a warranty that for many years to come we will be still excited by S. Marcus' ideas.

Thank you, Professor Marcus, and Happy Birthday to You !

Gheorghe PĂUN
May 1994

CONTENTS

Substitutions on Words and Languages; Applications to Cryptography

Adrian ATANASIU

Faculty of Mathematics, University of Bucharest

Str. Academiei 14, 70109 Bucureşti, Romania

Abstract. This paper investigates the operation of substituting subwords of a given word with other strings, an operation useful in cryptography. Some results and algorithms are presented on this topic. Then, this operation is extended to languages and a property of closure is verified. Some simple inequalities for complexity measures naturally associated with this encrypting method are given, too.

1. Preliminaries

To substitute some subwords of a word with other strings in the aim of hiding the original message is one of the well – known techniques of cryptography (see examples in [7]). In [1] and [2] the idea of substitution as a generalization of the insertion and deletion operations ([4]) was introduced. A substitution can be viewed as a production of the form $\alpha \to \beta$ where the words α, β are given or are elements of some previously defined languages.

In the sequel, the basic notions and notations necessary in the following sections will be presented. For formal languages details we refer to [5], [6]. An alphabet is a finite nonempty set; if $V = \{a_1, a_2, \ldots, a_n\}$ is an alphabet, then any sequence $w = a_{i_1} a_{i_2} \ldots a_{i_k}, 1 \leq i_j \leq n, 1 \leq j \leq k$, is called word (string) over V. Sometimes we shall write $w = w(1)w(2) \ldots w(k)$, with $w(j) = a_{i_j}, 1 \leq j \leq k$. The length of the word w is denoted by $|w|$. The empty word is denoted by ε, $|\varepsilon| = 0$. The set of all words over V is denoted by V^* and $V^+ = V^* - \{\varepsilon\}$. The four families in Chomsky hierarchy are denoted by $\mathcal{L}_i, i = 0, 1, 2, 3$.

For a finite set A denote by $card(A)$ the cardinality of A. For two words $x, y \in V^*$ we denote by $N_x(y)$ the number of occurences of x in y, that is

$$N_x(y) = card\{\alpha \mid y = \alpha x \beta, \alpha, \beta \in V^*\}.$$

Note that we count all different occurrences of x in y, including the overlapping ones. In [2] an algorithm to find this number is given. For $\alpha \in V^+$ we denote by $first(\alpha)$ the first symbol of α.

For $w, x, y \in V^*$, the *sequential substitution* of x with y is defined by

$$w(x \to y) = \{uyv \mid w = uxv\},$$

while the *parallel substitution* is defined by:

$$w(x \Rightarrow y) = \{z \mid z = z_0 y z_1 y \dots y z_n, n > 0 \text{ such that}$$
$$w = z_0 x z_1 x \dots x z_n, N_x(z_i) = 0, 0 \le i \le n\}.$$

For a language $L \subseteq V^+$ and $w, x, y \in V^*$, we denote by

$$L(x \to y) = \bigcup_{w \in L} w(x \to y), \qquad L(x \Rightarrow y) = \bigcup_{w \in L} w(x \Rightarrow y),$$

$$w(L \to y) = \bigcup_{x \in L} w(x \to y), \qquad w(L \Rightarrow y) = \bigcup_{x \in L} w(x \Rightarrow y),$$

$$w(x \to L) = \bigcup_{y \in L} w(x \to y), \qquad w(x \Rightarrow L) = \bigcup_{y \in L} w(x \Rightarrow y),$$

the natural extensions of the sequential and parallel substitution when a term of the operation is a language.

The sequential substitution has been investigated in [1], the parallel one in [2]. The sequential substitution corresponds to the usual rewriting in rewriting systems whereas the parallel one coresponds to the Indian type of parallel rewriting ([5]); note howewer that the language L considered above can be infinite.

In this paper we consider a generalization of the previous operations (for the case of strings only), namely with more substitution rules $x \to y$ used in parallel. Such a case is more closely related to the practical way of encrypting messages by various cryptographic systems.

2. Encryption rules and systems

Let V be a finite alphabet and $P \subseteq V^* \times V^*$ be a finite nonempty set of rewriting rules

$$P = \{x_i \to y_i \mid 1 \le i \le k\}.$$

For $w \in V^*$, the encryption of w by means of P is the set

$$w(P) = \{u_1 y_{i_1} u_2 y_{i_2} \dots u_r y_{i_r} u_{r+1} \mid w = u_1 x_{i_1} \dots u_r x_{i_r} u_{r+1},$$
$$1 \le i_j \le k, 1 \le j \le r, \text{and } N_{x_i}(u_j) = 0, 1 \le i \le k, 1 \le j \le r+1\}.$$

For $k = 1$ we obtain the parallel substitution on words.

Notations:

  – P: encryption formal key (**efk**);

- $x \to y$: encryption rule;
- (w, P): encryption formal system (**efs**) ;
- w: the clear-text; the elements of $w(P)$ are called crypto-texts.

Examples: (i) Any monoalphabetically encryption system (Caesar, afin, etc.) is an **efk**;

(ii) The substitutions in the sense used in Formal Language Theory are **efk** with $|x_i| = 1$ for all i.

3. Active and inactive encryption rules

Definition 1. Let $w \in V^*$ and P be an **efk**. A encryption rule $x \to y \in P$ is called *inactive* on w if $N_x(w) = 0$. Otherwise, the rule is called *active* on w.

Obviously, for practical purposes it is preferable to work with an **efk** without inactive rules.

For an **efs** (w, P), consider the set

$$\mathcal{E}_w(P) = \{R \mid R \subseteq P, w(P) = w(R)\} \tag{1}$$

Because $\mathcal{E}_w(P)$ is a finite and nonempty set $(P \in \mathcal{E}_w(P))$, it contains an element S with the property

$$card(S) = \min\{card(R) \mid R \in \mathcal{E}_w(P)\}.$$

It is clear that S has only active rules for w.

Remarks.

(i) The condition $R \subseteq P$ imposed in (1) is natural, but restrictive. If we ignore it, it is possible to find an **efk** P' with $card(P') < card(S)$ (S as above) and $w(P') = w(P)$. For example, let us consider the **efs** (w, P) where $w = abab, P = \{a \to xx, b \to y, aa \to \varepsilon, bb \to z\}$. It has as minimal active set of rules $S = \{a \to xx, b \to y\}$. However, $P' = \{ab \to xxy\}$ has only one rule and $w(P') = w(S)$.

(ii) Moreover, S is not necessarily unique. For example, if we take $w = abcd$, $P = \{a \to x, b \to y, c \to z, d \to t, ab \to xy, cd \to zt, abc \to xyz\}$, then there are two minimal sets of active rules in $\mathcal{E}_w(P)$, namely $S_1 = \{ab \to xy, cd \to zt\}$ and $S_2 = \{abc \to xyz, d \to t\}$.

An algorithm for constructing in linear time the set $Q = \{x \to y \mid x \to y \in P, N_x(w) > 0\}$, for a given **efk** (w, P), can be easily constructed. Algorithms of this type can be based, for example, on the algorithms in [3], [8]; the case $k = 1$ is treated also in [2].

In the following we consider that for an **efc** (w, P) all rules are active.

The encryption of w is unique if $card(w(P)) = 1$. In most classical cryptographic systems this is the case.

Proposition 1. *An* **efs** *(w, P) gives a unique encryption iff for no $i, j \in \{1, 2, \ldots, k\}$, the next situations are possible:*

 (i) $x_i = \alpha x_j \beta, \alpha\beta \neq \varepsilon$, or

 (ii) $w = u\alpha\beta\gamma v, x_i = \alpha\beta, x_j = \beta\gamma$.

When (i) or (ii) is true, more possibilities of substitution arise and the encryption of w is not unique.

If case (ii) with $i = j$ holds, then the problem of encryption with bordered words, discussed in [2], arises.

For an **efs** (w, P) with unique encryption, the substitution is reduced to a parallel one ([2]), as follows.

Let $\$_1, \$_2, \ldots, \$_k \notin V$ be k distinct new symbols (remember that $k = card(P)$) and denote $V' = V \cup \{\$_i \mid 1 \leq i \leq k\}$. If for $w \in V^*$, (w, P) is with unique encryption, then we obviously have

$$w(P) = w(x_1 \Rightarrow \$_1)(x_2 \Rightarrow \$_2)\ldots(x_k \Rightarrow \$_k)(\$_1 \Rightarrow y_1)(\$_2 \Rightarrow y_2)\ldots(\$_k \Rightarrow y_k).$$

Remarks.

(i) Because there is no overlapping, for every parallel substitution the obtained language contains only one word;

(ii) The order of the first k substitutions is not relevant and the assertion is true for the last k substitutions, too.

(iii) The need of k new symbols becomes more clear from the next example: Consider the **efs** (w, P) where $w = ay, P = \{a \rightarrow xyz, y \rightarrow a\}$. Then,

$$ay(a \Rightarrow xyz)(y \Rightarrow a) = xyzy(y \Rightarrow a) = \{xaza\};$$
$$ay(y \Rightarrow a)(a \Rightarrow xyz) = aa(a \Rightarrow xyz) = \{xyzxyz\};$$
$$ay(a \Rightarrow \$_1)(y \Rightarrow \$_2)(\$_1 \Rightarrow xyz)(\$_2 \Rightarrow a) =$$
$$= \$_1\$_2(\$_1 \Rightarrow xyz)(\$_2 \Rightarrow a) = \{xyza\};$$
$$ay(P) = \{xyza\}.$$

A counterpart of Proposition 1 can now be formulated as follows:

Proposition 2. *Let (w, P) be an* **efs***; it has the unique encryption property iff for any two distinct rules $x_i \rightarrow y_i, x_j \rightarrow y_j \in P$ the next assertions holds:*

 i) $card(w(x_i \Rightarrow \$)) = 1$, and

 ii) $N_{x_j}(w(x_i \Rightarrow \$)) = N_{x_j}(w)$, where $\$ \notin V$ is a new symbol.

Therefore, in the case of **efs** with unique encryption, the problem is reduced to an iterative application of parallel substitution with unbordered words. Moreover, from [2] it follows that the parallel substitutions can be applied as a sequence of sequential substitutions.

Another natural problem is that of correct decryption of the messages.

If $P = \{x_i \to y_i \mid 1 \leq i \leq k\}$ is an **efk**, we denote

$$P^{-1} = \{y_i \to x_i \mid 1 \leq i \leq k\}$$

and call this set *decryption formal key* (**dfc**).

For $w \in V^*$, the essential problem is the validity of the relation:

$$w \in \bigcup_{z \in w(P)} z(P^{-1}) \tag{2}$$

This is not a trivial question, because it is possible that (2) be not true; for example, if $w = ab, P = \{a \to b\}, P^{-1} = \{b \to a\}$, we obtain $w(P) = \{bb\}$, hence $z = bb$ and $ab \notin z(P^{-1}) = \{aa\}$.

The problem of correct decryption of a cryptotext can be solved as follows.

Theorem 1. *Consider an efs $(w, P), P = \{x_i \to y_i \mid 1 \leq i \leq k\}$ and denote $P_1 = \{x_i \to \$_i \mid 1 \leq i \leq k\}$, where $\$_1, \$_2, \ldots, \$_k$ are new symbols. The relation (2) is true iff there is $z' \in w(P_1)$, such that $z'(P^{-1}) = \emptyset$.*

Proof. ($\Longleftarrow$)   Let us suppose that a string $z' = u_1 \$_{i_1} u_2 \ldots u_n \$_{i_n} u_{n+1}$ as in the statement exists. Then $w = u_1 x_{i_1} u_2 \ldots u_n x_{i_n} u_{n+1}$ and $z' \in w(P_1)$ (P contains at least one active rule for w). Because $z'(P^{-1}) = \emptyset$, it follows that for all i we have $N_{y_i}(z') = 0$, that is (because $\$_i \notin V$) $N_{y_i}(u_j) = 0$ for all j. Consider the string $z = u_1 y_{i_1} u_2 \ldots u_n y_{i_n} u_{n+1}$. It follows that $w \in z(P^{-1})$ and, because $z \in w(P)$, relation (2) is verified.

($\Longrightarrow$)   Similarly. $\square$

4. Decomposable efs

Definition 2. The **efs** (w, P) is *decomposable* iff for all $P_1, P_2 \subseteq P$, such that $P_1 \neq P_2$, we have $w(P_1) \cap w(P_2) = \emptyset$.

There are non-decomposable **efk**. For example, if $P = \{b \to a, ab \to a\}$, $w = aab$, then we have only two nonempty subsetes of P, $P_1 = \{b \to a\}, P_2 = \{ab \to aa\}$, hence $w(P_1) = w(P_2) = w(P) = \{aaa\}$, hence (w, P) is not decomposable.

Remark. Because $P \subseteq P$, for a decomposable **efs** (w, P) it follows that for all $P_1 \subset P$, we have $w(P_1) \cap w(P) = \emptyset$.

Let $\$ \notin V$ be a new symbol and denote $V' = V \cup \{\$\}$.

As the set P is finite, the problem whether or not (w, P) is decomposable is obviously decidable. A simple algorithm for deciding this can be based on the following result.

Theorem 2. *The efs (w, P) is decomposable iff for all distinct rules $x \to y, x' \to y' \in P$ and for all $z \in w(x \Rightarrow \$)$ we have $N_{x'}(z) \neq 0$.*

Proof. ($\Longrightarrow$) Let us suppose that there are $x \to y, x' \to y' \in P$ and $z \in w(x \Rightarrow \$)$ such that $N_{x'}(z) = 0$. We will take $P_1 = \{x \to y\}$, $P_2 = \{x \to y, x' \to y'\}$ and we obtain $w(P_1) \subseteq w(P_2)$, hence $w(P_1) \cap w(P_2) \neq \emptyset$.
($\Longleftarrow$) Obvious. $\qquad\square$

5. Encryption on languages

Let $P = \{x_i \to y_i \mid 1 \leq i \leq k\}$ be an **efk**. We define the operation $C_P : V^* \longrightarrow 2^{V^*}$ by

$$C_P(w) = w(P),$$

and we extend this operation to languages in the natural way.

From now on we consider that a language $L \subseteq V^*$ is given. This language is called *the language of clear-texts* and $C_P(L)$ is *the language of crypto-texts*.

Remark. It is possible to exist words $w \in L$ for which P has no active rule. In this case, because $w(P) = \emptyset$, these words have no crypto-texts. For example, if $L = \{\alpha \mid \alpha \in \{a, b\}^*, N_a(\alpha) = N_b(\alpha)\}$ and $P = \{aa \to b\}$,, then we have $(ab)^i (ba)^j (P) = \emptyset$, for all $i, j \geq 0$.

Consequently, for a given language L there exists the possibility to add or to erase words which have no associated crypto-text. Because this looks unpleasant, in the following we shall consider only the case when for all $w \in L, w(P) \neq \emptyset$ (for every clear-text w, P contains at least one active rule).

This is not restrictive, because we always can add to P a "dummy" rule $\varepsilon \to \varepsilon$. If $P' = P \cup \{\varepsilon \to \varepsilon\}$, then for all $w \in L, w(P) = \emptyset$ implyes $w(P') = w$.

The converse implication is not always true. As an example, we can take $w = abab$, $P = \{a \to \varepsilon, b \to ab\}$. Then $P' = P \cup \{\varepsilon \to \varepsilon\}$ and $abab(P') = abab(P) = \{abab\}$.

A rule $x \to y \in P$ will be called *non-trivial* if $xy \neq \varepsilon$. An **efk** P is called *augmented* if $\varepsilon \to \varepsilon \in P$.

Theorem 3. *Let P be an **efk**. Then the families $\mathcal{L}_i, i = 0, 2, 3$, are closed under the operation C_P, but $\mathcal{L}_1$ is not closed. ($\mathcal{L}_1$ is closed under non-erasing **efk**, that is without rules of the form $x \to \varepsilon$, $x \neq \varepsilon$.)*

Proof. We shall prove the first assertion by constructing a transducer which performs the encryption operation.

Let us suppose that $P = \{x_i \to y_i \mid 1 \leq i \leq k\}$, with $|x_i| = n_i$, $1 \leq i \leq k$. We construct the transducer $M = (Q, V, \delta, q_0, F)$ where the application δ is defined as follows, for all $i, 1 \leq i \leq k$:

$$\begin{aligned}
&1) \quad \delta(q_0, a) = \{(q_0, a)\} \text{ for } a = first(x_i),\\
&2) \quad (q_{i,1}, \varepsilon) \in \delta(q_0, x_i(1)),\\
&3) \quad (q_{i,p+1}, \varepsilon) \in \delta(q_{i,p}, x_i(p+1)), \; p < n_i,
\end{aligned}$$

4) $\qquad (q_0, y_i) \in \delta(q_{i,n_i}, \varepsilon),$

5) $\qquad (q_0, x_i(1)\ldots x_i(p)) \in \delta(q_{i,p}, b),$ if $b \neq x_i(p+1),\ p < n_i,$

$\qquad\qquad$ and there is j such that $b = first(x_j),$

6) $\qquad (q_0, x_i(1)\ldots x_i(p)b) \in \delta(q_{i,p}, b),$ if $b \neq x_i(p+1),\ p < n_i,$

$\qquad\qquad$ and there is j such that $b \neq first(x_j),$

7) $\qquad (q_{j,1}, x_i(1)\ldots x_i(p)) \in \delta(q_{i,p}, x_i(p+1)),\ p < n_i,$

$\qquad\qquad$ and there is j such that $x_i(p+1) = x_j(1),$

8) $\qquad$ If $x_1 = \varepsilon, y_i \neq \varepsilon,$ then $(q_0, y_i) \in \delta(q_0, \varepsilon).$

Moreover, $Q = \{q_0\} \cup \{q_{i,p} \mid 1 \leq i \leq k, 1 \leq p \leq n_i\}$ and $F = \{q_0\}.$

From this construction, the equality $M(L) = \{w(P) \mid w \in L\}$ is easy to be proved. Therefore $M(L) = C_P(L).$

The families $\mathcal{L}_i, i = 0, 2, 3,$ are closed under arbitrary transducers, hence they are closed under the operation $C_P.$

A morphism $h : V^* \longrightarrow V^*$ can be simulated by the **efk** $P_h = \{a \to h(a) \mid a \in V\}.$ As $\mathcal{L}_1$ is not closed under erasing morphisms, the non-closure under C_P for arbitrary **efk** follows. On the other hand, by an easy modification of the previous construction, starting from a non-erasing **efk** P we can obtain a transducer M' which is ε-free; $\mathcal{L}_1$ is closed under such transducers, and this completes the proof. $\qquad\qquad\square$

Let $G = (N, T, S, P)$ be a Chomsky grammar; denote $V = N \cup T$ and consider P as **efk**. One can construct the languages $L_i, i \geq 0,$ as follows:

$$L_0 = \{S\}, \quad L_i = L_{i-1}(P),\ i > 0.$$

Then, the next equality is obvious:

$$L(G) = T^* \cap \bigcup_{i>0} L_i.$$

In the case of context-free grammars, a derivation based on encryption rules is a parallel one, at every step one level of a derivation tree being constructed.

For example, if $P = \{S \to aSbS, S \to \varepsilon\},$ then $w = abab$ can be obtained in only 3 steps:

$$aSbS \in L_1 = S(P),$$
$$abaSbS \in aSbS(P) \subseteq L_2 = L_1(P),$$
$$abab \in abaSbS(P) \subseteq L_3 = L_2(P).$$

6. Algorithms of encryption

The problem we try to solve in this section is that of splitting w into non-empty blocks $w_1, w_2, \ldots, w_m, m \geq 1$, with the property $w(P) = w_1(P)w_2(P) \ldots w_m(P)$, where P is an augmented set of active rules. We say that $(w_1, \ldots, w_m)$ is a *decomposition in blocks* of w. The case when $k = 1$ is studied in [2].

A necessary and sufficient condition for the existence of a decomposition in blocks of a nonempty word w is:

Proposition 3. *Let $w \in V^+$ and $w = w_1 w_2, w_i \neq \varepsilon, i = 1, 2$. Then $w(P) = w_1(P)w_2(P)$ iff for all $x \to y \in P, x \neq \varepsilon$, we have $N_x(w_1) + N_x(w_2) = N_x(w)$.*

In this case one can treat the operation of encryption in a sequential manner, block by block. Thus, it suffices to consider in encryption problems only the words w for which Proposition 3 is not true (that is with w reduced to one block only).

A decomposition in blocks $(w_1, w_2, \ldots, w_m)$ of w is *complete* iff for every $1 \leq i \leq m$, Proposition 3 is not true for w_i.

For every block w', component of w, we denote by $P_{w'} \subseteq P$ the set of active rules for w'.

Because $\varepsilon \to \varepsilon \in P_{w'}$ for all w', the next property holds:

Proposition 4. *Let $(w_1, w_2, \ldots, w_m)$ be a complete decomposition in blocks of w and $w' = w_i$ an arbitrary block of w. Then only one of the next two cases can arise:*

1. if $first(w') \cap first(x_i) = \emptyset$ for all $i, 1 \leq i \leq k$, and $x_i \neq \varepsilon$, then $|w'| = 1$ and $P_{w'} = \{\varepsilon \to \varepsilon\}$ (w' remains unchanged after encryption).

2. $|w'| \geq 1$ and $P_{w'} \neq \{\varepsilon \to \varepsilon\}$, otherwise.

Moreover, the case (2) appears for at least one block w_j.

Remark. The fact the case (2) is true at least once ensures the existence of an effective encryption for w.

In order to split w in a complete decomposition we can use the following algoritm **Decomp.**

Algoritm Decomp:

Input. $(w, P), w \in V^+, P = \{x_i \to y_i \mid 1 \leq i \leq k\}$ augmented and with all rules active,

$\quad\quad subst(k, n), n = |w|$, a predicate such that $subst(i, j) = 1$ iff x_i is a subword of w starting from the j-th position;

$\quad\quad vec(n)$;

Initialisation: $vec(i) = 0, 1 \leq i \leq n, DB := \emptyset$;

Output. The blocks of a complete decomposition of w;

1. for $p := 1$ to k do

$\quad\quad$ 1.1. for $j := 1$ to $n - |x_p|$ do

$\qquad$ 1.1.1. if $subst(p, j) = 1$ then begin
$\qquad\qquad$ $t := 1$
$\qquad\qquad$ while $t < |x_p|$ do
$\qquad\qquad\qquad$ $vec(j + t) := 1; t := t + 1;$
$\qquad\qquad$ repeat
$\qquad\qquad$ end
$\qquad$ 1.1.2. repeat
$\quad$ 1.2. repeat
2. $j := 1$
3. while $j \leq n$ do
$\quad$ 3.1. $p := 1$
$\quad$ 3.2. while $j + p \leq n$ and $vec(j + p) = 1$ do
$\qquad$ $p := p + 1$
$\quad$ repeat
$\quad$ 3.3. $DB := DB \cup \{w(j) \ldots w(j + p - 1)\}$
$\quad$ 3.4. $j := j + p$
$\quad$ 3.5. repeat
4. Stop

In this algorithm, after performing step (1), any maximal sequence of the form 01^* in table vec indicates a block in w on the corresponding entries; $vec(i) = 0$ means that a block begins on the i-th position. With step (3), the blocks are listed one by one. Every such a block is an elementary one (it cannot by splitten in other blocks), hence we have a complete decomposition.

The complexity of the algorithm **Decomp** is $O(n)$.

Theorem 4. *If (w, P_w) is an* **efs**, *$w \neq \varepsilon$, then there exists an unique complete decomposition in blocks of w.*

Proof. Follows from the algorithm **Decomp**. $\qquad\qquad\qquad\square$

In the following we consider only the case when w is a block (Proposition 3 is not true for w), and we look for the set $w(P_w)$ of all crypto-texts. The algorithm **Crypt** given below constructs this set:

Algorithm Crypt:
Input. $(w, P), P = \{x_i \to y_i \mid 1 \leq i \leq k\}$, all rules are active, $\varepsilon \to \varepsilon \notin P$,
$\qquad$ $poz(n), n = |w|$, a table of indexes,
$\qquad$ $crt(n)$, a table of flags,
$\qquad$ $reg(n, k)$, where every line i contains the indexes of rules which can be used starting from the i-th position of w.
Output. $w(P)$, the set of crypto-texts.
Initialisation: $poz(i) = 0, crt(i) = 1, 1 \leq i \leq n, w(P) = \emptyset$.
1. if $k = 0$ then goto 5
2. $i := 1; s := 1$

3. call $cr(i, s, poz, crt)$
4. for $i := n$ to 1 do
    4.1. if $poz(i) = 1$ then begin
        $s := s - |y_t|$, for $t = reg(i, crt(i) - 1)$
        if $reg(i, crt(i)) \neq 0$ then call $cr(i, s, poz, crt)$
            else $poz(i) := 0; crt(i) := 1$
    end
    else $s := s - 1$
    4.2. repeat
5. Stop

$cr(i, s, poz, crt)$
1. test:=false
2. while $i \leq n$ do
    2.1. if $reg(i, crt(i)) \neq 0$ then begin
    2.2.1. $p := reg(i, crt(i))$
    2.2.2. for $j := 1$ to $|y_p|$ do
        $z(s) := y_p(j); s := s + 1$
    2.2.3. $crt(i) := crt(i) + 1; poz(i) := 1;$
    2.2.4. test:=true; $i := i + |x_p|$
        end
    else
    2.2.5. $z(s) := w(i); i := i + 1; s := s + 1;$
    2.2. repeat
3. if test= true then $w(P) := w(P) \cup \{z\}$
4. Return

The algorithm **Crypt** is of backtracking type and its complexity is $O(n^2)$; we do not know a more performant algorithm for generating all crypto-texts, although probably such algorithms exist.

7. Some inequalities for a complexity measure

The next theorem gives an estimation of the complexity of the encryption method presented above.

Theorem 5. *Let (w, P_w) be an **efs**, $w \in V^+, P = \{x_i \rightarrow y_i \mid 1 \leq i \leq k\}$. If for every i we have $N_{x_i}(w) \neq 0$, then*

$$2 \leq \frac{\sum_{1 \leq i \leq k}(N_{x_i}(w) + |x_i|)}{k} \leq 1 + |w|,$$

$$\sum_{1 \leq i \leq k} N_{x_i}(w)|x_i| \leq \frac{(1 + |w|)^2 k}{4}.$$

Proof. The condition $N_{x_i}(w) \neq 0, 1 \leq i \leq k$, means that all rules are active.

Let us consider the case $k = 1$.

If $N_{x_1}(w) = 1$, then the relation $|x_1| \leq |w_1|$ is obvious. For $N_{x_1}(w) = 2$, the string x_1 must appear twice in w and these instances have to begin in different positions; therefore one obtains the relation $2|x_1| \leq 2(|w| - 1)$.

In general, we have the inequality $N_{x_1}(w)|x_1| \leq N_{x_1}(w)(|w| - N_{x_1}(w) + 1)$, hence $|x_1| \leq |w| - N_{x_1}(w) + 1$.

Let us consider this relation for an arbitrary $i, 1 \leq i \leq k$, and let sum up all these inequalities. We obtain

$$\sum_{1 \leq i \leq k} |x_i| \leq k(1 + |w|) - \sum_{1 \leq i \leq k} N_{x_i}(w),$$

hence the second inequality of the first relation in the theorem.

For the first part remark that if $|x_i| = 0$, then $N_{x_i}(w) = |w| + 1 \geq 2$, but if $|x_i| \neq 0$, then $N_{x_i}(w) \geq 1$.

In both cases, $N_{x_i}(w) + |x_i| \geq 2$ and by summation on i and dividing by k we obtain the first inequality of the first relation.

For the second relation we have

$$N_{x_i}(w)|x_i| \leq \frac{(N_{x_i}(w) + |x_i|)^2}{4} \leq \frac{(1 + |w|)^2}{4},$$

a relation which will be summed up on i. $\square$

References

1. A. Atanasiu, V. Mitrana, Substitution on words and languages, *Developments in Language Theory* (G. Rozenberg, A. Salomaa, eds.), World Sci. Publ., Singapore, 1994, 51 – 59.

2. A. Atanasiu, V. Mitrana, Parallel substitution on words and languages, *Proc of ROSYCS Symp.*, Iaşi, 1993.

3. A. Blumer, J. Blumer, A. Ehrenfeucht, D. Hausler, R. McConnell, Linear size finite automata for the set of all subwords of a word: An outline of results, *Bulletin of the EATCS*, 21 (1983), 12 – 20.

4. L. Kari, *On Insertion and Deletion in Formal Languages*, PhD. Thesis, Univ. of Turku, 1991.

5. Gh. Păun, *Recent Problems and Results in Formal Language Theory*, Editura Ştiinţifică şi Enciclopedică, Bucureşti, 1984 (in Romanian).

6. A. Salomaa, *Formal Languages*, Academic Press, New York, London, 1973.

7. A. Salomaa, *Public-key Cryptography*, Springer-Verlag, Heidelberg, 1990.

8. J.-C. Spehner, La reconnaisance des facteurs d'un mot dans un texte, *Theoretical Computer Science*, 48 (1986), 35 – 52.

Pocket Mathematics[1]

Cristian CALUDE
Computer Science Department, University of Auckland
Private Bag 92109, Auckland, New Zealand

Hermann MAURER
IICM (Institute f. Information Processing and Computer Supported Media)
Graz University of Technology, A-8010 Graz, Austria
and
Computer Science Department, University of Auckland
Private Bag 92109, Auckland, New Zealand

Abstract. Mathematics is in a dramatic and massive process of changing, mainly due to the advent of computers and computer science. Our aim is to present a *pocket* image of this phenomenon; a "case study" will give us the opportunity to describe some of these new ideas, problems, and techniques. Particularly, we will be concerned with foreseeable mutations in the interaction between deductive and experimental trends.

1. Introduction

The experimental trend and the deductive trend are interacting in the history of Mathematics. Their importance and influence vary from historical periods, countries, and even authors. For instance, Euclid, Hilbert, and Bourbaki can be safely considered champions of the deductive method, while Fermat or Euler are more representative for the experimental way of thinking. It is worth noticing that the deductive method has changed fairly little, say from Euclid's time, while the experimental component has evolved significantly, both in meaning and philosophy: it has got a completely new face in view of the development of computers.

This paper is aimed to give a *pocket* image of some new ideas, problems, and techniques in mathematics, with emphasis on mutations in the interaction between the deductive and experimental trends. Our "case study" pertains propositional tautologies, a completeley axiomatizable theory. This "toy universe" is rich enough to permit a non-trivial discussion of problems concerning proofs (nature, organization, utility), theorems (structure, decidability, complexity), theoretical credibility and feasibility.

---

[1]The work of the first author has been supported by Auckland University Research Grant A18/XXXXX/62090/3414012.

2. From empirical observations to formal systems

The fundamental faith in mathematics comes from the fact that virtually everything is **rigorously proved**. But, what do we mean by a "proof"? K. Devlin, in the introduction to the month's column *Computers and Mathematics* wrote [14]

> ...[we] mathematicians ... are somewhat schizophrenic when it comes to answering this question. ... we generally feel confident in our ability to tell a sound argument from an invalid one. Moreover, we tend to feel that it really is not an issue of judgement, and that for all their surface brevity, the proofs we construct and publish are, in an absolute sense, genuine *proofs*.

A good way to explain is *to do*. Our choice refers to the simplest way to analyse the mathematical thinking, i.e. by means of the model initiated more than a hundred of years ago by George Boole, currently referred as the *propositional calculus*. We are interested only in the "truth values" of propositions, and again our working hypothesis refers to the simplest case: propositions are only true or false, no other possibility is considered.[2]

We start with a (denumerable) set of *atomic propositions*. Denote by V this set. We add to V a new element, f, referring to it as the *universal false proposition*.

Using the usual propositional operations (disjunction, conjunction, negation, implication, etc.) we can form new propositions starting with the atomic ones. For the simplicity of the presentation we shall work with only one propositional operation – the *implication* (denoted by $\rightarrow$). Hence, we construct the "larger" set of propositions, call it P, defined by means of the following four rules:[3]

1. Every atomic proposition is a proposition, i.e. $V \subset P$.

2. The universal false proposition f belongs to P.

3. If x, y are arbitrary propositions, then $x \rightarrow y$ is a proposition.

4. Every proposition is obtained by rules 1-3.

Using only the implication and f doesn't really make our approach less general; indeed, all propositional operations can be "re-captured" as follows:

$$\text{negation: } \neg x = x \rightarrow f,$$

---

[2]It can be argued that even God is bound by logic. If God can lift any weight, then God is expressly prevented to create a weight so heavy that God cannot lift it. But God can do anything that does not involve a logical contradiction. (It seems that Einstein sympathised with this argument.) See also the discusssion in Wiener [41] and Odifreddi [32], [33].

[3]*Note for algebraists*: P is the free universal algebra of type $(0, 2)$ generated by V.

$$\text{disjunction: } x \cup y = (\neg x) \to y,$$

$$\text{conjunction: } x \cap y = \neg((\neg(x) \cup \neg(y))).$$

How do we know that the above formulas actually work?

To this aim we introduce the notion of interpretation. The set of truth values will be denoted by $\{0,1\}$ and we introduce on it the binary operation (called *truth implication*) which models the idea that an implication is false only in case the hypothesis is true but the conclusion is false:

$$\Longrightarrow: \{0,1\} \times \{0,1\} \to \{0,1\},$$

$$m \Longrightarrow n = \max\{1-m, n\}.$$

Clearly, $m \Longrightarrow n = 0$ iff $m = 1$ and $n = 0$.

An *interpretation* is a function

$$h : V \to \{0,1\},$$

i.e. a way the assign truth values to atomic propositions. We can extend this interpretation to the set of all propositions imposing the following two conditions:[4]

a) $h(f) = 0$,

b) $h(x \to y) = h(x) \Longrightarrow h(y)$, for all $x, y \in P$.

If h is an interpretation and $x \in P$, then the proposition x is *true under h* if $h(x) = 1$.

We can now compute the interpretations of the negation, disjunction, conjunction, according to a fixed h:

$$h(\neg x) = h(x \to f) = h(x) \Longrightarrow h(f) = h(x) \Longrightarrow 0 = 0 \text{ iff } h(x) = 1,$$

i.e. $h(\neg x) = 1 - h(x)$. Similarly,

$$h(x \cup y) = h((\neg x) \to y) = h(\neg x) \Longrightarrow h(y)$$

$$= (1 - h(x)) \Longrightarrow h(y) = \max\{1 - (1 - h(x)), h(y)\} = \max\{h(x), h(y)\},$$

$$h(x \cap y) = h(\neg((\neg(x) \cup \neg(y))))$$

$$= 1 - h(\neg(x) \cup \neg(y)) = 1 - \max\{h(\neg x),$$

$$h(\neg(y)\} = 1 - \max\{1 - h(x), 1 - h(y)\} = \min\{h(x), h(y)\},$$

---

[4] Algebraically, h is a morphism; as P is freely generated by V, h is uniquely determined by its values on generators, i.e. on V.

validating our claim.

The next step is to model the idea of "semantic consequence": the proposition $a \in P$ can be semantically deduced from the set of premises $X \subset P$ (or X is a semantic model for a) if every interpretation which makes **all** premises in X true, makes true x as well. Formally,

$$X \models a$$

if for every interpretation h such that $h(x) = 1$, for all $x \in X$, one has $h(a) = 1$.[5] In case $X = \emptyset$ we simple write $\models a$.

Example 2.1. *The following relations are true*

1. $\models a \to (b \to a)$, *for all $a, b \in P$.*

2. $\models (a \to (b \to c)) \to ((a \to b) \to (a \to c))$, *for all $a, b, c \in P$.*

3. $\models ((a \to f) \to f) \to a$, *for every $a \in P$.*

4. $\{a\} \models b \to a$, *for all $a, b \in P$.*

For instance, for the last relation we have to show that for every interpretation h such that $h(a) = 1$ one has $h(b \to a) = 1$. Indeed, $h(b \to a) = h(b) \implies h(a) = h(b) \implies 1 = 1$.

A special category of propositions is formed by "universal true propositions", i.e. propositions which are true with respect to all possible interpretations. We call them *tautologies*. The propositions $a \to (b \to a), (a \to (b \to c)) \to ((a \to b) \to (a \to c)), ((a \to f) \to f) \to a$ are all tautologies. Of course, not all propositions are tautologies; the extreme example is a proposition that is never true under any interpretation, for instance, $a \cap \neg a$.[6]

Example 2.2. *The following propositions are tautologies*

1. $a \to a$, *(identity principle)*,

2. $a \cup \neg a$, *(tertium non datur)*,

3. $(a \cap (a \to b)) \to b$, *(modus ponens)*,

4. $((a \to b) \cap (a \to \neg b)) \to \neg a$ *(negation principle)*,

---

[5] It is interesting to note that in LaTeX the symbol $\models$ is written $\models$.

[6] From a strict formal point of view, $a \cap \neg a$ is *not* a proposition in P, as $\cap, \neg$ are not admissible operators. Howevere, we shall use the formula $a \cap \neg a$ as an abbreviation for the proposition

$$(((a \to f) \to f) \to ((a \to f) \to f)) \to f.$$

5. $a \rightarrow (a \cup b)$, *(disjunction principle)*.

Several natural questions can be asked, for instance:

- Is there a compact way to "described" all and only all tautologies?

- What is the "structure" of the set of tautologies?

- Is it possible to "algorithmically" recognize a tautology? Is this a feasible task?

There are several possibilities to describe a set of propositions, specifically the set of tautologies. For our purpose the most interesting one is the deductive approach. The prototype of a deductive science is Euclid's geometry, developed around 300 B.C. Many of the facts about *geometry*[7] were collected by the Egyptians and Babylonians. The major step undertook by Euclid and his predecessors in Greece was to organise theses facts into a deductive science or axiomatic-deductive geometry.

The truth or falsity of most propositions in geometry cannot be seen directly from their meanings. The *axioms*, however, are special propositions whose truths are immediately recognized from their meanings; in fact, for a long period, this was the major criterion to select axioms (we shall return to this problem later). Starting with axioms, by a series of logical steps that we accept as propagating truth forward, we construct a "proof" by which we can arrive at the truth of other propositions called "theorems".[8]

Do we have a "solid" basis for recognizing the rules that allow us to propagate truth forward? This is a very delicate problem. For a long period Euclid's theory was considered the prototype of a perfect theory. However, in the nineteenth century people revealed flaws in Euclid's proofs, making essential use of "illustrated" figures.[9]

A fundamental change of view point has to be adopted: *deductions should be possible to carry out without reference to meanings*. In Euclid's case, proofs should read correctly with nonsense words substituted for "point", "line", "plane". The logical principles which mediate the steps in proofs should be stated in advance as *rules of inference*. So, the meanings of none of the words need to be considered in constructing proofs, the quality of being a valid proof depends then only on the form of the sentences. A valid proof has to be impersonal: whenever an alledged proof is submitted to a person who has previously been told the specifications of the system she/he should be able to *check* the proposed proof and decide whether it actually is a proof or not. No

---

[7] Earth measurement.

[8] Whose truth we might not have been ready to accept directly from their meanings.

[9] False "theorems" were discovered: "proofs" read just Euclid's proofs, except that some figures were "fudged" a little bit.

extra imagination or judgment is needed. In other terms, checking the validity of an alledged proof may be done by computer; this infinite class of yes-or-no questions is *algorithmically decidable.*[10]

In what follows we shall design an axiomatic system for tautologies. To this aim we "isolate" a few tautologies (called *axioms*) and a "deduction principle" with the aim of "deriving" all and only all tautologies. The axioms will be the first three tautologies in Example 2.1:

A1. $a \to (b \to a)$, for all $a, b \in P$.

A2. $(a \to (b \to c)) \to ((a \to b) \to (a \to c))$, for all $a, b, c \in P$.

A3. $((a \to f) \to f) \to a$, for every $a \in P$.

As a deduction rule we make use of the most fundamental principle (called *Modus Ponens*), modeling the following inference: if one proves y from x, and x has a proof, then y has a proof.

Modus Ponens : *For all $x, y \in P$, if x and $x \to y$, then y.*

We have got a "formal system". Within it we can discuss about "(formal) **proofs**".[11] Informally, a **proof** is just a finite sequence of propositions such that every element in the sequence is an axiom or can be deduced from propositions already in the sequence by *Modus Ponens.* Sometimes our **proofs** make use of extra hypotheses X; they will be called X**-proofs**.

Let X be a set of propositions and $a \in P$. An X**-proof** for a (i.e. a **proof** (within the system) of a from the set X of premises) is a sequence

$$x_1, x_2, \ldots, x_n$$

of elements in P such that $x_n = a$ and for all $1 \le i \le n$ one has:

- $x_i \in X$ or,

- x_i is an axiom, or

- there exist $1 \le k, l < i$ such that $x_j = x_k \to x_j$ (i.e. x_i can be deduced from x_k and x_j via *Modus Ponens*).

---

[10] This explains why the working mathematicians may differ (and, indeed, they do) in their views of what constitutes a rigorous proof, in spite of the fact that all of them believe in rigorous proofs.

[11] To distinguish between "proofs within our system" and "proofs outside the system", the first ones will be written in bold characters.

The proposition a is called an X-**theorem** in this case. Sometimes we write:

$$X \vdash a,$$

or simply

$$\vdash a,$$

in case $X = \emptyset$.

Example 2.3. *For all $a, b, c \in P$, the following relations are true:*

1. $\vdash a \rightarrow (b \rightarrow a)$,

2. $\vdash a \rightarrow a$,

3. $\{b\} \vdash a \rightarrow b$,

4. $\{a \rightarrow (c \rightarrow b), a \rightarrow c\} \vdash a \rightarrow b$.

Proof. The first proposition, $a \rightarrow (b \rightarrow a)$, is an axiom. For $a \rightarrow a$ we can write the following **proof**:

1. $a \rightarrow ((b \rightarrow a) \rightarrow a)) \rightarrow ((\rightarrow (b \rightarrow a)) \rightarrow (a \rightarrow a))$ (by A2.)

2. $a \rightarrow ((b \rightarrow a) \rightarrow a)$ (by A1.)

3. $(a \rightarrow (b \rightarrow a)) \rightarrow (a \rightarrow a)$ (by *Modus Ponens* from 2. and 1.)

4. $a \rightarrow (b \rightarrow a)$ (by A1.)

5. $a \rightarrow a$ (by *Modus Ponens*, from 4. and 3.).

The following sequence represents an $\{b\}$-**proof**:

1. $b \rightarrow (a \rightarrow b)$

2. b

3. $a \rightarrow b$.

Finally, the following sequence represents an $\{a \rightarrow (c \rightarrow b), a \rightarrow c\}$-**proof**:

1. $(a \rightarrow (c \rightarrow b)) \rightarrow ((a \rightarrow c) \rightarrow (a \rightarrow b))$

2. $a \rightarrow (c \rightarrow b)$

3. $(a \rightarrow c) \rightarrow (a \rightarrow b)$.

4. $a \rightarrow c$

5. $a \rightarrow b$.

$\square$

The following theorem, due to Herbrand [23], makes explicit the relation between the implication ($\rightarrow$), as an inner operator of the system, and the syntactical derivation ($\vdash$), the external deduction.

Theorem 2.4 [Deduction Theorem]. *Let $X \subset P$, and $a, b \in P$. The following statements are equivalent:*

a) $X \vdash a \rightarrow b$,

b) $X \cup \{a\} \vdash b$.

Proof. For the direct implication let $x_1, x_2, \ldots, x_n$ be an X-**proof** for $a \rightarrow b$. Then $x_1, x_2, \ldots, x_n, a, b$ is an $X \cup \{a\}$-**proof** for b.

We are proving the converse implication. Let $x_1, x_2, \ldots, x_n$ be an $X \cup \{a\}$-**proof** for b. We prove, by induction on i, that

$$X \vdash a \rightarrow x_i.$$

For $i = n$ we get the desired conclusion:

$$X \vdash a \rightarrow b,$$

as $x_n = b$.

There are four possible cases to be discussed:

- $x_i \in X$: since $\{x_i\} \vdash a \rightarrow x_i$ one deduces $X \vdash a \rightarrow x_i$, as $x_i \in X$.

- $x_i = a$: since $\vdash a \rightarrow a$, by Example 2.3, $X \vdash a \rightarrow a$.

- x_i is an axiom: one has $\vdash x_i$, so $\{x_i\} \vdash a \rightarrow x_i$, i.e. $X \vdash a \rightarrow x_i$.

- $x_k = x_j \rightarrow x_i, j, k < i$: by hypothesis, $X \vdash a \rightarrow x_j$ and $X \vdash a \rightarrow x_k$. By virtue of Example 2.3,

$$\{a \rightarrow x_j, a \rightarrow (x_j \rightarrow x_k)\} \vdash a \rightarrow x_i,$$

so $X \vdash a \rightarrow x_i$.

$\square$

Remark. There is a simpler, semantical analogue of the Deduction Theorem. It reads as following: *Let $X \subset P$, and $a, b \in P$. The following statements are equivalent:*

a) $X \models a \rightarrow b$,

b) $X \cup \{a\} \models b$.

Here are two more examples of X-**proofs**:

Example 2.5.

1. $\{f\} \vdash a$, for all $a \in P$,

2. $\{a, \neg a\} \vdash b$, for all $a, b \in P$.

Proof. Here is an $\{f\}$-**proof** for a:

1. f

2. $f \rightarrow ((a \rightarrow f) \rightarrow f)$

3. $(a \rightarrow f) \rightarrow f$

4. $((a \rightarrow f) \rightarrow f) \rightarrow a$

5. a.

Starting with the sequence

a. a

b. $a \rightarrow f$

c. f

and the above $\{f\}$-**proof**, i.e. steps 1.,2.,3.,4.,5. we get an arbitrary proposition b. $\qquad\square$

3. Adequacy problems

It's time to look critically at our system. Is it adequate? *Soundness* is the first required property, as we are interested to "describe" only tautologies. Specifically, the question reads: Is any **theorem** a tautology? A negative answer would ruin the whole construction.

We start proving that every X-**theorem** can be semantically deduced from X:

Proposition 3.1. *For all $X \subset P, a \in P$, if*

$$X \vdash a,$$

then

$$X \models a.$$

Proof. We use the definition of an X-**proof** inductively, noticing that all axioms are tautologies and *Modus Ponens* is an invariant rule.   □

To be really successful we need to prove the completeness of our system, i.e. a converse of Proposition 3.1. The following proof will give some more insight on the nature of tautologies.

Definition 3.2. A set $X \subset P$ is called *consistent* if it is free of contradictions; formally, if

$$X \nvdash f.$$

Example 3.3. *The empty set is consistent. The set $\{a, \neg a\}$ is not consistent.*

Proof. Indeed, if $\vdash f$, then, by Proposition 3.1, $\models f$, which is absurd as for every interpretation h one has $h(f) = 0$. By Example 2.5, $\{a, \neg a\} \vdash f$.   □

We shall prove now two technical results that are motivated by a typical algebraic construction: the embedding of a structure in a maximal structure of the same type.

Lemma 3.4. *The union of an increasing sequence (under set-theoretical inclusion) of consistent sets is still a consistent set.*

Proof. Let

$$B_1 \subset B_2 \subset \cdots \subset B_n \subset B_{n+1} \subset \cdots$$

be an increasing sequence of consistent sets and put

$$B = \bigcup_{n \geq 1} B_n.$$

If, by absurd, B is not consistent, then $B \vdash f$, i.e. there exists a finite set $X \subset B$ such that $X \vdash f$. So, $X \subset B_m$, for some natural $m \geq 1$ (as the sequence $(B_i)_{i \geq 1}$) is increasing). This contradicts the consistency of B_m.   □

Definition 3.5. A set $X \subset P$ is called *maximal consistent* if for every element $a \notin X$ the set $X \cup \{a\}$ is not consistent.

Proposition 3.6. *Every consistent set can be embedded into a maximal consistent set.*

Proof. The usual way to prove such a result is to invoke Zorn's Lemma.[12] We proceed *constructively*, i.e. introducing an enumeration technique usually

---

[12]Let X be a consistent subset of P. The set $\Gamma = \{T \subset P | X \subset T, T \nvdash f\}$ is non-empty ($X \in \Gamma$). More, Γ is inductively ordered: if $\{T_\alpha\}$ is a totally ordered family of elements of Γ and $T = \cup_\alpha T_\alpha$, then $X \subset T \subset P, T \nvdash f$ (as, if f is provable from T means that f is provable from a finite subset of T). Use now Zorn's Lemma (*if S is a partially ordered set in which each chain has an upper bound, then S contains a maximal element*) to assert the *existence* of a maximal element in Γ. In general, no claim of constructivity can be made for such a reasoning; see, for instance, the treatment in Barnes and Mack [3].

referred to as a *gödelization*. Assume that we have an one-one enumeration $v_i, i = 2, 3, \ldots$ of all atomic propositions. Then, we can construct an one-one function $g : P \to \mathbf{N}$ as follows:[13]

Put $v_1 = f$ and

$$g(v_i) = 2i + 1,$$

$$g(x \to y) = 2^{g(x)} \cdot 3^{g(y)}.$$

For instance, $g(f) = 0$,

$$g(v_1 \to (v_2 \to v_1)) = 2^{g(v_1)} \cdot 3^{g(v_2 \to v_1))}$$

$$= 2^1 \cdot 3^{2^{g(v_2)} 3^{g(v_1)}} = 2 \cdot 3^{2^2 \cdot 3^1} = 2 \cdot 3^4.$$

Let $X \subset P$ be a fixed consistent set. Using the above function g we define the following sequence of sets of propositions:

$$B_0 = X,$$

$$
\begin{aligned}
B_{n+1} &= B_n \cup \{g(n)\}, && \text{if } B_n \cup \{g(n)\} \text{ is consistent,} \\
&= B_n, && \text{otherwise.}
\end{aligned}
$$

Clearly, the sequence B_n is increasing and each B_n is consistent. So, by Lemma 3.4, $B = \bigcup_{n \geq 0} B_n$ is consistent as well. Since $B_0 = X \subset B$ the only fact it remains to be proven is the maximal consistency of B. Let $B \subset Y \subset P$ be such that $B \neq Y$, i.e. there exists a proposition

$$g(n) \in Y, g(n) \notin B.$$

From the relation $g(n) \notin B$ and the construction of B_{n+1} it follows that $g(n) \notin B_{n+1}$ – because $B_n \cup \{g(n)\}$ is not consistent, i.e.

$$B_n \cup \{g(n)\} \vdash f.$$

But, $B_n \subset Y$, $g(n) \in Y$, so $B_n \cup \{g(n)\} \subset Y$ and $Y \vdash f$, saying that Y is not consistent. $\square$

Maximal consistent sets are "fixed-points" of the operator generating **theorems** and they obey the Bivalence Principle.

Proposition 3.7. *If $X \subset P$ is a maximal consistent set, then*

---

[13] Assume that our enumeration $\{v_i\}$ was "computable", in the sense that there exists an *algorithm* computing v_i when presented i. Then, the function g is itself computable and given $i \in g(P)$ we can effectively discover the (unique) proposition $x \in P$ such that $g(x) = i$. We do not define the notion of algorithm; instead, we may think of an algorithm as a finite specification of a ste-by-step computation. A computer program is the most familiar instance of an algorithm.

1. $\{a \in P | X \vdash a\} = X$,

2. *for every* $a \in P$, *one and only one of the following relations is true:* $a \in X$ *or* $\neg a \in X$.

Proof. 1) Clearly, $X \subset \{a \in P | X \vdash a\}$. But

$$f \notin \{a \in P | X \vdash a\} = \{a \in P | \{b \in P | X \vdash b\} \vdash a\},$$

so $\{a \in P | X \vdash a\}$ is consistent. In view of the inclusion $X \subset \{a \in P | X \vdash a\}$ we can make use of the maximality to derive the equality.

2) If $a \notin X$, then $X \cup \{a\}$ is not consistent, i.e.

$$X \cup \{a\} \vdash f.$$

We use now the Deduction Theorem to get

$$X \vdash a \to f = \neg a.$$

By virtue of 1), $\neg a \in X$. If $\neg a \notin X$, then $X \cup \{\neg a\}$ is not consistent,

$$X \cup \{\neg a\} \vdash f,$$

so by the Deduction Theorem

$$X \vdash \neg a \to f = (a \to f) \to f = \neg\neg a.$$

By the axiom A3.

$$\neg\neg a \to a,$$

so $X \vdash a$, i.e. $a \in X$ by virtue of maximality. Of course, it is not the case that both a and $\neg a$ are in X, as X is consistent (see Example 2.5). $\square$

The next result shows that every maximal consistent set of propositions X has a model, i.e. there is an interpretation according to which all propositions in X are true.

Proposition 3.8. *Let X be a maximal consistent set. Then, c_X, the characteristic function of X (with respect to P) is an interpretation making true all propositions in X.*

Proof. Recall that $c_X : P \to \{0, 1\}$, $c_X(a) = 1$ iff $x \in X$. As X is maximal consistent, $X \nvdash f$, so $f \notin X$, i.e. $c_X(f) = 0$.

Take now $a, b \in P$. We shall prove that

$$c_X(a \to b) = c_X(a) \Longrightarrow c_X(b).$$

There are three cases to be analysed.

1. *If $b \in X$, then $c_X(b) = 1$, so $c_X(a) \implies c_X(b) = c_X(a) \implies 1 = 1$.* One has to prove that $c_X(a \to b) = 1$, i.e. $a \to b \in X$. We know that X is maximal consistent, so a fixed-point:

    $$X = \{c \in P | X \vdash c\}.$$

    By axiom A1., $\vdash b \to (a \to b)$, so

    $$X \vdash b \to (a \to b).$$

    By hypothesis, $b \in X$, so $X \vdash b$ and (by *Modus Ponens*) $X \vdash a \to b$. Again, by maximality, $a \to b \in X$.

2. *If $a \notin X$, then $c_X(a) = 0$, so $c_X(a) \implies c_X(b) = 0 \implies c_X(b) = 1$.* So, we have to prove again the relation $c_X(a \to b) = 1$. But $a \notin X$ implies, by Proposition 3.7, $\neg a \in X$. Using the Deduction Theorem (to $\{a, \neg a\} \vdash b$) we get

    $$\{\neg a\} \vdash a \to b.$$

    Since $\neg a \in X$, $X \vdash \neg a$, so $X \vdash a \to b$, i.e. $a \to b \in X$.

3. *If $a \in X$ and $b \notin X$, then $c_X(a) = 1, c_X(b) = 0$, so $c_X(a) \implies c_X(b) = 0$.* The relation $a \to b \notin X$ remains to be proven. Indeed, if $a \to b \in X, a \in X$, then $b \in X$, a contradiction.

□

Corollary 3.9. *If X is consistent, then there exists an interpretation $h : P \to \{0, 1\}$ such that $h(a) = 1$, for all $a \in X$.*

Proof. Embedd the given consistent set into a maximal consistent set and then use Proposition 3.8. □

We are now able to prove Post's Completeness Theorem [34], which guaranties that our system is completely adequate.

Lemma 3.10. *For every set of propositions X and every proposition a,*

$$X \models a \text{ iff } X \vdash a.$$

Proof. By Proposition 3.1 only the direct implication has to be proven. Assume that $X \models a$. We shall prove that $X \cup \{\neg a\}$ is not consistent. If it were consistent, then we would have, by Corollary 3.9, an interpretation h such that $h(b) = 1$, for all $b \in X \cup \{\neg a\}$, i.e.

$$h(\neg a) = 1,$$

and

$$h(b) = 1, \text{ for all } b \in X.$$

From $h(\neg a) = 1$ one deduces $h(a) = 0$, so we have contradicted the hypothesis $X \not\models a$.

From the inconsistency of the set $X \cup \{\neg a\}$ we deduce[14]

$$X \cup \{\neg a\} \vdash f.$$

Use again the Deduction Theorem

$$X \vdash \neg a \to f = \neg\neg a,$$

and the axiom A3. to get $X \vdash a$. $\qquad\qquad\square$

Taking $X = \emptyset$ in Lemma 3.10 we get

Theorem 3.11 [Completeness Theorem]. *For every proposition* a,

$$\models a \text{ iff } \vdash a.$$

Digression: *Three or many valued logics.* The proposition

$$(\neg a \to a) \to a$$

is clear a tautology (it seems to be discovered by Clavius, 1600 A.C.). If we switch the underlying logic, from binary, to, say ternary, we loose the tautological property. Indeed, assume we work with the ternary logic in which the truth values are $0, \frac{1}{2}$ (uncertain), 1. The implication interpretation will use the same formula, i.e. $m \implies n = \max\{1 - m, n\}$. This means that $\neg\frac{1}{2} = \frac{1}{2}$ and $\frac{1}{2} \implies \frac{1}{2} = \frac{1}{2}$. If the truth value of a is uncertain, then the proposition $(\neg a \to a) \to a$ is also uncertain.

4. The structure of tautologies

One reason why Boolean algebras are relevant to logic is that propositional operators have properties similar to Boolean operations. Based on this analogy we cannot ask questions such as "What is a proof?" or "How can we prove?"; instead, we can study the inner "structure" of provable propositions, that is, via the Completeness Theorem, of tautologies.

To every interpretation h we associate an equivalence relation $\overset{h}{\sim}$ defined on P as follows:

$$a \overset{h}{\sim} b \text{ iff } h(a) = h(b).$$

---

[14]Does it mean that actually we have got an $X \cup \{\neg a\}$ - **proof** for f or only an assertion telling that such a **proof** does exist?

In fact, $\overset{h}{\sim}$ is more than an equivalence relation, it is a *congruence*, in the sense that $\overset{h}{\sim}$ is compatible with the algebraic structure of P: If $a\overset{h}{\sim}b$ and $a'\overset{h}{\sim}b'$, then $a \to a'\overset{h}{\sim}b \to b'$. Indeed, from $h(a) = h(b), h(a') = h(b')$ we deduce

$$h(a \to a') = h(a) \implies h(a') = h(b) \implies h(b') = h(b \to b').$$

The intersection of congruences $\overset{h}{\sim}$, when h runs over all interpretations,

$$\sim = \bigcap_{h \text{ interpretation}} \overset{h}{\sim},$$

is still a congruence on P. The equivalence class of an element $a \in P$ is

$$[a] = \{b \in P | a\overset{h}{\sim}b, \text{ for every interpretation } h\}.$$

The family of all equivalence classes, $P/_\sim = \{[a]\}_{a\in P}$ can be endoweded, in a natural way, with the following Boolean operations:[15]

$$\neg[a] = [\neg a],$$

$$[a] \cup [b] = [\neg a \to b],$$

$$[a] \cap [b] = [\neg((\neg a) \cup (\neg b))].$$

These definitions are correct, i.e. they do not depend upon the chosen "names" for classes. For instance, if $a \sim b$, then $h(a) = h(b)$, for every interpretation h, so

$$h(\neg a) = h(a \to f) = h(a) \implies h(f) =$$

$$h(a) \implies 0 = h(b) \implies 0 = h(b \to f) = h(\neg b),$$

meaning that $[\neg a] = [\neg b]$. More, $(P/_\sim, \cup, \cap, \neg)$ is a Boolean algebra (called *Lindenbaum algebra*).[16]

---

[15] Recall that $\neg a$ is an abbreviation for the proposition $a \to f$.

[16] The following identities are satisfied for all $u, v, w \in P/_\sim$:

$$u \cap v = v \cap u, \quad u \cup v = v \cup u,$$

$$u \cap (v \cap w) = (u \cap v) \cap w, \quad u \cup (v \cup w) = (u \cup v) \cup w,$$

$$u \cap (u \cup v) = u, \quad u \cup (u \cap v) = u,$$

$$u \cap (v \cup w) = (u \cap v) \cup (u \cap w), \quad u \cup (v \cap w) = (u \cup v) \cap (u \cup w),$$

$$(u \cap \neg u) \cup v = v, \quad (u \cup \neg u) \cap v = v.$$

The distinguished element "1" of this Boolean algebra[17] is

$$\mathbf{Taut} = [a] \cup \neg[a] = [a] \cup [\neg a] = [a \cup \neg a],$$

and, as $h(a \cup \neg a) = 1$, for all $a \in P$, coincides with the set of all tautologies.

We make one more step further in our generalization: Consider an arbitrary Boolean algebra B endowed with the operations $\cup, \cap, \neg$, whose elements are identified with the propositions of some mathematical theory. Assume $F \subset B$ corresponds to the set of *provable* propositions (*theorems*). The common mathematical experience motivates the following two statements;

- If $s, t \in F$, then s **and** $t \in F$.

- If $s \in F$ and $t \in B$, then s **or** $t \in F$.

The above two properties are similar to properties defining the notion of *Boolean filter*. Is this only a superficial analogy? The argument for a negative answer is presented in the following

Theorem 4.1. *Let F be a subset of the Boolean algebra B. Then, the following two assertions are equivalent:*

1. *The set F is a filter.*[18]

2. *One has:*

    a. $1 \in F$.[19]

    b. *If $x \in F$ and $x \to y \in F$, then $y \in F$.*[20]

Proof. For the direct implication we assume that $x \in F$ and $x \to y \in F$. In view of the second property of a filter, if $p, q \in F$, then $p \cap q \in F$. A simple computation shows that $x \cap (x \to y) = x \cap (\neg x \cup y) = (x \cap \neg x) \cup (x \cap y) \in F$, i.e. $x \cap y \in F$. Finally, $y = y \cup (x \cap y)$ is in F as $x \cap y \in F$; we have used the third property of a filter.

Conversely, let $x, y \in F$. We have: $x = x \cap (x \cup y)$, so

$$\neg x = \neg x \cup \neg(x \cup y) = \neg x \cup (\neg x \cap \neg y).$$

Consequently,

$$1 = x \cup \neg x = x \cup (\neg x \cup (\neg x \cap \neg y)) = (x \cup (\neg x \cap \neg y)) \cup \neg x \in F.$$

---

[17] Recall that in every Boolean algebra the expression $x \cup \neg x$ does not depend upon the actual value of x; this is the element "1", or the maximal element of the algebra.

[18] That is, 1. $1 \in F$, 2. For all $x, y \in F, x \cap y \in F$, 3. For all $x \in F, y \in B, x \cup y \in F$.

[19] This condition says that all tautologies are provable.

[20] *Modus Ponens.*

But $x \in F$ and $1 \in F$, so $x \cup (\neg x \cap \neg y) \in F$ and

$$\neg x \cup ((\neg x \cap \neg y) \cup x) = \neg x \to ((\neg x \cap \neg y) \cup x) = 1 \in F.$$

So,

$$x \cup (\neg x \cap \neg y) = (x \cup \neg y) \cap (x \cup y) = x \cup \neg y = y \to x \in F.$$

Now we are using the second hypothesis, $y \in F$:

$$y \to (x \cap y) = \neg y \cup (x \cap y) = (\neg y \cup x) \cup (\neg y \cap x) = \neg y \cup x \in F,$$

so $x \cap y \in F$.

Let $x \in F$ and $y \in B$. In the above computation we substitute $\neg y$ for y and we obtain $x \cup \neg(\neg y) \in F$, i.e. $x \cup y \in F$. $\qquad\square$

We can now come back to our concrete example of Boolean algebra, Lindenbaum algebra $P/_\sim$. Take $X \subset P$ and

$$F(X) = \{[a] \in P/_\sim \,|\, X \vdash a\}.$$

Then $F(X)$ is a filter. Indeed, **Taut** $\in F(X)$ (if $a \in$ **Taut**, then $\models a$, so by the Completeness Theorem, $\vdash a$, so $X \vdash a$). Next take $[a] \in F(X)$ and $[a] \to [b] = [a \to b] \in F(X)$. This means that $X \vdash a, X \vdash a \to b$, so by *Modus Ponens*, $X \vdash b$, i.e. $[b] \in F(X)$.

So, from a structural point of view, $\{$**Taut**$\}$ is a filter in the Lindenbaum algebra $P/_\sim$; actually, it is an ultrafilter.

5. Ultrafilters and constructivity

Let B be a Boolean algebra. Filters in B which are maximal with respect to inclusion are called *ultrafilters*. It is not hard to show that *a filter F is an ultrafilter iff for every $x \in B$ either $x \in F$ or $\neg x \in F$, bot not both*; compare with Proposition 3.7. The key result on ultrafilters is the Ultrafilter Theorem (see, for a proof, Bell ans Slomson [4], Theorem 3.4, p.15; again, it is instructive to compare with Proposition 3.6):

Theorem 5.1. *Every filter in a Boolean algebra can be extended to an ultrafilter.*

To illustrate this situation we consider the Lindenbaum algebra $P/_\sim$; for every interpretation h define

$$F_h = \{[a] \in P/_\sim \,|\, h(a) = 1\}.$$

A simple argument shows that F_h is a filter, in fact, an ultrafilter.

These facts actually motivate another approach to the Completeness Theorem, a path followed by Rasiowa and Sikorski [36]. Bell and Slomson [4], p. 49, wrote:

> *The proofs of Post and Kalmár[21] both provide explicit recipes for constructing a proof of a given tautology. The proof that we have given, which is due to Rasiowa and Sikorski [1951], does not have this character, and since it depends on the ultrafilter theorem is not a constructive proof.*

This remark calls for a more detailed explanation. The problem under discussion is the following: Having a proposition a and *knowing* that a is a tautology, is it possible to get a **proof**, within the considered system, for a? As it stands, the above question has *always* a positive answer, by the Completeness Theorem, independently of the proof of this theorem. Indeed, a dovetailing algorithm[22] running through all possible proofs does the job, as *we know* that eventually the right **proof** will be discovered. In fact, this is exactly the algorithm rejected for the general problem discussed at the beginning[23]. The main difference lies in the *extra* information given in the weaker question: we know that a is a tautology. This is a quite subtle situation, in which the difference between a constructive proof and a non-constructive proof[24] affects very little the "numerical" content of the result. To get more insight on this phenomenon we make use of some rudiments of Constructive Mathematics. According to Bridges and Richman [6], p.1:

> *We engage in constructive mathematics from a desire to clarify the meaning of mathematical terminology and practice – in particular, the meaning of existence in a mathematical context. The classical mathematician, with the freedom of methodology advocated by Hilbert, perceives an object x to exist if he can prove the impossibility of its nonexistence; the constructive mathematician must be presented with an algorithm that constructs the object x before he will recognize that x exists.*

The essential difference between a classical and constructive approach to mathematics can be grasped by considering **binary sequences** generated by an algorithm. Let $b = b_1 b_2 \ldots b_n \ldots$ be a binary sequence and consider the following statements:

$$S(b) : b_n = 1, \text{ for some } n,$$

$$\neg S(b) : b_n = 0, \text{ for all } n.$$

Here $\neg S(b)$ is the denial of $S(b)$: under the assumption of $S(b)$ a contradictory statement (like $0 = 1$) holds. A constructive proof of $S(b) \vee \neg S(b)$ must

---

[21] See [25].

[22] A *British Museum algorithm*, following Chaitin.

[23] Having a proposition a, is it possible to algorithmically decide if a is a **theorem**?

[24] The proof discussed in this paper is only apparently constructive. It avoids the use of Zorn's Lemma, but makes essential use of the *embbeding*.

provide an algorithm showing that $b_n = 0$, for all n, or computing a positive integer n such that $b_n = 1$.

A **Brouwerian counterexample** to an assertion is a proof that the assertion implies some unacceptable principle in constructive mathematics. The most popular such principle is called the **Limited Principle of Omniscience, LPO**:

> *If (b_n) is a binary sequence, then either there exists n such that $b_n = 1$, or else $b_n = 0$, for all n.*

Clearly, **LPO** is simple the assertion

$$\forall b(S(b) \vee \neg S(b)).$$

Why is it constructively false? Just because it is equivalent to the **Halting Problem**, which cannot be solved algorithmically. Here is the outline of the argument. First we show that the **Halting Problem** is not decidable. Assume, for the sake of a contradiction, that there exists a **halting program** deciding if an arbitrary program eventually halts. The outputs, if any, for all our programs are supposed to be 0 or 1; also, we may asssume, without loss of generality, that the inputs for the programs are part of the programs themselves.

Construct, following Chaitin [9], the program (which essentially makes use of the **halting program**):

- read a natural N;

- generate all programs up to N bits in size;

- use the **halting program** to check for each generated program whether it halts;

- simulate the running of the above generated programs;

- make sure that the running time of the current program is bigger than the running time of all halting programs, generated above.

First, notice that the above program eventually halts for every natural N. How long is the above program ? It is about $\log_2 N$ bits. Indeed, the program consists of the input data N (which requires about $\log_2 N$ bits) and a constant part. Globally, the program has $\log_2 N + O(1)$ bits. For large enough N, the above program will belong to the set of programs having less than N bits (because $\log_2 N + O(1) < N$). Accordingly, the program will be generated by itself – at some stage of the computation. In this case we have got a contradiction, since the computation time for our program will be bigger than the computation time of itself!

The second step in our argument is a reduction: we prove that in case we assume **LPO**, then the **Halting Problem** is decidable. Indeed, let

$$\pi_1, \pi_2, \ldots, \pi_n, \ldots$$

be the set of all our programs and consider the following (computable) function μ:

$$\mu(m, k) = \begin{cases} 1, & \text{if } \pi_m(m) \text{ halts in time less than } k, \\ 0, & \text{otherwise.} \end{cases}$$

Applying **LPO** to the set of binary sequences

$$b_1^m, b_2^m, \ldots, b_i^m, \ldots,$$

where

$$b_i^m = \mu(m, i),$$

would solve the **Halting Problem**, which is impossible.

Markov's Principle, MP[25], which corresponds to our axiom A3., reads:

$$\neg\neg S(b) \Leftrightarrow S(b).$$

To illustrate **MP**[26] we consider an one-one enumeration of all possible proofs for tautologies:

$$p_1, p_2, \ldots$$

Let $a \in$ **Taut** and consider the predicate

$$Pred(a, i) = p_i \text{ is a proof for } a.$$

Clearly, for a fixed a, $Pred(a, i)$ is algorithmically decidable. Next, use **MP** to the statement

$$\exists i Pred(a, i),$$

saying that *it would be absurd to denny that there is a positive integer i such that $Pred(a, i)$.* From this fact we get no clue or computation bound for the construction of such an i.

To conclude, given a tautology a, we surely can get a **proof** for a; however, we can provide no indication concerning the number of proofs necessary to

---

[25] **MP** is rejected by Brouwer, but freely used by the Russian school in constructive mathematics.

[26] It is interesting to note, following Brouwer, that the statement

$$\neg\neg\neg A \Rightarrow \neg A,$$

is constructively meaningful. Indeed, under the assumption $\neg\neg\neg A$ we can prove $\neg a$ by deriving a contradiction from A: if A, then $\neg A$ is absurd, hence $\neg\neg A$, which contradicts $\neg\neg\neg A$.

inspect before getting the required **proof**: this state of affairs reflects the meaning of **MP**.

When considering the predicate calculus[27] we can prove a similar Completeness Theorem.[28] From a constructive point of view the situation is dramatically different: Church [12] has proven that *no proof of the Completeness Theorem for predicate calculus is constructive*. In this case the result has a devastating impact: *There is no algorithm testing the property of being a tautology, or equivalently, a theorem, for the predicate calculus.*

6. Decidability and complexity

The formulation of the negative result cited at the end of the above section leaves the impression that the property of being a **theorem** of the propositional calculus is algorithmically decidable. Is this true?

Indeed, the above decision problem is algorithmically decidable, by virtue of the Completeness Theorem. **Theorems** coincide with tautologies and testing if an arbitrary proposition is or is not a tautology is algorithmically decidable. Apparently, switching from **theorems** to tautologies doesn't help too much, as we replace the (potential infinite) search through all possible proofs by a search through all possible interpretations of propositions (an infinite set, as well). This is only a superficial feeling! If a contains n atomic propositions, then we don't have to go through all possible interpretations h, but to examine only the restriction of these interpretations to the set of atomic propositions in a. We have arrived at a finite set, containing 2^n elements.

The immediate question is: How difficult is to decide if an arbitrary proposition a is a **theorem**? To approach this question we will discuss briefly the class **P** of polynomial algorithms. The Euclidean algorithm (for computing the greatest common divisor of two positive integers) is an example of a polynomial algorithm, in the sense that the number of basic bit operations (the *time* used by the algorithm) is a polynomial function of the number of bits in the input.[29]

Sometimes we are not able to design a polynomial algorithm for a problem; at least, we can prove that a solution for the problem can be quickly recognized if some miraculously source furnishes it to us. A good example is the problem

---

[27] One augments the propositional calculus with the quantifier symbols $\exists$ (there exists) and $\forall$ (for all) and all necessary extra constructions. De Morgan gave the first example of a logically valid argument which cannot be expressed in the propositional calculus: *All horses are animals. Therefore all horses' heads are animals' heads.*

[28] Due to Gödel [18].

[29] If the two inputs have at most n digits, then the larger input is less than 2^n, so the number of steps is bounded by cn. Each step involves a division, i.e. about n^2 bit operations, which gives finally a cubic polynomial. In fact, by a more involved analysis one can show that the Euclidean algorithm works in time bounded by a quadratic function of the length of inputs.

of primality. It is not easy to determine if a positive integer having 1,000 digits is composite. But if we have got somehow two numbers and a claim that they multiply to the given number, then we can very easily check if the claim is correct or not. These two numbers form a *certificate* of their compositeness. This leads to the important class **NP** of algorithms running in nondeterministic polynomial time, i.e. algorithms working in polynomial time under the assumption that a certain certificate has been given. One of the most intriguing open problems in theoretical computer science pertains exactly the relation between **P** and **NP**: **P** =? **NP**.

Testing if an arbitrary proposition a is a **theorem** along the path suggested at the beginning of this section requires an exponential computation time. Is it possible to do it better? No one knows this. We can see readily that our problem is in co-**NP**,[30] as guessing an interpretation which makes a false solves very quickly the problem.

In fact the problem **P** = ? **NP** is really meta-mathematical! Indeed, assume an appropriate coding and measure of the size of proofs. So, we may have polynomial size proofs and exponential size proofs. The difference between **P** and **NP** – if any – may be seen as a difference between *constructing* a polynomial size proof and *verifying* a polynomial size proof. If **P** = **NP**, then they are the same.

Currently, there is a lot of work devoted to the problem **P** = ? **NP**. We will confine ourselves only to a single recent result, just because it uses a nonstandard approach and gives us a concrete example of a new kind of *axiom* or *hypothesis*. To this aim we consider the exponential deterministic time-complexity classes

$$E = DTIME\left(2^{\text{linear}}\right), \text{ and } E_2 = DTIME\left(2^{\text{polynomial}}\right).$$

There are several reasons for considering these classes (Lutz [27], [28]):

1)   Both classes E, E_2 have rich internal strutures.

2) E_2 is the smallest deterministic time complexity class known to contain **NP** and **PSPACE**.

3)   **P** $\subset E \subset E_2, E \neq E_2$, and E contains many **NP**-complete problems.

4)   Both classes E, E_2 have been proven to contain intractable problems.

In view of the property 2) there may be well a natural "notion of smallness" for subsets of E_2 such that **P** is a small subset of E_2, but **NP** is not. Similarly, it may be that **P** is a small subset of E, but that **NP**$\cap E$ is not! In the language

---

[30] co-**NP** is the class of sets X such that the predicate $x \notin X$ is in **NP**.

of constructive measure theory smallness can be translated by "measure zero" (with respect to the induced spaces E or E_2). One can prove that indeed **P** has constructive measure zero in E and E_2, Lutz [27]. This motivates Lutz [28] to adopt the following quantitative hypothesis:

The set **NP** *has not measure zero.*

This is a strong hypothesis, as it implies $\mathbf{P} \neq \mathbf{NP}$. It is consistent with Zimand [40] topological analysis (with respect to a natural, constructive topology, if $\mathbf{NP} \setminus \mathbf{P}$ is non-empty, then it is a *second Baire category* set, while **NP**-complete sets form a *first category* class) and appears to have more explanatory power than traditional, qualitative hypotheses. As currently we are unable to prove or disprove this conjecture, the best strategy seems to investigate it as a scientific hypothesis; its importance is to be evaluated in terms of the extent and credibility of its consequences.

Two more problems are quite relevant for our discussion. Both belong to number theory and are currently *open*. The *prime number problem* asks for an polynomial time algorithm to check whether an arbitrary number n is prime.[31] It is plain that this problem is in **NP**; Pratt [35] has shown that it is also in co-**NP**. Miller [31] has proven that this problem is in **P** if *one assumes the extended Riemann Hypothesis*.[32] The other problem, the *factorization problem* asks for non-trivial factors of the natural number n, if n is composite. It is basic for many public-key crypto-systems ("trapdoor ones") and it is widely believed to be *intractable*. See more in Salomaa [38].[33]

It is interesting to note that:

- Much security is essentially based on a problem *believed* to be intractable, but concerning which very little is known.

- The *theoretical ignorance* supports two schools in Computer Science, the automatic proving systems based on resolution principles in AI (a school which is largely based on the belief that $\mathbf{P} = \mathbf{NP}$) and the public-key cryptography school (which assumes the opposite relation, i.e. $\mathbf{P} \neq \mathbf{NP}$).

---

[31] It should be emphasized that one is looking for a polynomial time algorithm in the number of digits representing the number n.

[32] The function

$$\zeta(s) = 1 + \frac{1}{2^s} + \frac{1}{3^s} + \frac{1}{4^s} + \cdots$$

has all non-real zeros on the axis $x = \frac{1}{2}$.

[33] Actually, we do not even know if this problem is **NP**-complete.

7. Experimental mathematics = mathematics for the future ?

Church's theorem concerning the impossibility to prove constructively the completensss for the predicate calculus is just a first result in a long list of theorems about the limits of mathematics.

A really impressive remark made by Bridges [5] is relevant for our discussion. Consider the following function F, defined on the set $\mathbf{N}$ of natural numbers:

$$F(n) = \begin{cases} 1, & \text{if the Continuum Hypothesis is true,} \\ 0, & \text{if the Continuum Hypothesis is false.} \end{cases}$$

Deep work by Gödel [19] and Cohen [13] shows that neither the Continuum Hypothesis[34] nor its negation can be proved within Zermelo-Fraenkel set theory augmented with the axiom of choice. According to classical logic, F is computable because there exists an algorithm that computes it: that algorithm is either the one which always produces 0, or else the one which always produces 1. The trouble is we cannot know the correct one! And, as the Continuum Hypothesis is independent of the axioms of Zermelo-Fraenkel set theory augmented with the axiom of choice – the standard framework for mathematics – **we will never know which of the two algorithms actually is the one that computes** F.

The deepest result marking the limits of mathematics was discovered by Gödel [18]; we will present it in the stronger, information-theoretic variant due to Chaitin [9], [7], [37]:

- *An n-bit formal axiomatic system cannot enable one to exhibit any specific object with program-size complexity greater than* $n + c$.[35]

- *There exists an exponential diophantine equation*[36]

$$P(n, x, y_1, y_2, \ldots, y_m) = 0,$$

such that every n-bit formal axiomatic system cannot enable one to determine more than $n + c'$ *naturals k for which the equation*

$$P(k, x, y_1, y_2, \ldots, y_m) = 0$$

has an infinity of solutions.

---

[34] There is no cardinal number strictly in between aleph-null, the cardinal of the the set of natural numbers, and aleph-one, the cardinal of the set of reals.

[35] The program-size complexity of a finite object, e.g. a binary string, is a measure of the difficulty of specifying that object.

[36] That is an equation which is built by means of addition, mutiplication, and exponentiation of non-negative integer constants and variables.

The above results support Chaitin's claim that randomness has pervaded the inner structure of Mathematics![37] A complementary conclusion can be derived from another analysis of Gödel Incompleteness Theorem. In Calude, Jürgensen, Zimand [8] one proves that, in a quite general topological sense, incompleteness is a rather common phenomenon: *with respect to any reasonable topology the set of true and unprovable statements of a recursively enumerable, consistent, and rich enough theory is dense, and in many cases even co-rare.* These results show that the significance of axioms and proofs should be accordingly "modified". This point of view is consistent with the opinions expressed (thirty years ago) by Gödel [20], [21]:

> *... besides mathematical intuition there exists another (though only probable) criterion of truth of mathematical axioms, namely their fruitfulness in mathematics, and one may add, possibly also in [4] physics... The simplest case of an application of the criterion under discussion arises when some ... axiom has number-theoretical consequences verifiable by computation up to any given integer.*

> *... axioms need not be evident in themselves, but rather their justification lies (exactly as in physics) in the fact that they make it possible for these "sense perceptions" to be deduced ... I think that ... this view has been largely justified by subsequent developments, and it is to be expected that it will be still more so in the future. It has turned out that the solution of certain arithmetical problems requires the use of assumptions essentially transcending arithmetic ... Of course, under these circumstances mathematics may lose a good deal of its "absolute certainty"; but, under the influence of the modern criticism of the foundations, this has already happened to a large extent ...*

The above discussion leads naturally to the question: How should one do Mathematics? According to Chaitin [10]

> *... elementary number theory and the rest of mathematics should be pursued more in the spirit of experimental science, and ... [one] should be willing to adopt new principles.*

A new tendency in (the Philosophy of) Mathematics called **Experimental Mathematics** is emerging.[38] The emphasis on observational and experimental is not a new idea in the history of Mathematics; the novelty comes from

---

[37]Note that the above assertion does not mean a "mandate for revolution, anarchy, and license".

[38]There are several journals using in their titles the adjective *experimental*, for instance, the *Journal of Experimental Mathematics*.

the way and scale of experiments. This is possible due to the advent of computers; for a detailed analysis see S. Marcus [29], [30]. We have computer proofs for Gödel Incompletenss Theorem (Ammon [1]), computer proofs in Number Theory (Andrews, Ekhand, Zeilberger [2]), computer proofs for identities (Ekhand, Tre [15]). Computers were used in one of the technical steps of Louis de Branges' proof of the Bieberbach conjecture. Franz Mertens, a contemporary of Riemann, proposed a conjecture that involves only naturals; if true, this conjecture would have provided strong evidence that Riemann Hypothesis was also true. Mertens' conjecture was tested and proven true for at least the first 10 billion of naturals. However, a much larger computation revealed in 1984 that for numbers of the order of magnitute of

$$10^{(10^{70})}$$

the pattern guessed by Mertens vanishes! Recently, Chaitin [11] showed that it is possible to write down executable programs (in C and *Mathematica*) that embody the constructions in the proofs of theorems in algorithmic information theory.

The utility of proofs in today, and, especially, tomorrow Mathematics is currently an object of debates, sometimes rather hectic (see, for instance, Horgan paper "The death of proof" [24], and one of the replies it generated, "The immortality of proof", by Kranz [26]). An important direction of this discussion is centered around the advent of a technique, developed by Lazlo Babai team, that offers not certainty, but only a statistical probability truth.

> *The philosophical cost of this efficient method is that we lose the absolute certainty of a Euclidean proof... But if you do have doubts, will you bet with me?*

says Babai.

Zeilberger [39], in a more radical attitude wrote about the **day after tomorrow**:

> *There are writings on the wall that, now that the silicon savior has arrived, a new testament is going to be written. Although there will always be a small group of "rigorous" old-style mathematicians (e.g. [16]* [39]*) who will insist that the true religion is theirs and that the computer is a false Messiah, they may be viewed by future mainstream mathematicians as a fringe set of harmless eccentrics, as mathematical physicists are viewed by regular physicists today. ...*

---

[39] Jaffe and Quinn distinguish between "Theoretical Mathematics" (referring to the speculative and intuitive work) and "Rigorous Mathematics" (the proof-oriented phase) in an attempt to build a framework assuring a positive role for speculation and experiment.

I speculate that ... [transparent proofs] will "trivialize" large parts of mathematics by reducing mathematical truths to routine, albeit possibly very long and exorbitantly expensive to check "proof certificates". These proof certificates would also enable us, by plugging in random values, to assert "probable truths" very cheaply.

I can envison an abstract of a paper, c. 2100, that reads, "We show in a certain precise sense that the Goldbach conjecture is true with probability larger than 0.99999 and that its complete truth could be determined with abudget of 10 billion".

We believe that there is a lot of exageration in saying that proofs are dead. *We will always need proofs! The problem is that sometimes we cannot afford them.*

References

1. K. Ammon, An automatic proof of Gödel's incompleteness theorem, *Artificial Intelligence*, 61 (1993), 291 – 306.

2. G. E. Andrews, S. B. Ekhand, D. Zeilberger, A short proof of Jacobi's formula for the number of representations of an integer as a sum of four squares, *Amer. Math. Monthly*, 100 (1993), 274 – 276.

3. D. W. Barnes, J. M. Mack, *An Algebraic Introduction to Mathematical Logic*, Springer-Verlag, New York, Heidelberg, Berlin, 1975.

4. J. L. Bell, A. B. Slomson, *Models and Ultraproducts: An Introduction*, North-Holland, Amsterdam, Oxford, New York, 3rd revised printing, 1974.

5. D. S. Bridges, *Computability – A Mathematical Sketchbook*, Springer-Verlag, Berlin, 1994.

6. D. S. Bridges, F. Richmanm, *Varieties of Constructive Mathematics*, Cambridge, University Press, Cambridge, 1987.

7. C. Calude, *Information and Randomness. An Algorithmic Perspective*, Springer-Verlag, Heidelberg, 1994.

8. C. Calude, H. Jürgensen, M. Zimand, Is independence an exception?, *Appl. Math. Comput.* (in press).

9. G. J. Chaitin, *Information-Theoretic Incompleteness*, World Scientific, Singapore, New Jersey, Hong Kong, 1992.

10. G. J. Chaitin, Randomness in arithmetic and the decline and fall of reductionism in pure mathematics, *EATCS Bull.*, 50 (1993), 314 – 328.

11. G. J. Chaitin, *The Limits of Mathematics – Course Outline & Software*, IBM Watson Center, Yorktown Heights, December 12, 1993.

12. A. Church, A note on the entscheidungsproblem, *J. Symbolic Logic*, 1 (1936), 40 – 41, 101 – 102.

13. P. J. Cohen, *Set Theory and the Continuum Hypothesis*, Benjamin, New York, 1966.

14. K. Devlin, Introduction to the column "Computers and Mathematics", *Notices Amer. Math. Soc.*, 39 (1992), 1065 – 1066.

15. S. B. Ekhand, S. Tre, A purely verification proof of the first Rogers - Ramanujan identity, *J. Combin. Theory*, Ser. A, 54 (1990), 309 – 311.

16. A. Jaffe, F. Quinn, "Theoretical mathematics": toward a cultural synthesis of mathematics and theoretical physics, *Bull. Amer. Math. Soc.*, 29 (1993), 1 – 13.

17. K. Gödel. Die Vollständigkeit der Axiome des logischen Funktionenkalkúlus, *Monatsh. Math. Phys.*, 37 (1930), 582 – 591.

18. K. Gödel, Über formal unenscheidbare Sätze der Principia Mathematica und verwandter Systeme I, *Monatsh. Math. Phys.*, 38 (1931), 173 – 198.

19. K. Gödel, *The Consistency of the Continuum Hypothesis*, Princeton University Press, Princeton, 1940.

20. K. Gödel, Russell's mathematical logic, in *Philosophy of Mathematics* (P. Benacerref, H. Putnam, eds.), Prentice-Hall, Englewood Cliffs, New Jersey, 1964, 211 – 232.

21. K. Gödel. What is Cantor's continuum problem ? in *Philosophy of Mathematics* (P. Benacerref, H. Putnam, eds.), Prentice-Hall, Englewood Cliffs, New Jersey, 1964, 258 – 273.

22. P. R. Halmos, *Lectures on Boolean Algebras*, Van Nostrand, New Jersey, 1963.

23. J. Herbrand, Sur la théorie de la démonstration, *C. R. Acad. Sci. Paris*, 126 (1928), 1274 – 1276.

24. J. Horkan, The death of proof, *Scientific American*, 269 (1993), 74 – 82.

25. L. Kalmár, Über die axiomatisierbarkeit des Aussagenkalkülus, *Acta Sci. Math. (Szeged)*, 7 (1934-5), 222 – 243.

26. S. G. Kranz, The immortality of proof, *Notices Amer. Math. Soc.*, 41 (1994), 10 – 13.

27. J. H. Lutz, Almost everywhere high nonuniform complexity, *J. Comput. System Sci.*, 44 (1992), 220 – 258.

28. J. H. Lutz, The quantitative structure of exponential time, *Proceedings of the Eighth Annual Structure in Complexity Theory Conference*, (San Diego, CA, May 18–21, 1993), IEEE Computer Society Press, 1993, 158 – 175.

29. S. Marcus, *The Mathematical Shock*, Albatros Publ. House, Bucharest, 1987 (in Romanian).

30. S. Marcus, *Controversies in Science and Engineering*, Technical Publ. House, Bucharest, 1990 (in Romanian).

31. G. L. Miller, Riemann's hypothesis and tests of primality, *J. Comput. System Sci.*, 13(1976), 300 – 317.

32. P. Odifreddi, *La prova di dio*, manuscript, January 1994.

33. P. Odifreddi, *Ultrafiltri, dittatori e dei*, manuscript, January 1994.

34. E. Post. Introduction to a general theory of elementary propositions, *Amer. J. Math.*, 43 (1921), 1963 – 1985.

35. V. Pratt, Every prime has a succinct certificate, *SIAM J. Comput.*, 4(1975), 214-220.

36. H. Rasiowa, R. Sikorski, A proof of the completeness theorem of Gödel, *Fund. Math.*, 37 (1951), 193 – 200.

37. G. Rozenberg, A. Salomaa, *Cornerstones of Undecidability*, Prentice-Hall, 1994.

38. A. Salomaa, *Public-Key Cryptography*, Springer-Verlag, Berlin, 1990.

39. D. Zeilberger, Theorems for a price: Tomorrow's semi-rigorous mathematical culture, *Notices Amer. Math. Soc.*, 40 (1993), 878 – 891.

40. M. Zimand, If not empty, $NP \backslash P$ is topologically large, *Theoret. Comput. Sci.*, 119 (1993), 293 – 310.

41. N. Wiener, *God and Golem*, MIT Press, Cambridge, Ma., 1064.

Feedback, Iteration, and Repetition[1]

Virgil Emil CĂZĂNESCU
Faculty of Mathematics, University of Bucharest
Str. Academiei 14, 70109 Bucureşti, Romania

Gheorghe ŞTEFĂNESCU
Institute of Mathematics, Romanian Academy of Sciences
P.O. Box 1-764, 70700 Bucureşti, Romania

Abstract. This paper provides a comparison of three looping operations: Kleene's repetition ('star'), Elgot's iteration ('dagger') and feedback ('uparrow'). The comparison is based on an algebraic study of an algebra for flowgraphs (this is a generic name for digraph models like: automata, nets, flowchart schemes, etc.), called *biflow*. Equivalent presentations of biflows and biflows over algebraic or matrix theories are given using these operations. Finally, there are given extensions of these algebras to cope with axiomatisations of the regular languages and regular trees.

1. Introduction

Different characterizations of regular languages were given in the early book of Marcus, [14]. Here we deal with algebraic presentations of regular languages, regular trees and flowgraphs (automata, nets, flowchart schemes, etc.).

In order to get an algebraic theory of computation one needs an axiomatic looping operation. This may be Kleene's repetition (cf. [3], for example), Elgot's iteration [8] or feedback [15], [18]. The proper acyclic context for repetition seems to be a matrix theory (such a theory is equivalent with the theory of matrices over a semiring [9]), for iteration an algebric theory in the sense of Lawvere and for feedback a (symmetric) strict monoidal category in the sense of MacLane [13].

The equational axioms for the looping operation are not easily codified. A *regular algebra* cf. Conway [3] is a structure which satisfies all the identities (written in terms of union, composition, repetition and constants 0,1) which

---

[1] This paper was written in 1988 [5]. We have inserted here a few footnotes and references to update the relationship of the results in this paper to other ones that have appeared in the meantime.

are valid in the algebras of regular events. The theory of matrices over a regular algebra is a matrix theory, but the axioms for repetition are yet unknown.[2] This algebra is intended as a model for the input-output behaviour of nondeterministic computation.

An *iteration theory* cf. Bloom, Elgot anf Wright [2] is a structure which satisfies all the identities (written in terms of tupling, composition, iteration and constants $I_a, 0_a, \pi_i^a$) which are valid in the theories of regular trees. The axiomatisation for iteration theories was found by Esik [10]. An iteration theory is an algebraic theory in which an iteration operation is given and satisfies certain axioms. This algebra is intended as a model for the input behaviour of deterministic computation (we use the name 'input behaviour' insted of the 'strong behaviour' name used by Elgot).

A *biflow* (or *aα-flow*) is a structure which satisfies all the identities (written in terms of separated sum, composition, feedback and constants $I_a, {}^a X^b$) which are valid in the algebras of flowchart schemes. An axiomatisation for biflows is given in [18], [4]. A biflow is a symmetric strict monoidal category in which a feedback operation is given and satisfies certain axioms. This model is more related with the algorithms themselves than with their behaviours.

It is well known that we have some natural inclusions

> matrix theories $\subseteq$ algebraic theories $\subseteq$ (symmetric) strict monoidal categories

and the inclusions are strict. It is also known that

> matrix theories of regular algebras $\subseteq$ iteration theories over matrix theories $\subseteq$ biflows over matrix theories

and

> iteration theories $\subseteq$ biflows over algebraic theories

(It seems likely that one can prove that the above inclusions are strict, –this was proved by Esik for the latter case.)

The aim of this paper is to give a translation between iteration and feedback operations. (Another one was previously given in [15], [4].) Via this translation the axioms of iteration in an axiomatic system for biflows over algebraic theories (previously called 'algebraic theories with iterate') are translated in terms of feedback one-by-one.

---

[2]In the meantime Krob [12] published proofs of two conjectures of Conways describing equational axiomatisations of regular algebras. Independently, Bloom and Esik in [1] gave another equational axiomatisation more closed to the axiom systems presented in this paper (i.e., they use the axioms of biflows over matrix theories completed with a weaker equational version of functoriality of finite relations).

When we combine the present translation with the translation between iteration and repetition operations given in [15], [17] we get an easy and natural translation between feedback, iteration and repetition operations. This is used to give certain axiomatic systems for biflows over algebraic and matrix theories. More importantly, this translation is used in the concluding remarks to emphasize some new advantages of the use of feedback over the use of iteration or repetition than those initially given in [18].

2. Biflows and biflows over algebraic or matrix theories

We assume the reader is familiar with the calculus of symmetric strict monoidal categories (cf. [13], [7], for example), algebraic theories (cf. [8], [7]) and matrix theories (cf. [9], [7]).

TABLE 1.

B1	$(f \cdot g) \cdot h = f \cdot (g \cdot h)$	B2	$\mathsf{I}_a \cdot f = f = f \cdot \mathsf{I}_b$
B3	$(f + g) + h = f + (g + h)$	B4	$\mathsf{I}_0 + f = f = f + \mathsf{I}_0$
B5	$\mathsf{I}_a + \mathsf{I}_b = \mathsf{I}_{a+b}$	B6	$(f + g) \cdot (u + v) = f \cdot u + g \cdot v$
			for $a \xrightarrow{f} b \xrightarrow{u} c,\ a' \xrightarrow{g} b' \xrightarrow{v} c'$
B7	${}^a\mathsf{X}^b \cdot {}^b\mathsf{X}^a = \mathsf{I}_{a+b}$	B8	${}^a\mathsf{X}^0 = \mathsf{I}_u$
B9	${}^a\mathsf{X}^{b+c} = ({}^a\mathsf{X}^b + \mathsf{I}_c) \cdot (\mathsf{I}_b + {}^a\mathsf{X}^c)$	B10	$(f + g) \cdot {}^b\mathsf{X}^d = {}^a\mathsf{X}^c \cdot (g + f)$
			for $f : a \to b, g : c \to d$
B11	$\mathsf{T}_0 = \mathsf{I}_0$	B12	$\mathsf{T}_a \cdot f = \mathsf{T}_b$
B13	$\vee_a \cdot f = (f + f) \cdot \vee_b$	B14	$\mathsf{I}_{a+b} = (\mathsf{I}_a + \mathsf{T}_{b+a} + \mathsf{I}_b) \cdot \vee_{a+b}$
B15	$\perp^0 = \mathsf{I}_0$	B16	$f \cdot \perp^b = \perp^a$
B17	$f \cdot \wedge^b = \wedge^a \cdot (f + f)$	B18	$\wedge^{a+b} \cdot (\mathsf{I}_a + \perp^{a+b} + \mathsf{I}_b) = \mathsf{I}_{a+b}$

Let us consider a category $(T, \cdot, \mathsf{I}_a)$ having as objects the elements of a monoid $(M, +, 0)$. That is, the composition satisfies B1 and B2 in Table 1. The application of a function f to an element x is written xf and the composite of $f : A \to B$ and $g : B \to C$ is written in the diagramatic order $f \cdot g$ (or fg).

A category as above is a *strict monoidal category* (*smc*, for short) if a sum $+ : T(a, b) \times T(c, d) \to T(a + c, b + d)$ is given which obeys axioms B3–B6. An smc is a *symmetric strict monoidal category* (*ssmc*, for short) if some constants ${}^a\mathsf{X}^b \in T(a + b, b + a)$ are given that obey the axioms B7–B10.

A symmetric strict monoidal category T is an *algebraic theory* if some constants $\mathsf{T}_a \in T(0, a)$ and $\vee_a \in T(a + a, a)$ are given that obey the axioms

B11–B14. In an algebraic theory, defined as above, a tupling operation $\langle\,,\,\rangle$: $T(a,c) \times T(b,c) \to T(a+b,c)$ and some constants denoted $\langle a,b,c\rangle \in T(b,a+b+c)$ may be introduced as follows

$$\langle f,g\rangle = (f+g) \cdot \vee_c \qquad \langle a,b,c\rangle = \top_a + I_b + \top_c$$

An algebraic theory may equivalently be introduced as a category T as above in which a tupling $\langle\,,\,\rangle$ and some constants $\langle a,b,c\rangle$ are given fulfilling the axioms T1–T3 below.

T1 $\langle 0,a,0\rangle = I_a$;

T2 $\langle a,b,c\rangle \cdot \langle d,a+b+c,e\rangle = \langle d+a,b,c+e\rangle$;

T3   for every $f \in T(a,c)$ and $g \in T(b,c)$ the morphism $\langle f,g\rangle$ is the unique $h \in T(a+b,c)$ such that $\langle 0,a,b\rangle \cdot h = f$ and $\langle a,b,0\rangle \cdot h = g$.

It follows that $T(0,a)$ contains a unique element, denoted $\top_a$. In a such defined algebraic theory the sum of $f : a \to b$ and $g : c \to d$ is $\langle f \cdot \langle 0,b,d\rangle,\ g \cdot \langle b,d,0\rangle\rangle$ and $\vee_a = \langle I_a, I_a\rangle$. We mention that every algebraic theory is an ssmc, where ${}^a\mathsf{X}^b = \langle\langle b,a,0\rangle, \langle 0,b,a\rangle\rangle$.

An algebraic theory T is a *matrix theory* if some constants $\bot^a \in T(a,0)$ and $\wedge^a \in T(a,a+a)$ are given fulfilling the axioms B15–B18. In a matrix theory T, defined as above, a target-tupling $[\,,\,] : T(a,b) \times T(a,c) \to T(a,b+c)$ and some constants $[a,b,c] \in T(a+b+c,b)$ may be introduced as follows

$$[f,g] = \wedge^a \cdot (f+g) \qquad [a,b,c] = \bot^a + I_b + \bot^c$$

In a matrix theory T we may also define a union operation $\cup : T(a,b) \times T(a,b) \to T(a,b)$ and some constants $0_b^a \in T(a,b)$ as follows

$$f \cup g = \wedge^a \cdot (f+g) \cdot \vee_b \qquad 0_b^a = \bot^a \cdot \top_b$$

and a matrix-building operation which maps a quadruple of morphisms $f : a \to c, g : a \to d, h : b \to c$ and $i : b \to d$ into $\begin{bmatrix} f & g \\ h & i \end{bmatrix} \in T(a+b,c+d)$ defined to be either

$$\langle [f,g],[h,i]\rangle \quad \text{or} \quad [\langle f,h\rangle,\langle g,i\rangle]$$

In a matrix theory, for any four objects a,b,c and d, there is a unique way to write any morphism j in $T(a+b,c+d)$ as $j = \begin{bmatrix} f & g \\ h & i \end{bmatrix}$ with f,g,h and i as above. It follow that $(T(a,a),\cup,\cdot,0_a^a,I_a)$ is a semiring. Actually, a matrix theory over the monoid of natural numbers may also be presented as the theory of matrices over a semiring, see [9].

Let us consider the following axiomatic systems F1–F2, I1–I4 and R1–R3 given in Table 2.[3] The price we have to pay is the complication of the axioms that replace functoriality and of the corresponding proofs.

- Suppose T is a symmetric strict monoidal category. Let $\uparrow^a \_\_ : T(a+b, a+c) \to T(b,c)$, for any a, b and c objects in T be a 'feedback operation' (the result is written: $\uparrow^a f$). (Actually, this is a 'family' of feedback operations indexed by a, b, c. Similar comments apply to iteration and repetition to be introduced below.) We consider several requirements on this operation: F1 consists of the following 7 axioms $F1_1$–$F1_7$ and F2 of the axioms $F2_1$–$F2_5$.

- Suppose that T is an algebraic theory. Let $\dagger : T(a, a+b) \to T(a, b)$, for any a and b objects in T, be an 'iteration operation' (the result is written: $f^\dagger$). Four systems of equations involving iteration I1–I4 are given below.

- Finally, suppose that T is a matrix theory. Let $* : T(a, a) \to T(a, a)$, for any object a in T, be a 'repetition operation' (the result is written: f^*). R1–R3 below are three systems of equations involving this operation.

A morphism $y : a \to b$ is called

- $\uparrow$-*functorial* if for every $f : a + c \to a + d$ and $g : b + c \to b + d$ the equality $f \cdot (y + I_d) = (y + I_c) \cdot g$ implies $\uparrow^a f = \uparrow^b g$;

- $\dagger$-*functorial* if for every $f : a \to a + c$ and $g : b \to b + c$ the equality $f \cdot (y + I_c) = y \cdot g$ implies $f^\dagger = y \cdot g^\dagger$;

- $*$-*functorial* if for every $f : a \to a$ and $g : b \to b$ the equality $f \cdot y = y \cdot g$ implies $f^* \cdot y = y \cdot g^*$;

---

[3] The interest in these axiom systems comes from the following results.

- **Axiomatisation of flowgraphs** [18], [4], [19]: The axioms of biflows (B1–B10 + $F1_1$–$F1_7$) give a correct and complete axiomatisation for flowgraphs (i.e., automata, nets, flowchart schemes, etc.) over bijections. Adding axiomatisations of certain classes of relations as in [7], [19] we get axiomatisations for various classes of deterministic and nondeterministic flowgraphs.

- **Axiomatisation of the input behaviour (regular trees)** [16]: The axioms for biflows over algebraic theories completed with the condition that all finite functions be functorial give a correct and complete axiomatisation for the input behaviour.

- **Axiomatisation of the input-output behaviour (regular events)** [17], [19]: The axioms for biflows over matrix theories completed with the demand that all finite relations be functorial give a correct and complete axiomatisation for the input-output behaviour.

The last two types of results may be refined to get 'equational axiomatisations' as in [10], [12], [1]

TABLE 2.

$F1_1$ $\quad \uparrow^a ({}^a\mathsf{X}^a) = \mathsf{I}_a$	$F2_1$ $\quad \uparrow^a ({}^a\mathsf{X}^a \cdot (\mathsf{I}_a + f)) = f$
$F1_2$ $\quad \uparrow^b \uparrow^a f = \uparrow^{a+b} f$	$F2_2$ $\quad \uparrow^b \uparrow^a f = \uparrow^{a+b} f$
$F1_3$ $\quad \uparrow^{a+b} (({}^a\mathsf{X}^b + \mathsf{I}_c) \cdot f \cdot ({}^b\mathsf{X}^a + \mathsf{I}_d)) = \;\; = \uparrow^{b+a} f$	$F2_3$ $\quad \uparrow^{a+b} (({}^a\mathsf{X}^b + \mathsf{I}_c) \cdot f \cdot ({}^b\mathsf{X}^a + \mathsf{I}_d)) = \;\; = \uparrow^{b+a} f$
$F1_4$ $\quad (\uparrow^a f) \cdot g = \uparrow^a (f \cdot (\mathsf{I}_a + g))$	$F2_4$ $\quad \uparrow^a (f + \mathsf{T}_d) = \uparrow^a f + \mathsf{T}_d$
$F1_5$ $\quad g \cdot (\uparrow^a f) = \uparrow^a ((\mathsf{I}_a + g) \cdot f)$	$F2_5$ $\quad \uparrow^a \langle f, g \rangle = g \cdot \langle \uparrow^a \langle f, \mathsf{I}_a + \mathsf{T}_c \rangle, \mathsf{I}_c \rangle$
$F1_6$ $\quad \uparrow^a f + g = \uparrow^a (f + g)$	$\qquad$ for $f : a \to a + c, g : b \to a + c$
$F1_7$ $\quad \uparrow^a \mathsf{I}_a = \mathsf{I}_0$	

$I1_1$ $\quad (f \cdot (\vee_a + \mathsf{I}_b))^\dagger = f^{\dagger\dagger}$	$I2_1$ $\quad f \cdot \langle f^\dagger, \mathsf{I}_b \rangle = f^\dagger$
$I1_2$ $\quad (f \cdot (g + \mathsf{I}_c))^\dagger = f \cdot \langle (g \cdot f)^\dagger, \mathsf{I}_c \rangle$	$I2_2$ $\quad (f \cdot (\vee_a + \mathsf{I}_b))^\dagger = f^{\dagger\dagger}$
$\qquad$ for $f : a \to b + c, g : b \to a$	$I2_3$ $\quad g \cdot (f \cdot (g + \mathsf{I}_c))^\dagger = (g \cdot f)^\dagger$
$I1_3$ $\quad (f \cdot (\mathsf{I}_a + g))^\dagger = f^\dagger \cdot g$	$\qquad$ for $f : a \to b + c, g : b \to a$
	$I2_4$ $\quad (f \cdot (\mathsf{I}_a + g))^\dagger = f^\dagger \cdot g$

$I3_1$ $\quad (\mathsf{T}_a + \mathsf{I}_a)^\dagger = \mathsf{I}_a$	$I4_1$ $\quad (\mathsf{T}_a + f)^\dagger = f$
$I3_2$ $\quad \langle f, g \rangle^\dagger = \langle f^\dagger \cdot \langle h, \mathsf{I}_c \rangle, h \rangle$	$I4_2$ $\quad \langle f, g \rangle^\dagger = \langle f^\dagger \cdot \langle h, \mathsf{I}_c \rangle, h \rangle$
$\qquad$ where $h = (g \cdot \langle f^\dagger, \mathsf{I}_{b+c} \rangle)^\dagger$	$\qquad$ where $h = (g \cdot \langle f^\dagger, \mathsf{I}_{b+c} \rangle)^\dagger$
$I3_3$ $\quad ({}^a\mathsf{X}^b \cdot f \cdot ({}^b\mathsf{X}^a + \mathsf{I}_c))^\dagger = {}^a\mathsf{X}^b \cdot f^\dagger$	$I4_3$ $\quad ({}^a\mathsf{X}^b \cdot f \cdot ({}^b\mathsf{X}^a + \mathsf{I}_c))^\dagger = {}^a\mathsf{X}^b \cdot f^\dagger$
$I3_4$ $\quad (f \cdot (\mathsf{I}_a + g))^\dagger = f^\dagger \cdot g$	$I4_4$ $\quad (f + \mathsf{T}_c)^\dagger = f^\dagger + \mathsf{T}_c$

$R1_1$ $\quad (f \cup g)^* = (f^* \cdot g)^* \cdot f^*$	$R2_1$ $\quad f^* = \mathsf{I}_a \cup f \cdot f^*$
$R1_2$ $\quad (f \cdot g)^* = \mathsf{I}_a \cup f \cdot (g \cdot f)^* \cdot g$	$R2_2$ $\quad (f \cup g)^* = (f^* \cdot g)^* \cdot f^*$
	$R2_3$ $\quad (f \cdot g)^* \cdot f = f \cdot (g \cdot f)^*$

$R3_1$ $\quad (0_a^a)^* = \mathsf{I}_a$	
$R3_2$ $\quad \begin{bmatrix} f & g \\ h & i \end{bmatrix}^* = \begin{bmatrix} x & y \\ z & w \end{bmatrix}$	
$\qquad$ where $w = (h \cdot f^* \cdot g \cup i)^*$	
$\qquad$ and $x = f^* \cup f^* \cdot g \cdot w \cdot h \cdot f^*$	
$\qquad\qquad y = f^* \cdot g \cdot w$	
$\qquad\qquad z = w \cdot h \cdot f^*$	
$R3_3$ $\quad ({}^a\mathsf{X}^b \cdot f \cdot {}^b\mathsf{X}^a)^* = {}^a\mathsf{X}^b \cdot f^* \cdot {}^b\mathsf{X}^a$	

A *biflow* is by definition an ssmc in which a feedback is given fulfilling the axioms $F1_1$–$F1_7$. A *biflow over an algebraic theory* (resp. *over a matrix theory*) is an algebraic theory (resp. a matrix theory) considered with the natural structure of ssmc and in which a feedback is given fulfilling the axioms $F1_1$–$F1_7$.

Proposition 1. *Suppose T is an algebraic theory with a given iteration operation. Then the four axiomatic systems* I1, I2, I3 *and* I4 *are equivalent.*

3. Iteration and feedback in algebraic theories

Let T be an algebraic theory and let $\mathbf{It}(T)$ (resp. $\mathbf{Fd}(T)$) be the set of all iteration operations (resp. feedback operations) defined on T. We define two functions

$$\alpha : \mathbf{Fd}(T) \to \mathbf{It}(T) \quad \text{and} \quad \beta : \mathbf{It}(T) \to \mathbf{Fd}(T)$$

as follows

- $\uparrow\!\alpha$ is the iteration operation that maps an $f \in T(a, a + b)$ into $\uparrow^a \langle f, I_a + \top_b \rangle$;

- $\dagger\!\beta$ is the feedback operation that for a, b and c objects in T maps $f = \langle f_1, f_2 \rangle \in T(a + b, a + c)$, with $f_1 : a \to a + c$ and $f_2 : b \to a + c$, into $f_2 \langle f_1^\dagger, I_c \rangle$.

Let

- $\mathbf{Fd}_r(T)$ (resp. $\mathbf{Fd}_i(T)$) be the subset of all the feedback operations in $\mathbf{Fd}(T)$ that obey the axioms $F1_4$–$F1_6$ (resp. $F2_5$) and

- $\mathbf{It}_r(T)$ be the subset of all the iteration operations in $\mathbf{It}(T)$ that obey the axiom $I3_4$.

Finally, let us consider the restrictions

$$\alpha_r . \mathbf{Fd}_r(T) \to \mathbf{It}_r(T) \text{ and } \beta_r : \mathbf{It}_r(T) \to \mathbf{Fd}_r(T)$$

and

$$\alpha_i : \mathbf{Fd}_i(T) \to \mathbf{It}(T) \text{ and } \beta_i : \mathbf{It}(T) \to \mathbf{Fd}_i(T)$$

Theorem 2. *Suppose T is an algebraic theory. Then:*
a) The restrictions $\alpha_i, \beta_i, \alpha_r$ and β_r are (totally defined) bijective functions. Moreover, α_i is the inverse of β_i and α_r of β_r.
b) For $k \in [4]$, $\dagger$ satisfies $I4_k$ iff $\dagger\beta$ satisfies $F2_k$.
c) For $k \in [4]$, $\dagger$ satisfies $I3_k$ iff $\dagger\beta$ satisfies $F1_k$.
d) y is $\dagger$-functorial iff y is $\dagger\beta$-functorial.

Corollary. *For an algebraic theory with an iteration or a feedback operation, the axiomatic systems F1, F2, I1, I2, I3 and I4 are equivalent.*

4. Repetition, iteration and feedback in matrix theories

Let T be a matrix theory and $\mathbf{Rp}(T)$ be the set of all the repetition operations defined on T. We use the translations in [17]

$$\sigma : \mathbf{It}(T) \to \mathbf{Rp}(T) \quad \text{and} \quad \tau : \mathbf{Rp}(T) \to \mathbf{It}(T)$$

defined by

- $\dagger\sigma$ is the repetition operation that for an object a in T maps $f \in T(a,a)$ into $[f, \mathsf{I}_a]^\dagger$; and

- $*\tau$ is the iteration operation that for a and b objects in T maps $f = [f_1, f_2] \in T(a, a+b)$, with $f_1 : a \to a$ and $f_2 : a \to b$, into $f_1^* \cdot f_2$.

Finally, let us consider the restrictions

$$\sigma_r : \mathbf{It}_r(T) \to \mathbf{Rp}(T) \text{ and } \tau_r : \mathbf{Rp}(T) \to \mathbf{It}_r(T)$$

induced by σ and τ.

Theorem 4. *Suppose T is a matrix theory. Then:*
a) The restrictions σ_r and τ_r are (totally defined) bijective functions. Moreover, σ_r is the inverse of τ_r.
b) For $k \in [3]$, $*$ satisfies R3$_k$ iff $*\tau$ satisfies I3$_k$.
c) For $k \in [3]$, $*$ satisfies R2$_k$ iff $*\tau$ satisfies I2$_k$.
d) For $k \in [2]$, $*$ satisfies R1$_k$ iff $*\tau$ satisfies I1$_k$.
e) y is $*$-functorial iff y is $*\tau$-functorial.

Corollary. *a) The restrictions $\alpha_r \cdot \sigma_r$ and $\tau_r \cdot \beta_r$ are (totally defined) bijective functions. Moreover, $\alpha_r \cdot \sigma_r$ is the inverse of $\tau_r \cdot \beta_r$.*
b) For $k \in [3]$, $*$ satisfies R3$_k$ iff $*\tau\beta$ satisfies F1$_k$.
c) y is $*$-functorial iff y is $*\tau\beta$-functorial.

Corollary. *For a matrix theory with a repetition, an iteration or a feedback operation, the axiomatic systems F1, F2, I1, I2, I3, I4, R1, R2 and R3 are equivalent.*

5. Proofs

Proof of Proposition 1:

(I1 $\Leftrightarrow$ I2)

It is easy to see that I1 and I2 are equivalent.

Indeed, $I1_2$ for $g = I_a$ gives $I2_1$; moreover, by $I1_2$ and $I2_1$ we get

$$
\begin{aligned}
g(f(g + I_c))^\dagger &= gf\langle (gf)^\dagger, I_c\rangle \\
&= (gf)^\dagger
\end{aligned}
$$

hence $I1_2$ also implies $I2_3$.

The converse implication '$I2_1 + I2_3$ implies $I1_2$' follows using $I2_1$ and $I2_3$ in

$$
\begin{aligned}
(f(g + I_c))^\dagger &= f(g + I_c)\langle (f(g + I_c))^\dagger, I_c\rangle \\
&= f\langle g(f(g + I_c))^\dagger, I_c\rangle \\
&= f\langle (gf)^\dagger, I_c\rangle
\end{aligned}
$$

(I3 $\Leftrightarrow$ I4) First, $I3_1$ and $I3_4$ imply $I4_1$ and $I3_4$ implies $I4_4$. Hence I3 implies I4.

For the converse, first note that $I4_1$ implies $I3_1$. Then as in [11] we prove that $I3_4$ follows from I4.

Indeed, assume $f : a \to a + b$ and $g : b \to c$. Then using $I4_1$

$$
\begin{aligned}
((\mathsf{T}_{a+b} + g)\langle (f + \mathsf{T}_c)^\dagger, I_{b+c}\rangle)^\dagger &= (\mathsf{T}_b + g)^\dagger \\
&= g
\end{aligned}
$$

and using $I4_2$ we get

$$
\begin{aligned}
\langle f + \mathsf{T}_c, \mathsf{T}_{a+b} + g\rangle^\dagger &= \langle (f + \mathsf{T}_c)^\dagger \langle g, I_c\rangle, g\rangle \\
&= \langle f^\dagger g, g\rangle
\end{aligned}
$$

Using $I4_3$ we get

$$
\langle f + \mathsf{T}_o, \mathsf{T}_{a+b} + g\rangle^\dagger = {}^a\mathsf{X}^b\langle \mathsf{T}_{b+a} + g, f^a\mathsf{X}^b + \mathsf{T}_c\rangle^\dagger.
$$

As $(\mathsf{T}_{b+a} + g)^\dagger = \mathsf{T}_a + g$ and

$$
\begin{aligned}
(f^a\mathsf{X}^b + \mathsf{T}_c)\langle \mathsf{T}_a + g, I_{a+c}\rangle &= f\langle I_a + \mathsf{T}_c, \mathsf{T}_a + g\rangle \\
&= f(I_a + g)
\end{aligned}
$$

using $I4_2$ we get

$$
\begin{aligned}
\langle f^\dagger g, g\rangle &= {}^a\mathsf{X}^b\langle (\mathsf{T}_a + g)\langle (f(I_a + g))^\dagger, I_c\rangle, (f(I_a + g))^\dagger\rangle \\
&= \langle (f(I_a + g))^\dagger, g\rangle
\end{aligned}
$$

hence $I3_4$ holds. Consequently $I3$ and $I4$ are equivalent.

(I1 $\Rightarrow$ I3) In the next proof of $I3$ from $I1$ we also use $I2$. As $I2_1$ implies $I3_1$ and $I2_3$ implies $I3_3$ we only need to include from [16] a proof of $I3_2$:

$$\begin{aligned}
\langle f,g\rangle^\dagger &= (\langle f,g\rangle(I_a + T_{b+a} + I_{b+c})(\vee_{a+b} + I_c))^\dagger && \text{using } I1_1 \\
&= (\langle f,g\rangle(I_a + T_b + I_{b+c})(I_{a+b} + T_a + I_{b+c}))^{\dagger\dagger} && \text{using } I1_3 \\
&= ((\langle f,g\rangle((I_a + T_b) + I_{b+c}))^\dagger(T_a + I_{b+c}))^\dagger && \text{using } I1_2 \\
&= (\langle f,g\rangle(((I_a + T_b)\langle f,g\rangle)^\dagger, I_{b+c})(T_a + I_{b+c}))^\dagger \\
&= (\langle f\langle f^\dagger, I_{b+c}\rangle, g\langle f^\dagger, I_{b+c}\rangle\rangle(T_a + I_{b+c}))^\dagger && \text{using } I2_1 \\
&= (\langle f^\dagger, g\langle f^\dagger, I_{b+c}\rangle\rangle((T_a + I_b) + I_c))^\dagger && \text{using } I1_2 \\
&= \langle f^\dagger, g\langle f^\dagger, I_{b+c}\rangle\rangle\langle((T_a + I_b)\langle f^\dagger, g\langle f^\dagger, I_{b+c}\rangle\rangle)^\dagger, I_c\rangle \\
&= \langle f^\dagger, g\langle f^\dagger, I_{b+c}\rangle\rangle\langle(g\langle f^\dagger, I_{b+c}\rangle)^\dagger, I_c\rangle && \text{using } I2_1 \\
&= \langle f^\dagger\langle(g\langle f^\dagger, I_{b+c}\rangle)^\dagger, I_c\rangle, (g\langle f^\dagger, I_{b+c}\rangle)^\dagger\rangle
\end{aligned}$$

(I3 $\Rightarrow$ I1) As $I3$ and $I4$ are equivalent we shall use axioms from $I4$, too. First, for every $g : b \to a$ and $v : a \to a + b + c$ we show that

$$v^\dagger\langle(gv^\dagger)^\dagger, I_c\rangle = (v(\langle I_a, g\rangle + I_c))^\dagger \tag{0.1}$$

$$(gv^\dagger)^\dagger = g(v(\langle I_a, g\rangle + I_c))^\dagger \tag{0.2}$$

As $((g + T_{b+c})\langle v^\dagger, I_{b+c}\rangle)^\dagger = (gv^\dagger)^\dagger$ using $I3_2$ it follows that

$$\langle v, g + T_{b+c}\rangle^\dagger = \langle v^\dagger\langle(gv^\dagger)^\dagger, I_c\rangle, (gv^\dagger)^\dagger\rangle$$

On the other hand, using $I3_3$ we get

$$\langle v, g + T_{b+c}\rangle^\dagger = {}^aX^b\langle T_b + g + T_c, v({}^aX^b + I_c)\rangle^\dagger.$$

As $(T_b + g + T_c)^\dagger = g + T_c$ and $v({}^aX^b + I_c)\langle g + T_c, I_{a+c}\rangle = v(\langle I_a, g\rangle + I_c)$ using $I3_2$ we get

$$\langle v, g + T_{b+c}\rangle^\dagger = {}^aX^b\langle(g + T_c)\langle(v(\langle I_a, g\rangle + I_c))^\dagger, I_c\rangle, (v(\langle I_a, g\rangle + I_c))^\dagger\rangle$$

therefore

$$\langle v^\dagger\langle(gv^\dagger)^\dagger, I_c\rangle, (gv^\dagger)^\dagger\rangle = \langle(v(\langle I_a, g\rangle + I_c))^\dagger, g(v(\langle I_a, g\rangle + I_c))^\dagger\rangle$$

hence we get (1) and (2).

From (1) for $v := T_a + f$ where $f : a \to b + c$ we get $I1_2$ and from (2) for $v := f : a \to a + a + b$ and $g := I_a$ we get $I1_1$.

Proof of Theorem 2:

a) Note that $\uparrow := \dagger\beta$ satisfies $F2_5$; indeed,

$$
\begin{aligned}
g\langle \uparrow^a \langle f, l_a + \top_c \rangle, l_c \rangle
&= g\langle (l_a + \top_c)\langle f^\dagger, l_c \rangle, l_c \rangle \\
&= g\langle f^\dagger, l_c \rangle \\
&= \uparrow^a \langle f, g \rangle
\end{aligned}
$$

Consequently β_i is totally defined.

Obviously $\dagger = \dagger\beta\alpha$. For the converse, note that $(\uparrow \alpha\beta)^a$ maps $\langle f_1, f_2 \rangle \in T(a+b, a+c)$ (with $f_1 : a \to a+c$ and $f_2 : b \to a+c$) in $f_2\langle \uparrow^a \langle f_1, l_a + \top_c \rangle, l_c \rangle$. Hence $\uparrow = \uparrow \alpha\beta$ for a $\uparrow \in \mathbf{Fd}_i(T)$.

For the second restriction, note that $\dagger$ satisfies $I3_4$ iff $\uparrow := \dagger\beta$ satisfies $F1_4$. Indeed, $\uparrow$ satisfies $F1_4$ iff for every $f = \langle f_1, f_2 \rangle : a+b \to a+c$ (with $f_1 : a \to a+c$ and $f_2 : b \to a+c$) and $g : c \to d$ the term

$$
(\uparrow^a f)g = f_2\langle f_1^\dagger, l_c \rangle g = f_2\langle f_1^\dagger g, g \rangle
$$

is equal to

$$
\begin{aligned}
\uparrow^a (f(l_a + g))
&= \uparrow^a \langle f_1(l_a + g), f_2(l_a + g) \rangle \\
&= f_2(l_a + g)\langle (f_1(l_a + g))^\dagger, l_d \rangle \\
&= f_2\langle (f_1(l_a + g))^\dagger, g \rangle
\end{aligned}
$$

Consequently if an $\dagger$ satisfies $I3_4$, then the corresponding $\uparrow$ satisfies $F1_4$ and if an $\uparrow$ satisfies $F1_4$, then using $l_a + \top_c$ for f_2 above we conclude that the corresponding $\dagger$ satisfies $I3_4$. Hence we have got a bijective correspondence between $\mathbf{It}_r(T)$ and the subset of all the feedbacks in $\mathbf{Fd}(T)$ that satisfies $F2_5 + F1_4$.

The conclusion follows if we show that $F2_5 + F1_4$ is equivalent to $F1_{4-6}$. This equivalence may be proved as follows:

- $F2_5$ implies $F1_5$:

    If $f = \langle f_1, f_2 \rangle : a + b \to a + c$ (with $f_1 : a \to a + c$ and $f_2 : b \to a + c$) and $g : d \to b$, then by a double application of $F2_5$ we get

$$
\begin{aligned}
\uparrow^a ((l_a + g)f)
&= \uparrow^a \langle f_1, gf_2 \rangle \\
&= gf_2\langle \uparrow^a \langle f_1, l_a + \top_c \rangle, l_c \rangle \\
&= g \cdot \uparrow^a \langle f_1, f_2 \rangle \\
&= g \cdot \uparrow^a f
\end{aligned}
$$

- $F2_5 + F1_4$ implies $F1_6$:

If $f = \langle f_1, f_2 \rangle : a + b \to a + c$ (with $f_1 : a \to a + c$ and $f_2 : b \to a + c$) and $g : d \to e$, then using in turn F2$_5$, F1$_4$ and again F2$_5$ we get

$$
\begin{aligned}
\uparrow^a (f + g) &= \uparrow^a \langle f_1 + \mathsf{T}_e, f_2 + g \rangle \\
&= (f_2 + g)\langle \uparrow^a \langle f_1 + \mathsf{T}_e, \mathsf{l}_a + \mathsf{T}_{c+e} \rangle, \mathsf{l}_{c+e} \rangle \\
&= (f_2 + g)\langle \uparrow^a \langle f_1, \mathsf{l}_a + \mathsf{T}_c \rangle + \mathsf{T}_e, \mathsf{l}_{c+e} \rangle \\
&= (f_2 + g)(\langle \uparrow^a \langle f_1, \mathsf{l}_a + \mathsf{T}_c \rangle, \mathsf{l}_c \rangle + \mathsf{l}_e) \\
&= f_2 \langle \uparrow^a \langle f_1, \mathsf{l}_a + \mathsf{T}_c \rangle, \mathsf{l}_c \rangle + g \\
&= \uparrow^a f + g
\end{aligned}
$$

- F1$_{4-6}$ implies F2$_5$:

  If $f : a \to a + c$ and $g : b \to a + c$, then

$$
\begin{aligned}
\uparrow^a \langle f, g \rangle &= \uparrow^a [(\mathsf{l}_a + g)(\langle f, \mathsf{l}_a + \mathsf{T}_c \rangle + \mathsf{l}_c)(\mathsf{l}_a + \vee_c)] \\
&= g(\uparrow^a \langle f, \mathsf{l}_a + \mathsf{T}_c \rangle + \mathsf{l}_c) \vee_c \\
&= g \langle \uparrow^a \langle f, \mathsf{l}_a + \mathsf{T}_c \rangle, \mathsf{l}_c \rangle
\end{aligned}
$$

b) Let $\uparrow$ and $\dagger$ be two corresponding operations, i.e. $\uparrow = \dagger\beta$. The equivalence for $k = 1$, say for $f : b \to c$ holds by

$$
\begin{aligned}
(\mathsf{T}_a + f)^\dagger &= \uparrow^a \langle \mathsf{T}_a + f, \mathsf{l}_a + \mathsf{T}_c \rangle \\
&= \uparrow^a ({}^a\mathsf{X}^a(\mathsf{l}_a + f))
\end{aligned}
$$

For $k = 2$, note that if $f : a \to a+b+c, g : b \to a+b+c$ and $i : d \to a+b+c$, then

$$
\uparrow^{a+b} \langle f, g, i \rangle = i\langle \langle f, g \rangle^\dagger, \mathsf{l}_c \rangle
$$

and

$$
\begin{aligned}
\uparrow^b \uparrow^a \langle f, g, i \rangle &= \uparrow^b (\langle g, i \rangle \langle f^\dagger, \mathsf{l}_{b+c} \rangle) \\
&= \uparrow^b \langle g \langle f^\dagger, \mathsf{l}_{b+c} \rangle, i \langle f^\dagger, \mathsf{l}_{b+c} \rangle \rangle \\
&= i \langle f^\dagger, \mathsf{l}_{b+c} \rangle \langle h, \mathsf{l}_c \rangle \\
&= i \langle \langle f^\dagger \langle h, \mathsf{l}_c \rangle, h \rangle, \mathsf{l}_c \rangle
\end{aligned}
$$

where $h = (g \langle f^\dagger, \mathsf{l}_{b+c} \rangle)^\dagger$. Consequently $\uparrow$ satisfies F2$_2$ iff $\dagger$ satisfies I4$_2$.

For $k = 3$, note that if $f = \langle f_1, f_2 \rangle : b + a + c \to b + a + d$ (with $f_1 : b + a \to b + a + d$ and $f_2 : c \to b + a + d$), then

$$
\begin{aligned}
\uparrow^{a+b} (({}^a\mathsf{X}^b + \mathsf{l}_c)f({}^b\mathsf{X}^a + \mathsf{l}_d)) &= \uparrow^{a+b} \langle {}^a\mathsf{X}^b f_1({}^b\mathsf{X}^a + \mathsf{l}_d), f_2({}^b\mathsf{X}^a + \mathsf{l}_d) \rangle \\
&= f_2({}^b\mathsf{X}^a + \mathsf{l}_d)\langle ({}^a\mathsf{X}^b f_1({}^b\mathsf{X}^a + \mathsf{l}_d))^\dagger, \mathsf{l}_d \rangle \\
&= f_2 \langle {}^b\mathsf{X}^a({}^a\mathsf{X}^b f_1({}^b\mathsf{X}^a + \mathsf{l}_d))^\dagger, \mathsf{l}_d \rangle
\end{aligned}
$$

and

$$\uparrow^{b+a} f = f_2\langle f_1^\dagger, \mathsf{I}_d\rangle$$

Since $^a\mathsf{X}^b \cdot {}^b\mathsf{X}^a = \mathsf{I}_{a+b}$ it follows that $\mathsf{I}4_3$ is equivalent to $\mathsf{F}2_3$.

For $k = 4$, note that the axioms $\mathsf{F}2_4$ and $\mathsf{I}4_4$ may be written as

$$\uparrow^a (f(\mathsf{I}_{a+c} + \top_d)) = (\uparrow^a f)(\mathsf{I}_c + \top_d)$$

and

$$(f(\mathsf{I}_{a+b} + \top_c))^\dagger = f^\dagger(\mathsf{I}_b + \top_c)$$

respectively. Now the equivalence of $\mathsf{F}2_4$ and $\mathsf{I}4_4$ directly follows from the above proof of the equivalence of $\mathsf{F}1_4$ and $\mathsf{I}3_4$.

c) The proof of c) is covered by the above proof of b).

d) Suppose that $y : a \to b$ is $\dagger gger$-functorial and $f = \langle f_1, f_2\rangle : a+c \to a+d$ (with $f_1 : a \to a + d$ and $f_2 : c \to a + d$) and $g = \langle g_1, g_2\rangle : b + c \to b + d$ (with $g_1 : b \to b + d$ and $g_2 : c \to b + d$) are such that

$$f(y + \mathsf{I}_d) = (y + \mathsf{I}_c)g$$

Then $f_1(y + \mathsf{I}_d) = yg_1$ and $f_2(y + \mathsf{I}_d) = g_2$. By the $\dagger$-functoriality of y we get $f_1^\dagger = yg_1^\dagger$. Hence

$$\begin{aligned}
\uparrow^a f &= f_2\langle f_1^\dagger, \mathsf{I}_d\rangle \\
&= f_2\langle yg_1^\dagger, \mathsf{I}_d\rangle \\
&= f_2(y + \mathsf{I}_d)\langle g_1^\dagger, \mathsf{I}_d\rangle \\
&= g_2\langle g_1^\dagger, \mathsf{I}_d\rangle \\
&= \uparrow^b g
\end{aligned}$$

Conversely, suppose that $y : a \to b$ is $\uparrow$-functorial and $f : a \to a + c$ and $g : b \to b + c$ are such that

$$f(y + \mathsf{I}_c) = yg$$

Then

$$\begin{aligned}
\langle f, \mathsf{I}_a + \top_c\rangle(y + \mathsf{I}_c) &= \langle f(y + \mathsf{I}_c), y + \top_c\rangle \\
&= \langle yg, y + \top_c\rangle \\
&= (y + \mathsf{I}_a)\langle g, y + \top_c\rangle
\end{aligned}$$

By the $\uparrow$-functoriality of y we get $\uparrow^a \langle f, \mathsf{I}_a + \top_c\rangle = \uparrow^b \langle g, y + \top_c\rangle$. As

$$\begin{aligned}
\uparrow^a \langle f, \mathsf{I}_a + \top_c\rangle &= (\mathsf{I}_a + \top_c)\langle f^\dagger, \mathsf{I}_c\rangle \\
&= f^\dagger
\end{aligned}$$

and

$$\uparrow^b \langle g, y + \top_c \rangle = (y + \top_c)\langle g^\dagger, I_c \rangle$$
$$= yg^\dagger$$

the result follows.

Proof of Theorem 4:

  a) Note that $\dagger := *\tau$ satisfies I3$_4$. Indeed, if $f = [f_1, f_2] : a \to a + b$ (with $f_1 : a \to a$ and $f_2 : a \to b$) and $g : b \to c$, then

$$(f(I_a + g))^\dagger = [f_1, f_2 g]^\dagger$$
$$= f_1^* f_2 g$$
$$= f^\dagger g$$

Consequently τ_r is totally defined. Obviously $* = *\tau\sigma$. For the converse, note that $\dagger\sigma\tau$ maps $f = [f_1, f_2] = [f_1, I_a](I_a + f_2) \in T(a, a + b)$ (with $f_1 : a \to a$ and $f_2 : a \to b$) in $[f_1, I_a]^\dagger f_2$. Hence $\dagger = \dagger\sigma\tau$, for $\dagger \in \mathbf{It}_r(T)$.

  b) Let $\dagger$ and $*$ be corresponding operations, i.e. $\dagger = *\tau$. The equivalence in the case $k = 1$ holds by

$$(\top_a + I_a)^\dagger = [0_a^a, I_a]^\dagger$$
$$= (0_a^a)^* I_a$$
$$= (0_a^a)^*$$

  For $k = 2$ note that if $f = [f_1, f_2, f_3] : a \to a + b + c$ (with $f_1 : a \to a, f_2 : a \to b$ and $f_3 : a \to c$) and $g = [g_1, g_2, g_3] : b \to a + b + c$ (with $g_1 : b \to a, g_2 : b \to b$ and $g_3 : b \to c$), then

$$\langle f, g \rangle^\dagger = \begin{bmatrix} f_1 & f_2 & f_3 \\ g_1 & g_2 & g_3 \end{bmatrix}^\dagger$$
$$= \begin{bmatrix} f_1 & f_2 \\ g_1 & g_2 \end{bmatrix}^* \begin{bmatrix} f_3 \\ g_3 \end{bmatrix}$$

and

$$h := (g\langle f^\dagger, I_{b+c} \rangle)^\dagger$$
$$= ([g_1 \ \ g_2 \ \ g_3] \begin{bmatrix} f_1^* f_2 & f_1^* f_3 \\ I_b & 0 \\ 0 & I_c \end{bmatrix})^\dagger$$
$$= [g_1 f_1^* f_2 \cup g_2 \ \ g_1 f_1^* f_3 \cup g_3]^\dagger$$
$$= w(g_1 f_1^* f_3 \cup g_3)$$

where $w = (g_1 f_1^* f_2 \cup g_2)^*$, hence

$$\langle f^\dagger \langle h, I_c \rangle, h \rangle = \begin{bmatrix} f_1^* f_2 h \cup f_1^* f_3 \\ h \end{bmatrix}$$

$$= \begin{bmatrix} f_1^* f_2 w g_1 f_1^* \cup f_1^* & f_1^* f_2 w \\ w g_1 f_1^* & w \end{bmatrix} \begin{bmatrix} f_3 \\ g_3 \end{bmatrix}$$

Consequently, if $*$ satisfies R3$_2$ then $\dagger$ satisfies I3$_2$.

Conversely, if $\dagger$ satisfies I3$_2$, then from the above computation it follows that

$$\begin{bmatrix} f_1 & f_2 \\ g_1 & g_2 \end{bmatrix}^* \begin{bmatrix} f_3 \\ g_3 \end{bmatrix} = \begin{bmatrix} f_1^* f_2 w g_1 f_1^* \cup f_1^* & f_1^* f_2 w \\ w g_1 f_1^* & w \end{bmatrix} \begin{bmatrix} f_3 \\ g_3 \end{bmatrix}$$

Applying this first for $f_3 = I_a, g_3 = 0_a^b$ and then for $f_3 = 0_b^a, g_3 = I_b$ we get R3$_2$.

For $k = 3$, note that if $f = [f_1, f_2] : b + a \to b + a + c$ (with $f_1 : b + a \to b + a$ and $f_2 : b + a \to c$), then

$$({}^a\mathsf{X}^b f({}^b\mathsf{X}^a + I_c))^\dagger = [{}^a\mathsf{X}^b f_1 \cdot {}^b\mathsf{X}^a, {}^a\mathsf{X}^b f_2]^\dagger$$

$$= ({}^a\mathsf{X}^b f_1 \cdot {}^b\mathsf{X}^a)^* \cdot {}^a\mathsf{X}^b f_2$$

and

$$^a\mathsf{X}^b f^\dagger = {}^a\mathsf{X}^b f_1^* f_2$$

Since $^b\mathsf{X}^a \cdot {}^a\mathsf{X}^b = I_{a+b}$ it follows that R3$_3$ and I3$_3$ are equivalent.

c) Let $\dagger$ and $*$ be corresponding operations. For $k = 1$, note that if $f = [f_1, f_2] : a \to a + b$ (with $f_1 : a \to a$ and $f_2 : a \to b$), then

$$f^\dagger = f_1^* f_2$$

and

$$f\langle f^\dagger, I_b \rangle = f_1 f_1^* f_2 \cup f_2$$

$$= (f_1 f_1^* \cup I_a) f_2$$

Hence R2$_1$ and I2$_1$ are equivalent.

For $k = 2$, note that if $f = [f_1, f_2, f_3] : a \to a + a + b$ (with $f_1 : a \to a, f_2 : a \to a$ and $f_3 : a \to b$), then

$$f^{\dagger\dagger} = [f_1^* f_2, f_1^* f_3]^\dagger$$

$$= (f_1^* f_2)^* f_1^* f_3$$

and

$$(f(\vee_a + \mathsf{I}_b))^\dagger = [f_1 \cup f_2, f_3]^\dagger$$
$$= (f_1 \cup f_2)^* f_3$$

Hence R2$_2$ and I2$_2$ are equivalent.

For $k = 3$, suppose that $f = [f_1, f_2] : a \to b + c$ (with $f_1 : a \to b$ and $f_2 : a \to c$) and $g : b \to a$. Then

$$g(f(g + \mathsf{I}_c))^\dagger = g[f_1 g, f_2]^\dagger$$
$$= g(f_1 g)^* f_2$$

and

$$(gf)^\dagger = [gf_1, gf_2]^\dagger$$
$$= (gf_1)^* gf_2$$

show that R2$_3$ and I2$_3$ are equivalent.

d) The case $k = 1$ is covered by c). For $k = 2$, note that if $f = [f_1, f_2] : a \to b + c$ (with $f_1 : a \to b$ and $f_2 : a \to c$) and $g : b \to a$, then

$$(f(g + \mathsf{I}_c))^\dagger = [f_1 g, f_2]^\dagger$$
$$= (f_1 g)^* f_2$$

and

$$f\langle (gf)^\dagger, \mathsf{I}_c \rangle = [f_1, f_2]\langle (gf_1)^* gf_2, \mathsf{I}_c \rangle$$
$$= f_1(gf_1)^* gf_2 \cup f_2$$
$$= (\mathsf{I}_a \cup f_1(gf_1)^* g)f_2$$

Hence R1$_2$ and I1$_2$ are equivalent.

e) Suppose that $y : a \to b$ is $*$-functorial and $f = [f_1, f_2] : a \to a + c$ (with $f_1 : a \to a$ and $f_2 : a \to c$) and $g = [g_1, g_2] : b \to b + c$ (with $g_1 : b \to b$ and $g_2 : b \to c$) are such that

$$f(y + \mathsf{I}_c) = yg$$

Then $f_1 y = yg_1$ and $f_2 = yg_2$. By the $*$-functoriality of y we get $f_1^* y = yg_1^*$. Consequently,

$$yg^\dagger = yg_1^* g_2$$
$$= f_1^* yg_2$$
$$= f_1^* f_2$$
$$= f^\dagger$$

Conversely, suppose that $y : a \to b$ is $\dagger$-functorial and $f : a \to a$ and $g : b \to b$ are such that

$$fy = yg$$

Then

$$
\begin{aligned}
[f, y](y + \mathsf{l}_b) &= [fy, y] \\
&= [yg, y] \\
&= y[g, \mathsf{l}_b]
\end{aligned}
$$

hence

$$[f, y]^\dagger = y[g, \mathsf{l}_b]^\dagger$$

showing that $f^* y = y g^*$.

6. Concluding remarks

We conclude here be pointing some advantages of the use of feedback over the use of iteration or repetition.

Firstly, the proper acyclic context for the use of feedback is a symmetric strict monoidal category, for iteration it is an algebraic theory and for repetition it is a matrix theory. Hence the feedback operations may be used in a more general context than iteration or repetition operations.

Secondly, in the context of matrix theories there is a bijection between the repetition operations and the iteration operations that *obey* the axiom $\mathrm{I3}_4$. Hence the iteration operations are more expressive than the repetition ones since they display some properties of the looping operations that are hidden by the repetition operations. Analogously, in the context of algebraic theories there is a bijection between the iteration operations and the feedback operations that *obey* the axiom $\mathrm{F2}_5$. Hence the feedback operations are more expressive that the iteration or repetition ones since they display some properties of the looping operations that are hidden by the other ones.

Finally, let us note that some properties are easier to express in terms of feedback, e.g. the property expressed by the 'matrix formula' $\mathrm{R3}_2$ or by the 'paring axiom' $\mathrm{I3}_2$ is expressed in terms of feedback as $\mathrm{F1}_2$.[4]

---

[4] The comparison of the axiom systems that we have displayed in this paper enlightens the role of soms 'misterious' axioms as $\mathrm{R1}_1$–$\mathrm{R1}_2$ used in the setting of regular algebras (resp. of the axioms $\mathrm{I3}_1$–$\mathrm{I3}_4$ of 'theories with iterate' used in the setting of iteration theories). Namely, they provide a combination of complete axioms for acyclic behaviour given by the matrix theory rules (resp. algebraic theory rules) with complete axioms for cyclic flowgraphs, but *not* for their behaviour. Clearly, something is missing here: we need a device that allow us to cope with the behaviour of cyclic processes. (In our study such a device is provided by the functoriality rule.)

References

1. S. L. Bloom, Z. Esik, Equational axioms of regular sets, *Mathematical Structures in Computar Science*, 1993.

2. S. L. Bloom, C. C. Elgot, J. B. Wright, Vector iteration in pointed algebraic theories, *SIAM Journal of Computing*, 9 (1980), 525 – 540.

3. J. Conway, *Regular Algebra and Finite Machines*, Chapman and Hall, London, 1971.

4. V. E. Căzănescu, Gh. Ştefănescu, A formal representation of flowchart schemes *Analele Universitătii Bucuresti, Matematică - Informatică*, 37 (1988), 33 – 51.

5. V. E. Căzănescu, Gh. Ştefănescu, *Feedback, iteration and repetition*, Preprint Series in Mathematics No. 42/1988, The National Institute for Scientific and Technical Creation, Bucharest 1988.

6. V. E. Căzănescu, Gh. Ştefănescu, A formal representation of flowchart schemes II, *Studii şi Cercetări Matematice*, 41 (1989), 151 – 167.

7. V. E. Căzănescu, Gh. Ştefănescu, Towards a new algebraic foundation of flowchart scheme theory, *Fundamenta Informaticae*, 13 (1990), 171 – 210.

8. V. E. Căzănescu, Gh. Ştefănescu, Classes of finite relations as initial abstract data types I, *Discrete Mathematics*, 90 (1991), 233 – 265.

9. C. C. Elgot, Manadic computation and iterative algebraic theories, *Proceedings Logic Colloquium '73*, pages 175 – 230, North-Holland, 1975, Studies in Logic and the Foundations of Mathematics, Volume 80.

10. C. C. Elgot, Matricial theories, *Journal of Algebra*, 42 (1976), 391 – 421.

11. Z. Esik, Identities in iterative and rational algebraic theories, *Computational Linguistic and Computational Languages*, 7 (1980), 183 – 207.

12. Z. Esik, Algebra of iteration theories, *Journal of Computer and System Sciences*, 27 (1983), 291 – 303.

13. D. Krob, Complete systems of B-rational identities, *Theoretical Computer Science*, 89 (1991), 207 – 343.

14. S. MacLane, *Categories for the working mathematician*, Springer–Verlag, 1971.

15. S. Marcus, *Gramatici şi automate finite*, Editura Academiei R. P. Româ-
ne, 1964.

16. Gh. Ştefănescu, An algebraic theory of flowchart schemes, in *Proceedings 11-th Colloquium on Trees in Algebra and Programming, CAAP
'86* (P. Franchi-Zannettacci, ed.), *Lecture Notes in Computer Science*
214, Springer–Verlag, 1986, 60 – 73.

17. Gh. Ştefănescu, On flowchart theories I: The deterministic case, *Journal
of Computer and Systems Sciences*, 35 (1987), 163 – 191.

18. Gh. Ştefănescu, On flowchart theories II: The nondeterministic case,
Theoretical Computer Science, 52 (1987), 307 – 340.

19. Gh. Ştefănescu, Feedback theories (a calculus for isomorphism classes
of flowchart schemes), *Revue Roumaine de Mathematiques Pures et Ap-
plique*, 35 (1990), 73 – 79 (Early distributed as *Preprint Series in Mathematics*, The National Institute for Scientific and Technical Creation,
Bucharest, No. 24/April 1986).

20. Gh. Ştefănescu, *Determinism and nondeterminism in program scheme
theory; algebraic aspects*, Ph. D. Thesis, University of Bucharest, 1991
(in Romanian).

Grammar Systems:
a Multi-Agent Framework for
Natural Language Generation[1]

Erzsébet CSUHAJ-VARJÚ
Computer and Automation Institute
Hungarian Academy of Science
H-1111 Budapest, Kende u. 13-17, Hungary

Abstract. We present a multi-agent framework for generating natural languages, motivated by grammar systems from formal language theory. The model gives a unified approach to describe different aspects and levels of natural language generation, from generating sentences to discourse and text generation.

1. Natural language processing

The main concern of natural language processing (NLP) is the computational study of language use. The area deals with the analysis and the design of computational agents that use natural languages in order to issue, acquire and change information in the interest of changing the state of the surrounding world (including other agents). In contrasts with linguistics, philosophy and psycholinguistics, which also study questions connected with natural languages, the main emphasis in NLP is in finding computational models. Agents assumed to have intelligent behaviour. Thus, important notions like action have an outstanding role in approaching natural languages by tools of artificial intelligence (AI). For example, in such sense, one of the central topics, natural language generation (NLG) can be considered as a particular kind of action planning.

Language generation has a very rich history in NLP. Starting from different points of view, there have been many approaches to NLG. An example is to view natural language generation as an attempt to achieve communicative goals by using language. Another one is to view language generation as a structure mapping where an input conceptual structure is mapped into a linguistic structure. This case corresponds to a process of decision-making

---

[1] Research supported by Hungarian Research Foundation OTKA no. 2571 and 4295 and EC Cooperative Action IC 1000 "ALTEC"

under constraints or as something in between a goal-satisfaction or rule satisfaction process. According to another approach, natural language generation is based on two main parts: a strategic, or what-to-say component and a tactical, or how-to-say component. Another point of classification in language generation is the distinction between sentence generation and text (discourse) generation. The early research was concerned with single sentence generation: direct translation of formal representations, elaboration and testing of grammars and study of lexical decision criteria. This situation in the eightees changed: the work was concerned with generation of discources and texts. The appearance of multi-expert systems and the developments in distributed artificial intelligence motivated new architectures that gave new launch to language generation. Current language generation work focuses on the view of language as action; it deals with problems of constructing systems that can generate appropriate linguistic actions. We follow this line of ideas by proposing a multi-agent framework for modelling natural language generation. We consider natural language generation action as a planned or an emergent action performed by some agent(s) of some interacting multiagent systems where agents are represented by (usually generative) grammars (rule-based systems). The proposed model unifies some advantages of the previous approaches and provides tools for handling different levels and aspects of language generation in an integrated way.

In order to get a better understanding of the roots of our ideas, we briefly sketch main characteristics of multi-agent systems (MA-systems) of distributed and decentralized artificial intelligence (DAI) and grammar systems of formal language theory. (For current trends of natural language processing the reader is referred to [20]).

2. Multi-agent systems

The theory of multi-agent systems is in the focus of the current research in distributed artificial intelligence. The area is dealing with intelligent behaviour among collections of autonomous agents; how they can coordinate their knowledge, goals, skills and plans, jointly to take actions or to solve problems. The agents may have and may be working toward a single global goal, or they may have and may be working toward separate individual goals that interact. They share knowledge about problems and solutions and about the process of coordination. There are cases where there is no possibility for global control, globally consistent knowledge, globally shared goals, even global representation of a system. Such special systems are open systems. Open systems are composed of independently developed parts in continuous evolution. They are concurrent and asynchronous, have decentralized control based on debate and negotiations, and exhibit many local inconsistences. Open systems consist of agents with bounded knowledge and bounded influence; they have no fixed global boundaries visible to the agents constituting the system. (For further details the interested reader is referred to [2], [3], [15].)

Theory of autonomous agents with emergent functionality belongs to another mainstream of current AI, namely, to decentralized artificial intelligence ([13], [4], [5], [17]). In this case the functionality of the agent is viewed as an emergent property of its intensive interaction with its dynamic environment. Agents are constructed from modules obtained by task-level decomposition. The communication among modules is reduced to the minimum and there is no global representation or a global planner of the activity of an agent. The activity of an agent emerges by the interaction of the behaviours of the modules. Each autonomous agent accomplishes its own individual task or a global task.

For building our linguistic model we shall use characteristic features of multi-agent systems from both distributed and decentralized artificial intelligence.

3. Grammar systems

Natural language generation is supposed to be based on higly elaborated formalisms. To find appropriate formal (mathematical) tools for our model, we turn to grammar systems that has been a dynamically evolving area of recent formal language theory, and that realizes generative paradigms of variants of multi-agent systems. For further details and motivations concerning the topic the interested reader is referred to [12], [21], [10], and [16]. The notion of the grammar system means a finite set of generative (usually, context-free) grammars that cooperate in the interest of deriving some languages. The area concentrates on that questions if cooperation increases the generative capacity of grammars or not and how to describe languages, arising from cooperation, by systems of generative grammars which are, from syntactic point of view, as simple as possible.

The first variant, motivated by two-level substitution mechanism, was the cooperating grammar system introduced in [18]. An extensive study of the topic has been launched after relating the notion to the blackboard model of problem solving and defining a generalized version, called cooperating/distributed grammar system (CD grammar system) ([7], [8]). The CD grammar system is a finite set of context-free grammars which sequentially generate a shared a common sential form to obtain words of a common language. The context-free grammars correspond to the agents (the independent knowledge sources), the current sentential form to the blackboard (the global database with information concerning the problem solving), a derivation step to a contribution to problem solving and the generated language to the problem solution(s). Terminal sets correspond to acceptance fields; how grammars (agents) relate to the accepted problem solution or behaviour.

Since 1988 there have been a lot of variants of grammar systems examined: grammars cooperating by recognition of dynamic start/stop context conditions, grammars allowed to perform a limited number of consecutive derivation steps during the generation, grammars with different levels of competence, with hypothesis, with external-internal control mechanisms, and with additional communication tools to help cooperation. Besides sequential models, grammars functioning in parallel way have been studied as well (teams, parallel communicating grammar systems, etc.). Each of the above types of grammar systems corresponds to some variant of multi-agent systems and reflects to vital questions and problems.

To give some insight about formalisms, we present the formal definition of three variants of grammar systems that correspond to models of different levels and aspects of language generation: sentence generation, discourse (text) generation and language generation as a social action.

Throughout we assume the reader is familiar with formal language theory. For further details the reader should consult with [23].

We first recall the definition of a CD grammar system with dynamic start/ stop context conditions from [11]. The idea is simple: there are some start/stop context conditions associated to each cooperating grammar. Before entering the derivation, the grammar checks if the current sentential form satisfies its start context condition. If the check is succesful then the grammar continues the context-free derivation. It can stop with the generation if some of its stop context conditions hold. The model is strongly motivated by sentence generation: It is enough to think of that during the process of formulating a grammatical sentence we must keep some conventions concerning the context of the current sentential form (for example, sentences in languages with fix word order have to follow the word order, etc.), that is we check if some local and/or global context conditions hold or not.

Definition 1. A CD grammar system *with dynamic start/stop context conditions* (a DCD grammar system, for short) is an $(n + 2)$-tuple

$$\Gamma = (T, G_1, G_2, \ldots, G_n, S),$$

where

- $G_i = (N_i, T_i, P_i, \pi_i, \rho_i)$ is a component grammar of Γ with start condition π_i and stop condition ρ_i, for $1 \leq i \leq n$, where

- (N_i, T_i, P_i) is an incomplete context-free grammar with nonterminal set N_i, terminal set T_i and production set P_i, for $1 \leq i \leq n$,

- π_i and ρ_i are predicates on $V_i^* = (N_i \cup T_i)^*$, for $1 \leq i \leq n$,

- $T \subseteq \bigcup_{i=1}^{n} T_i$, is the set of terminals of Γ,

- $S \in N_i$ for some i, $1 \leq i \leq n$. S is the startsymbol of Γ.

The language $L(\Gamma)$ generated by Γ is the set of all words $z \in T^*$ for which there is a derivation $S = w_0 \Rightarrow^*_{G_{i_1}} w_1 \Rightarrow^*_{G_{i_2}} w_2 \Rightarrow^*_{G_{i_3}} \cdots \Rightarrow^*_{G_{i_r}} w_r = z$ such that, for $1 \leq j \leq r$, $\pi_{i_j}(w_{j-1}) = true$ and $\rho_{i_j}(w_j) = true$.

Let us have an example.

Example 1. Let $\Gamma_1 = (\{a, b, c\}, G_1, G_2, S)$, where

- $G_1 = (\{S, A, B\}, \{a, b, c\}, \{S \rightarrow abc, S \rightarrow AB, A \rightarrow aA'b, B \rightarrow B'c\}$, $\pi_1, \rho_1)$, where π_1=true iff either S or symbols A and B both occur in the current sentential form and ρ_1=true in all cases.

- $G_2 = (\{S, A, B\}, \{a, b, c\}, \{A' \rightarrow A, B' \rightarrow B\}, \pi_2, \rho_2)$, where π_2=true iff symbols A' and B' both occur in the current sentential form and ρ_2=true in all cases.

The language generated by Γ_1 is $L(\Gamma_1) = \{a^n b^n c^n \mid n \geq 1\}$ that is a non-context-free context sensitive language. Thus, cooperation results in considerable increment of generative capacity even in the case of very simple components.

As it can be guessed from the above example, according to different choices of predicates, we can obtain different powerful subclasses of the context-sensitive language class. Derivation steps correspond to actions; some of them are planned (in the case of context check) and some of them are emergent (determined by the symbols constituting the sentential form). It is easy to observe that DCD grammar systems model distributed text generation, too.

Discourse generation and text generation are based on both serial and parallel actions. Besides common generation, some additional communication of agents is presupposed.

Such cases are modelled by parallel communicating grammar systems ([22]). Originally, the notion was introduced to model multi-board (classroom) architecture of problem solving. In this model, each component grammar works simultaneously, rewriting its own sentential form. A universal clock synchronizes the derivation of the components, that is, every component has to perform a derivation step in each time unit. Components cooperate in the interest of solving a common task (generating languages). From time to time they communicate by issuing communication symbols, by sending their own current sentential form and by receiving the current sentential form(s) of another grammar(s). The language identifying the task solution is the language generated by a distinguished component, called the master grammar.

Definition 2. A *parallel communicating grammar system* (a PC grammar system, for short) of degree n, $n \geq 1$, is an $(n+3)$-tuple $\Gamma = (N, K, T, G_1, \ldots, G_n)$, where

- $G_i = (N \cup K, T, P_i, S_i), 1 \leq i \leq n$, are usual Chomsky grammars, called the components of Γ, where

- N is the nonterminal alphabet, T is the terminal alphabet, $K = \{Q_1, Q_2, \ldots, Q_n\}$, is the set of query symbols. N, T, K are mutually disjoint. The i-th query symbol, Q_i belongs to component G_i, respectively. P_i is the set of productions and S_i is the startsymbol.

We denote by $V_\Gamma = N \cup T \cup K$.

Generation in PC grammar systems is realized via both componentwise derivation steps and communication steps.

Given a PC grammar system $\Gamma = (N, K, T, G_1, \ldots, G_n)$, as above, for two n-tuples $(x_1, x_2, \ldots, x_n)$, $(y_1, y_2, \ldots, y_n)$, $x_i, y_i \in V_\Gamma^*$, $1 \leq i \leq n$, we write $(x_1, \ldots, x_n) \Longrightarrow (y_1, \ldots, y_n)$ if one of the next two cases holds:

- There is no query symbol occurring in $x_1, \ldots, x_n$. We perform a componentwise derivation. If x_i, $1 \leq i \leq n$, is a terminal word, then $y_i = x_i$. If x_i contains at least one nonterminal, then $x_i \Longrightarrow_{G_i} y_i$.

- (ii) There is some query symbol occurring in some x_i, for $1 \leq i \leq n$. Then a communication step is performed: each appearance of Q_j in x_i is replaced by x_j, providing x_j does not contain query symbols. Sentential form x_i (containing query symbols) is modified only if all its occurrences of query symbols refer to sentential forms without occurrences of query symbols. In a communication step, the communicated string x_j replaces the query symbol Q_j and after that the grammar G_j resumes working from its axiom. The communication has priority to the effective rewriting. If some query symbols are not satisfied at a given communication step, then they will be satisfied at the next one (providing they ask for strings without query symbols in that moment) and so on. No rewriting is possible if at least one query symbol is present.

As usual, by $\Longrightarrow^*$ we shall denote the reflexive transitive closure of $\Longrightarrow$, that is the sequences of derivation and communication steps.

The language $L(\Gamma)$ generated by a PC grammar system Γ, as above, is
$$L(\Gamma) = \{x \in T^* \mid (S_1, S_2, \ldots, S_n) \Longrightarrow^* (x, \alpha_2, \ldots, \alpha_n), \alpha_i \in V_\Gamma^*, 2 \leq i \leq n\}.$$

Example 2. Let $\Gamma_2 = \{A, B\}, \{Q_2\}, \{a, b, c\}, G_1, G_2)$, where

- $G_1 = (\{A, B, Q_2\}, \{a, b, c\}, \{A \to aAc, A \to aQ_2c\}, A)$, and

- $G_2 = (\{A, B, Q_2\}, \{a, b, c\}, \{B \to bB, B \to b\}, B)$.

The language generated by Γ_2 is $L(\Gamma_2 = \{a^n b^n c^n | n \geq 1\}$, that is the same language that was generated by Γ_1 in the previous example.

As in the case of DCD grammar systems, PC grammar systems are very powerful devices.

PC grammar system models distributed text generation in an elegant way. It corresponds to that case if agents prepare a text in a distributed way and from time to time they change some parts with each other.

Besides text generation, PC grammar systems have nice applications in sentence generation, too. For example, it is a well-known fact that there are some parts (phrases) of the sentence that can be generated simultaneously for some time but to continue the generation they have to be inserted in a fixed part of the sentence structure.

Language generation is also a social action. An example for modelling text generation by teams being organized into local hierarchies is the stratified grammar system ([9]). Originally, the concept was constructed to model Minsky's society of mind, that understands the human mind as a society of small agents organized into agencies and divisions ([19]). Component grammars of the stratified grammar system are clustered in sets, called strata. There is a linear ordering of these strata is given. The work of the system starts with the first stratum in this ordering and continues from stratum to stratum, until a terminal string is obtained. The use of a stratum means to use exactly one rule from each production set on that stratum. Thus, when a task is to be solved, an agent (as representant of an agency) takes this task and, if not succeeding to solve it, it splits the task in sub-tasks which will be approached by agents in another stratum. The process continues until the complete solution of the task is produced.

Definition 3. A stratified grammar system of degree $n, n \geq 1$ (an ST grammar system, for short), is an $n + 3$-tuple $\Gamma = (N, T, S, P_1, P_2, \ldots, P_n)$, where

- N is the nonterminal vocabulary, T is the terminal vocabulary, $S \in N$ is the axiom and $P_1, P_2, \ldots, P_n$ are sets of sets of production rules of generative grammars,

- $P_i = \{P_{i,1}, P_{i,2}, \ldots, P_{i,k_i}\}, 1 \leq i \leq n$, with $k_1 = 1$ and $k_i \geq 1, 2 \leq i \leq n$ (each $P_{i,j}$ is a set of production rules over $N \cup T$). Each P_i is called stratum.

The formal concept of the derivation in ST grammar systems is as follows: For $x, y \in (N \cup T)^*$ and for a stratum $P_i, 1 \leq i \leq n$, we write $x \Longrightarrow_{P_i} y$ iff: $x = x_1 A_{j_1} x_2 A_{j_2} x_3 \ldots x_{k_i} A_{j_{k_i}} x_{k_i+1}, y = x_1 w_{j_1} x_2 w_{j_2} x_3 \ldots x_{k_i} w_{j_{k_i}} x_{k_i+1}, x_t \in$

$(N \cup T)^*$, $1 \le t \le k_i + 1$, $A_{j_r} \to w_{j_r} \in P_{i,j_r}$, $1 \le r \le k_i$, and $\{j_1, j_2, \ldots, j_{k_i}\} = \{1, 2, \ldots, k_i\}$.

Denoting by $\Longrightarrow_{P_i}^*$ the reflexive transitive closure of $\Longrightarrow_{P_i}$, the language $L(\Gamma)$ generated by Γ is $L(\Gamma) = \{x \in T^* \mid S \Longrightarrow_{P_1}^* x_1 \Longrightarrow_{P_2}^* x_2 \Longrightarrow_{P_3}^* \cdots \Longrightarrow_{P_t}^* x_t = x, 1 \le t \le n\}$.

Example 3. Let $\Gamma_3 = (\{S, A, B\}, \{a, b, c\}, S,$
$\{\{S \to AB\}\}, \{\{A \to aAb, A \to ab\}, \{B \to cB, B \to c\}\}$.
Then $L(\Gamma_3) = \{a^n b^n c^n \mid n \ge 1\}$. Thus, stratified grammar systems are very powerful generative devices, too.

Stratified grammar systems produce powerful language classes with interesting structural properties of words.

In the following we introduce our framework for natural language generation that is a developed version of the model we introduced in [6].

4. The model for natural language generation

We consider natural language as behaviour of a world (a family) of multi-agent symbol systems that interact in a nonsimple way. These systems are complex systems of Simon, that is " in such systems the whole is more than the sum of the parts, not in an ultimate, metaphysical sense but in the important pragmatic sense that, given the properties of the parts and the laws of their interaction, it is not trivial matter to infer the properties of the whole." ([24]). The number of multi-agent systems in the MA-world is not fixed, depending on the current situation, some new members can join it and some can leave it. There is a clock associated with the MA-world measuring absolute time. A finite number of multi-agent systems is said to be a fragment of the world. Fragments can be taken into account according to a period determined by absolute time units or without time factor. Each multi-agent system is represented by some grammar system: agents correspond to grammars. Grammar systems can be either from formal language theory (generative grammars) or can be systems of grammars known in natural language processing, constructed according to ideas of building generative grammar systems. Each grammar system has its own competence, responsibility and boundaries that determines its activities. Moreover, there is an own clock associated to each grammar system, too, and each component grammar is allowed to perform a derivation step (an action) in each time unit according to this clock. Some clocks are synchronized, some of them work in asynchronous way. Clocks with negative time (going back in time) are allowed to exist, too. Active periods of the grammar systems are limited in absolute time; grammar systems can born and die. They can interact, migrate and can change their own components. Each grammar system determines a behaviour that is the set of words generated by the grammars (according to the clock of the system). The behaviour of a fragment is the set of languages generated by the constituent grammar systems. Behaviours can be relativized according to time and to other well-defined criteria.

The components of the grammar system, organization and the form of cooperation can be chosen according to the purpose of that the grammar system is intended to use.

The above multi-agent approach gives a flexible tool for modelling different levels and aspects of natural language generation. It provides a unified treatment for handling both pure syntactic questions and such features of language that, in traditional approach, have semantic explanation or are determined by social nature of language. Grammar systems from the above multi-agent world can belong to sentence generation, to agents (human and artificial beings), to societies of linguistic agents, etc. Therefore the same formalism can be used for generating discources, texts, sentences, description of natural language development, etc.

In the following we illustrate our ideas by some linguistic examples. It is obvious that coordinated and cooperative activities of simple grammars (a grammar system) can help in modularized sentence generation. But, our approach provides some additional possibilities. An interesting example is the problem of ungrammatical sentences. Grammars are for identifying grammatical sentences (correct sentences). However, people (agents) having the competence of language generation often communicate ungrammatical sentences. Moreover, the notion of ungrammatical can change during time. One of the main efforts in NLG is to construct grammars which generate only correct sentences or to associate with the grammar precise descriptions of the criteria of grammatical correctness. By our framework, ungrammatical sentences are sentential forms which are generated by the grammar system but do not belong to any language over the acceptence field (the terminal set) of the system. Moreover, any change in the acceptance field implies a change of the criteria of correctness. In this case a special fragment is taken from the MA-world, namely, a grammar system that generates the sentences constructed from English words. According to time relativization, we can follow the changes of correctness of sentences through time.

Similar interesting example is the question of style. There are words, phrases, sentences, texts, etc. that some people prefer to use and there are words, phrases, etc. which are characteristic for people who use them. These features can be explained in the above multi-agent model in the following natural way: Different agents (human or artificial beings) can determine different grammar systems and fragments. Because of grammar systems can be active only for a limited period, therefore, during a fixed period of time, some phrases can be very fashionable or some of them can go out from fashion.

The above multi-agent model provides an interpretation of learning/forgetting languages as well. This is again that case if we form a fragment by associating grammar systems to human (artificial) beings from the MA-world. (For example, each person is associated with a fragment of grammar systems where the grammar systems are able to generate the sentences, discources and texts constructed from English words.) If some new grammar systems join the fragment over that the human (artificial) being manipulates, then a learning process is realized. If some grammar systems are in an inactive state, we are witnesses of a forgetting process.

Another interesting property, the grammatical interference corresponds to that case if some grammar system in the fragment is replaced by another one which is almost of the same range of activity but its deviance does not come to light in each case.

If we consider fragments of grammar systems that belong to a society of people, we obtain explanation for development of natural languages. Because of some grammar systems can come into being and some come to an end, therefore fragments change through time.

5. An application

In the following we shall illustrate our ideas in natural language generation by a simple example similar to that one we used in [6]. We do not restrict ourselves to generative grammars but use some another types of grammars well-known in NLG. Moreover, our example demonstrates only some features of our framework. (For further details concerning these grammars the reader is referred to [1] and [14].) We consider generation as an immediate verbalization of the parts of computable conceptual structures in situations that are predictable in advance. Generation is a complex realization of progressive, cooperative and distributed activities where, besides linguistic structures, grammar systems the linguistic MA-system (how to say) are processing partial conceptual structures which are computed by grammar systems of the conceptual MA-system (what to say). Our model does not divide sharply strategic (what to say) and tactical (how-to say) component. Although the formulation starts by content determination, information flow is not serial. Both the linguistic MA-system and the conceptual MA-system can run simultaneously and provide a feedback. If the linguistic MA-system is in function, then the conceptual MA-system can be active and add more conceptual structures. For example, it may happen that specified information is not sufficient to identify the sentence uniquely, or unspecified but required information is missing. To avoid these situations, leading to the successive specification of the complete sentence structure, the linguistic MA-system has to provide a feedback for the selection of what is missing or what to say next by the conceptual MA-system. Generation also requires particular needs upon syntactic description and processing in a parallel fashion. When the whole syntactic structure of an utterance is built, it should be possible to decide for every partial structure whether it is locally complete. One should not assume that the chronological order in which syntactic parts are attached during generation, corresponds to linear order of the resulting utterance.

In the following we shall follow the derivation process of sentence "He bought a pencil from Jane." We consider such case where grammar systems in the MA-systems are represented by cooperating/distributed grammars associated with dynamic start/stop context conditions and by parallel communicating grammar systems. Start/stop conditions are context conditions in a general sense that they encode/refer to verbalized information/or information being to be verbalized that is necessary on that level of generation for continuation of the generation process. Start conditions implicitly presume a minimal competence : the grammar system can enter the derivation if it is able to contribute the generation process. Notice that contribution does not necessarily mean real development, hesitations and corrections are also included. Stop conditions are of two types: either they express that the grammar (the grammar system) is not able to continue the derivation (for example, the verbalization of the information is locally complete on that level) or they express that the generation is on a level that is sufficient to start with another grammar systems. Moreover, we assume that grammar systems, depending on the current need in the progress of generation, can run both in sequential and in parallel fashion.

In our example we assume that semantic and discourse information is encoded in the same notation. To use a uniform representation for the content, structure, and lexical items in the sentence we use the functional unification grammar, slightly different from unification grammar, which is a well-suited framework for investigating the interaction between the grammatical issues and the content planning issues.

The syntactic ordering restrictions are given by patterns in structures. The complete sentence is constructed by unifying structures together where the pattern slot determines the syntactic order of the constituents.

```
(S (FIRST-NP (np)
MAIN-V (verb ROOT x TENSE y NUMBER Z)
NUMBER = NUM(FIRST-NP) = NUM(MAIN-VERB)
OBJ (np)
MOD (pp)
PATTERN (FIRST-NP, MAIN-VERB, OBJ, MOD))
(NP DET (art)
HEAD (noun)
PATTERN (ART NOUN ... MOD))
(NP PRO (pro)
PATTERN (PRO))
(NP NAME (name)
```

PATTERN (name))
(PP **PREP** (prep)
POBJ (np)
PATTERN (**PREP POBJ**))

In our example the following grammar systems cooperate : a case grammar (representing the conceptual MA-system), a syntactic grammar (providing the connection and feedback between the conceptual MA-system and the linguistic MA-system), a functional unification grammar (determining basic syntactic structure of the sentence), grammars in the reference MA-system, lexical MA-system, morphological MA-system (all of them are subsystems of the linguistic MA-system and are responsible for reference, linearization, inflection, etc.).

The generation starts by functioning of the conceptual MA-system. In our example, a case grammar is activated that produces a conceptual output as follows:

(S **TENSE** past
AGENT NUMBER Singular
AGENT PERSON 3
VOICE active
ACTION TYPE buy1
AGENT John1
THEME pencil10
FROM POSSESSION Jane1)

The output satisfies some stop conditions associated by the case grammar (specified information are locally complete) and it corresponds to start conditions of the syntactic grammar. The syntactic grammar maps the output structure to a correct structure defined by the functional unification grammar. This is done by using unification operations that equate roles like **AGENT** with **FIRST_NOUN**.

For example, if a choice has to be done between active and passive forms, then following sentence forms that map the case roles to the desired syntactic positions.

(SF **FIRST-NP**(
NP **REF**= ˆ **AGENT**)
OBJ (NP **REF**= ˆ **THEME**)
VOICE active)
(SF **FIRST-NP**(
NP **REF**= ˆ **THEME**)
AUX be
MODS (PP **PREP** by
POBJ (NP **REF**= ˆ **AGENT**)
VOICE passive)

By unifying one of the active and passive structures into the conceptual structure, the new structure will be:

(S **TENSE** past
AGENT NUMBER Singular
AGENT PERSON 3
VOICE active
ACTION TYPE buy1
AGENT John1
THEME pen10
FROM POSSESSION Mary1
FIRST-NP (NP **REF**= ˆ **AGENT**)
OBJ (NP **REF**= ˆ **THEME**))

The overall structure of the sentence has been determined, but none of the subconstituents of the structure have been planned.

The output structure is taken by a grammar based lexical analyzer which plans how to realize each slot-value pair in the structure. For instance, the pair **ACTION TYPE**/buy1 can be realized using the main verb with root *buy*.

The next necessary step is the tense analysis that is done by a separate grammar system that then simply unifies its results back into the structure form being constructed.

MAIN-VERB (
verb **ROOT** buy
TENSE past
NUM Singular)

The generation continues by activation of reference grammar system. If it is decided that the **AGENT**/John1 will be realized as noun phrase as (NP **REF** John1) in the **FIRST-NP** slot, then grammars in the system might choose to realize this as a pronoun unifying in the structure (NP **PRO** he). Similarly, they realize **THEME**/pencil 1 pair in NP in the **OBJ** slot. The reference grammar system might reason that this object has not been introduced before and choose to introduce it with an indefinite noun phrase e.g. (NP **DET** a **HEAD** pencil).

Finally, once all these choices are made, the remaining details of the sentence structure are determined by unifications with the proper syntactic rules in the linguistic MA-system to produce a final representation of the sentence such as:

(S **FIRST-NP** (NP **PRO** he
AGENT NUMBER Singular
AGENT PERSON 3
REFERENCE John1

```
PATTERN (PRO))
MAIN-VERB (verb ROOT buy
TENSE past
NUM 3)
OBJ (NP DET a
HEAD pencil)
REF pencil10)
PATTERN (DET HEAD))
MODS (PP PREP from
POBJ (NP name Jane
REF Jane1)
PATTERN (PREP POBJ))
PATTERN (FIRST-NP, MAIN-VERB, OBJ, MOD)))
```

There have remained processes which perform the inflection and the linearization. They are performed by means of the grammar systems in the morphological MA-system. Since all the orderings and word choice decisions have been determined, the output structure would be *He bought a pencil from Jane.*

The above method can be used to support more complex types of reasoning needed to generate coherent situations and texts. Each component needs to specify only information relevant to its choice; a syntactic decision, a semantic decision, a lexical decision, or a combination of these. Every conceptual or linguistic part can be observed as an interactive segment which tries to verbalize itself as locally and as independently as possible. Based upon this, cooperative and distributed organization can be realized.

References

1. J. Allen, *Natural Language Understanding*, The Benjamin/Cummings Publ. Co., California, 1987.

2. A. H. Bond, L. Gasser (eds.), *Readings in Distributed Artificial Intelligence*, Morgan Kaufmann, San Mateo, California, 1988.

3. A. H. Bond, L. Gasser (eds.), An analysis of problems and research in distributed artificial intelligence. Chapter 1, in *Readings in Distributed Artificial Intelligence*, Morgan Kaufmann, San Mateo, California, 1988.

4. R. A. Brooks, Intelligence without representation, *Artificial Intelligence*, 47 (1991), 139 – 159.

5. R. A. Brooks, *Intelligence without reason*, AI Laboratory (AI Memo No. 1293), MIT, Cambridge, Mass., 1991.

6. E. Csuhaj-Varjú, R. Abo-Alez, Multi-agent systems in natural language processing, in *TWLT6. Natural Language Parsing. Methods and formalisms*, ACL/SIGPARSE Workshop (K. Sikkel, A. Nijholt, eds.), Enschede, University of Enschede, 1993, 129 – 137.

7. E. Csuhaj-Varjú, J. Dassow, On cooperating/distributed grammar systems, *J. of Inf. Processing and Cybernetics*, 26 (1990), 49 – 63.

8. E. Csuhaj-Varjú, J. Kelemen, Cooperating grammar systems: a syntactical framework for blackboard model of problem-solving, in *Artificial Intelligence and Information-Control Systems of Robots'89* (I. Plander, ed.), Elsevier, Amsterdam, 1989, 121 – 127.

9. E. Csuhaj-Varjú, J. Dassow, J. Kelemen, Gh. Păun, Stratified grammar systems, *Computers and Artificial Intelligence*, accepted.

10. E. Csuhaj-Varjú, J. Dassow, J. Kelemen, Gh. Păun, *Grammar Systems*, Gordon and Breach Publ. House, London, 1994.

11. E. Csuhaj-Varjú, J. Dassow, Gh. Păun, Dynamically controlled cooperating/distributed grammar systems, *Information Sciences*, 69 (1993), 1 – 25.

12. J. Dassow, J. Kelemen, Cooperating/distributed grammar systems: a link between formal languages and artificial intelligence, *EATCS Bulletin*, 45 (1991), 131 – 145.

13. Y. Demazeau, J.-P. Müller, Decentralized artificial intelligence, in *Decentralized A.I.* (Y. Demazeau, J.-P. Müller, eds.), North Holland, Amsterdam, 1990.

14. M. A. K. Halliday, *An Introduction to Functional Grammar*, Edward Arnold Publishers, London, 1985.

15. C. E. Hewitt, Offices are open systems, *ACM Trans. on Office Information Systems*, 4 (1986), 271 – 287.

16. J. Kelemen, Syntactical models of distributed cooperative systems, *J. of Experimental and Theoretical Artificial Intelligence*, 3 (1991), 1 – 10.

17. P. Maes, Designing autonomous agents, *Robotics and Autonomous Systems*, 6 (1990), 1 – 2.

18. R. Meersman, G. Rozenberg, Cooperating grammar systems, *Proc. of Symp. MFCS'78*, Springer-Verlag, Berlin, 1978, 364 – 373.

19. M. Minsky, *The Society of Mind*, Simon & Schuster, New York, 1988.

20. F. C. N. Pereira, B. J. Grosz., eds., *Natural Language Processing*, Special volume of *Artificial Intelligence*, 63 (1993), 1 - 2.

21. G. Păun, Formal grammars and cognitive architectures, in *Foundamentals of Artificial Intelligence Research*, (Ph. Jorrand, J. Kelemen, eds.), Springer-Verlag, Berlin, 1991, 48 - 58.

22. Gh. Păun, L. Sântean, Parallel communicating grammar systems: the regular case, *Ann. Univ. Bucuresti, Mat.-Inform.*, 38 (1989), 55 - 63.

23. A. Salomaa, *Formal Languages*, Academic Press, New York, 1973.

24. H. A. Simon, *The Sciences of the Artificial* (2nd edition), The MIT Press, Cambridge, Massachusetts, 1982.

Normal Forms for Contextual Grammars[1]

Andrzej EHRENFEUCHT

Department of Computer Science, University of Colorado at Boulder
Boulder, CO 80309, USA

Gheorghe PĂUN

Institute of Mathematics of the Romanian Academy of Sciences
PO Box 1 – 764, 70700 Bucureşti, Romania

Grzegorz ROZENBERG

Department of Computer Science, Leiden University
PO Box 9512, 2300 RA Leiden, The Netherlands
and
Department of Computer Science, University of Colorado at Boulder
Boulder, CO 80309, USA

Abstract. Two normal form theorems for contextual grammars with regular choice are given. The first one concerns the (dynamic) use of productions in derivations when a contextual grammar is executed in the external mode. The second one concerns the (static) relationships between the productions and so it applies to both the external and the internal execution of contextual grammars.

Using the first normal form, a new (more elegant) proof of the linearity of the external languages of contextual grammars with regular choice is given.

1. Introduction

Contextual grammars were introduced in [2] based on linguistic motivations. Since then it has been demonstrated that contextual grammars play fundamental role in formal language theory (see, e.g., [1], [3], [5], [6], [7], [8], etc.).

A *contextual production* is of the form $\pi = (D, u\$v)$, where D is a language (called the *selector* of π), u, v are words and $\$$ is a reserved symbol (the words u and v are called the *left* and the *right context* of π, the word $u\$v$ is called the

---

[1]Research supported by ESPRIT Basic Research Working Group ASMICS II

context of π). For a word w one may consider applying π to w either *externally* or *internally*. If $w \in D$, then π can be applied externally to w yielding the word uwv (w gets "surrounded" by the context words: the left context u on the left and the right context v on the right). If w is of the form $w_1 w_2 w_3$ and $w_2 \in D$, then π can be applied internally to w yielding a word $w_1 u w_2 v w_3$ (a subword w_2 of w gets "surrounded" by the context words u and v).

A contextual grammar G consists essentially of a finite set of axioms A and a finite set P of contextual productions. We say that a grammar G is *with regular choice* if all the selectors in its productions are regular sets. An *external derivation* (*internal derivation*) in G is a sequence of words $w_0, w_1, \ldots, w_n$, with $n \geq 0$, where w_0 is an axiom and for each $0 \leq i \leq n$ there is a production π in P such that π applied externally (applied internally, respectively) to w_{i-1} yields w_i. The *external language* (*internal language*) of G consists of all words appearing in external derivations (internal derivations, respectively) of G.

In this paper we investigate normal forms for contextual grammars.

The first of them concerns the structure of (the use of productions in the) external derivations. We demonstrate that each external language L can be generated by a contextual grammar G such that for each $w \in L$ there exists an external derivation $w_0, w_1, \ldots, w_n = w$, where if $\pi_i = (D_i, u_i \$ v_i)$ and $\pi_{i+1} = (D_{i+1}, u_{i+1} \$ v_{i+1})$ are productions applied externally to w_i and w_{i+1}, respectively, then $\{u_i\} D_i \{v_i\} \subseteq D_{i+1}$; we say that (π_i, π_{i+1}) is a *matching pair* of productions. Hence if (π_i, π_{i+1}) is a matching pair, then *whenever* π_i can be externally applied to a word z yielding the word z', then π_{i+1} can be externally applied to z'. This *matching normal form* is then used to give a very simple proof of the fact that the languages externally generated by contextual grammars with regular choice are linear.

The second normal form concerns the structure of selectors of productions in a contextual grammar. We demonstrate that for each contextual grammar G there is a contextual grammar G' such that for any two productions $\pi_1 = (D_1, u_1 \$ v_1)$ and $\pi_2 = (D_2, u_2 \$ v_2)$ of P either $D_1 = D_2$ or $D_1 \cap D_2 = \emptyset$, and both the internal and the external languages of G and G' are equal. Thus the union of all selectors (for all productions) from G' is partitioned by the family of all selectors from all productions of G'.

This *disjoint-equal normal form* is "static" in nature: it concerns the apriori given structure of productions. Note that if a contextual grammar G is in this normal form, then the only nondeterminism in external derivations comes from the fact that one may have different productions with the same selectors. (If we additionally require that different productions have different selectors, and there is one axiom only, then G generates a sequence of words.)

At the end of the paper we also consider a combination of these two normal forms.

2. Contextual grammars; the need of normal forms

We begin by giving some basic notions and notations to be used in this paper (we refer the reader to [9] for the basic notions of formal language theory that are not explicitly introduced in this paper). For an alphabet V, V^* denotes the free monoid generated by V; λ is the empty word and $V^+ = V^* - \{\lambda\}$. For a regular expression E, LE is the language denoted by E, and $\mathcal{A}L$ is the minimal deterministic (total) finite automaton recognizing LE. For $L_1, L_2 \subseteq V^*$, $L_1 \backslash L_2$ and L_2/L_1 denote respectively the left and the right quotient of L_2 with respect to L_1, hence

$$L_1 \backslash L_2 = \{w \in V^* \mid uw \in L_2 \text{ for some } u \in L_1\},$$
$$L_2/L_1 = \{w \in V^* \mid wu \in L_2 \text{ for some } u \in L_1\}.$$

A *contextual grammar with arbitrary choice* [2] is a triple

$$G = (V, A, P),$$

where V is an alphabet, A is a finite set of strings over V, and P is a finite set of *productions*, where each production is of the form

$$\pi = (D, u\$v),$$

where D is a language over V, u, v are strings over V, and $\$$ is a reserved symbol not in V. D is called the *selector* and $u\$v$ the *context* of π.

For $\pi = (D, u\$v) \in P$ and $x \in D$ the result of applying externally π to x is denoted by $\pi(x)$, i.e. $\pi(x) = uxv$; we also write $x \Longrightarrow_\pi uxv$ or $x \Longrightarrow uxv$. Then, the *external language* generated by G is

$$L_{ex}(G) = A \cup \{y \in V^* \mid w = x_1 \Longrightarrow \ldots \Longrightarrow x_k = y, w \in A, k \geq 1\}.$$

Hence one begins with a string in A and repeatedly adjoins contexts (u, v), providing that the selections of the productions providing the contexts allows that. More specifically, we can write

$y \in L_{ex}(G)$ iff   either $y \in A$ or
         $y = u_n \ldots u_1 w v_1 \ldots v_n$, with $n \geq 1$,
         where $w \in A \cap D_1$, for some $(D_1, u_1\$v_1) \in P$,
         and for each $2 \leq i \leq n, u_{i-1} \ldots u_1 w v_1 \ldots v_{i-1} \in D_i$
         for some $(D_i, u_i\$v_i) \in P$.

Hence the generation process reminds the one used in linear grammars: symbols are added at the ends of the current string. However, a linear grammar proceeds in the opposite direction, by introducing first the extreme symbols and then moving stepwise towards the center. Thus, we could try to "reverse" an external derivation δ in a contextual grammar,

$$\delta \ : \ w \Longrightarrow u_1 w v_1 \Longrightarrow u_2 u_1 w v_1 v_2 \Longrightarrow \ldots \Longrightarrow u_n \ldots u_1 w v_1 \ldots v_n,$$

and to associate with it an equivalent derivation in a linear grammar,

$$S \Longrightarrow u_n \overline{D}_n v_n \Longrightarrow \ldots \Longrightarrow u_n \ldots u_1 \overline{D}_1 v_1 \ldots v_n \Longrightarrow u_n \ldots u_1 w v_1 \ldots v_n,$$

where $\overline{D}_i, 1 \le i \le n$, are symbols associated to the selectors D_i involved in productions used in δ (i.e. for all $2 \le i \le n, u_{i-1} \ldots u_1 w v_1 \ldots v_{i-1} \in D_i$ and $(D_i, u_i \$ v_i) \in P$). However, this idea may not work in general without modifying the generated language, because a rule $\overline{D}_{i+1} \to u_i \overline{D}_i v_i$ assumes that every string $u_i x v_i$, with $x \in D_i$ belongs to D_{i+1}.

This is illustrated by the following example. Consider $G = (\{a, b, c, d, e\}, \{ab\}, P)$, with P containing the productions

$$\pi_1 = (\{ab\}, a\$b),$$
$$\pi_2 = (\{ab, aabb\}, c\$c),$$
$$\pi_3 = (\{cabc\}, d\$d),$$
$$\pi_4 = (\{caabbc\}, e\$e).$$

There are only two maximal derivations in G (i.e. derivations that cannot be continued anymore):

$$\delta_1 \ : \ ab \Longrightarrow_{\pi_1} aabb \Longrightarrow_{\pi_2} caabba \Longrightarrow_{\pi_4} ecaabbce,$$
$$\delta_2 \ : \ ab \Longrightarrow_{\pi_2} cabc \Longrightarrow_{\pi_3} dcabcd.$$

Reversing them we get

$$\delta_1' \ : \ S \Longrightarrow e \overline{D}_4 e \Longrightarrow ec \overline{D}_2 ce \Longrightarrow eca \overline{D}_1 bce \Longrightarrow ecaabbce,$$
$$\delta_2' \ : \ S \Longrightarrow d \overline{D}_3 d \Longrightarrow dc \overline{D}_2 cd \Longrightarrow dcabcd.$$

Continuing from $dc \overline{D}_2 cd$ in δ_2' with $\overline{D}_2 \Longrightarrow a \overline{D}_1 b \Longrightarrow aabb$ as in δ_1', we obtain the string $dcaabbcd$ which is not in $L_{ex}(G)$!

This leads us to consider the following property. Let $G = (V, A, P)$ be a contextual grammar, and let $\pi_1 = (D_1, u_1 \$ v_1), \pi_2 = (D_2, u_2 \$ v_2)$ be two productions of P. We say that the ordered pair (π_1, π_2) is *matching* if and only if for every $x \in D_1$ we have $\pi_1(x) \in D_2$. A derivation in G is *matching* if and only if every two consecutive productions π_i, π_{i+1} used in it form a matching pair. A contextual grammar G is in the *matching normal form* if for every $x \in L_{ex}(G)$ there is a matching derivation in G.

As should be clear from the above discussion, with each matching derivation we can associate an equivalent linear derivation; this leads to the following theorem. Note that the selection sets D_i in productions can be arbitrary languages. Since contextual grammars with arbitrary choice can generate arbitrarily complex languages (even non-recursively enumerable), the following result is somewhat surprising.

Theorem 1. *If G is a contextual grammar in the matching normal form, then $L_{ex}(G)$ is a linear language.*

Proof. Let $G = (V, A, P)$ with $A = \{w_1, \ldots, w_k\}$, and $P = \{\pi_1, \ldots, \pi_n\}$, where, for each $1 \leq i \leq n$, $\pi_i = (D_i, u_i\$v_i)$. With each set D_i we associate a nonterminal $\overline{D}_i$. Then let G' be the linear grammar

$$G' = (\{\overline{D}_i \mid 1 \leq i \leq n\} \cup \{S\}, V, S, P'),$$

where P' contains the following productions:

1. $S \rightarrow w_i$, for $1 \leq i \leq k$,

        $S \rightarrow u_i\overline{D}_iv_i$, for $1 \leq i \leq n$,
2. $\overline{D}_i \rightarrow w_j$, for each $1 \leq i \leq n$, and $1 \leq j \leq k$, such that $w_j \in D_i$,
3. $\overline{D}_j \rightarrow u_i\overline{D}_iv_i$, for each matching pair (π_i, π_j), where $1 \leq i, j \leq n$.

We will prove now that $L(G) = L(G')$.

($\subseteq$) Let $z \in L(G)$ and consider a matching derivation for z in G,

$$w_i \Longrightarrow u_{j_1}w_iv_{j_1} \Longrightarrow u_{j_2}u_{j_1}w_iv_{j_1}v_{j_2} \Longrightarrow \ldots \Longrightarrow u_{j_m}\ldots u_{j_1}w_iv_{j_1}\ldots v_{j_m} = z,$$

which is using the productions $\pi_{j_1} = (D_{j_1}, u_{j_1}\$v_{j_1}), \ldots, \pi_{j_m} = (D_{j_m}, u_{j_m}\$v_{j_m})$ such that $w_i \in D_{j_1}$, $u_{j_s}\ldots u_{j_1}w_iv_{j_1}\ldots v_{j_s} \in D_{j_{s+1}}, 1 \leq s \leq m - 1$. The pairs $(\pi_{j_s}, \pi_{j_{s+1}}), 1 \leq s \leq m - 1$, are matching, hence the rules $\overline{D}_{j_{s+1}} \rightarrow u_{j_{s+1}}\overline{D}_{j_s}v_{j_{s+1}}, 1 \leq s \leq m - 1$, are in P'; P' contains also the rule $S \rightarrow u_{j_m}\overline{D}_{j_m}v_{j_m}$ and, because $w_i \in D_{j_1}$, the rule $\overline{D}_{j_1} \rightarrow w_i$. Consequently we have the following derivation in G':

$$S \Longrightarrow u_{j_m}\overline{D}_{j_m}v_{j_m} \Longrightarrow u_{j_m}u_{j_{m-1}}\overline{D}_{j_{m-1}}v_{j_{m-1}}v_{j_m} \Longrightarrow \ldots$$

$$\ldots \Longrightarrow u_{j_m}\ldots u_{j_1}\overline{D}_{j_1}v_{j_1}\ldots v_{j_m} \Longrightarrow u_{j_m}\ldots u_{j_1}w_iv_{j_1}\ldots v_{j_m} = z.$$

Thus $z \in L(G')$.

($\supseteq$) Take $z \in L(G')$ produced by a derivation in G'

$$S \Longrightarrow u_{j_m}\overline{D}_{j_m}v_{j_m} \Longrightarrow u_{j_m}u_{j_{m-1}}\overline{D}_{j_{m-1}}v_{j_{m-1}}v_{j_m} \Longrightarrow \ldots$$

$$\ldots \Longrightarrow u_{j_m}\ldots u_{j_1}\overline{D}_{j_1}v_{j_1}\ldots v_{j_m} \Longrightarrow u_{j_m}\ldots u_{j_1}w_iv_{j_1}\ldots v_{j_m} = z.$$

The used rules are $S \to u_{j_m} \overline{D}_{j_m} v_{j_m}, \overline{D}_{j_1} \to w_i$, and $\overline{D}_{j_{s+1}} \to u_{j_s} \overline{D}_{j_s} v_{j_s}, 1 \leq s \leq m - 1$. The rule $\overline{D}_{j_1} \to w_i$ is introduced in P' only when $w_i \in D_{j_1}$ and $\overline{D}_{j_{s+1}} \to u_{j_s} \overline{D}_{j_s} v_{j_s}$ corresponds to a matching pair $(\pi_{j_s}, \pi_{j_{s+1}}), 1 \leq s \leq m - 1$. Consequently, $w_i \in D_{j_1}, u_{j_1} w_i v_{j_1} \in D_{j_2}, \ldots, u_{j_s} \ldots u_{j_1} w_i v_{j_1} \ldots v_{j_s} \in D_{j_{s+1}}, \ldots$, and $u_{j_{m-1}} \ldots u_{j_1} w_i v_{j_1} \ldots v_{j_{m-1}} \in D_{j_m}$. Consequently we have the following derivation in G:

$$w_i \Longrightarrow u_{j_1} w_i v_{j_1} \Longrightarrow u_{j_2} u_{j_1} w_i v_{j_1} v_{j_2} \Longrightarrow \ldots \Longrightarrow u_{j_m} \ldots u_{j_1} w_i v_{j_1} \ldots v_{j_m} = z.$$

Thus $z \in L(G)$. $\square$

Note that iff the selectors appearing in the productions of G are not recursive, then the construction from the proof of Theorem 1 is not effective.

Two contextual grammars G_1, G_2 are *externally equivalent* if and only if $L_{ex}(G_1) = L_{ex}(G_2)$.

3. The matching normal form theorem

Consider the contextual grammar

$$G = (\{a, b, c, d\}, \{ab\}, P),$$

with the productions

$$\pi_1 = (a^+ b^+, a\$b),$$
$$\pi_2 = (a^+ b^+ c^*, \$c),$$
$$\pi_3 = (\{a^n b^m c^m \mid n, m \geq 1\}, d\$d).$$

Then
$$L_{ex}(G) = \{a^n b^n c^m \mid n \geq 1, m \geq 0\} \cup \{da^n b^n c^n d \mid n \geq 1\},$$

which is a non-context-free (and hence non-linear) language. Thus according to Theorem 1 we cannot find matching derivations for all strings in $L_{ex}(G)$, and this is true for all grammars externally equivalent with G. We note that D_1 and D_2 (in π_1, π_2) are regular while D_3 is linear. We will show now that when all sets D_i in a grammar are regular (we say then that such a grammar is *with regular choice*, or that it is an *rc contextual grammar*), then an externally equivalent grammar in the matching normal form exists. Hence, by Theorem 1, it is the selector of the production π_4 in the grammar G above that is responsible for the non-linearity of $L_{ex}(G)$.

When specifying the productions $\pi_i = (D_i, u_i \$ v_i)$ of an rc contextual grammar, we shall represent the languages D_i by regular expressions, thus writing $\pi_i = (E_i, u_i \$ v_i)$, for E_i a regular expression such that $D_i = LE_i$. Sometimes we shall identify the regular expressions and the languages they represent, that is $(E_i, u_i \$ v_i)$ and $(LE_i, u_i \$ v_i)$ will represent the same production.

The family of languages externally generated by rc contextual grammars is denoted by $EC(REG)$.

Given a contextual grammar $G = (V, A, P)$, a grammar $G' = (V, A, P')$ with $P \subseteq P'$ is called an *extension* of G.

Theorem 2. *For every rc contextual grammar G there is an externally equivalent rc contextual grammar G' in the matching normal form; moreover, G' is an extension of G.*

We shall present the construction of G' after establishing a series of preliminary lemmas (whenever possible, they are stated for arbitrary contextual grammars rather than for rc contextual grammars only).

Lemma 1. *If $(D_1, u\$v)$ is a production of a contextual grammar $G = (V, A, P)$ and $D_2 \subseteq D_1$, then $L_{ex}(G) = L_{ex}(G')$ where $G' = (V, A, P \cup \{(D_2, u\$v)\})$.*

Proof. Obvious, because the use of the production $(D_2, u\$v)$ can be replaced by the use of $(D_1, u\$v)$. $\square$

For productions $\pi_1 = (D_1, u_1\$v_1), \pi_2 = (D_2, u_2\$v_2)$ of a contextual grammar $G = (V, A, P)$, denote

$$M[\pi_1, \pi_2] = D_1 \cap u_1 \backslash D_2 / v_1.$$

Lemma 2. *For π_1, π_2 as above, the pair $(\pi_{1,2}, \pi_2)$, with $\pi_{1,2} = (M[\pi_1, \pi_2], u\$v)$ is matching.*

Proof. By the definition of $M[\pi_1, \pi_2]$ we have $\pi_1(x) \in D_2$ for all $x \in M[\pi_1, \pi_2]$. As $\pi_1(x) = u_1 x v_1 = \pi_{1,2}(x)$, the lemma holds. $\square$

Lemma 3. *If $G = (V, A, P)$ is a contextual grammar, and $\pi_1, \pi_2 \in P$, with $\pi_1 = (D_1, u_1\$v_1)$, then $G' = (V, A, P \cup \{\pi_{1,2}\})$, with $\pi_{1,2} = (M[\pi_1, \pi_2], u_1\$v_1)$, is a contextual grammar externally equivalent with G.*

Proof. By definition, $M[\pi_1, \pi_2] \subseteq D_1$, hence the lemma follows from Lemma 1. $\square$

We move now to establishing those preliminary results (necessary in the proof of Theorem 2) which hold only for rc contextual grammars.

A deterministic total finite automaton without final states is called a *transition system*. Hence, such a transition system is a 4-tuple $A = (V, Q, \delta, q_{in})$, where V is an alphabet, Q is the set of states, $q_{in} \in Q$ is the initial state, and $\delta : Q \times V \longrightarrow Q$ is a transition function.

Two transition systems $A_i = (V_i, Q_i, \delta_i, q_{in,i}), i = 1, 2$, are said *equal* if and only if $V_1 = V_2$ and there is a bijection $\varphi : Q_1 \longrightarrow Q_2$ such that

1. $\varphi(q_{in,1}) = q_{in,2}$,
2. $\delta_1(q, a) = q'$ iff $\delta_2(\varphi(q), a) = \varphi(q')$ for all $a \in V_1$ and all $q, q' \in Q_1$.

Let $\mathcal{T}$ be a finite set of transition systems over the same alphabet V. The *closure* of $\mathcal{T}$, denoted $cl(\mathcal{T})$, is the smallest set $\mathcal{T}'$ of transition systems containing $\mathcal{T}$ and closed under the following two operations.

1. *Taking subsystems* determined by setting any state to be initial.

   Hence for $\mathcal{A} = (V, Q, \delta, q_{in})$ and $q_0 \in Q$, we define $sub(\mathcal{A}, q_0) = (V, Q', \delta', q_0)$, where $Q' = \{q \in Q \mid$ there is $u \in V^*$ such that $\delta(q_0, u) = q\}$ (the set of all states reachable from q_0), and $\delta : Q' \times V \longrightarrow Q'$, is defined by $\delta'(q, a) = \delta(q, a)$ for all $q \in Q'$ and all $a \in V$ (the restriction of δ to $Q' \times V$).

2. *The reachable product.*

   For $\mathcal{A}_i = (V, Q_i, \delta_i, q_{in,i}), i = 1, 2$, the reachable product of $\mathcal{A}_1, \mathcal{A}_2$ is the transition system $\mathcal{A}_1 \otimes \mathcal{A}_2 = (V, Q_{1,2}, \delta_{1,2}, (q_{in,1}, q_{in,2}))$, where $Q_{1,2} = \{(q_1, q_2) \mid$ there is $u \in V^*$ such that $\delta_1(q_{in,1}, u) = q_1$, and $\delta(q_{in,2}, u) = q_2\}$ (the set of pairs in $Q_1 \times Q_2$ reachable from $q_{in,1}, q_{in,2}$ in the two transition systems by the same string in V^*), $\delta_{1,2}((q_1, q_2), a) = (\delta_1(q_1, a), \delta_2(q_2, a))$ for $(q_1, q_2) \in Q_{1,2}, a \in V$.

Here are some properties of these operations.

Lemma 4. *The reachable product is commutative and associative.*

Proof. Follows directly from our definition of equality of two isomorphic transition systems. $\square$

Lemma 5. *If $\mathcal{A}_i = (V, Q_i, \delta_i, q_{in,i}), i = 1, 2$, are two transition systems and $q_1 \in Q_1, q_2 \in Q_2$, then*

$$sub(\mathcal{A}_1, q_1) \otimes sub(\mathcal{A}_2, q_2) = sub(\mathcal{A}_1 \otimes \mathcal{A}_2, (q_1, q_2)).$$

Proof. This follows directly from our definition of the equality of transition systems and from the fact that each $\mathcal{A}_i$ is deterministic and total. $\square$

Corollary. *Every $\mathcal{B} \in cl(\mathcal{T})$ is of the form*

$$\mathcal{B} = sub(\mathcal{A}_{i_1} \otimes \mathcal{A}_{i_2} \otimes \ldots \otimes \mathcal{A}_{i_m}, (q_{i_1}, q_{i_2}, \ldots, q_{i_m})),$$

where $m \geq 1$, each $\mathcal{A}_{i_j} \in \mathcal{T}$, and each q_{i_j} is a state of $\mathcal{A}_{i_j}$ for each $1 \leq j \leq m$.

Lemma 6. *Given a transition system $\mathcal{B} = (V, Q, \delta, q_{in})$, there are only finitely many deterministic finite automata whose underlying transition systems are equal to $\mathcal{B}$.*

Proof. $\mathcal{B}$ is the underlying transition system of a finite automaton $\mathcal{A}$ if and only if $\mathcal{A} = (V, Q, \delta, q_{in}, F)$ with $F \subseteq Q$. Hence there are $2^{card(Q)}$ such automata (we have included the case $F = \emptyset$). $\qquad\square$

The following result plays a crucial role in the proof of Theorem 2.

Lemma 7. *If $\mathcal{T}$ is a finite set of transition systems, then $cl(\mathcal{T})$ is finite.*

Proof. Let $\mathcal{T} = \{\mathcal{A}_1, \ldots, \mathcal{A}_n\}$, where, for each $1 \le i \le n$, $\mathcal{A}_i = (V, Q_i, \delta_i, q_{in,i})$, and let $\mathcal{B} \in cl(\mathcal{T})$. According to the above corollary, $\mathcal{B}$ is a subsystem of the product $\mathcal{C} = \mathcal{A}_{i_1} \otimes \mathcal{A}_{i_2} \otimes \ldots \otimes \mathcal{A}_{i_m}$ of some $m \ge 1$ elements of $\mathcal{T}$.

Let m_0 be the smallest such m, for the given $\mathcal{B}$. Consider the initial state of $\mathcal{B}$, say $(q_{i_1,j_1}, q_{i_2,j_2}, \ldots, q_{i_{m_0},j_{m_0}})$ where $q_{i_k,j_k} \in Q_{i_k}$ for each $1 \le k \le m_0$.

Claim. *For no k, l such that $1 \le k < l \le m_0$ we have $i_k = i_l$ and $j_k = j_l$.*

Proof of the claim. As all $\mathcal{A}_i \in \mathcal{T}$ are deterministic and total, if $i_k = i_l, j_k = j_l$, then

$$\delta_{i_k}(q_{i_k,j_k}, u) = \delta_{i_l}(q_{i_l,j_l}, u),$$

for all $u \in V^*$ (what happens on coordinates i_k, i_l is identical). Therefore we can define an isomorphism φ from $Q_{\mathcal{B}}$, the set of states of $\mathcal{B}$, to a set $Q'_{\mathcal{B}}$ of $(m_0 - 1)$-tuples, by

$$\varphi(q_{i_1,s_1}, \ldots, q_{i_k,s_k}, \ldots, q_{i_{l-1},s_{l-1}}, q_{i_l,s_l}, q_{i_{l+1},s_{l+1}}, \ldots, q_{i_{m_0},s_{m_0}}) =$$
$$= (q_{i_1,s_1}, \ldots, q_{i_k,s_k}, \ldots, q_{i_{l-1},s_{l-1}}, q_{i_{l+1},s_{l+1}}, \ldots, q_{i_{m_0},s_{m_0}})$$

(we skip the coordinate l, because $q_{i_k,s_k} = q_{i_l,s_l}$).

Consequently, $\mathcal{B}$ is equal to a transition system $\mathcal{B}'$ which is a subsystem of the product of $m_0 - 1$ elements of $\mathcal{T}$, contradicting the fact that m_0 is minimal.

This claim implies that every $\mathcal{A}_i$ in $\mathcal{T}$ can appear in the product $\mathcal{C}$ at most $card(Q_i)$ times, and so the constant m_0 is bounded by

$$M_0 = \sum_{i=1}^{n} card(Q_i).$$

Thus, each $\mathcal{B} \in cl(\mathcal{T})$ is a subsystem of a product $\mathcal{A}_{i_1} \otimes \ldots \otimes \mathcal{A}_{i_m}$ with $m \le m_0$, which implies that $cl(\mathcal{T})$ is finite. $\qquad\square$

We relate now the operations used for defining $cl(\mathcal{T})$ to the construction of the set $M[\pi_1, \pi_2]$ as in Lemmas 2, 3.

Lemma 8. *Let $\pi_1 = (E_1, u_1\$v_1)$, $\pi_2 = (E_2, u_2\$v_2)$ be productions in an rc contextual grammar $G = (V, A, P)$, and let $\mathcal{A}_1, \mathcal{A}_2$ be the underlying transition systems of the deterministic total finite automata AE_1, AE_2 recognizing LE_1 and LE_2, respectively. There is an automaton $\mathcal{B}$ accepting $M[\pi_1, \pi_2]$ such that its underlying transition system $\mathcal{A}$ is a subsystem of $\mathcal{A}_1 \otimes \mathcal{A}_2$.*

Proof. Let $\mathcal{AE}_i = (V, Q_i, \delta_i, q_{in,i}, F_i)$, for $i = 1, 2$; hence $\mathcal{A}_i = (V, Q_i, \delta_i, q_{in,i})$. Let $\mathcal{B} = (V, Q, \delta, q_{in}, F)$ be the deterministic finite automaton recognizing $M[\pi_1, \pi_2] = LE_1 \cap u_1 \backslash LE_2 / v_1$ where:

$$Q = \{(q_1, q_2) \quad | \quad \text{there is } u \in V^* \text{ such that}$$
$$\delta_1(q_{in,1}, u) = q_1, \delta_2(q_{in,2}, u_1 u) = q_2\}$$

(all pairs of states reachable by the same input word in $\mathcal{A}_1$ from $q_{in,1}$ and in $\mathcal{A}_2$ from $\delta_2(q_{in,2}, u_1)$),

$$q_{in} = (q_{in,1}, \delta_2(q_{in,2}, u_1)),$$
$$F = \{(q_1, q_2) \mid q_1 \in F_1, \delta(q_2, v_1) \in F_2\},$$
$$\delta((q_1, q_2), a) = (\delta_1(q_1, a), \delta_2(q_2, a)), (q_1, q_2) \in Q, a \in V.$$

Clearly $L(\mathcal{B}) = M[\pi_1, \pi_2]$.

Ignoring the final states of $\mathcal{B}$, we obtain a transition system $\mathcal{A}$ which is clearly equal to $\mathcal{A}_1 \otimes sub(\mathcal{A}_2, \delta_2(q_{in,2}, u_1)) = sub(\mathcal{A}_1 \otimes \mathcal{A}_2, (q_{in,1}, \delta_2(q_{in,2}, u_1)))$. Hence the lemma holds. $\quad\square$

For productions $\pi_i = (E_i, u_i \$ v_i), i = 1, 2$, in an rc contextual grammar, we write

$$\pi_1 \subseteq \pi_2 \quad \text{iff} \quad LE_1 \subseteq LE_2 \text{ and } (u_1, v_1) = (u_2, v_2),$$
$$\pi_1 \equiv \pi_2 \quad \text{iff} \quad LE_1 = LE_2 \text{ and } (u_1, v_1) = (u_2, v_2).$$

Moreover, let $m[\pi_1, \pi_2]$ be a regular expression for the language $M[\pi_1, \pi_2]$ (clearly, $M[\pi_1, \pi_2]$ is a regular set).

Proof of Theorem 2. Let $G = (V, A, P)$ be an rc contextual grammar. We construct a sequence $G_1, G_2, \ldots, G_n$ of rc contextual grammars $G_i = (V, A, P_i), 1 \leq i \leq n$, as follows:

1. $P_1 = P$,
2. (C1) If there are $\pi_1 = (E_1, u_1 \$ v_1), \pi_2 = (E_2, u_2 \$ v_2)$ in P_i
   such that for each $\pi_3 \in P_i$ we have $\pi_3 \not\equiv (m[\pi_1, \pi_2], u_1 \$ v_1)$, then
   $$P_{i+1} = P_i \cup \{m[\pi_1, \pi_2], u_1 \$ v_1)\},$$
   go to 2;
3. (C2) Else $n = i$, stop.

The grammar we look for is $G' = G_n$ given by this construction.

Claim 1. (Correctness of the definition) *There is an i such that (C2) holds (hence the procedure terminates).*

Proof. Let $\mathcal{T}$ be the set of all transition systems that underlie the deterministic finite automata $\mathcal{AE}$, for productions $(E, u \$ v)$ in P. This is a finite set.

By Lemma 8, for each production $(E', u'\$v')$ in P_i, $1 \leq i \leq n$, the underlying transition system of $\mathcal{A}E'$ is in $cl(\mathcal{T})$. By Lemma 7, this set is finite. By Lemma 6, the set of finite automata corresponding to transition systems in $cl(\mathcal{T})$ is also finite. Therefore each P_i is a subset of a fixed finite set of productions, and so the construction terminates.

Claim 2. *For every production $\pi_3 \in P_n$ there is $\pi_1 \in P$ such that $\pi_3 \subseteq \pi_1$.*

Proof. We shall prove by induction on i that for each $\pi_3 \in P_i$ there is $\pi_1 \in P$ such that $\pi_3 \subseteq \pi_1$.

For $i = 1$ the statement trivially holds, $\pi_3 \subseteq \pi_3 \in P_1 = P$.

Assume that the statement is true for all $i \leq j$ for some $j \geq 1$, and consider P_{j+1}.

Each $\pi_3 \in P_{j+1}$ is either in P_j, and then by the inductive assumption $\pi_3 \subseteq \pi_1 \in P$, or $\pi_3 \in P_{j+1} - P_j$. In the latter case $\pi_3 = (m[\pi_4, \pi_2], u_1\$v_1)$ for some $\pi_4, \pi_2 \in P_j$. From the construction of $M[\pi_4, \pi_2]$ it follows $\pi_3 \subseteq \pi_4$, and by the inductive assumption we have $\pi_4 \subseteq \pi_1$ for $\pi_1 \in P$; consequently, $\pi_3 \subseteq \pi_1 \in P$, which concludes the proof of Claim 2.

Claim 3. $L_{ex}(G_n) = L_{ex}(G)$.

Proof. From the construction, for all $1 \leq i \leq n-1$, $P_{i+1} = P_i \cup \{(m[\pi_1, \pi_2], u_1\$v_1)\}$ for some $\pi_1, \pi_2 \in P_i$, hence by Lemma 3 we have $L_{ex}(G_i) = L_{ex}(G_{i+1})$. This implies that $L_{ex}(G_i) = L_{ex}(G_1) = L_{ex}(G)$, for all $i = 1, 2, \ldots, n$.

Claim 4. *For every $z \in L_{ex}(G_n)$ there is a matching derivation in G_n producing z.*

Proof. Since $z \in L_{ex}(G_n) = L_{ex}(G)$, there is a derivation for z in G,

$$w_j \Longrightarrow_{\pi_1} u_1 w_j v_1 \Longrightarrow_{\pi_2} \cdots \Longrightarrow_{\pi_m} u_m \ldots u_1 w_j v_1 \ldots v_m = z,$$

where $\pi_k = (E_k, u_k\$v_k)$ for $1 \leq k \leq m$, $w_j \in A \cap LE_1$ and $u_{k-1} \ldots u_1 w_j v_1 \ldots v_{k-1} \in LE_k$ for all $2 \leq k \leq m$.

Now starting with productions $\pi_1, \pi_2, \ldots, \pi_m$, we construct (backwards, starting from m) a sequence of productions $\pi'_1, \ldots, \pi'_m$ in P_n, as follows:

1. $\pi'_m = \pi_m$,

2.   for each $2 \leq i \leq m$, π'_{i-1} is a production $\pi_{0,i-1}$ of P_n such that

$$\pi_{0,i-1} \equiv (m[\pi_{i-1}, \pi'_i], u_{i-1}\$v_{i-1}).$$

Since the condition (C2) from the construction of P_n is satisfied when P_n is obtained, a production $\pi_{0,i-1}$ as above exists in P_n, and so π'_{i-1} can be constructed.

Now, starting from w_j and using the productions $\pi'_1, \pi'_2, \ldots, \pi'_m$, in this order, a derivation for z is obtained in G_n. By the definition of $\pi'_1, \ldots, \pi'_m$, this is a matching derivation ($m[\pi_{i-1}, \pi_i']$ ensures that $u_{i-1}xv_{i-1} \in LE_i'$, for $\pi_i' = (E_i', u_i\$v_i)$ for all $x \in M[\pi_{i-1}, \pi_i']$).

Consequently

(i) $\qquad$ G' exists $-$ by Claim 1;

(ii) $\qquad$ G' is an extension of G $-$ by construction;

(iii) $\qquad$ G' is externally equivalent with G $-$ by Claim 3;

(iv) $\qquad$ G' is in the matching normal form $-$ by Claim 4.

This concludes the proof of Theorem 2. $\qquad\qquad\qquad\qquad\qquad\qquad$ $\square$

Corollary 1. $EC(REG) \subseteq LIN.$

Proof. This follows directly from Theorems 1 and 2. $\qquad\qquad\qquad\qquad$ $\square$

This basic relationship for the theory of contextual languages is also proved in [4], [6] by rather ad-hoc combinatorial constructions, while the above proof follows from the analysis of the similarity of derivations in linear grammars and in contextual grammars.

In [6] one considers one-sided contextual grammars, that is grammars $G = (V, A, P)$ with all productions in P of the form $(D, \$v), D \subseteq V^*, v \in V^*$. We use $1REC(REG)$ to denote the family of languages generated by one-sided rc contextual grammars (the additional letter R indicates that we use *right* one-sided contexts).

It is easy to see that the considerations from the proof of Theorem 2 go through also for one-sided contexts, and that the proof of Theorem 1 shows that $L_{ex}(G)$ is regular if G is a one-sided rc contextual grammar in the matching normal form. Consequently, we get the following result.

Corollary 2. $1REC(REG) \subseteq REG.$

4. A static normal form

The previous normal form refers to the relationship between the productions used in a derivation, hence it has a dynamic character. We consider now a relationship between the selectors of the productions from a contextual grammar.

A contextual grammar $G = (V, A, P)$ with $P = \{\pi_1, \ldots, \pi_n\}$ where, for each $1 \leq i \leq n, \pi_i = (D_i, u_i\$v_i)$ is said to be in the *disjoint-equal normal form* if for all $i, j \in \{1, \ldots, n\}$, either $D_i = D_j$ or $D_i \cap D_j = \emptyset$.

This property is sometimes explicitely, sometimes implicitely formulated in the definition of a contextual grammar, whereas in other cases it is, explicitely or implicitely, ignored. As we shall prove below, for rc contextual grammars such a distinction is not significant (from the generative point of view).

As mentioned in the introduction, for a contextual grammar $G = (V, A, P)$ one can also consider the language generated by *internal application* of productions. Then one considers the following derivation relation: for $x, y \in V^*$ we write $x \longrightarrow y$ if and only if $x = x_1 x_2 x_3$ with $x_1, x_2, x_3 \in V^*$, $y = x_1 u x_2 v x_3$, and there is $\pi = (D, u\$v)$ in P with $x_2 \in D$ (the context (u, v) is applied to the subword x_2 providing that $x_2 \in D$). Then the *internal language* generated by G is

$$L_{in}(G) = A \cup \{y \in V^* \mid w \longrightarrow x_1 \longrightarrow \ldots \longrightarrow x_k = y, w \in A, k \geq 1\}.$$

Two contextual grammars G_1, G_2 are *internally equivalent* if $L_{in}(G_1) = L_{in}(G_2)$.

Theorem 3. *For every contextual grammar G there is a contextual grammar G' in the disjoint-equal normal form such that G' is both externally and internally equivalent with G.*

Before giving the proof of this theorem we give a general auxiliary result.

Lemma 9. *If in a contextual grammar $G = (V, A, P)$ we replace a production $\pi = (D, u\$v)$ with a set of productions*

$$(D_1, u\$v), (D_2, u\$v), \ldots, (D_k, u\$v), k \geq 2,$$

such that $\bigcup_{i=1}^{k} D_i = D$, then the obtained grammar, $G' = (V, A, P')$ is externally and internally equivalent with G.

Proof. ($\subseteq$) Every (internal or external) derivation step in G that is using a production $\pi' \neq \pi$, is also a derivation step in G'. If in a derivation step $x \Longrightarrow y$ (or $x \longrightarrow y$) π is used, then there is $i, 1 \leq i \leq k$, such that $x \in D_i$, hence $x \Longrightarrow y$ (or $x \longrightarrow y$) is also a derivation step in G' which is using the production $(D_i, u\$v)$.

($\supseteq$) If in a derivation step a production different from π is used, then this is also a derivation step in G. If in a derivation step a production $(D_i, u\$v)$ is used, then $x \in D_i \subseteq D$, and so this is a derivation step in G using π. $\qquad\square$

Proof of Theorem 3. Let $G = (V, A, P)$ be a contextual grammar with $P = \{\pi_1, \ldots, \pi_n\}$, where $\pi_i = (D_i, u_i\$v_i)$ for each $1 \leq i \leq n$. A contextual grammar $G' = (V, A, P')$ is constructed as follows.

For each partition $\{T_1, T_2\}$ of the set $\{1, 2, \ldots, n\}$ with $T_1 \neq \emptyset$ consider the set

$$D(T_1, T_2) = \bigcap_{i \in T_1} D_i - \bigcup_{i \in T_2} D_i \qquad (*)$$

Let $M_1, M_2, \ldots, M_q$ be the non-empty sets of the form $(*)$ for all possible partitions $\{T_1, T_2\}$ of $\{1, 2, \ldots, n\}$.

For each set M_i there is at least one D_j such that $M_i \subseteq D_j$. We define then the set P' of productions as follows:

$$(M_i, u_j\$v_j) \in P' \quad \text{iff} \quad M_i \subseteq D_j, 1 \le i \le q, 1 \le j \le n.$$

We will prove now that the contextual grammar $G' = (V, A, P')$ satisfies the statement of the theorem.

Claim 1. $\bigcup_{i=1}^{q} M_i = \bigcup_{i=1}^{n} D_i$.

Proof. Since every M_i is included in some D_j, the inclusion $\subseteq$ follows. Conversely, for $x \in \bigcup_{i=1}^{n} D_i$, let $T_1 = \{i \mid x \in D_i\}$ and $T_2 = \{1, 2, \ldots, n\} - T_1$. Clearly, $T_1 \ne \emptyset$ and $x \in \bigcap_{i \in T_1} D_i - \bigcup_{i \in T_2} D_i = M_k$ for some k where $1 \le k \le q$. Thus also the inclusion $\supseteq$ holds.

Claim 2. *For every $1 \le i \le q$ and every $1 \le j \le n$, either $M_i \subseteq D_j$ or $M_i \cap D_j = \emptyset$.*

Proof. If $M_i = \bigcap_{j \in T_1} D_j - \bigcup_{j \in T_2} D_j$, for some T_1, T_2 as above, then $M_i \subseteq D_j$, for each $j \in T_1$, and $M_i \cap D_j = \emptyset$ for each $j \in T_2$.

Claim 3. *The sets $M_1, \ldots, M_q$ are pairwise disjoint.*

Proof. By induction on n (the number of productions in P).

For $n = 1$ the claim trivially holds.

Assume that the claim holds for all $n \le m$ for some $m \ge 1$, and let $n = m + 1$.

Now let $\mathcal{M}_m$ be the family of nonempty sets denoted by all expressions of the form $(*)$ which do not involve D_{m+1}. By inductive assumption, the sets in $\mathcal{M}_m$ are pairwise disjoint. Let $\mathcal{M}_{m+1}$ be the family of nonempty sets denoted by all expressions of the form $(*)$ – hence also by expressions involving D_{m+1}. For each set M of the form

$$M = (D_{i_1} \cap D_{i_2} \cap \ldots \cap D_{i_r}) - (D_{j_1} \cup D_{j_2} \cup \ldots \cup D_{j_s}),$$

with $\{i_1, i_2, \ldots, i_r, j_1, j_2, \ldots, j_s\} = \{1, 2, \ldots, m\}$ and $r + s = m$, by considering D_{m+1} we can define

$$M_{left} = (D_{i_1} \cap \ldots \cap D_{i_r} \cap D_{m+1}) - (D_{j_1} \cup \ldots \cup D_{j_s}),$$

and

$$M_{right} = (D_{i_1} \cap \ldots \ldots D_{i_r}) - (D_{j_1} \cup \ldots \cup D_{j_s} \cup D_{m+1}).$$

Obviously, $M_{left} \subseteq M$ and $M_{right} \subseteq M$ (hence if M is empty, then both M_{left} and M_{right} are empty).

Consider now an ordered pair of sets from $\mathcal{M}_{m+1}$. Such a pair is in one of the following four forms:

$$(M_{left}, M'_{left}), \ (M_{left}, M'_{right}), \ (M_{right}, M'_{right}), \ (M_{left}, M_{right}),$$

for $M, M' \in \mathcal{M}_m$. By the induction assumption, M and M' are disjoint, hence also each of the first three pairs of sets above is disjoint. By Claim 2 we know that $M_{left} \subseteq D_{m+1}$ and $M_{right} \cap D_{m+1} = \emptyset$, hence also the sets M_{left}, M_{right} are disjoint. This completes the proof of Claim 3.

Consequently, the productions in G' have the desired property (note that one may have productions $(M, u\$v), (M', u'\$v')$ with $M = M'$; this happens when $M = M_i = M'$ for $M_i \subseteq D_j, M_i \subseteq D_k$; then both $(M_i, u_j\$v_j)$ and $(M_i, u_k\$v_k)$ are in P').

From Claims 1 and 2 it follows that for every $1 \leq i \leq n$, there are $M_{i_1}, \ldots, M_{i_k}$ such that $D_i = \bigcup_{j=1}^{k} M_{i_j}$. By Lemma 9, if we remove $(D_i, u_i\$v_i)$ and replace it by productions $(M_{i_j}, u_i\$v_i), 1 \leq j \leq k$, then neither the internally nor the externally generated language will change. Replacing in this way all productions of G leads to the use of all the sets $M_1, \ldots, M_q$. In this way G', which is both internally and externally equivalent to G is obtained. $\square$

In the above construction, we move from sets D_i in productions of P, to sets of the form $(*)$ in productions of P'. If selectors of G are in a family F which is not closed under the operations involved in expressions of the form $(*)$, then the selectors of G' may not be in F anymore. However, for $F = REG$ we have the following result.

Corollary. *For every rc contextual grammar G there is an rc contextual grammar G' in the disjoint-equal normal form such that G' is both internally and externally equivalent with G.*

The form of contexts (one- or two-sided) plays no role in the proof of Theorem 3, hence Theorem 3 and its corollary hold also for one-sided contextual grammars.

At the first sight, the two normal forms, Theorem 2 and Theorem 3, are somewhat contradictory: the proof of Theorem 2 introduces new productions, with selectors included into the selectors of old productions, whereas the proof of Theorem 3 splits the selectors of productions removing in this way possible matching relations. However, it turns out that the two normal forms can be combined (for rc contextual grammars).

Given a contextual grammar G we will use $match(G)$ to denote an arbitrary but fixed grammar G' satisfying the statement of Theorem 2 (hence $match(G)$ is externally equivalent with G and in the matching normal form), and we will use $disj(G)$ to denote an arbitrary but fixed grammar G' satisfying the statement of Theorem 3 (hence G' is externally equivalent with G and in disjoint-equal normal form).

Theorem 4. *For every rc contextual grammar G there is an rc contextual grammar G' externally equivalent with G such that G' is both in the matching normal form and in the disjoint-equal normal form.*

Proof. Let $G = (V, A, P)$ with $P = \{\pi_1, \ldots, \pi_n\}$ where $\pi_i = (E_i, u_i\$v_i)$ for each $1 \leq i \leq n$.

Let $\mathcal{T}$ be the set of underlying transition systems of given deterministic automata for $LE_1, LE_2, \ldots, LE_k$.

As we have seen in the proof of Theorem 2, the transition systems associated with productions in $match(G_0)$ are in $cl(\mathcal{T})$.

Claim 1. *The transition systems underlying the finite automata recognizing the selectors in the productions of $disj(G_0)$ are elements of $cl(\mathcal{T})$.*

Proof. The productions in $disj(G_0)$ are of the form $(M, u\$v)$, with M a set of the form $(*)$, that is

$$M = \bigcap_{i \in T_1} LE_i - \bigcup_{i \in T_2} LE_i,$$

where $\{T_1, T_2\}$ is a partition of the set $\{1, 2, \ldots, n\}$, $T_1 \neq \emptyset$. Let CLE_i denote the complement of LE_i. We have

$$M = (\bigcap_{i \in T_1} LE_i) \cap (\bigcap_{i \in T_2} CLE_i).$$

If R_1, R_2 are two regular languages recognized by the deterministic finite automata $\mathcal{B}_1, \mathcal{B}_2$ where $\mathcal{B}_i = (V, Q_i, \delta_i, q_{in,i}, F_i)$ for $i = 1, 2$, then $R_1 \cap R_2$ is recognized by the product automaton $\mathcal{B}_{1,2} = (V, Q_{1,2}, \delta_{1,2}, (q_{in,1}, q_{in,2}), F_1 \times F_2)$ with $\delta_{1,2}((q_1, q_2), a) = (\delta_1(q_1, a), \delta_2(q_2, a))$ for all $q_1 \in Q_1, q_2 \in Q_2$ and $a \in V$, and $Q_{1,2}$ contains all reachable pairs of states. Consequently, the transition system associated to $\mathcal{B}_{1,2}$ is the reachable product of the transition systems underlying $\mathcal{B}_1$ and $\mathcal{B}_2$.

Moreover, if $\mathcal{B} = (V, Q, \delta, q_{in}, F)$ is a deterministic total finite automaton for a language L, then the complement of L is recognized by $\mathcal{B}' = (V, Q, \delta, q_{in}, Q-F)$, therefore by an automaton with the same underlying transition system. Consequently, a set M given above is recognized by a finite automaton with the underlying transition system equal to $\mathcal{A}'_1 \otimes \mathcal{A}'_2 \otimes \ldots \otimes \mathcal{A}'_n$, where $\mathcal{A}'_1, \ldots, \mathcal{A}'_n$ are the underlying transition systems of the deterministic finite automata $\mathcal{A}_1, \ldots, \mathcal{A}_n$, recognizing the languages $LE_1, \ldots, LE_n$, respectively.

We construct now a sequence of grammars, $G_1, G_2, \ldots, G_m$, as follows:

1. $G_1 = G$,
2. (C1) If G_i is not in the matching normal form, then
$$G_{i+1} = match(G_i), \text{ go to 2,}$$
   (C2) Else go to 3;
3. (C3) If G_i is not in the disjoint-equal normal form, then
$$G_{i+1} = disj(G_i), \text{ go to 2,}$$
   (C4) Else $m = i$, stop.

By Lemma 8 and Claim 1 above, every G_i corresponds to a transition system in $cl(\mathcal{T})$. Moreover, if in Step 2 or in Step 3 above we construct G_{i+1} different from G_i, then G_{i+1} has strictly more productions than G_i. This implies that the procedure terminates (since $cl(\mathcal{T})$ and the set of deterministic finite automata with the transition systems in $cl(\mathcal{T})$ are finite, (C4) must be eventually fulfilled). On the other hand, the procedure terminates if and only if the currently constructed grammar is both in the disjoint-equal normal form and in the matching normal form. From the proofs of Theorems 2 and 3 we know that $L_{ex}(G_0) = L_{ex}(match(G_0)) = L_{ex}(disj(G_0))$. Consequently, if we set $G' = G_m$, then G' satisfies the statement of the theorem. $\square$

Note that the statement of Theorem 4 does not require that G' is an extension of G (compare this with Theorem 2).

References

1. A. Ehrenfeucht, Gh. Păun, G. Rozenberg, On representing recursively enumerable languages by internal contextual languages, manuscript, 1994.

2. S. Marcus, Contextual grammars, *Rev. Roum. Math. Pures Appl.*, 14 (1969), 1525 – 1534.

3. Gh. Păun, *Contextual Grammars*, The Publ House of the Romanian Academy of Sciences, Bucharest, 1982 (in Romanian).

4. Gh. Păun, On some open problems about Marcus contextual grammars, *Intern. J. Computer Math.*, 17 (1985), 9 – 23.

5. Gh. Păun, Marcus contextual grammars. After 25 years, *Bulletin EATCS*, 52 (Febr. 1994), 263 – 273.

6. Gh. Păun, G. Rozenberg, A. Salomaa, Contextual grammars: erasing, determinism, one-sided contexts, *Developments in Language Theory* (G. Rozenberg, A. Salomaa, eds.), World Sci. Publ., Singapore, 1994, 370 – 388.

7. Gh. Păun, G. Rozenberg, A. Salomaa, Contextual grammars: parallelism and blocking of derivations, *Fundamenta Informaticae*, to appear.

8. Gh. Păun, G. Rozenberg, A. Salomaa, Marcus contextual grammars: modularity and leftmost derivation, in the present volume, 375 – 392.

9. A. Salomaa, *Formal Languages*, Academic Press, New York, London, 1973.

Control Mechanisms on
#-Context-Free Array Grammars[1]

Rudolf FREUND

Institute for Computer Languages, Technical University Wien
Resselgasse 3, 1040 Wien, Austria

Abstract. Like in the string case, also for two-dimensional array grammars we obtain regular, context-free, and monotonic grammars by imposing specific restrictions on the corresponding array productions. The families of regular, context-free, monotonic, and recursively enumerable (r.e. for short) two-dimensional array languages form a Chomsky-like hierarchy. Yet if we consider #-context-free array productions with the left hand side consisting of one non-terminal symbol surrounded by some blank symbols #, but with no restrictions imposed on the right hand side, then in contrast to the string case these #-context-free two-dimensional array productions are more powerful than the restricted monotonic context-free array productions usually considered in the literature.

Whereas in the string case programmed grammars without appearance checking, matrix grammars without appearance checking, and ordered grammars using arbitrary context-free productions cannot generate every recursively enumerable string language, in this paper we show that (two-dimensional) programmed array grammars without appearance checking, matrix array grammars without appearance checking, and ordered array grammars using #-context-free two-dimensional array productions can already generate any r.e. two-dimensional array language (which is not true any longer when using context-free two-dimensional array productions only).

1. Introduction

Usually in the theory of two-dimensional array grammars only array languages of equivalence classes of connected arrays are considered ([1], [9], [11]). By imposing specific restrictions on the two-dimensional array productions, regular, context-free, and monotonic two-dimensional array grammars are obtained. The corresponding families of (two-dimensional) array languages form

---

[1]Research carried out during the author's visit at the University Magdeburg

97

a Chomsky-hierarchy like in the string case. Yet these results are obtained with a very restricted form of context-free two-dimensional array productions, i.e. with the right hand side being a finite connected pattern of non-blank symbols only. In the one-dimensional case, these restricted context-free array productions allow the generation of regular one-dimensional array languages only ([7]). Hence in this paper we investigate the generative power of #--context-free two-dimensional array productions (i.e. of two-dimensional array productions with the left hand side consisting of one non-terminal symbol surrounded by some blank symbols #, but with no restrictions imposed on the right hand side) in combination with well-known control mechanisms for regulated rewriting ([2]), i.e. in (two-dimensional) programmed array grammars, matrix array grammars, and ordered array grammars. In the string case, the additional use of λ-rules of the form $A \to \lambda$ increases the generative power of monotonic context-free productions in such a way that programmed grammars with appearance checking and matrix grammars with appearance checking using arbitrary context-free productions allow the generation of any r.e. string language, which is not possible with ordered grammars or with programmed grammars without appearance checking respectively matrix grammars without appearance checking ([2]). In contrast to the string case, the additional use of blank rules of the form $A \to \#$ in an even more astonishing way increases the generative power of context-free two-dimensional array productions: From the results shown in [7] we know that the generative power of matrix array grammars without and even with appearance checking using monotonic context-free array productions only in some sense is rather small (most of the results proved in [7] for the one-dimensional case can immediately be taken over for the two-dimensional case, too), e. g. there are monotonic array languages that cannot be generated by matrix array grammars with appearance checking using monotonic context-free array productions; yet in this paper we will prove that (two-dimensional) matrix array grammars without appearance checking, programmed array grammars without appearance checking, and ordered array grammars using #-context-free two-dimensional array productions can already generate any r.e. two-dimensional array language (using other proof techniques, in [5] it could only be shown that matrix array grammars *with* appearance checking and programmed array grammars *with* appearance checking can generate any r.e. array language).

2. String languages prerequisites

The reader is assumed to be familiar with the basic notions and results of formal language theory (e. g. see [10]). We only recall the following notions:

By $\mathbf{N}$ we denote the set of natural numbers, i.e. $\mathbf{N} = \{1, 2, \ldots\}$, and by $\mathbf{Z}$ the set of integers.

For an alphabet V, by V^* we denote the free monoid generated by V under the operation of concatenation; the *empty string* is denoted by λ, and $V^* - \{\lambda\}$ is denoted by V^+. Any subset of V^+ is called a *λ-free (string) language*. The length of $x \in V^*$ is denoted by $|x|$.

A *(string) grammar* is a quadruple $G = (V_N, V_T, P, S)$, where V_N and V_T are finite sets of non-terminal respectively terminal symbols with $V_N \cap V_T = \emptyset$, P is a finite set of productions $\alpha \to \beta$ with $\alpha \in V^+$ and $\beta \in V^*$, where $V = V_N \cup V_T$, and $S \in V_N$ is the start symbol. For $x, y \in V^*$ we say that *y is directly derivable from x in G*, denoted by $x \Longrightarrow_G y$, if and only if for some $\alpha \to \beta$ in P and $u, v \in V^*$ we get $x = u\alpha v$ and $y = u\beta v$. Denoting the reflexive and transitive closure of the derivation relation $\Longrightarrow_G$ by $\Longrightarrow_G^*$, the *(string) language generated by G* is

$$L(G) = \{w \in V_T^* \mid S \Longrightarrow_G^* w\}.$$

A production $\alpha \to \beta$ in P is called

- *monotone* if $|\alpha| \le |\beta|$,

- *context-free* if $\alpha \in V_N$,

- *λ-free context-free* if $\alpha \in V_N$ and $|\beta| \ge 1$,

- *regular* if it is of the form $A \to a$ or of the form $A \to aB$, where $A, B \in V_N$ and $a \in V_T$.

The grammar G is called an *arbitrary, monotone, context-free, λ-free context-free* respectively *regular* grammar, if every production in P is monotone, context-free, λ-free context-free respectively regular (we also say that G respectively the productions in P are of type $ENUM$, MON, CF, $CF - \lambda$, and REG). The families of λ-free (string) languages generated by arbitrary, monotone, context-free, λ-free context-free, respectively regular grammars are denoted by $L(ENUM)$, $L(MON)$, $L(CF)$, $L(CF - \lambda)$, respectively $L(REG)$. The following relations are known as the Chomsky-hierarchy ([10]):

$$L(REG) \subsetneq L(CF) = L(CF - \lambda) \subsetneq L(MON) \subsetneq L(ENUM).$$

Each context-free language in $L(CF)$ can be generated by a context-free grammar G not using λ-rules of the form $A \to \lambda$ with $A \in V_N$, i.e. allowing λ-rules does not increase the generative power of context free grammars in comparison with the generative power of λ-free context-free grammars (which implies $L(CF) = L(CF - \lambda)$).

Each arbitrary language L in $L(ENUM)$ can be generated by a grammar G in *Kuroda normal form*, which means that all productions in G are of the following forms:

$$A \to XY, \; AD \to XY, \text{ where } A, B, X, Y \in V_N, \text{ or}$$
$$A \to a, \text{ where } A \in V_N \text{ and } a \in V_T \cup \{\lambda\}.$$

For $L \in L(MON)$ productions of the form $A \to \lambda$, $A \in V_N$, can be omitted, and for $L \in L(CF)$ also productions of the form $AD \to XY$, $A, B, X, Y \in V_N$, are not needed.

3. Arrays and array grammars

In this section we introduce the definitions and notations for arrays and array grammars ([3], [4], [5], [6], [9], [11], [12]).

Let V be a finite alphabet. An *array* $\mathcal{A}$ over V is a function $\mathcal{A} : \mathbf{Z}^2 \to V \cup \{\#\}$ with finite support $supp(\mathcal{A})$, where

$$supp(\mathcal{A}) = \{v \in \mathbf{Z}^2 \mid \mathcal{A}(v) \neq \#\};$$

$\# \notin V$ is called the *background* or *blank symbol*. We usually shall write

$$\mathcal{A} = \{(v, \mathcal{A}(v)) \mid v \in supp(\mathcal{A})\}.$$

The set of all arrays over V shall be denoted by V^{*2}. The *empty array* in V^{*2} with empty support shall be denoted by Λ. Moreover, we define $V^{+2} = V^{*2} - \{\Lambda\}$. Any subset of V^{+2} is called a *(Λ-free) array language*.

Let $v \in \mathbf{Z}^2$. Then the *translation* $\tau_v : \mathbf{Z}^2 \to \mathbf{Z}^2$ is defined by $\tau_v(w) = w + v$ for all $w \in \mathbf{Z}^2$, and for any array $\mathcal{A} \in V^{*2}$ we get $(\tau_v(\mathcal{A}))(w) = \mathcal{A}(w - v)$ for all $w \in \mathbf{Z}^2$.

Usually ([9], [11] and [12]) arrays are regarded as equivalence classes of arrays with respect to linear translations, i.e. only the relative positions of the symbols different from $\#$ in the plane are taken into account.

The equivalence class $[\mathcal{A}]$ of an array $\mathcal{A} \in V^{*2}$ is defined by

$$[\mathcal{A}] = \{\mathcal{B} \in V^{*2} \mid \mathcal{B} = \tau_v(\mathcal{A}) \text{ for some } v \in \mathbf{Z}^2\}.$$

The set of all equivalence classes of arrays over V with respect to linear translations shall be denoted by $\left[V^{*2}\right]$.

Example 1. Let $V = \{a, b\}$, $\mathcal{A} : \mathbf{Z}^2 \to \{\#, a, b\}$, $\mathcal{A}(0, 0) = \mathcal{A}(1, 0) = b$ and $\mathcal{A}(0, 1) = a$. Then

$$supp(\mathcal{A}) = \{(0, 0), (0, 1), (1, 0)\},$$

and we also write

$$\mathcal{A} = \{((0, 0), b), ((0, 1), a), ((1, 0), b)\}.$$

Moreover,

$$[\mathcal{A}] = \{\{((i, j), b), ((i, j + 1), a), ((i + 1, j), b)\} \mid (i, j) \in \mathbf{Z}^2\}.$$

In a more depictive way, this array in $\left[\{a,b\}^{*2}\right]$ can be described by the following pattern:

$$a$$
$$b \quad b$$

$\square$

In order to be able to define the important notion of connectedness of arrays we need the following definitions:

An (undirected) *graph* g is an ordered pair (K, E), where K is a finite set of nodes and E is a set of undirected edges $\{x, y\}$ with $x, y \in K$. A sequence of different nodes $x_0, x_1, \ldots, x_m$, $m \geq 1$, is called a path of length m in g with the starting-point x_0 and the ending-point x_m, if for all i with $1 \leq i \leq m$ an edge $\{x_{i-1}, x_i\}$ in E exists. A graph g is said to be *connected*, if for any two nodes $x, y \in K$, $x \neq y$, a path in g with starting point x and ending point y exists. Observe that a graph $(\{x\}, \emptyset)$ with only one node and an empty set of edges is connected, too.

Let W be a non-empty finite subset of $\mathbf{Z}^2$. For any $k \in \mathbf{N} \cup \{0\}$, a graph $g_k(W) = (W, E_k)$ can be assigned to W such that E_k for $v, w \in W$ contains the edge $\{v, w\}$ if and only if $0 < \|v - w\| \leq k$, where the norm $\|u\|$ of a vector $u \in \mathbf{Z}^2$, $u = (u(1), u(2))$, is defined by $\|u\| = \max\{|u(1)|, |u(2)|\}$. Then W is said to be *k-connected* if $g_k(W)$ is a connected graph. Observe that W is 0-connected if and only if $card(W) = 1$, where $card(W)$ denotes the number of elements in the set W.

Now let V be a finite alphabet and $\mathcal{A}$ an array over V, $\mathcal{A} \neq \Lambda$. Then $\mathcal{A}$ is said to be *k-connected* if $g_k(supp(\mathcal{A}))$ is a connected graph. Obviously, if $\mathcal{A}$ is k-connected then $\mathcal{A}$ is m-connected for all $m > k$, too. The *norm of* $\mathcal{A}$ is the smallest integer $k \geq 0$ such that $\mathcal{A}$ is k-connected, and is denoted by $\|\mathcal{A}\|$. Observe that $\|\mathcal{A}\| = 0$ if and only if $card(supp(\mathcal{A})) = 1$.

Example 2. Obviously, the array

$$\mathcal{A} = \{((0,0), b), ((0,1), a), ((1,0), b)\}$$

in $\{a, b\}^{*2}$ is k-connected for every $k \geq 1$, and therefore $\|\mathcal{A}\| = 1$. $\square$

An *array production* p over V is a triple $(W, \mathcal{A}, \mathcal{B})$, where $W \subset \mathbf{Z}^2$ is a finite set and $\mathcal{A}$ and $\mathcal{B}$ are mappings from W to $V \cup \{\#\}$. Moreover we say that the array $\mathcal{D}_2 \in V^{*2}$ is *directly derivable* from the array $\mathcal{D}_1 \in V^{*2}$ by the array production $(W, \mathcal{A}, \mathcal{B})$ if and only if there exists a vector $v \in \mathbf{Z}^2$ such that $\mathcal{D}_1(w) = \mathcal{D}_2(w)$ for all $w \in \mathbf{Z}^2 - \tau_v(W)$ as well as $\mathcal{D}_1(w) = \mathcal{A}(\tau_{-v}(w))$ and $\mathcal{D}_2(w) = \mathcal{B}(\tau_{-v}(w))$ for all $w \in \tau_v(W)$, i.e. the subarray of $\mathcal{D}_1$ corresponding to $\mathcal{A}$ is replaced by $\mathcal{B}$, thus yielding $\mathcal{D}_2$. We also write $\mathcal{D}_1 \Longrightarrow_p \mathcal{D}_2$.

In contrast to the representation of an array $\mathcal{A} \in V^{*n}$, which is uniquely described by $\{(v, \mathcal{A}(v)) \mid v \in supp(\mathcal{A})\}$ (i.e. by listing all positions v in $\mathbf{Z}^2$

occupied by a non-blank symbol $\mathcal{A}(v) \in V$ together with this symbol $\mathcal{A}(v)$), in an array production $(W, \mathcal{A}, \mathcal{B})$ over V all positions in W together with their associated symbols must be listed for representing $\mathcal{A}$ respectively $\mathcal{B}$ by

$$\mathcal{A} = \{(v, \mathcal{A}(v)) \mid v \in W\} \text{ and } \mathcal{B} = \{(v, \mathcal{B}(v)) \mid v \in W\}.$$

Therefore the norm of the array production $(W, \mathcal{A}, \mathcal{B})$ is defined to be the norm of W, i.e.

$$\|(W, \mathcal{A}, \mathcal{B})\| = \|W\|.$$

As can already be seen from the definitions of an array production, the conditions for an application to an array $\mathcal{D}$ and the result of an application to $\mathcal{D}$, an array production

$$(W, \mathcal{A}, \mathcal{B})$$

is a representative for the infinite set of equivalent array productions of the form

$$(\tau_v(W), \tau_v(\mathcal{A}), \tau_v(\mathcal{B}))$$

with $v \in \mathbf{Z}^2$, i.e. only the relative positions of the elements of W are important for the effect of the array production $(W, \mathcal{A}, \mathcal{B})$ on an underlying array. Hence, without loss of generality, in the sequel we shall assume $(0, 0) \in W$ and moreover $\mathcal{A}((0, 0)) \neq \#$. Moreover, we often will omit the set W, because it can be reconstructed uniquely from the description of the two mappings $\mathcal{A}$ and $\mathcal{B}$ by

$$\mathcal{A} = \{(v, \mathcal{A}(v)) \mid v \in W\} \text{ and } \mathcal{B} = \{(v, \mathcal{B}(v)) \mid v \in W\}.$$

Thus in the sequel we will represent the array production $(W, \mathcal{A}, \mathcal{B})$ also by writing $\mathcal{A} \to \mathcal{B}$, i.e.

$$\{(v, \mathcal{A}(v)) \mid v \in W\} \to \{(v, \mathcal{B}(v)) \mid v \in W\}.$$

An *array grammar* is a quintuple

$$G = (V_N, V_T, P, \{(v_S, S)\}, \#),$$

where V_N is the alphabet of *non-terminal symbols*, V_T is the alphabet of *terminal symbols*, $V_N \cap V_T = \emptyset$, $\# \notin V_N \cup V_T$; P is a finite non-empty set of array productions over $V_N \cup V_T$, $\{(v_S, S)\}$ is the *start array* (S is the *start symbol* and v_S is the *start vector*).

We say that the array $\mathcal{D}_2 \in V^{*2}$ is *directly derivable* from the array $\mathcal{D}_1 \in V^{*2}$ in G, denoted $\mathcal{D}_1 \Longrightarrow_G \mathcal{D}_2$, if and only if there exists an array production $p = (W, \mathcal{A}, \mathcal{B})$ in P such that $\mathcal{D}_1 \Longrightarrow_p \mathcal{D}_2$. Let $\Longrightarrow_G^*$ be the reflexive transitive closure of $\Longrightarrow_G$. Then the *array language generated by* G, $L(G)$, is defined by

$$L(G) = \{\mathcal{A} \in V_T^{*2} \mid \{(v_S, S)\} \Longrightarrow_G^* \mathcal{A}\}.$$

The corresponding array language of equivalence classes with respect to linear transformations is $[L(G)] = \{[\mathcal{A}] \mid \mathcal{A} \in L(G)\}$.

The norm of the array grammar G is defined to be the maximum of the norm of the array productions in P, i.e.

$$\|G\| = \max\{\|p\| \mid p \in P\}.$$

Let $G = (V_N, V_T, P, \{(v_S, S)\}, \#)$ be an array grammar. An array production $p = (W, \mathcal{A}, \mathcal{B})$ in P is called

- *monotonic*, if $supp(\mathcal{A}) \subseteq supp(\mathcal{B})$;

- *#-context-free*, if $card(supp(\mathcal{A})) = 1$;

- *context-free*, if $card(supp(\mathcal{A})) = 1$, $\mathcal{A}((0,0)) \in V_N$, $\|W\| = 1$, and $supp(\mathcal{B}) = W$ ($supp(\mathcal{B}) = W$ also implies that p is monotonic);

- *regular*, if

    (a) $W = \{(0,0), v\}$ for some $v \in U$, where $U = \{(i_1, i_2) \mid |i_1| + |i_2| = 1\}$, and $\mathcal{A} = \{((0,0), B), (v, \#)\}$, $\mathcal{B} = \{((0,0), a), (v, C)\}$, $B, C \in V_N$ and $a \in V_T$, **or**
    (b) $W = \{(0,0)\}$, $\mathcal{A} = \{((0,0), B)\}$, $\mathcal{B} = \{((0,0), a)\}$, where $B \in V_N$ and $a \in V_T$.

The grammar G is called an *arbitrary, #-context-free, monotonic, context-free,* respectively *regular* array grammar, if every production in P is an arbitrary, #-context-free, monotonic, context-free, respectively regular array production (we also say that G respectively the productions in P are of type $ENUMA$, $\# - CFA$, $MONA$, CFA, and $REGA$). The corresponding families of Λ-free array languages shall be denoted by $L(ENUMA)$, $L(\# - CFA)$, $L(MONA)$, $L(CFA)$, and $L(REGA)$, the corresponding families of array languages of equivalence classes of arrays shall be denoted by $[L(ENUMA)]$, $[L(\# - CFA)]$, $[L(MONA)]$, $[L(CFA)]$, and $[L(REGA)]$.

Collecting the results about the different families of array languages from [1], [9], [11], [3], [4], and [6], we obtain the following proposition:

Proposition 1. *(Chomsky-hierarchy of two-dimensional array languages)*

$$L(REGA) \subsetneq L(CFA) \subsetneq L(MONA) \subsetneq L(ENUMA) \ and$$
$$L(REGA) \subsetneq L(CFA) \subsetneq L(\# - CFA) \subsetneq L(ENUMA).$$

The same hierarchy holds true for the families of array languages of equivalence classes of arrays with respect to linear translations:

$$[L(REGA)] \subsetneq [L(CFA)] \subsetneq [L(MONA)] \subsetneq [L(ENUMA)] \ and$$
$$[L(REGA)] \subsetneq [L(CFA)] \subsetneq [L(\# - CFA)] \subsetneq [L(ENUMA)].$$

An arbitrary array grammar $G = (V_N, V_T, P, \{(v_S, S)\}, \#)$ is said to be in *Kuroda normal form*, if all array productions in P are of the following forms:

$$\{((0,0), A), (v, D)\} \to \{((0,0), X), (v, Y)\},$$
$$\text{where } A, X, Y \in V_N \text{ and } D \in V_N \cup \{\#\}, \text{ or}$$
$$\{((0,0), A)\} \to \{((0,0), a)\}, \text{ where } A \in V_N \text{ and } a \in V_T \cup \{\#\}.$$

As we shall show in the fifth section, for each array grammar G' we can effectively construct an array grammar G in Kuroda normal form such that $L(G) = L(G')$.

Example 3. Consider the array grammar

$$G_1 = (\{S, T\}, \{a\}, P_1, \{((0,0), S)\}, \#)$$

with P_1 containing the productions

$$(\{(0,0), (1,1)\}, \{((0,0), S), ((1,1), \#)\}, \{((0,0), a), ((1,1), T)\}),$$
$$(\{(0,0), (1,1)\}, \{((0,0), T), ((1,1), \#)\}, \{((0,0), \#), ((1,1), T)\}), \text{ and}$$
$$(\{(0,0)\}, \{((0,0), T)\}, \{((0,0), a)\});$$

in a more depictive way these three array productions can be represented by

$$S\ \begin{matrix}\#\\ \end{matrix} \to \begin{matrix}T\\a\end{matrix}\ , \qquad T\ \begin{matrix}\#\\ \end{matrix} \to \begin{matrix}T\\\#\end{matrix}\ , \quad and \quad T \to a.$$

As all the array productions in P_1 are $\#$-context-free,

$$L(G_1) = \{\{((0,0), a), ((k,k), a)\} \mid k \in \mathbf{N}\} \in L(\# - CFA),$$

but obviously $L(G_1) \notin L(MONA)$, because there is no $k \geq 1$ such that all arrays in $L(G_1)$ are k-connected (whereas for every monotonic array grammar G we have $\|\mathcal{A}\| \leq \|G\|$ for every array $\mathcal{A} \in L(G)$).
As $\|\{(0,0)\}\| = 0$ and $\|\{(0,0), (1,1)\}\| = 1$, we obtain $\|G_1\| = 1$.   □

If only one-dimensional structures are generated by an array grammar, in special cases the resulting arrays can be interpreted as strings: Let $\mathcal{A} \in V^{+2}$ be an array with

$$\mathcal{A} = \{((i_k, 0), a_k) \mid a_k \in V,\ i_k \in \mathbf{Z},\ 1 \leq k \leq m,\ m \geq 1, \text{ and } i_1 < \ldots < i_m\}$$

Then the string image of $\mathcal{A}$ is defined by

$$str(\mathcal{A}) = a_1 \ldots a_m.$$

For any set $L \subseteq V^{+2}$ of arrays, where $str(\mathcal{A})$ is defined for every array $\mathcal{A}$ in L, we define

$$str(L) = \{str(\mathcal{A}) \mid \mathcal{A} \in L\}.$$

With respect to the generation of one-dimensional patterns, the generative power of context-free array grammars is very restricted. According to the results proved in [7] we obtain the following proposition:

Proposition 2. *Let G be a context-free array grammar such that $str(L(G))$ is well defined; then $str(L(G)) \in L(REG)$. On the other hand, for every regular string language $L \in L(REG)$ there exists a context-free array grammar G such that $str(L(G)) = L$.*

Whereas the string immage of an array language generated by a context-free array grammar can only be a regular string language, every context-free string language has a representation as the string image of a #-context-free array grammar.

Proposition 3. *For every context-free string language $L \in L(CF)$ there exists a #-context-free array grammar G such that $str(L(G)) = L$.*

Proof. Let $G = (V_N, V_T, P, S)$ be a context-free string grammar in Kuroda normal form. Then $str(L(G')) = L(G)$ for the #-context-free array grammar

$$
\begin{aligned}
G' &= (V_N, V_T, P', \{((0,0), S)\}, \#) \text{ with} \\
P' &= \{X\# \to \#X \mid X \in V_N\} \cup \\
&\quad \{A\# \to BC \mid A \to BC \in P, \ A, B, C \in V_N\} \cup \\
&\quad \{A \to a \mid A \to a \in P, \ A \in V_N, \ a \in V_T\}.
\end{aligned}
$$

The array productions of the form

$$X\# \to \#X, \ X \in V_N,$$

guarantee that there is enough place for the application of the array productions of the form $A\# \to BC$. $\square$

As can be seen from the construction of the #-context-free grammar G' in the proof of proposition 2, for every string $a_1 \ldots a_n \in L(G)$ with $n \geq 2$ we obtain infinitely many arrays $\{((0,0), a_1), ((i_2, 0), a_2), \ldots, ((i_n, 0), a_n)\}$ in $L(G')$ with $0 < i_2 < \ldots < i_n$, all of them yielding the same string image $a_1 \ldots a_n$. In the underlying arrays, the symbols appear in the right order, but are separated by an arbitrary number of blank symbols. In general, for non-regular context-free string languages L this side effect in representing L as the string image of an array language generated by a #-context-free array grammar cannot be avoided, e. g. even for the context-free string language $L_0 = \{a^n b^n \mid n \geq 1\}$ no #-context-free array grammar G with $str(L(G)) = L_0$ exists such that every array in $L(G)$ is 1-connected. On the other hand, in the following two examples we shall show that even non-context-free string languages can be obtained as the string images of array languages generated by #-context-free array grammars.

Example 4. Consider the #-context-free array grammar

$$G_2 = (\{A, B, C, L, S, T, U, V\}, \{a, b\}, P_2, \{((0,0), S)\}, \#) \quad \text{with}$$
$$P_2 = \{S\# \to LT, T\# \to bC, C\# \to \#C, C \to a, T\# \to UC, U\# \to \#V,$$
$$V\# \to \#T, L \to a, L\# \to aB, B\# \to \#B, \#B \to Ab, \#A \to A\#,$$
$$A\# \to aB, A \to a\}.$$

Then

$$L(G_2) = \{\{((0,0), a), ((2n-1), b)\} \cup \{((i_k, 0), a), ((j_k, 0), b) \mid$$
$$1 \leq k \leq m,\ 0 < i_1 < \ldots < i_m < j_1 < \ldots < j_m < 2n - 1\} \cup$$
$$\{((h_l, 0), a) \mid 1 \leq l \leq n,\ 2n - 1 < h_1 < \ldots < h_n\} \mid 0 \leq m < n\},$$

which implies

$$str(L(G_2)) = \{a^{m+1} b^{m+1} a^n \mid 0 \leq m < n\}.$$

The main idea of G_2 is that the non-terminal symbol L, which is generated at the origin $(0,0)$ and finally goes to a, establishes a left boundary for all other symbols generated by array productions in G_2. Each time the array productions $U\# \to \#V$, $V\# \to \#T$, and $T\# \to UC$ are applied sequentially, the non-terminal symbol U is pushed two positions to the right and, moreover, a non-terminal symbol C is generated, which on an arbitrary position to the right finally goes to a. After the application of the array production $T\# \to bC$ the $2n - 2$ positions i, $1 \leq i \leq 2n - 2$, are filled with $m \leq n - 1$ terminal symbols a on the left and m terminal symbols b on the right hand side of this bounded space. $\square$

Whereas in the previous example we only needed a #-context-free array grammar with norm 1, in the following example we need a #-context-free array grammar with norm 3.

Example 5. Consider the #-context-free array grammar G_3 with

$$G_3 = (\{S_0, S, A, B, C\}, \{a, b, c\}, P_3, \{((-1, 0), S)\}, \#),$$
$$P_3 = \{\#\#\#S_0 \to ASbc, \#\#\#S \to ASbB, S \to \#, \#A \to A\#,$$
$$A \to a, C\# \to \#C, C \to c\} \cup$$
$$\{\{((0,0), B), ((2,0), \#)\} \to \{((0,0), \#), ((2,0), B)\}\} \cup$$
$$\{\{((0,0), B), ((3,0), \#)\} \to \{((0,0), \#), ((3,0), C)\}\}.$$

The main idea of the #-context-free array grammar G_3 is that by the array productions $\#\#\#S_0 \to ASbc$, on the positions $(-2,0)$ and $(-1,0)$ a hurdle of length two is established, which can only be taken by using

$$\{((0,0), B), ((3,0), \#)\} \to \{((0,0), \#), ((3,0), C)\},$$

but not by applying

$$\{((0,0), B), ((2,0), \#)\} \to \{((0,0), \#), ((2,0), B)\}.$$

Hence it is easy to verify that

$$
\begin{aligned}
L(G_3) \;=\; & \{\{((l_k,0), a) \mid 1 \le k \le n,\ i_1 < \ldots < i_n < -2n-1\} \cup \\
& \{((-2k,0), b) \mid 1 \le k \le n\} \cup \\
& \{((j_k,0), c) \mid 1 \le k \le n,\ -1 = j_1 < \ldots < j_n\} \mid n \ge 1\}
\end{aligned}
$$

and therefore

$$str(L(G_3)) = \{a^n b^n c^n \mid n \ge 1\}.$$

$\square$

The #-sensibility used in the productions of the #-context-free array grammar in the previous example induces a relatively high generative power of even regular and context-free array grammars with respect to the generation of sets of specific two-dimensional patterns, which is shown in the following two examples:

Example 6. The set of solid squares over the one-letter alphabet $\{a\}$ is a regular array language ([12]), i.e. $\{\{((i,j), a) \mid 0 \le i, j \le k\} \mid k \ge 0\} \in [L(REGA)]$.

For the proofs in the succeeding sections we need an even more elaborated construction, because we want to mark the edges as well as the middle of a square, yet we confine ourselves to construct a context-free array grammar, which is sufficient for our purposes and allows us to obtain a rather small and depictive array grammar.

Example 7. We consider the following set Q of squares filled with symbols b and with a side length $4m+3$, $m \ge 1$, the middle of the squares lying in the origin $(0,0)$ being marked with the symbol s, the edges of the squares marked by lines of thickness one with symbols e, and the left upper corner marked with the symbol h :

$$
\begin{aligned}
Q \;=\; & \{((0,0), s), ((-k,k), h)\} \cup \\
& \{(v, e) \mid v \in \mathbf{Z}^2,\ \|v\| = k,\ v \ne (-k,k)\} \cup \\
& \{(v, b) \mid v \in \mathbf{Z}^2,\ 0 < \|v\| < k\} \mid k = 2m+1 \text{ for some } m \ge 1\}
\end{aligned}
$$

Q is generated by the context-free array grammar

$$G_4 = (V_4, \{b, e, h, s\}, P_4, \{((0,0), S)\}, \#)$$

with

$$V_4 = \{S', S, B, E, H, R_1, D_1, L_1, U_1, R_2, D_2, L_2, U_2\}$$

and $P_4 = P_0 \cup P_4^t$, where

$$P_4^t = \{S \to s, \ B \to b, \ E \to e, \ H \to h\}$$

contains the terminal productions for deriving the terminal symbols s, b, e, and h, and

$$P_0 = \{s_1, s_2, h\} \cup \{r_i, d_i, l_i, u_i \mid 1 \le i \le 4\}$$

contains the array productions depicted in the following:

s_1

```
#                                     R_1
#               #   #                 B                      B   B
#   #   #   #                         B   B   B   B
    #   S'  #                 ⟶             B   S   B
    #   #   #   #                         B   B   B   B
#   #               #                 B   B                      B
```

s_2

```
#                                     R_2
#               #   #                 B                      B   B
#   #   #   #                         B   B   B   B
    #   S'  #                 ⟶             B   S   B
    #   #   #   #                         B   B   B   B
#   #               #                 B   B                      B
```

r_1

```
    #                     B
    R_1  #   #    ⟶       B   B   R_1
    #                     B
```

r_2

```
        #   #             B               B   B
R_1  #   #   #    ⟶       B   B   B   B
#           #             B               D_1
```

d_1

$$
\begin{array}{ccc}
 & D_1 & \# \\
\# & \# & \\
 & \# &
\end{array}
\longrightarrow
\begin{array}{ccc}
 & B & B \\
B & B & \\
 & D_1 &
\end{array}
$$

d_2

$$
\begin{array}{ccc}
\# & D_1 & \# \\
 & \# & \\
 & \# & \\
\# & \# & \# \\
 & \# &
\end{array}
\longrightarrow
\begin{array}{ccc}
B & B & B \\
 & B & \\
 & B & \\
L_1 & B & B \\
 & B &
\end{array}
$$

l_1

$$
\begin{array}{ccc}
 & \# & \\
\# & \# & L_1 \\
 & \# &
\end{array}
\longrightarrow
\begin{array}{ccc}
 & B & \\
L_1 & B & B \\
 & B &
\end{array}
$$

l_2

$$
\begin{array}{cccc}
\# & & \# & \\
\# & \# & \# & L_1 \\
 & \# & \# &
\end{array}
\longrightarrow
\begin{array}{cccc}
U_1 & & & B \\
 & B & B & B & B \\
B & B & & & B
\end{array}
$$

u_1

$$
\begin{array}{ccc}
 & \# & \\
 & \# & \# \\
\# & U_1 &
\end{array}
\longrightarrow
\begin{array}{ccc}
 & U_1 & \\
 & B & B \\
B & B &
\end{array}
$$

u_2

$$
\begin{array}{ccc}
\# & & \\
\# & & \\
\# & \# & \\
 & \# & \\
 & \# & \\
\# & U_1 & \#
\end{array}
\longrightarrow
\begin{array}{ccc}
R_1 & & \\
B & & \\
B & B & \\
 & B & \\
 & B & \\
B & B & B
\end{array}
$$

u_3

$$
\begin{array}{ccc}
\# & & \\
\# & & \\
\# & \# & \\
 & \# & \\
 & \# & \\
\# & U_1 & \#
\end{array}
\longrightarrow
\begin{array}{ccc}
R_2 & & \\
B & & \\
B & B & \\
 & B & \\
 & B & \\
B & B & B
\end{array}
$$

r_3

$$\begin{array}{ccc} R_2 & \# & \# \\ & \# & \end{array} \longrightarrow \begin{array}{ccc} E & E & R_2 \\ & B & \end{array}$$

r_4

$$\begin{array}{cccc} R_2 & \# & \# & \# \\ \# & & & \# \end{array} \longrightarrow \begin{array}{cccc} E & E & E & E \\ B & & & D_2 \end{array}$$

d_3

$$\begin{array}{cc} & D_2 \\ \# & \# \\ & \# \end{array} \longrightarrow \begin{array}{cc} & E \\ B & E \\ & D_2 \end{array}$$

d_4

$$\begin{array}{cc} \# & D_2 \\ & \# \\ & \# \\ \# & \# \end{array} \longrightarrow \begin{array}{cc} B & E \\ & E \\ & E \\ L_2 & E \end{array}$$

l_3

$$\begin{array}{ccc} & \# & \\ \# & \# & L_2 \end{array} \longrightarrow \begin{array}{ccc} & & B \\ L_2 & E & E \end{array}$$

l_4

$$\begin{array}{cccc} \# & & & \# \\ \# & \# & \# & L_2 \end{array} \longrightarrow \begin{array}{cccc} U_2 & & & B \\ E & E & E & E \end{array}$$

u_4

$$\begin{array}{cc} \# & \\ \# & \# \\ U_2 & \end{array} \longrightarrow \begin{array}{cc} U_2 & \\ E & B \\ E & \end{array}$$

h

$$\begin{array}{cc} \# & \\ \# & \\ \# & \\ U_2 & \# \end{array} \longrightarrow \begin{array}{cc} H & \\ E & \\ E & \\ E & B \end{array}$$

By first applying s_2, we have to proceed with applying r_3, r_4, d_3, d_4, l_3, l_4, u_4, and h, which yields a square of side length 7 represented by the following pattern (observe that the non-terminal symbol S lies in the origin $(0,0)$):

$$
\begin{array}{ccccccc}
H & E & E & E & E & E & E \\
E & B & B & B & B & B & E \\
E & B & B & B & B & B & E \\
E & B & B & S & B & B & E \\
E & B & B & B & B & B & E \\
E & B & B & B & B & B & E \\
E & E & E & E & E & E & E
\end{array}
$$

By applying the terminal productions in P_4^t to this array we obtain a square of side length 7, filled with symbols b, the middle of the square lying in the origin $(0,0)$ being marked with the symbol s, the edges of the squares marked by lines of thickness one with symbols e, and the left upper corner marked with the symbol h; this square - the smallest one in $L(G_4)$ - can be represented by the following pattern:

$$
\begin{array}{ccccccc}
h & e & e & e & e & e & e \\
e & b & b & b & b & b & e \\
e & b & b & b & b & b & e \\
e & b & b & s & b & b & e \\
e & b & b & b & b & b & e \\
e & b & b & b & b & b & e \\
e & e & e & e & e & e & e
\end{array}
$$

If we first apply the array production s_1, then r_1, r_2, d_1, d_2, l_1, l_2, u_1, and u_2 can be applied repeatedly until instead of u_2 we apply u_3, which - by applying the array productions r_3, r_4, d_3, d_4, l_3, l_4, u_4, and h - allows us to finish the generation of a square of side length $4m+3$, $m \geq 2$, filled with symbols B, the middle of the square lying in the origin $(0,0)$ being marked with the symbol S, the edges of the squares marked by lines of thickness one with symbols E, and the left upper corner marked with the symbol H. Applying the terminal productions in P_4^t to this array we obtain the corresponding terminal array in $L(G_4)$, i.e. a square of side length $4m+3$, $m \geq 2$, filled with symbols b, the middle of the square lying in the origin $(0,0)$ being marked with the symbol s, the edges of the squares marked by lines of thickness one with symbols e, and the left upper corner marked with the symbol h. $\qquad\Box$

4. Control mechanisms

In this section we introduce the notions for the specific control mechanisms we deal with in this paper, i.e. *ordered grammars, programmed grammars, and matrix grammars.* For detailed informations concerning these control mechanisms as well as many other interesting results about regulated rewriting in the theory of string languages the reader is referred to [2].

An *ordered (string) grammar* is a construct

$$G_O = (V_N, V_T, (P, <), S)$$

where V_N and V_T are disjoint alphabets of non-terminal respectively terminal symbols, $S \in V_N$ is the start symbol, P is a finite set of (string) productions over $V_N \cup V_T$, and $<$ is a partial order relation on the productions in P. For $v, w \in (V_N \cup V_T)^*$ we define $v \Longrightarrow_{G_O} w$ if and only if there exists a production $p \in P$ such that w is the result of the application of p to v, whereas no other production $q \in P$ with $q > p$ is applicable to v. With $\Longrightarrow_{G_O}^*$ denoting the reflexive and transitive closure of the derivation relation $\Longrightarrow_{G_O}$ the string language generated by G_O is

$$L(G_O) = \{w \in V_T^* \mid S \Longrightarrow_{G_O}^* w\}.$$

A *programmed (string) grammar (or graph controlled (string) grammar) with appearance checking* is a construct

$$G_P = (V_N, V_T, (R, L_i, L_f), S);$$

V_N and V_T are disjoint alphabets of non-terminal respectively terminal symbols; $S \in V_N$ is the start symbol; R is a finite set of rules r of the form $(l(r) : p(l(r)), \sigma(l(r)), \varphi(l(r)))$, where $l(r) \in Lab(G_P)$, $Lab(G_P)$ being a set of labels associated (in a one-to-one manner) to the rules r in R, $p(l(r))$ is a string production over $V_N \cup V_T$, $\sigma(l(r)) \subseteq Lab(G_P)$ is the *success field* of the rule r, and $\varphi(l(r))$ is the *failure field* of the rule r; $L_i \subseteq Lab(G_P)$ is the set of initial labels, and $L_f \subseteq Lab(G_P)$ is the set of final labels.

For $r = (l(r) : p(l(r)), \sigma(l(r)), \varphi(l(r)))$ and $v, w \in (V_N \cup V_T)^*$ we define $(v, l(r)) \Longrightarrow_{G_P} (w, k)$ if and only if

- **either** $p(l(r))$ is applicable to v, the result of the application of the production $p(l(r))$ to v is w, and $k \in \sigma(l(r))$,

- **or** $p(l(r))$ is not applicable to v, $w = v$, and $k \in \varphi(l(r))$.

The (string) language generated by G_P is

$$L(G_P) = \{w \in V_T^* \mid (S, i) \Longrightarrow_{G_P} (w_1, l_1) \Longrightarrow_{G_P} \ldots (w_k, l_k), \ k \geq 1,$$
$$w_j \in (V_N \cup V_T)^* \text{ and } l_j \in Lab(G_P) \text{ for } 1 \leq j \leq k,$$
$$w_k = w, \ i \in L_i, \ l_k \in L_f\}.$$

If the failure fields $\varphi(l(r))$ are empty for all $r \in R$, then G_P is called a *programmed grammar without appearance checking*.

A *matrix grammar* is a construct

$$G_M = (V_N, V_T, (M, F), S)$$

where V_N and V_T are disjoint alphabets of non-terminal respectively terminal symbols, $S \in V_N$ is the start symbol, M is a finite set of matrices, $M = \{m_i \mid 1 \le i \le n\}$, where the matrices m_i are sequences of the form $m_i = (m_{i,1}, \ldots, m_{i,n_i})$, $n_i \ge 1$, $1 \le i \le n$, and the $m_{i,j}$, $1 \le j \le n_i$, $1 \le i \le n$, are productions over $V_N \cup V_T$, and F is a subset of $\bigcup_{1 \le i \le n, 1 \le j \le n_i} \{m_{i,n_i}\}$.

- For $m_i = (m_{i,1}, \ldots, m_{i,n_i})$ and $v, w \in (V_N \cup V_T)^*$ we define $v \Longrightarrow_{m_i} w$ if and only if there are $w_0, w_1, \ldots, w_{n_i} \in (V_N \cup V_T)^*$ such that $w_0 = v$, $w_{n_i} = w$, and for each $j, 1 \le j \le n_i$,

- **either** w_j is the result of the application of $m_{i,j}$ to w_{j-1},

- **or** $m_{i,j}$ is not applicable to w_{j-1}, $w_j = w_{j-1}$, and $m_{i,j} \in F$.

The language generated by G_M is

$$L(G_M) = \{w \in V_T^* \mid S \Longrightarrow_{m_{i_1}} w_1 \ldots \Longrightarrow_{m_{i_k}} w_k = w,$$
$$w_j \in (V_N \cup V_T)^*, m_{i_j} \in M \text{ for } 1 \le j \le k\}.$$

If $F = \emptyset$ then G_M is called a *matrix (string) grammar without appearance checking*.

An ordered (string) grammar, a programmed (string) grammar, respectively a matrix (string) grammar is said to be of type $ENUM$, MON, CF, $CF - \lambda$, respectively REG, if every production appearing in this grammar is of the corresponding type, i.e. an arbitrary, monotonic, context-free, λ-free context-free, respectively regular production. For $X \in \{ENUM, MON, CF, CF - \lambda, REG\}$ by

$$O(X), \ P_{ac}(X), \ M_{ac}(X), \ P(X), \ M(X)$$

we denote the λ-free (string) languages generated by ordered grammars, programmed grammars with appearance checking, matrix grammars with appearance checking, programmed grammars without appearance checking, respectively matrix grammars without appearance checking of type X.

In the following we list some of the most important results known ([2], [8]) for the control mechanisms defined above:

$$L(X) = Y(X) \text{ for } X \in \{REG, MON, ENUM\},$$

$$\text{and } Y \in \{O, P_{ac}, P, M_{ac}, M\};$$
$$L(CF - \lambda) \subsetneq P(CF - \lambda) = M(CF - \lambda) \subsetneq$$
$$P_{ac}(CF - \lambda) = M_{ac}(CF - \lambda) \subsetneq L(MON);$$
$$P(CF - \lambda) = M(CF - \lambda) \subsetneq P(CF) = M(CF) \subsetneq$$
$$P_{ac}(CF) = M_{ac}(CF) = L(ENUM);$$
$$L(CF - \lambda) = L(CF) \subsetneq O(CF - \lambda) \subseteq O(CF) \subsetneq L(ENUM).$$

The definitions of ordered grammars, programmed grammars, and matrix grammars can immediately be taken over for array grammars by taking array productions instead of string productions in the definitions given above, e. g. an *ordered array grammar* is a construct

$$G = (V_N, V_T, (P, <), \{(v_S, S)\}, \#),$$

where V_N, V_T, P, and $\{(v_S, S)\}$ are defined as for an array grammar and $<$ is a partial order relation on the array productions in P etc.

An ordered array grammar, a programmed array grammar, respectively a matrix array grammar is said to be of type $ENUMA$, $\# - CFA$, $MONA$, CFA, respectively $REGA$, if every array production appearing in this grammar is of the corresponding type, i.e. an arbitrary, monotonic, context-free, #-context-free, respectively regular array production. For $X \in \{ENUMA, \# - CFA, MONA, CFA, REGA\}$ by

$$O(X), \ P_{ac}(X), \ M_{ac}(X), \ P(X), \ M(X)$$

we denote the Λ-free array languages generated by ordered array grammars, programmed array grammars with appearance checking, matrix array grammars with appearance checking, programmed array grammars without appearance checking, respectively matrix array grammars without appearance checking of type X.

In the following we give some examples elucidating the control mechanisms defined above.

Example 8. Consider the context-free programmed array grammar without appearance checking

$$G_5 = (\{S, A, B, C\}, \{a, b, c\}, (R, \{1\}, \{9\}), \{((0,0); S)\}, \#)$$

with R containing the following rules:

$$(1 : S\# \to AB, \{2\}, \emptyset),$$
$$(2 : B\# \to BB, \{2,3\}, \emptyset),$$

$$(3 : B\# \rightarrow BC, \{4,7\}, \emptyset),$$
$$(4 : \#A \rightarrow Aa, \{5\}, \emptyset),$$
$$(5 : B \rightarrow b, \{6\}, \emptyset),$$
$$(6 : C\# \rightarrow cC, \{4,7\}, \emptyset),$$
$$(7 : A \rightarrow a, \{8\}, \emptyset),$$
$$(8 : B \rightarrow b, \{9\}, \emptyset),$$
$$(9 : C \rightarrow c, \{9\}, \emptyset).$$

By the rules labelled $1, 2$, and 3 we can produce an array of the form

$$\{((0,0), A), ((n+1, 0), C)\} \cup \{((i, 0), B) \mid 1 \le i \le n\}, \; n \in \mathbf{N}.$$

Repeatedly using the rules labelled $4, 5$, and 6, for every non-terminal symbol B, which goes to b, a terminal symbol a on the left side as well as a terminal symbol c on the right side are introduced from A respectively C. The last terminal symbol a, b, respectively c finally is obtained by applying the rules labelled $7, 8$, respectively 9, where every derivation ends. Hence we obtain

$$L(G_5) = \{\{(((-i+1, 0), a), ((i, 0), b), ((n+i, 0), c) \mid 1 \le i \le n\} \mid n \in \mathbf{N}\}$$

and therefore

$$str(L(G_5)) = \{a^n b^n c^n \mid n \ge 1\},$$

which is the same (non-context-free) string language already obtained by the #-context-free array grammar G_3, whereas $L(G_5)$ itself cannot be generated by a #-context-free array grammar. $\square$

Whereas in the string case the control mechanism of an ordering on the productions does not increase the generative power of regular grammars, there are regular ordered array grammars generating array languages that cannot even be generated by (#-)context-free array grammars (compare with Lemma 8 in [3]):

Example 9. According to [12], the set R_H of hollow rectangles of thickness one over the one-letter alphabet $\{a\}$ cannot be generated by a context-free array grammar.

Yet the following regular ordered array grammar G_6 generates R_H, i.e.

$$R_H \in [O(REGA)].$$

We take the ordered array grammar

$$G_6 \;=\; (\{S, A, B, C, D, Q\}, \{a\}, (P_6, <), \{((0,0), S)\}, \#),$$

$$P_6 = \left\{ \begin{matrix} \# \\ S \end{matrix} \to \begin{matrix} S \\ a \end{matrix}, \begin{matrix} \# & \# \\ S & \end{matrix} \to \begin{matrix} a & A \\ a & \end{matrix}, A\# \to aA, \right.$$

$$\begin{matrix} A & \# \\ & \# \end{matrix} \to \begin{matrix} a & a \\ & B \end{matrix}, \begin{matrix} B \\ \# \end{matrix} \to \begin{matrix} a \\ B \end{matrix}, \begin{matrix} B \\ \# & \# \end{matrix} \to \begin{matrix} a \\ C & a \end{matrix},$$

$$\left. \#C \to Ca, \#C \to Da, \begin{matrix} \# \\ D \end{matrix} \to \begin{matrix} Q \\ a \end{matrix}, D \to a \right\}.$$

The order relation $<$ only consists of

$$D \to a < \begin{matrix} \# \\ D \end{matrix} \to \begin{matrix} Q \\ a \end{matrix},$$

which guarantees that $D \to a$ is only applied when no blank symbol appears above the non-terminal symbol D, or otherwise the (forced) application of

$$\begin{matrix} \# \\ D \end{matrix} \to \begin{matrix} Q \\ a \end{matrix}$$

introduces the trap symbol Q.

The derivation of a rectangle of side lengths n and m, $n, m \geq 3$, proceeds as follows:

The left vertical line of the hollow rectangle is generated by using $n - 2$ times the rule

$$\begin{matrix} \# \\ S \end{matrix} \to \begin{matrix} S \\ a \end{matrix}.$$

After applying the rule

$$\begin{matrix} \# & \# \\ S & \end{matrix} \to \begin{matrix} a & A \\ a & \end{matrix},$$

the upper horizontal line of the rectangle is generated by using $m - 2$ times the rule

$$A\# \to aA.$$

The generation of the right vertical line of the rectangle starts with the application of the array production

$$\begin{matrix} A & \# \\ & \# \end{matrix} \to \begin{matrix} a & a \\ & B \end{matrix},$$

whereafter we can proceed with repeatedly applying

$$\begin{matrix} B \\ \# \end{matrix} \to \begin{matrix} a \\ B \end{matrix}.$$

By applying

$$\begin{matrix} B & & \\ \# & \# \end{matrix} \rightarrow \begin{matrix} & a \\ c & a \end{matrix}$$

the generation of the lower horizontal line is started, which proceeds by repeatedly applying

$$\#C \rightarrow Ca.$$

The final array production

$$D \rightarrow a$$

can only be applied, if with the non-terminal D we have arrived exactly below the starting point of our derivation; otherwise the trap symbol Q is introduced by the application of

$$\begin{matrix} \# \\ D \end{matrix} \rightarrow \begin{matrix} Q \\ a \end{matrix} \,,$$

which is forced by the order relation $<$. Hence we conclude

$$L(G_6) \;=\; \{\{((0,j),a),((i,n-1),a),((m-1,j+1),a),((i+1,0),a)\,| \\ 0 \leq j \leq n-2,\ 0 \leq i \leq m-2\}\,|\,n \geq 3,\ m \geq 3\}$$

and therefore

$$[L(G_6)] = R_H.$$

$\square$

For the generation of the set S_H of hollow squares (compare with Lemma 1 in [3]) regular array productions are not sufficient, i.e. S_H can only be generated by a context-free matrix array grammar with appearance checking:

Example 10. We consider the context-free matrix array grammar with appearance checking

$$G_7 = (\{S, U, R, D, L, Q\}, \{a\}, (M_7, F_7), \{((0,0), S)\}, \#)$$

with M_7 and F_7 containing the following matrices:

$$\left(\begin{matrix} \# & \\ S & \# \end{matrix} \rightarrow \begin{matrix} & U \\ a & R \end{matrix} \right),$$

$$\left(\begin{matrix} \# \\ U \end{matrix} \rightarrow \begin{matrix} U \\ a \end{matrix} \,, R\# \rightarrow aR \right),$$

$$\left(\begin{matrix} \# & \# \\ U \end{matrix} \rightarrow \begin{matrix} a & D \\ a \end{matrix} \,, R\# \rightarrow aL \right),$$

$$\left(D\# \to aD, \ \frac{\#}{L} \to \frac{L}{a} \right),$$

$$\left(\frac{\#}{L} \to \frac{Q}{L}, L \to a, D \to a \right);$$

$$F_7 = \{ \frac{\#}{L} \to \frac{Q}{L} \}.$$

After using the initial matrix

$$\left(\begin{matrix} \# & \\ S & \# \end{matrix} \to \begin{matrix} & U \\ a & R \end{matrix} \right),$$

the generation of the hollow square of side length $n \geq 3$ proceeds as follows: By the matrix

$$\left(\frac{\#}{U} \to \frac{U}{a}, \ R\# \to aR \right)$$

the left vertical line and the lower horizontal line grow in a synchronized manner. After the application of the matrix

$$\left(\begin{matrix} \# & \# \\ U & \end{matrix} \to \begin{matrix} a & D \\ a & \end{matrix}, \ R\# \to aL \right),$$

the upper horizontal line and the right vertical line are grown in a synchronized manner. If L has arrived just below D, the terminating matrix

$$\left(\frac{\#}{L} \to \frac{Q}{L}, \ L \to a, D \to a \right)$$

can be applied by skipping the array production

$$\frac{\#}{L} \to \frac{Q}{L}$$

in the appearance checking mode and finally deriving the last two terminal symbols a. If this terminating matrix is applied too early, the application of the array production

$$\frac{\#}{L} \to \frac{Q}{L}$$

is possible, which introduces the trap symbol Q and therefore prohibits the derivation of wrong terminal arrays.

Hence we conclude

$$L(G_7) \ = \ \{\{((0,i),a),((i,n-1),a),((n-1,i+1),a),((i+1,0),a) \mid$$
$$0 \leq i \leq n-2\} \mid n \geq 3\}$$

and therefore

$$[L(G_7)] = S_H.$$

$\square$

The previous two examples reveal an important difference between the applicability of a context-free string production to an underlying string and the applicability of a context-free array production to an underlying array: Whereas a context-free string production $A \to w$ is applicable to the underlying string if and only if the non-terminal symbol A appears in this string, the applicability of a context-free array production $(W, \mathcal{A}, \mathcal{B})$ with $\mathcal{A}((0,0)) = A$ to an underlying array not only depends on the occurrence of the non-terminal symbol A in the underlying array, but also on the "availability" of blank symbols in the neighbourhood of A on the relative positions $v \in W - \{(0,0)\}$. This #-sensing ability is the basis of the main results we will prove in the following section, i.e. in contrast to the string case, even #-context-free programmed array grammars *without* appearance checking, #-context-free matrix array grammars *without* appearance checking, and #-context-free ordered array grammars can generate any r.e. Λ-free array language.

5. Results

The following results directly follow from the definitions:

Lemma 1. *For all $X, Y \in \{REGA, CFA, \# - CFA, MONA, ENUMA\}$ with $L(X) \subseteq L(Y)$ as well as for all $U \subset \{P, P_{ac}, M, M_{ac}, O\}$*

$$U(X) \subseteq U(Y).$$

Lemma 2. *For every $X \in \{REGA, CFA, \# - CFA, MONA, ENUMA\}$*

$$L(X) \subseteq P(X) \subseteq P_{ac}(X),$$
$$L(X) \subseteq M(X) \subseteq M_{ac}(X), \ and$$
$$L(X) \subseteq O(X).$$

Proof. Let $G = (V_N, V_T, P, \{(v_S, S)\}, \#)$ be an array grammar of type X with $P = \{p_i \mid 1 \leq i \leq n\}$ for some $n \in \mathbf{N}$.

1. Let

$$G_P = (V_N, V_T, (R, L_i, L_f), \{(v_S, S)\}, \#)$$

be the programmed array grammar with

$$R = \{(i : p_i, \sigma(i), \varphi(i)) \mid 1 \leq i \leq n\},$$
$$\sigma(i) = \{i \mid 1 \leq i \leq n\} \text{ and } \varphi(i) = \emptyset \text{ for all } i \text{ with } 1 \leq i \leq n,$$

as well as

$$L_i = L_f = \{i \mid 1 \le i \le n\}.$$

By construction, G_P again is of type X. Moreover, it is easy to see that $L(G_P) = L(G)$, which proves $L(X) \subseteq P(X)$.

As any programmed array grammar without appearance checking by definition is a programmed array grammar with appearance checking, too, we immediately obtain

$$L(X) \subseteq P(X) \subseteq P_{ac}(X).$$

2. Let

$$G_M = (V_N, V_T, M, \{(v_S, S)\}, \#)$$

be the matrix array grammar with

$$M = \{(p_i) \mid 1 \le i \le n\}.$$

By construction G_M is again of type X. Obviously $L(G_M) = L(G)$ and therefore $L(X) \subseteq M(X)$. As any matrix array grammar without appearance checking by definition is a matrix array grammar with appearance checking, too, we immediately obtain

$$L(X) \subseteq M(X) \subseteq M_{ac}(X).$$

3. Let

$$G_O = (V_N, V_T, (P, <), \{(v_S, S)\}, \#)$$

be the ordered array grammar with the empty order relation $<$. Then obviously $L(G_O) = L(G)$ and therefore

$$L(X) \subseteq O(X).$$

$\square$

Lemma 3. *For every* $X \in \{REGA, CFA, \# - CFA, MONA, ENUM\}$, $M(X) \subseteq P(X)$ *and* $M_{ac}(X) \subseteq P_{ac}(X)$.

*Proof.*Let

$$G_M = (V_N, V_T, (M, F), \{(v_S, S)\}, \#)$$

be a matrix array grammar of type X with

$$M = \{m_i \mid 1 \le i \le n\} \text{ and } m_i = (m_{i,1}, ..., m_{i,k_i}),$$

where $n, k_1, ..., k_n \in N$ and the $m_{i,j}$ with $1 \le i \le k_i$, $1 \le i \le n$, are array productions of type X.

Then an equivalent programmed array grammar G_P with $L(G_P) = L(G_M)$ can be defined as follows:

$$
\begin{aligned}
G_P &= (V_N, V_T, (R, L_i, L_f), \{(v_S, S)\}, \#), \\
Lab(R) &= \{(i,j) \mid 1 \le j \le k_i,\ 1 \le i \le n\}, \\
L_i &= L_f = \{(i,1) \mid 1 \le i \le n\}, \\
R &= \{(i,j) : m_{i,j}, S_{i,j}, F_{i,j}) \mid 1 \le j \le k_i,\ 1 \le i \le n\}, \text{ where} \\
&\quad S_{i,j} = \{(i, j+1)\} \text{ for } 1 \le j < k_i,\ 1 \le i \le n, \\
&\quad S_{i,k_i} = \{(m,1) \mid 1 \le m \le n\} \text{ for } 1 \le i \le n, \\
&\quad F_{i,j} = \begin{cases} S_{i,j} & \text{if } m_{i,j} \in F \\ \emptyset & \text{if } m_{i,j} \notin F \end{cases} \quad \text{for } 1 \le j \le k,\ 1 \le i \le n.
\end{aligned}
$$

The set of initial labels L_i guarantees that the simulation of a derivation in G_M by a derivation in G_P can start with the first production in any arbitrary matrix of M, whereas the set of final labels L_f guarantees that the simulation of a derivation in G_M by a derivation in G_P can stop after the last production in any arbitrary matrix of M. By the rules

$$\{((i,j) : m_{i,j}, S_{i,j}, F_{i,j}) \mid 1 \le j \le k_i\}$$

any arbitrary derivation by the matrix m_i in G_M can be simulated by the corresponding sequence of array productions in G_P; moreover, the application of $m_{i,j}$ can be skipped in the appearance checking mode in G_P if and only if $m_{i,j}$ appears in F (which means that its application can be skipped in the appearance checking mode in G_M).

As a final observation we mention that, if G_M is a matrix array grammar without appearance checking, i.e. $F = \emptyset$, then by the construction given above G_P is (a programmed array grammar) without appearance checking, too, which completes the proof. $\qquad\square$

Whereas the proofs of the previous lemmas did not depend on the specific type of the underlying array productions, because of the very restricted forms of regular array productions the technique used in the proof of the following lemma does not work for the type $REGA$:

Lemma 4. *For every* $X \in \{CFA, \# - CFA, MONA, ENUMA\}$

$$O(X) \subseteq M_{ac}(X).$$

Proof. Let

$$G_O = (V_N, V_T, (P, <), \{(v_S, S)\}, \#)$$

be an ordered array grammar of type X. Then a matrix array grammar with appearance checking

$$G_M = (V_N \cup \{Q\}, V_T, (M, F), \{(v_S, S)\}, \#)$$

of type X with $L(G_M) = L(G_O)$ can be defined as follows:

For each array production $p \in P$ with $p = (W_p, \mathcal{A}_p, \mathcal{B}_p)$ we introduce the new array production

$$p^- = (W_p, \mathcal{A}_p, \{(v, Q) \mid v \in W_p\})$$

with the trap symbol Q appearing on the right hand side of the production.

Moreover, for each $p \in P$ let

$$P_p^- = \{q \in P \mid q > p\} = \{q_{p,1}, ..., q_{p,n_p}\}.$$

Then the applicability of the rule p can be checked by checking the applicability of every rule in P_p^- before applying p, i. e. we define

$$M = \{(q_{p,1}^-, ... q_{p,n_p}^-, p) \mid p \in P\}$$

and

$$F = \{p^- \mid p \in P\}.$$

It is easy to verify that according to these constructions we obtain $L(G_M) = L(G_O)$. $\qquad\qquad\square$

From now on we shall restrict our attention to the types $ENUMA$ and $\# - CFA$ in order to establish our main result stated in theorem 4, i.e.

$$X(\# - CFA) = Y(ENUMA)$$

for every $X \in \{P, P_{ac}, M, M_{ac}, O\}$ and every $Y \in \{L, P, P_{ac}, M, M_{ac}, O\}$.

Lemma 5. *For each array grammar $G = (V_N, V_T, P, \{(v_s, S)\}, \#)$ there exists an equivalent array grammar $G' = (V_N', V_T, P', \{(v_s, S^*)\}, \#)$ such that every array production in P' is one of the following forms:*

1. $X \to Y$, where $X \in V_N$, $Y \in V_N \cup V_T \cup \{\#\}$;

2. $\{((0,0), A), (v, D)\} \to \{((0,0), X), (v, Y)\}$, where $A \in V_N$, $D, X, Y \in V_N \cup \{\#\}$, and $\|v\| = 1$.

Proof. First of all, we can introduce a new non-terminal symbol $[a]$ for each terminal symbol $a \in V_T$ and consider the homomorphism $h : V_N \cup V_T \to V_N \cup \{[a] \mid a \in V_T\}$ with $h(X) = X$ for all $X \in V_N$ and $h(a) = [a]$ for all $a \in V_T$. Then instead of G we consider

$$G'' = (V_N \cup h(V_T), V_T, h(P) \cup \{([a] \to a) \mid a \in V_T\}, \{(v_s, S)\}, \#),$$

where the productions in $h(P)$ are obtained from the productions in P by replacing each terminal symbol a by the corresponding non-terminal symbol $[a]$. Obviously, $L(G'') = L(G)$.

The array grammar $G'' = (V_N'', V_T, P'', \{(v_s, S)\}, \#)$ now can be represented in such a way that $P'' = P_1 \cup P_2$, where $P_1 \cap P_2 = \emptyset$ and P_1 contains exactly those rules in P'' being already in the desired forms. Let

$$P_2 = \{p_i \mid 1 \le i \le m\}, \text{ where for } 1 \le i \le m$$
$$p_i = (W_i, \mathcal{A}_i, \mathcal{B}_i),$$
$$W_i = \{w_{i,j} \mid 0 \le j \le m_i\}, \; w_{i,0} = (0,0), \; m_i \ge 2,$$
$$\mathcal{A}_i = \{(w, \mathcal{A}_i(v)) \mid v \in W_i\},$$
$$\mathcal{B}_i = \{(w, \mathcal{B}_i(v)) \mid v \in W_i\}.$$

Without loss of generality, we may also assume $\mathcal{A}_i(w_{i,0}) \in V_N$.

For each W_i and $w_{i,j} \ne (0,0)$ in W_i, let $g_{i,j}$ be a path from $w_{i,0}$ to $w_{i,j}$ such that

$$g_{i,j} = (w_{i,j,0}, w_{i,j,1}, ..., w_{i,j,m_{i,j}}) \text{ with}$$
$$w_{i,j,0} = w_{i,0}, \; w_{i,j,m_{i,j}} = w_{i,j}, \text{ and } \|w_{i,j,k} - w_{i,j,k-1}\| = 1, \; 1 \le k \le m_{i,j};$$

then each $p_i \in P_2$ is replaced by a new set of productions with norm 1 :

$$\mathcal{A}_i(w_{i,0})^* \to [\mathcal{A}_i(w_{i,0}), i, 1, f, 0]^*,$$
$$\{((0,0), [X, i, j, f, k]^*), (w_{i,j,k+1} - w_{i,j,k}, Y)\} \; \to$$
$$\{((0,0), X), (w_{i,j,k+1} - w_{i,j,k}, [Y, i, j, f, k+1]^*)\}),$$
$$0 \le k < m_{i,j}, \; 1 \le j \le m_i, \; X, Y \in V_N \cup \{\#\};$$
$$[\mathcal{A}_i(w_{i,j}), i, j, f, m_{i,j}]^* \to [\mathcal{B}_i(w_{i,j}), i, j, b, m_{i,j}]^*, \; 1 \le j \le m_{i,j};$$
$$\{((0,0), [X, i, j, b, k]^*), (w_{i,j,k-1} - w_{i,j,k}, Y)\} \to$$
$$\{((0,0), X), (w_{i,j,k} - w_{i,j,k-1}, [Y, i, j, b, k-1]^*)\},$$
$$m_{i,j} \ge k \ge 1, \; 1 \le j \le m_i, \; X, Y \in V_N \cup \{\#\};$$
$$[\mathcal{A}_i(w_{i,0}), i, j, b, 0]^* \to [\mathcal{A}_i(w_{i,0}), i, j+1, f, 0]^*, \; 1 \le j < m_i;$$
$$[\mathcal{A}_i(w_{i,0}), i, m_i, b, 0]^* \to \mathcal{B}_i(w_{i,0})^*.$$

Now let P_2' denote the set of all array productions obtained by the procedure described above and V_2' denote the set of all new non-terminal symbols introduced in these array productions. We now are able to define $G' = (V_N', V_T, P', \{(v_s, S^*)\}, \#)$ by

$$V_N' = V_N'' \cup V_2' \cup \{X^* \mid X \in V_N''\} \cup \{\#^*, \#'\} \quad \text{and}$$
$$P' = P_1' \cup P_2' \cup P_3',$$
$$P_1' = \{X^* \to Y^* \mid X \to Y \in P_1, \; X \in V_N, \; Y \in V_N \cup \{\#\}\} \cup$$
$$\{\{((0,0), A^*), (v, D)\} \to \{((0,0), X^*), (v, Y)\} \mid$$

$$\{((0,0),A),(v,D)\} \to \{((0,0),X),(v,Y)\} \in P_1,$$
$$A \in V_N, \ D, X, Y \in V_N \cup \{\#\}, \ \|v\| = 1\} \cup$$
$$\{A \to a \mid A \to a \in P_1, \ A \in V_N, \ a \in V_N \cup \{\#\}\};$$
$$P_3' = \{\{((0,0),X^*),(v,Y)\} \to \{((0,0),X),(v,Y^*)\} \mid$$
$$X \in V_N, \ Y \in V_N \cup \{\#\}, \ \|v\| = 1\} \cup$$
$$\{\{((0,0),\#^*),(v,Y)\} \to \{((0,0),\#'),(v,Y^*)\} \mid$$
$$Y \in V_N \cup \{\#\}, \ \|v\| = 1\} \cup \{\#^* \to \#, \#' \to \#\}.$$

Terminal symbols do not appear in any other array productions in P'' than in the terminal array productions of the form $A \to a$, $A \in V_N$, $a \in V_T$; hence as soon as any position in an array derivable from the start array $\{(v_s, S^*)\}$ in G' is occupied by a terminal symbol, no other array production in P' can involve this position any more. Thus without loss of generality we can assume that in a derivation of an array in $L(G')$ the terminal array productions are only applied in the last stage of this derivation, i.e. after the first application of a terminal array production no other array productions than terminal array productions will be applied during the rest of the derivation.

The second observation is that in any array derivable from the start array $\{(v_s, S^*)\}$ in G' exactly one non-terminal symbol is marked by a star, until we apply the array production $\#^* \to \#$. This guarantees the correct simulation of the array productions from P'' by the corresponding (sequence of) array productions in P', because no interferences are possible. In conclusion, we finally obtain $L(G') = L(G'') = L(G)$. $\qquad\square$

Corollary 1. *For every arbitrary array grammar G there exists an equivalent array grammar G' in Kuroda normal form such that $L(G') = L(G)$.*
Proof. Let
$$G = (V_N, V_T, P, \{(v_S, S)\}, \#)$$
be an arbitrary array grammar; because of lemma 5, without loss of generality we can already assume all array productions in P to be of the following forms:

1. $X \to Y$, where $X \in V_N$ and $Y \in V_N \cup V_T \cup \{\#\}$;

2. $\{((0,0),A),(v,D)\} \to \{((0,0),X),(v,Y)\}$, where $A \in V_N$, $D, X, Y \in V_N \cup \{\#\}$, and $\|v\| = 1$.

We now define an array grammar
$$G' = (V_N', V_T, P', \{(v_S, S)\}, \#)$$
in Kuroda normal form such that $L(G') = L(G)$:
Adding a new non-terminal B to V_N yields V_N', i.e.
$$V_N' = V_N \cup \{B\}.$$

Moreover, we define the homomorphism

$$h : V_N \cup \{\#\} \to V_N \cup \{B\} \text{ with } h(X) = X \text{ for all } X \in V_N \text{ and } h(\#) = B.$$

The new set of array productions P' then can be defined as follows:

$$
\begin{aligned}
P' \;=\; &\{A \to a \mid A \to a \in P \text{ for } A \in V_N \text{ and } a \in V_N \cup \{\#\}\} \cup \{B \to \#\} \cup \\
&\{((0,0), X), (v, D)\} \to \{((0,0), Y), (v, D)\} \mid \\
&\quad X \to Y \in P \text{ for } X, Y \in V_N, \; D \in V_N, \; \|v\| = 1\} \cup \\
&\{((0,0), X), (v, \#)\} \to \{((0,0), Y), (v, B)\} \mid \\
&\quad X \to Y \in P \text{ for } X, Y \in V_N, \; \|v\| = 1\} \cup \\
&\{((0,0), A), (v, D)\} \to \{((0,0), h(X)), (v, h(Y))\} \mid \\
&\quad \{((0,0), A), (v, D)\} \to \{((0,0), X), (v, Y)\} \in P \text{ for } \\
&A \in V_N, \; D, X, Y \in V_N \cup \{\#\}\}
\end{aligned}
$$

By the construction given above, all array productions are in the desired forms, i.e. G' is in Kuroda normal form. All array productions from P are also covered by P' : The terminal array productions $A \to a$, $A \in V_N$, $a \in V_T \cup \{\#\}$, can immediately be taken over from P to P'; the array productions $X \to Y$ in P, $X, Y \in V_N$, are replaced by suitable array productions with arbitrary context; blank symbols on the right hand side of the remaining other array productions in P are replaced by the new symbol B in the array productions in P'; by the array production $B \to \#$ the non-terminal symbol B can be erased again. Obviously, according to these considerations we can conclude that $L(G) = L(G')$. $\qquad\square$

Theorem 1. $P_{ac}(ENUMA) \subseteq ENUMA.$

Proof. Let

$$G_P = (V_N, V_T, (R, L_i, L_f), \{(v_S, S)\}, \#)$$

be an arbitrary programmed array grammar, where without loss of generality we assume $Lab(R) = \{i \mid 1 \le i \le n\}$ for some $n \in \mathbf{N}$, i.e.

$$R = \{(i : p(i), \sigma(i), \varphi(i)) \mid 1 \le i \le n\}.$$

Moreover, we denote $\|G\| = \max\{\|p(i)\| \mid 1 \le i \le n\}$ and $p(i) = (W_i, A_i, B_i)$, $1 \le i \le n$.

We now construct an array grammar

$$G = (V_N', V_T, P, \{(v_S, S')\}, \#)$$

with $L(G) = L(G_P)$:

First we take the array productions in

$$P_0 = \{s_1, s_2, h\} \cup \{r_i, d_i, l_i, u_i \mid 1 \leq i \leq 4\}$$

from Example 7, which allow us to generate squares of side length $4m + 3$, $m \in N$, with S marking the middle of the square lying in v_s, the edges of the square marked by lines of thickness one with symbols E, the left upper corner marked with the symbol H, and the rest of the square filled with symbols B.

As already shown in Example 7, the smallest array generated by the array productions in P_0 can be represented by the following picture (observe that the symbol S now marks the position v_S):

$$
\begin{array}{ccccccc}
H & E & E & E & E & E & E \\
E & B & B & B & B & B & E \\
E & B & B & B & B & B & E \\
E & B & B & S & B & B & E \\
E & B & B & B & B & B & E \\
E & B & B & B & B & B & E \\
E & E & E & E & E & E & E
\end{array}
$$

The squares generated by the array productions in P_0 establish the working area where we will simulate the derivations possible in G_P. In this working area the blank symbol $\#$ is represented by the symbol B; hence we need the following homomorphism h mapping $\#$ to B :

$$h : V_N \cup V_T \cup \{\#\} \rightarrow V_N \cup V_T \cup \{B\},$$
$$h(X) = X \text{ for all } X \in V_N \cup V_T \text{ and } h(\#) = B.$$

The simulation of a derivation of an array in $L(G_P)$ within the working area generated by the array productions in P_0 and enclosing all positions reached during this derivation is initiated by the array productions

$$H \rightarrow H_i \quad \text{for } 1 \leq i \leq n \text{ and } i \in L_i.$$

For each i, $1 \leq i \leq n$, with $\sigma(i) \neq \emptyset$, we introduce the set P_i containing the following array productions (observe that throughout this paper without loss of generality we assume $\mathcal{A}_i((0,0)) \neq \#$):

$$
\begin{array}{ccc}
H_i & & H_i^\sigma \\
B & \rightarrow & B_i^\sigma
\end{array} \; ;
$$

$$
X_i^\sigma Y \rightarrow X Y_i^\sigma, \qquad
\begin{array}{c} X_i^\sigma \\ Y \end{array} \rightarrow \begin{array}{c} X \\ Y_i^\sigma \end{array} \qquad \text{for } X, Y \in V_N \cup V_T \cup \{B\};
$$

$$YX_i^\alpha \to Y_i^\alpha X, \qquad \begin{array}{c} Y \\ X_i^\alpha \end{array} \to \begin{array}{c} Y_i^\alpha \\ X \end{array} \qquad \text{for } X, Y \in V_N \cup V_T \cup \{B\};$$

$$\begin{array}{c} H_i^\sigma \\ B_i^\alpha \end{array} \to \begin{array}{c} H_j \\ B \end{array} \qquad \text{for } j \in \sigma(i);$$

$$\{((0,0), \mathcal{A}_i((0,0))_i^\sigma)\} \cup \{(w, h(\mathcal{A}_i(w))) \mid w \in W_i - \{(0,0)\}\} \cup U \to$$
$$\{((0,0), (h(\mathcal{B}_i((0,0))))_i^\alpha)\} \cup \{(w, h(\mathcal{B}_i(w))) \mid w \in W_i - \{(0,0)\}\} \cup U$$

for $U \in U_i^\sigma$, where we define

$$U_i^\sigma = \{\{(v, X_v) \mid v \in Z_i\} \mid X_v \in V_N \cup V_T \cup \{B\} \text{ for all } v \in Z_i\} \text{ and}$$
$$Z_i = \{v \mid v \in \mathbf{Z}^2 - W_i, \|v\| \le 2\,\|G\|\}.$$

The additional sets U in the productions above guarantee that symbols from $V_N \cup V_T$ are only generated at a distance of at least $\|G\|$ from the edges of the square representing the working area, which guarantees that checking the applicability of an array production $p(i)$ (which will be done below for array productions with $\varphi(i) \ne \emptyset$) is not affected by the limitations of the working area established by the edge symbols E. If G_P is a programmed array grammar without appearance checking, we only have to add the final set of array productions P_{n+1} containing the following array productions:

$$H_i \to T_1 \text{ for } 1 \le i \le n \text{ and } i \in L_f,$$
$$T_1 EE \to \#T_1 E, \quad T_1 E\# \to T_2\#\#,$$
$$\#T_2 \to T_2\#, \quad \begin{array}{cc} T_2 & \\ E & B \end{array} \to \begin{array}{cc} \# & \\ \# & T_B \end{array},$$
$$T_B X \to \#T_X \quad \text{for } X \in V_T \cup \{B\},$$
$$T_a X \to aT_X \quad \text{for } X \in V_T \cup \{B\}, \text{ and } a \in V_T,$$
$$T_B E \to T_2\#, \quad \begin{array}{cc} T_2 & \\ E & E \end{array} \to \begin{array}{cc} \# & \\ \# & T_3 \end{array},$$
$$T_3 EE \to \#T_3 E, \quad T_3 E\# \to \#\#\#.$$

By the array productions in P_{n+1}, from the top to the bottom each row of the square representing our working area is scanned from the left to the right in such a way that only the terminal symbols remain at their positions, whereas the non-terminal symbols B and E are erased, i.e. finally a terminal array can be derived.

If G_P works in the appearance checking mode, then for each i, $1 \le i \le n$, with $\varphi(i) \ne \emptyset$ we also have to add the set P_i' of array productions, which allow us to check that $p(i)$ is not applicable to the current array over $V_N \cup V_T$ embedded in the working area. Like before with the final set P_{n+1}, from the top to the bottom we scan each row of the working area from the left to the right and at each position occupied by the symbol $\mathcal{A}_i((0,0))$ we check the (non-)applicability of the array production $p(i)$. P_i' for $\varphi(i) \neq \emptyset$ contains the following array productions:

$$\begin{array}{c} H_i \\ B \end{array} \rightarrow \begin{array}{c} H_i^\varphi \\ B_i^\varphi \end{array}, \quad B_i^\varphi E \rightarrow B_i^\rho E;$$

$$X_i^\varphi Y \rightarrow X Y_i^\varphi \quad \text{for } X, Y \in V_N \cup V_T \cup \{B\} \text{ and } Y \neq \mathcal{A}_i((0,0));$$

$$X_i^\varphi \mathcal{A}_i((0,0)) \rightarrow X \mathcal{A}_i((0,0))_i^\delta \quad \text{for } X \in V_N \cup V_T \cup \{B\};$$

$$\{((0,0), \mathcal{A}_i((0,0))_i^\delta\} \cup U \rightarrow \{((0,0), \mathcal{A}_i((0,0))_i^\varphi)\} \cup U$$

$$\text{for } U \in U_i^\varphi, \text{ where we define}$$

$$U_i^\varphi = \{\{(v, X_v) \mid v \in W_i - \{(0,0)\}\} \mid$$

$$X_v \in V_N \cup V_T \cup \{B\} \text{ for all } v \in W_i - \{(0,0)\} \text{ and}$$

$$X_{v_0} \neq h(\mathcal{A}_i(v_0)) \text{ for some } v_0 \in W_i - \{(0,0)\}\};$$

(observe that by the array productions in the P_i, $1 \leq i \leq n$, the symbol $\mathcal{A}_i((0,0)) \neq \#$ can only appear in a position with a distance of at least $\|G\|$ from the edges of the working area)

$$Y X_i^\rho \rightarrow Y_i^\rho X \quad \text{for } X, Y \in V_N \cup V_T \cup \{B\};$$

$$\begin{array}{cc} E & B_i^\rho \\ & B \end{array} \rightarrow \begin{array}{cc} E & B \\ & B_i^\varphi \end{array}; \quad \begin{array}{cc} E & B_i^\rho \\ & E \end{array} \rightarrow \begin{array}{cc} E & B_i^\beta \\ & E \end{array}; \quad \begin{array}{c} B \\ B_i^\beta \end{array} \rightarrow \begin{array}{c} B_i^\beta \\ B \end{array};$$

$$\begin{array}{c} H_i^\varphi \\ B_i^\beta \end{array} \rightarrow \begin{array}{c} H_j \\ B \end{array} \quad \text{for } j \in \varphi(i).$$

Collecting all sets of array productions defined above we obtain

$$P = P_0 \cup P_{n+1} \cup \bigcup_{1 \leq i \leq n, \sigma(i) \neq \emptyset} P_i \cup \bigcup_{1 \leq i \leq n, \varphi(i) \neq \{\}} P_i'.$$

All non-terminal symbols occuring in the array productions in P are covered by

$$\begin{aligned} V_N' \; = \; & \{S', R_1, D_1, L_1, U_1, R_2, D_2, L_2, U_2, B, E, H\} \cup V_N \cup \\ & \{H_i, H_i^\sigma, H_i^\varphi, B_i^\beta \mid 1 \leq i \leq n\} \cup \\ & \{X_i^k \mid X \in V_N \cup V_T \cup \{B\}, 1 \leq i \leq n, k \in \{\sigma, \alpha, \varphi, \delta, \rho\}\} \cup \\ & \{T_x \mid x \in \{1, 2, 3\} \cup V_T \cup \{B\}\}. \end{aligned}$$

$\square$

One of the main components of the previous proof, namely the introduction of a working area using the construction of specific squares like in example 7, is also an important part of the proofs of the two succeeding theorems, where we will show that already #-context-free matrix array grammars without appearance checking respectively #-context-free ordered array grammars can generate any (Λ-free) r.e. array language.

Theorem 2. $L(ENUM) \subseteq M(\# - CFA)$.

Proof. Let

$$G = (V_N, V_T, P, \{(v_S, S)\}, \#)$$

be an arbitrary array grammar, which by corollary 1 without loss of generality can be assumed to be in Kuroda normal form. We now construct a matrix grammar without appearance checking

$$G_M = (V_N', V_T, M, \{(v_S, S')\}, \#)$$

with $L(G_M) = L(G)$:

Like in the proof of theorem 1 we take the set of array productions P_0 defined in Example 7 in order to generate suitable working areas allowing us to simulate derivations possible in G within this working area by using only #-context-free array productions in matrices, but without taking advantage of the appearance checking mode. Hence we first define

$$M_0 = \{(p) \mid p \in P_0\}.$$

Depending on the form of the array production $p \in P$ we now define a suitable matrix m_p for the simulation of the application of p in a derivation in G by the application of m_p in a derivation in G_M :

$$
\begin{aligned}
M_1 \;=\; & \{(H \to H_p, \; B \to \#, \; p, \; H_p \to H) \mid p \in P \text{ and} \\
& p = (\{(0,0), v\}, \{((0,0), A), (v, \#)\}, \{((0,0), X), (v, Y)\}) \\
& \text{for } A, X, Y \in V_N \text{ and } v \in \mathbf{Z}^2 \text{ with } \|v\| = 1\}, \\
M_2 \;=\; & \{(H \to H_p, \; D \to \#, \; p, \; H_p \to H) \mid p \in P \text{ and} \\
& p = (\{(0,0), v\}, \{((0,0), A), (v, \#)\}, \{((0,0), X), (v, Y)\}) \\
& \text{for } A, D, X, Y \in V_N \text{ and } v \in \mathbf{Z}^2 \text{ with } \|v\| = 1\}, \\
M_3 \;=\; & \{(H \to H_p, \; p, \; H_p \to H) \mid p \in P \text{ and} \\
& p = (\{(0,0)\}, \{((0,0), A)\}, \{((0,0), a)\}) \\
& \text{for } A \in V_N \text{ and } a \in V_T\}, \\
M_4 \;=\; & \{(H \to H_p, \; A \to B, \; H_p \to H) \mid p \in P \text{ and} \\
& p = (\{(0,0)\}, \{((0,0)A)\}, \{((0,0), \#)\}) \text{ for } A \in V_N\}.
\end{aligned}
$$

For finishing the derivation of a terminal array in G_M we need the matrices in M_5 :

$$M_5 = \{(H \to H_t), (H_t \to H_t, B \to \#), (H_t \to H_t, E \to \#), (H_t \to \#)\}.$$

As the application of productions p in P can only be simulated in G_M as long as the non-terminal symbol H occurs in the underlying array, the application of the array production $H \rightarrow H_t$ terminates the simulation, whereafter only the erasing of the non-terminal symbols B and E and finally of H_t itself is possible.

Collecting all sets of matrices defined above as well as all the non-terminal symbols occurring in array productions within these matrices we obtain

$$M = \bigcup_{0 \leq i \leq 5} M_i$$

as well as

$$V_N' = \{S', R_1, D_1, L_1, U_1, R_2, D_2, L_2, U_2, B, E, H, H_t\} \cup \{H_p \mid p \in P\} \cup V_N.$$

As it is easy to see, all derivations possible in G can be simulated in G_M leading to the same terminal arrays and on the other hand no other terminal arrays than those from $L(G)$ can be derived in G_M, we conclude $L(G_M) = L(G)$. $\square$

Theorem 3. $L(ENUMA) \subseteq O(\# - CFA)$.

Proof. Let

$$G = (V_N', V_T, P, \{(v_S, S)\}, \#)$$

be an arbitrary array grammar which by Corollary 1 without loss of generality can be assumed to be in Kuroda normal form. We now construct an ordered array grammar

$$G_O = (V_N, V_T, (P', <), \{(v_S, S')\}, \#)$$

with $L(G_O) = L(G)$. The construction is based on the following ideas:

– Like in the proofs of the preceeding theorems a working area is established by the set of array productions P_0 (for the definition of P_0 see Example 7).

– The simulation of the application of an array production in P by array productions in P' is controlled by suitable control variables H_x in the left upper corner of the square representing the working area as well as by the order relation $<$ on the array productions in P'.

– Controlling the applicability of the array productions in P' by the order relation $<$ is achieved by using array productions introducing a trap symbol F as array productions that are forced to be applied before a specific production itself can be applied.

Besides $S(\in V_N)$ as well as B and E, from the array productions in P_0 we obtain the set of non-terminal symbols

$$V_0 = \{S', R_1, D_1, L_1, U_1, R_2, D_2, L_2, U_2\}.$$

The control variables in the left upper corner of the square representing the working area are taken from the set

$$V_H = \{H, H_t\} \cup \{H_p^1, H_p^2 \mid p \in P\}.$$

In addition we will also use the trap symbol F as well as the non-terminal symbols A_p^1 and A_p^2 for $A \in V_N$ and $p \in P$, which alltogether yields

$$V_N' = V_N \cup V_0 \cup V_H \cup \{A_p^1, A_p^2 \mid A \in V_N, \ p \in P\} \cup \{B, E, F\}.$$

The array productions, which introduce the trap symbol F and therefore block the derivation of a terminal array, are taken from the set

$$
\begin{aligned}
P_F &= \{A_p^1 \to F, A_p^2 \to F \mid A \in V_N, p \in P\} \cup \\
&\quad \{X \to F \mid X \in V_0 \cup V_H \cup \{B, E\}\} \cup P_F', \text{ where} \\
P_F' &= \{(\{(0,0), v\}, \{((0,0), A), (v, \#)\}, \{((0,0), F), (v, F)\}) \mid \\
&\quad A \in V_N, v \in \mathbf{Z}^2 \text{ with } \|v\| = 1\}.
\end{aligned}
$$

Depending on the form of the array production p in P we now define a set P_p of array productions (that allows us to simulate the application of p in a derivation in G by the application of a suitable sequence of the array productions in P_p within the underlying working area) as well as for every array production q in P_p a suitable set of array productions $P_q^F \subseteq P_F$ with $q < r$ for every $r \in P_q^F$ (in order to guarantee that the derivation in G_O is blocked by the introduction of the trap symbol F when we try to apply the array production $q \in P_p$ at the wrong moment); in the following we will only state P_q^F if it is not empty:

1. For $p = (\{(0,0), v\}, \{((0,0), A), (v, \#)\}, \{((0,0), X), (v, Y)\})$
   with $A, X, Y \in V_N$ and $v \in \mathbf{Z}^2$ with $\|v\| = 1$ we define

$$
\begin{aligned}
P_p &= \{H \to H_p^1, A \to A_p^1, H_p^1 \to H_p^2, B \to B_p^2, B_p^2 \to \#, \\
&\quad (\{(0,0), v\}, \{((0,0), A_p^1), (v, \#)\}, \{((0,0), X), (v, Y)\}), H_p^2 \to H\}
\end{aligned}
$$

as well as

$$
\begin{aligned}
P_{A \to A_p^1}^F &= \{X \to F \mid X \in V_0 \cup (V_H - \{H_p^1\}) \cup \{A_p^1\}\}, \\
P_{B \to B_p^2}^F &= \{X \to F \mid X \in V_0 \cup (V_H - \{H_p^2\}) \cup \{B_p^2\}\} \cup P_F', \\
P_{H_p^2 \to H}^F &= \{A_p^1 \to F, B_p^2 \to F\} \cup P_F'.
\end{aligned}
$$

By $P_{A \to A_p^1}^F$ it is guaranteed that only after the application of $H \to H_p^1$ the array production $A \to A_p^1$ can be applied at most once. If $H_p^1 \to H_p^2$ is applied immediately after $H \to H_p^1$, then only the application of $H_p^2 \to H$ makes sense, because after applying $B \to B_p^2$ and $B_p^2 \to \#$ only array productions from P_F', which introduce the trap symbol F, are applicable. But after the application of the sequence of array productions $H \to H_p^1$, $H_p^1 \to H_p^2$, $H_p^2 \to H$ the underlying array has not been changed, whereas by applying the array productions in P_p in the sequence as they are listed above in the definition of the set P_p, then exactly one application of the array production p in a derivation in G has been simulated in G_O. Observe that the derivation in G_O is also blocked, if A_p^1 and B_p^2 are not derived at suitable positions.

2. For $p = (\{(0,0), v\}, \{((0,0), A), (v, D)\}, \{((0,0), X), (v, Y)\})$ with $A, D, X, Y \in V_N$ and $v \in \mathbf{Z}^2$ with $\|v\| = 1$ we define

$$\begin{aligned}
P_p \quad = \quad &\{H \to H_p^1, A \to A_p^1, H_p^1 \to H_p^2, D \to D_p^2, D_p^2 \to \#, \\
&\{(0,0), v\}, \{((0,0), A_p^1), (v, \#)\}, \{((0,0), X), (v, Y)\}), H_p^2 \to H\}
\end{aligned}$$

as well as

$$\begin{aligned}
P_{A \to A_p^1}^F &= \{X \to F \mid X \in V_0 \cup (V_H - \{H_p^1\}) \cup \{A_p^1\}\}, \\
P_{D \to D_p^2}^F &= \{X \to F \mid X \in V_0 \cup (V_H - \{H_p^2\}) \cup \{D_p^2\}\} \cup P_F', \\
P_{H_p^2 \to H}^F &= \{A_p^1 \to F, D_p^2 \to F\} \cup P_F'.
\end{aligned}$$

Similar considerations as in the first case show that applying the array productions from P_p in the sequence as they are listed above in the definitions of the set P_p allows the simulation of the application of the array production p in a derivation in G by G_O, whereas the choice of the sets $P_{A \to A_p^1}^F$, $P_{D \to D_p^2}^F$, and $P_{H_p^2 \to H}^F$ blocks parasitic derivations.

3. For $p = (\{(0,0)\}, \{((0,0), A)\}, \{((0,0), a)\})$ with $A \in V_N$ and $a \in V_T$ we define

$$\begin{aligned}
P_p &= \{H \to H_p^1, p, H_p^1 \to H\} \text{ and} \\
P_p^F &= \{X \to F \mid X \in V_0 \cup (V_H - \{H_p^1\})\}.
\end{aligned}$$

4. For $p = (\{(0,0)\}, \{((0,0), A)\}, \{((0,0), \#)\})$ with $A \in V_N$ we define

$$\begin{aligned}
p' &= (\{(0,0)\}, \{((0,0), A)\}, \{((0,0), B)\}) \text{ as well as} \\
P_p &= \{H \to H_p^1, p', H_p^1 \to H\} \text{ and} \\
P_p^F &= \{X \to F \mid X \in V_0 \cup (V_H - \{H_p^1\})\}.
\end{aligned}$$

Whereas in the first two cases the application of the array production $H \to H_p^1$ leads to the simulation of at most one application of p, in the case of an array production of the form $A \to a$ with $A \in V_N$ and $a \in V_T$ respectively of the form $A \to \#$ with $A \in V_N$, after the application of $H \to H_p^1$ the array production p respectively p' can be applied arbitrarily often until $H_p^1 \to H$ is applied.

If non-terminal symbols from V_N do not appear within the working area any more, the derivation of the terminal array embedded in the working area can be initiated by applying the array production $H \to H_t$, whereafter the non-terminal symbols B and E and finally H_t itself can be erased:

$$P_t = \{H \to H_t, B \to \#, E \to \#, H_t \to \#\} \text{ and}$$
$$P_{H \to H_t}^F = \{X \to F \mid X \in V_N\},$$
$$P_{B \to \#}^F = P_{E \to \#}^F = \{X \to F \mid X \in V_0 \cup V_N \cup (V_H - \{H_t\})\},$$
$$P_{H_t \to \#}^F = \{B \to F, E \to F\}.$$

Collecting all the sets of array productions defined above we obtain

$$P' = P_0 \cup P_F \cup P_t \cup \bigcup_{p \in P} P_p \qquad .$$

and the order relation determined by the sets P_q^F, $q \in P'$, defined above, i.e. for $q, r \in P'$ the relation $q < r$ holds if and only if $r \in P_q^F$. Hence, we have completely specified the #-context-free ordered array grammar G_O; according to the comments given above it is easy to see that $L(G_O) = L(G)$, which completes the proof. $\square$

In the following theorem we summarize the most important results we proved in this paper.

Theorem 4. $X(\# - CFA) = Y(ENUMA)$ *for every* $X \in \{P, P_{ac}, M, M_{ac}, O\}$ *and every* $Y \in \{L, P, P_{ac}, M, M_{ac}, O\}$.

Proof. By Lemma 2 and Theorem 1 we obtain

$$L(ENUMA) \subseteq P(ENUMA) \subseteq P_{ac}(ENUMA) \subseteq L(ENUMA)$$

and therefore $L(ENUMA) = P(ENUMA) = P_{ac}(ENUMA)$
By Lemma 2, Lemma 3, and Theorem 1 we obtain

$$L(ENUMA) \subseteq M(ENUMA) \subseteq M_{ac}(ENUMA) \subseteq$$
$$\subseteq P_{ac}(ENUMA) \subseteq L(ENUMA)$$

and therefore $L(ENUMA) = M(ENUMA) = M_{ac}(ENUMA)$, too.
By Lemma 2, Lemma 4, and the previous observation we also get

$$L(ENUMA) \subseteq O(ENUMA) \subseteq M_{ac}(ENUMA) = L(ENUMA)$$

and therefore $L(ENUMA) = O(ENUMA)$.

Collecting all these results for the type $ENUMA$ yields

$$L(ENUMA) = Y(ENUMA) \text{ for every } Y \in \{P, P_{ac}, M, M_{ac}, O\}.$$

As obviously $L(\# - CFA) \subseteq L(ENUMA)$, from Lemma 1 we know that

$$U(\# - CFA) \subseteq U(ENUMA) \text{ for every } U \in \{P, P_{ac}, M, M_{ac}, O\}.$$

Together with Theorem 2 as well as Lemma 2 and Lemma 3 respectively Theorem 3 and Lemma 4 this implies

$$L(ENUMA) \subseteq M(\# - CFA) \subseteq M_{ac}(\# - CFA) \subseteq$$
$$\subseteq M_{ac}(ENUMA) = L(ENUMA)$$

and

$$L(ENUMA) \subseteq M(\# - CFA) \subseteq P(\# - CFA) \subseteq$$
$$\subseteq P_{ac}(ENUMA) = L(ENUMA)$$

respectively

$$L(ENUMA) \subseteq O(\# - CFA) \subseteq M_{ac}(\# - CFA) \subseteq$$
$$\subseteq M_{ac}(ENUMA) = L(ENUMA).$$

Combining all these results for the types $ENUMA$ and $\# - CFA$ we obtain

$$X(\# - CFA) = Y(ENUMA)$$

for every $X \in \{P, P_{ac}, M, M_{ac}, O\}$ and every $Y \in \{L, P, P_{ac}, M, M_{ac}, O\}$, which completes the proof. $\square$

Corollary 2. $[X(\# - CFA)] = [Y(ENUMA)]$ *for every* $X \in \{P, P_{ac}, M, M_{ac}, O\}$ *and* $Y \in \{L, P, P_{ac}, M, M_{ac}, O\}$.

6. Summary

Whereas matrix array grammars without and even with appearance checking using context-free array productions only cannot even generate all monotonic array languages (which follows from the results proved in [7], in this paper we have shown that (two-dimensional) matrix array grammars without appearance checking, programmed array grammars without appearance checking, and ordered array grammars using #-context-free two-dimensional array productions can already generate any r.e. two-dimensional array language which contradicts the results obtained in the string case.

The main results of this paper, i.e. Theorems 1 to 4, are based on the construction of suitable working areas, i.e. specific squares that can be generated even by using context-free array productions only (see Example 7). Constructing suitable working areas for the one-dimensional case is a straight-forward exercise, so the proofs of these theorems can immediately be adapted for the one-dimensional case. Yet if these theorems should also be proved for higher dimensions (i.e. for n-dimensional arrays with $n \geq 3$) by using the proof techniques presented in this paper, then the construction of suitable working areas (i.e. specific n-dimensional hyper-cubes) by using n-dimensional context-free array productions only or at least by using n-dimensional (#-)context-free matrix array grammars respectively n-dimensional (#-)context-free ordered array grammars remains as a non-trivial task for future research.

In [2] many other control mechanisms were introduced; the investigation of these mechanisms for the regulated rewriting of arrays using context-free respectively #-context-free (two-)dimensional array productions also remains for future research and might reveal some other interesting features of (families of) array languages in contrast to (families of) string languages.

References

1. C. R. Cook, P. S.-P. Wang, A Chomsky hierarchy of isotonic array grammars and languages, *Computer Graphics and Image Processing*, 8 (1978), 144 – 152.

2. J. Dassow, Gh. Păun, *Regulated rewriting in Formal Language Theory*, Springer-Verlag, Berlin, Heidelberg, 1989.

3. J. Dassow, R. Freund, G. Păun, Cooperating array grammar systems, *submitted*, 1993.

4. R. Freund, *N-dimensionale Sprachen*, Thesis, Technical University Wien, 1982.

5. R. Freund, *Regulated rewriting of arrays*, "1. Automatentag", Magdeburg, 1991.

6. R. Freund, Aspects of n-dimensional Lindenmayer systems, in *Developments in Language Theory* (G. Rozenberg, A. Salomaa, eds.), World Sci. Publ., Singapore, 1994, 250 – 261..

7. R. Freund, G. Păun, One-dimensional matrix array grammars, *J. Inform. Process. Cybernet., EIK*, 29 (6) (1993), 1 – 18.

8. D. Hauschildt, M. Jantzen, Petri net algorithms in the theory of matrix grammars, *submitted*, 1993.

9. A. Rosenfeld, *Picture Languages*, Academic Press, Reading, MA, 1979.

10. A. Salomaa, *Formal Languages*, Academic Press, New York, London, 1973.

11. P. S.-P. Wang, Some new results on isotonic array Grammars, *Information Processing Letters*, 10 (1980), 129 – 131.

12. Y. Yamamoto, K. Morita, K. Sugata, Context-sensitivity of two-dimensional regular array grammars, in *Array Grammars, Patterns and Recognizers* (P. S.-P. Wang, ed.), World Sci. Publ. Series in Computer Science, Vol. 18, Singapore, 1989.

Infinite Hierarchies of Some Types
of Contextual Languages

Gianina GEORGESCU
Faculty of Mathematics, University of Bucharest
Str. Academiei 14, 70109 Bucureşti, Romania

Abstract. We introduce and investigate from the point of view of connectedness several syntactic measures for some families of contextual languages. It is show that these measures induce infinite hierarchies of languages on the related families.

1. Introduction

The contextual grammars were introduced in [2] and they are based on the operation of adjoining contexts (pairs of strings) to strings or to parts of strings. In the last years, many researchers have investigated these grammars because the contextual grammars raise many theoretical problems and provide hints for application. For example, the study of recursion in language theory can be considered from the point of view of addition of the contexts, the bottom-up parsing can be examined from the point of view of erasing contexts etc. (scc [5]).

In the present paper several syntactical measures (many of them introduced here) are examined for various classes of contextual grammars. These measures are studied from the point of view of their connectedness (see [1]). The connectedness of a measure related to a given family of languages implies the existence of an infinite hierarchy of languages in that family (see the definitions in the next section). This is the case for most measures we consider here.

2. Definitions

For a vocabulary V we denote by V^* the free monoid generated by V under the operation of concatenation; the null element of V^* is denoted by λ. The length of $x \in V^*$ is denoted by $|x|$. The number of occurrences of a symbol a in a string x is denoted by $|x|_a$.

A *general contextual grammar* is a quadruple $G = (V, B, C, \varphi)$, where V is a finite non-empty alphabet, B is a finite language over V, $C \subseteq V^* \times V^* \times V^* \longrightarrow 2^C$ is the *selection mapping*.

The language generated by G, denoted $L(G)$, is the smallest set $L \subseteq V^*$ which includes B and has the next property: if $x \in L, x = x_1 x_2 x_3$, with $x_1, x_2, x_3 \in V^*$, and $(u, v) \in \varphi(x_1, x_2, x_3)$, then $x_1 u x_2 v x_3 \in L$. We also use the notation $x \Longrightarrow y$ for $x, y \in V^*$ if $x = x_1 x_2 x_3, y = x_1 u x_2 v x_3$ for some $(u, v) \in C, x_1, x_2, x_3 \in V^*$ such that $(u, v) \in \varphi(x_1, x_2, x_3)$. Then

$$L(G) = \{w \in V^* \mid x \overset{*}{\Longrightarrow} w, \text{ for some } x \in B\}.$$

A contextual grammar as above is said to be an *internal contextual grammar with choice* if the mapping φ has the following property:

$$\varphi(x_1, x_2, x_3) = \varphi(x_1', x_2, x_3') \text{ for all } x_1, x_1', x_2, x_3, x_3' \in V^*.$$

When the mapping φ is defined by $\varphi(x) = C$ for all $x \in V^*$, then the grammar G is called *internal contextual* (without choice).

A contextual grammar as above is called *external contextual with choice* if the mapping φ has the following property: $\varphi(x_1, x_2, x_3) = \emptyset$ for all $x_1, x_2, x_3 \in V^*$ with $x_1 x_3 \neq \lambda$ (the contexts can be added only at the ends of the strings).

If in an external grammar we have $\varphi(x) = C$ for all $x \in V^*$, then we say that the grammar is a *simple contextual grammar* (without choice).

When defining a grammar without choice, the mapping φ will be omitted.

We shall also distinguish between internal and external generated languages by writing $L_{in}(G)$, $L_{ex}(G)$, respectively.

We shall denote by E, EC, I, IC, T the families of languages generated by external simple contextual, by external contextual with choice, by internal contextual (without choice), by internal contextual with choice, and by (general) contextual grammars respectively.

We denote by $1X$ the family of languages generated by grammars of type X with contexts of the form (λ, v) only, and by $11X$ the family generated when both right contexts (λ, v) and left contexts (u, λ) are allowed (but no contexts (u, v) with $u \neq \lambda, v \neq \lambda$), $X \in \{E, EC, I, IC, T\}$.

A *(general) contextual grammar with erased contexts* is a construct $G = (V, B, C_1, C_2, \varphi, \delta)$, where (V, B, C_1, φ) is a usual (general) contextual grammar, $C_2 \subseteq V^* \times V^*$ and $\delta : V^* \times V^* \times V^* \longrightarrow 2^{C_2}$; the contexts in C_2 are erased and δ selects the contexts to be erased in the following way: for $x, y \in V^*$ we write $x \Longrightarrow y$ iff either

$$(1) \qquad x = x_1 x_2 x_3, y = x_1 u x_2 v x_3, (u, v) \in C_1, (u, v) \in \varphi(x_1, x_2, x_3),$$

$$\text{or } (2) \qquad x = x_1 u x_2 v x_3, y = x_1 x_2 x_3, (u, v) \in C_2, (u, v) \in \delta(x_1, x_2, x_3).$$

A *(general) contextual grammar with erasing contexts* is a construct $G = (V, B, C_1, C_2, \varphi, \gamma)$, where (V, B, C_1, φ) is a usual (general) contextual grammar, $C_2 \subseteq V^* \times V^*$ and $\gamma : V^* \times V^* \times V^* \longrightarrow 2^{C_2}$; the strings accepted by contexts in C_2 according to γ can be erased from the generated string in the following way: for $x, y \in V^*$ we write $x \Longrightarrow y$ iff either

(1) $\qquad x = x_1 x_2 x_3, y = x_1 u x_2 v x_3, (u, v) \in C_1, (u, v) \in \varphi(x_1, x_2, x_3),$

or (2) $\qquad x = x_1 u x_2 v x_3, y = x_1 u v x_3, (u, v) \in C_2, (u, v) \in \gamma(x_1, x_2, x_3).$

For a family X of contextual languages, $X \in \{E, EC, I, IC, T\}$ we denote by X_d the corresponding family generated by grammars with erased contexts and by X_g the family obtained when erasing contexts are used.

For a (general) contextual grammar $G = (V, B, C, \varphi)$ we define (see [4])

$$LCon(G) = max\{|uv| \mid (u, v) \in C\},$$

$$TCon(G) = \sum_{(u,v) \in C} |uv|,$$

$$Ass(G) = sup\{card \ \varphi(x) \mid x \in V^*\}.$$

These measures are defined for languages in the natural way:

$$M(L) = inf\{M(G) \mid L = L(G)\}, \ M \in \{LCon, TCon, Ass\}.$$

We extend these measures to families of grammars with erased and erasing contexts in the following way:

For a general contextual grammar with erased contexts $G = (V, B, C_1, C_2, \varphi, \delta)$ we define:

$$E_d Con(G) = card(C_2),$$

$$LE_d Con(G) = max\{|uv| \mid (u, v) \in C_2\},$$

$$TE_d Con(G) = \sum_{(u,v) \in C_2} |uv|,$$

$$Ass_d(G) = sup\{card \ \delta(x) \mid x \in V^*\}.$$

For a general contextual grammar with erasing contexts $G = (V, B, C_1, C_2, \varphi, \gamma)$ we define:

$$E_g Con(G) = card(C_2),$$

$$LE_g Con(G) = max\{|uv| \mid (u, v) \in C_2\},$$

$$TE_g Con(G) = \sum_{(u,v) \in C_2} |uv|,$$

$$Ass_g(G) = sup\{card\ \gamma(x) \mid x \in V^*\}.$$

We extend as above these measures to languages.

Given a measure $M : \mathcal{L}(X) \longrightarrow \mathbf{N}$ of syntactic complexity of languages in a family $\mathcal{L}(X)$ (generated by grammars in the class X), we say that M is *connected* on $\mathcal{L}(X)$ if for each $n \geq 1$ there is $L_n \in \mathcal{L}(X)$ such that $M(L_n) = n$.

Remark. If $M : \mathcal{L}(X) \longrightarrow \mathbf{N}$ is a connected measure for the family $\mathcal{L}(X)$, then there are the classes $\mathcal{L}_n, n \geq 1$, of languages of complexity at most n, such that

$$\mathcal{L}_1 \subset \mathcal{L}_2 \subset \ldots \subset \mathcal{L}_n \subset \ldots \subset \mathcal{L}(X)$$

thus, the measure M induces an infinite hierarchy on $\mathcal{L}(X)$.

3. Results

Theorem 1. *The measures $LCon$ and $TCon$ are connected on the family I.*

Proof. Let us consider the languages L_n for $n \geq 1$:

$$L_n = \{a^n\}^+$$

generated by the internal contextual grammars $G_n = (\{a\}, \{a^n\}, \{(\lambda, a^n)\})$. Hence, $LCon(L_n) \leq n, TCon(L_n) \leq n$.

If $G'_n = (\{a\}, B, C, \varphi)$ is an arbitrary grammar generating L_n, then each string $x \in B \subseteq L_n$ must be of the form $x = a^{kn}, k \geq 1$. If $(u, v) \in C$ and there are x_1, x_2, x_3 such that $(u, v) \in C, x_1 x_2 x_3 = a^{kn} \in L_n$, then $y = x_1 u x_2 v x_3 \in L_n$, $y = a^{ln}, l \geq k$. Thus, $|uv| = (l - k)n$. As L_n is infinite, there is at least a context $(u, v) \in C$ such that $l - k > 0$, hence $|uv| \geq n$, and thus $LCon(G'_n) \geq n, TCon(G'_n) \geq n$. It follows that $LCon(L_n) \geq n, TCon(L_n) \geq n$, and the proof is over. $\square$

Theorem 2. *The measure Ass is connected on IC.*

Proof. Let us consider the language $L_n, n \geq 1$ generated with the grammar

$$G = (\{a, b, c, d\}, \{abab\}, C, \varphi),$$

with

$$C = \{((c^i d)^2, (c^i d)^2) \mid 1 \leq i \leq n\} \cup \{(ab, ab)\},$$

$$\varphi(b^s a^s) = C, \text{ for every } s \geq 1.$$

Obviously, $Ass(L_n) \leq n + 1$.

Now, let G' be an arbitrary grammar generating L_n:

$$G' = (\{a, b, c, d\}, B', C', \varphi').$$

Denote

$$l_0 = max\{|\alpha| \mid \alpha \in B'\},$$
$$t_0 = max\{t \mid (a^t b^t, a^t b^t) \in C'\},$$
$$s_0 = max\{l_0, t_0\}.$$

We suppose that for every $s > s_0$, for every $t \in N, (a^t b^t, a^t b^t) \notin \varphi'(b^s a^s)$.

Let us consider the string $w = a^{2s_0} b^{2s_0} a^{2s_0} b^{2s_0} \in L_n$. Then, there is the string $w' \in L_n, w' = a^r b^r a^r b^r$ such that $w' \Longrightarrow_{G'} w$. But then it follows that $(a^{2s_0-r} b^{2s_0-r}, a^{2s_0-r} b^{2s_0-r} \in \varphi'(b^r a^r)$. We deduce that $r < s_0$, hence $s_0 < 2s_0 - r$. But $s_0 \geq t_0$, so $2s_0 - r > t_0 = max\{t \mid (a^t b^t, a^t b^t) \in C'\}$, contradiction. Therefore, there is $s > s_0$, there is $t \in N$ such that

$$(a^t b^t, a^t b^t) \in \varphi'(b^s a^s) \qquad (1)$$

Let us consider the strings:

$$w_i = a^s (c^i d)^2 b^s a^s (c^i d)^2 b^s, 1 \leq i \leq n.$$

Clearly $w_i \in L_n$, but because $s > s_0$, it follows that $w_i \notin B'$. Then, there is $w' \in L_n$ such that $w' \Longrightarrow_{G'} w_i$.

It is easy to see that $w' = a^s b^s a^s b^s$. But then

$$((c^i d)^2 b^t, a^t (c^i d)^2) \in \varphi'(b^{s-t} a^{s-t}), t \geq 0, s - t \geq 1 \qquad (2)$$

Suppose that $t \geq 1$. Consider the string $a^{s-t} b^{s-t} a^{s-t} b^{s-t}$ from which we can derive the string $a^{s-t} (c^i d)^2 b^s a^s (c^i d)^2 a^{s-t}$ which is not in $L(G)$ for $t \geq 1$. It follows that $t = 0$ and therefore

$$((c^i d)^2, (c^i d)^2) \in \varphi'(b^s a^s), \qquad (3)$$

From (1) and (3) we deduce that $card(\varphi'(b^s a^s)) \geq n + 1$, which implies that $Ass(G') \geq n + 1$, for every grammar G' generating L_n.

It follows that $Ass(L_n) = n + 1$. $\qquad \square$

In [5] it is proved that $E_g = E, EC_g = EC$. In conclusion, $E_g Con_X(L) = 0, TE_g Con_X(L) = 0, LE_g Con_X(L) = 0$, for every $L \in X$, and for every family of languages $X \in \{E_g, EC_g\}$.

Theorem 3. *For every $L \in X$ where $X \in \{1T_g, 11T_g, T_g\}$ we have* $E_g Con(L) = 1, LE_g Con(L) = 0, TE_g Con(L) = 0, Ass_g(L) = 1.$

Proof. Let us consider a language L in a family $X \in \{1T_g, 11T_g, T_g\}$, and let $G = (V, B, C_1, C_2, \varphi, \gamma)$ be a grammar generating L.

We consider the selection mapping

$$\gamma' : V^* \times V^* \times V^* \longrightarrow 2^{C'_2}$$

with $C_2' = \{(\lambda, \lambda)\}$ where:

$$\gamma'(x_1, x_2, x_3) = \gamma(x_1, x_2, x_3) - $$
$$-\{(u, v) \mid (u, v) \in C_2, uv \neq \lambda, (u, v) \in \gamma(x_1, x_2, x_3)\}$$

If there are x_1, x_2, x_3, u, v such that $(u, v) \in C_2, uv \neq \lambda, (u, v) \in \gamma(x_1, x_2, x_3)$ then we put

$$\gamma'(x_1 u, x_2, v x_3) = \{(\lambda, \lambda)\}.$$

If we have in G

$$x \Longrightarrow_G y, x = x_1 u x_2 v x_3, (u, v) \in \gamma(x_1, x_2, x_3)$$

then $(\lambda, \lambda) \in \gamma'(x_1 u, x_2, v x_3)$ and also we have in G':

$$x_1 u \lambda x_2 \lambda v x_3 \Longrightarrow_{G'} x_1 u v x_3.$$

If there is a derivation in G':

$$y \Longrightarrow z, y = y_1 y_2 y_3, z = y_1 y_3, (\lambda, \lambda) \in \gamma'(y_1, y_2, y_3)$$

then we have in G one of the following cases:

- $(\lambda, \lambda) \in \gamma(y_1, y_2, y_3)$ and hence we deduce that:

$$y \Longrightarrow_G z$$

- $y_1 = x_1 u, y_3 = v x_3, (u, v) \in \gamma(x_1, y_2, x_3)$ and then:

$$y = x_1 u y_2 v x_3 \Longrightarrow_G x_1 u v x_3 = y_1 y_3 = z,$$

With this facts we have that $L(G) = L(G')$ where $G' = (\Sigma, B, C_1, \{(\lambda, \lambda)\}, \varphi, \gamma')$, and the theorem is proved. $\square$

Theorem 4. *The measures Ass_g and $E_g Con$ are connected on the family IC_g.*

Proof. For $n \geq 1$ let us consider the grammar

$$G = (\{a, b_1, \ldots, b_n\}, B, C_1, C_2, \varphi, \gamma)$$

defined by:

$$B = \{ab_i ab_i \mid 1 \leq i \leq n\},$$
$$C_1 = \{(ab_i, a), (\lambda, b_i) \mid 1 \leq i \leq n\},$$
$$C_2 = \{(b_i, b_i) \mid 1 \leq i \leq n\},$$
$$\varphi(b_i^s a^s) = \{(ab_i, a)\}, 1 \leq i \leq n, s \geq 1,$$
$$\varphi(b_i a^k b_i) = \{(\lambda, b_i)\}, 1 \leq i \leq n, k \geq 1,$$
$$\gamma(a^s) = C_2, s \geq 1.$$

We can show that

$$L(G) \;=\; \bigcup_{i=1}^{n} \{a^p b_i^p a^p b_i^q \mid p \geq 1, q \geq 1\} \cup$$

$$\cup \bigcup_{i=1}^{n} \{a^p b_i^p b_i^q \mid p \geq 1, q \geq 1\}.$$

We deduce that $Ass_g(L(G)) \leq n,\ E_g Con(L(G)) \leq n$. Let

$$G' = (\{a, b_1, \ldots, b_n\}, B', C_1', C_2', \varphi', \gamma')$$

be a grammar generating $L(G)$. Let i be a fixed integer, $1 \leq i \leq n$.

Consider the strings $w = ab_i b_i^m$. For arbitrarily large m, $w \notin B'$, and thus there is $w' \in L(G')$ such that:

$$w' \Longrightarrow_{G'} w \qquad (1)$$

If $w' = ab_i b_i^q$, then there is a context $(\lambda, b_i^l) \in C_1'$ such that $(\lambda, b_i^l) \in \varphi(a^s b_i^t)$, $l \geq 1, 0 \leq s < t \leq 2$ (if $s = 1$ then $t = 2$). But then, because the string $a^2 b_i^2 a^2 b_i^2$ is in $L(G')$, we have in G' the following derivation:

$$a^2 b_i^2 a^2 b_i^2 \Longrightarrow_{G'} a^2 b_i^{2+l} a^2 b_i^2, l \geq 1$$

The derived string is not in $L(G)$, hence the string w' have the form:

$$w = ab_i ab_i^m, m \geq 1$$

and the substring a bordered by the two symbols b_i must be erased. It follows that $\gamma(a) \neq \emptyset$.

If $(\lambda, \lambda) \in \gamma(a)$ then the string $b_i ab_i$ can be derived from $ab_i ab_i$ in G', but this string is not in $L(G)$.

Thus, there is a context $(u, v) \in C_2', (u, v) \in \gamma(a)$ such that $u = u'b_i$ or $v = b_i v'$ for every $i, 1 \leq i \leq n$. Therefore, we deduce that $Ass_g(G') \geq n$, for every grammar G' generating L.

In conclusion, $Ass_g(L(G)) = n, E_g Con(L(G)) = n$. $\qquad\square$

Theorem 5. *The measures $LE_g Con$ and $TE_g Con$ are connected on the family IC_g.*

Proof. Let $n \geq 1$ be an integer and let us consider the grammar

$$G = (\{a, b, c\}, \{b^n cb^n ab, bcb\}, \{(b, b), (\lambda, b)\}, \{(b^n, \lambda)\}, \varphi, \gamma)$$

where

$$\varphi(c) = \{(b, b)\}$$

$$\varphi(a) = \{(\lambda, b)\}$$

$$\gamma(c) = \{(b^n, \lambda)\}$$

The derivations in G are of the one of the following form, depending on the beginning axiom:

- $b^n cb^n ab \overset{*}{\Longrightarrow} b^{n+i} cb^{n+i} ab^j \Longrightarrow b^{2(n+i)} ab^j \overset{*}{\Longrightarrow} b^{2(n+i)} ab^{j+k}$,
  $i \geq 0, j \geq 1, k \geq 0$

- $bcb \overset{*}{\Longrightarrow} b^j cb^j \Longrightarrow b^{2j}, j \geq n$.

Thus:

$$L(G) \;\; = \;\; \{b^i cb^i ab^j \mid i \geq n, j \geq 1\} \cup \{b^{2i} ab^j \mid i \geq n, j \geq 1\} \cup$$
$$\cup \{b^i cb^i \mid i \geq 1\} \cup \{b^{2i} \mid i \geq n\}$$

and $LE_g Con(L(G)) \leq n, TE_g Con(L(G)) \leq n$.

Assume that $L(G) = L(G')$ for some

$$G' = (\{a, b, c\}, B', C'_1, C'_2, \varphi', \gamma').$$

Let us consider the string $w = b^{2i} ab^j$ with large enough i, j such that $w \notin B'$. Then there is a string $w' \in L(G')$ such that

$$w' \Longrightarrow_{G'} w \qquad (1)$$

We can consider the following cases:

- $w' = b^{2s}, n \leq s \leq i$; then there is a context $(b^p, ab^q) \in C'_1$ such that $(b^p, ab^q) \in \varphi'(b^j), j \geq 1$. Using this context to string $b^j cb^j ab \in L(G)$ we obtain the derivation:

$$b^j cb^j ab \Longrightarrow_{G'} b^{p+j} ab^q cb^j ab.$$

But the derived string is not in $L(G)$.

- $w' = b^{2s} ab^p$; then there is a context $(b^r, b^q) \in \varphi'(b^{r_1} ab^{q_1}), r + q \geq 1$. Using this context we obtain the derivation:

$$b^t cb^t ab^t \Longrightarrow_{G'} b^t cb^{t+r} ab^{t+q} \in L(G'), \; t \geq max(r_1, q_1, n)$$

It follows that $r = 0$, which implies $s = i$. For large enough i we can find in every derivation of w in G' the sequence $w' \Longrightarrow w'' \Longrightarrow^* w$, where $w' = b^{2s} ab^p, s < i$, or $w' = b^s cb^s ab^p$, case which will be discussed below. In the first case, we observe that a context of the form $(b^r, b^q) \in$

$\varphi'(b^{r_1}ab^{q_1}), e \geq 1$, is used at the step $w' \Longrightarrow w''$. But then we obtain in G' the derivation:

$$b^t cb^t ab^t \Longrightarrow b^t cb^{t+r} ab^{t+q}, \ r \geq 1, t \geq max\{r_1, q_1, n\}$$

The derived string is not in $L(G)$.

- $w' = b^s cb^s ab^p$ for some $s \geq n$ and $p \geq 1$.

Thus, in the derivation (1) the symbol c is erased. This implies that there is a context $(a^q, a^r) \in \gamma'(a^t ca^t)$, $q, r, t \geq 0$. Suppose that $q + r < n$ and $q \leq r$. We can obtain in G' the derivation:

$$b^{r+t} cb^{r+t} \Longrightarrow_{G'} b^{2r}, r < n$$

The string b^{2r}, $r < n$ is not in $L(G)$ hence $r + q \geq n$ and $LE_g Con(G') \geq n$, $TE_g Con(G') \geq n$ for every grammar G' generating $L(G')$. $\qquad\square$

Theorem 6. *The measure $E_d Con$ is connected on the family E_d.*

Proof. Let $n \geq 1$ be an integer. Take

$$G = (\{a, b, c, d\}, \{a^i db^i \mid 1 \leq i \leq n\}, \{(c, \lambda), (d, d)\}, \{(d, b^i d) \mid 1 \leq i \leq n\}).$$

From [5] (Theorem 6, Section 6) we deduce that

$$L_{ex}(G) = \bigcup_{i=1}^{n} \{d^{i_1} c^{j_1} \ldots d^{i_k} c^{j_k} a^i db^i d^{i_1 + \cdots + i_k} \mid i_s \geq 0, j_s \geq 0,$$

$$1 \leq s \leq k, k \geq 0\} \cup$$

$$\cup \bigcup_{i=1}^{n} \{d^{i_1} c^{j_1} \ldots d^{i_k} dc^{j_k} a^i d^{i_1 + \cdots + i_k} \mid i_s \geq 0, j_s \geq 0,$$

$$1 \leq s \leq k, k \geq 0\},$$

and $L_{ex}(G) \in E_d - EC$.

It follows that $E_d Con(L_{ex}(G)) \leq n$. Let $G' = (\{a, b, c, d\}, R', C'_1, C'_2)$ be an arbitrary grammar that generates $L_{ex}(G)$.

Take an $i, 1 \leq i \leq n$. The strings $dc^j a^i$ are in $L_{ex}(G')$ for all $j \geq 0$, and moreover, these strings are in $Min_0(L(G'))$. Hence, we deduce that there is $j \geq 0$ and the string $x = dc^j a^i db^i d \in L_{ex}(G')$ such that $x \Longrightarrow_{G'} dc^j a^i$. This derivation can be obtained only by erasing the context $(u, v), uv = db^i d$. So, for every $i, 1 \leq i \leq n$, there is a context $(u, v) \in C'_2$ such that $uv = db^i d$. Thus, we have $E_d Con(G') \geq n$ for every grammar G' generating $L_{ex}(G)$, hence $E_d Con(L_{ex}(G)) = n$. $\qquad\square$

Corollary 6.1. *For every integer $n \geq 2$ there is a language $L_n \in E_d$ such that $LE_dCon(L_n) = n, TE_dCon(L_n) = n$.*

Proof. For $n \geq 2$ take the grammar:

$$G = (\{a, b, c, d\}, \{ab^{n-1}\}, \{(c, \lambda), (d, d)\}, \{(\lambda, b^{n-1}d)\}).$$

As in the above theorem we deduce that:

$$\begin{aligned}
L_n = L_{ex}(G) \quad = \quad & \{d^{i_1}c^{j_1} \ldots d^{i_k}c^{j_k}ab^{n-1}d^{i_1+\cdots+i_k} \mid i_s \geq 0, j_s \geq 0, \\
& \qquad 1 \leq s \leq k, k \geq 0\} \cup \\
& \{d^{i_1}c^{j_1} \ldots d^{i_k}dc^{j_k}ad^{i_1+\cdots+i_k} \mid i_s \geq 0, j_s \geq 0, \\
& \qquad 1 \leq s \leq k, k \geq 0\}
\end{aligned}$$

and $L_n \in E_d \dot{-} EC$. We also have that $LE_dCon(L_n) \leq n, TE_dCon(L_n) \leq n$. If $G' = (\{a, b, c, d\}, B', C_1', C_2')$ is an arbitrary grammar generating L_n, we deduce also (as in the above theorem) that there is an erased context $(u, v) \in C_2'$ such that $uv = b^{n-1}d$, thus $LE_dCon(G') \geq n, TE_dCon(G') \geq n$ for every grammar G' generating L_n, which means that $LE_dCon(G') = n, TE_dCon(G') = n$. $\square$

Theorem 7. *If $L \in E_d$ is a language such that $LE_dCon = 1$ or $TE_dCon = 1$, then $L \in E$.*

Proof. Let $L \in E_d$ be a language such that $LE_dCon = 1$ and $G = (V, B, C_1, C_2)$ a grammar that generates it.

Suppose that $C_2 \neq \emptyset$. Then, if $(u, v) \in C_2$ then $u \in V, v = \lambda$ or conversely. Let $V_1 = \{a \in V \mid (a, \lambda) \in C_2 \text{ or } (\lambda, a) \in C_2\}$. We construct the grammar $G' = (V, B', C')$ in the following way.

First, we consider the finite substitution $\sigma : V^* \longrightarrow V_1^*$ defined by

$$\sigma(a) = \left\{ \begin{array}{ll} \{a, \lambda\}, & a \in V_1 \\ \{a\}, & a \in V - V_1 \end{array} \right.$$

We notice that:

- if $x \in L$ and $y \in \sigma(x)$, then y is obtained from x by erasing some symbols from V_1 corresponding to some erased contexts from C_2, hence $y \in L$.

- if $(u, v) \in C_2$ and $x \in \sigma(u), y \in \sigma(v), z \in L$, then $uzv \in L$ but also $xzy \in L$.

Now, we put:

$$B' = B \cup \{x \mid \text{ there is } y \in B \text{ such that } x \in \sigma(y)\},$$
$$C' = C \cup \{(u, v) \mid \text{ there is } (x, y) \in C_2 \text{ such that } u \in \sigma(x), v \in \sigma(y)\}.$$

Obviously, B' and C' can be effectively obtained, because B and C_2 are finite. With this facts, we can deduce that $L(G') = L(G)$. $\qquad\square$

Theorem 8. *For every language $L \in EC_d$, $Ass_d(L) \leq 1$.*

Proof. Let $L \in EC_d$ be a language generated with the grammar

$$G = (V, B, C_1, C_2, \varphi, \delta), C_2 \neq \emptyset$$

We suppose that $Ass_d(G) \geq 2$. We construct the grammar $G' = (V, B', C'_1, C'_2, \varphi', \delta')$ in the following way:

$$B' = B,$$
$$C'_1 = C_1,$$
$$\varphi' = \varphi.$$

Let $z \in V^*$ be a string such that $card(\delta(z)) \geq 2$. If $(u, v) \in \delta(z)$ such that $uzv \in L$ then we put $\delta'(z) = \{u, v)\}$. The other contexts in $\delta(z)$ are useless (they cannot yield to other strings in L except z).

If there is no context $(u, v) \in \delta(z)$ such that $uzv \in L$, then we put $\delta'(z) = \emptyset$. It is obvious that $L(G) = L(G')$ and $Ass_d(G') \leq 1$. $\qquad\square$

Theorem 9. *The measure E_dCon is connected on the family I_d.*

Proof. For $n \geq 1$ we consider the grammar $G = (V, B, C_1, C_2)$, where:

$$V = \{a_1, a_2, \ldots, a_{2n+1}, b'_2, \ldots, b'_{2n+1}\},$$
$$B = \{\lambda\},$$
$$C_1 = \{(a_1, a_2 a'_2), (a_3 a'_3, a_4 a'_4), \ldots, (a_{2n+1} a'_{2n+1}, \lambda)\},$$
$$C_2 = \{(a'_2, a'_3), (a'_4, a'_5), \ldots, (a'_{2n}, a'_{2n+1})\}.$$

We observe that for every $w \in L_{in}(G)$:

$$| w |_{a_1} = | w |_{a_2},$$
$$| w |_{a_3} = | w |_{a_4}, \qquad\qquad (1)$$
$$\cdots$$
$$| w |_{a_{2n-1}} = | w |_{a_{2n}}.$$

Let be $w \in L_{in}(G) \cap a_1^+ a_2^+ \ldots a_{2n+1}^+$. Because $a'_2, \ldots, a'_{2n+1}$ do not appear in w, this means that they have been erased by $\{(a'_2, a'_3), \ldots, (a'_{2n}, a'_{2n+1})\}$, hence we have a string w' with

$$| w' |_{a'_2} = | w' |_{a'_3},$$
$$\cdots$$
$$| w' |_{a'_{2n}} = | w' |_{a'_{2n+1}},$$
$$w' \overset{*}{\Longrightarrow} w$$

But

$$| \, w' \, |_{a_2'} = | \, w' \, |_{a_2},$$

$$\dots$$

$$| \, w' \, |_{a_{2n+1}'} = | \, w' \, |_{a_{2n+1}}.$$

We deduce that

$$| \, w' \, |_{a_1} = | \, w' \, |_{a_2} = \dots | \, w' \, |_{a_{2n+1}}$$

and hence $w = a_1^m a_2^m \dots a_{2n+1}^m$ for some $m \geq 1$.

Conversely, we have:

$$\lambda \overset{*}{\Longrightarrow} a_1^m (a_2 a_2')^m, \dots, (a_{2n} a_{2n}')^m (a_{2n+1} a_{2n+1}')^m \overset{*}{\Longrightarrow} a_1^m a_2^m \dots a_{2n+1}^m.$$

Hence,

$$L_{in}(G) \cap a_1^+ a_2^+ \dots a_{2n+1}^+ = \{ a_1^m a_2^m \dots a_{2n+1}^m \mid m \geq 1 \} \qquad (2)$$

Now, let $G' = (V', B', C_1', C_2')$ be a grammar that generates $L_{in}(G)$. Let us consider the string $w = a_1^m a_2^m \dots a_{2n+1}^m$ for some large enough m such that this string is not an axiom. Then, there is an axiom $w_0 \in B'$ such that:

$$D : w_0 \overset{*}{\Longrightarrow} w \qquad (3)$$

Suppose that there is a string w' such that

$$D : w_0 \overset{*}{\Longrightarrow} w' \overset{*}{\Longrightarrow} w$$

and in w' the order $a_1, a_2, \dots, a_{2n+1}$ is disturbed so that $w' = w_1 a_i^p w_2 a_j^q w_3$ with $i > j$. Then, the a_j's must be erased for obtaining w. Thus, we can find a derivation of w from w_0 such that the intermediated strings keep the order $a_1, a_2, \dots, a_{2n+1}$ (such that a_i cannot appear before a_j for $i > j$). We can suppose that (3) is such a derivation.

If $a_1^m a_2^m \dots a_{2n+1}^m$ is obtained by erasing some a_i's or by adding some a_j's, then (2) do not fulfilled. Thus, because $|w|_{a_j} = |w|_{a_{j+1}}, j = 1, \dots, 2n - 1$, we deduce that there is w_j' such that $w_j' = w_1 a_j^t (a_{j+1} a_{j+1}')^t w_2$ and w_j' appears in the derivation (3):

$$D : w_0 \overset{*}{\Longrightarrow} w_j' \overset{*}{\Longrightarrow} w \qquad (4)$$

But then, the a_{j+1}''s can be erased, thus there is a context $(u, v) \in C_2'$ such that

$$u = u_1 a_{j+1}' u_2 \ \text{ or } \ v = v_1 a_{j+1}' v_2 \qquad (5)$$

Suppose that there is $(u, v) \in C_2'$ such that

$$u = u_1 a_i' u_2 a_j' u_3, \ i < j, 2 \leq i, j \leq 2n - 1 \qquad (6)$$

and the order $a_1, a_2, \ldots, a_{2n+1}$ is kept. Then u is a substring of string z in $L_{in}(G)$ of the form:

$$z = a_1^{p_1}(a_2 a_2')^{p_2}, \ldots, (a_{2n+1} a_{2n+1}')^{p_{2n+1}}$$

and

$$u = u_1 a_i' u_2' a_j a_j' u_3.$$

Thus, by applying this erased context, the number of a_j's decreases. The same thing happens if we have

$$v = v_1 a_i v_2 a_j v_3, \ i < j, 2 \le i, j \le 2n - 1 \qquad (7)$$

Thus, for every $j = 2, \ldots, 2n - 1$ there is a context $(u, v) \in C_2'$ such that we have (5) and the relations (6) and (7) are false, hence in such a context can appear almost two symbols a_i, a_j. It follows that $card(C_2') \ge n$, which implies $E_d Con(G') \ge n$ for every grammar G' generating $L_{in}(G)$, thus $E_d Con(L_{in}(G)) = n$. $\qquad\square$

Corollary 9. *For every $n \ge 2$, there is a language $L_n \in I_d$ such that $LE_d Con(L_n) = n$.*

Proof. For $n \ge 2$ we consider the language L_n generated by the grammar:

$$G = (\{a, b, c, d, e\}, \{\lambda\}, \{(a, bc^{n-1}), (de, \lambda)\}, \{(c^{n-1}, e)\})$$

As in the above theorem we can prove that $L_{in}(G) = L_n \cap a^+ b^+ d^+ = \{a^m b^m d^m \mid m \ge 1\}, L_n \in I_d - T$.

If $G' = (\{a, b, c, d, e\}, B', C_1', C_2')$ is an arbitrary grammar that generates L_n, then we can deduce that c^{n-1} and e must appear in a context from C_2', hence $LE_d Con(G') \ge n, TE_d Con(G') \ge n$. In conclusion, $LE_d Con(L_n) = n, TE_d Con(L_n) = n$. $\qquad\square$

4. Final remarks

There are many other problems related to the study of measures of syntactic complexity which remain to be considered also for the previous measures. We mention only two of them.

For a measure $M : \mathcal{L}(X) \longrightarrow \mathbf{N}$ (where X is a family of grammars and $\mathcal{L}(X)$ is the family of generated languages) define

$$M^{-1}(L) = \{G \in X \mid L(G) = L, M(G) = M_X(L)\}$$

the set of minimal grammars with respect to M. Two measures M_1, M_2 are *incompatible* if there is a language L such that

$$M_1^{-1}(L) \cup M_2^{-1}(L) = \emptyset$$

(they cannot be simultaneously minimized). Otherwise, M_1, M_2 are said to be *compatible*.

Given two classes X_1, X_2 of grammars, $X_1 \subset X_2$, and a measure M of syntactic complexity we say that M has the the property of *simple fidelity* iff there is $L \in L(X_1)$ such that

$$M_{X_1}(L) > M_{x_2}(L).$$

What about the compatibility and the fidelity of the measures investigated in the previous sections ?

It also remains to be investigated the syntactic complexity of the extended contextual grammars with erased and erasing contexts (in which some symbols in the alphabet are used only in the process of derivation; see [5]).

References

1. J. Gruska, Descriptional complexity of context-free languages, *Proc. Math. Found. Comp. Sci. Symp.*, High Tatras, 1973, 71 – 83.

2. S. Marcus, Contextual grammars, *Rev. Roum. Math. Pures Appl.*, 14, 10 (1969), 1525 – 1534.

3. G. Păun, *Contextual Grammars*, The Publ House of the Romanian Academy of Sciences, Bucureşti, 1982 (in Romanian).

4. G.Păun, Further remarks on the syntactic complexity of Marcus contextual languages, *Ann. Univ. Bucharest, Ser. Matem.-Inform.*, 3 (1990-1991), 72 – 82.

5. G. Păun, G. Rozenberg, A. Salomaa, Contextual grammars: Erasing, determinism, one-sided contexts, in *Developments in Language Theory* (G. Rozenberg, A. Salomaa, eds.), World Sci. Publ., Singapore, 1994, 370 – 388.

Lower Bounds on Systolic Array Computations and the Optimality of Kung's Convolution Algorithm

Juraj HROMKOVIČ[1], Juraj PROCHÁZKA[2]
Department of Mathematics and Informatics
University of Paderborn, 4790 Paderborn, Germany

Abstract. It is proved that the Kung's systolic algorithm for the multiplication of two polynomials is area-optimal in the class of all VLSI algorithms and time optimal in the class of algorithms on one-dimensional systolic array. Thus, Kung's algorithm is also area-time (AT) and area-time squared (AT^2) optimal in the class of one-dimensional systolic array algorithms.

1. Introduction

One of the most intensively investigated areas of complexity theory is the study and the comparison of the computational power of distinct interconection networks as candidates for the use as parallel architectures for existing parallel computers. There are several approaches enabling to compare the efficiency and the "suitability" of different parallel architectures from distinct point of views. One extensively used approach deals with the possibility to simulate one network by another without any essential increase of computational complexity (parallel time $- T$, number of processors - P). Such efficient simulation is mostly obtained by some suitable embedding of one network to another one (an overview of this research direction can be found in [18], [20]). Another approach searching for the best (most effective) structures of interconection networks is the study of the complexity of the realization of fundamental communication tasks like routing (for some overview see [18]) or broadcast and gossip (for some overview see [5], [6]).

The approach considered here for measuring the computational power of interconetion networks is to investigate which class of computing problems can be computed by a given class of networks. Obviously, this question is

[1] This author was partially supported by Leibniz program of DFG.

[2] On the leave from the Commenius University, 842 15 Bratislava, Slowakia. This author was partially supported by MSV SR grant and by EC Cooperative Action IC 1000: project ALTEC.

reasonable only by additional restrictions on the networks because each class of networks with unbounded number of processors or with powerful processors (equivalent to a sequential machine) can recognize all recursive sets. These restrictions considered are mostly of two kinds. The first kind of restrictions is given on the regularity of the "global" behavior of the computations and the second kind of restrictions bounds the computational sources like time (T) or the number of processors (P). The most used restriction of the first type has been introduced by Kung [15], who defined so-called *systolic computation*. A synchronized computation is systolic if it consists only of the periodic repetition of simple computation and communication steps of simple (small) processors with finite memory. The concept of systolic computations has revived the interest of formal language theorists to investigate the power of such regular structures as arrays and complete binary trees according to the language recognition (see, for instance [12], [1], [14], [3], [2], [13], [4]).

The contribution of this paper lies on the border of formal language theory and complexity theory, and it is devoted to the study of the simplest parallel architecture – one-dimensional systolic arrays (See figure 1).

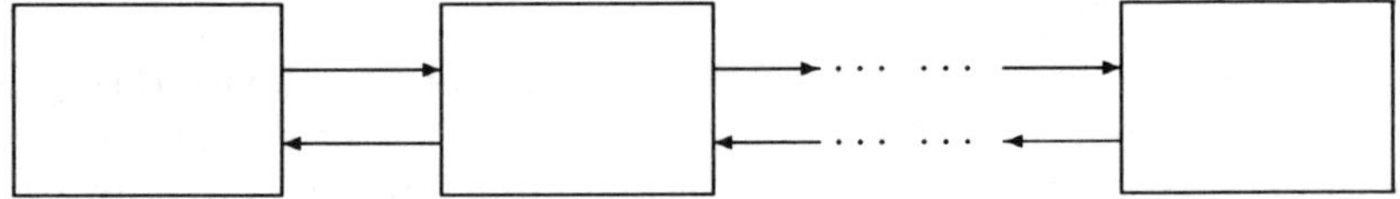

Fig. 1.

First, using and formalizing a lower bound method on the area complexity of VLSI computations from [22], [23], we prove that there are problems for which the simplest architecture — one dimensional systolic arrays is the best one in some sense. More precisely, each architecture of bounded degree computing convolution (multiplication of two polynomials) needs asympthotically the same number of processors as one-dimensional arrays use to compute this task. Thus, no increase of the "descriptional complexity" of networks can decrease the number of processors needed to compute convolution on one-dimensional systolic arrays. Secondly, combining some well-known ideas we present a lower bound method on the time complexity of one-dimensional systolic arrays (1SA). We illustrate the use of this method to show that Kung's convolution algorithm on 1SA is time optimal in the class of 1SA-algorithms. But, the main point is that we believe that the presented simple lower bound methods can be used to prove several results of the optimality of different algorithms for language recognition on systolic arrays.

Now, we give more details about our effort in this paper.

H. T. Kung [16] designed an algorithm for the multiplication of two polynomials (the convolution problem) on one-dimensional systolic array. This systolic system uses a linear number of processors ($P = O(n)$, where n is the maximum degree of the polynomials) and a linear time ($T = O(n)$). Another 1SA-algorithms with the same asympthotical complexities has been developed in [21]. The aim of this paper is to show that these algorithms are *area-optimal* in the class of all VLSI-algorithms and *time-optimal* in the class of all VLSI algorithms on one-dimensional arrays.

Note. By VLSI algorithms we denote semilective VLSI circuits [23], where each input variable enters exactly once into a processor of the circuit; and the time moment together with the input processor in which the input variable enters are fixed over all inputs (for formal definition look for instance [7]).

To show this optimality we will use the *communication complexity* introduced by Yao [24]. It is well known that the communication complexity of a computing problem P provides a direct lower bound on the area needed to compute P by any VLSI algorithm [22], [23], and that the communication complexity squared provides a lower bound on the area-time squared (AT^2) complexity of VLSI algorithms [22], [23]. Since the communication complexity of the convolution (polynomial multiplication) problem is in $O(n^{1/2} log\, n)$ [18], the communication complexity has not helped to prove the efficiency of the Kung's algorithm.

We shall overcome this difficulty by using the following two results:

(1) one-way communication complexity (a special case of communication complexity) provides a direct lower bound on the area complexity of VLSI algorithms (see, for instance [23]), and

(2) we prove here that each one-dimensional systolic array algorithm computing a problem with a linear one-way communication complexity must have a linear number of processors, and it works in a linear time.

Since the one-way communication complexity of a problem may be much greater than the communication complexity of this problem (and this is also our case for the convolution problem), one-way communication complexity can help to get reasonable lower bounds, even though communication complexity provides only some trivial (far from the upper bounds) lower bounds.

So, to get the optimality of Kung's algorithm among one-dimensional array algorithms (and the area optimality among all VLSI algorithms) it is sufficient to prove a linear lower bound on one-way communication complexity of the convolution problem.

That, what we shall really do in this paper, is to prove a linear lower bound on the one-way information content (introduced in [23]) of the multiplication of two polynomials over $\mathbf{Z}_2$, which provides direct lower bound on the one-way communication complexity of this computing problem [10]. Before starting the technical proofs, let us give the basic definitions and notations needed.

A *computing problem of n inputs and m outputs $P_{n,m}$* is a set of m Boolean functions $\{h_1, \ldots, h_m\}$, where $h_i : \{0,1\}^n \longrightarrow \{0,1\}$ for each $i = 1, \ldots, m$, and each h_i is defined over the same set of the input variables $X = \{x_1, \ldots, x_n\}$. We say that $P_{n,m}$ *depends on all input variables* if for every $i \in \{1, \ldots, n\}$ there is $j \in \{1, \ldots, m\}$ and vectors $\alpha = (\alpha_1, \alpha_2, \ldots, \alpha_{i-1}, 0, \alpha_{i+1}, \ldots, \alpha_n)$, $\beta = (\alpha_1, \alpha_2, \ldots, \alpha_{i-1}, 1, \alpha_{i+1}, \ldots, \alpha_n) \in \{0,1\}^n$ such that $f_j(\alpha) \neq f_j(\beta)$. In this case we also say that the Boolean function f_j *depends on the variable x.*

So, the multiplication of two polynomials of the maximal degree $n - 1$ over $\mathbf{Z}_2$ is the computing problem of $2n$ inputs and $m = 2n - 1$ outputs $P_{2n,m} = \{f_{2n}^1, f_{2n}^2, \ldots, f_{2n}^m\}$, where

$$f_{2n}^i(a_0, a_1, \ldots, a_{n-1}, b_0, b_1, \ldots, b_{n-1}) = \sum_{\substack{j+k=i \\ 0 \leq j,k \leq n-1}} a_j \cdot b_k (mod\ 2)$$

for $i = 0, \ldots, 2n - 2$.

The informal definition of one-way communication complexity is connected with the following computing model. Let C_1 and C_2 be two abstract computers with an unbounded computing power. Let the input variables are partitioned according to a partition π between the two computers C_1 and C_2. Now C_1 and C_2 together have to compute the outputs for any actual input, where C_i gets always only the actual values of the input variables assigned to C_i. Obviously, C_i (for $i = 1, 2$) can compute directly only the outputs depending on the subset of variables assigned to C_i.

The computation is realized in the following way: the computer C_1 sends a message to the computer C_2, and (after receiving the message) the computer C_2 computes the outputs. The length of this message maximized over all inputs is *one-way communication complexity of the given problem according to the considered partition π.* To get the one-way communication complexity of the given problem one has to take the minimum of the one-way communication complexities over all partitions that divide the input variables in so called *almost balanced* way ("almost balanced" will be defined in the next paragraph).

In [23] one-way information content is used instead of one-way communication complexity in order to get some lower bounds on VLSI computations. We prefer this approach also here by showing the direct relation between one-way information content and complexity of VLSI computations instead to combine the facts that one-way information provides a lower bound on one-way communication complexity [10] and that one-way communication complexity provides some lower bounds on VLSI computations. Using this approach we do not need to give the formal definition of one-way communication complexity here, and it is sufficient to deal only with one-way information content.

Definition 1.1. An *almost balanced partition* π of the set of input variables $X = \{x_1, \ldots, x_n\}$ is a pair $(\pi_L(X), \pi_R(X))$, where

(i) $\pi_L(X) \cup \pi_R(X) = X$,

(ii) $\pi_L(X) \cap \pi_R(X) = \emptyset$, and

(iii) $\lceil n/3 \rceil \leq |\pi_L(X)|, |\pi_R(X)| \leq \lceil 2n/3 \rceil$.

Definition 1.2. Let $Bal(X)$ denote the set of all almost balanced partitions of X. Let $P_{n,m} = \{f_1, \ldots, f_m\}$ be a problem with the set of input variables $X = \{x_1, \ldots, x_n\}$, and let $\pi \in Bal(X)$. We say that *an input assignment α for $P_{n,m}$* is a mapping from X to $\{0, 1\}$ giving a Boolean value to each input variable; and we say that *an input assignment $\alpha_L(\alpha_R)$ restricted to $\pi_L(x)(\pi_R(x))$* is a mapping from $\pi_L(X)$ to $\{0, 1\}$ (from $\pi_R(X)$ to $\{0, 1\}$), where $\alpha_L(X) = \alpha(X)$ for all $x \in \pi_L(X)(\alpha_R(y) = \alpha(y)$ for all $y \in \pi_R(X))$.

Let $\gamma : \pi_L(X) \to \{0, 1\}, \delta : \pi_R(X) \to \{0, 1\}$ be two input assignments for a $\pi \in Bal(X)$. Then $\pi^{-1}(\gamma, \delta)$ denotes an input assignment $\omega : X \longrightarrow \{0, 1\}$ such that $\omega(x) = \gamma(x)$ for each $x \in \pi_L(X)$, and $\omega(y) = \delta(y)$ for each $y \in \pi_R(X)$.

Note, that in this notation $\pi^{-1}(a_L, a_R)$ denotes the original input assignment α. Let, for a problem P and an input $\alpha \in \{0, 1\}^+$, $P(\alpha)$ denote the corresponding output from $\{0, 1\}^l$.

Definition 1.3. We say that a set $\mathcal{A}_\pi^P \subseteq \{a_L : \pi_L(X) \to \{0, 1\}\}$ is a *one-way fooling set according to a problem $P_{n,m}$ and a partition π* if for any distinct α and β in $\mathcal{A}_\pi^P$ there exists an input assignment $\gamma : \pi_R(X) \longrightarrow \{0, 1\}$ such that $P_{n,m}(\pi^{-1}(\alpha, \gamma))$ and $P_{n,m}(\pi^{-1}(\beta, \gamma))$ differ on some output variable $y \in \{y_1, \ldots, y_m\}$ which depends on at least one input variable in $\pi_R(X)$.

Definition 1.4. Let P_n be a problem defined on a set of input variables X and let $\pi \in Bal(X)$. We say that *one-way information content of P_n according to a partition π*, denoted by $1\mathbf{I}(P_n, \pi)$, is logarithm, base 2, of the largest one-way fooling set for P_n and π.

Finally, we say that $1\mathbf{I}(P_n) = \min\{1\mathbf{I}(P_n, \pi) | \pi \in Bal(X)\}$ is *one-way information content* of P_n.

This paper is organized as follows. Section 2 generally shows how one-way information content can provide lower bounds on the complexity of VLSI computations, and especially on 1SA-computations. Section 3 proves the lower bound on the one-way information content of the convolution, which together with the results of Section 2 shows the optimality of Kung's convolution algorithm in the sense mentioned above.

2. Lower bound methods

The aim of this section is to show which lower bounds on VLSI computations, and especially 1SA-computations, can be provided by the one-way information content $1I(P)$ of some computing problem P. First, we show that $1I(P)/2$ is a lower bound on the number of processors of any VLSI-circuit computing P. This fact is carefully explained in [23], but we give a complete proof of it in our notation here in order to make this paper selfcontained. Combining the ideas from [11], [8] we show that each computing problem P fulfilling a natural additional condition requires $\Omega(1I(P))$ time to be computed on one-dimensional arrays.

Here, we consider the fundamental binary model of VLSI circuits ([23]) viewed as directed graphs, where:

(a) each processor (node) is simple, without any local memory

(b) the indegree of each processor is bounded by 2 and the outdegree of each processor is bounded by 2

(c) each edge corresponding to a communication link transports a Boolean value

(d) the circuit works in a synchronized way, i.e., in each step each processor using the Boolean values on its input edges computes Boolean output for its output edges

(e) for each input (output) variable there is a fixed pair (i, p) specifying that input (output) value of the considered variable will be available on the external port of processor p in the i-th synchronized time unit

(f) each processor has at most one external input or output port.

For more details of the definition of VLSI circuits one can consult [23], [22], [7] for instance. We note that the following lower bounds techniques are working also if one considers the so-called word-model of VLSI circuits, where each link transfers a binary word of a fixed length d and processors having a local memory of size d work over the 2^d values corresponding to these words. The only one change in the following lower bounds would be for such a model in the constant (depending on d only) hidden in $\Omega(1I(P))$.

We start to show how $1I(P)$ provides lower bounds on the number of processors. In what follows we consider only non-degenerated computing problems $P = \{f_1, \ldots, f_m\}$, where each Boolean function $f \in P$ depends on at least one input variable.

Theorem 2.1. [23] *Let P be a computing problem of n input variables in X. Then every VLSI-circuit computing P has*

$$1I(P)/2$$

processors.

Proof. Let R be a VLSI-circuit computing P. Obviously, R must read all n inputs before R gives all outputs. We distinguish two possibilities according to the way in which the input variables are read.

(i) Let there be a time unit k in which R reads at least $m \geq \lfloor n/3 \rfloor$ input values. Since each processor can read only one value in one time unit, R must have at least m processors. Clearly $m \geq 1\mathrm{I}(P)$ because $1\mathrm{I}(P') \leq n/3$ for every problem P' of n variables.

(ii) Let, in each time unit, at most $\lfloor n/3 \rfloor - 1$ input variables be read. Then, there exists a time unit d such that after this time unit $m_1 \geq \lfloor n/3 \rfloor$ input variables were read and $m_2 \geq \lfloor n/3 \rfloor$ input variables were still not read. Thus, the d-th time unit defines an almost balanced partition $\pi = (\pi_L(X), \pi_R(X))$, where $\pi_L(X)$ are input variables read until the time unit d and $\pi_R(X)$ are input variables read after the time unit d. Let $\mathcal{A}_\pi^P$ be a one-way fooling set according to P and π of the cardinality $2^{1\mathrm{I}(P,\pi)}$.

Now, we want to prove that the number of global states of R is at least $|\mathcal{A}_\pi^P|$. A *global state* of R is a sequence of all Boolean values appearing on all edges (links) of R (Note, that this is the only information saved by R in any time moment because no processor has an own local memory). Thus, the number of global states of R is $2^{E(R)}$, where $E(R)$ is the number of edges of R. If $P(R)$ denotes the number of processors of R, then we have that the number of global states of R is at least $2^{P(R)/2}$ because each processor hat at most two output edges.

Let us assume that $|\mathcal{A}_\pi^P| > 2^{P(R)/2}$. Then, there are $\alpha, \beta \in \mathcal{A}_\pi^P$ and $\gamma \in \{0,1\}^{m_2}$ such that:

1. R reaches the same global state S after reading α of the input $\pi^{-1}(\alpha, \gamma)$ and after reading β of the input $\pi^{-1}(\beta, \gamma)$ in the time unit d, and

2. $P(\pi^{-1}(\beta, \gamma))$ and $P(\pi^{-1}(\alpha, \gamma))$ differ on some output variable depending on at least one input variable in $\pi_R(X)$.

Obviously, this is the contradiction because R starting from the same global state S and getting the same rest γ of the inputs $\pi^{-1}(\beta, \gamma)$ and $\pi^{-1}(\alpha, \gamma)$ must produce the same output values for variables computed after time unit d for both inputs (R has no possibility more to distinguish the inputs $\pi^{-1}(\beta, \gamma)$ and $\pi^{-1}(\alpha, \gamma)$). Clearly, each output value of a variable depending on some input variable in $\pi_R(X)$ is computed after the time unit d.

Thus, $|\mathcal{A}_\pi^P| \geq 2^{P(R)/2}$ which implies

$$P(R) \geq \left(log_2(|\mathcal{A}_\pi^P|)\right)/2 \geq 1\mathrm{I}(P, \pi)/2 \geq 1\mathrm{I}(P)/2.$$

$\square$

Next, we use $I1(P)$ to get lower bounds on the time complexity of 1SA-computations. Note, that 1SA-circuit is a VLSI circuit having the structure depicted in figure 1.

Lemma 2.2. *Let P be a computing problem of n variables, and let P contain a Boolean function f depending on all input variables. Then each 1SA-circuit computing P works in time at least*

$$1I(P)/12.$$

Proof. Let R be a 1SA-circuit computing P in time $T(R)$. Following Theorem 2.1 we know $P(R) \geq 1I(P)/2$. Let us assume that R is a 1SA-circuit with minimal number of processors computing P in time $T(R)$. Let p be a processor of R producing the output value of the function $f \in P$ depending on all variables. This implies that all processors of R having at least one external input port are in the distance at most $T(R)$ from p (see figure 2).

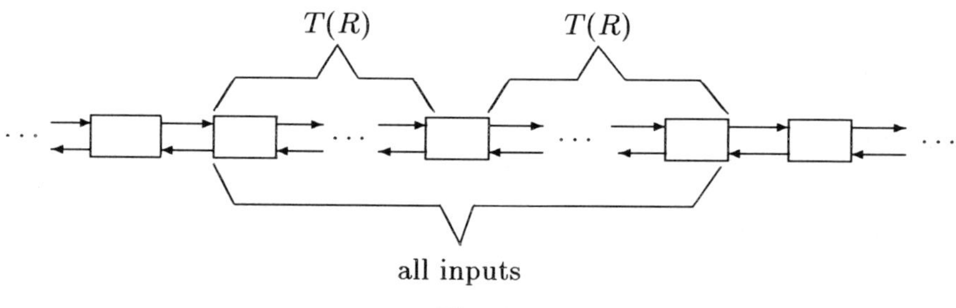

Fig. 2.

Further, all processors producing outputs depending at least on one input variable are in the instance at most $2T(R)$ from p (if not, all inputs are in the distance greater than $T(R)$ from a given output processor, and its output cannot depend on any input). From the same reason we can conclude all processor of R are in the distance at most $3T(R)$ from p because in the opposite case we can remove some processors (in the distance greater than $3T(R)$) from R which contradicts to the assumption of the minimality of R according to the number of processors. Thus, we have $6 \cdot T(R) \geq A(R)$ which implies $T(R) \geq A(R)/6 \geq 1I(P)/12.$ $\qquad\square$

3. The optimality of Kung's algorithm

Here, we prove a linear lower bound on the one-way information content of the convolution. This lower bound together with the results of Section 2 provide the proof of the optimality of Kung's algorithm in the class of 1SA-algorithms.

First, we state some useful technical lemmas. The first lemma gives us a general strategy how to find a one-way communication complexity (one-way information content) of the problem $P_{n,m}$ with n inputs and m outputs.

Lemma 3.1. *Let $P_{n,m} = \{f_n^1, f_n^2, \ldots, f_n^m\}$ be a computing problem (for $m, n \in \mathbf{N}$), where f_n^i be a Boolean function of n variables $x_1, \ldots, x_n$ for each $i = 1, \ldots, m$. Let $1\mathbf{I}(f_n^i, \pi)$ be the one-way information content according to a Boolean function f_n^i and a partition π.*

Let, for a nondecreasing function $h : \mathbf{N} \to \mathbf{N}$ and each $i = 1, \ldots, m$,

$$\mathcal{P}_h(f_n^i) = \{\pi \in Bal(X) | 1I(f_n^i, \pi) \geq h(n)\}.$$

If $\displaystyle\bigcup_{i=1}^{m} \mathcal{P}_h(f_n^i) = Bal(X)$, then

$$1\mathbf{I}(P_{n,m}) \geq h(n).$$

Proof. Obvious. Note, that $1\mathbf{I}(P_{n,m}) = min\{1\mathbf{I}(P_{n,m}, \pi) | \pi \in Bal(X)\}$. To show that $1\mathbf{I}(P_{n,m}) \geq h(n)$ it is sufficient to show that for each $\pi' \in Bal(X)$: $1\mathbf{I}(P_{n,m}, \pi') \geq h(n)$. Let π' be an arbitrary almost balanced partition. Then following our assumption, there exists j that $\pi' \in \mathcal{P}_h(f_n^j)$, i.e. $1I(f_n^j, \pi') \geq h(n)$. Obviously any fooling set for π' and f_n^j is also the fooling set for π' and $P_{n,m}$, and so $1\mathbf{I}(P_{n,m}, \pi') \geq h(n)$. $\square$

In the next Lemma 3.3 we shall show that, for getting the one-way information content of the size m for one item f_{2n}^i of the convolution according to a partition π, it can be helpful (it is sufficient) to find m elementary conjunctions of f_{2n}^i such that each one of the two variables in each of these m elementary conjunctions is assigned to another computer by the partition π. To be precise, let us formalize this idea.

Definition 3.2. **(Separated pair)** Let $P_{2n,m} = \{f_{2n}^1, f_{2n}^2, \ldots, f_{2n}^m\}$ be the convolution problem and let $X = \{a_0, a_1, \ldots, a_{n-1}, b_0, b_1, \ldots, b_{n-1}\}$ be its set of input variables. Let $\pi = (\pi_L(X), \pi_R(X))$ be an almost balanced partition of X. Let us denote $A = \{a_0, a_1, \ldots, a_{n-1}\}$ and $B = \{b_0, b_1, \ldots, b_{n-1}\}$. For any $j, k \in \{0, \ldots, n-1\}$ the pair (a_j, b_k) is called *a separated pair according to π* if $(a_j, b_k) \in S$, where

$$S = (A \cap \pi_L(X)) \times (B \cap \pi_R(X)) \cup (A \cap \pi_R(X)) \times (B \cap \pi_L(X)).$$

We call S *the set of separated pairs according to π*. Informally: a pair (x_i, x_j), where $x_i, x_j \in X$, is called separated, when x_i, x_j belong not only to the different classes A and B (in our case x_i, x_j are coefficients of different polynomials $a(x), b(x)$) but also they belong to the different classes $\pi_L(X), \pi_R(X)$

of the almost balanced partition π. It is clear that for each $\pi \in Bal(X)$ the set S of separated pairs is nonempty.

Lemma 3.3. *Let $m \leq n$. Let $i \in \{0, \ldots, 2n-2\}$, and let $f_{2n}^i(a_0, \ldots, a_{n-1}, b_0, \ldots, b_{n-1}) = c_i$. Let $\pi \in Bal(X)$ and let m pairs (a_j, b_k) that occur as the multiplications (elementary conjunctions) $a_j b_k$ in c_i are separated. Then there exists a one-way fooling set $\mathcal{A}(f_{2n}^i, \pi)$ according to f_{2n}^i and π with the cardinality 2^m.*

Proof. Let $\{x_1, \ldots, x_m\} \subseteq \pi_L(X), \{y_1, \ldots, y_m\} \subseteq \pi_R(X)$, and let for each $j \in \{1, \ldots, m\}, x_j y_j$ be an elementary conjunction of f_{2n}^i. Without loss of generality let us assume that $\pi_L(X) = \{x_1, \ldots, x_m, z_{m+1}, \ldots, z_{|\Pi_L(X)|}\}$. We set $\mathcal{A}(f_{2n}^i, \pi) = \{(\alpha_1, \ldots, \alpha_{|\Pi_L(X)|})$
$|\alpha_{m+1} = \alpha_{m+2} = \ldots = \alpha_{|\pi_L(X)|} = 0$, and $\alpha_i \in \{0,1\}$ for $i = 1, \ldots, m\}$. Obviously, $|\mathcal{A}(f_{2n}^i, \pi)| = 2^m$.

Now, we prove that $\mathcal{A}(f_{2n}^i)$ is a one-way fooling set according to f_{2n}^i and π. Let $\alpha, \beta \in \mathcal{A}(f_{2n}^i, \pi), \alpha \neq \beta, \alpha = (\alpha_1, \ldots, a_{|\pi_L(X)|}), \beta = (\beta_1, \ldots, \beta_{|\pi_L(X)|})$. Without loss of generality we may assume that there exists $t \leq m$ such that $a_t = 1$ and $\beta_t = 0$. Then we consider the following input assignment $\gamma \in \{0,1\}^{|\pi_R(X)|}$ restricted to $\pi_R(X) = \{y_1, \ldots, y_m, u_{m+1}, \ldots, u_{|\pi_R(X)|}\} : \gamma = (\gamma_1, \ldots, \gamma_m, \ldots, \gamma_{|\pi_R(X)|})$ where $\gamma_t = 1$ and $\gamma_1 = \ldots = \gamma_{t-1} = \gamma_{t+1} = \ldots = \gamma_{|\pi_R(X)|} = 0$. Obviously, $1 = f_{2n}^i(\pi^{-1}(\alpha, \gamma)) \neq f_{2n}^i(\pi^{-1}(\beta, \gamma)) = 0$, which completes the proof. $\square$

In what follows, we shall say, for each $f_{2n}^i(a_0, \ldots, a_{n-1}, b_0, \ldots, b_{n-1}) = c_i = \sum_{j+k=i} a_j b_k$ for any $i \in \{0, \ldots, 2n-1\}$, that f_{2n}^i *contains the pair* (a_j, b_k) if $a_j b_k$ is an elementary conjunction of f_{2n}^i. To estimate the lower bound on the maximal number of separated pairs contained in one element c_i of the convolution P_{2n} for any almost balanced partion π, we need a lower bound estimation for the size of the set S of separated pairs. First we give a lower bound on the number of separated pairs according to any fixed partition.

Lemma 3.4. *Let $\pi \in Bal(X)$. If S is the set of separated pairs according to π, then*

$$|S| \geq n^2/12.$$

Proof. Remember that $S = (A \cap \pi_L(X)) \times (B \times \pi_R(X)) \cup (A \cup \pi_R(X)) \times (B \cap \pi_L(X))$ for $A = \{a_0, a_1, \ldots, a_{n-1}\}$ and $B = \{b_0, b_1, \ldots, b_{n-1}\}$ (Definition 3.2). We can see that there exists at least one pair of sets $(D, F), (D, F) \in \{(A, \pi_L(X)), (A, \pi_R(X)), (B, \pi_L(X)), (B, \pi_R(x))\}$ such that $|D \cap F| \geq n/2$ (if such a pair does not exist, then $|X| < 2n$, and we have got the contradiction). Without loss of generality we suppose that $|A \cap \pi_L(X)| \geq n/2$. Let us now estimate the size of $B \cap \pi_R(X)$. Using the facts

$$\pi_R(X) = (A \cap \pi_R(X)) \cup (B \cap \pi_R(X)), \text{ and}$$
$$|\pi_R(X)| = |A \cap \pi_R(X)| + |B \cap \pi_R(X)| \geq 2n/3,$$

we get

$$|B \cap \pi_R(X)| \geq 2n/3 - |A \cap \pi_R(X)| \geq n/6.$$

It is evident that $(A \cap \pi_L(X)) \times (B \cap \pi_R(X)) \subseteq S$ and so $|S| \geq |A \cap \pi_L(X)| * |B \cap \pi_R(X)| \geq n^2/12$, which completes the proof. $\square$

Lemma 3.5. *Let P_{2n} be the convolution problem. Then for any almost balanced partition $\pi = (\pi_L(X), \pi_R(X))$ of X there exists at least one element f_{2n}^i of the convolution P_{2n}, that contains at least $n/24$ separated pairs (a_j, b_k) according to π.*

Proof. We prove Lemma 3.5 by contradiction. Let us suppose that there exists an almost balanced partition π, for which each convolution element c_i contains less than $n/24$ separated pairs according to π. Let us define a special matrix $D = [d_{i,j}]$ for $i, j = 0, \ldots, n - 1$ where

$$d_{i,j} = \begin{cases} 1 & if \ (a_i, b_j) \in S. \\ 0 & if \ (a_i, b_j) \notin S. \end{cases}$$

Clearly, the number of 1's of D is the number of separated pairs of D.

We consider the set $\mathcal{D}$ of diagonals of matrix D

$$\mathcal{D} = \{D_i | D_i = \{d_{j,k} | j + k = i, 0 \leq j, k \leq n, d_{j,k} \in \{0, 1\}\}, i = 0, \ldots, 2n - 2\}.$$

The diagonal $D_i \in \mathcal{D}$ coincide with the element c_i of the convolution. From the precondition the number of 1's in each diagonal D_i is less then $n/24$. The number of diagonals is $2n - 1$ and so the number of 1's in the matrix D is less then

$$(2n - 1) * n/24 < n^2/12.$$

Since this contradicts to Lemma 3.4 the proof of Lemma 3.5 is completed. $\square$

As a consequence of the previous lemmas we can state the main theorem:

Theorem 3.6. *Let $P_{2n,m}$ be the convolution problem for any $n \in \mathbf{N}, m = 2n - 1$. Then*

$$1\mathbf{I}(P_{2n,m}) \geq n/24.$$

Proof. To prove this theorem it is sufficient to prove $1\mathbf{I}(P_{2n,m}, \pi) \geq n/24$ for any $\pi \in Bal(X)$, where X is the set of input variables for $P_{2n,m}$. Let π

be any partition from $Bal(X)$. By Lemma 2.5 there exists $i \in \{0, \ldots, m-1\}$ such that f^i_{2n} contains at least $n/24$ separated pairs. Then Lemma 3.3 provides $1\mathbf{I}(f^i_{2n}, \pi) \geq n/24$.

Thus, we have proved that, for each $\pi' \in Bal(X)$, there exists $i \in \{0, \ldots, m-1\}$ that $1\mathbf{I}(f^i_{2n}, \pi') \geq n/24$. Applying Lemma 3.1 we get $1\mathbf{I}(P_{2n,m}) \geq n/24$. $\square$

Corollary 3.7. *Each VLSI circuit computing the convolution problem $P_{2n,m}$ must have at least $n/48$ processors.*

Proof. Corollary 3.7 follows directly from Theorem 3.6 and Theorem 2.1 because $P_{2n,m}$ depends on all input variables. $\square$

Corollary 3.8. *Any one-dimensional array computing the convolution problem $P_{2n,m}$ works in time $\Omega(1\mathbf{I}(P_{2n,m})) = \Omega(n)$.*

Proof. The assertion follows from Theorem 3.6, Lemma 2.2, and from that fact that $P_{2n,m}$ contains a Boolean function depending on all inputs variables. $\square$

4. Conclusion

Finally, we can conclude that Kung's one-dimensional systolic array algorithm (linear systolic system (LSS)) for the convolution problem is assymptotically $P^r T^s$-optimal (P is the number of processors and T stands for the time) for any nonnegative integers r, s in the class of one-dimensional systolic array algorithms. There are two interesting points on this fact.

1° Any complicated architecture (note that one-dimensional array is the simplest parallel architecture) cannot compensate for the number of processors of the one-dimensional array computing the convolution problem. Thus, the convolution problem has the nice property that it can be solved in optimal area on the simplest parallel architecture.

2° The Kung's algorithm [16], [17] for the convolution problem has a nice, regular flow of input data distributed "regularly" over the one-dimensional array. Generally the theoretical model of VLSI circuit allows a lot of irregularities (for each variable an input processor and the time in which the variable enters the circuit can be chosen completely arbitrarily). But no use of these irregularities can decrease the time or the area complexity of the computation.

We conclude this paper noting that Section 2 provides a useful framework for proving the optimality of 1SA-algorithms for different computing problems including the problem of language recognition. So, the study of the one-way information content of distinct problems in the relation to 1SA-algorithms may be of interest. Another direction for further research may be a search for another, special lower bound method for special classes of systolic networks (algorithms). One step in this direction can be found in [8], where systolic computations on complete binary trees are considered.

References

1. C. Choffrut, K. Culik II, On real-time cellular automata and trellis automata, *Acta Informatica*, 21 (1984), 393 – 407.

2. K. Culik II, J. Gruska, A. Salomaa, Systolic automata for VLSI on balanced trees, *Acta Informatica*, 18 (1983), 335 – 344.

3. K. Culik II, A. Salomaa, D. Wood, Systolic tree acceptors, *R. A. I. R. O. Theoretical Informatics*, 18 (1984), 53 – 69.

4. J. Gruska, Syntesis, structure and power of systolic computations, *Th. Computer Sci.*, 71 (1990), 44 – 77.

5. S. M. Hedetniemi, S. T. Hedetniemi, A. L. Liestmann, A survey of gossiping and broadcasting in communication networks, *Networks*, 18 (1988), 319 – 349.

6. J. Hromkovič, R. Klasing, B. Monien, R. Peine, Dissemination of information in interconection networks (broadcasting & gossiping), in *Combinatorial Network Theory* (Frank Hsu, Ding – Zhu Du, eds.), Science Press, AMS 1994.

7. J. Hromkovič, Some complexity aspects of VLSI computations. Part 1. A framework for the study of information transfer in VLSI circuits, *Computers and Artificial Intelligence*, 7, 3 (1988), 229 – 252.

8. J. Hromkovič, Some complexity aspects of VLSI computations. Part 2. Topology of circuits and information transfer, *Computers and Artificial Intelligence*, 7, 4 (1988), 289 – 302.

9. J. Hromkovič, Some complexity aspects of VLSI computations. Part 5. Nondeterministic and probabilistic VLSI circuits, *Computers and Artificial Intelligence*, 8, 2 (1989), 169 – 188.

10. J. Hromkovič, Some complexity aspects of VLSI computations. Part 6. Communication complexity, *Computers and Artificial Intelligence*, 8, 3 (1989), 209 – 225.

11. J. Hromkovič, J. Procházka, Branching programs as a tool for proving lower bounds on VLSI computations and optimal algorithms for systolic arrays, *Proc. 13th MFCS Symposium, LNCS* 324, Springer-Verlag, 1988, 360 – 370.

12. O. H. Ibarra, S. M. Kim, Characterizations and computational complexity of systolic trellis automata, *Theoretical Computer Science*, 29 (1984), 123 – 153.

13. O. H. Ibarra, S. M. Kim, S. Moran, Sequential machine characterizations of trellis and cellular automata and applications, *SIAM J. Comput.*, 14 (1985), 426 – 447.

14. O. H. Ibarra, M. A. Palis, S. M. Kim, Fast parallel language recognition by cellular automata, *Theoretical Computer Science*, 41 (1985), 231 – 246.

15. H. T. Kung, Let's design algorithms for VLSI systems, in *Proc. of the Caltech Conference of VLSI* (CL. L. Seifz, ed), Pasadena, California 1979, 65 – 90.

16. H. T. Kung, Use of VLSI in algebraic computation, Some suggestions, *Proc. SYMSAC'81*, ACM Symp., Snowbird 1981, 218 – 222.

17. H. T. Kung, *Why systolic architectures*, Technical report, CMU-CS-81-148, Carnegie – Mellon Univ., Comp. Science Dept., Nov. 1981.

18. F. T. Leighton, *Introduction to Parallel Algorithms and Architectures*, Morgan Kaufmann Publishers, Inc., San Mateo, California 1992.

19. R. Lidl, H. Niederreiter, *Finite Fields*, in *Encyclopedia of Mathematics and its Applications*, Vol. 20 (G.-C. Rota, ed.), Addison-Wesley Publ. Comp., 1983.

20. B. Monien, I. H. Sudborough, Embedding one interconection network in another, *Computing Suppl.*, 7 (1990), 257 – 282.

21. J. Procházka, Systolic systems for polynomial GCD computation, *Journal of Inf. Process. Cybern. EIK*, 26 (1990), 5 – 18.

22. C. D. Thompson, *A complexity theory for VLSI*, Doctoral dissertation, CMU-CS-80-140, Comp. Science Dept. Carnegie-Mellon University, Pittsburgh, 1980.

23. J. D. Ullman, *Computational Aspects of VLSI*, Computer Science Press, Rockville, MD, 1984.

24. A. C. Yao, Some complexity questions related to distributed computing, *Proc. 11th Annual ACM STOC*, ACM 1979, 209 – 213.

25. A. C. Yao, The entropic limitations of VLSI computations, *Proc. 13th Annual ACM STOC*, ACM 1981, 308 – 311.

On Contextual Grammars
with Parallel Derivation

Lucian ILIE

Faculty of Mathematics, University of Bucharest

Str. Academiei 14, 70109 Bucureşti, Romania

Abstract. We investigate some problems concerning the generative power of contextual grammars with parallel derivation, mainly when the selection of contexts is limited to strings in sets of a given type (finite, regular, context-free, etc.). Certain problems remained open in [8] are solved.

1. Introduction

The contextual grammars were introduced in [3] and they are based on the phenomenon, much investigated in descriptive linguistics [2], of accepting a string by a context or a context by a string. Discussion about the subject can be found also in [4].

In the twenty five years since they have been introduced, the whole program usual in formal language theory has been put in work about contextual grammars. Many variants have been considered, their generative power and properties have been investigated (necessary conditions, characterizations, closure and decidability properties, descriptional complexity, regulated rewriting, grammar forms, and so on and so forth). The reader can find a description of the domain at the level of 1981 in the monograph [5]; an updated survey appears in [6].

From two sources, Lindenmayer systems and grammar systems, both of them so intimately related with contextual grammars, naturally arises the idea to consider contextual grammars with parallel derivation, namely with the parallelism restricted in the style of step limitation of derivation in grammar systems. Specifically, we can consider contextual grammars such that in each derivation step exactly k, at least k, at most k, or an arbitrary number of contexts are adjoined simultaneously, or the derivation is totally parallel (the whole current string is splitted into substrings to which contexts are adjoined).

In the present paper, we refer to part of these variants, answering some of the problems remained open in [8].

2. Basic definitions

A (general) contextual grammar is a quadruple $G = (V, B, C, \varphi)$, where V is a finite non-empty alphabet, B is a finite language over V, $C \subseteq V^* \times V^*$ is a finite set of *contexts* over V (V^* is the free monoid generated by V; its identity is denoted by λ and $V^* - \{\lambda\} = V^+$), and $\varphi : V^* \times V^* \times V^* \longrightarrow 2^C$ is the *selection mapping*.

The language generated by G, denoted $L(G)$, is the smallest set $L \subseteq V^*$ which includes B and has the following property: if $x \in L, x = x_1 x_2 x_3$, with $x_1, x_2, x_3 \in V^*$, and $(u, v) \in \varphi(x_1, x_2, x_3)$, then $x_1 u x_2 v x_3 \in L$. (The context (u, v) is added to x, to obtain $x_1 u x_2 v x_3$, if and only if it is selected by the mapping φ; this selection depends on the whole string x, in the specified decomposition.)

A contextual grammar as above is said to be an *internal contextual grammar with choice* [7] if the mapping φ has the following property:

$$\varphi(x_1, x_2, x_3) = \varphi(x_1', x_2, x_3'), \text{ for all } x_1, x_1', x_2, x_3, x_3' \in V^*.$$

(In words, the selection of contexts does not depend on the left and right strings; we assume then the mapping φ as defined on V^*, hence of only one argument.)

When the mapping φ is defined by $\varphi(x) = C$ for all $x \in V^*$, then the grammar G is simply called *internal contextual* (without choice; it can be also considered a general grammar without choice).

We shall denote by IC the family of languages generated by internal contextual grammar with choice and by REG, CF, CS, RE the families of regular, context-free, context-sensitive, and recursively enumerable languages in the Chomsky hierarchy; by FIN we shall denote the family of finite languages.

Various restrictions of the mapping φ have been considered (see references in [5], [6]), the most natural being either to define the mapping φ only on a finite subset of V^* (hence to take $\varphi(x) = \emptyset$ for other strings) or to define it uniformly on regular subsets of V^*, namely to consider the following equivalence relation for strings $x, y \in V^*$,

$$x \equiv_\varphi y \text{ iff } \varphi(x) = \varphi(y),$$

and to impose the condition that all its equivalence classes are, for instance, regular languages. In such a case, the grammar is said to be *with regular choice*.

In general, if the languages $\varphi^{-1}(D)$, for all $D \subseteq C$ belong to a given family F of languages, then we say that the grammar is *with F choice*. The coresponding family of languages generated by internal contextual grammars is denoted by $IC(F)$.

3. Parallel contextual grammars. The main result

The grammars we consider here are internal contextual grammars with choice, but the way of using them is different from that presented in the previous section (and similar to those usual in grammar systems area [1]). For a grammar $G = (V, B, C, \varphi)$ and two strings $x, y \in V^*$ we define the following five derivation relations (k is a given positive integer);

$$
\begin{aligned}
x \Longrightarrow^{=k} y \quad &\text{iff} \quad x = x_1 z_1 x_2 z_2 \ldots x_k z_k x_{k+1}, \\
&\qquad y = x_1 u_1 z_1 v_1 x_2 u_2 z_2 v_2 \ldots x_k u_k z_k v_k x_{k+1}, \\
&\qquad x_i \in V^*, 1 \le i \le k+1, z_i \in V^*, 1 \le i \le k, \\
&\qquad (u_i, v_i) \in \varphi(z_i), 1 \le i \le k; \\
x \Longrightarrow^{\le k} y \quad &\text{iff} \quad x \Longrightarrow^{=k'} y \text{ for some } k' \le k; \\
x \Longrightarrow^{\ge k} y \quad &\text{iff} \quad x \Longrightarrow^{=k'} y \text{ for some } k' \ge k; \\
x \Longrightarrow^* y \quad &\text{iff} \quad x \Longrightarrow^{=k} y \text{ for some } k \ge 0; \\
x \Longrightarrow^t y \quad &\text{iff} \quad x = z_1 z_2 \ldots z_k, z_i \in V^*, 1 \le i \le k, k \ge 1; \\
&\qquad y = u_1 z_1 v_1 u_2 z_2 v_2 \ldots u_k z_k v_k, \\
&\qquad (u_i, v_i) \in \varphi(z_i), 1 \le i \le k.
\end{aligned}
$$

For $f \in \{*, t\} \cup \{\le k, = k, \ge k \mid k \ge 1\}$ the language generated by a grammar G in the mode f is defined by

$$
\begin{aligned}
L_f(G) \quad = B \cup \quad &\{x \in V^* \mid w \Longrightarrow^f w_1 \Longrightarrow^f \ldots \Longrightarrow^f w_m = x; \\
&m \ge 1, w \in B, w_i \in V^*, 1 \le i \le m\}.
\end{aligned}
$$

The family of languages $L_f(G)$, generated by grammars G with choice restricted to a given family F of languages, is denoted by $PIC(F, f)$. In what follows, F will be one of the families FIN, REG, CF, CS, RE.

In [8] it is proved that $IC(FIN) \subset IC(REG) \subset IC(CF) \subset IC(CS) \subset IC(RE)$ (Theorem 7), and a similar result is supposed to be true, but it is left open, for parallel derivation. For $f \in \{*, = 1, \ge 1\} \cup \{\le k \mid k \ge 1\}$, and for F any family of languages, it is also proved in the same paper (Theorem 1), that $PIC(F, f) = IC(F)$, hence for these values of f the problem is solved.

In the following, we shall solve the problem for $f \in \{= k, \ge k \mid k \ge 2\}$. Our ideas are similar enough to those of Theorem 7 in [8], but we shall avoid too many references and present here the proof with all details. Because the inclusions $PIC(F, f) \subseteq PIC(F', f)$, for $F \subseteq F'$ two arbitrary families and for all modes f of derivation, are obvious, we shall prove in the considered cases only the strictness.

Lemma 1. $PIC(REG, f) - PIC(FIN, f) \ne \emptyset$, for $f \in \{= k, \ge k \mid k \ge 2\}$.

Proof. Take

$$
G_1 \quad = \quad (\{a, b, c\}, \{(ababc)^{k-1}abab\}, \{(a, a), (b, b), (\lambda, \lambda)\}, \varphi),
$$

$$\varphi(ab^n a) = \{(a,a),(\lambda,\lambda)\}, n \geq 1,$$
$$\varphi(ba^n b) = \{(b,b),(\lambda,\lambda)\}, n \geq 1.$$

We obtain

$$\begin{aligned} L_{=k}(G_1) \quad = \quad & \{a^{n_1}b^{m_1}a^{n_1}b^{m_1}ca^{n_2}b^{m_2}a^{n_2}b^{m_2}c\ldots ca^{n_k}b^{m_k}a^{n_k}b^{m_k} \mid \\ & n_i \geq 1, m_i \geq 1 \text{ for all } 1 \leq i \leq k\} \\ & \in PIC(REG, = k). \end{aligned}$$

We assume that $L_{=k}(G_1) = L_{=k}(G)$ for some $G = (\{a,b,c\}, B, C, \varphi)$ with $\varphi^{-1}(D)$ finite for all $D \subseteq C$.

Observe that the symbols c must appear from the beginning in B, else when we introduce a symbol c, we can introduce an arbitrary number of symbols c obtaining a string not in $L_{=k}(G_1)$, a contradiction.

Let us take $w = a^{n_1}b^{m_1}a^{n_1}b^{m_1}c\ldots ca^{n_k}b^{m_k}a^{n_k}b^{m_k}$ with arbitrarily large $n_i, m_i, 1 \leq i \leq k$. There is a $w' \in L_{=k}(G)$ with $w' \Longrightarrow^{=k} w$ and, using the above remark, we must have $w' = a^{n'_1}b^{m'_1}a^{n'_1}b^{m'_1}c\ldots ca^{n'_k}b^{m'_k}a^{n'_k}b^{m'_k}$ with $n'_i \leq n_i, m'_i \leq m_i$, for all $1 \leq i \leq k$. We shall suppose that at least one of these $2k$ inequalities is proper. Therefore, we have three cases, but, before treating them, we make an observation: we cannot add contexts around a string containing an occurrence of the symbol c. This is obvious because such a context can increase only the number of occurrences of the symbols being beside that c (else, we must have $(u,v) \in \varphi(a^i b^m cw)$, with m arbitrarily large, or $(u,v) \in \varphi(wca^n b^i)$, with n arbitrarily large, both posibilities being in contradiction with the finiteness of $\varphi^{-1}(D)$ for $(u,v) \in D)$. So, if the number of occurrences of the symbol b in the left of a symbol c is increased (the same reasoning could be made for the a beside a c) its pair must be increased (we consider the underlined occurrences of the symbol b in $\ldots ca^{n'_i}\underline{b}^{m'_i}a^{n'_i}\underline{b}^{m'_i}\ldots$ as being paired), but, if the number of occurrences of another symbol b is increased instead of that, we obtain a string not in $L_{=k}(G_1)$, a contradiction. Therefore, the reasoning can be made for every part separately; between two consecutively occurrences of the symbol c, before the first, or after the last occurrence of the symbol c.

Now, the cases are:

1. If there is some $i, 1 \leq i \leq k$, with $n'_i < n_i, m'_i = m_i$, then the derivation $w' \Longrightarrow^{=k} w$ must use some context $(a^{n_i-n'_i}, a^{n_i-n'_i}) \in \varphi(a^i b^m a^j), i,j \geq 0, m$ arbitrarily large, a contradiction with the finiteness of $\varphi^{-1}(D)$, for $(a^{n_i-n'_i}, a^{n_i-n'_i}) \in D$.

2. If there is some $i, 1 \leq i \leq k$, with $n'_i = n_i, m'_i < m_i$, then we obtain a similar contradiction.

3. If there is some $i, 1 \leq i \leq k$, with $n'_i < n_i, m'_i < m_i$, then some context $(a^{n_i-n'_i}b^{m_i-m'_i}, a^{n_i-n'_i}b^{m_i-m'_i}) \in \varphi(b^{m'_i}a^{n'_i})$ must be used. As n_i, m_i are arbitrarily large and $n_i - n'_i, m_i - m'_i$ must be bounded (the set C is finite), we obtain that n'_i, m'_i are arbitrarily large, again a contradiction with the finiteness of $\varphi^{-1}(D)$, for $(a^{n_i-n'_i}b^{m_i-m'_i}, a^{n_i-n'_i}b^{m_i-m'_i}) \in D$.

In conclusion $L_{=k}(G_1) \notin PIC(FIN, = k)$.

For the case of the derivation mode $\geq k$, it is obvious that $L_{\geq k}(G_1) = L_{=k}(G_1)$ (at most k contexts different from (λ, λ) can be adjoined at the same time), and the proof is analogous. $\qquad\square$

Lemma 2. $PIC(CF, f) - PIC(REG, f) \neq \emptyset$, for $f \in \{= k, \geq k \mid k \geq 2\}$

Proof. Let us consider

$$
\begin{aligned}
G_2 \;=\; & (\{a, b, c, d, e\}, \{(abccabd)^{k-1}abccab\}, \\
& \quad \{(\lambda, a), (a, a), (b, b), (e, e), (\lambda, \lambda)\}, \varphi), \\
& \varphi(ab^n cca) = \{(a, a), (\lambda, \lambda)\}, n \geq 1, \\
& \varphi(bcca^n b) = \{(b, b), (\lambda, \lambda)\}, n \geq 1, \\
& \varphi(bc) = \{(\lambda, a), (\lambda, \lambda)\}, \\
& \varphi(a^m b^m caca^n b^n) = \{(e, e), (\lambda, \lambda)\}, m, n \geq 1.
\end{aligned}
$$

We obtain

$$
\begin{aligned}
L_{=k}(G_2) \;-\; & \{w_1 d w_2 d \ldots d w_k \mid k \geq 1, \\
& w_i \in \{a^n b^m cca^n b^m \mid n, m \geq 1\} \cup \{a^n b^m ca^p ca^n b^m \mid n, m, p \geq 1\} \\
& \cup \{e^j a^n b^n ca^p ca^n b^n e^j \mid j, n, p \geq 1\} \text{ for all } 1 \leq i \leq k\} \in \\
& \in PIC(CF, = k).
\end{aligned}
$$

Assume that $L_{=k}(G_2) = L_{=k}(G)$ for some $G = (\{a, b, c, d, e\}, B, C, \varphi)$ with $\varphi^{-1}(D)$ regular for all $D \subseteq C$. Again, the symbols d must appear from the beginning in B, else, when a symbol d is introduced, an arbitrary number of symbols d could be introduced, obtaining a string not in $L_{=k}(G_2)$, a contradiction. Moreover, in a derivation in G, the number of occurrences of the symbols a, b, or e which are in pairs cannot be increased by adjoining contexts around a d. (We consider the underlined occurrences of the symbol a (or b, or c) in $\ldots e^j \underline{a}^n b^n ca^p c\underline{a}^n b^n e^j \ldots$ (or $\ldots e^j a^n \underline{b}^n ca^p ca^n \underline{b}^n e^j \ldots$ or $\ldots \underline{e}^j a^n b^n ca^p ca^n b^n \underline{e}^j \ldots$, respectively, as being paired). We consider only the case of strings of the form $a^n b^m cca^n b^m$ being in the left-hand side of a d. (The argument is analogous for the other two forms and for the right-hand side.) First, such a context cannot increase the number of further occurrences of the symbol a (or b) from d (we mean the underlined occurrences of the symbol a in $\ldots \underline{a}^n b^m cca^n b^m d \ldots$) because, in that case, the number of nearer occurrences of the symbol a (or b, respectively; we mean the underlined occurrence of the symbol a in $\ldots a^n b^m cc\underline{a}^n b^m d \ldots$) could not be increased, so we would obtain a string not in $L_{=k}(G_2)$, a contradiction. If the number of nearer occurrences of the symbol a (or b) is increased, then its pair must be increased too, and, if the number of others occurrences of the symbol a (or b, respectively) is increased instead of that, the obtained string is not in $L_{=k}(G_2)$, the same contradiction. Therefore, we can make the reasoning separately between two occurrences of the symbol d. Specifically, if we have a derivation $w \Longrightarrow^{=k} w'$ where $w = w_1 d w_2 d \ldots d w_k$ and $w' = w_1' d w_2' d \ldots d w_k'$, in fact, we have $w_i \Longrightarrow^{=1} w_i'$, $1 \leq i \leq k$ and we shall work in this mode in the following.

So, if we have the derivation $w \Longrightarrow^{=1} w'$ where $w = e^q a^n b^n ca^p ca^n b^n e^q$ then $w' = e^{q'} a^{n'} b^{n'} ca^{p'} c\, a^{n'} b^{n'} e^{q'}$ with $n = n'$. (If $n < n'$ then $(a^{n'-n} b^{n'-n}, a^{n'-n} b^{n'-n}) \in \varphi(b^n ca^p ca^n)$ and we can obtain also $e^q a^{n+1} bb^n ca^p ca^n ab^{n+1} e^q \Longrightarrow^{=1} w''$, $w'' = e^q a^{n+1} b\, a^{n'-n} b^{n'-n} b^n ca^p ca^n a^{n'-n} b^{n'-n} ab^{n+1} e^q$, and, for every string $w = w_1 d w_2 d \ldots d w_k$ such that there is some $i, 1 \leq i \leq k$, with $w_i = w''$, we have $w \notin L_{=k}(G_2)$, a contradiction.) Consequently, infinitely many strings of the form w' are obtained starting from strings of the form $a^n b^m ca^p ca^n b^m$, $n, m \geq 1, p \geq 0$. Taking a derivation of such a w', we consider the step when the first extreme occurrence of the symbol e is introduced, $a^n b^m ca^p ca^n b^m \Longrightarrow^{=1} e^q a^{n'} b^{m'} ca^{p'} ca^{n'} b^{m'} e^q$. Obviously, we must have $n' = n, m' = m, p' = p$. Looking at the form of $L_{=k}(G_2)$ it follows that $m = n$, hence the context (e^q, e^q) belongs to a set $D \subseteq C$ such that $\varphi^{-1}(D) \cap \{a^n b^m ca^p ca^n b^m \mid n, m, p \geq 1\} = \{a^n b^n ca^p ca^n b^n \mid n, p \geq 1\}$. As $\varphi^{-1}(D) \in REG$, the last equality is imposible. In conclusion $L_{=k}(G_2) \notin PIC(REG, = k)$.

For the mode $\geq k$, we obviously have $L_{\geq k}(G_2) = L_{=k}(G_2)$, and the proof is similar. $\qquad\qquad\square$

Lemma 3. $PIC(CS, f) - PIC(CF, f) \neq \emptyset$, *for $f \in \{= k, \geq k \mid k \geq 2\}$.*

Proof. Consider now

$$
\begin{aligned}
G_3 \;=\; & (\{a, b, c, d\}, \{(cbacd)^{k-1}cbac\}, \{(\lambda, a), (a, \lambda), (c, c), (\lambda, \lambda)\}, \varphi), \\
& \varphi(cb) = \{(\lambda, a), (\lambda, \lambda)\}, \\
& \varphi(b) = \{(a, \lambda), (\lambda, \lambda)\}, \\
& \varphi(caba^{2^n} c) = \{(c, c), (\lambda, \lambda)\}, n \geq 1.
\end{aligned}
$$

We obtain

$$
\begin{aligned}
L_{=k}(G_3) = \;\; & \{w_1 d w_2 d \ldots d w_k \mid k \geq 1, \\
& w_i \in \{cba^n c \mid n \geq 1\} \cup \{ca^n ba^m c \mid n, m \geq 1\} \cup \\
& \cup \{c^j a^n ba^{2^m} c^j \mid n, m \geq 1, j \geq 2\} \text{ for all } 1 \leq i \leq k\} \in \\
& \in PIC(CS, = k).
\end{aligned}
$$

Assume that $L_{=k}(G_3) = L_{=k}(G)$, with $G = (\{a, b, c, d\}, B, C, \varphi)$, $\varphi^{-1}(D) \in CF$ for all $D \subseteq C$. Like in the previous proofs, the symbols d must appear from the beginning in B (we cannot add a symbol d by a context), and the number of occurrences of the symbol c cannot be increased by introducing a context around a symbol d. We take now a string $w = w_1 d w_2 d \ldots d w_k$ with $w_i = c^2 a^n b a^{2^m} c^2$. As the number of occurrences of the symbol a between b and c^2 cannot be increased, w must be obtained from a string $w' = w'_1 d w'_2 d \ldots d w'_k$ with $w'_i = c a^{n'} b a^{m'} c$ by adjoining the context (c, c). In fact, we have a derivation $c a^n b a^{2^m} c \Longrightarrow^{=1} c^2 a^n b a^{2^m} c^2$, hence $(c, c) \in \varphi(c a^n b a^{2^m} c)$. Let $D \subseteq C$ be the set of contexts which contains (c, c). Because $\varphi^{-1}(D) \in CF$, then there exist some strings $c a^{n'} b a^{m'} c \in \varphi^{-1}(D)$, with $m' \neq 2^p, p \geq 0$, (otherwise $\varphi^{-1}(D)$ cannot be context-free). But, the derivation $c a^{n'} b a^{m'} c \Longrightarrow^{=1} c^2 a^{n'} b a^{m'} c^2$ is also posible and if it is made between two occurrences of the symbol d (or before the first or after the last occurrence of the symbol d), the obtained string is not in $L_{=k}(G_3)$, a contradiction. In conclusion, $L_{=k}(G_3) \notin PIC(CF, = k)$.

For the mode $\geq k$, we have $L_{\geq k}(G_3) = L_{=k}(G_3)$, and we can prove in the same way that $L_{\geq k}(G_3) \notin PIC(CF, \geq k)$. $\qquad\square$

Lemma 4. $PIC(RE, f) - PIC(CS, f) \neq \emptyset$, *for* $f \in \{= k, \geq k \mid k \geq 2\}$.

Proof. Let $L \subseteq V^+$ be a language such that $L \in RE - CS$, and $b, c, d \notin V$ three new symbols. Consider

$$
\begin{aligned}
G_L \;=\; & \{V \cup \{b, c, d\}, \{cca_1 cbcca_2 cb \ldots bcca_k c \mid a_i \in V, 1 \leq i \leq k\}, \\
& \{(\lambda, a) \mid a \in V\} \cup \{(d, d)\}, \varphi), \\
& \varphi(cc) = \{(\lambda, a) \mid a \in V\}, \\
& \varphi(cwc) = \{(d, d)\}, w \in L.
\end{aligned}
$$

Obviously, $L_{=k}(G_L) \in PIC(RE, = k)$. By Theorem 4 in [8] $PIC(CS, f) \subseteq CS$ for all modes f, hence $L_{=k}(G_L) \in CS$. However,

$$
\begin{aligned}
L_{=k}(G_L) \cap \{cdc\} V^* (\{cdbcdc\} V^*)^{k-1} \{cd\} \;=\; \\
= \{cdc\} L (\{cdbcdc\} L)^{k-1} \{cd\} \notin CS,
\end{aligned}
$$

a contradiction which proves the relation $PIC(RE, = k) - PIC(CS, = k) \neq \emptyset$. Because $L_{\geq k}(G_L) = L_{=k}(G_L)$ the proof is finished. $\qquad\square$

Combining lemmas 1, 2, 3, 4 we obtain our main result.

Theorem 1. $PIC(FIN, f) \subset PIC(REG, f) \subset PIC(CF, f) \subset PIC(CS, f) \subset PIC(RE, f)$ *for* $f \in \{= k, \geq k \mid k \geq 2\}$.

Remark. It is proved in [8] that $PIC(CS, t) \subset PIC(RE, t)$, but for others inclusions the corresponding problem remains *open* for the mode t of derivation.

References

1. E. Csuhaj-Varju, J. Dassow, J. Kelemen, Gh. Păun, *Grammar Systems*, Gordon and Breach, 1994.

2. S. Marcus, *Algebraic Linguistics. Analytical Models*, Academic Press, New York, 1967.

3. S. Marcus, Contextual grammars, *Rev. Roum. Math. Pures Appl.*, 14, 10 (1969), 1525 – 1534.

4. S. Marcus, Deux types nouveaux de grammaires génératives, *Cah. Ling. Th. Appl.* 6 (1969), 69 – 74.

5. Gh. Păun, *Contextual Grammars*, The Publ. House of the Romanian Academy of Sciences, Bucureşti, 1982 (in Romanian).

6. Gh. Păun, Marcus contextual grammars. After 25 years, *Bulletin EATCS*, 52 (February 1994), 263 – 273.

7. Gh. Păun, X. M. Nguyen, On the inner contextual grammars, *Rev. Roum. Math. Pures Appl.*, 25, 4(1980), 641 – 651.

8. Gh. Păun, G. Rozenberg, A. Salomaa, Contextual grammars: parallelism and blocking of derivation, *Fundamenta Inform.*, to appear.

On Transitive Cofinal Automata

Masami ITO, Msashi KATSURA
Faculty of Science, Kyoto Sangyo University
Kyoto 603, Japan

0. Introduction

In this paper, a special class of automata, called transitive cofinal automata, is dealt with. First, we determine the structure of a transitive cofinal automaton and then investigate the structure of $V_X(TC)$, i.e. the class of all transitive cofinal X-automata, and its subclass $V_X(STC)$, i.e. the class of all strictly transitive cofinal X-automata. As has been seen in [4], the class $V_X(Au)$ of all X-automata is considered as a partially ordered set (or briefly a poset). Consequently, $V_X(TC)$ and $V_X(STC)$ can be considered as subposets of $V_X(Au)$.

Our main purpose is to investigate subclasses of $V_X(TC)$ and $V_X(STC)$ which form lattices. Lattices in $V_X(STC)$ are directly dealt with. On the other hand, for an investigation on lattices in $V_X(TC)$, we introduce a poset, called a weighted poset, and study its subposets which form lattices. Using some results on a weighted poset, we povide a method for obtaining some kinds of subclasses of $V_X(TC)$ which form maximal lattices in $V_X(TC)$.

1. Strongly cofinal automata

In this section, we provide some properties of strongly cofinal automata. First, we expect that, for related definitions and notations, the reader will refer to [4]. Furthermore, for elementary notions on lattice theory, see [1]. We begin with the following definition.

Definition 1.1. Let $A = (S, X)$ be an automaton. If the following condition is satisfied, then A is called a *cofinal automaton*: For any $s, t \in S$, there exists $p \in X^*$ such that $sp^A = tp^A$.

The following result can easily be proved.

Proposition 1.2. *Let $A = (S, X)$ be a cofinal automaton. Then there exists some $p \in X^*$ such that $Sp^A = \{sp^A \mid s \in S\}$ is a singleton.*

In what follows, the notation $Sp^A = s$ will be often used instead of $Sp^A = \{s\}$ when Sp^A is a singleton.

Remark 1.3. A cofinal automaton has been already defined under the name of a directable automaton in [2]. In this paper, we use the name of a cofinal automaton instead of that of a directable automaton. Because, we have already studied systematically this automaton under the name of a cofinal automaton. (See [4,5].)

Definition 1.4. A cofinal automaton is called a *strongly cofinal automaton*, if it is strongly connected.

Let $V_X(Au)$, $V_X(S)$, $V_X(Cf)$ and $V_X(Scf)$ be, respectively, the classes of all X-automata, strongly connected X-automata, cofinal X-automata and strongly cofinal X-automata. Note that isomorphic automata are considered to be equal. We are mostly interested in the structures of these classes under the following partial order: $B \leq A$ iff B is a homomorphic image of A.

The following result plays a fundamental role in this paper. Dang Huu Dao [3] obtained a similar result about the endomorphism semigroup of a directable automaton.

Lemma 1.5. *Let $A = (S, X)$ and $B = (T, X)$ be strongly cofinal automata such that $B \leq A$. Then $Hom(A, B)$ is a singleton.*

Proof. Let $h, h' \in Hom(A, B)$. Since A is strongly cofinal, for any $s \in S$ there exists $p \in X^*$ such that $s = Sp^A$. Thus $h(s) = h(Sp^A) = h(S)p^B = Tp^B$ where $h(S) = \{h(s) \mid s \in S\}$. Note that Tp^B is a singleton. By the same way, we have $h'(s) = Tp^B$. Thus for any $s \in S$ we have $h(s) = h'(s)$. $\square$

Corollary 1.6. *Let $A = (S, X)$ be a strongly cofinal automaton and let $h \in Aut(A)$. Then for any $s \in S$, we have $h(s) = s$.*

In what follows, the unique element of $Hom(A, B)$ will be often denoted by $h_{A,B}$ when A and B are strongly cofinal automata such that $Hom(A, B) \neq \emptyset$.

For the proofs of the following results and for related results, see [4].

Proposition 1.7 *For any X, the classes $V_X(S), V_X(Cf)$ and (Scf) are strong classes.*

Proposition 1.8. *For any X, $V_X(Scf)$ is a lattice and neither $V_X(Au)$ nor $V_X(Cf)$ is a lattice. If $|X| = 1$, then $V_X(S)$ forms a lattice. If $|X| \geq 2$, then $V_X(S)$ does not form a lattice.*

Proposition 1.9. *Let $V_X(P)$ be one of $V_X(Au)$, $V_X(S)$ and $V_X(Cf)$. Then for any $A, B \in V_X(P)$, $[A \circ B]_{V(P)} \neq \emptyset$ where $[A \circ B]_{V(P)}$ means the set of all minimal upper bounds of $\{A, B\}$ in $V_X(P)$.*

2. Transitive automata and quasiperfect automata

In this section, we define a transitive automaton and a quasiperfect automaton, and provide some properties of these automata.

Definition 2.1. Let $A = (S, X)$ be an automaton. Then A is called a *transitive automaton* if $Aut(A)$ is transitive on S, i.e. for any $s, t \in S$, there exists $h \in \mathrm{Aut}(A)$ such that $t = h(s)$.

The proof of the following lemma is not difficult and so omitted.

Lemma 2.2. *Let A be a transitive automaton. Then all connected subautomata of A are strongly connected and isomorphic to each other.*

Definition 2.3. A transitive automaton is called *quasiperfect* if it is strongly connected.

Let $V_X(Tr)$ and $V_X(Qp)$ be, respectively, the classes of all transitive X-automata and all quasiperfect X-automata. The proof of the following result can be found in [4].

Proposition 2.4. $V_X(Qp)$ *forms a lattice. Moreover, it is not a strong class if $|X| \geq 2$.*

Definition 2.5. Let A be an automaton whose connected components (i.e. maximal connected subautomata of A) are $A_1, A_2, \cdots, A_{r-1}$ and A_r. Then we denote $A = A_1 + \cdots + A_r$. Moreover, if $A = B + B_1 + \cdots + B_{r-1}$ and B_i is isomorphic to B for each $i, 1 \leq i \leq r - 1$, then we denote $A = rB$.

The following results can easily be proved by Lemma 2.2.

Lemma 2.6. *An automaton $A = (S, X)$ is a transitive automaton iff there exists some $r \in \mathbf{N}$ and some $B \in V_X(Qp)$ such that $A = rB$ where $\mathbf{N}$ is the set of all positive integers.*

Lemma 2.7. *Let $r, r' \in \mathbf{N}$ and let $B, B' \in V_X(Qp)$. Then $r'B' \leq rB$ iff $r' \leq r$ and $B' \leq B$.*

Corollary 2.8. $V_X(Tr)$ *forms a lattice. As a poset, $V_X(Tr)$ is isomorphic to the direct product of $\mathbf{N}$ and $V_X(Qp)$.*

It can easily be seen that, for any X, there exists two automata A and A' such that $A \in V_X(Tr), A' \leq A$ and $A' \notin V_X(Tr)$. Thus we have the following.

Proposition 2.9. $V_X(Tr)$ *is not a strong class.*

3. Permutation automata

In Masunaga et al. [6], it is shown that the class of all homomorphic images of quasiperfect X-automata coincides with $V_X(Cp)$, the class of all connected permutation X-automata. In this section, we investigate the structure of $V_X(Cp)$ as a poset.

Definition 3.1. An automaton $A = (S, X)$ is called a *permutation automaton* if x^A induces a permutation on S for any $x \in X$.

Definition 3.2. Let $A = (S, X)$ be an automaton. For $p, q \in X^*$, we denote $p \sim q$ iff we have $sp^A = sq^A$ for any $s \in S$. Then the relation $\sim$ is a congruence one on X^*. The quotient monoid $C(A) = X^*/\sim$ is called the *characteristic semigroup* of A. For $p \in X^*$, we denote by $\bar{p}$ the equivalence class by $\sim$ containing p.

The following result [6] can easily be proved.

Lemma 3.3. *Let $A = (\dot{S}, X)$ be an automaton. Then $C(A)$ is a group iff A is a permutation automaton.*

Definition 3.4. Let $A = (S, X)$ be a connected permutation automaton. Then the automaton $\bar{A} = (C(A), X)$ is called the *quasiperfect automaton* associated with A where $\bar{p}x^{\bar{A}} = \overline{px}$ for any $(\bar{p}, x) \in C(A) \times X$. Since the relation $\sim$ is a congruence one, this state transition function is well defined.

The proof of the following result [6] can easily be carried out by using Lemma 3.3.

Proposition 3.5. *Let $A = (S, X)$ be a connected permutation automaton. Then, $\bar{A} = (C(A), X)$ is a qusiperfect qutomaton.*

The proof of the first part of the following proposition can be found in [6].

Proposition 3.6. *Let $A = (S, X)$ be a connected permutation automaton and $\bar{A} = (C(A), X)$ be the qusiperfect automaton associated with A. Then $A \leq \bar{A}$ holds. Moreover, if $B = (T, X)$ is a quasiperfect automaton such that $A \leq B$, then we have $\bar{A} \leq B$.*

Proof of the second part. First, we show that, for any $(s, t) \in S \times T$, there exists some $g \in Hom(B, A)$ such that $g(t) = s$. Let $g' \in Hom(B, A)$, let $t' \in T$ and let $g'(t') = s$. Since B is transitive, there exists $k \in Aut(B)$ such that $k(t) = t'$. It is easy to see that $g'k \in Hom(B, A)$ and $g'k(t) = g'(t') = s$. Next, we define a mapping h of T into $C(A)$ as follows: Fix an element t_0 in T. Since B is strongly connected, for any $t \in T$ there exists $p \in X^*$ such that $t = t_0 p^B$. Let $h(t_0 p^B) = \bar{p}$. Asssume $t_0 p^B = t_0 q^B$. As has been shown above, for any $s \in S$ there exists $g \in Hom(B, A)$ such that $g(t_0) = S$. Thus we have $sp^A = g(t_0)p^A = g(t_0 p^B) = g(t_0 q^B) = g(t_0)q^A = sq^A$. This means that $\bar{p} = \bar{q}$. Hence h is well defined. It is obvious that h is surjective. For any $(t_0 p^B, x) \in T \times X$, we have $h((t_0 p^B)x^B) = h(t_0(px)^B) = \overline{px} = \bar{p}x^{\bar{A}} = h(t_0 p^B)x^{\bar{A}}$. This means that $h \in Hom(B, \bar{A})$. $\qquad\square$

Now, we prove the following. Note that the second part of the statement can be found in [6].

Proposition 3.7. *(i) An automaton $A = (S, X)$ is a permutation automaton iff A is a homomorphic image of a transitive automaton. (ii) An automaton $A = (S, X)$ is a connected permutation automaton iff A is a homomorphic image of a quasiperfect automaton.*

Proof of the 'if' part of (i). First, we prove that a homomorphic image of a permutation automaton is also a permutation automaton. Let $B = (T, X)$ be a permutation automaton such that $A \leq B$ and $h \in Hom(B, A)$. For any $s \in S$, there exists $t \in T$ such that $h(t) = s$. Since B is a permutation automaton, for any $x \in X$ there exists $t' \in T$ such that $t'x^B = t$. We have $h(t')x^A = h(t'x^B) = h(t) = s$. This means that x^A is a permutation on S, i.e. A is a permutation automaton. Since it is easy to see that a transitive automaton is a permutation automaton, the 'if' part of (i) is now obvious.
Proof of the 'if' part of (ii). A homomorphic image of a connected automaton is always connected. Hence, the conclusion follows from the above.
Proof of the 'only if' part of (ii). Obvious from Proposition 3.6.
Proof of the 'only if' part of (i). We can denote $A = A_1 + A_2 + \cdots + A_r$ where each $A_i(1 \leq i \leq r)$ is a connected permutation automaton. Since $A_i \leq \bar{A}_i(1 \leq i \leq r)$ and $V_X(Qp)$ is a lattice, there exists a quasiperfect automaton B such that $A_i \leq B$ for any $i(1 \leq i \leq r)$. It is easy to see that $A \leq rB$. $\qquad\square$

Corollary 3.8. *$V_X(Cp)$, the class of all connected permutation X-automata, and $V_X(Pm)$, the class of all permutation X-automata, are the minimum strong classes containing, respectively, $V_X(Qp)$ and $V_X(Tr)$.*

Proposition 3.9. *Let $A, B \in V_X(Pm)$. Then $[A \circ B]_{V(Pm)} = [A \circ B]_{V(Au)} \neq \emptyset$. Let $A, B \in V_X(Cp)$. Then $[A \circ B]_{V(Cp)} = [A \circ B]_{V(S)} = [A \circ B]_{V(Au)} \neq \emptyset$.*

Proof. By the result in [4], we know that $[A \circ B]_{V(Au)} \subseteq \{C \mid C$ is a subautomaton of $A \times B\}$ and that $[A \circ B]_{V(Au)} \neq \emptyset$. However, it is easy to see that any (connected) subautomaton of $A \times B$ is also a (connected) permutation automaton. $\qquad\square$

Proposition 3.10. *For any X, $V_X(Pm)$ does not form a lattice.*

Proof. Let A, A', B and B' be the following permutation automata.
$A = (\{a, b_1, b_2\}, X), ax^A = a, b_1x^A = b_2, b_2x^A = b_1$ for any $x \in X$.
$A' = (\{a, b_1, b_2, b_3\}, X), ax^{A'} = a, b_1x^{A'} = b_2, b_2x^{A'} = b_3, b_3x^{A'} = b_1$ for any $x \in X$.
$B = (\{a_1, a_2, b_1, b_2, b_3\}, X), a_1x^B = a_2, a_2x^B = a_1, b_1x^B = b_2, b_2x^B = b_3, b_3x^B = b_1$ for any $x \in X$.
$B' = (\{a, b_1, b_2, \ldots, b_6\}, X), ax^{B'} = a, b_1x^{B'} = b_2, \ldots, b_5x^{B'} = b_6, b_6x^{B'} = b_1$ for any $x \in X$.
Then it can easily be seen that $B, B' \in [A \circ A']_{V(Pm)}$. $\qquad\square$

Proposition 3.11. *Let $|X| \geq 2$. Then $V_X(Cp)$ does not form a lattice.*

Proof. See the proof of Theorem 3.2 in [4].   □

The following result can easily be proved.

Proposition 3.12. *Let $|X| = 1$. Then $V_X(Cp) = V_X(Qp) = V_X(S)$ forms a lattice. As a poset, it is isomorphic to $\mathbf{N}$ where the partial order is defined as follows: $r' \leq r$ holds iff r is divisible by r'.*

The following result is useful.

Proposition 3.13. *Let $A, A' \in V_X(Cp)$ and let $B \in [A \circ B]_{V(Cp)}$. Then $\bar{B} = [\bar{A} \circ \bar{A}']_{V(Qp)}$.*

Proof. Since $V_X(Cp)$ is a strong class, B is a connected subautomaton of $A \times A'$. Any connected subautomaton of $\bar{A} \times \bar{A}'$ is isomorphic to $[\bar{A} \circ \bar{A}']_{V(Qp)}$ (See [4]). Since $A \times A'$ is a homomorphic image of $\bar{A} \times \bar{A}'$, we conclude that $B \leq [\bar{A} \circ \bar{A}']_{V(Qp)}$. Thus, by Proposition 3.6 we have $\bar{B} \leq [\bar{A} \circ \bar{A}']_{V(Qp)}$. Now, we show the converse. $\bar{B}$ is a quasiperfect automaton such that $A, A' \leq \bar{B}$. Hence, by proposition 3.6, we have $\bar{A}, \bar{A}' \leq \bar{B}$. Thus we have $[\bar{A} \circ \bar{A}'] \leq \bar{B}$.   □

4. Transitive cofinal automata

In this section, we define a transitive cofinal automaton. Assume that $A = (S, X)$ is a cofinal automaton.

Definition 4.1. Let $S_f = \{s \in S \mid$ there exists some $p \in X^*$ such that $Sp^A = s\}$. Then S_f is called the *strongly cofinal part* of S (with respect to A).

The following lemma can easily be proved.

Lemma 4.2. *Let $A = (S, X)$ be a cofinal automaton. Then for any $(s, x) \in S_f \times X$, we have $sx^A \in S_f$. Moreover, for any $s, t \in S_f$, there exists $p \in X^*$ such that $t = sp^A = tp^A$.*

Definition 4.3. Let $A = (S, X)$ be a cofinal automaton. Then, the automaton $A_f = (S_f, X)$ is called the *strongly cofinal part* of A where $sx^{A_f} = sx^A$ for any $(s, x) \in S_f \times X$.

By Lemma 4.2, we have the following.

Lemma 4.4. *Let $A = (S, X)$ be a cofinal automaton. Then $A_f = (S_f, X)$ is strongly cofinal.*

Remark 4.5. In [3], Dang Huu Dao called A_f the strongly connected part of a directable automaton A, and he used this subautomaton for an investigation of the characteristic semigroup and the endomorphism semigroup of A.

The following result, which is a special case of a theorem in [3], can easily be proved by a similar way to the proof of Lemma 1.5.

Lemma 4.6. *Let $A = (S, X)$ be a cofinal automaton and $h \in Aut(A)$. Then $h(s) = s$ for any $s \in S_f$.*

Corollary 4.7. *Let $h \in Aut(A)$ and let $s \in S$. Then $s \in S_f$ holds iff $h(s) \in S_f$ holds.*

From the above result, for any $h \in Aut(A), h|_{S_f}$ equals the identity on S_f and $h|(S - S_f)$ is a permutation on $S - S_f$ where $h|_K$ means the restriction of h to K.

Definition 4.8. A cofinal automaton $A = (S, X)$ is called a *transitive cofinal automaton* (or briefly a TC automaton) if either $\{h|_{(S-S_f)} \mid h \in Aut(A)\}$ is transitive on $S-S_f$, i.e. for any $s, t \in S-S_f$ there exists $h \in Aut(A)$ such that $t = h(s)$, or $S - S_f = \emptyset$, i.e. A is strongly cofinal. A transitive cofinal automaton $A = (S, X)$ is called a *strictly transitive cofinal automaton* (or briefly an STC automaton) if it is not strongly cofinal.

Lemma 4.9. *Let $A = (S, X)$ be an STC automaton. Then, we have the following two results: (i) There exists $(s, x) \in (S-S_f) \times X$ such that $sx^A \in S_f$. (ii) Let $(s, x) \in (S - S_f) \times X$. If $sx^A \in S_f$, then $(S - S_f)x^A = sx^A$.*

Proof. (i) Let $t \in S - S_f$. Then there exists $p = x_1 x_2 \cdots x_r \in X^*$ such that $tp^A \subset S_f$ where $r \geq 1$ and $x_i \in X(1 \leq i < r)$. It is obvious that there exists some $k(1 \leq k \leq r)$ such that $t(x_1 x_2 \ldots x_{k-1})^A \in S - S_f$ and $t(x_1 x_2 \ldots x_{k-1} x_k)^A \in S_f$. Let $s = t(x_1 x_2 \ldots x_{k-1})^A$ and let $x = x_k$. Then we have $s \in S - S_f$ and $sx^A \in S_f$. (ii) Let $t \in S - S_f$. Since A is an STC automaton, there exists some $h \in Aut(A)$ such that $t = h(s)$. By Lemma 4.4, we have $tx^A = h(s)x^A = h(sx^A) = sx^A$. Thus $(S - S_f)x^A = sx^A$ holds. $\square$

Definition 4.10. Let $A = (S, X)$ be an STC automaton. Then $X_t = X - \{x \in X \mid (S - S_f)x^A \in S_f\}$ is called the *transitive part* of X (with respect to A). Furthermore, $S_t = S - S_f$ is called the *transitive part* of S (with respect to A).

By Lemma 4.9, we have the following.

Lemma 4.11. *Let $A = (S, X)$ be an STC automaton such that $X_t \neq \emptyset$. Then for any $(s, x) \in S_f \times X_f$ we have $sx^A \in S_t$.*

Definition 4.12. Let $A = (S, X)$ be an STC automaton such that $X_t \neq \emptyset$. Then, the automaton $A_t = (S_t, X_t)$ is called the *transitive part* of A where $sx^{A_t} = sx^A$ for any $(s, x) \in S_t \times X_t$.

The proofs of the following three lemmas are not difficult.

Lemma 4.13. *Let $A = (S, X)$ be an STC automaton such that $X_t \neq \emptyset$. Then $A_t = (S_t, X_t)$ is a transitive automaton.*

Lemma 4.14. *Let $|X| = 1$. Then $V_X(TC)$ and $V_X(STC)$ are totally ordered sets and the former is a strong class.*

Lemma 4.15. *Let $|X| \leq 2$. Then $V_X(TC)$ and $V_X(STC)$ are not strong classes.*

Lemma 4.16. *Let $A = (S, X)$ and $B = (T, X)$ be STC automata such that $B \geq A$. Then for any $h \in Hom(A, B), h(S_f) = T_f$ holds. Hence $B_f \leq A_f$.*

Proof. Let $s \in S_f$. Then there exists $p \in X^*$ such that $Sp^A = s$. Hence $h(s) = h(Sp^A) = h(S)p^B = Tp^B$. This means that $h(s) \in T_f$. Since B_f is strongly connected, we have $h(S_f) = T_f$. $\square$

Lemma 4.17. *Let $A = (S, X)$ and $B = (T, X)$ be STC automata such that $B \leq A$. Then the transitive part of X w.r.t. A coincides with the transitive part of X w.r.t. B.*

Proof. Let $h \in Hom(A, B)$ and let $Sx^A = s$ where $(s, x) \in S_f \times X$. Then we have $Tx^B = h(S)x^B = h(Sx^A) = h(s)$. This means that the transitive part of X w.r.t. B is included in that w.r.t. A. Conversely, let $h(s) = t$ with $s \in S$ and $t \in T_t$. Then, by lemma 4.16, we have $s \in S_t$. Let x be contained in the transitive part of X w.r.t. A. Then we have $sx^A \in S_t$. By Lemma 2.2, there exists $p \in X^*$ such that $(sx^A)p^A = s$. Thus we have $t = h(s) = h(s(xp)^A) = h(s)(xp)^B = t(xp)^B = (tx^B)p^B$. Hence $tx^B \in T_t$. This means that x is contained in the transitive part of X w.r.t. B. $\square$

The following result follows directly from the above lemma.

Corollary 4.18. *Let $|X| \geq 2$. Then $V_X(TC)$ and $V_X(STC)$ do not form lattices.*

In what follows, we assume always that $|X| \geq 2$.

5. Indexed automata and chain compositions

In the present section, we introduce the notions of an indexed automaton and a chain composition, and determine the structure of TC-automata.

Definition 5.1. Let $B = (T, X)$ be an automaton and W be a nonempty set. A mapping of W into T is called *W-index mapping* on B.

Definition 5.2.   Let $B = (T, X) \in V_X(Scf)$, Let W be a nonempty set and Let f be a W-index mapping on B. Then a pair $\langle B, f \rangle$ is called a *W-indexed automaton*. Let $\langle B, f \rangle$ and $\langle B', f' \rangle$ be W-indexed automata.

If $f' = h_{B,B'}f$ holds, then $h_{B,B'}$ is called a *homomorphism* of $\langle B, f\rangle$ onto $\langle B', f'\rangle$ and we denote $\langle B', f'\rangle \leq \langle B, f\rangle$. Moreover, $\langle B, f\rangle$ and $\langle B', f'\rangle$ are said to be isomorphic to each other if $\langle B, f\rangle \leq \langle B', f'\rangle$ and $\langle B', f'\rangle \leq \langle B, f\rangle$. By $V_X(Ind,\ W)$ we denote the set of all isomorphic classes of W-indexed automata. $V_X(Ind,\ W)$ is considered as a poset by homomorphism relation.

Definition 5.3. Let U be a nonempty finite set and let $\langle B, f\rangle$ be an X-indexed automaton where $B = (T, X)$ is a strongly cofinal automaton. Then a chain composition of $\langle B, f\rangle$ and U, denoted by $A = \langle B, f, U\rangle$ is the automaton $A = (T \bigcup U, X)$ defined as $tx^A = tx^B$ for any $(t, x) \in T \times X$ and $Ux^A = f(x)$ for any $x \in X$. Now, assume $Y \subseteq X, Y \neq \emptyset$ and $X - Y \neq \emptyset$. Let $C = (U, Y)$ be an automaton and $\langle B, f\rangle$ be an $(X - Y)$-indexed automaton where $B = (T, X)$ is a strongly cofinal automaton. Then a chain composition of $\langle B, f\rangle$ and C, denoted by $A = \langle B, f, U\rangle$ is the automaton $A = (T \bigcup U, X)$ defined as $tx^A = tx^B$ for any $(t, x) \in T \times X$, $Uz^A = f(z)$ for any $z \in X - Y$, and $uy^A = uy^C$ for any $(u, y) \in U \times Y$.

The following result indicates the structure of STC automata.

Theorem 5.4. *An automaton $A = (S, X)$ is an STC automaton iff A is a chain composition of an indexed automaton and a nonempty finite set (or a transitive automaton).*

Proof of the 'if' part. Let $A = (T \bigcup U, X)$ be a chain composition of an indexed automaton $\langle B, f\rangle$ and a set U (or a transitive automaton $C = (U, Y)$) where $B = (T, X)$ is a strongly cofinal automaton. Then it is obvious that A is a cofinal automaton which is not strongly cofinal and $(T \cup U)_f = T, (T \cup U)_t = U$. Let h be an arbitrary permutation on U (when U is a set) or $h \in Aut(C)$ (when C is a transitive automaton). We define a mapping $\bar{h}$ of $T \cup U$ onto itself as $\bar{h}(t) = t$ for any $t \in T$ and $\bar{h}(u) = h(u)$ for any $u \in U$. Then it can easily be seen that $\bar{h} \in Aut(A)$. This implies that $\{g|_U \mid g \in Aut(A)\}$ is transitive on U. Hence A is an STC automaton.
Proof of the 'only if' part. Let $A = (S, X)$ be an STC automaton. If $X_t = \emptyset$, then it can easily be seen that $A = \langle A_f, f, S_t\rangle$ where $f(x) = S_t x^A$ for any $x \in X$. If $X_t \neq \emptyset$, then it can easily be seen that $A = \langle A_f, f, A_t\rangle$ where $f(z) = S_t z^A$ for any $z \in X - X_t$. $\qquad\square$

Let Y be a subset of X such that $X - Y \neq \emptyset$. Moreover, let $V_X(TC, Y) = \{A \in V_X(TC) \mid X_t = Y \text{ or } X_t = \emptyset\}$ and let $V_X(STC, Y) = \{A \in V_X(STC) \mid X_t = Y\}$.

The following result is a restatement of the above theorem.

Corollary 5.5. *If $Y = \emptyset$, then $V_X(STC, Y) = \{\langle B, f, U\rangle \mid \langle B, f\rangle \in V_X(Ind, X) \text{ and } U \text{ is a nonempty finite set }\}$. If $Y \neq \emptyset$, then $V_X(STC, Y) =$*

$$\{\langle B, f, C \rangle \mid \langle B, f \rangle \in V_X(Ind, X - Y), C \in V_Y(Tr)\} = \{\langle B, f, rC \rangle \mid \langle B, f \rangle \in V_X(Ind, X - Y), r \in \mathbf{N}, C \in V_Y(Qp)\}.$$

Proposition 5.6a. *Let* $Y \neq \emptyset$ *and let* $A = \langle B, f, rC \rangle$, $A' = \langle B', f', r'C' \rangle \in V_X(STC, Y)$ *where* $r, r' \in \mathbf{N}$ *and* $C, C' \in V_Y(Qp)$. *Then* $A' \leq A$ *iff* $\langle B', f' \rangle \leq \langle B, f \rangle$, $r' \leq r$ *and* $C' \leq C$.

Proof. Let $B = (T, X)$, let $B' = (T', X)$, let $rC = (U, Y)$ and let $r'C' = (U', Y)$.

Proof of the 'if' part. By Lemma 2.7, $Hom(rC, r'C') \neq \emptyset$. Let $g \in Hom(rC, r'C')$ and let k be a mapping of $T \bigcup U$ into $T' \bigcup U'$ defined as $k(t) = h_{B,B'}(t)$ for any $t \in T$ and $k(u) = g(u)$ for any $u \in U$. Then it is obvious that k is a surjection. It is also obvious that $k(t)x^{A'} = k(tx^A)$ for any $(t, x) \in T \times X$ and $k(u)y^{A'} = k(uy^A)$ for any $(u, y) \in U \times Y$. Let $(u, z) \in U \times (X - Y)$. Then since $k(u)z^{A'} \in T'$ and $uz^A \in T$, we have $k(u)z^{A'} = f'(z) = h_{B,B'}f(z) = h_{B,B'}(uz^A) = k(uz^A)$. Consequently, we have $k \in Hom(A, A')$.

Proof of the 'only if' part. Let $k \in Hom(A, A')$. By Lemma 4.16, we have $B' \leq B$, i.e., $k|_T = H_{B,B'}$. Also by Lemma 4.16, there exists a subautomaton $D = (V, Y)$ of rC such that $k|_V \in Hom(D, rC')$. Clearly, D is of type $r''C$ where $r' \leq r'' \leq r$. Moreover, since $C, C' \in V_Y(Qp)$, it is obvious that $C' \leq C$. For any $z \in X - Y, h_{B,B'}f(z) = h_{B,B'}(Vz^A) = k(Vz^A) = k(V)z^{A'} = U'z^{\overline{A}'} = f'(z)$. This means that $\langle B', f' \rangle \leq \langle B, f \rangle$. $\qquad\square$

Proposition 5.6b. *Let* $Y = \emptyset$ *and let* $A = \langle B, f, U \rangle$, $A' = \langle B', f', U' \rangle \in V_X(STC, Y)$. *Then* $A' \leq A$ *iff* $\langle B', f' \rangle \leq \langle B, f \rangle$ *and* $|U'| \leq |U|$.

Proof. The same way as above. $\qquad\square$

Corollary 5.7. *If* $Y \neq \emptyset$, *then we have* $V_X(STC, Y) \simeq V_X(Ind, X - Y) \times V_X(Tr) \simeq V_X(Ind, X - Y) \times \mathbf{N} \times V_X(Qp)$. *If* $Y = \emptyset$, *then we have* $V_X(STC, Y) \simeq V_X(Ind, X) \times \mathbf{N}$. *Here the notation* $\simeq$ *denotes the poset isomorphism relation.*

By the above result, we can insist that the essential part of the partial order structure of $V_X(STC, Y)$ is that of $V_X(Ind, X - Y)$.

Note that $V_X(Ind, X - Y)$ can be considered as a subclass of $V_X(Au)$ (more exactly, of $V_X(STC)$). See the following.

Proposition 5.8. *Let* O_Y *be the one state* Y*-automaton (when* $Y \neq \emptyset$*) or the set of one element (when* $Y = \emptyset$*). Then, as a poset,* $V_X(Ind, X - Y)$ *is isomorphic to* $\{\langle B, f, O_Y \rangle \in V_X(STC, X) \mid \langle B, f \rangle \in V_X(Ind, X - Y)\}$ *by the isomorphism* $\langle B, f \rangle \rightarrow \langle B, f, O_Y \rangle$.

6. Lattices in $V_X(STC)$

In this section, we determine all lattices in $V_X(STC)$. To this end, we introduce the notion of W-index system. We begin with the following proposition.

Proposition 6.1. *Let* $\langle B, f_B \rangle, \langle B', f_{B'} \rangle \in V_X(Ind, W)$ *and let* $D = [B \circ B']_{V(Scf)}$. *Then the following conditions are equivalent.*
(1) There exists a lattice in $V_X(Ind, W)$ *which contains* $\langle B, f_B \rangle$ *and* $\langle B', f_{B'} \rangle$.
(2) $\{\langle B, f_B \rangle, \langle B', f_{B'} \rangle\}$ *has an upper bound in* $V_X(Ind, W)$.
(3) There exists a W-*index mapping* f_D *on* D *such that* $f_B = h_{D,B} f_D$ *and* $f_{B'} = h_{D,B'} f_D$.
(4) For any $w \in W$, *there exists an element* v *of the state set of* D *such that* $h_{D,B}(v) = f_B(w)$ *and* $h_{D,B'}(v) = f_{B'}(w)$
(5) $(f_B(w), f_{B'}(w))$ *is an element of the state set of the unique strongly connected subautomaton of* $B \times B'$ *for any* $w \in W$.

Proof. $(1) \rightarrow (2)$. Obvious.
$(2) \rightarrow (3)$. Let $\langle D', f_{D'} \rangle$ be an upper bound of $\{\langle B, f_B \rangle, \langle B', f_{B'} \rangle\}$. Then we have $f_B = h_{D',B} f_{D'}, f_{B'} = h_{D',B'} f_{D'}$ and $D \leq D'$. Let $f_D = h_{D',D} f_{D'}$. Then by Lemma 1.5, we have $f_B = h_{D',B} f_{D'} = h_{D,B} h_{D',D} f_{D'} = h_{D,B} f_D$ and $f_{B'} = h_{D,B'} f_D$.
$(3) \rightarrow (1)$. It can easily be seen that $\{\langle D, f_D \rangle, \langle B, f_B \rangle, \langle B', f_{B'} \rangle, \langle O_X, f_O \rangle\}$ forms a lattice where O_X means the one state X-automaton and f_O is the trivial W-index mapping on O_X.
$(3) \leftrightarrow (4)$. Obvious.
$(4) \leftrightarrow (5)$. By [4], D can be considered as the unique strongly connected subautomaton of $B \times B'$, and $h_{D,B}$ and $h_{D,B'}$ are projections. $\square$

From the above result, we have the following.

Proposition 6.2. *If one of the conditions of Proposition 6.1 is satisfied, then* $\langle D, f_D \rangle = [\langle B, f_B \rangle \circ \langle B', f_{B'} \rangle]_{V(Ind,W)}$. *Otherwise,* $\{\langle B, f_B \rangle, \langle B', f_{B'} \rangle\}$ *has no upper bound in* $V_X(Ind, W)$. $\square$

Proposition 6.3. *Let* $A = \langle B, f_B, C \rangle$ *and* $A' = \langle B', f_{B'}, C' \rangle$ *be elements of* $V_X(STC, Y)$ *where* C *and* C' *are trasitive* Y-*automata (when* $Y \neq \emptyset$) *or nonempty finite sets (when* $Y = \emptyset$). *Let* $D = [B \circ B']_{V(Scf)}$. *Then following conditions are equivalent.*
(1) There exists a lattice in $V_X(STC, Y)$ *which contains* A *and* A'.
(2) There exists a lattice in $V_X(Ind, X - Y)$ *which contains* $\langle B, f_B \rangle$ *and* $\langle B', f_{B'} \rangle$.
(3) $\{\langle B, f_B \rangle, \langle B', f_{B'} \rangle\}$ *has an upper bound in* $V_X(Ind, X - Y)$.
(4) There exists an $(X - Y)$-*index mapping* f_D *on* D *such that* $f_B = h_{D,B} f_D$ *and* $f_{B'} = h_{D,B'} f_D$.
(5) For any $z \in X - Y$, *there exists an elemet* v *of the state set of* D *such that* $h_{D,B}(v) = f_B(z)$ *and* $h_{D,B'}(v) = f_{B'}(z)$.
(6) $(f_B(z), f_{B'}(z))$ *is an element of the state set of the unique strongly connected subautomaton of* $B \times B'$ *for any* $z \in X - Y$.
(7) $(f_B(z), f_{B'}(z))$ *is an element of the state set of the unique strongly connected subautomaton of* $B \times B'$ *for any* $z \in X - Y$.

Proof. (1) $\leftrightarrow$ (2). Obvious.

(6) $\leftrightarrow$ (7). We can assume that D is a subautomaton of $A \times A'$. Then it is obvious that D coincides with the unique strongly connected subautomaton of $A \times A'$. $\qquad\square$

Thus we have the following results.

Proposition 6.4a. *Assume that $Y \neq \emptyset$. Let $A = \langle B, f_B, rC \rangle$ and $A' = \langle B', f_B, r'C' \rangle$ be elements of $V_X(STC, Y)$ where $r, r' \in \mathbf{N}$ and $C, C' \in V_X(Qp)$. Let $D = [B \circ B']_{V(Scf)}$. If one of the conditions of Proposition 6.3 is satisfied, then $[A \circ A']_{V(STC,Y)} = \langle D, f_D, max\{r, r'\}[C \circ C']_{V(Qp)} \rangle$. Otherwise $\{A, A'\}$ has no upper bound in $V_X(STC, Y)$.*

Proposition 6.4b. *Assume that $Y = \emptyset$. Let $A = \langle B, f_B, U \rangle$ and $A' = \langle B', f_B, U' \rangle$ be elements of $V_X(STC, Y)$. Let $D = [B \circ B']_{V(Scf)}$. If one of the conditions of Proposition 6.3 is satisfied, then $[A \circ A']_{V(STC,Y)} = \langle D, f_D, max\{U, U'\} \rangle$ where $max\{U, U'\}$ means the set whose cardinality equals $max\{|U|, |U'|\}$. Otherwise, $\{A, A'\}$ has no upper bound in $V_X(STC, Y)$.*

Definition 6.5. Let M be a subclass of $V_X(\text{Scf})$ and let W be a nonempty set. Assume that, for each $B \in M$, a W-index mapping f_B is given. Then $F = \{f_B \mid B \in M\}$ is called a W-index system on M if $f_{B'} = h_{B,B'} f_B$ holds for any $B, B' \in M$ such that $B' \leq B$. For a W-index system $F = \{f_B\}$ on M, we denote $\langle M, F \rangle = \{\langle B, f_B \rangle \mid B \in M\}$.

The following theorem is now obvious.

Theorem 6.6. *The set of all lattices in $V_X(Ind, W)$ coincides with the set $\{\langle M, F \rangle \mid M$ is a lattice in $V_X(Scf)$ and F is a W-index system on M $\}$.*

Definition 6.7. Assume $Y = \emptyset$. Let M be a subclass of $V_X(\text{Scf})$, let $F = \{f_B\}$ be an X-index system on M, and let K be a subset of $\mathbf{N}$. Then $\langle M, F, K \rangle = \{\langle B, f_B, C \rangle \mid B \in M$ and C is a set such that $|C| \in K\}$ is called the *chain composition* of $\langle M, F \rangle$ and K. Now, assume $Y \neq \emptyset$. Let M be a subclass of $V_X(\text{Scf})$, Let $F = \{f_B\}$ be an $(X - Y)$-index system on M and let K be a subclass of $V_X(Tr)$. Then $\langle M, F, K \rangle = \{\langle B, f_B, C \rangle \mid B \in M$ and $C \in K\}$ is called the *chain composition* of $\langle M, F \rangle$ and K.

Lemma 6.8. *Let M be a lattice in $V_X(Scf)$ and let F be an $(X-Y)$-indexed system on M, i.e. $\langle M, F \rangle$ is a lattice in $V_X(Ind, X - Y)$. Moreover, let K be a subset or $\mathbf{N}$ (when $Y = \emptyset$) or a lattice in $V_X(Tr)$ (when $Y \neq \emptyset$). Then the chain composition $\langle M, F, K \rangle$ forms a lattice.*

Proof. In general, if L_1 and L_2 are lattices, then the direct product $L_1 \times L_2$ is also a lattice. The lemma is obvious from this fact. $\qquad\square$

The proof of the following lemma is not difficult and so omitted.

Lemma 6.9. *Let L be a lattice in $V_X(Scf)$, let $M = \{A_f | A \in L\}$ and let $\overline{M} = \{B \in V_X(Scf)|$ there exists $B' \in M$ such that $B \le B'\}$. Then $\overline{M}$ forms a lattice. Moreover, there exists a subset Y of X and an $(X-Y)$-index system F on $\overline{M}$ such that $L \subseteq \langle \overline{M}, F, V_Y(Tr) \rangle$ or $L \subseteq \langle \overline{M}, F, N \rangle$.*

Note that, in the above, M is not necessarily a lattice.

Lemma 6.10. *There exists a sequence of elements of $V_X(Scf)$, $A_1 \le A_2 \le \dots \le A_i \le A_{i+1} \le \dots$, such that $\overline{\{A_i \mid i \in \mathbf{N}\}} = \{A \in V_X(Scf) \mid$ there exists some $i \in \mathbf{N}$ such that $A \le A_i\} = V_X(Scf)$.*

Proof. Since $V_X(Scf)$ is a countable set, we can assume that $V_X(Scf) = \{B_1, B_2, \dots, B_i, B_{i+1}, \dots\}$. Let $A_1 = B_1$ and $A_{i+1} = [A_i \circ B_{i+1}]_{V(Scf)}$ for any $i \in \mathbf{N}$. Then we have $A_i \le A_{i+1}(i \in \mathbf{N})$ and $\overline{\{A_i \mid i \in \mathbf{N}\}} = V_X(Scf)$. $\square$

The following result is fundamental for an investigation of the structure of a class of TC automata.

Proposition 6.11. *Let M be a subclass of $V_X(Scf)$ which forms a lattice and let $\{f_B | B \in M\}$ be a W-index system on M. Then there exists a W-index system $\{g_B | B \in V_X(Scf)\}$ on $V_X(Scf)$ such that $g_B = f_B$ for any $B \in M$. Furthermore, if $\overline{M} = V_X(Scf)$, then the above W-index system is uniquely determined.*

Proof. It can easily be seen that $\overline{M}$ forms a lattice. Let $B \in \overline{M}$. Then there exists $B' \in M$ such that $B < B'$. Let $g_B(w) = h_{B',B} f_B(w)$ for any $w \in W$. Then $g_B(w)$ is well defined for any $B \in M$ and $w \in W$, and $\{g_B \mid B \in \overline{M}\}$ becomes a W-index system on $\overline{M}$ such that $g_B = f_B$ for any $B \in M$. Moreover, if $\overline{M} = V_X(Scf)$, then the above W-index system on $V_X(Scf)$ is the unique extesion of $\{f_B \mid B \in M\}$. This completes the proof of the second part of the proposition.

From the above consideration, to prove the first part of the proposition, it is enough to assume that M is a strong subclass of $V_X(Scf)$. Furthermore, we can assume $W = \{w\}$ without loss of generality. By Lemma 6.10, there exists a sequence of elements of $V_X(Scf)$, $A_1 \le A_2 \le \dots \le A_i \le \dots$, such that $\overline{\{A_i \mid i \in \mathbf{N}\}} = V_X(Scf)$. It is easy to see that, for any $i \in \mathbf{N}$, the set $\{B \in M \mid B \le A_i\}$ forms a lattice. Hence it has a maximum element B_i. Let $S_{i,j}$ and T_i be the subsets of the state set of $A_i(j, j \in \mathbf{N}, i \le j)$ defined as $S_{i,i} = h_{A_i,B_i}^{-1}(f_{B_i}(w))$, $S_{i,j} = h_{A_j,A_j}(S_{j,j})$ and $T_i = \bigcap_{j=i}^{\infty} S_{i,j}$. It is obvious that $S_{i,j} \ne \emptyset$ for any $i, j \in \mathbf{N}(i \le j)$. Moreover, we have $h_{A_i,B_i}(S_{i,j}) = h_{A_i,B_i} h_{A_j,A_j}(S_{j,j}) = h_{A_j,B_i}(S_{j,j}) = h_{B_j,B_i} h_{A_j,B_j}(S_{j,j}) = h_{B_j,B_i}(f_{B_j}(w)) = f_{B_i}(w)$. Hence $S_{ikj} \subseteq S_{i,i}$. Let $i \le j \le k$. Then we have $S_{i,k} = h_{A_k,A_i}(S_{k,k}) = h_{A_j,A_i} h_{A_k,A_j}(S_{k,k}) = h_{A_j,A_i}(S_{j,k}) \subseteq h_{A_j,A_i}(S_{j,j}) = S_{i,j}$. Moreover, note that the state set of A_i is finite. Thus, $T_i \ne \emptyset$ for any $i \in \mathbf{N}$. It is easy to see that $h_{A_j,A_i}(T_j) = T_i$ for any $i, j \in \mathbf{N}(i \le j)$. For any $i \in \mathbf{N}$, we choose inductively an element $t_i \in T_i$ as follows: Choose an element $t_1 \in T_1$. Assume that $t_{i-1} \in T_{i-1}$ is chosen. Then, choose $t_i \in T_i \cap h^{-1}_{A_i,A_{i-1}}(t_{i-1})$. Now, we define a $\{w\}$-index mapping g_B for any $B \in V_X(Scf)$ as follows: If $B \leq A_i$, then $g_B(w) = h_{A_i,B}(t_i)$. Note that $h_{A_j,A_i}(t_j) = t_i$ for any $i, j \in \mathbf{N}(i \leq j)$. Let $B \leq A_i \leq A_j(i \leq j)$. Then $h_{A_j,B}(t_j) = h_{A_i,B}h_{A_j,A_i}(t_j) = h_{A_i,B}(t_i)$. This means that g_B is well defined. Let $B \in M$ and let $B \leq B_i$. Then $g_B(w) = h_{A_i,B}(t_i) = h_{B_i,B}h_{A_i,B_i}(t_i) = h_{B_i,B}(f_{B_i}(w)) = f_B(w)$. Hence $\{g_B\}$ is an extension of $\{f_B\}$. Finally, we show that $\{g_B\}$ is a $\{w\}$-index system on V_X(Scf). Let $B' \leq B \leq A_i$. Then $h_{B,B'}(g_B(w)) = h_{B,B'}h_{A_i,B}(t_i) = h_{A_i,B'}(t_i) = g_{B'}(w)$. This completes the proof of the proposition. $\qquad\square$

Corollary 6.12. *The set of all maximal lattices in $V_X(Ind, W)$ coincides with the set $\{\langle V_X(Scf), F, N\rangle \mid F$ is an W-index system on $V_X(Scf)\}$.*

Thus we have the following theorem.

Theorem 6.13. *The set of all maximal lattices in $V_X(STC)$ coincides with the set $\{\langle V_X(Scf), F, N\rangle \mid F$ is an X-index system on $V_X(Scf)\} \cup \{\langle V_X(Scf), F, V_Y(Tr)\rangle \mid Y \subseteq X, Y \neq \emptyset, X - Y \neq \emptyset$ and F is an $(X - Y)$-index system on $V_X(Scf)\}$.*

7. Construction of maximal lattices in $V_X(STC)$

Now, we give a method to construct all maximal lattices in $V_X(STC)$. By Theorem 6.13, to this end, it is sufficient to give a method to construct all W-index systems on $V_X(Scf)$ where W is nonempty suset of X. Hence we consider a method to construct all W-index systems on $V_X(STC)$ for a nonempty finite set W.

Method 7.1. *Let A_i be the least upper bound of $\{B = (T, K) \in V_X(\text{Scf}) \mid |T| \leq i\}$, i.e. A_i is the unique strongly connected subautomaton of the direct product of all elements of the set $\{B = (T, X) \in V_X(Scf) \mid |T| \leq i\}$. Then $A_1 \leq A_2 \leq \ldots \leq A_i \ldots$ and $\overline{\{A_i \mid i \in \mathbf{N}\}} = V_X(Scf)$.*
(1) For the one state automaton $A_1 = (\{t_1\}, X)$, Let $w_1 = t_1$ for any $w \in W$. Assume that an element w_{n-1} of the state set of A_{n-1} is chosen for any $w \in W$.
(2) Compute A_n and $h_{A_n,A_{n-1}}$.
(3) For every $w \in W$, choose an arbitrary element $w_n \in h^{-1}_{A_n,A_{n-1}}(W_{n-1})$.
(4) Let $B = (T, X) \in V_X(Scf)$ such that $|T| = n$. Compute $h_{A_n,B}$ and define the W-index mapping f_B on B by $f_B(w) = h_{A_n,B}(w_n)$ for any $w \in W$. Then, $\{f_B\}$ is a W-index system on $V_X(Scf)$.
Conversely, any W-index system on $V_X(Scf)$ can be constructed by this method. The proof can easily be carried out by Proposition 6.11.

Next, we consider an algorithm to decide, for a given finite subset K of $V_X(Sfc)$, whether or not there exists a lattice in $V_X(STC)$ which contains K.

By Lemmata 6.8 and 6.9, to this end, it is sufficient to consider an algorithm to decide, for a given finite subset M of $V_X(Ind, W)$, whether there exists a lattice in $V_X(Ind, W)$ which contains M. However, such an algorithm is easily obtained from Proposition 6.1. For example:

Proposition 7.2. *Let K be a finite subset of $V_X(STC)$ and let $M = \{B_1, B_2, \ldots, B_r\} = \{A_f | A \in K\}$. Then there exists a lattice which contains K iff the following conditions are satisfied:*
(1) The transitive part of X w.r.t. all A in K are coincedent, i.e. there exists $Y \subseteq X$ such that $K \subseteq V_X(STC, Y)$.
(2) Let $\langle B, f, C \rangle, \langle B, f', C' \rangle \in K$. Then $f = f'$, i.e. for any $B_i \in M$, there exists one and only one $(X - Y)$-index system $\{f_{B_i}\}$ such that $K \subseteq \{\langle B_i, f_{B_i}, V_Y(Tr) \rangle \mid 1 \leq i \leq r\}$ or $K \subseteq \{\langle B_i, f_{B_i}, \mathbf{N} \rangle \mid 1 \leq i \leq r\}$.
(3) $(f_{B_1}(z), f_{B_2}(z), \ldots, f_{B_r}(z))$ is an element of the state set of the unique strongly connected subautomaton of $B_1 \times B_2 \times \ldots \times B_r$ for any $z \in X - Y$. $\square$

If there exists a lattice which contains K, then we can give a method to construct all maximal lattices in $V_X(STC)$ which contain K by Method 7.1 with a slight change.

For an infinite subset K of $V_X(STC)$, we have no algorithm to decide whether or not there exists a lattice which contains K. Also, we gave no method to construct a maximal lattice which contains K (See the proof of Propositions 6.11). However, we shall provide afterward a method to construct all maximal lattices in $V_X(TC)$ which contain the infinite subset $V_X(Scf)$. And also, maximal lattices in $V_X(TC)$ which contain an infinite lattice $\langle V_X(Scf), F, V_Y(Tr) \rangle$ or $\langle V_X(Scf), F, \mathbf{N} \rangle$.

Now, we show that the cardinality of the set of all maximal lattices in $V_X(STC)$ is continuous.

Lemma 7.3. *Let $B = (T, X) \in V_X(Scf)$ and let $n \in \mathbf{N}$. Then there exists $B' \in V_X(Scf)$ such that $B \leq B'$ and $h^{-1}_{B', B}(t) = n$ for any $t \in T$.*

Proof. Let $|T| = 1$. Then we define an automaton $B' = (T', X)$ as follows: $T' = \{1, 2, \ldots, n\}$, $z \in X$, $iz^{B'} = i + 1$ for $i \in \{1, 2, \ldots, n - 1\}$, $nz^{B'} = 1$ and $T'x^{B'} = 1$ for any $x \in X - \{z\}$. Then it is easy to see that B' satisfies the conclusion. Next, Let $|T| \geq 2$. Since B is cofinal, there exists $z \in X$ and $t_0, t_1, t_2 \in T$ such that $t_1 \neq t_2$ and $t_1 z^B = t_2 z^{B'} = t_0$. Then we define an automaton $B' = (T', X)$ as follows: $T' = T \times \{1, 2, \ldots, n\}$, $(t_1, 1)z^{B'} = (t_0, 1), (t_2, n)z^{B'} = (t_0, n), (t_1, i + 1)z^{B'} = (t_0, i)$ and $(t_2, i)z^{B'} = (t_0, i + 1)$ for $i = 1, 2, \ldots, n-1$, and $(t, j)x^{B'} = (tx^B, j)$ for $(t, j, x) \in T \times \{1, 2, \ldots, n\} \times X - \{t_1, t_2\} \times \{1, 2, \ldots, n\} \times \{z\}$. Since B is a strongly connected automaton, for any $t \in T - \{t_0\}$ there exists $p_t = x_1 x_2 \ldots x_{r-1} x_r \in X^*$ such that $t_0(x_1 x_2 \ldots x_i)^B \neq t_0$ for $i = 1, 2, \ldots, r - 1$ and $t_0(p_t)^B = t$. Moreover, let $p_{t_0} = \wedge$ where $\wedge$ is the identity element of X^*. Then it can easily be seen that $(t_0, i)(p_t)^{B'} = (t, i)$

for any $(t, i) \in T'$. Since B is strongly cofinal, there exists $q \in X^*$ such that $Tq^B = t_1$. It can easily be seen that $T'(qz(p_{t_1}z)^{n-2})^{B'} = (t_0, 1)$. This means that B' is cofinal. Also, we have $(t_0, 1)((p_{t_2}z)^{i-1}p_t)^{B'} = (t, i)$ for any $(t, i) \in T'$. It follows from the above that B' is strongly connected. Let h be a mapping of T' onto T such that $h((t, i)) = t$ for any $(t, i) \in T'$. It is easy to see that h is a homomorphism and $h^{-1}(t) = n$ for any $t \in T$. This completes the proof of the lemma. $\qquad\square$

Theorem 7.4. *Let W be a finite nonempty set and $\mathcal{L}$ be the set of all maximal lattices in $V_X(Ind, W)$ Then, $|\mathcal{L}| = \aleph$.*

Proof. By Lemma 6.10, there exists a sequence of elements of $V_X(Scf)$, $A_1 \leq A_2 \leq \ldots \leq A_i \leq \ldots$, such that $\overline{\{A_i \mid i \in \mathbf{N}\}} = V_X(Scf)$. Then, by using Proposition 6.11, we have $|\mathcal{L}| \leq \aleph_0^{\aleph_0} = \aleph$. Now, we prove that $|\mathcal{L}| \geq \aleph$. By Lemma 7.3, there exists a subsequence $\{B_i = (T_i, X) \mid i \in \mathbf{N}\}$ of $\{A_i \mid i \in \mathbf{N}\}$ such that $\overline{\{B_i \mid i \in \mathbf{N}\}} = V_X(Scf)$, $|T_1| \geq 2$ and $|h_{B_{i+1}, B_i}^{-1}(t)| \geq 2$ for any $i \in \mathbf{N}$ inductively as follows:

(1) $g_1(0)$ and $g_1(1)$ are arbitrary elements of T_1 such that $g_1(0) \neq g_1(1)$.

(2) $g_{i+1}(a_1, a_2, \ldots, a_i, 0)$ and $g_{i+1}(a_1, a_2, \ldots, a_i, 1)$ are elements of $h_{B_{i+1}, B_i}^{-1}(g_i(a_1, a_2, \ldots, a_i))$ such that $g_{i+1}(a_1, a_2, \ldots, a_i, 0) \neq g_{i+1}(a_1, a_2, \ldots, a_i, 1)$ for any $i \geq 1$.

We define a mapping k_i of $\mathcal{P} = \{(a_1, a_2, \ldots, a_i, \ldots) \mid a_k \in \{0, 1\}\}$ into the set of all W-index system on B_i for any $i \in \mathbf{N}$ as $k_i(a_1, a_2, \ldots, a_i, \ldots)(w) = g_i(a_1, a_2, \ldots, a_i)$ for any $w \in W$.

Then it is easy to see that $\{k_i \mid i \in \mathbf{N}\}$ induces a mapping of $\mathcal{P}$ into the set of all W-index system on $\{B_i \mid i \in \mathbf{N}\}$. Since a W-index system on $\{B_i \mid i \in \mathbf{N}\}$ is uniquely extended to a W-index system on $V_X(Scf)$, we get a mapping of $\mathcal{P}$ into $\mathcal{L}$. It is easy to see that this mapping is an injection. Therefore, $|\mathcal{L}| \geq 2^{\mathbf{N}} = \aleph$. $\qquad\square$

Corollary 7.5. *The cardinality of the set of all maximal lattices in $V_X(Scf)$ is continuous.*

Remark 7.6. Using results in Section 10, we can prove that the cardinality of the set of all maximal lattices is $V_X(Scf)$ is also continuous.

8. Weighted posets

Before dealing with lattices in $V_X(TC)$, we define, in this section, a weighted poset and provide some properties of weighted posets.

Definition 8.1. A poset S is called a *weighted poset* if S satisfies the following conditions: (i) S is a countable set. (ii) $\{b \in S \mid b \leq a\}$ is a finite set for any $a \in S$.

The following lemma can easily be verified.

Lemma 8.2. *Let S be a weighted poset. Then we have the following results:*
(1) Let $L \subseteq S$ and $a, a' \in L$. Then $|[a \circ a']_L| \geq 1$ iff $\{a, a'\}$ has at least one upper bound in L where $[a \circ a']_L$ means the set of all minimal upper bound of $\{a, a'\}$ in L.
(2) Let L be a lower semilattice in S. Then, for any $a, a' \in L$, we have $|[a \circ a']_L| \leq 1$.
(3) Let L be a lower semilattice in S. Then L forms a lattice iff, for any $a, a' \in L, \{a, a'\}$ has at least one upper bound in L.
(4) Let $L \subseteq S$ and $a, a' \in L$. Then $|[a * a']_L| \geq 1$ iff $\{a, a'\}$ has at least one lower bound in L where $[a * a']_L$ means the set of all maximal lowe bounds of $\{a, a'\}$ in L.
(5) Let L be an upper semilattice in S. Then L forms a lattice iff, for any $a, a' \in L$, we have $[a * a']_L \leq 1$.
(6) Let L be an upper semilattice in S. Then L forms a lattice iff, for any $a, a' \in L, \{a, a'\}$ has at least one lower bound in L.
(7) Let L be a subset of S which has a minimum element. Then L forms a lattice iff L is an upper semilattice.

By using the Zorn's lemma, we can prove the following.

Proposition 8.3. *Let S be a weighted poset. Then for any lattice L in S, there exists at least one maximal lattice in S which contains L. Moreover, if for any $a \in S$, there exists some $b \in S$ such that $a \leq b$ and $a \neq b$, then any maximal lattice in S is an infinite set.*

Note that $V_X(Au)$ is a weighted poset with the minimum element. Since any subposet of a weighted poset is also a weighted poset, any subclass of $V_X(Au)$ is a weighted poset.

It can easily be seen that, if S is a weighted poset with the minimum element 0, then any maximal lattice in S contains 0.

9. Maximal lattices in weighted posets

Definition 9.1. Let S be a poset and let $R \subseteq S$. Then we denote $\bar{R} = \{a \in S \mid$ there exists $b \in R$ such that $a \leq b\}$. R is called a *strong subset* of S if $\bar{R} = R$.

In this section, we assume that S is a weighted poset with the minimum element 0, R is a strong subset of S and $Q = S - R$ forms a lattice. Our purpose is to investigate the structure of S and to consider a method to construct maximal lattices in S which contain Q.

Definition 9.2. Let $r \in R$. Then the set of all minimal elements of $\{q \in Q \mid r \leq q\}$ is denoted by $\tilde{r}$. r is called an *element with the admissible property* (or briefly an AP element) of R if $|\tilde{r}| \geq 1$, i.e., there exists some $q \in Q$ such that $r \leq q$. If $|\tilde{r}| = 1$, then r is called an *element with the minimal* *property* (or briefly an MP element) and the unique element of $\tilde{r}$ is also denoted by $\tilde{r}$.

Let R_A and R_M be the sets of, respectively, all AP elements and all MP elements. The following lemmas can easily be verified.

Lemma 9.3. *Let $r \in R$. Then $r \in R_A$ iff there exists a lattice $L \subseteq S$ such that $r \in L$ and $L \not\subseteq R$.*

Lemma 9.4. *(i) Let $r, r' \in R_M$ and $r' \leq r$. Then for any $q \in \tilde{r}$, there exists $q' \in \tilde{r'}$ such that $q' \leq q$. (ii) Let $r, r' \in R_M$ and $r' \leq r$. Then, $\tilde{r'} \leq \tilde{r}$.*

Lemma 9.5. *Let $r, r' \in R_A$. Then $[r \circ r']_S = [r \circ r']_R \cup (\{q'' \in Q \mid q''$ is a minimal element of $\{[q \circ q']_Q \mid q \in \tilde{r}, q' \in \tilde{r'}\}\} = \{q'' \in Q \mid$ there exists $r'' \in [r \circ r']_R$ such that $r'' \leq q''\})$.*

Lemma 9.6. *Let $r, r' \in R_A$ and $r'' \in [r \circ r']_R$. Then for any $q'' \in \tilde{r''}$, there exists $q \in \tilde{r}$ and $q' \in \tilde{r'}$ such that $[q \circ q']_Q \leq q''$.*

Lemma 9.7. *(i) Let $q \in Q$ and $r \in R_A$. Then $[q \circ r]_S = \{q'' \in Q \mid q''$ is a minimal element of $\{[q \circ q']_Q \mid q' \in \tilde{r}\}\}$ (ii) Let $q \in Q$ and $r \in R_M$. Then $[q \circ r]_S = [q \circ \tilde{r}]_Q$.*

Definition 9.8. Let P be a subset of R which contains 0. Then P is called a *lattice generating set* (or briefly an LGS) if $P \cup Q$ forms a lattice. A maximal element of the set of all LGS's is called a *maximal* LGS.

By Proposition 6.3, for any LGS P, there exists at least one maximal LGS which contains P.

Proposition 9.9. *Let $r \in R$. Then $r \in R_M$ iff there exists an LGS which contains r.*

Proof of the 'if' part. Let P be an LGS which contains r. By Lemma 9.3, $r \in R_A$. Now, suppose that $r \notin R_M$. Then there exists $q, q' \in \tilde{r}$ such that $q \neq q'$. Since $[q \circ q']_Q \leq [q \circ q']_{P \cup Q}$ and $[q \circ q']_Q \in Q$, we have $[q \circ q']_{P \cup Q} \in Q$. On the other hand, $r \leq [q \circ q']_{P \cup Q} \leq q, q'$. This contradicts the minimality of q and q' in Q. Therefore, $r \in R_M$.
Proof of the 'only if' part. It can easily be seen that $\{0, r\} \cup Q$ forms a lattice. $\qquad\square$

The proof of the following lemma is not difficult and so it is omitted.

Lemma 9.10. *Let $P \subseteq R_M$. Then P is an LGS iff the following condition is satisfied: For any $p, p' \in P$, if $[p \circ p']_P \neq \emptyset$, then $|[p \circ p']_P| = 1$ and $[p \circ p']_P \leq [\tilde{p} \circ \tilde{p'}]_Q$.*

Lemma 9.11. *Let $P \subseteq R_M$. Then P is an LGS iff the following condition is satisfied: $P \cap F$ is an LGS for any finite strong subset F of R.*

Proof of the 'if' part. Let $p, p' \in P$ and let $[p \circ p']_P \neq \emptyset$. Assume that $r, r' \in [p \circ p']_P$. Let $F = \overline{\{r, r'\}}$. It is obvious that $r, r' \in [p \circ p']_{P \cap F}$. Therefore, by Lemma 9.10, $r = r' = [p \circ p']_{P \cap F}$ and $[p \circ p']_{P \cap F} \leq [\tilde{p} \circ \tilde{p'}]_Q$. Consequently, we have $|[p \circ p']_P| = 1$ and $[p \circ p']_P \leq [\tilde{p} \circ \tilde{p'}]_Q$. By Lemma 9.10, P is an LGS. *Proof of the 'only if' part.* Let $p, p' \in P \cap F$ and $[p \circ p']_{P \cap F} \neq \emptyset$. Assume $r, r' \in [p \circ p']_{P \cap F}$. Note that $[p \circ p']_{P \cap F} \neq \emptyset$ implies $[p \circ p']_P \neq \emptyset$. Since P is an LGS , by Lemma 9.10, we have $|[p \circ p']_P| = 1$ and $[p \circ p']_P \leq [\tilde{p} \circ \tilde{p'}]_Q$. Because of $[p \circ p']_P \leq r, r' \in F = \bar{F}$, we have $[p \circ p']_P \in P \cap F$. Thus we have $r = r' = [p \circ p']_P = [p \circ p']_{P \cap F}$. Moreover, we have $[p \circ p']_{P \cap F} \leq [\tilde{p} \circ \tilde{p'}]_Q$. Therefore, by Lemma 9.10, $P \cap F$ is an LGS. $\qquad\square$

Now, we consider a method to construct maximal lattices in S which contain Q, i.e. a method to construct maximal LGS 's.

Method 9.12. *Let f be a bijective mapping of $\mathbf{N}$ onto R_M. We determine a subset O_i of R_M for any $i \in \mathbf{N}$ as follows: (1) $O_1 = \{f(1)\}$. Note that, by Proposition 9.9, there exists an LGS P_1 such that $O_1 \subseteq P_1$. (2) Assume that O_{i-1} is determined for $i \geq 2$. If there exists an LGS P_i such that $O_{i-1} \cup \{f(i)\} \subseteq P_i$, then $O_i = O_{i-1} \cup \{f(i)\}$. Otherwise, $O_i = O_{i-1}$. By Lemma 9.11, P_i can be chosen as a subset of $\overline{O_{i-1} \cup \{f(i)\}}$. (3) Let $P_f = \cup_{i=1}^{\infty} O_i$.*

It is easy to see that there exists an LGS P_i such that $O_i \subseteq P_i \subseteq \bar{O}_i$ and $P_i \cap \{f(j) \mid j \leq i\} = O_i$ for any $i \in \mathbf{N}$. Also, we can see easily that $P_f \cap \{f(j) \mid j \leq i\} = O_i$ for any $i \in \mathbf{N}$.

Theorem 9.13. *Method 9.12 is a method to construct all maximal LGS's.*

Proof. First, we prove that, for any bijection f of $\mathbf{N}$ onto R_M, P_f is a maximal LGS. Let $p, p' \in P_f$ and let $[p \circ p']_{P_f} \neq \emptyset$. Assume $r, r' \in [p \circ p']_{P_f}$. Then there exists a sufficiently large $i \in \mathbf{N}$ such that $p, p', r, r' \in O_i \subseteq P_i$ where P_i is an LGS. Since P_i is an LGS, by Lemma 9.10 we have $r = r' = [p \circ p']_{P_i} \leq [p \circ p']_Q$. Therefore, by using Lemma 9.10 again, P_f becomes an LGS. Now, we show the maximality of P_f. Let P be an LGS such that $P_f \subseteq P$. Then, for any $f(i) \in P - P_f, O_{i-1} \cup \{f(i)\}$ is contained in an LGS P. Hence $f(i)$ must be contained in O_i. Thus we have $P - P_f$. Consequently, P_f is a maximal LGS. Now, we prove that, for any maximal LGS $P(\subseteq R_M)$, there exists a bijection f of $\mathbf{N}$ onto R_M such that $P = P_f$. To this end, we define the following set $\mathcal{H} = \{T \mid T \in R_M$ and, for any finite subset F of R_M, there exists an LGS P_F such that $T \cap F \subseteq P_F\}$. Note that, by using the Zorn's lemma, we can prove that for any $T' \in \mathcal{H}$ there exists a maximal element T in $\mathcal{H}$ such that $T' \subseteq T$. Let T be a maximal element in $\mathcal{H}$ and $r \in R_M - T$. Since $T \cup \{r\} \notin \mathcal{H}$, there exists a finite set F of R_M such that there exists no LGS which contains $(T \cup \{r\}) \cap F$. By $T \in \mathcal{H}$, we have $r \in F$. Consequently, there exists no LGS which contains $(T \cap F) \cup \{r\}$. This insists that there exists a finite nonempty subset F_r of T such that any LGS which contains F_r does not contain r. Now, we prove that there exists a bijection f of $\mathbf{N}$ onto R_M such that $T = P_f$. Let g be a bijection of $\mathbf{N}$ onto $2\mathbf{N} = \{2i \mid i \in \mathbf{N}\}$ and let h be a bijection of $\mathbf{N}$ onto $R_M - T$. We extend g to an injection of R_M into $\mathbf{N}$ as follows: $g(h(1)) = \max\{g(t) \mid t \in F_{h(1)}\} + 1$ and $g(h(i)) = \max\{\max\{g(t) \mid t \in F_{h(1)}\} + 1, g(h(i-1)) + 2\}$ for $i \geq 2$. Let g' be the order preserving bijection of $g(R_M)$ onto $\mathbf{N}$ and let $f = (g'g)^{-1}$. Then f is a bijection of $\mathbf{N}$ onto R_M. It can easily be seen that $T = P_f$. We are ready to complete the proof of the theorem. Let P be a maximal LGS. Since $P \in \mathcal{H}$, there exists a maximal element T in $\mathcal{H}$ such that $P \subseteq T$. We have proved that, in this case, there exists a bijection f of $\mathbf{N}$ onto R_M such that $T = P_f$. Hence we have $P \subseteq P_f$. Since P_f is a maximal LGS , we have $P = P_f$. This completes the proof of the theorem. $\qquad\square$

For the later use, we consider from now on the following special case:
For any $r, r' \in R_M, r' \leq r$ iff $\tilde{r}' \leq \tilde{r}$.

Remark 9.14. It is easy to see that above condition implies that for any $r, r' \in R_M, r' = r$ iff $\tilde{r}' \leq \tilde{r}$.

Definition 9.15. Let $r, r' \in R_M$. Then a pair (r, r') is called a *very good pair* if $\{r, r'\}$ has no upper bound in R_M. (r, r') is called a *good pair* if $|[r \circ r']_{R_M}| = 1$ and $[r \circ r']_{R_M} = [r \circ r']_Q$. Otherwise, (r, r') is called a *bad pair*.

The following result can easily be proved.

Lemma 9.16. *(1) If (r, r') is a very good pair in R_M, then $[r \circ r']_{R_M \cup Q} = [r \circ r']_Q$.*
(2) If (r, r') is a good pair in R_M, then $[r \circ r']_{R_M \cup Q} = [r \circ r']_{R_M}$.
(3) If (r, r') is a bad pair in R_M, then $|[r \circ r']_{R_M \cup Q}| \geq 2$.

Proposition 9.17. *Let P be a subset of R_M which contains 0. Then P is an LGS iff the following conditions are satisfied: For any good pair (r, r') in P, if $[r \circ r']_{R_M} \notin P$, then, $\{r, r'\}$ has no upper bound in P. For any bad pair (r, r') in P, $\{r, r'\}$ has no upper bound in P.*

Proof. Proof of the 'if' part is easy. So, we prove only the 'only if' part. Assume that there exist a good pair (r, r') and $p' \in P$ such that $[r \circ r']_{R_M} \notin P$ and $r, r' \leq P'$. Since $P = [r \circ r']_{P \cup Q} \leq p' \in P$, we have $p \in P$. Therefore, $[r \circ r']_{R_M} \leq p$ and $[r \circ r']_{R_M} \neq p$. Consequently, by Lemma 9.4, we have $[\tilde{r} \circ \tilde{r}']_Q = \widetilde{[r \circ r']_{R_M}} \leq \tilde{p}$. On the other hand, since $r, r' \leq [\tilde{r} \circ \tilde{r}']_Q$, we have $p = [r \circ r']_{P \cup Q} \leq [\tilde{r} \circ \tilde{r}']_Q$ and thus $\tilde{p} \leq [\tilde{r} \circ \tilde{r}']_Q$. Hence we have $\tilde{p} = [\tilde{r} \circ \tilde{r}']_Q = \widetilde{[r \circ r']_{R_M}}$. By Remark 9.14, we have $p = [r \circ r']_{R_M}$. However, this is a contradiction. Now, we assume that there exist a bad pair (r, r') and $p' \in P$ such that $r, r' \leq p'$. Since $p = [r \circ r']_{P \cup Q} \leq p' \in p$, we have $p \in P$. Let t be an element of $[r \circ r']_{R_M}$ such that $t \leq p$. Then $\tilde{t} \leq \tilde{p}$. On the other hand, since $r, r' \leq \tilde{t}$ and $\tilde{t} \in Q$, we have $p = [r \circ r']_{P \cup Q} \leq \tilde{t}$. Hence $\tilde{p} \leq \tilde{t}$ and $\tilde{p} = \tilde{t}$. By Remark 9.14, we have $t = p$. We show that $[r \circ r']_{R_M}$ is a singleton. Let $u \in [r \circ r']_{R_M}$ and $u \neq p$. Since $r, r' \leq \tilde{u} \in Q, p = [r \circ r']_{P \cup Q} \leq \tilde{u}$ holds. Therefore, $\tilde{p} \leq \tilde{u}$. By Remark 9.14, we have $p \leq u$. However, this contradicts the fact $p \in [r \circ r']_{R_M}$. Consequently, we have $p = [r \circ r']_{R_M}$. Next, by $p \leq [\tilde{r} \circ \tilde{r}']_Q$, we have $\tilde{p} \leq [\tilde{r} \circ \tilde{r}']_Q$. On the other hand, from the fact that $\tilde{p} \in Q$ and $r, r' \leq \tilde{p}$, we have $\tilde{r}, \tilde{r}' \in \tilde{p}$. Hence $[\tilde{r} \circ \tilde{r}']_Q \leq \tilde{p}$ holds. This means that $[r \circ r']_{R_M}$ is a singleton and $\widetilde{[r \circ r']}_{R_M} = [\tilde{r} \circ \tilde{r}']_Q$. This contradicts the assumption that (r, r') is a bad pair. $\square$

The following results can easily be verified by using Proposition 9.17.

Lemma 9.18. *An intersection of any number of LGS's is also an LGS.*

Theorem 9.19. *Let $T \subseteq R_M$. Assume that T is contained in an LGS. Then there exists the minimum LGS T' which contains T.*

We can construct the above T' by the following method:

Proposition 9.20. *Let $T \subseteq R_M$. Let $T_1 = T$ and let $T_i = \{[t \circ t']_{R_M} \mid t, t' \in T_{i-1}, (t, t')$ is a good pair and there exists $t'' \in T$ such that $t, t' \leq t''\}$ for $i \geq 2$. Let $T' = \cup_{i=1}^{\infty} T_i$. If T' is an LGS, then T' is the minimum LGS which contains T. If T' is not an LGS, then there exists no LGS which contains T.*

Note that, if $T_j \subseteq \cup_{i=1}^{j-1} T_i$ for some $j \in \mathbf{N}$, then $T_k \subseteq \cup_{i=1}^{j-1} T_i$ for any $j \in \mathbf{N}$ such that $j \leq k$. When T is finite, the above method ends in finite steps. Hence the above method gives an algorithm to construct the minimum LGS which contains T if it exists. Also, it gives an algorithm to decide whether or not there exists an LGS which contains T.

Remark 9.21. In general, Lemma 9.18 and Theorem 9.19 do not hold when we do not require the condition of the special case. Let $S = \{0, 1, \ldots, 7\}$ be a poset defined by $0 < 1 < 3$, $0 < 2 < 3 < 4 < 5 < 7$ and $4 < 6 < 7$. Then $R = R_M = \{0, 1, \ldots, 6\}$ and $Q = \{7\}$. Consider $T = R_M - \{3\}$ and $T' = R_M - \{4\}$. Then, T and T' are LGS 's. However, $T \cap T' = R_M - \{3, 4\}$ is not an LGS. This indicates, at the same time, that there does not exists the minimum LGS which contains $T \cap T'$ is contained in an LGS.

10. Structure of $V_X(TC)$

In Section 6, the structures of maximal lattices in $V_X(STC)$ are made clear using the notions of indexed automaton and index system. However, the situation is more complicated in the case of $V_X(TC)$. Form now on, we investigate the structures of lattices, especially maximal lattices, in $V_X(TC)$. To this end, some results in Section 9 will be applied.

For a subset Y of $X(X - Y \neq \emptyset)$ and an $(X - Y)$-index system $F = \{f_B\}$ on $V_X(Scf)$, we denote by $M(F)$, the set $\langle V_X(Scf), F, V_Y(Tr)\rangle \cup V_X(Scf)$ (when $Y \neq \emptyset$) or $\langle V_X(Scf), F, \mathbf{N})\rangle \cup V_X(Scf)$ (when $Y = \emptyset$).

Lemma 10.1. *Let L be a lattice in $V_X(TC)$. Then, there exist a subset Y of $X(X - Y \neq \emptyset)$ and an $(X - Y)$-index system F on $V_X(Scf)$ such that $L \subseteq M(F)$.*

Proof. When $L \subseteq V_X(Scf)$, for any $(X - Y)$-index system F on $V_X(Scf)$ we hav $L \subseteq M(F)$. Now, assume that $L \cap V_X(STC) \neq \emptyset$. By Lemma 4.17, we can easily see that, for any $A, A' \in L \cap V_X(STC)$, the transitive parts of X w.r.t. A and A' are coincident. By Y, we denote this transitive part of X. Let $O_{X,Y} = (\{s, t\}, X)$ be the automaton such that $sx^{O_{X,Y}} = s \ (x \in X)$, $ty^{O_{X,Y}} = t \ (y \in Y)$ and $tz^{O_{X,Y}} = s \ (z \in X - Y)$. Then $O_{X,Y} \in V_X(STC)$ and $O_{X,Y} \leq A$ for any $A \in L \cap V_X(STC)$. Hence $(L \cap V_X(STC)) \cup \{O_{X,Y}\}$ forms a lattice in $V_X(STC)$. Hence by Theorem 6.13, there exists an $(X - Y)$-index system F on $V_X(Scf)$ such that $L \subseteq M(F)$. $\qquad\qquad\square$

From the above, to deal with lattices in $V_X(TC)$, it is sufficient to consider lattices in $M(F)$ for a subset Y of X and an $(X - Y)$-index system F on $V_X(Scf)$.

For an X-automaton $A = (S, X)$ and a nonempty subset Y of X, we denote by A_Y the Y-automaton $A_Y = (S, Y)$ such that $sy^{A_Y} = sy^A$ for any $(s, y) \in S \times Y$.

Definition 10.2. Assume that $\emptyset \neq Y \subseteq X$ and $X - Y \neq \emptyset$. Let $B = (T, X) \in V_X(Scf)$, let f be an $(X - Y)$-index mapping on B and let $D = (V, Y)$ be a subautomaton of $B_Y = (T, Y)$. Then D is called an *f-admissible part* of B if $D \in V_Y(Cp)$ and $Vz^B = f(z)$ for any $z \in X - Y$. Now, assume $Y = \emptyset$. Let $B = (T, X) \in V_X(Scf), d \in T$ and f be an X-index mapping on B. Then d is called an *f-admissible part* of B if $dx^B = f(x)$ for any $x \in X$.

Definition 10.3. Let $B = (T, X) \in V_X(Scf)$ and let f be an $(X - Y)$-index mapping on B. Then B is called a *strongly cofinal automaton with the f-admissible property* (or briefly an f-AP automaton) if B has at least one f-admissible part. Let $F = \{f_B \mid B \in V_X(Scf)\}$ be an $(X - Y)$-index system on $V_X(Scf)$. Then an f_B-AP automaton is called an *F-AP automaton*. We denote by $V_X(F\text{-}AP)$ the set of all F-AP automata.

Lemma 10.4. *There exists $B \in V_X(Scf)$ satisfying the following conditions: For any nonempty subset Y of $X \ (X - Y \neq \emptyset)$ and for any $(X - Y)$-index mapping f on B, B has no f-admissible part.*

Proof. Let $B = (\{a, b, c\}, X)$ be an automaton defined as follows: $ax^B = b$, $bx^B = c$ for any $x \in X$, $cz^B = a$ for some $z \in X$ and $cx^B = b$ for any

$x \in X - \{z\}$.

Then it can easily be seen that $B \in V_X(Scf)$ and B satisfies the condition of the lemma.   □

The following results can easily be proved.

Lemma 10.5. *Let $Y = \emptyset$, let $A = \langle B, f, rC \rangle \in V_X(STC)$ ($r \in \mathbf{N}, C \in V_Y(Qp)$ and let $B' \in V_X(Scf)$. Then $B' \leq A$ holds iff the following conditions are satisfied: (i) $B' \leq B$. (ii) There exists an $(h_{B,B'}f)$-admissible part D of B' such that $D \leq C$.*

Lemma 10.6. *Let $Y = \emptyset$, let $A = \langle B, f, U \rangle \in V_X(STC)$ and let $B' \in V_X(Scf)$. Then $B' \leq A$ holds iff the following conditions are satisfied: (i) $B' \leq B$. (ii) B' is an an $(h_{B,B'}f)$-AP automaton.*

Corollary 10.7. *Let F be an $(X - Y)$-index system on $V_X(Scf)$ and let $B \in V_X(Scf)$. Then the following two conditions are equivalent: (1) There exists an STC automaton A which is included in $M(F)$ and $B \leq A$. (2) B is an F-AP automaton.*

Let F be an $(X - Y)$-index system on $V_X(Scf)$. Then $S = M(F)$, $R = V_X(Scf)$ and $Q = \langle V_X(Scf), F, V_Y(Tr) \rangle$ (or $Q = \langle V_X(Scf), F, \mathbf{N} \rangle$) satisfy the assumption of Section 9. From the above result, we have $R_A = V_X(F\text{-}AP)$. It remains to determine R_M, the set of all MP elements.

First, consider the case $Y = \emptyset$.

The proof of the following result is easy.

Lemma 10.8. *Let $F = \{f_B\}$ be an X-index system on $V_X(Scf)$. Then any F-AP automaton B is also an MP element and $\tilde{B} = \langle B, f_B, 0 \rangle$ where 0 means the set of one element.*

By the above result and Lemma 4.16, we can see that, for any $B, B' \in V_X(F\text{-}AP)$, $B' \leq B$ iff $\tilde{B}' \leq \tilde{B}$. Hence $R_A = R_M = V_X(F\text{-}AP)$ satisfies the condition of the special case given in Section 9.

The following lemma can also be proved easily.

Lemma 10.9. *Let $F = \{f_B\}$ be an X-index sytem on $V_X(Scf)$. Then any pair (B, B') in $V_X(F\text{-}AP)$ is a good or very good pair.*

Now, we prove the following.

Theorem 10.10. *Let $F = \{f_B\}$ be an X-index system on $V_X(Scf)$. If $V_X(F\text{-}AP) \neq V_X(Scf)$, then the set of all maximal lattices in $M(F)$ coincides wiht the set $\{\langle V_X(Scf), F, \mathbf{N} \rangle \cup V_X(F\text{-}AP), V_X(Scf)\}$. If $V_X(F\text{-}AP) = V_X(Scf)$, then $M(F)$ forms a lattice.*

Proof. Let $V_X(F\text{-}AP) \neq V_X(Scf)$. First, we prove that $V_X(Scf)$ is a maximal lattice in $M(F)$. Assume that there exists some lattice L in $M(F)$ such that $V_X(Scf) \subseteq L$ and $V_X(Scf) \neq L$. Then there exist $A = \langle B, f_B, U \rangle \in L - V_X(Scf)$ and $B' \in V_X(Scf) - V_X(F\text{-}AP)$ such that $B' \leq A$. However, in this case, by Corollary 10.7, $B' \in V_X(F\text{-}AP)$ and this is a contradiction. Therefore, $V_X(Scf)$ is a maximal lattice in $M(F)$. Now, let K be a maximal lattice in $M(F)$ such that $K \nsubseteq V_X(Scf)$. By a similar way to the above, we can show easily that $K \subseteq \langle V_X(Scf), F, \mathbf{N} \rangle \cup V_X(F\text{-}AP)$. Moreover, by Lemmas 9.17 and 10.9, $V_X(F\text{-}AP)$ becomes an LGS in $M(F)$. Thus $\langle V_X(Scf), F, \mathbf{N} \rangle \cup V_X(F\text{-}AP)$ forms a lattice and coincides with K. Next let $V_X(F\text{-}AP) = V_X(Scf)$. By the latter half of the above discussion, $\langle V_X(Scf), F, \mathbf{N} \rangle \cup V_X(F\text{-}AP) = \langle V_X(Scf), F, \mathbf{N} \rangle \cup V_X(Scf) = M(F)$ forms a lattice. $\qquad\square$

The first case of the above theorem really occurs. Now, we determine the second case.

The following lemma can be proved almost automatically.

Lemma 10.11.   *Let $W = \{w_1, w_2, \ldots, w_r\}$, let $W' = \{w'_1, w'_2, \ldots, w'_r\}$, and let $p_1, p_2, \ldots, p_r \in X^*$. For a W-index sytem $\{f_B \mid B \in V_X(Scf)\}$ on $V_X(Scf)$, we define a W'-index mapping g_B for any $B \in V_X(Scf)$ as follows: $g_B(w'_1) = f_B(w_i)p_i^B$ for any $i(1 \leq i \leq r)$ and any $B \in V_X(Scf)$. Then $\{g_B\}$ is an W'-index system on $V_X(Scf)$.*

Let $W = \{w\}$ be a singleton. Then by Proposition 6.11, there exists a W-index system $\{g_B\}$ on $V_X(Scf)$. For every $B \in V_X(Scf)$, we define an X-index mapping f_B on B as $f_B(x) = g_B(w)x^B$ for any $x \in X$. Then by the above lemma, $F = \{f_B\}$ is an X-index system on $V_X(Scf)$. It can easily be seen that $g_B(w)$ is an f_B-admissible part of B for any $B \in V_X(Scf)$.

We can determine the case when $M(F)$ is a lattice as follows:

Theorem 10.12.   *Let $W = \{w\}$ be a singleton, let $\{g_B\}$ be a W-index system on $V_X(Scf)$ and let $F = \{f_B\}$ be an X-index system on $V_X(Scf)$ defined as $f_B(x) = g_B(w)x^B$ for any $x \in X$. Then $M(F)$ forms a lattice. Conversely, if F is an X-index sytem on $V_X(Scf)$ and $M(F)$ forms a lattice, then F can be constructed as above.*

Proof. The first part of the theorem follows directly from the above remark and Theorem 10.10. We prove the second part. Let $F = \{f_B\}$ be an X-index sytem on $V_X(Scf)$ such that $M(F)$ forms a lattice. Now we construct a $\{w\}$-index sytem $\{g_B\}$ on $V_X(Scf)$. Let $A_1 \leq A_2 \leq \ldots A_i \leq \ldots$ be a sequence of elements of $V_X(Scf)$ such that $\{A_i | i \in \mathbf{N}\} = V_X(Scf)$. Let $S_{i,j}$ and T_i be the subsets of the state set of A_i $(i, j \in \mathbf{N}, \; i \leq j)$ defined as $S_{i,i} = \{d | d$ is an f_{A_i}-admissible part of $A_i\}$, $S_{i,j} = h_{A_j, A_i}(S_{j,j})$ and $T_i = \cap_{j=i}^{\infty} S_{i,j}$. It is obvious that $S_{i,j} \supseteq S_{i,k}$ $(i \leq j \leq k)$ and $S_{i,j} \neq \emptyset$ $(i \leq j)$. Moreover, since the state set of A_i is finite, we have $T_i \neq \emptyset$ for any $i \in \mathbf{N}$. It is easy to see that $h_{A_j, A_i}(T_j) = T_i$ for any $i, j \in \mathbf{N}$ $(i \leq j)$. For any $i \in \mathbf{N}$, we choose an element $t_i \in T_i$ inductively as follows: Choose any element $t_1 \in T_1$. Assume that $t_{i-1} \in T_{i-1}$ is chosen for $i \geq 2$. Then choose $t_i \in T_i \cap h^{-1}_{A_i, A_{i-1}}(t_{i-1})$. For any $B \in V_X(Scf)$, we define a $\{w\}$-index mapping g_B as follows: If $B \leq A_i$, then $g_B(w) = h_{A_i, B}(t_i)$.

It is easy to see that g_B is well defined and $\{g_B\}$ is a $\{w\}$-index system on $V_X(Scf)$. Note that t_i is an f_{A_i}-admissible part of A_i for any $i \in \mathbf{N}$. In other words, $t_i x^{A_i} = f_{A_i}(x)$ for any $i \in \mathbf{N}$ and $x \in X$. Hence if $B \leq A_i$, then $g_B(w)x^B = h_{A_i, B}(t_i)x^B = h_{A_i, B}(t_i x^{A_i}) = h_{A_i, B} f_{A_i}(x) = f_B(x)$. This completes the proof of the second part of the theorem. $\qquad\square$

Remark 10.13. In the above theorem, we consider only the case $Y = \emptyset$. However, by using Lemma 10.4, it can easily be seen that, if $Y \neq \emptyset$, then $M(F)$ does not form a lattice for any $(X - Y)$-index system F on $V_X(Scf)$. In fact, in this case, threre is no lattice which contains strictly $V_X(Scf)$ in $M(F)$. Consequently, $V_X(Scf)$ is a maximal lattice in $M(F)$. From this fact and Theorem 10.10, it follows that, for any index (X-index or $(X - Y)$-index) system F on $V_X(Scf)$, a maximal lattice in $M(F)$ which contains $V_X(Scf)$ can be uniquely determined, i.e. $V_X(Scf)$ or $M(F)$. Note that $V_X(Scf)$ is not a maximal lattice in $V_X(TC)$ though it becomes a maximal lattice in some $M(F)$.

Finally, consider the case $Y \neq \emptyset$.

Definition 10.14. Let B be an f-AP automaton. Then we denote by $\underset{\sim}{B}$ the set of all minimal elements of $\{\bar{D} \in V_Y(Qp) | D$ *is an* f-*admissible part of* $B\}$ where $\bar{D}$ means the quasiperfect automaton associated with D. B is called a *strongly cofinal automaton with the* f-*minimal property* (or briefly an f-MP automaton) if B is an f-AP automaton and $|\underset{\sim}{B}| = 1$. In this case, the unique element of B is called the *quasiperfect automaton associated with* B (with respert to f) and also denoted by B. Let $F = \{f_B\}$ be an $(X - Y)$-index system on $V_X(Scf)$. Then an f_B-MP automaton is called an F-MP automaton. We denote by $V_X(F\text{-}MP)$ the set of all F-MP automata.

Let F be an $(X - Y)$-index system on $V_X(Scf)$ where $Y \neq \emptyset$. Let $S = M(F)$, let $R = V_X(Scf)$ and let $Q = \langle V_X(Scf), F, V_Y(Tr) \rangle$, and consider the situation of Section 9. We have shown that $R_A = V_X(F\text{-}AP)$. As in Section 9, by $\tilde{B}$ we denote the set of all minimal elements of $\{A \in \langle V_X(Scf), F, V_Y(Tr) \rangle \mid B \leq A\}$ for any $B \in V_X(F\text{-}AP)$.

The following lemma can easily be proved.

Lemma 10.15. *Let* $B \in V_X(F\text{-}AP)$. *Then* $\tilde{B} = \{\langle B, f_B, C \rangle | C \in \underset{\sim}{B}\}$. *Consequently,* B *is an MP element iff* B *is an F-MP automaton.*

By the above result, we have $R_M = V_X(F\text{-}MP)$. Hence we are ready to apply Method 9.12 for obtaining all maximal LGS 's in $M(F)$. Now, let $F =$

$\{f_B \,|\, B \in V_X(Scf)\}$ be an $(X - Y)$-index system such that the set $\{f_B(z) \,|\, z \in X - Y\}$ is explicitly given for any $B \in V_X(Scf)$. Then it is not difficult to prove that there exists an algorithm to decide whether or not $B \in R_M$ for a given $B \in V_X(Scf)$ by using the results of the present section and Section 3. Consequently, for any $n \in \mathbf{N}$ we can obtain the set $R_M^{(n)} = \{B \in R_M \mid |B| \leq n\}$ where $|B|$ denotes the cardinality of the state set of B. Note that $R_M = \cup_{n=1}^{\infty} R_M^{(n)}$ holds. Moreover, let f be a bijective mapping of $\mathbf{N}$ onto R_M such that the set $\{f(i) \mid 1 \leq i \leq n\}$ is explicitly given for any $n \in \mathbf{N}$. We say that Method 9.12 is *practical* if there exists an algorithm for obtaining O_i for each $i \in \mathbf{N}$. We shall show the following.

Theorem 10.16. *Under the above assumptions on F and f, Method 9.12 is practical.*

Proof. Since $O_1 = \{f(1)\}$, there is no problem for $i = 1$. Assume that O_{i-1} can be determined for some $i \in \mathbf{N}$ $(i \geq 2)$. Let $n = \max\{|f(i)|, |B| \mid B \in O_{i-1}\}$. Then $\overline{O_{i-1} \cup \{f(i)\}} \subseteq R_M^{(n)}$. Since we can decide whether or not $B \leq B'$ for any $B, B' \in R_M^{(n)}$, $\overline{O_{i-1} \cup \{f(i)\}}$ can be determined. Let $O_{i-1} \cup \{f(i)\} \subseteq T \subseteq \overline{O_{i-1} \cup \{f(i)\}}$. For any $B, B' \in T$, we can determine easily $[B \circ B']_T$. Moreover, by Lemma 10.15 and the results of [4], we can compute $[B \circ B']_Q$ where $Q = \langle V_X(Scf), F, V_Y(Tr)\rangle$. It is not difficult to test whether or not $[B \circ B']_T \leq [B \circ B']_Q$ when $|[B \circ B']_T| = 1$. Hence by Lemma 9.10, we can decide whether or not T is an LGS. Consequently, we can carry out Method 9.12. Namely, $O_i = O_{i-1} \cup \{f(i)\}$ if there exists some LGS P_i such that $O_{i-1} \cup \{f(i)\} \subseteq P_i \subseteq \overline{O_{i-1} \cup \{f(i)\}}$, and $O_i = O_{i-1}$ otherwise. This completes the proof of the theorem. $\qquad\square$

To conclude this section, note the following. By Lemma 10.15 and Lemma 4.16, we have $B' \leq B$ iff $\tilde{B}' \leq \tilde{B}$ for any $B, B' \in V_X(F\text{-}AP)$. This means that $R_M = V_X(F\text{-}AP)$ satisfies the condition of the special case given in Section 9. Hence we can apply the discussion in the last part of Section 9 to a finite subset of $V_X(Scf)$. Namely, we have an algorithm to decide whether or not there exists the minimum lattice K in $V_X(TC)$ which contains $\langle V_X(Scf), F, V_X(Tr)\rangle \cup T$ for a given finite subset T of $V_X(Scf)$. Furthermore, when there exists such a K, we can provide a constructin method for it.

11. Conclusion

We have dealt in this paper with $V_X(TC)$, i.e. the class of all transitive cofinal automata. First, we determined the structure of transitive cofinal automata. And then we determined all maximal lattices in $V_X(STC)$. Finally, we investigated lattices in $V_X(TC)$ by using some results on lattices in weighted posets. For any X-index system F on $V_X(Scf)$, we could determine all maximal lattices in $M(F)$. However, for an $(X - Y)$-index system F on $V_X(Scf)$

where $Y \neq \emptyset$, we could deteremine only all maximal lattices in $M(F)$ which contains $\langle V_X(Scf), F, V_X(Tr) \rangle$ or $V_X(Scf)$. To conclude this paper, we wish to pose the following open problem: For any $(X-Y)$-index system F on $V_X(Scf)$, determine all maximal lattices in $M(F)$.

References

1. G. Birkhoff, *Lattice Theory*, Providence, RI, 1967.

2. J. Cerný, A. Pirická, B. Rosenauerová, On directable automata, *Kybernetika*, 7 (1972), 289 – 294.

3. Dang Huu Dao, Az irányitható automaták félcsoportjairól (On the semi-groups of directable automata, in Hungarian), *Automataeleeméleti Füzetek*, Budapest, 1978, 1 – 28.

4. M. Ito, Some classes of automata as partially ordered sets, *Math. Systems Theory*, 15 (1982), 357 – 370.

5. M. Ito, G. Tanaka. Cartesian composition of classes of automata, *Papers on Automata Theory III*, K. Marx Univ. of Economics, Dep. of Math., Budapest, 1981, No DM 81-2, 53 – 75.

6. Y. Masunaga, S. Noguchi, J. Oizumi, A structure theory of automata characterized by groups, *J. Comput. System. Sci.*, 7 (1973), 300 – 305.

Algebraic Foundations for Montague Grammars[1]

Helmut JÜRGENSEN
Department of Computer Science, The University of Western Ontario
London, Ontario, N6A 5B7 Canada

Katrin TENT
Department of Mathematics, Notre Dame University
Notre Dame, Indiana, 46556 USA

Abstract. We establish the precise connection between Montague grammars, context-free grammars and partial sorted algebras. Moreover, using Montague translations, we formulate the linguistic problem of universal grammar in mathematical terms.

1. Introduction

Montague grammars were introduced as a universal formal tool by which to describe structural aspects of natural languages, in particular the connection between syntactical and semantical structure. The linguistic theory of *universal grammar* postulates the existence of a universal structural characterization of all *possible human languages*. In [12] and [13] it is demonstrated how Montague translations can be applied to construct a fragment of a universal grammar for a finite sample of structurally quite different languages; this is achieved by building intertranslatable grammars for all the languages involved. In essence, this can be viewed as a step towards establishing the *mathematical* viability of the linguistic theory.

The underlying mathematical problem can be phrased as follows: *Given a class of formal systems for the description of languages and given an arbitrary set of languages described by such systems and having a common semantics, is there always a formal system of the same kind describing all languages in the set? And if so, can one construct this system assuming that the languages are given constructively ?* For the discussion in linguistics, a positive answer to these mathematical questions could point to ways in which to approximate a *universal grammar*, while a negative answer – in view of [12] and [13] the

---

[1] This work was supported by the Natural Sciences and Engineering Council of Canada under Grant OGP0000243.

far less likely case in our opinion – would point out limitations of the theory of universal grammar.

The present paper – intended as a step towards answering these purely mathematical questions – establishes the algebraic context in which the problem of universal grammar can be studied for the class of Montague grammars. In Section 2, we summarize the required algebraic background regarding partial and sorted algebras. In Section 3, we provide basic facts concerning Montague grammars. The connection is established in Section 4, where we show that Montague grammars and total Peano algebras are, algebraically, the same objects. This connection should turn out to be useful as it makes classical tools of universal algebra and category theory applicable to Montague grammars. In Sections 5 and 6, we briefly discuss the mathematical formulation of the techniques used in [12] and [13]; we do not, however, provide an answer to the problem of universal grammar – but we plan and hope to settle this in the near future. In Section 7, we describe the connection between Montague grammars and context-free grammars in the sense of Chomsky. We show that these classes of grammars only differ in the amount of detailed structural information they provide, but not really in terms of their generative power. The proofs involve ideas taken from the theory of tree automata. Thus, an answer to the problem of universal grammar obtained for Montague grammars would carry over to context-free grammars in the sense of Chomsky as well.

Beyond linguistics, our considerations are applicable or related to work on artificial languages, like programming languages or pictorial languages (see [2], for example).

2. Partial algebras; basic notions

In this section we briefly review some basic notions from universal algebra, in particular from the theory of partial algebras and algebras with sorts. For more details, we refer to the books [5], [1] and [11]. With the application of this theory to Montague grammars in mind, we restrict our attention to algebras with only finitary operation symbols. For the same reason we modify the notation of [1] and [11] slightly – but without serious implications – so as to simplify the transition between these theories.

We use the symbols $\mathbf{N}$ and $\mathbf{N_0}$ to denote the sets of positive and of non-negative integers, respectively. Mappings are written on the left with the exception of morphism which we prefer to write on the right.

Definition 2.1. A *similarity type* is a pair (Ω, ν) with Ω a set of *operation symbols* and $\nu : \Omega \to \mathbf{N_0}$ the *arity function*. A *partial algebra* of similarity type (Ω, ν) is a quadruple $\mathbf{A} = (A, \mathcal{F}^A, \Omega, \nu)$ where A is the *carrier set* of $\mathbf{A}$ with $A \cap \Omega = \emptyset$ and $\mathcal{F}^A = \{F_\omega^A \mid \omega \in \Omega\}$ is a family of *partial operations* such that, for $\omega \in \Omega$, F_ω^A is a partial mapping of $A^{\nu(\omega)}$ into A. The algebra $\mathbf{A}$ is said to be *total* if each F_ω^A is total.

To keep the notation concise, we use typographical variants of letters and corresponding superscripts and subscripts to identify the various parts of an object – a partial algebra in this case. Thus, if $\mathbf{B}$ is a partial algebra of similarity type (Ω, ν), then B is the carrier set and $\mathcal{F}^B$ is the set of operations F_ω^B with $\omega \in \Omega$.

In this paper, with the theory of Montague grammars in mind, we only consider algebras with finitary operation symbols. This assumption simplifies certain algebraic constructions significantly. Some of the proofs in this paper rely on this assumption and would need to be re-examined without it.

Among the various options for defining the notion of morphism for partial algebras we choose the one of [1], Definition 2.1.1, p. 24. Let $\mathbf{A}$ and $\mathbf{B}$ be two partial algebras of the same similarity type (Ω, ν). A *morphism* of $\mathbf{A}$ to $\mathbf{B}$ is a mapping ϕ of A into B which satisfies the following condition for all $\omega \in \Omega$ and $a_1, \ldots, a_{\nu(\omega)} \in A$:

> *Whenever $F_\omega^A(a_1, \ldots, a_{\nu(\omega)})$ exists then $F_\omega^B(a_1\phi, \ldots, a_{\nu(\omega)}\phi)$ exists and is equal to $F_\omega^A(a_1, \ldots, a_{\nu(\omega)})\phi$.*

In the case of total algebras this condition reduces to the usual condition for morphism s.

The morphism ϕ of $\mathbf{A}$ to $\mathbf{B}$ is an *isomorphism* if there is a morphism ψ of $\mathbf{B}$ to $\mathbf{A}$ such that $\phi\psi$ is the identity mapping of $\mathbf{A}$ and $\psi\phi$ is the identity mapping of $\mathbf{B}$. An *endomorphism* is a morphism of a partial algebra to itself; *automorphisms* are endomorphisms which are also isomorphisms. *Monomorphisms* and *epimorphisms* are defined in the usual category theory sense via right and left cancellation, respectively. A *bimorphism* is a morphism which is both a monomorphism and an epimorphism. One proves that the monomorphisms are exactly the injective morphisms; every surjective morphism is an epimorphism; epimorphisms need not be surjective and bimorphisms are not necessarily isomorphisms [1].

Let $\mathbf{A}$ and $\mathbf{B}$ be as before. A morphism ϕ is said to be *full* if, for every $\omega \in \Omega$ and every $a_1, \ldots, a_{\nu(\omega)} \in A$, the following property obtains:

> *If $F_\omega^B(a_1\phi, \ldots, a_{\nu(\omega)}\phi)$ is defined and in $A\phi$ then there exist $a_1', \ldots,$ $a_{\nu(\omega)}' \in A$ such that $F_\omega^A(a_1', \ldots, a_{\nu(\omega)}')$ is defined and $a_i\phi = a_i'\phi$ for $i = 1, \ldots, \nu(\omega)$.*

A morphism ϕ is said to be *closed* if, for every $\omega \in \Omega$ and every $a_1, \ldots, a_{\nu(\omega)} \in A$, the following property obtains:

> *If $F_\omega^B(a_1\phi, \ldots, a_{\nu(\omega)}\phi)$ is defined then $F_\omega^A(a_1, \ldots, a_{\nu(\omega)})$ is defined.*

Every closed morphism is full. The compositon of morphisms preserves closedness but not necessarily fullness (see [1]). For any given similarity type (Ω, ν), the class of all partial algebras of similarity type (Ω, ν) forms a category.

We also need the notion of a heterogeneous partial algebra. Intuitively, in such an algebra the carrier set A is subdivided into a family of pairwise disjoint subsets, the *sorts*. For the partial operations, rules are given which govern their action on the sorts. We choose to use the slightly more general approach of [1], p. 40, which defines sorted partial algebras as follows.

Definition 2.2. A *sorted partial algebra* is a quintuple

$$\mathcal{A} = (\mathbf{A}, \sigma, \mathbf{S}, \Omega, \nu)$$

with the following properties:

(a) $\mathbf{A}$ and $\mathbf{S}$ are partial algebras of similarity type (Ω, ν).

(b) The carrier set S of $\mathbf{S}$ is non-empty.

(c) σ is a morphism of $\mathbf{A}$ to $\mathbf{S}$.

The algebra $\mathbf{S}$ is called the *sort algebra of $\mathcal{A}$*. The carrier set of $\mathbf{A}$ is the *carrier set of $\mathcal{A}$*. The sorted partial algebra $\mathcal{A}$ is a *heterogeneous partial algebra* if the domain of every non-nullary operation of $\mathbf{S}$ is a singleton set. In this case, the algebra $\mathbf{S}$ is called a *heterogeneous sort algebra*. The sorted partial algebra $\mathcal{A}$ is said to be a *total sorted algebra* if σ is closed.

Let $\mathcal{A} = (\mathbf{A}, \sigma, \mathbf{S}, \Omega, \nu)$ be a sorted partial algebra. For each element $a \in A$, the morphism σ determines its *sort $a\sigma$*. Now consider $\omega \in \Omega$ and $a_1, \ldots, a_{\nu(\omega)}, a \in A$. Suppose, that F_ω^A is defined on $(a_1, \ldots, a_{\nu(\omega)})$ and $F_\omega^A(a_1, \ldots, a_{\nu(\omega)}) = a$. Then $F_\omega^S(a_1\sigma, \ldots, a_{\nu(\omega)}\sigma)$ is defined and equal to $a\sigma$. Thus, F_ω^S determines the sort of the result of F_ω^A from the sorts of its arguments.

For example, in a typical programming language setting – in the part of a compiler concerning arithmetic – one has *variables* of types *integer* and *real*. Restricted to these types, a typical implementation of arithmetic can be described as follows: The set A consists of the disjoint union of a finite set A_I of binary representations of integers and a finite set A_R of binary floating point representations of real numbers[2]. The set of sorts S would include the elements I and R denoting the sorts of integers and reals, respectively. For the binary operation symbol $+$, the algebra $\mathbf{S}$ would provide

$$F_+^S(R, R) = F_+^S(I, R) = F_+^S(R, I) = R$$
$$\text{and} \quad F_+^S(I, I) = I,$$

---

[2] Only finitely many different numbers can be represented if one takes the usual approach to computer arithmetic, exlcuding arbitrary precision or implicit representations as used in computational algebra. This point is not really essential for our example, however.

expressing the usual type conversion rules. For $a \in A$, one has $\sigma(a) = I$ if $a \in A_I$ and $\sigma(a) = R$ if $a \in A_R$. In the algebra $\mathbf{A}$, $F_+^A = (a_1, a_2)$ would yield the corresponding representations of the sum of the values of a_1 and a_2, as long as it is in A. Of course, $F_+^A(a_1, a_2)$ could be undefined.

As another example, consider the abstract linguistic notions[3] of an *object specifier, determinate object,* and *indeterminate object.* We also consider the notions of a *determinator* and an *indeterminator.* The idea is that a determinator or indeterminator together with an object specifier will result in a determinate or indeterminate object, respectively. Let O, O_D, O_I, D, I denote the notions of object specifier, determinate object, indeterminate object, determinator, and indeterminator, respectively. Let $\circ$ denote the operation of "putting things together" mentioned above. The carrier set of our sort algebra $\mathbf{S}$ would contain the set $\{O, O_D, O_I, D, I\}$ and, in $\mathbf{S}$, the interpretation of $\circ$ could be

$$F_\circ^S(x, y) = \begin{cases} O_D, & \text{if } x = D \text{ and } y = O, \\ O_I, & \text{if } x = I \text{ and } y = O, \\ \text{undefined}, & \text{otherwise.} \end{cases}$$

In the algebra $\mathbf{A}$ we could have words like 'the,' 'a,' and 'house' map onto D, I, and O by σ, respectively. With $F_\circ^A$ interpreted as interpretation, we classify 'the house' and 'a house' as determinate and indeterminate objects, respectively.

Clearly, this example is an unnatural simplification of linguistical methods. Its only intent is to make the connection between the formal notation employed in this paper and the ideas of structural linguistics apparent.

We need to extend the notion of morphism from partial algebras to sorted partial algebras. Such morphisms need to "translate" sorts and sort restrictions.

Definition 2.3. Let $\mathcal{A} = (\mathbf{A}, \sigma, \mathbf{S}, \Omega, \nu)$ and $\mathcal{B} = (\mathbf{B}, \tau, \mathbf{T}, \Omega, \nu)$ be sorted partial algebras. A *morphism* of $\mathcal{A}$ to $\mathcal{B}$ is a pair (ϕ, ψ) with the following properties:

(a) ϕ is a morphism of $\mathbf{A}$ to $\mathbf{B}$.

(b) ψ is a morphism of $\mathbf{S}$ to $\mathbf{T}$.

(c) $\phi\tau = \sigma\psi$.

The notions of *isomorphism, endomorphism, automorphism, monomorphism, epimorphism,* and *bimorphism* for sorted partial algebras are defined analogously to the ones for partial algebras defined above. Thus, for example,

---

[3]The particular ones in this example may not be very useful or typical for linguistics; they were invented for this example.

a morphism (ϕ, ψ) of $\mathcal{A}$ to $\mathcal{B}$ is an isomorphism if there is a morphism (ϕ', ψ') of $\mathcal{B}$ to $\mathcal{A}$ such that $(\phi, \psi)(\phi', \psi')$ is the identity morphism.

The properties postulated in Definition 2.3 imply, intuitively, that the sort assignment in $\mathcal{B}$ is compatible with the one induced by ψ from the sort assignment in $\mathcal{A}$. Note that the definition of [1] corresponding to Definition 2.3 concerns the special case of $\mathcal{S} = \mathcal{T}$ with ψ the identity mapping. The class of sorted partial algebras of a given similarity type (Ω, ν), forms a category, denoted by $\mathbf{sALG}(\Omega, \nu)$. For $i = 1, 2, 3$, let $\mathcal{A}_i$ be an sorted partial algebra in this category and, for $i = 1, 2$, let (ϕ_i, ψ_i) be a morphism of $\mathcal{A}_i$ to $\mathcal{A}_{i+1}$. Then the composite morphism $(\phi_1, \psi_1)(\phi_2, \psi_2)$ mapping $\mathcal{A}_1$ to $\mathcal{A}_3$ is given by $(\phi_i \phi_2, \psi_1 \psi_2)$.

In the category $\mathbf{sALG}(\Omega, \nu)$, *multiple pullbacks* exist: Let I be an arbitrary non-empty set. Let $\mathcal{A}$ and, for $i \in I$, $\mathcal{A}_i$ be sorted partial algebras of type (Ω, ν). Suppose that, for each $i \in I$, there is a morphism (ϕ_i, ψ_i) of $\mathcal{A}_i$ to $\mathcal{A}$. Then there is a sorted partial algebra $\mathcal{P}$ of type (Ω, ν) and, for each $i \in I$, there is a morphism (ϕ_i', ψ_i') of $\mathcal{P}$ to $\mathcal{A}_i$ such that the following conditions are satisfied:

(i) For all $i, j \in I$ one has $(\phi_i', \psi_i')(\phi_i, \psi_i) = (\phi_j', \psi_j')(\phi_j, \psi_j)$.

(ii) If $\hat{\mathcal{P}}$ is a sorted partial algebra and if, for $i \in I$, there are morphisms $(\hat{\phi}_i', \hat{\psi}_i')$ of $\hat{\mathcal{P}}$ to $\mathcal{A}_1$ such that, for all $i, j \in I$ one has $(\hat{\phi}_i', \hat{\psi}_i')(\phi_i, \psi_i) = (\hat{\phi}_j', \hat{\psi}_j')(\phi_j, \psi_j)$, then there is a unique morphism (ϕ, ψ) of $\hat{\mathcal{P}}$ to $\mathcal{P}$ such that $(\hat{\phi}_i', \hat{\psi}_i') = (\phi, \psi)(\phi_i', \psi_i')$.

The algebra $\mathcal{P}$ together with the family $\{(\phi_i', \psi_i')\}_{i \in I}$ is uniquely determined up to isomorphism, and is the multiple pullback of the family $\{(\phi_i, \psi_i)\}_{i \in I}$.

In the following definition we introduce the counterpart of 'term algebras' for the context of sorted partial algebras:

Definition 2.4. Let $\mathcal{A} = (\mathbf{A}, \sigma, \mathbf{S}, \Omega, \nu)$ be a sorted partial algebra and let $X \subseteq A$. Then $\mathcal{A}$ is said to be a *partial Peano algebra with Peano basis X* if the following properties obtain:

(a) For every $\omega \in \Omega$ and every $a_1, \ldots, a_{\nu(\omega)} \in A$, if $F_\omega^A(a_1, \ldots, a_{\nu(\omega)})$ is defined then $F_\omega^A(a_1, \ldots, a_{\nu(\omega)}) \notin X$.

(b) For every $\omega, \omega' \in \Omega$ and every $a_1, \ldots, a_{\nu(\omega)}, a_1', \ldots, a_{\nu(\omega')}' \in A$, if $F_\omega^A(a_1, \ldots, a_{\nu(\omega)})$ and $F_{\omega'}^A(a_1', \ldots, a_{\nu(\omega')}')$ are defined and $F_\omega^A(a_1, \ldots, a_{\nu(\omega)}) = F_{\omega'}^A(a_1', \ldots, a_{\nu(\omega')}')$ then $\omega = \omega'$ and $a_i = a_i'$ for $i = 1, \ldots, \nu(\omega)$.

(c) X is a set of generators of A.

A partial Peano algebra which is total as a sorted algebra is called a *Peano algebra* or a *similarity type A*.

In essence and intuitively, the similarity type As play the rôle of absolutely free objects in the category of sorted partial algebras. The situation is more complicated, however – far more complicated than in the case of total homogeneous algebras. A very thorough analysis of the problem is provided in [1].

3. Montague grammars, basic facts

In the definitions of this section we review [8]. However, we take the liberty to simplify the notation and to omit details in cases of little mathematical consequence. We use the following simplified notion of a disambiguated Montague grammar :

Definition 3.1. A *disambiguated Montague grammar* is a quintuple $G = (\Delta, \Gamma, \mathcal{X}, \nu, \mathcal{S})$ with the following properties:

(1) Δ is a non-empty set, the set of *names of syntactic categories*[4].

(2) Γ is a non-empty set and (Γ, ν) is a similarity type.

(3) $\mathcal{X} = \{X_\delta \mid \delta \in \Delta\}$ is a family of pairwise disjoint sets, some of which may be empty.

(4) $\mathcal{S} = \{S_\gamma \mid \gamma \in \Gamma\}$ is a family of partial mappings S_γ of $\Delta^{\nu(\gamma)}$ into Δ, the set of *syntax rules*.

(5) $\Gamma \cap \Delta = \emptyset$ and $\Gamma \cap X_\delta = \emptyset$ for all $\delta \in \Delta$.

G is said to be *finite* if Δ, Γ, and all the sets X_δ for $\delta \in \Delta$ are finite.

Let $G = (\Delta, \Gamma, \mathcal{X}, \nu, \mathcal{S})$ be a disambiguated Montague grammar and let $X = \bigcup_{\delta \in \Delta} X_\delta$. The set X is called the *dictionary* of G and the elements of X are called *basic expressions*. Let $\mathbf{A} = \mathbf{A}(G)$ be the absolutely free total algebra of type (Γ, ν) generated by X. Let $A = A(G)$ be the carrier set of $\mathbf{A}$. We can identify $\mathbf{A}$ with the term algebra generated by X, thus letting[5] $\mathcal{F}^A = \Gamma$. By the syntax rules in $\mathcal{S}$, *correct sentences* can be distinguished from incorrect

---

[4] The term 'category' as used in this context – or in linguistics in general – has nothing to do with the mathematical term 'category' used before in this paper. This terminological confusion is unfortunate, but inevitable. We shall keep the notions separated by referring to the linguistic variant as 'syntactic category' while every other usage of the word 'category' refers to the mathematical meaning.

[5] In the usual definition of Montague grammars one has an additional set of operations, interpreting the symbols in Γ, which is used to build complex structures from simpler ones. In the case of disambiguated Montague grammars, this set is redundant as the set Γ takes its rôle.

ones. The quadruple $(\Delta, \mathcal{S}, \Gamma, \nu)$ is a partial algebra $\mathbf{D}(G)$ of similarity type (Γ, ν), the *algebra of syntactic categories of G*.

We now construct the family of syntactic categories defined by a disambiguated Montague grammar. This will then allow us to obtain the language defined by such a grammar. To do so we start with the dictionary and, from there, recursively build more complicated structures using the operation symbols in Γ. Some of the constructs thus obtained may not be acceptable according to the syntax rules and are removed from the process. The rest are assigned to syntactic categories according to the syntax rules.

Definition 3.2. Let $G = (\Delta, \Gamma, \mathcal{X}, \nu, \mathcal{S})$ be a disambiguated Montague grammar. The family $\mathcal{C} = \mathcal{C}(G) = \{C_\delta \mid \delta \in \Delta\}$ of *syntactic categories* C_δ of G is defined as follows:

(a) For all $\delta \in \Delta$ one has $X_\delta \subseteq C_\delta$.

(b) For $\gamma \in \Gamma$ and $\delta_i \in \Delta$, $c_i \in C_{\delta_i}$ with $i = 1, \ldots, \nu(\gamma)$, $\gamma(c_1, \ldots, c_{\nu(\gamma)})$ is an element of $C_{S_\gamma(\delta_1, \ldots, \delta_{\nu(\gamma)})}$ if and only if $S_\gamma(\delta_1, \ldots, \delta_{\nu(\gamma)})$ is defined.

(c) For $\delta \in \Delta$, C_δ is the smallest subset of A which satisfies conditions (a) and (b).

The construction of the syntactic categories C_δ for $\delta \in \Delta$ is controlled by $\mathcal{S}$. Initially, the basic expressions are assigned to the syntactic categories. Some of the sets X_δ may be empty because there may be syntactic categories containing no basic expressions. Now, using elements already constructed, we build new elements in the absolutely free algebra $\mathbf{A}(G)$. Thus, for $\gamma \in \Gamma$ and $c_1, \ldots, c_{\nu(\gamma)}$ already constructed, we consider the term $\gamma(c_1, \ldots, c_{\nu(\gamma)})$ in $\mathbf{A}(G)$. Suppose that the syntactic category of c_i is δ_i, for $i = 1, \ldots, \nu(\gamma)$. The term is discarded if $S_\gamma(\delta_1, \ldots, \delta_{\nu(\gamma)})$ is undefined. Otherwise it is assigned to the syntactic category thus determined by S_γ.

Intuitively, an operation symbol γ can sometimes be applied to a $\nu(\gamma)$-tuple

$$(c_1, \ldots, c_{\nu(\gamma)}) \in A$$

without regard to whether or not the arguments or the result are syntactically (or semantically) correct. The syntax rules in $\mathcal{S}$ 'sort' a subset of A into syntactic categories. In particular, we imply that the elements of the syntactic categories are precisely the correct parts of the language.

Note that in the original setting of [8], one syntactic category is singled out as that of declarative sentences. However, mathematically this does not seem important; hence, to simplify the notation, we omit this part of the definition of Montague grammars.

Definition 3.3. Let $G = (\Delta, \Gamma, \mathcal{X}, \nu, \mathcal{S})$ be a disambiguated Montague grammar. The *language* of G is the set $L = L(G) = \bigcup_{\delta \in \Delta} C_\delta$.

A language L presented in this way by a disambiguated Montague grammar can be viewed, essentially, as a language in the common sense of the word together with all the necessary information to understand its phrases at least at the syntactical level. In the terminology of Chomsky grammars, instead of just providing the elements of the language, we provide their derivations. Thus, with an element of L we have all the structural information required to construct it.

Proposition 3.1. *Let* $G = (\Delta, \Gamma, \mathcal{X}, \nu, \mathcal{S})$ *be a disambiguated Montague grammar.*

(1) If the sets Γ and $\Delta(X) = \{\delta \mid \delta \in \Delta, X_\delta \neq \emptyset\}$ are recursively enumerable and if the mappings ν and S_γ for $\gamma \in \Gamma$ are recursive then the set $\Delta_\infty = \{\delta \mid \delta \in \Delta, C_\delta \neq \emptyset\}$ is recursively enumerable.

(2) If the sets Γ, Δ, and X_δ for $\delta \in \Delta$ are recursively enumerable and if the mappings ν and S_γ for $\gamma \in \Gamma$ are recursive then L and every C_δ for $\delta \in \Delta$ are recursively enumerable.

(3) If the sets Δ and X_δ for $\delta \in \Delta$ are recursively enumerable and if the mappings S_γ for $\gamma \in \Gamma$ are recursive with recursive domains then the following two questions are decidable:

(a) Given $x \in A(G)$ and $\delta_0 \in \Delta$, is $x \in C_{\delta_0}$?

(b) Given $x \in A(G)$, is $x \in L$?

Proof. The recursive enumeration will, in step i, have obtained a finite subset Δ_i of Δ_∞, and a finite subset Γ_i of Γ. It will also be maintaining a finite set P_i of *active computations* and a finite list L_i of *attempted computations*. Initially, $\Gamma_0 = \Delta_0 = P_0 = L_0 = \emptyset$. In step 0 we start the enumeration of Γ and $\Delta(X)$; in subsequent steps we continue these enumerations. In general, in step i, we run these enumerations for a fixed amount of time. Every new γ obtained in this way is added to Γ_i to result in Γ_{i+1}. Every δ found is kept temporarily in a set Δ'. For every $\gamma \in \Gamma_i$ and $\delta_1, \ldots, \delta_{\nu(\gamma)} \in \Delta_i$, we check in L_i whether a computation of $S_\gamma(\delta_1, \ldots, \delta_{\nu(\gamma)})$ has been attempted. If no, such a computation is now started, that is, it is added to P_i and the information about this fact is added to L_i. Let the resulting set of active computations be called P_i' and the resulting list of attempted computations be L_{i+1}.

We now continue every computation in P_i' for a fixed amount of time, starting it if required. Those computations that halt within this time are removed from P_i', and their results are added to Δ'. The resulting set of still active computations is P_{i+1}. Finally, let $\Delta_{i+1} = \Delta_i \cup \Delta'$. This completes step i. This proves the first statement.

The proof of the second statement is analogous. Instead of enumerating $\Delta(X)$ one enumerates C_δ. At step i, enumerations of the sets X_δ with $\delta \in \Delta_i$ are carried out or continued to obtain increasingly larger finite parts of these sets. Whenever it has been determined by some computation in P_i that $S_\gamma(\delta_1, \ldots, \delta_{\nu(\gamma)}) = \delta$ with $\gamma \in \Gamma_i$ and $\delta_1, \ldots, \delta_{\nu(\gamma)} \in \Delta_i$, then we generate $\gamma(x_1, \ldots, x_{\nu(\gamma)})$ as element of C_δ for all $x_i \in C_{\delta_i}$ known to this moment, where $i = 1, \ldots, \nu(\gamma)$. With some careful bookkeeping, no element of L will be missed and each element will be in its proper syntactic category.

We now turn to the proof of the third statement. Let $x \in A(G)$ be given. We use induction on the depth of nested operations in x to prove that it is decidable whether $x \in L$ and, if $x \in C_\delta$ for some $\delta \in \Delta$, then δ can be computed from x.

If the depth is 0, then $x \in X$ and $x \in L$ by definition. As Δ and each set X_δ with $\delta \in \Delta$ is recursively enumerable, and as the sets X_δ are pairwise disjoint, one can compute the unique δ such that $x \in X_\delta$. As $X_\delta \subseteq C_\delta$, we only need to compary δ with δ_0 to decide whether $x \in C_{\delta_0}$.

Now suppose that $x \notin X$, that is, the nesting depth is greater than 0. Thus $x = \gamma(x_1, \ldots, x_{\nu(\gamma)})$ for some $\gamma \in \Gamma$ and $x_1, \ldots, x_{\nu(\gamma)} \in A(G)$. For $i = 1, \ldots, \nu(\gamma)$, the nesting depth of x_i is strictly less than that of x. Hence, by induction assumption, we can decide if $x_i \in L$ and, if so, determine the unique $\delta_i \in \Delta$ such that $x_i \in C_{\delta_i}$. If $x_i \notin L$ then $x \notin L$ and $x \notin C_{\delta_0}$. Suppose now that each $x_i \in L$ and that the corresponding δ_i have been computed. Decide whether $(\delta_1, \ldots, \delta_{\nu(\gamma)})$ is in the domain of S_γ. If no, $x \notin L$. If yes, we have $x \in L$ and compute $\delta = S_\gamma(\delta_1, \ldots, \delta_{\nu(\gamma)})$ with $x \in C_\delta$. To decide whether $x \in C_{\delta_0}$ we only need to compare δ and δ_0. $\qquad\square$

We also need to define the notion of morphisms of disambiguated Montague grammars. At this point, we provide a definition which is mainly motivated by straightforward algebraic considerations. This definition is expanded later to accomodate ideas from a linguistic context.

Definition 3.4. Let $G = (\Delta_G, \Gamma, \mathcal{X}_G, \nu, \mathcal{S}_G)$ and $H = (\Delta_H, \Gamma, \mathcal{X}_H, \nu, \mathcal{S}_H)$ be two disambiguated Montague grammars. A *morphism* of G to H is a pair (ϕ, ψ) such that ϕ is a morphism of $\mathbf{A}(G)$ to $\mathbf{A}(H)$, ψ is a morphism of $\mathbf{D}(G)$ to $\mathbf{D}(H)$ and $X_{G,\delta}\phi \subseteq C_{H,\delta\psi}$ for all $\delta \in \Delta_G$.

Morphisms of disambiguated Montague grammars can be viewed as a simple language translation mechanism for languages with essentially the same structure. Basic expressions of the source language may become derived expressions in the target language. Moreover, syntactic categories separated in the source language may get merged in the target language. The general structure, however, as expressed in the syntactic categories is preserved.

As before in the case of algebras, one defines the notions of *isomorphism, endomorphism, automorphism, monomorphism, epimorphism,* and *bimorphism* of disambiguated Montague grammars by the standard category theory approach.

Proposition 3.2. *Let $G = (\Delta_G, \Gamma, \mathcal{X}_G, \nu, \mathcal{S}_G)$ and $H = (\Delta_H, \Gamma, \mathcal{X}_H, \nu, \mathcal{S}_H)$ be two disambiguated Montague grammars and let (ϕ, ψ) be a morphism of G to H. Then $C_{G,\delta}\phi \subseteq C_{H,\delta\psi}$ for all $\delta \in \Delta_G$.*

Proof. Let $\delta \in \Delta_G$ and $x \in C_{G,\delta}$. We use induction on the depth of nested operations in x.

If the depth is 0, then $x \in X_{G,\delta}$ and $x\phi \in X_{G,\delta}\phi \subseteq C_{H,\delta\psi}$ by Definition 3.4.

Now suppose that $x \notin X_{G,\delta}$, that is, $x = \gamma(x_1, \ldots, x_{\nu(\gamma)})$ for some $\gamma \in \Gamma$ and some $x_1, \ldots, x_{\nu(\gamma)} \in L$. For each i, $i = 1, \ldots, \nu(\gamma)$, there is a unique $\delta_i \in \Delta_G$ such that $x_i \in C_{G,\delta_i}$. Moreover, the nesting depth of each x_i is strictly less than that of x. Thus, by induction assumption, $x_i\phi \in C_{H,\delta_i\psi}$.

As $x \in C_{G,\delta}$, $S_{G,\gamma}(\delta_1, \ldots, \delta_{\nu(\gamma)})$ is defined and equal to δ. As ψ is a morphism of $\mathbf{D}(G)$ into $\mathbf{D}(H)$ also $S_{H,\gamma}(\delta_1\psi, \ldots, \delta_{\nu(\gamma)}\psi)$ is defined and equal to $\delta\psi$. This proves that $x\phi = \gamma(x_1\phi, \ldots, x_{\nu(\gamma)}\phi) \in C_{H,\delta\psi}$. $\square$

Corollary 3.1. *Let $G = (\Delta_G, \Gamma, \mathcal{X}_G, \nu, \mathcal{S}_G)$ and $H = (\Delta_H, \Gamma, \mathcal{X}_H, \nu, \mathcal{S}_H)$ be two disambiguated Montague grammars and let (ϕ, ψ) be a morphism of G to H. Then $L(G)\phi \subseteq L(H)$.*

Corollary 3.2. *The disambiguated Montague grammars form a category.*

Proof. Let $G = (\Delta_G, \Gamma, \mathcal{X}_G, \nu, \mathcal{S}_G)$ be a disambiguated Montague grammar. Let ϕ be the identity mapping of $\mathbf{A}(G)$ and ψ the identity mapping of Δ_G. Then (ϕ, ψ) is the identity morphism of G. Now, let $H = (\Delta_H, \Gamma, \mathcal{X}_H, \nu, \mathcal{S}_H)$ and $K = (\Delta_K, \Gamma, \mathcal{X}_K, \nu, \mathcal{S}_K)$ be disambiguated Montague grammars and let (ϕ_H, ψ_H) and (ϕ_K, ψ_K) be homomorpisms of G to H and of H to K, respectively. Consider $(\phi, \psi) = (\phi_H, \psi_H)(\phi_K, \psi_K) = (\phi_H\phi_k, \psi_H\psi_K)$. Then ϕ is a morphism of $\mathbf{A}(G)$ to $\mathbf{A}(K)$ and ψ is a morphism of $\mathbf{D}(G)$ to $\mathbf{D}(K)$. By Proposition 3.2, one has $X_{G,\delta}\phi = X_{G,\delta}\phi_H\phi_K \subseteq C_{H,\delta\psi_H}\phi_K \subseteq C_{K,\delta\psi_H\psi_K} = C_{K,\delta\psi}$ as required. $\square$

4. Montague grammars as sorted partial algebras

The standard notation for Montague grammars and even our simplified notation for disambiguated Montague grammars obscures their close relationship to sorted partial algebras, objects that have been studied extensively in universal algebra (see [1]). In this section we explain the connection between disambiguated Montague grammars and sorted partial algebras.

Theorem 4.1. *Let **MontG** and **PAlg** be the categories of disambiguated Montague grammars and (total) Peano algebras, respectively. There are* *functors* $\Phi : \mathbf{MontG} \to \mathbf{PAlg}$ *and* $\Psi : \mathbf{PAlg} \to \mathbf{MontG}$ *having the following properties:*

(1) *For every disambiguated Montague grammar* G, $G\Phi\Psi$ *and* G *are isomorphic.*

(2) *For every Peano algebra* $\mathcal{A}$, $\mathcal{A}\Psi\Phi$ *and* $\mathcal{A}$ *are isomorphic.*

(3) Φ *preserves isomorphisms.*

(4) *For every disambiguated Montague grammar* G, *the carrier set of* $G\Phi$ *is equal to* $L(G)$.

(5) *For every Peano algebra* $\mathcal{A}$, *the language* $L(\mathcal{A}\Psi)$ *is equal to the carrier set of* $\mathcal{A}$.

Proof. We first define Φ. Let $G = (\Delta, \Gamma, \mathcal{X}, \nu, \mathcal{S})$ be a disambiguated Montague grammar. We construct a sorted partial algebra

$$G\Phi = (\mathbf{L}(G), \sigma_G, \mathbf{D}(G), \Gamma, \nu)$$

as follows. The sort algebra is $\mathbf{D}(G) = (\Delta, \mathcal{S}, \Gamma, \nu)$. The partial algebra $\mathbf{L}(G)$ has $L = L(G)$ as its carrier set. For $x \in L$ define $x\sigma_G$ by $x \in C_{x\sigma_G}$. As the syntactic categories form a partition of L, σ_G is a well-defined total mapping of L into Δ.

For each operation symbol $\gamma \in \Gamma$ we now define the partial operation F_γ^L in the algebra $\mathbf{L}(G)$. For $x_1, \ldots, x_{\nu(\gamma)} \in L$, let F_γ^L be defined on $(x_1, \ldots, x_{\nu(\gamma)})$ if and only if $S_\gamma(x_1\sigma_G, \ldots, x_{\nu(\gamma)}\sigma_G)$ is defined and, if it is defined, the image is $\gamma(x_1, \ldots, x_{\nu(\gamma)})$. Let $\mathcal{F}^L = \{F_\gamma^L \mid \gamma \in \Gamma\}$ and $\mathbf{L}(G) = (L, \mathcal{F}^L, \Gamma, \nu)$. Then σ_G is a closed morphism of $\mathbf{L}(G)$ to $\mathbf{D}(G)$. Hence $G\Phi$ is a total sorted algebra. Moreover, $G\Phi$ is a Peano algebra with Peano basis X. Statement (4) is true by the definition of Φ.

Let H be a disambiguated Montague grammar, and let (ϕ, ψ) be a morphism of G to H. Let $(\phi, \psi)\Phi = (\phi|_{L(G)}, \psi)$ where $\phi|_{L(G)}$ is the restriction of ϕ to $L(G)$. Clearly, $(\phi, \psi)\Phi$ is a morphism of $G\Phi$ to $H\Phi$.

Now assume, that (ϕ, ψ) is an isomorphism. Thus, there is a morphism (ϕ', ψ') of H to G such that $(\phi, \phi)(\phi', \psi') = (\phi\phi', \psi\psi')$ is the identity morphism of G. We verify that

$$(\phi, \psi)\Phi(\phi', \psi')\Phi = (\phi|_{L(G)}\phi'|_{L(H)}, \psi\psi')$$

is the identity morphism of $G\Phi$. By Corollary 3.1, $L(G)\phi \subseteq L(H)$ and $L(H)\psi \subseteq L(G)$. Therefore, $x\phi = x\phi|_{L(G)}$ is in the domain of $\phi'|_{L(H)}$ for every $x \in L(G)$, and thus $x\phi|_{L(G)}\phi'|_{L(H)} = x$. Thus, $\phi|_{L(G)}\phi'|_{L(H)}$ is the identity morphism of $\mathbf{L}(G)$. By assumption, $\psi\psi'$ is the identity morphism of $\mathbf{D}(G)$. This proves that Φ preserves isomorphisms.

We now turn to the construction of Ψ. Let $\mathcal{A} = (\mathbf{A}, \sigma, \mathbf{S}, \Gamma, \nu)$ be a total Peano algebra with Peano basis X, where X is a subset of the carrier set A of $\mathbf{A}$ and where

$$\mathbf{A} = (A, \mathcal{F}^A, \Gamma, \nu) \text{ and } \mathbf{S} = (S, \mathcal{F}^S, \Gamma, \nu).$$

We construct a disambiguated Montague grammar

$$\mathcal{A}\Psi = (\Delta, \Gamma, \mathcal{X}, \nu, \mathcal{F}^S)$$

as follows. Let $\Delta = S$, that is, we identify the the sorts of $\mathcal{A}$ with the names of syntactic categories of $\mathcal{A}\Psi$ and, thus, we define $\mathbf{D}(\mathcal{A}\Psi)$ as $\mathbf{S}$. For $\delta \in \Delta$, let $X_\delta = X \cap \delta\sigma^{-1}$ and let $\mathcal{X} = \{X_\delta \mid \delta \in \Delta\}$.

Note that $\mathbf{A}$ can be considered as a partial Peano algebra with a single sort. Hence there is an absolutely free total algebra $\hat{\mathbf{A}}$ which is a completion of $\mathbf{A}$ (see [1], p. 80–82). Moreover, $\hat{\mathbf{A}}$ is uniquely determined up to isomorphim and isomorphic with the absolutely free total algebra[6] of type (Γ, ν) generated by X. Let $\hat{A}$ be the carrier set of $\hat{\mathbf{A}}$. Then, without loss of generality A can be considered as a subset of $\hat{A}$. Clearly, the construct $\mathcal{A}\Psi$ is a disambiguated Montague grammar and one has $L(\mathcal{A}\Psi) \subseteq \hat{A}$. We define $\mathbf{A}(\mathcal{A}\Psi)$ as $\hat{\mathbf{A}}$.

We now show that $A = L(\mathcal{A}\Psi)$. First, consider $x \in A$. If $x \in X$ then $x \in X_\delta$ with $x\sigma = \delta$ and, thus, $x \in C_{\mathcal{A}\Psi, \delta}$. If $x \notin A$ then $x = \gamma(x_1, \ldots, x_{\nu(\gamma)})$ for for some $\gamma \in \Gamma$ and some $x_1, \ldots, x_{\nu(\gamma)} \in A$ and $S_\gamma(x_1\sigma, \ldots, x_{\nu(\gamma)}\sigma)$ is defined and equal to some $\delta \in S = \Delta$ [1]. Let $\delta_i = x_i\sigma$ for $i = 1, \ldots, \nu(\gamma)$. By induction assumption, $x_i C_{\mathcal{A}\Psi, \delta_i}$ and, hence $x \in C_{\mathcal{A}\Psi, \delta}$. This proves $A \subseteq L(\mathcal{A}\Psi)$.

Second, for the converse, consider $x \in C_{\mathcal{A}\Psi, \delta}$ for some $\delta \in \Delta = S$. If $x \in X_\delta$, then $x \in A$ as $X_\delta \subseteq X \subseteq A$. Suppose that $x \notin X_\delta$. Thus, there is an operation symbol $\gamma \in \Gamma$ and there are $\delta_1, \ldots, \delta_{\nu(\gamma)} \in \Delta = S$ such that $x = \gamma(x_1, \ldots, x_{\nu(\gamma)})$ with $x_i \in C_{\mathcal{A}\Psi, \delta_i}$ for $i = 1, \ldots, \nu(\gamma)$. By induction assumption $x_i \in A$ for all i. Moreover, $S_\gamma(\delta_1, \ldots, \delta_{\nu(\gamma)})$ is defined and equal to δ. As σ is closed, $\gamma(x_1, \ldots, x_{\nu(\gamma)}) \in A$. This proves Statement (5).

It follows from this proof of (5) that $x \in C_{\mathcal{A}\Psi, \delta}$ if and only if $x \in A$ and $x\sigma = \delta$.

Now suppose that $\mathcal{B} = (\mathbf{B}, \tau, \mathbf{T}, \Gamma, \nu)$ is a total Peano algebra with Peano basis Y and (ϕ, ψ) is a morphism of $\mathcal{A}$ to $\mathcal{B}$. Define $(\phi, \psi)\Psi$ as $(\hat{\phi}, \psi)$ where $\hat{\phi}$ is the extension of ϕ to a morphism of $\mathbf{A}(\mathcal{A}\Psi)$ to $\mathbf{A}(\mathcal{B}\Psi)$. This extension exists and is unique.

---

[6] As we consider finitary operation symbols only, some of the constructions are simpler than those in [1], and $\hat{\mathbf{A}}$ is just the term algebra of type (Γ, ν) generated by X. For any given $\gamma \in \Gamma$ and $x_1, \ldots, x_{\nu(\gamma)} \in A$, we can, therefore, identify $x = F_\gamma(x_1, \ldots, x_{\nu(\gamma)}) \in A$ with the corresponding term $\hat{x} = \gamma(\hat{x}_1, \ldots, \hat{x}_{\nu(\Gamma)})$ where $\hat{x} = x$ for all $x \in X$. We use this identification in the sequel without special mention.

Now consider $x \in X_\delta = X \cap \delta\sigma^{-1}$. As $X \subseteq A$, x is in the domain of ϕ and $x\hat\phi = x\phi \in B = L(\mathcal{B}\Psi)$. Using the fact that (ϕ, ψ) is a morphism of $\mathcal{A}$ to $\mathcal{B}$, one verifies that $x\phi \in C_{\mathcal{B}\Psi, \delta\psi}$. This proves that $(\phi, \psi)\Psi$ is a morphism of $\mathcal{A}\Psi$ to $\mathcal{B}\Psi$.

To complete the proof of (1), consider a disambiguated Montague grammar $G = (\Delta, \Gamma, \mathcal{X}, \nu, \mathcal{S})$. Construct $G\Phi$ as above and let $G\Phi\Psi = (\Delta', \Gamma', \mathcal{X}', \nu', \mathcal{S}')$. By construction, $\Delta' = \Delta$, $\Gamma' = \Gamma$, $\mathcal{X}' = \mathcal{X}$, $\nu' = \nu$, $\mathcal{S}' = \mathcal{S}$, and there is an isomorphism of $\mathbf{A}(G)$ to $\mathbf{A}(G\Phi\Psi)$. Together with the identity morphism of $\mathbf{D}(G)$ this is an isomorphism of G to $G\Phi\Psi$. Note that this isomorphism is actually the identity if, in the constructions, we work within the term algebra of type (Γ, ν) generated by X.

Finally, to complete the proof of (2), consider a Peano algebra $\mathcal{A} = (\mathbf{A}, \sigma, \mathbf{S}, \Gamma, \nu)$ with Peano basis X. Construct $\mathcal{A}\Psi$ as above and let $\mathcal{A}\Psi\Phi = (\mathbf{A}', \sigma', \mathbf{S}', \Gamma', \nu')$. By construction one has $\Gamma' = \Gamma$, $\nu' = \nu$, and $\mathbf{S}' = \mathbf{S}$. Moreover, $A = L(\mathcal{A}\Psi) = A'$ where A' is the carrier set of $\mathbf{A}'$ and $\sigma = \sigma'$. $\square$

In Statements (1) and (2), identity instead of isomorphism can be achieved if all the constructions are carried out within a fixed term algebra.

5. Polynomial morphisms; some linguistic background

While the above definitions of morphisms of disambiguated Montague grammars and of sorted partial algebras are most natural from a purely algebraic point of view, they need to be expanded in order to model certain linguistic facts. Indeed, assume that two languages L_1 and L_2 are to be compared ('languages' taken in an informal sense!). It is certainly not reasonable to assume that these languages have the same syntactic categories, that their dictionaries are in one-to-one correspondence, or that their sentences are syntactically the same. On the other hand, we do assume that somehow both languages can essentially express the same ideas. Thus, loosely speaking, every sentence and every syntactical construct of one language would have its counterpart in the other one – though possibly not via direct correspondence of basic operations and syntactic categories. Therefore, one needs to consider a different kind of morphisms, that of polynomial morphisms.

In the present section of this paper, we provide a definition of polynomial morphisms and state some of their basic properties. The linguistic interpretation is then re-considered in the next section.

Recall that the elements of a total Peano algebra $\mathcal{A} = (\mathbf{A}, \sigma_A, \mathbf{S}, \Omega, \nu)$ with Peano basis X can be considered as terms or *polynomials* over the similarity type (Ω, ν) with unknowns in X. Let $\mathcal{B} = (\mathbf{B}, \sigma_B, \mathbf{S}, \Omega, \nu)$ be a sorted partial algebra with the same sort algebra. If $p(x_1, \ldots, x_n)$ is a polynomial with the n distinct unknowns $x_1, \ldots, x_n$ and if $b_1, \ldots, b_n$ are elements of $\mathcal{B}$ – not necessarily distinct – then

$$p(x_1, \ldots, x_n)[a_1, \ldots, a_n] = p(a_1, \ldots, a_n)$$

is the image of $p(x_1, \ldots, x_n)$ under the partial morphism of $\mathcal{A}$ into $\mathcal{B}$ which maps x_i onto a_i for $i = 1, \ldots, n$. Hence, the polynomial $p(x_1, \ldots, , x_n)$ can be considered as an n-ary operation in every sorted partial algebra with sort algebra $\mathcal{S}$.

Definition 5.1. Let $\mathcal{A} = (\mathbf{A}, \sigma_A, \mathbf{S}_A, \Omega_A, \nu_A)$ and $\mathcal{B} = (\mathbf{B}, \sigma_B, \mathbf{S}_B, \Omega_B, \nu_B)$ be sorted partial algebras. A *polynomial morphism* of $\mathcal{A}$ into $\mathcal{B}$ is a triple $\phi = (\phi_\Omega, \phi_S, \chi)$ of mappings with the following properties:

(a) ϕ_Ω is a mapping of Ω_A such that, for every $\omega \in \Omega_A$, $\phi_\Omega(\omega)$ is a $\nu_A(\omega)$-ary polynomial $p_\omega(x_1, \ldots, x_{\nu_A(\omega)})$ over (Ω_2, ν_2).

(b) ϕ_S is a mapping of $\mathbf{S}_A$ into $\mathbf{S}_B$ such that, for all $\omega \in \Omega_A$ and for all elements $s_1, \ldots, s_{\nu_A(\omega)}$ of $\mathbf{S}$, the existence of $\mathcal{F}_\omega^{S_A}(s_1, \ldots, s_{\nu_A(\omega)})$ implies that also

$$p_\omega(s_1\phi_S, \ldots, s_{\nu_A(\omega)}\phi_S)$$

exists and that it is equal to $\mathcal{F}_\omega^{S_A}(s_1, \ldots, s_{\nu_A(\omega)})\phi_S$.

(c) χ is a mapping of $\mathbf{A}$ into $\mathbf{B}$ such that, for all $\omega \in \Omega_A$ and for all elements $a_1, \ldots, a_{\nu_A(\omega)}$ of $\mathbf{A}$, the existence of $\mathcal{F}_\omega^A(a_1, \ldots, a_{\nu_A(\omega)})$ implies that also

$$p_\omega(a_1\chi, \ldots, a_{\nu_A(\omega)}\chi)$$

exists and that it is equal to $\mathcal{F}_\omega^A(a_1, \ldots, a_{\nu_A(\omega)})\chi$.

(d) $\sigma_A\phi_S = \chi\sigma_B$.

Lemma 5.1. *The sorted partial algebras with polynomial morphisms form a category.*

The proof of Lemma 5.1, being a simple application of the definition, is omitted. Using the functors of Theorem 4.1, one introduces the notion of *polynomial morphisms* of disambiguated Montague grammars as an approximation of the notion of language translation. One shows that the disambiguated Montague grammars with polynomial morphisms form a category and that there is a functorial connection between it and the category of total Peano algebras with polynomial morphisms which is induced by the functors of Theorem 4.1.

6. Comparison of languages through translations

In [12] and [13] one proposes to use language translations as a mechanism for the approximation or construction of a 'universal grammar.' In this section we follow that approach and describe a possible formal definition of that construction. The ideas developed in this section are still speculative and parts of the mathematical model may still have to be changed to match the linguistic facts.

Intuitively, a *translation* between two languages should be semantic preserving. This requirement immediately introduces several serious difficulties. The proposals of [12], [13], and [6] address this problem by giving the semantics a syntactic framework – this is very much in the spirit of Montague's original ideas. The suggested framework is essentially as follows: We are given two languages L_1 and L_2 ('languages' taken in an informal sense!). For these we suppose we have two disambiguated Montague grammars G_1 and G_2, respectively, and an abstract general semantics expressed as another disambiguated Montague grammar G together with two polynomial morphisms ϕ_i, $i = 1, 2$, which for every sentence of L_i determine its *meaning* in G. Linguistically, disambiguation means that ϕ_1 and ϕ_2 must be injective[7].

A *translation* from G_1 to G_2 would be a polynomial morphism ϕ of G_1 into G_2 such that the following diagram commutes.

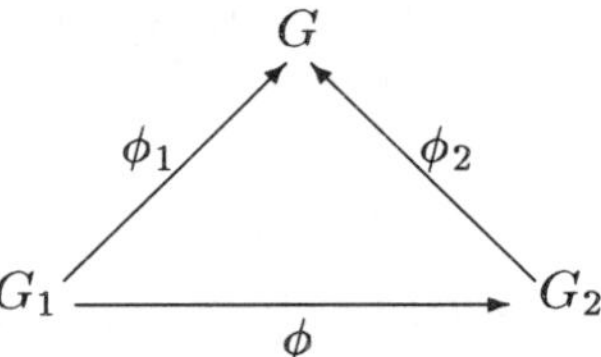

Some of the subtle linguistic problems with this formulation of the notion of translation are pointed out in [12] and [13]. If the diagram above commutes then ϕ is injective. In real linguistic situations this rarely happens. Indeed, a translation is usually not injective implying that the translation reveals hidden ambiguities in G_2, that is, G_2 is not really disambiguated as far as semantics is concerned. Similarly, a translation from L_2 to L_1 could reveal hidden ambiguities in G_1.

To resolve this problem, one constructs a common grammar H for L_1 and L_2 – a step towards a universal grammar – such that the structures of L_1 and

---

[7]As a basic linguistic – or philosophical – axiom one usually assumes that every human language is capable of expressing every possible 'meaning.' This would imply that ϕ_1 and ϕ_2 are also surjective. This requirement seems to be too strong, mathematically, and we are still discussing weaker assumptions which would, nevertheless, reflect the philosophical position. For the intuitive discussion in this part of the paper we make the rather vague assumption that the images of ϕ_1 and ϕ_2 have a 'very large' intersection.

L_2 are explained by H and H is disambiguated[8].

The disambiguated Montague grammar H would have the following properties. There are surjective polynomial morphisms ϕ'_i, $i = 1, 2$, and an injective polynomial morphism ϕ^H such that the following diagram commutes.

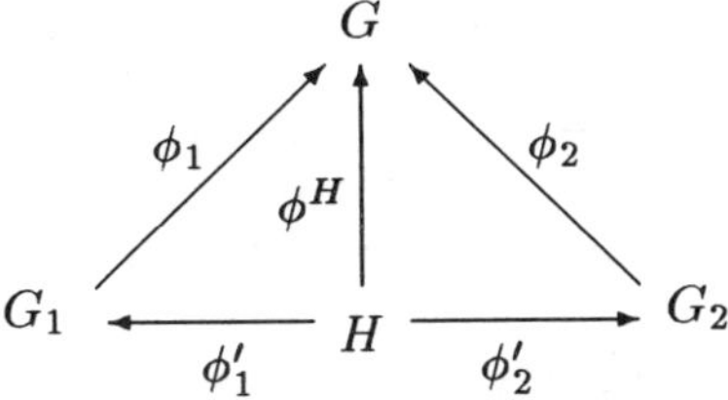

Moreover, H would have to have certain universality properties (similar to those of a pullback).

Whether this is the right mathematical model for the linguistic facts is still an unresolved matter. However, we believe that the results of this paper, placing the problem in its proper algebraic context, will help to resolve this question.

7. Montague grammars and context-free grammars

In this section we determine the connection between Montague grammars and grammars in the sense of Chomsky[9]. Chomsky grammars are string rewriting systems with a few additional properties. Among the various kinds of Chomsky grammars, we only consider context-free grammars in the sequel.

If X is any set then let X^* denote the set of all words over X, including the *empty word* ϵ. With concatenation of words as multiplication, X^* is the free monoid generated by X.

Definition 7.1. A *context-free grammar* is a quadruple $H = (N, T, P, R)$ such that N is a finite non-empty set, the *alphabet of nonterminal*, T is a finite, non-empty set with $T \cap N = \emptyset$, the *alphabet of terminal symbols*, $R \in N$ is the *start symbol*, and P is a finite set of *production rules* of the form $A \to u$ with $A \in N$ and $u \in (N \cup T)^*$.

In order to achieve the comparison with disambiguated Montague grammars in all generality, we need the notion of a *generalized context-free grammar*. For its definition one drops all finiteness conditions in Definition 7.1

---

[8] We see that the term 'disambiguated' really has two meanings, the mathematical one derived from the notion of freeness in algebra and the linguistic one which seems to imply the existence of a notion of degree of disambiguation.

[9] We assume that the reader is familiar with basic properties of Chomsky grammars. Any book on formal languages or the theory of computer science would serve as a reference for introductory information on this subject, for example [14].

Let $H = (N, T, P, R)$ be a generalized context-free grammar. On $(N \cup T)^*$, the set P of production rules defines the relation $\Longrightarrow_H$, or just $\Longrightarrow$ when H is understood, by

$$v \Longrightarrow w \text{ if and only if } \exists v_1, v_2, A, u \ (v = v_1 A v_2 \wedge A \to u \in P \wedge w = v_1 u v_2)$$

for $v, w \in (N \cup T)^*$. Let $\Longrightarrow^*$ be the reflexive and transitive closure of $\Longrightarrow$. One has $v \Longrightarrow^* w$ for $v, w \in (N \cup T)^*$ if and only if there is an $n \in \mathbf{N}_0$ and there are words $v_0, \ldots, v_n \in (N \cup T)^*$ such that

$$v = v_0 \Longrightarrow v_1 \Longrightarrow \cdots \Longrightarrow v_{n-1} \Longrightarrow v_n = w.$$

Any such sequence $(v_0, v_1, \ldots, v_n)$ is called a *derivation* of w from v. The *language generated by H* is the set $L(H)$ of all words $w \in T^*$ such that $R \Longrightarrow^* w$.

Suppose that $D_{A,w} = (v_0, \ldots, v_n)$ is a derivation of w from A with $A \in N$ and $w \in (N \cup T)^*$. With $D_{A,w}$ one associates the corresponding *derivation tree* $t(D_{A,w})$.

To represent (ordered) trees with node labels, we use the following notation: The empty tree is represented by (). A tree consisting of single labelled node only is represented by that label. A tree with root label x and maximal subtrees $t_1, \ldots, t_n$ (in this order) is represented by $x(\hat{t}_1, \ldots, \hat{t}_n)$ where, for $i = 1, \ldots, n$, $\hat{t}_i$ represents t_i. In the sequel we do not distinguish between trees and their representations.

The *yield* of such a tree t is a word $yield(t)$ over the node labels obtained as follows. If $t = ()$ then $yield(t) = \epsilon$. If t is a single node labelled by x then $yield(t) = x$. If $t = x(t_1, \ldots, t_n)$ then $yield(t) = yield(t_1) \cdots yield(t_n)$.

The tree $t(D_{A,w})$ is constructed recursively. The tree corresponding to v_0 consists of a single node labelled by A as $v_0 = A$; it is given by the expression A. Now consider the step from v_{i-1} to v_i and suppose it is achieved using the rule $B \to u$. Let the tree corresponding to v_{i-1} be given and represented by an expression of the form $A(\ldots, B, \ldots)$, where B in this expression corresponds to the occurrence of B in v_{i-1} which is going to be replaced – and is a leaf node of the tree. Replace this leaf node – or the occurrence of B in the expression – by the tree represented by the expression $B(u_1, \ldots, u_k)$ where $u_1, \ldots, u_k \in N \cup T$ and $u = u_1 \cdots u_k$. The derivation tree represents the derivation uniquely up to equivalence of derivations (see [14], for example). Its yield is the word w.

For a word in $L(H)$, its derivation trees for derivations from the start variable describe the word's syntactical structure with respect to the given grammar. If there is only one derivation tree for every word in $L(H)$ then the grammar is said to be *unambiguous*. For $A \in N$, let $T_A(H)$ be the set of derivation trees of the words in T^* from the symbol A.

We now proceed to describe the connection between Montague grammars and context-free grammars. Let $G = (\Delta, \Gamma, \mathcal{X}, \nu, \mathcal{S})$ be a disambiguated Montague grammar. We construct a generalized context-free grammar $H(G) = (N, T, P, R)$ from G. For each $\delta \in \Delta$ and $\gamma \in \Gamma$, let $[\delta, \gamma]$ be a new symbol and let R be a symbol distinct from these and from all other symbols. Let

$$N = \Delta \cup \{[\delta, \gamma] \mid \delta \in \Delta, \gamma \in \Gamma\} \cup \{R\}.$$

Let $T = \bigcup_{\delta \in \Delta} X_\delta$. In P, we have four kinds of production rules.

(1) $\delta \to [\delta, \gamma] \in P$ if and only if δ is in the image of S_γ.

(2) $[\delta, \gamma] \to \delta_1 \cdots \delta_{\nu(\gamma)} \in P$ for all $\delta_1, \ldots, \delta_{\nu(\gamma)} \in \Delta$ such that $S_\gamma(\delta_1, \ldots, \delta_{\nu(\gamma)})$ is defined and equal to δ.

(3) $\delta \to x \in P$ for $\delta \in \Delta$ and $x \in X_\delta$.

(4) $R \to \delta \in P$ for $\delta \in \Delta$

In order for $H(G)$ to be generalized context-free grammar, we assume without loss of generality that $T \cap N = \emptyset$.

Theorem 7.1. *Let $G = (\Delta, \Gamma, \mathcal{X}, \nu, \mathcal{S})$ be a disambiguated Montague grammar, and let $H(G) = (N, T, P, R)$ be the generalized context-free grammar constructed above. For each $\delta \in \Delta$, there is a bijection from C_δ onto the set $T_\delta(H(G))$. Moreover, there is a bijection from the language $L(G)$ onto the set $T_R(H(G))$. The grammar $H(G)$ is a context-free grammar if and only if G is finite.*

Proof. With each $x \in L(G)$ we associate a tree $\tau(x)$ as follows. Consider $x \in L(G)$. If $x \in X$, then there is a unique $\delta \in \Delta$ such that $x \in X_\delta$, and the corresponding tree $\tau(x)$ is $\delta(x)$. Suppose that $x \notin X$. Then there is a unique $\delta \in \Delta$ such that $x \in C_\delta \setminus X_\delta$. Moreover, there is a unique $\gamma \in \Gamma$ and there are unique $x_1, \ldots, x_{\nu(\gamma)} \in L(G)$ and unique $\delta_1, \ldots, \delta_{\nu(\gamma)} \in \Delta$ such that $S_\gamma(\delta_1, \ldots, \delta_{\nu(\gamma)}) = \delta$ and $x_i \in C_{\delta_i}$ for $i = 1, \ldots, \nu(\gamma)$. Define $\tau(x)$ as $\delta([\delta, \gamma](\tau(x_1), \ldots, \tau(x_{\nu(\gamma)})))$.

Clearly, for each $\delta \in \Delta$, τ maps C_δ into the set $T_\delta(H(G))$. One shows by induction that τ is injective. For each $x \in L(G)$, let $\hat{\tau}(x)$ be the tree $R(\tau(x))$. Then $\hat{\tau}$ is an injective mapping of $L(G)$ into $T_R(H(G))$.

On the other hand, let t be any derivation tree in $T_\delta(H(G))$ with $\delta \in \Delta$. There are two possibilities. Either $t = \delta(x)$ for some $x \in X_\delta$, hence $x \in L(G)$ and $\tau(x) = t$, or $t = \delta([\delta, \gamma](t_1, \ldots, t_{\nu(\gamma)}))$ with $\gamma \in \Gamma$ and each t_i a derivation tree of some x_i from some δ_i for $i = 1, \ldots, \nu(\gamma)$. Moreover, $S_\gamma(\delta_1, \ldots, \delta_{\nu(\gamma)}) = \delta$ and $\delta([\delta, \gamma](\delta_1, \ldots, \delta_{\nu(\gamma)}))$ is a derivation tree of $\delta_1 \cdots \delta_{\nu(\gamma)}$ from δ. By induction $x_i \in C_{\delta_i}$ for $i = 1, \ldots, \nu(\gamma)$ and $t_i = \tau(x_i)$. Thus $t = \tau(x)$ where

220   H. Jürgensen and K. Tent

$x = \gamma(x_1, \dots, x_{\nu(\gamma)})$. This shows that τ maps each C_δ onto $T_\delta(H(G))$. As a consequence, also $\hat{\tau}$ is surjective.

For the last statement, note that N is finite if and only Δ and Γ are finite, and T is finite if and only if X is finite. Moreover, in that case also P is finite. $\square$

The construction of a generalized context-free grammar from a disambiguated Montague grammar shown above clarifies two important points. First, Montague grammars separate the syntactic structure from its written or spoken representation[10]. In Chomsky grammars, on the other hand, these issues are mixed from the start – derivation trees are inferred objects. This reflects clearly the differences in the underlying philosophy. Second, however, items important to linguistic theory take spots of similar importance in either approach. The syntactic categories, expressed by Δ, and the syntactic constructions, expressed by Γ, have their counterparts as *the* nonterminal symbols – in addition to R which is of technical relevance only. Thus, important aspects of syntax are equally represented in either formalism. Structural details, however, are *forgotten* by Chomsky grammars at an earlier stage than by Montague grammars.

We now consider a converse of the above construction. We start with a generalized context-free grammar $H = (N, T, P, R)$ and construct a disambiguated Montague grammar $G(H) = (\Delta, \Gamma, \mathcal{X}, \nu, \mathcal{S})$ from it. The main idea of the construction is that the nonterminal symbols should play the rôle of the names of the syntactic categories and also of the operation symbols, such that applying a rule $A \to u_1 \cdots u_i \in P$ with $u_1, \dots, u_i \in N \cup T$ would correspond applying an operation A to $(u_1, \dots, u_i)$. The main problem is that A would not have a fixed arity. To solve this we introduce the notion of a *homogeneous generalized context-free grammar* and show that, for every generalized context-free grammar, a homogeneous generalized context-free grammar can be found which has – in a sense to be defined – the same derivation trees.

Definition 7.2. A generalized context-free grammar $H = (N, T, P, R)$ is said to be *homogeneous* if P has the following property: For all $A \in N$, if $A \to u \in P$ and $A \to v \in P$ then $|u| = |v|$.

Lemma 7.1. *Let $H = (N, T, P, R)$ be a generalized context-free grammar. There is a homogeneous generalized context-free grammar $H' = (N', T, P', R)$ with $N \subseteq N'$ such that $L(H) = L(H')$ and, for every $A \in N$, there is a bijection of $T_A(H)$ onto $T_A(H')$. Moreover, H' is a homogeneous context-free grammar if and only if H is a context-free grammar.*

Proof. The proof is based on an idea used to show that the context-free languages are the yields of the forests recognized by finite tree automata [4].

---

[10] To be precise, they do so when considered without the additional modifications as discussed in the linguistics literature.

Consider $A \in N$. If there is a rule $A \to w \in P$ then we introduce a new symbol $[A, i]$ with $i = |w|$. Let

$$N' = N \cup \left\{ [A, i] \mid A \in N, i \in \mathbf{N}_0, \exists w \in (N \cup T)^* \; (A \to w \in P \text{ and } i = |w|) \right\}.$$

The new set P' of rules is given by

$$\begin{aligned} P' \;=\; & \{A \to [A, i] \mid A, [A, i] \in N'\} \cup \\ & \cup \{[A, i] \to w \mid [A, i] \in N', w \in (N \cup T)^i, A \to w \in P\}. \end{aligned}$$

Let $H' = (N', T, P', R)$.

If $u_1 A u_2 \Longrightarrow_H u_1 w u_2$ with $u_1, u_2 \in (N \cup T)^*$ and $A \to w \in P$ then $u_1 A u_2 \Longrightarrow_{H'} u_1 [A, i] u_2 \Longrightarrow_{H'} u_1 w u_2$ with $i = |w|$. Thus, for every derivation with respect to H there is a corresponding derivation with respect to H' in which every derivation step with respect to H is replaced by two steps with respect to H' as shown.

Conversely, let

$$v = v_0 \Longrightarrow_{H'} v_1 \Longrightarrow_{H'} v_2 \Longrightarrow_{H'} \cdots \Longrightarrow_{H'} v_{n-1} \Longrightarrow_{H'} v_n = w$$

be a derivation with respect to H' such that $v, w \in (N \cup T)^*$. By the definition of P', a nonterminal $A \in N$ can only be written in two steps, first using $A \to [A, i]$ for some i and then, possibly several steps later, $[A, i] \to u$ for some u such that $A \to u \in P$ and $|u| = i$. As v and w contain only symbols in $N \cup T$, for any step involving a rule $A \to [A, i]$ in the above derivation there is also a step in which the corresponding occurrence of $[A, i]$ is rewritten. As H' is a generalized context-free grammar, we may re arrange the derivation steps in such a way that these two steps succeed each other. This can be performed for all derivation steps resulting in an equivalent derivation with respect to H'. By combining successive pairs of steps involving rules of the forms $A \to [A, i]$ and $[A, i] \to u$ into single steps involving the corrsponding rules $A \to u$, one obtains a derivation of w from v with respect to H. This completes the proof of the first two statements.

The last statement follows from the fact that N' and P' are finite if and only if N and P are finite. $\qquad\square$

Theorem 7.2. *Let $H = (N, T, P, R)$ be a homogeneous generalized context-free grammar. There is a disambiguated Montague grammar $G(H) = (\Delta, \Gamma, \mathcal{X}, \nu, \mathcal{S})$ such that $t \in L(G(H)) \setminus X$ if and only if $t \in T_A(H)$ for some $A \in N$.*

Proof. Without loss of generality we may assume that, for every $A \in N$ there is a rule in P with A on its left hand side[11]. Let $\Gamma = N$ and, for $A \in \Gamma$, let $\nu(A) = |u|$ where $A \to u \in P$. As H is homogeneous, ν is well-defined.

---

[11] The standard proof of this fact for context-free grammar s (see [14], for example) can be modified to deal with generalized context-free grammar s – at the cost of constructivity, of course.

For $x \in N \cup T$, let δ_x be a new symbol, and let $\Delta = \{\delta_x \mid x \in N \cup T\}$. Let $\mathcal{X} = \{X_\delta \mid \delta \in \Delta\}$ where X_{δ_x} is empty for $x \in N$ and equal to $\{x\}$ for $x \in T$.

For $A \in N$, the partial function S_A is given as follows. Let $\delta_1, \ldots, \delta_{\nu(A)} \in \Delta$. Then $S_A(\delta_1, \ldots, \delta_{\nu(A)})$ is defined and equal to δ_A if and only if there is a rule $A \to u_1 \cdots u_{\nu(A)}$ in P with $u_1, \ldots, u_{\nu(A)} \in N \cup T$ such that $\delta_i = \delta_{u_i}$ for $i = 1, \ldots, \nu(A)$. This completes the definition of $G = G(H)$.

Note that $C_{\delta_x} = X_{\delta_x} = \{x\}$ for all $x \in T$. Indeed, suppose that there is a $t \in C_{\delta_x} \setminus X_{\delta_x}$ for some $x \in T$. Then $t = A(t_1, \ldots, t_{\nu(A)})$ for some uniquely determined $A \in \Gamma$ and $t_i \in C_{\delta_i}$ for $i = 1, \ldots, \nu(A)$ such that $S_A(\delta_1, \ldots, \delta_{\nu(A)}) = \delta_x$. By the definition of S_A one has $x = A \in N$, a contradiction.

Consider $t \in L(G)$. Then there is a unique $x \in N \cup T$ such that $t \in C_{\delta_x}$. We show, using induction on the nesting depth, that either $t = x \in T$ or $x \in N$ and $t \in T_x(H)$.

By the above, if $x \in T$ then $t = x$. Suppose now that $x \in N$. As $X_{\delta_x} = \emptyset$ it follows that $t = A(t_1, \ldots, t_{\nu(A)})$ for some uniquely determined $A \in \Gamma$ and $t_i \in C_{\delta_i}$ for $i = 1, \ldots, \nu(A)$ such that $S_A(\delta_1, \ldots, \delta_{\nu(A)})$ is defined and equal to δ_x, hence $x = A$. For $i = 1, \ldots, \nu(A)$, let $x_i \in N \cup T$ be such that $\delta_{x_i} = \delta_i$. As S_A is defined on $(\delta_1, \ldots, \delta_{\nu(A)})$ and equal to δ_A, there is a derivation rule $A \to x_1 \cdots x_{\nu(A)}$ in P. For $i = 1, \ldots, \nu(A)$, if $x_i \in T$ then $t_i = x_i$; if $x_i \in N$ then, by induction assumption, $t_i \in T_{x_i}(H)$. This proves that $t \in T_x(H) = T_A(H)$.

For the converse, consider a derivation tree t from $A \in N$ to some word containing only terminal symbols. We use induction on the height of t. The corresponding derivation must have at least one step. Let $A \to u_1 \cdots u_{\nu(A)}$ be the rule applied in the first step, where $u_1, \ldots, u_{\nu(A)} \in N \cup T$. For $i = 1, \ldots, \nu(A)$, if $u_i \in T$ then u_i is a leaf node t_i of t; if $u_i \in N$ then u_i is the root label of a derivation tree t_i from u_i to a terminal word with respect to H. By induction assumption, as the height of t_i is strictly smaller than that of t, $t_i \in C_{\delta_{u_i}}$. Moreover, $S_A(\delta_{u_1}, \ldots, \delta_{u_{\nu(A)}})$ is defined and equal to δ_A. Therefore, $t = A(t_1, \ldots, t_{\nu(A)}) \in C_{\delta_A}$. $\qquad\square$

Together, these results corroborate a statement made earlier: The main difference between disambiguated Montague grammars and context-free grammars is that the former maintain complete structural information about sentences in the language while the latter discard this information during the derivation process. The above contructions show how this structural information can be removed from a disambiguated Montague grammar to arrive at a corresponding context-free grammar and how, starting from a context-free grammar, this information can be re-introduced to arrive at a disambiguated Montague grammar. These constructions are not really inverses of each other because they introduce technical artifacts – the symbols $[\delta, \gamma]$ in the first contruction, the symbols $[A, i]$ and the singleton dictionary sets in the second one. However, essentially the following weaker kind of equivalence is achieved. Let G be a disambiguated Montague grammar and H a generalized context-free grammar. Then the derivation trees of $H(G)$ and the words in $L(G) \setminus X$ are in one-to-one correspondence. Moving on to $G(H(G))$ one gets a one to one correspondence between the languages $L(G)$ and $L(G(H(G)))$, but some syntactic categories have been split. This continues in further two-step iterations. On the other hand, starting from H, making H homogeneous doubles the heights of derivation trees. The construction of $G(H)$ yields exactly these trees. The construction of $H(G(H))$ introduces additional nonterminals which, again double the heights of derivation trees. This is continued in further iteration steps.

These problems can be avoided by more careful constructions that would take the special properties of $H(G)$ and $G(H)$ into account.

References

1. P. Burmeister, *A Model Theoretic Oriented Approach to Partial Algebras*, Akademie-Verlag, Berlin, 1986.

2. S.-K. Chang, Icon semantics – A formal approach to icon system design, *International J. of Pattern Recognition and Artificial Intelligence*, 1 (1987), 103 – 120.

3. D. R. Dowty, R. F. Wall, S. Peters, *Introduction to Montague Semantics*, D. Reidel Publishing Co., Dordrecht, 1981.

4. F. Gécseg, M. Steinby, *Tree Automata*, Akadémiai Kiadó, Budapest, 1984.

5. G. Grätzer, *Universal Algebra*, D. van Nostrand Company, Inc., Princeton, New Jersey, 1968.

6. J. Landsbergen, Montague grammar and machine translation, in *Linguistic Theory and Computer Applications* (Whitelock et al., eds.), Academic Press, New York, 1987, 113 – 147.

7. S. MacLane, *Categories for the Working Mathematician*, Springer-Verlag, New-York, 1971.

8. R. Montague, Universal grammar, *Theoria*, 36 (1970), 373 – 398. Reprinted in [10].

9. R. Montague, H. Schnelle, *Universale Grammatik*, Vieweg, Braunschweig, 1972.

10. R. Montague, *Formal Philosophy. Selected Papers of Richard Montague*, Edited and with an introduction by R. H. Thomason, Yale University Press, New Haven, 1974.

11. H. Reichel, *Initial Computability, Algebraic Specifications, and Partial Algebras*, Akademie-Verlag, Berlin, 1987.

12. K. Tent, *Die Anwendung von Montague-Übersetzungen in der Universalienforschung*, Dissertation, Universität Kiel, 1988.

13. K. Tent, The application of Montague translations in universal research and typology, *Linguistics and Philosophy*, 13 (1990), 661 – 686.

14. D. Wood, *Theory of Computation*, Harper & Row, New York, 1987.

On the Defect Effect
of Many Identities in Free Semigroups[1]

Juhani KARHUMÄKI

Department of Mathematics, University of Turku
SF 20500 Turku, Finland

Wojciech PLANDOWSKI

Institute of Computer Science, Warsaw University
02-097 Banacha 2, Warsaw, Poland

0. Introduction

One of the fundamental properties of free semigroups is stated in Defect Theorem: If n words of a free semigroup satisfies a nontrivial identity, they can be expressed as products of $n - 1$ words. Actually this theorem has different formulations; the above one emphasizes a combinatorial point of view, cf. [4], another an algebraic one cf. [2], [7].

A natural question is: What happens if the set $X = \{x_1, \ldots, x_n\}$ of n words in a free semigroup satisfies two (independent) identities? Can these words be stated in terms of $n - 2$ words ? The well-known answer is "no", cf. Section 1. On the other hand, considering a generalization of the combinatorial defect theorem, it is possible to find necessary conditions for n words to be expressable by $n - t$ $(t - 2, \ldots, n-1)$ words, cf. [4]. In particular, for $t = n - 1$ (e.g. X is periodic) such a condition is that the following graph G_X associated with X is connected. The vertices of G_X correspond to words of X and there exists an edge between x_i and x_j iff $x_i X^* \cap x_j X^* \neq \emptyset$.

In this paper we search for how many independent identities, words in X can satisfy without forcing the defect effect of a certain order t. In particular we concentrate to the extreme cases when $t = 2$ or $t = n - 1$. The former corresponds to the fact that the identities imply only the smallest possible defect effect, while the latter means that the identities are still satisfied by a nonperiodic set of words.

We consider the above problems both in free monoids and free semigroups. In free semigroups we show the following two results. First, for each natural number n we construct a set of $3n+2$ words such that they are not expressable as products of $3n$ words but still satisfy $\Omega(n^2)$ independent equations. Second, we construct a nonperiodic set of $O(n)$ words satisfying $\Omega(n^3)$ independent equalities. For free monoids we show that the above lower bounds are $\Omega(n^3)$

---

[1]This work was supported by the Academy of Finland under the grant 11181.

and $\Omega(n^4)$, respectively. Note, that the systems of equations must be solved in a sufficiently large structures, for example in the case of the first lower bound in a free semigroup containing at least $3n + 1$ generators.

The proofs of the above results utilize ideas of [6] where the sizes of independent systems of equations in free monoids and semigroups, among the other things, are studied. Of course, the system is independent if it is not equivalent to any of its subsystems. By the validity of the Ehrenfeucht Conjecture, cf. [1], [5], [8], we know that each independent system of equations with a finite number of unknowns in a free monoid or semigroup is finite, although no upper bound for its size is known.

1. Preliminaries

Free *monoids* and *semigroups* generated by a (not necessarily finite) alphabet Σ are denoted by Σ^* and $\Sigma^+ = \Sigma^* - \{1\}$, respectively. An *equation* with variables $X = \{x_1, \ldots, x_n\}$ is a pair $(u, v) \in X^+ \times X^+$, denoted by $u = v$. A *solution* of the equation $u = v$ in Σ^* (resp. Σ^+) is a morphism $h : X^* \to \Sigma^*$ (resp. $h : X^+ \to \Sigma^+$) satisfying $h(u) = h(v)$. Hence, a solution can be identified with an n-tuple of words. System of equations as well as their solutions are defined in a natural way.

Two systems of equations are *equivalent* iff they have exactly the same solutions. A system is *independent* iff it is not equivalent to any of its proper subsystems.

Our interest is in solutions of systems of equations, that is in (ordered) finite sets of words. Hence, we define a *degree* of a set of words $X = \{x_1, \ldots, x_n\}$, as

$$deg(X) = \min\{|F| \mid X \subseteq F^*\}.$$

where vertical bars denote the cardinality of a set. We say that X is *periodic* iff its degree equals 1.

With the above terminology Defect Theorem can be stated as follows:

Defect Theorem: *Any solution of a nontrivial equation with n variables is of degree at most $n - 1$.*

The fact that the degree of solutions of two independent equations need not diminish by two is seen as follows: Consider the pair

$$
\begin{aligned}
xzy &= yzx \\
xz^2y &= yz^2x
\end{aligned}
$$

of equations. Clearly, it has a solution $x = y = \alpha$, $z = \beta$ which can be chosen to be of degree two in a free monoid or semigroup containing at least two generators. However, this system is independent since the triple

$$x = aba, z = b, y = a$$

is a solution of the first but not of the second equation, while the triple

$$x = abba, z = b, y = a$$

shows the reverse.

We do not know any system of three independent equations with three variables having a nonperiodic solution in a free semigroup. The results in [9] may be helpful here.

We conclude this section by introducing, for each $t \geq 1$, a function $F_t :$ $\mathbf{N} \to \mathbf{N} \cup \{\infty\}$ as follows

$$F_t(n) = \begin{cases} 1 & \text{if } n < t \\ \sup\{|S| \mid \begin{array}{l} S \text{ is an independent system of} \\ \text{equations with } n \text{ variables having} \\ \text{a solution of degree } n - t\} \end{array} & \text{otherwise.} \end{cases}$$

Clearly, the above functions depend also on structures where the equations are solved, i.e. in each case we have two families of these mappings, one for free monoids and another for free semigroups. It is also worth noticing that although, as we mentioned, there does not exist an infinite independent system of equations in these structures, we cannot be sure whether the values $F_t(n)$ are finite.

Informally, $F_t(n)$ measures the maximal size of independent systems of equations of n variables having only the defect of order t, e.g. having a solution of degree $n-t$. Consequently, the value $t = 1$ corresponds to the minimal defect effect while the value $t = n - 2$ corresponds to the case of having nonperiodic solutions. By our example of this section we have $F_1(3) \geq 2$.

2. $F_t(n)$ in free semigroups

In this section we search for lower bounds for the values $F_t(n)$ in free semigroups. In particular, we prove nontrivial lower bounds for the extreme cases $t = 1$ and $t = n - 2$.

Theorem 1. $F_1(n) = \Omega(n^2)$ *in free semigroups.*

Proof. Define $X = \{x, y\} \cup \{u_i, v_i, w_i \mid i = 1, \ldots, n\}$, as the set of variables and consider the system S of equalities containing the following equations

$$x u_j w_k v_j y \;=\; y u_j w_k v_j x, \qquad \text{for } j, k = 1, \ldots, n.$$

Clearly, $|S| = n^2$ and the number of variables is $3n + 2$.

We have to show that:
(i) S has a solution of degree $3n + 1$,
(ii) S is independent.

Condition (i) is easily fulfilled: Choose $x = y$ when all equations of S become trivial, so that a required solution can be found in a free semigroup having $3n + 1$ generators.

Condition (ii) is a simple modification of constructions in [6]. We have to show that for fixed j and k there exists a solution of the system

$$S(j,k) = S - \{xu_j w_k v_j y = yu_j w_k v_j x\}$$

which is not a solution of the whole S. It is a matter of simple calculations that the following evaluation of the unknowns works here:

$$(\alpha) \begin{cases} y &= b \\ x &= b^2 ab \\ u_t &= \begin{cases} ba & \text{if } t = j \\ bab & \text{otherwise,} \end{cases} \\ w_t &= \begin{cases} bab^2 & \text{if } t = k \\ b & \text{otherwise,} \end{cases} \\ v_t &= \begin{cases} ba & \text{if } t = j \\ a & \text{otherwise.} \end{cases} \end{cases}$$

$\square$

Theorem 1 yields immediately:

Corollary 2. *For each natural number n there exist systems of equations S_1 and S_2 with $O(n)$ variables such that*

(i) $|S_2| = \Omega(n^2)$,
(ii) $S_1 \cup S_2$ is independent,
(iii) the maximal degrees of solutions of S_1 and S_2 are the same.

Intuitively, the above corollary tells that for certain equations one can add step by step more and more new constraints without obtaining any new defect effect. More precisely, this can be done at least $\Omega(n^2)$ times in an equation containing $O(n)$ variables.

For the other extreme we have a better lower bound.

Theorem 3. $F_{n-2}(n) = \Omega(n^3)$ *in a free semigroup.*

Proof. Define $X = \{x_i, y_i, u_i, w_i, v_i \mid \text{for } i = 1, \ldots, n\}$ as the set of variables and consider the system S of equations containing the following equations

$$x_i u_j w_k v_j y_i = y_i u_j w_k v_j x_i, \qquad \text{for } i, j, k = 1, \ldots, n$$

This is obtained from the system of the previous proof by replacing variables x, y by new $2n$ variables x_i, y_i respectively. Clearly, S has n^3 equations with $5n$ variables. To prove independence of the system it is enough to extend the evaluation (α) from the previous proof in the following way:

$$
x_t = \begin{cases} b^2ab & \text{if } t = i \\ a & \text{otherwise,} \end{cases}
$$
$$
y_t = \begin{cases} b & \text{if } t = i \\ a & \text{otherwise.} \end{cases}
$$

and directly check that it satisfies all equations from S, except $x_i u_j w_k v_j y_i = y_i u_j w_k v_j x_i$. Fix now i, j and k. The evaluation above is nonperiodic and it is a solution of the system $S - \{x_i u_j w_k v_j y_i = y_i u_j w_k v_j x_i\}$, which is independent, and consists of $n^3 - 1$ equations with $5n$ variables, i.e. it is a system we are looking for. $\qquad\square$

Remark. Essentially in the same way we proved Theorem 3 we can prove more general result:

$$
F_t(3n + 2t) \;\geq\; tn^2, \qquad \text{for } n, t \geq 1
$$

3. $F_t(n)$ for free monoids

In this section we look for bounds for $F_t(n)$ in free monoids. Clearly, the lower bound results of Section 1 holds here, too. Moreover, these results can be improved, due to the fact that a possibility to give a variable the value 1 is a powerful tool when constructing independent systems of equations.

Theorem 4. $F_1(n) = \Omega(n^3)$ *in free monoids.*

Proof. Define $X = \{y\} \cup \{x_i, u_i, v_i, \bar{x}_i, \bar{u}_i, \bar{v}_i, \tilde{x}_i, \tilde{u}_i, \tilde{v}_i \mid i = 1, \ldots, n\}$ and consider the following system S of equations:

$$
yx_i u_j v_k \bar{x}_i \bar{u}_j \bar{v}_k \tilde{x}_i \tilde{u}_j \tilde{v}_k \;=\; x_i u_j v_k \bar{x}_i \bar{u}_j \bar{v}_k \tilde{x}_i \tilde{u}_j \tilde{v}_k y, \text{for } i, j, k = 1, \ldots, n. \quad (*)
$$

Clearly, $|S| = n^3$ and $|X| = 9n + 1$.

We have to show that
(i) S has a solution of degree $9n$ and that
(ii) S is independent.

The first claim is clear: Set $y = 1$, when $(*)$ reduces to a trivial identity, and thus possesses a solution of degree $9n$ in a monoid generated by $9n$ elements.

The claim (ii) is again a modification of a construction in [6]. Let for fixed i, j and k

$$
S(i, j, k) = S - \{yx_i u_j v_k \bar{x}_i \bar{u}_j \bar{v}_k \tilde{x}_i \tilde{u}_j \tilde{v}_k = x_i u_j v_k \bar{x}_i \bar{u}_j \bar{v}_k \tilde{x}_i \tilde{u}_j \tilde{v}_k y\}.
$$

Then the following evaluation of unknowns yields a solution of $S(i,j,k)$, but not of S:

$$(\beta) \begin{cases} y & = & ababa \\ x_t = u_t = v_t & = & \begin{cases} ab & \text{if } t = i \\ 1 & \text{otherwise,} \end{cases} \\ \bar{x}_t = \bar{u}_t = \bar{v}_t & = & \begin{cases} a & \text{if } t = j \\ 1 & \text{otherwise,} \end{cases} \\ \tilde{x}_t = \tilde{u}_t = \tilde{v}_t & = & \begin{cases} ba & \text{if } t = k \\ 1 & \text{otherwise.} \end{cases} \end{cases}$$

Under this evaluation the equation in $S - S(i,j,k)$ is of the form

$$yx_i^3 u_j^3 v_k^3 \;=\; x_i^3 u_j^3 v_k^3 y$$

and is not satisfied, while the other equations are of the form

$$yx_i^s u_j^s v_k^s \;=\; x_i^s u_j^s v_k^s y, \qquad \text{for } s \le 2$$

and are satisfied. $\qquad\qquad\qquad\qquad\qquad\qquad\qquad\qquad\qquad\qquad$ $\square$

As a counterpart of the corollary of the previous section we now obtain:

Corollary 5. *For each natural number n there exist systems of equations S_1 and S_2 with $O(n)$ variables such that*

(i) $|S_2| = \Omega(n^3)$,
(ii) $S_1 \cup S_2$ is independent,
(iii) the maximal degrees of solutions of S_1 and S_2 are the same.

As in the previous section the lower bound from Theorem 4 can be improved in the case when $t = n - 2$.

Theorem 6. $F_{n-2}(n) = \Omega(n^4)$ *in free monoids.*

Proof. Here the proof is a straightforward modification of that of Theorem 4. Indeed, replace X from the proof of Theorem 4 by

$$X' = (X - \{y\}) \cup \{y_i \mid i = 1, \ldots, n\},$$

that is take n copies of the variable y. The set of equations (*) is modified analogously: in both sides y ranges simultaneously from y_1 to y_n. Let S' be the resulted system. Then clearly, $|S'| = n^4$ and $|X'| = 10n$.

Now, for fixed t from 1 to n we extend the evaluation (β) in the proof of Theorem 4 as follows

$$y_t = \begin{cases} ababa & \text{if } t = l \\ 1 & \text{otherwise.} \end{cases}$$

Then, essentiallly as in the previous proof we conclude that S' is independent, by concluding that the above evaluation is a solution for

$$S' - \{y_t x_i u_j v_k \bar{x}_i \bar{u}_j \bar{v}_k \tilde{x}_i \tilde{u}_j \tilde{v}_k = x_i u_j v_k \bar{x}_i \bar{u}_j \bar{v}_k \tilde{x}_i \tilde{u}_j \tilde{v}_k y_t\}$$

but not for S'. Since this solution can be chosen to be nonperiodic the proof is completed. $\square$

There is a general alternate way of proving Theorem 6:
Assume that we know that there exists a system of $I(n)$ independent equations in a *free monoid*. Then by the method used to reduce the generalized Ehrenfeucht Conjecture to ordinary one, cf. [3], one can easily conclude that $F_n(2n) \geq I(n)$, and therefore $F_t(2n) \geq I(n)$ for $t \geq n$. This method uses heavily the empty word, and thus cannot be extended to free semigroups.

Remark. As in the previos section we can generalize Theorem 6 in the following way:

$$F_t(9n + t) \quad \geq \quad tn^3, \qquad \text{for } n, t \geq 1$$

4. Concluding remarks

The defect theorems are sometimes considered as versions of dimension properties of free monoids: Dependancy of words imply that they belong to a smaller monoid (which can be chosen free). Our results, in particular Corollaries 2 and 5, shows that such dimension properties in free monoids are actually very weak.

We conclude with a few open problems. We already mentioned as an open problem, whether $F_1(3) \geq 3$ in a free semigroup. As another ones we ask, whether the lower bounds of Theorems 1, 3, 4, 6 can be improved exponential.

References

1. M. H. Albert, J. Lawrence, A proof of Ehrenfeucht's Conjecture, *Theoret. Comp. Science* , 41 (1985), 121 – 123.

2. J. Berstel, D. Perrin, J. F. Perrot, A. Restivo, Sur le Theoreme des defaut, *J. Algebra*, 60 (1979), 169 – 180.

3. K. Culik II, J. Karhumäki, System of equations over a free monoid and Ehrenfeucht's Conjecture, *Discrete Math.*, 43 (1983), 139 – 153.

4. T. Harju, J. Karhumäki, On the defect theorem and simplifiability, *Semigroup Forum*, 33 (1986), 199 – 217.

5. J. Karhumäki, On recent trends in formal language theory, *Lect. Notes in Computer Science* 267, Springer-Verlag (1987), 136 – 162.

6. J. Karhumäki, W. Plandowski, On the size of independent systems of equations in semigroups, manuscript, 1993.

7. M. Lothaire, *Combinatorics on words*, Addison-Wesley Publishing Company, Massachussets, 1983.

8. A. Salomaa *Jewels of Formal Languages*, Computer Science Press, Potomac, Maryland, 1981.

9. J.-C. Spehner, *Quelques Problémes d'Extension, de Conjugaison et de Presentation des Sous-Monoides d'Un Monoide Libre*, PhD Thesis, Université Paris VII, 1976.

Aperiodic Languages and Generalizations[1]

Lila KARI, Gabriel THIERRIN

Department of Mathematics, University of Western Ontario
London, Ontario, N6A 5B7, Canada

Abstract. For every integer $k \geq 0$, a class of languages, called k-aperiodic languages, is defined, generalizing the class of aperiodic languages. Properties of these classes are investigated, in particular the operations under which they are preserved. A characterization of the syntactic monoid of a k-aperiodic language is also obtained.

1. Introduction

Let X be a finite alphabet and let X^* be the free monoid generated by X. Any subset of X^* is called a language.

A language L over X is called *aperiodic* or *noncounting* ([1]) if there exists an integer $n \geq 0$ such that for all $x, y, z \in X^*$, $xy^n z \in L$ if and only if $xy^{n+1} z \in L$.

The language L is called *left aperiodic or left-noncounting* ([4]) if there exists an integer $n \geq 0$ such that for all $y, z \in X^*$, $y^n z \in L$ if and only if $y^{n+1} z \in L$.

The integer n, that is dependent on L, is called the *order* of the aperiodic or left-aperiodic language L. From the definition we see that every aperiodic language over X is a left-aperiodic language over X (see [6]).

Aperiodic and left-aperiodic languages differ by the fact that in the first case there is no restriction on the prefix x and that in the second case x is reduced to the empty word. It is therefore natural to consider cases that are situated between these two extremes. This is done in the following by putting conditions on the length of the prefix x.

Let k be a non-negative integer. A language L is called *k-aperiodic* if there exists an integer $n \geq 0$ such that for all $x, y, z \in X^*$ with $|x| \leq k$, $xy^n z \in L$, if and only if $xy^{n+1} z \in L$.

Section 2 contains definitions and some preliminary results. It is shown for example that there exists an infinite hierarchy of k-aperiodic languages. A family of right congruences is defined and used to characterize k-aperiodic languages as unions of classes of these right congruences.

---

[1]This research was supported by Grant OGP0007877 of the Natural Sciences and Engineering Research Council of Canada

Section 3 deals with closure properties of aperiodic and k-aperiodic languages under several operations such as catenation, boolean operations, morphism, insertion and deletion.

The notion of *right syntactic congruence* of a k-aperiodic language is defined and investigated in Section 4. Based on this notion, the syntactic monoid of a k-aperiodic language is defined, and a complete characterization of monoids which are syntactic monoids of k-aperiodic languages is obtained.

2. Definitions and preliminary results

Throughout this paper X will denote a finite alphabet with $\operatorname{card}(X) \geq 2$, and X^* will be the free monoid generated by X. The elements of X^* will be called words and any subset of X^* will be called a language. For a word $u \in X^*$, $|u|$ will denote the length of u. The empty word will be denoted by 1.

Definition 2.1. A language L is called k-*aperiodic* if there exists an integer $n \geq 0$ such that for all $x, y, z \in X^*$ with $|x| \leq k$, $xy^n z \in L$ if and only if $xy^{n+1} z \in L$.

Left-aperiodic languages are 0-aperiodic languages and aperiodic languages are k-aperiodic languages for all $k \geq 0$.

The number n is called the *order* of the k-aperiodic language L. Since all the numbers $n' \geq n$ can also be considered as the order of L, the order of L is in fact a subset of natural numbers.

Let AP and AP_k be respectively the family of the aperiodic and the family of k-aperiodic languages. Clearly

$$AP \subseteq \cdots \subseteq AP_{k+1} \subseteq AP_k \subseteq \cdots \subseteq AP_1 \subseteq AP_0$$

Proposition 2.1. *The preceding hierarchy is strict, that is, we have:*

$$AP \subset \ldots \subset AP_{k+1} \subset AP_k \subset \ldots \subset AP_1 \subset AP_0$$

Proof. Let $L_k = \{a^{k+1} b^{2n} \mid n \geq 1\}$. Then $L_k \in AP_k$ and $L_k \notin AP_{k+1}$.

Indeed, we will show that if $m > k + 1$, then L_k is k-aperiodic of order m.

If $xy^m z$ is a word in L_k, with $|x| \leq k$, then necessarily $x = a^i$, $i \leq k$, $y = a^j b^p$, $j \geq 1$. As no word of the form $a^i (a^j b^p)^m b^{2n-pm}$, $m > k + 1$, belongs to L_k, it follows that L_k is k-aperiodic.

Suppose now that L_k is $(k + 1)$- aperiodic of order $m \geq 0$. This implies, in particular, that if the word $xy^m z \in L_k$, with $x = a^{k+1}$, $y = b$, $z = b^{2n-m}$ then also the word $xy^{m+1} z = a^{k+1} b^{2n+1}$ belongs to L_k- a contradiction. Consequently, L_k is not $(k + 1)$-aperiodic. $\qquad\square$

The k-aperiodic languages can also be defined by using binary relations.

For words $u, v \in X^*$, consider the following three conditions, where k is a fixed non negative integer:

(i) $u = v$;

(ii) $u = xy^n z$ and $v = xy^{n+1}z$ for some $x, z \in X^*$, $y \in X^+$, $|x| \leq k$;

(iii) $u = xy^{n+1}z$ and $v = xy^n z$ for some $x, z \in X^*$, $y \in X^+$, $|x| \leq k$.

For $u, v \in X^*$ define the relation $u \leftrightarrow_{k,n} v$ if and only if one of the above three conditions hold and let $\sim_{k,n}$ denote the transitive closure of $u \leftrightarrow_{k,n} v$. Clearly, for each k and n, $\sim_{k,n}$ is an equivalence relation that is right compatible and hence a right congruence. The relation $\sim_n$ defined by $u \sim_n v$ if and only if $u \sim_{k,n} v$ for every k is a congruence relation (see [1]).

Proposition 2.2. *A language L is k-aperiodic if and only if it is a union of right congruence classes of $\sim_{k,n}$ for some n.*

Proof. Let L be a k-aperiodic language. In order to prove that L is a union of classes of $\sim_{k,n}$ we have to show that if L contains a word u, it contains also all the words v belonging to the same class as u. This follows immediately as $u \in L$ and $u \sim_{k,n} v$ imply $v \in L$.

On the other hand, if L is a union of classes of $\sim_{k,n}$ then, from the definition of $\sim_{k,n}$ it easily follows that L is k-aperiodic. $\qquad\square$

3. Operations with aperiodic languages

In this section we investigate closure properties of the family of aperiodic (k-aperiodic, left aperiodic) languages under basic operations such as boolean operations, catenation, right/left quotient, insertion and deletion.

The study reveals intriguing differences between these apparently similar language families. It turns out that the family of aperiodic languages is closed under all the above listed operations, while for example, the family of left or k- aperiodic languages is not closed under deletion and left quotient. On the other hand, as the conditions imposed on left and k-aperiodic languages affect only the prefix of the words, these families are closed under right quotient.

It is still an open question whether or not the insertion of two left aperiodic (k-aperiodic) languages remains left aperiodic (k-aperiodic).

Proposition 3.1. *If A, B are k-aperiodic languages over X, then AB is k-aperiodic.*

Proof. We may assume that the orders of A and B are respectively $n_1 \geq 1$ and $n_2 \geq 1$. Let $m = n_1 + n_2 + 1$ and let $xv^m u \in AB$ with $|x| \leq k$.

(1) If $xv^m u = (xv^m u_1)(u_2)$, where $u_1, u_2 \in X^*$, $xv^m u_1 \in A$, $|x| \leq k$ and $u_2 \in B$ then, since A is k-aperiodic of order n_1 and hence also of order m, it follows that $xv^{m+1}u_1 \in A$, that is, $xv^{m+1}u \in AB$.

(2) If $xv^m u = xv^{n_1+n_2+1}u = (xv^{n_1}w_1)(w_2 u)$ where $w_1, w_2 \in X^*$, $xv^{n_1}w_1 \in A$ and $w_2 u \in B$, then, since A is k-aperiodic and $|x| \leq k$, $xv^{n_1+1}w_1 \in A$. It follows that $xv^{m+1}u \in AB$.

(3) If $xv^m u = (xv^i v_1)(v_2 v^{m-i-1} u)$ where $v_1, v_2 \in X^*$, $v_1 v_2 = v$, $i < n_1$, $xv^i v_1 \in A$ and $v_2 v^{m-i-1} u \in B$, then $m - i - 1 \geq n_2$ and

$$v_2 v^{m-i-1} u = (v_2 v_1)(v_2 v_1) \cdots (v_2 v_1) v_2 u$$

$$= (v_2 v_1)^{m-i-1} v_2 u \in B$$

Since B is k-aperiodic, we have $(v_2 v_1)^{m-i} v_2 u \in B$. It follows that

$$xv^{m+1} u = (xv^i v_1)(v_2 v^{m-i} u) \in AB$$

(4) If $xv^m u = (x_1)(x_2 v^m u)$ where $x_1, x_2 \in X^*$, $x = x_1 x_2$, $x_1 \in A$, $x_2 v^m u \in B$. Since B is k-aperiodic and $|x_2| \leq |x| \leq k$, then $x_2 v^{m+1} u \in B$ and $xv^{m+1} u = (x_1)(x_2 v^{m+1} u) \in AB$. $\square$

Proposition 3.2. *The family of k-aperiodic languages is closed under catenation and the boolean operations of union, intersection and complementation.*

Proof. The closure under catenation has been proved in the preceding proposition and it is easy to see the closure under union and intersection (and hence under complementation). $\square$

Recall that a nonempty language $L \subseteq X^+$ is called a *prefix (suffix) code* if $L \cap LX^+ = \emptyset$ ($L \cap X^+ L = \emptyset$). This means that for any $x \in L$, $xy \notin L$ ($yx \notin L$) for all $y \in L^+$.

Proposition 3.3. *Let X be an alphabet and let $A, B \subseteq X^*$. If AB is k-aperiodic of order n and B is a suffix code, then A is k-aperiodic of order n.*

Proof. If A is in the set $\{\emptyset, \{1\}\}$, then the proposition is trivially true. Hence we may assume A is not in $\{\emptyset, \{1\}\}$.

Assume AB is k-aperiodic of order n. Let $xy^n z \in A$, $|x| \leq k$, $x, y, z \in X^*$. Then $xy^n zb \in AB$, where $b \in B$. Since AB is k-aperiodic of order n, we have $xy^{n+1} zb \in AB$. Now, since B is a suffix code by assumption, we have $xy^{n+1} z \in A$. Similarily, we can show that $xy^{n+1} z \in AB$, $|x| \leq k$, implies $xy^n z \in A$. Hence A is k-aperiodic of order n. $\square$

Corollary. *Let $A \in X^*$. If A is a suffix code then A^2 is k-aperiodic if and only if A is k-aperiodic.*

Proof. It follows from the preceding Proposition and Proposition 3.1. $\square$

As we will see in the following, aperiodicity is preserved even when we consider an operation which generalizes the catenation operation.

Let u, v be words over an alphabet X. The *insertion* of v into u is defined as (see [2], [3]):

$$u \leftarrow v = \{u_1 v u_2 \mid u = u_1 u_2, u_1, u_2 \in X^*\}.$$

The operation can be easily extended to languages,

$$L_1 \leftarrow L_2 = \bigcup_{u \in L_1, v \in L_2} (u \leftarrow v).$$

Proposition 3.4. *The family of aperiodic languages is closed under insertion.*

Proof. Let L_1, L_2 be aperiodic languages of order n_1, respectively n_2. Choose $m = 2n_1 + n_2 + 1$ and let $xy^m z \in L_1 \leftarrow L_2$. This means that $xy^m z = uwv$ where $uv \in L_1$, $w \in L_2$.

One of the following cases can occur:

A. y^m is a subword of w.

Then $w = \alpha y^m \beta \in L_2$ which implies $\alpha y^{m+1} \beta \in L_2$, that is, $xy^{m+1} z \in L_1 \leftarrow L_2$.

B. w is a subword of y^m and y^m (possibly) overlaps with u and v. Then at least one of the following must happen:

– the length of the overlap between y^m and w is bigger than $|y| \times n_2$.
– the length of the overlap between y^m and u is bigger than $|y| \times n_1$.
– the length of the overlap between y^m and v is bigger than $|y| \times n_1$.

Indeed, if none of these happens then we have

$$|y^m| = m \times |y| = \text{sum of overlaps with } u, w, v \leq |y| \times (2n_1 + n_2)$$

– a contradiction.

Now, assume that the first case happens. This means that $w = \alpha y^{n_2} \beta$ which implies that $\alpha y^{n_2+1} \beta \in L_2$. This, in turn, implies that $xy^{m+1} z \in L_1 \leftarrow L_2$.

In the other cases, one can reason in a similar way.

C. y^m overlaps with w and v.

Then, one of the folowing cases must hold:

– the length of the overlap between y^m and w is bigger than $|y| \times n_2$
– the length of the overlap between y^m and v is bigger than $|y| \times n_1$.

(Otherwise, we would have that

$$|y^m| = m \times |y| = \text{sum of overlaps with } w, v \leq |y| \times (n_2 + n_1),$$

– a contradiction.)

Assume that the first case holds. We can reason as in case B) to see that this leads to the desired conclusion.

D. The word y^m overlaps with w and u. This case is similar to the preceding one. $\square$

The family of aperiodic languages is closed under right/left quotient. This result will be obtained as a consequence of a more general one which states that, by deleting any language from an aperiodic one, the result is still aperiodic. Before that, we need to introduce the definition of *deletion*, which is an operation generalizing the right/left quotient of languages.

Let u, v be two words over the alphabet X. The *deletion* of v from u is defined as (see [2], [3]):

$$u \rightarrow v = \{w \in X^* \mid w = u_1 u_2, u = u_1 v u_2\}.$$

The operation can be extended to languages in the natural fashion.

Proposition 3.5. *If L_1 is an aperiodic language and L_2 is an arbitrary language, then the deletion of L_2 from L_1, $L_1 \rightarrow L_2$, is an aperiodic language.*

Proof. Let L_1 be an aperiodic language of order n and let $m = 2n + 2$.

Let $xy^m z$ be a word in $L_1 \rightarrow L_2$. Then, $xy^m z = uv$, where there exists $w \in L_2$ such that $uwv \in L_1$.

One of the following case holds:

A. $x_1 w x_2 y^m \in L_1$ (w has been erased from the x-part). Then, as L_1 is aperiodic, $x_1 w x_2 y^{m+1} z \in L_1$ which implies $x_1 x_2 y^{m+1} z \in L_1 \rightarrow L_2$.

B. $xy^m z_1 w z_2 \in L_1$ – similar to A.

C. $xy^i y_1 w y_2 y^j z \in L_1$, where $i + j + 1 = m$, $y = y_1 y_2$.

At least one of the following cases must hold:

$-$ i is greater than n

$-$ j is greater than n

(If none of these happens, then $m = i + j + 1 \leq n + n + 1 = 2n + 1$ – a contradiction.)

Assume, for example, that $i > n$. Then, $xy^{i+1} y_1 w y_2 y^j z \in L_1$, which implies $xy^{i+1} y_1 y_2 y^j z \in L_1 \rightarrow L_2$, that is, $xy^{m+1} z \in L_1 \rightarrow L_2$.   □

Corollary. *The family of aperiodic languages is closed under right/left quotient.*

Proof. It follows from the preceding proposition and by noticing that, if $\#$ is a letter which does not belong to X, the right/left quotient can be obtained as particular cases of deletion. Indeed, we have:

$$L_1/L_2 = L_1\# \rightarrow L_2\# \text{ and } L_2 \backslash L_1 = \# L_1 \rightarrow \# L_2,$$

for all $L_1, L_2 \subseteq X^*$.   □

The following examples show that the families of left aperiodic and k-aperiodic languages are closed under neither deletion, nor left quotient.

Example 1. Let $L_1 = \{ab^{2n}\mid n \geq 1\}$ and $L_2 = \{a\}$. Both languages are left aperiodic but the deletion of L_2 from L_1 (which in this case coincides with the left quotient $L_2 \backslash L_1$),

$$L_1 \rightarrow L_2 = \{b^{2n}\mid n \geq 1\},$$

is not a left aperiodic language.

Example 2. Consider the k-aperiodic languages

$$L_1 = \{d^{k+1}a^m b^n c^n \mid n, m \geq 1\} \text{ and } L_2 = da^*b,$$

where $k > 0$. The deletion of L_2 from L_1 is

$$L_1 \rightarrow L_2 = \{d^k b^{n-1} c^n \mid n \geq 1\},$$

which is not a k-aperiodic language.

Example 3. Let $k \geq 0$ and consider the languages

$$L_1 = \{a^{k+1}b^{2n}\mid n \geq 1\}, \quad L_2 = \{a\}.$$

According to Proposition 2.1 the language L_1 is k-aperiodic and L_2 is k-aperiodic being finite. However, the left quotient $L_2 \backslash L_1 = \{a^k b^{2n}\mid n \geq 1\}$ is not k-aperiodic.

The situation changes if we consider right quotient instead of left quotient. As the conditions for left aperiodic languages and k-aperiodic languages affect only the prefix of the words, these families are still closed under right quotient. In fact, a more general result holds.

Proposition 3.6. *If L_1 is a k-aperiodic language, $k \geq 0$, and L_2 is an arbitrary language, then the right quotient L_1/L_2 is a k-aperiodic language.*

Proof. Let L_1 be a k-aperiodic language of order m. We shall show that L_1/L_2 is k-aperiodic of the same order.

Indeed, let $xy^m z \in L_1/L_2$, $|x| \leq k$. This implies there exists $v \in L_2$ such that $xy^m zv$ is in L_1. From the k-aperiodicity of L_1 we deduce that $xy^{m+1}zv \in L_1$, which further implies $xy^{m+1}z \in L_1/L_2$. The other implication can be proved analogously. $\qquad\square$

We conclude this section with the remark that the family of k-aperiodic languages is not closed under morphisms. For example, consider the language $L = \{a^{k+1}b^{2n}\mid n \geq 1\}$ and the morphism h defined as $h(a) = 1$ and $h(b) = b$. L is k-aperiodic but $h(L)$ is not.

4. Syntactic monoids of k-aperiodic languages

This section is devoted to the study of connections between syntactic congruences and k-aperiodic languages. Moreover, we introduce and investigate the notion of right syntactic congruence of a k-aperiodic language. Based on this notion, a complete characterization of monoids which are syntactic monoids of k-aperiodic languages is obtained.

Let M be a monoid and let $L \subseteq M$. If $u \in M$, then:

$$u^{-1}L = \{x \in M \mid ux \in L\}.$$

The relation R_L defined by

$$u \equiv v\ (R_L) \Leftrightarrow u^{-1}L = v^{-1}L$$

is a right congruence called the *right principal congruence* associated to the subset L.

The right principal congruence can also be defined by:

$$u \equiv v\ (R_L) \Leftrightarrow \forall x, y \in M,\ (ux \in L \text{ iff } vx \in L).$$

The relation P_L defined by:

$$u \equiv v\ (P_L) \Leftrightarrow \forall x, y \in M,\ (xuy \in L \text{ iff } xvy \in L)$$

is a congruence called the *principal congruence* of the language L. If P_L is the identity relation, then L is called a *disjunctive subset*.

If the monoid M is the free monoid X^* and L is a language over X, then R_L and P_L are called respectively the *right syntactic congruence* and the *syntactic congruence* of the language L. The quotient monoid $\mathrm{syn}(L) = X^*/P_L$ is called the *syntactic monoid* of the language L.

Recall that a language L is regular iff the index of R_L is finite.

Proposition 4.1. *A language L over X is k-aperiodic if and only if there exists $n > 0$ such that*

$$xu^n \equiv xu^{n+1}\ (R_L)\ \ \forall u, x \in X^*, |x| \le k$$

Proof. This follows from the fact that, if $|x| \le k$, then $z \in (xu^n)^{-1}L$ if and only if $xu^n z \in L$, hence if and only if $xu^{n+1}z \in L$. $\qquad\square$

Proposition 4.2. *If a language L over X is k-aperiodic, then every class of R_L is a k-aperiodic language.*

Proof. Let A be a class modulo R_L. By Proposition 4.1, there exists $n > 0$ such that $xu^n \equiv xu^{n+1}\ (R_L)$ for all $u, x \in X^*$ with $|x| \le k$. Since R_L is a right congruence, this implies $xu^n y \equiv xu^{n+1} y \ (R_L)$. It follows then that $xu^n y \in A$ if and only if $xu^{n+1} y \in A$. Hence A is k-aperiodic. $\qquad\square$

Proposition 4.3. *Let L be a regular language over X. Then L is k-aperiodic if and only if every class of R_L is a k-aperiodic language.*

Proof. If L is k-aperiodic, the aperiodicity of every class of R_L follows from Proposition 4.1.

Suppose now that every class of R_L is k-aperiodic. The language L is a union of classes A_i of R_L, and since L is regular, the number of these classes is finite, say m. Consequently, we can write $L = \bigcup_{i=1}^{m} A_i$. Since the union of a finite number of k-aperiodic languages is k-aperiodic, it follows that L itself is k-aperiodic. $\qquad\square$

A monoid M is called an *aperiodic* or *combinatorial* monoid if there exists a positive integer n such that $u^n = u^{n+1}$ for all $u \in M$ ([5], [7], [8]). A finite monoid is aperiodic if and only if all its subgroups are trivial. A language L over X is aperiodic if and only if its syntactic monoid is aperiodic.

A right congruence R of X^* is called a *k-aperiodic congruence* iff there exists a positive integer n such that $xu^n \equiv xu^{n+1} \ (R)$ for all $u, x \in X^*$ with $|x| \le k$.

Lemma 4.1. *Let L be a k-aperiodic language over X. Then*
(i) The syntactic right congruence R_L is a k-aperiodic right congruence.
(ii) If T is a congruence of X^* such that $P_L \subseteq T \subseteq R_L$, then $P_L = T$.

Proof. *(i)* This follows immediately from Proposition 4.1.

(ii) If $u \equiv v \ (T)$, then, since T is a congruence, $xuy \equiv xvy \ (T)$ for all $x, y \in X^*$. Since L is a union of classes of R_L and $T \subseteq R_L$, it follows that L is also a union of classes of T. Hence $xuy \in L$ implies $xvy \in L$ and vice versa. Therefore $u \equiv v \ (P_L)$ which means $T \subseteq P_L$. Consequently, we have $P_L = T$. $\qquad\square$

If M is a monoid, a right congruence R over M is called *strict* if, for every congruence R' of M, the relation $R' \subseteq R$ implies that R' is the identity relation.

A monoid M is called a *strict (k,n)-aperiodic monoid* where k and n are positive integers if the following conditions are satisfied:
(i) M is finitely generated;
(ii) M contains a strict right conguence R;
(iii) M contains a finite set G of generators such that

$$xu^n \equiv xu^{n+1} \ (R)$$

for all $u, x \in M$ with $x = g_1 g_2 \cdots g_m, \ g_i \in G, \ m \le k$.

Proposition 4.4. *Let L be a k-aperiodic language over the alphabet X and let $syn(L)$ be its syntactic monoid. Then $syn(L)$ is a strict (k,n)-aperiodic monoid for some positive integer n. Furthermore $syn(L)$ contains a disjunctive subset D that is a union of classes of R.*

Proof. If R_L is the syntactic right congruence of L, then by Lemma 4.1, R_L is a k-aperiodic right congruence and $P_L \subseteq R_L$. Hence there exists a positive integer n such that $xu^n \equiv xu^{n+1}(R_L)$ for every $u, x \in X^*$ with $|x| \le k$.

The right congruence R_L induces on $syn(L) = X^*/P_L$ a right congruence R that is strict by Lemma 4.1, (ii). If $X = \{x_1, x_2, \cdots, x_r\}$ and if $g_i = [x_i]$ is the class of x_i modulo P_L, let $G = \{g_1, g_2, \cdots, g_r\}$. Clearly, if $[x]$ denotes the class of x modulo P_L, we have

$$[x][u]^n \equiv [x][u]^{n+1} \ (R)$$

for every $[u], [x] \in syn(L)$ such that $[x] = g_{i_1} g_{i_2} \cdots g_{i_m}$, $g_{i_j} \in G$ and $m \le k$. Let $D = \{\ [x] \ | \ x \in L\}$ be the subset consisting of all the classes $[x]$ of P_L containing words of L. Since $syn(L) = X^*/P_L$, D is a disjunctive subset of $syn(L)$ and a union of classes of R. $\qquad\qquad\square$

Proposition 4.5. *Let M be a strict (k,n)-aperiodic monoid with the strict right congruence R and containing a disjunctive subset D that is a union of classes of R. Then the monoid M is isomorphic to the syntactic monoid of a k-aperiodic language over an alphabet X.*

Proof. The monoid M, being finitely generated, contains a finite set G of generators. Let $X = G$, let X^* be the free monoid generated by X and let ϕ be the canonical homomorphism of X^* onto M. If $L = \phi^{-1}(D)$, then X^*/P_L is isomorphic to M because D is a disjunctive subset of M. Therefore M is isomorphic to the syntactic monoid $syn(L)$ of the language L.

Since R is a strict right congruence of M, $xu^n \equiv xu^{n+1} \ (R)$ for all $u \in M$, $x = x_{i_1} x_{i_2} \cdots x_{i_m}$, $x_{i_j} \in G = X$ and $m \le k$. Since D is a union of classes of R, then $R \subseteq R_D$ and $xu^n \equiv xu^{n+1} \ (R_D)$ for all $u \in M$ and x satisfying the above condition. Therefore $yv^n \equiv yv^{n+1} \ (R_L)$ for all $v \in X^*$ and $y \in X^*$ with $|y| \le k$. By Proposition 4.1, this implies that L is k-aperiodic. $\qquad\square$

References

1. J. A. Brzozowski, K. Čulik II, A. Gabrielian, Classification of noncounting events, *J. Comp. Syst. Sci.*, 5 (1971), 41 – 53.

2. L. Kari, Insertion and deletion of words: determinism and reversibility, *Proceedings of MFCS'93, Lecture Notes in Computer Science* 711, Springer-Verlag, 1993, 315 – 327.

3. L. Kari, *On Insertion and Deletion in Formal Languages*, Ph.D. thesis, University of Turku, Finland, 1991.

4. H. J. Shyr, G. Thierrin, Left-noncounting languages, *Intern. J. Comp. and Information Sci.*, 4 (1975), 95 – 102.

5. H. J. Shyr, *Free Monoids and Languages*, Lectures Notes, National Chung-Hsing University, Hon Min Book Company, Taichung, 1991.

6. R. McNaughton, S. Papert, *Counter-Free Automata*, MIT Press, 1971.

7. G. Lallement, *Semigroups and Combinatorial Applications*, Wiley, New York, 1979.

8. J. E. Pin, *Varieties of Formal Languages*, Foundations of Computer Science, Plenum Press, New York, 1986.

A Mathematical Model of Personal Pronouns

Manfred KUDLEK

Hamburg University, Computer Science Department
Vogt-Köln-Str. 30, 2000 Hamburg 54, Germany

1. Introduction

An approach to a precise mathematical model for the description of personal pronouns in natural languages is presented in this paper, such that the category of personal pronouns can be seen as one of several universal categories in natural languages.

The first step is the description of a communication situation with normally one speaker (first person), several listeners, the audience (second persons), and also several other persons or things (third persons), and the definition of a mathematical personal pronoun.

The second step then is the encoding of this situation by a word or several words over some alphabet. Normally, such an encoding is not unique and may depend on the communication situation. There may exist several encodings for the same mathematical personal pronoun, e.g. possessive pronouns and forms for different cases, and one expression may also encode several mathematical personal pronouns.

The third step is a presentation of certain relations between mathematical personal pronouns, describing actions with several participants, and their encoding.

2. The basic communication model

A normal situation of communication among men includes a single speaker and not a choir (first person), an audience consisting of one or several listeners (second persons), and a group of persons or things spoken about (third persons). Usually, the speaker receives information about the audience and other persons or things by seeing them, and sends information to the audience. This situation can be described in the following simplest communication model using sets for the different participants in the communication process:

$$\begin{array}{ll}
1 \text{ sender (speaker, } 1^{st} \text{ person)} & \{s\} \\
\text{several receivers (audience, } 2^{nd} \text{ persons)} & R \\
\text{several others (thirds, } 3^{rd} \text{ persons)} & T
\end{array}$$

with an 1-way communication channel for receiving visual information by s about R and T, represented by a visibility relation σ, and another 1-way audio communication channel for sending information from s to R, represented by a relation $\tau = \{s\} \times R$,

$$\sigma \subseteq R \times \{s\} \cup T \times (\{s\} \cup R) \text{ with } R \times \{s\} \subseteq \sigma.$$

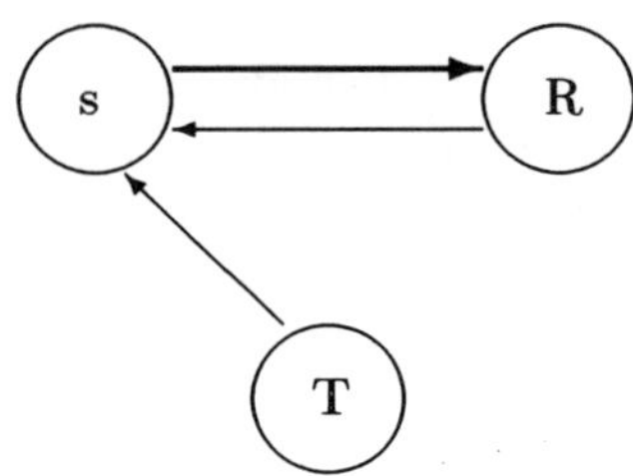

In a more general situation not all members of T can be seen by s, thus causing a partition of T into 2 disjoint sets T_0 (not seen by s) and T_1 (seen by s).

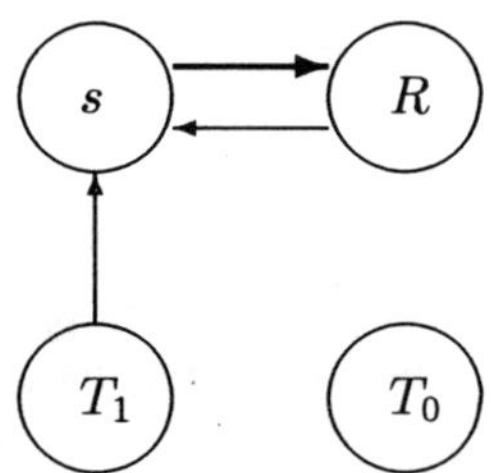

Related to this distinction is another one, defined by distance from the speaker: *here (at me), there (at you), over there (at them), further away.*

In a still more general situation R can also receive visual information about T, thus partitioning T into 4 disjoint sets. This can be described by

$$T_{00} = \{t \in T \mid \neg(t, s) \in \sigma \wedge \neg \exists r \in R : (t, r) \in \sigma\}$$
$$T_{01} = \{t \in T \mid \neg(t, s) \in \sigma \wedge \exists r \in R : (t, r) \in \sigma\}$$
$$T_{10} = \{t \in T \mid (t, s) \in \sigma \wedge \neg \exists r \in R : (t, r) \in \sigma\}$$
$$T_{11} = \{t \in T \mid (t, s) \in \sigma \wedge \exists r \in R : (t, r) \in \sigma\}$$

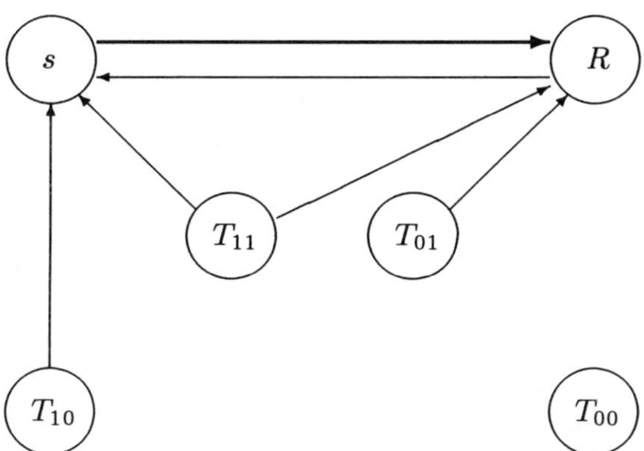

A **mathematical personal pronoun** can now be defined simply as some subset $P \subseteq \{s\} \cup R \cup T$.

The visibility relation will give s information for the encoding of the mathematical personal pronouns. In a strict sense, s also has to receive information about the subset of T seen by all $r \in R$. But for simplicity this fact will be neglected in this context.

3. Features of mathematical personal pronouns

In many natural languages the elements of $\{s\} \cup R \cup T$ have a number of features, e.g. *(animate, inanimate)*, *(female, male, neuter)*, or degrees of social rank. In some natural languages several such features are present. The features can be modelled at best by finite sets $C_i, 1 \leq i \leq k$. The elements of such sets are usually called **classes**, and for simplicity they can just be enumerated from 1 to $m_i : C_i = \{1, \cdots, m_i\}$.

The properties of elements $p \in \{s\} \cup R \cup T$ are given by feature functions f_i which may be assumed to be surjective

$$f_i : \{s\} \cup R \cup T \longrightarrow C_i, \ 1 \leq i \leq k.$$

Mathematically, all k features may be combined into one by considering the Cartesian product

$$C = C_1 \times \cdots \times C_k \text{ with elements } (j_1, \cdots, j_k).$$

For linguistic reasons, however, only the model with several features will be presented. Some examples of such features are:

$$C = \{1\} \qquad \text{no distinction by gender or social rank (Chinese)}$$
$$C = \{1,2\} \qquad \{female, male\} \text{ (Arabic)}$$
$$\{animate, inanimate\}$$
$$C = \{1,2,3\} \qquad \{female, male, neuter\} \text{ (German)}$$
$$C = \{1,2,3,4,5,6\} \quad \text{6 classes (Swahili)}$$

The feature functions introduced, however, are not sufficient for a description of the features of an entire mathematical personal pronoun P. Therefore, the definition has to be generalized. This can be done by generalizing the f_i from elements $p \in \{s\} \cup R \cup T$ to subsets:

$$F_i : 2^{\{s\} \cup R \cup T} \to C_i$$

with several possibilities to generalize from one element to a subset, e.g.

$$F_i(P) = min\{f_i(p) \mid p \in P\} \text{ or } F_i(P) = max\{f_i(p) \mid p \in P\}.$$

4. Cardinality

The mathematical personal pronoun P introduced so far allows an arbitrary number of different possibilities. In natural languages, however, these are put into a few categories (or mathematical equivalence classes) only, usually defined by **number (cardinality)**, the most common ones being *singular, dual, (trial), plural*. Normally, only the following distinctions between such cardinalities are important, with the number of equivalence classes (see below) given in the 3rd column:

≥ 1	no distinction	3
$(1, > 1)$	singular, plural	9
$(1, 2, > 2)$	singular, dual, plural	14
$(1, 2, 3, > 3)$	singular, dual, trial, plural	21

Possible mathematical personal pronouns depending on their cardinalities will be considered below. To simplify the notation, r, t will be written for $p \in R$, $p \in T$, respectively.

4.1. Singular

In this case there are only 3 possibilities, given in the following list with some English encoding and a short notation in the 1st column:

s	$\{s\}$	I
r	$\{r\}$	you
t	$\{t\}$	he/she/it

4.2. Dual

There are 5 possibilities in the case of dual, 4 of them distinguished in a number of Amerindian languages. The 1st column gives a short notation again.

sr	$\{s, r\}$	we both inclusive (the addressee)
st	$\{s, t\}$	we both exclusive (the addressee)
rr	$\{r, r'\}$	you both
rt	$\{r, t\}$	both you and he
tt	$\{t, t'\}$	they

4.3. Trial

In this case, rather rare in natural languages, the following pronouns are possible:

$\{s, t, t'\}$	we excl.
$\{s, r, t\}$	we all
$\{s, r, r'\}$	we incl.
$\{r, r', r''\}$	you
$\{r, r', t\}$	you all
$\{r, t, t'\}$	you all
$\{t, t', t''\}$	they

4.4. Plural

For simplicity only the case of > 2 with 6 equivalence classes will be presented, giving also a short notation in the 1st, and special situations in the 5th column.

sT	$s \in P, P \cap R = \emptyset, P \cap T \neq \emptyset$	we excl.	$P = \{s\} \cup T$
sR	$s \in P, P \cap R \neq \emptyset, P \cap T = \emptyset$	we incl.	$P = \{s\} \cup R$
sRT	$s \in P, P \cap R \neq \emptyset, P \cap T \neq \emptyset$	we all	$P = \{s\} \cup R \cup T$
R	$s \notin P, P \cap R \neq \emptyset, P \cap T = \emptyset$	you	$P = R$
RT	$s \notin P, P \cap R \neq \emptyset, P \cap T \neq \emptyset$	you all	$P = R \cup T$
T	$s \notin P, P \cap R = \emptyset, P \cap T \neq \emptyset$	they	$P = T$

In natural languages there is usually no distinction between RT and R, and between sRT and sR.

5. Encoding of mathematical personal pronouns

A mathematical personal pronoun defined in the previous sections, or more precisely, its equivalence classes according to cardinality, is mapped onto one word or several words over some alphabet V, or onto a finite set of such words. This encoding may depend on several relations based on features of the different participants in the communication, and on syntactical or semantic categories.

In the simplest case the encoding is a function

$$c : \{s\} \cup R \cup T \to V^* \quad \text{or} \quad c : \{s\} \cup R \cup T \to 2^{V^*}$$

In the general case the encoding c may depend on the communication situation, or more precisely on the features of the different participants in the communication. This means that there are several such encodings depending on $f(s)$, $F(R)$, and $F(T)$, giving functions $c_{(f(s),F(R),F(T))}$.

Furthermore, the encoding may depend on syntactical or even semantic categories i, like cases. This gives functions $c_{(f(s),F(R),F(T)),i}$.

In the simplest situation the encoding is independent of such features and categories, giving a function c.

The following example is from Classical Arabic giving the encodings of pronouns as prefixes and suffixes of verbs in the indicative imperfect tense. The feature set is $C = \{1,2\}$ for $\{male, female\}$ with $F(P) = min\{f(p) \mid p \in P\}$, with short notations for singular, dual, and plural.

Sing.	$c(P)$	Dual	$c(P)$	Plur.	$c(P)$
t, $f(t) = 1$	y - u	tt, $F(P) = 1$	y - āni	T, $F(P) = 1$	y-ūna
2	t - u	2	t - āni	2	y - na
r, $f(r) = 1$	t - u	rr,rt, $F(P) \leq 2$	t - āni	R,RT, $F(P) = 1$	t-ūna
2	t-īna			2	t - na
s, $f(s) \leq 2$	' - u			sR,sT,sRT, $F(P) \leq 2$	n - u

The second example is from *Potowatomi* [1], [3], an Algonquian language, and presents the possessive pronouns, again as prefixes and suffixes. There is no distinction of gender.

Sing.	$c(P)$	Plur.	$c(P)$
r	k -	R,RT	k - wa
s	n -	sR,sRT	k - nan
		sT	n - nan
t	w -	T	w - wa

The encoding in achieved by the following algorithm for prefixes (pref) and suffixes (suff):

Begin
If $P \cap R \neq \emptyset$ then pref $= k$
else if $s \in P$ then pref $= n$ else pref $= w$
if $card(P) > 1$ then
if $s \in P$ then suff $= nan$ else suff $= wa$
End.

Example: *n-čiman-nan $=$ our (excl.) canoe.*

The next example is from German and presents different encodings c_i for mathematical pronouns according to linguistic case (nominative, dative, accusative) and possessive. The features set is $C = \{1, 2, 3\}$ for *male, female, neuter.*

P	Nom.	Dat.	Acc.	Poss.
s, $f(s) \leq 3$	ich	mir	mich	mein
r, $f(s) \leq 3$	du	dir	dich	dein
t, $f(t) = 1$	er	ihm	ihn	sein
2	sie	ihr	sie	ihr
3	es	ihm	es	sein
sR,ST,sRT	wir	uns	uns	unser
R,RT	ihr	euch	euch	euer
T	sie	ihnen	sie	ihr

In a more complex case the encoding may depend on the feature of the speaker, giving a function $c_{f(s)}$. This can be found in the incomplete example from Classical Mixtec [4].

	r				t			
	man	boy	woman	girl	man	boy	woman	girl
man	dzi				ye	dacu		
boy			do			dacu		
woman			dzi		dzu	dzuq		
girl							yco	yco

Other possibilities are $c_{F(R)}$, $c_{(f(s),F(R))}$, being important for languages with several social ranks.

Theoretically, also $c_{F(T)}$, $c_{(f(s),F(T))}$, and $c_{(f(s),F(R),F(T))}$ are possible.

To illustrate this, a simple theoretical example is presented. In this example there is only one feature $\{male, female, nonhuman\}$, abbreviated by $\{m, f, n\}$. The encoding of P depends on $f(s)$, $F(R)$, and $F(T)$. F is defined by

$$F(P) = \begin{cases} m & \text{if } \exists p \in P : f(p) = m \\ f & \text{if } \neg\exists p \in P : f(p) = m \wedge \exists p \in P : f(p) = f \\ n & \text{if } \neg\exists p \in P : f(p) = m \wedge \neg\exists p \in P : f(p) = f \wedge \\ & \quad \wedge \exists p \in P : f(p) = n \end{cases}$$

with $f(s) \in \{m, f\}$ and $F(R) \in \{m, f\}$.

This gives 4 functions $c_{(m,m)}$, $c_{(m,f)}$, $c_{(f,m)}$, and $c_{(f,f)}$ which have to be used for the encoding in the corresponding situations.

6. Relations between personal pronouns

In the previous sections only isolated pronouns have been considered, either as mathematical objects or as encodings. There are however also relations between personal pronouns, ranging in arity from 1 to some n. This relations are important for verbs with their participants in actions. Verbs or verb forms with 1 participant are usually called (not in the mathematical but in the linguitic sense) **intransitive**, those with 2 **transitive** (also **reflexive** in some situations). To intransitive verb forms belong also **passive** forms. Most natural languages have special encodings for these situations. There exist also natural languages with special encodings for verb forms with 3 or even 4 participants.

Mathematically, these are just relations on the Cartesian products

$$R_k \subseteq (\{s\} \cup R \cup T\})^k \text{ with elements } (P_1, \cdots, P_k).$$

6.1. Unary relations

Unary relations ($k = 1$) are just the mathematical personal pronouns themselves. In natural languages they are realized for instance as **subjects** in 1-referent actions (active or passive), or possessors.

6.2. Binary relations

Binary relations $R_2 \subseteq (\{s\} \cup R \cup T)^2$ are common for most natural languages describing for instance 2-referent actions.

The first component P_1 is called **subject**, the second one P_2 **object** in a binary relation.

The relations can be classified in the following way:

$$
\begin{aligned}
&P_1 \cap P_2 = \emptyset && \text{transitive} \\
&P_1 \cap P_2 \neq \emptyset \wedge P_1 = P_2 && \text{pure reflexive} \\
&P_1 \cap P_2 \neq \emptyset \wedge P_1 \neq P_2 \wedge P_1 \subset P_2 && \text{reflexive} \\
&P_1 \cap P_2 \neq \emptyset \wedge P_1 \neq P_2 \wedge P_2 \subset P_1 && \text{reflexive} \\
&P_1 \cap P_2 \neq \emptyset \wedge P_1 \not\subset P_2 \wedge P_2 \not\subset P_1 && \text{(incomparable)}
\end{aligned}
$$

This yields, with the short notation introduced in section 4, the following possibilities for transitive actions (only singular and plural) (from space shortage reason, the table is splitted into two parts):

	s	r	t	sT	sR
s		(s,r)	(s,t)		
r	(r,s)	(r,r')	(r,t)	(r,sT)	(r,sR')
t	(t,s)	(t,r)	(t,t')	(t,sT')	(t,sR)
sT		(sT,r)	(sT,t')		
sR		(sR,r')	(sR,t)		
sRT		(sRT,r')	(sRT,t')		
R	(R,s)	(R,r')	(R,t)	(R,sT)	(R,sR')
RT	(RT,s)	(RT,r')	(RT,t')	(RT,sT')	(RT,sR')
T	(T,s)	(T,r)	(T,t')	(T,sT')	(T,sR)

	sRT	R	RT	T
s		(s,R)	(s,RT)	(s,T)
r	$(r,sR'T)$	(r,R')	$(r,R'T)$	(r,T)
t	(t,sRT')	(t,R)	(t,RT')	(t,T')
sT		(sT,R)	(sT,RT')	(sT,T')
sR		(sR,R')	$(sR,R'T)$	(sR,T)
sRT		(sRT,R')	$(sRT,R'T')$	(sRT,T')
R	$(R,sR'T)$	(R,R')	$(R,R'T)$	(R,T)
RT	$(RT,sR'T')$	(RT,R')	$(RT,R'T')$	(RT,T')
T	(T,sRT')	(T,R)	(T,RT')	(T,T')

where r', t', R', or T' indicate that in the corresponding pronouns either $t' \notin P_j$ ($j = 1,2$), $P_1 \cap P_2 \cap T = \emptyset$, $r' \notin P_j$ ($j = 1,2$), or $P_1 \cap P_2 \cap R = \emptyset$.

The distinction of different subsets of the addressed group R is rather theoretical, however.

6.3. Ternary relations

As there are too many possibilities for characterizing ternary relations only **transitive** ones will be introduced. R_3 is called such if

$$P_1 \cap P_2 = P_1 \cap P_3 = P_2 \cap P_3 = \emptyset.$$

With only singular and plural, excluding different subsets of R, the following triples are possible:

(s,r,t)	(s,r,T)	(s,R,t)	(s,R,T)	(s,t,t')	(s,t,T')	(s,T,t')	(s,T,T')
(r,t,t')	(r,t,T')	(r,T,t')	(r,T,T')	(R,t,t')	(R,t,T')	(R,T,t')	(R,T,T')
(t,t',t'')	(t,t',T'')	(t,T',t'')	(t,T',T'')	(T,t',t'')	(T,t',T'')	(T,T',t'')	(T,T',T'')

An example in English with 3 participants is:
You give *me her* book.

7. Encoding of binary relations

There exist many possibilities for the encoding of binary relations between mathematical personal pronouns. Only some will be considered.

In the simplest case the encoding of the mathematical personal pronouns is unique, and it is also used for the encoding of personal pronouns in binary relations, yielding

$$c(P_1, P_2) = (c(P_1), c(P_2)).$$

Combined with a verb V, either isolated or affixed, this gives the possibilities (all permutations)

$$c(P_1) - c(P_2) - V, \ c(P_1) - V - c(P_2), \ V - c(P_1) - c(P_2),$$
$$c(P_2) - c(P_1) - V, \ c(P_2) - V - c(P_1), \ \text{and} \ V - c(P_2) - c(P_1).$$

Reflexive forms can also be encoded by using some special word ρ giving $c(P) - \rho - V$ and its permutations.

In the next case the encoding of binary relations is related to the encoding of unary relations. Here there exist 2 encodings of unary relations, c and c'. They can be also used to encode the subject in active and inactive (passive) actions with 1 participant.

If the active participant of 1-participant actions is encoded by $c(P)$ (for **nominative**) and the participants of 2-participant actions are encoded by $(c(P_1), c'(P_2))$, this situation is called a **nominative-accusative** structure.

If the active participant of 1-participant actions is encoded by $c(P)$ (for **nominative**) and the participants of 2-participant actions are encoded by $(c'(P_1), c(P_2))$, this situation is called a **nominative-ergative** structure.

There is also the possibility that two encodings c and c' are used for 1-participant actions (active and passive for instance), and the 2-participant actions are encoded again by $(c(P_1), c'(P_2))$ or $(c'(P_1), c(P_2))$.

An example for a natural language with a nominative-accusative structure is German, encoding the subject $c(P_1)$ in nominative, and the object $c'(P_2)$ in accusative:

$$c(P_1) - V \ \text{and} \ c(P_1) - V - c'(P_2).$$

An example for a natural language with a nominative-ergative structure is Quiché [5], a language spoken in Guatemala. In this language the personal pronouns are encoded by prefixes:

Sing.	$c(P)$	$c'(P)$	Plur.	$c(P)$	$c'(P)$
s	nu, v	i, in	sR, sRT, sT	qa, q	oh
r	a, av	at	R, RT	i, iv	iš
t	u, r	$\emptyset$	T	ke, k	e

where the second variants have to be used before vowels.

1-participants forms (active or passive) are $c(P) - V$, and 2-participant (transitive) forms are $c'(P_2) - c(P_1) - V$.

Example: *keloq'on* = they love, *kiloq'oš* = I am loved, *katnuloq'oh* = I love you.

Some natural languages use an entire different encoding of binary relations. The next example is from Potowatomi [3] again.

The encoding starts with the question which kind of participants is present in the action : R, s, and T ? (in this order), marked by prefixes k, n, and w, respectively. The next fact to be encoded is the direction of the action, namely $s \to R$, $R \to s$, $s \to T$, $T \to s$, $R \to T$, $T \to R$, $T \to T'$, and $T' \to T$, where T' stands for more distant participants. This is encoded by suffixes un, uy, a, uk, a, uk, a, and uko, respectively. Finally, the cardinality of the entire group $G = P_1 \cup P_2$ of participants has to be encoded asking $card(G) = 2$, $card(G) > 2$? (in this order). In the second case further questions, $s \in G$, $R \subseteq G$, $T \subseteq G$? are put (in this order), encoded by suffixes mun, nan for s, wa for R, and wa, k for T, respectively.

All forms are presented in the following (splitted) table:

	r	R,RT	sR,sRT	s
r				k - ∅
R,RT				
sR,sRT				
s	k - un	k - un-um		
sT	k - un-mun	k - un-mun		
t	k - uk	k - uk-wa	k - uk-nan	n - uk
T	k - uko-k	k - uk-wa-k	k - uk-nan-uk	n - uko-k

	sT	t	T
r	k - uy-mun	k - a	k - a-k
R,RT	k - uy-mun	k - a-wa	k - a-wa-k
sR,sRT		k - a-mun	k - a-mun
s		n - a	n - a-k
sT		n - a-mun	n - a-mun
t	n - uk-nan	w - a-n w - uko-n	(w - a-n) (w - uko-n)
T	n - uk-nan-uk	w - a-wa-n w - uk-wa-n	(w - a-wa-n) (w - uk-wa-n)

Example: *n-wapm-uk-nan-uk = they see us (excl.)*, *k-wapm-a-mun = we (incl.) see him.*

256   M. Kudlek

The last example is from Quechua [2], the second official language of Peru. The personal pronouns can be encoded by suffixes being used for 1-participant forms:

Sing.	$c(P)$	Plur.	$c(P)$
s	-ni	sT	-niku
r	-nki	sR,(sRT)	-nchik
t	-n	R,(RT)	-nkichik
		T	-nku

Some, but not all, 2-participant relations can be encoded by suffixes indicating the direction of the action, and by suffixes for participants. The directions $s \to R$, $R \to T$, $T \to s$, and $T \to R$ are encoded by the suffixes *yki*, *wan*, *wan*, and *su*, respectively. All possible forms are given in:

	s	st	sR	r	R	t	T
s				-yki	-yki-chik		
sT				-yki-ku			
sR							
r	-wan-ki	-wan-kiku					
R	-wan-kichik						
t	-wan	-wan-ku	-wan-chik	-sun-ki	-sun-kichik		
T							

Example: *pukllaniku = we (excl.) are playing, qayasunkichik = he is calling you.*

In an extreme case all (P_1, P_2) may be encoded differently.

References

1. L. Bloomfield, *The Menomini Language*, Yale Univ. Press, Newhaven, London, 1962.

2. R. Hartmann (ed.), '*rimaykullayki*', Reimer, Berlin, 1985.

3. C. F. Hockett, What Algonquian is really like, *IJAL*, 32, 1 (1966), 59 – 73.

4. Antonio de los Reyes, *Arte en Lengua Mixteca*, México, 1593.

5. Fray Francisco Ximénez, *Arte de las Tres Lenguas Cakchiquel, Quiché y Tzutujil*, Guatemala, 1701.

Foundations of a Mathematical Semiotics

Robert MARTY
Department of Mathematics, University of Perpignan
Av. de Villeneuve, 66025 Perpignan, France

0. Introduction

According to C. S. Peirce, we have a possible classification of sciences in :
-"Mathematics, the study of ideal constructions without reference to their
real existence,
- Empirics, the study of phenomena with the purpose of identifying their
forms with those mathematics has studied,
- Pragmatics, the study of how we ought to behave in the ligth of the truths
of empirics." ([14], p. 1122)
We can put together this text with the conclusion of S. Marcus book "Se-
miotique formelle du folklore" [9]:
"Les Mathématiques et la Théorie des langages contribuent de par leur nature à la découverte des fonctions sémiotiques des objets qui nous entourent".
When we know, in other respects, Marcus constant preoccupation of connecting structural formal research and automatic treatment of data the parallel
is complet. The existence and the learning of mathematics are justified only
by their ability to give form to the phenomena, that is to say to create scientific cognition, with the possibility to allow effective actions on the real world.
This conception of the role of mathematics is available for every phenomenon:
gravity just as well as morphology of the tales, chemistry just as well as com-
binatory of ideas, biology just as well as functionning of the signs in social
life, etc... There is no banning of investing every field of the human sciences
with mathematical formalisms, it's even recommand in a good scientific moral.
S. Marcus and his students have illustrated with more success this scientific
principles formalizing daringly linguistics, of course but also theater, poetry,
folklore, economics, etc... In many aspects, this is a work of pionners. We can
see today, notably in the works of R. Thom and J. Petitot, that this way is
really heuristic and prolific.

In addition, we can specify our comparison in the linguistic and semiotic
areas. For instance, S. Marcus introduce explicitly the reader and the reader's
interpretations in the field of its investigations, considering their particular
grammar. That is a very semiotic point of view : "Les invariants repérés par
l'analyse et la grammaire élaborée à partir d'eux [...] ne sont plus considérés
comme immanents au texte, mais expriment un rapport entre texte et lecteur"

[9]. It's a way of formulating the necessity of taking as objects of knowledge the triadic sign constituted by the different elements of the text, the objects represented and the interpretants suggested by the text to the reader. In other words, the semiotic phenomena (in triadic meaning) must be put at the center of the cognitive process.

We would like to show, in this article, that a formal treatment of the semiotic phenomena is possible and that such a treatment allows us to reach the very grammar of the phenomena. To that end we extend Peirce's works in phenomenology and semiotics. Our tools are essentially category theory and functors, tools very close to the use of homological algebra by I. Gorun [9] and R. Ceterchi [5]. We obtain a general methodology for formalizing the functionning of every system of signs.

1. Perception

Any semiotic phenomenon, defined as a phenomenon in which the present thing is as valid as a missing one, assumes a sign as "a concrete subject which represents" [CP 1-540]. This means that we cannot approach semiotics without taking into account the perception of this concrete subject. This compels us to support at least an embryo of formal perception theory.

We shall take as a starting point the perceptual fact, which Peirce calls a "percipuum". It is not necessary to consider exclusively the fact as a current event ; it is enough for the fact to happen and be memorized, in other words, to belong to the experience of one subject, at least.

For Peirce, a "percipuum" is the juxtaposition of a percept and of a perceptual judgement. This analysis is confirmed, essentially, by the experiences which underline the fact that perception is a selection process during which a subject chooses, not only the percept elements but the manner in which they are put together in order to form the perceived collective totalities. Furthermore, the exemple of ambivalent pictures shows that two perceptual judgements can be associated with a same group of stimuli which lead us to form two distinct totalities, possibly present in the mind. We may call "perceptive configuration" the result of the selection and of this stimuli arrangement. The case of ambivalent pictures shows that the same "bundle" of stimuli can be organized in two different manners by the same subject so as to form two distinct perceptive configurations. This will enable us to understand and to formalize the fact that in the semiotic phenomenon there can be present to the mind of a subject, not only the concrete thing that represents but also the one missing from the field of present experience.

More precisely, every stimulus produces a corresponding "quality of feeling" and these simple qualities of feelings created by the outside word are selected according to their "pregnance" and "forcefulness" that is to say according to the subject's more or less developed receptivity based on his previous experiences or on the intrinsic capacity of the stimulus to impose itself on the subject's perception by its own power. Perceptual judgements are produced in the subject's own interior world and, in essence, they consist of bundles of qualities of feelings which constitute a sort of unit of a superior order. Accordingly, we formalize the perception phenomena considering abstract sets corresponding to the qualities of feelings on the one hand, and bundles of these qualities of feelings which are linked together by a complex group of relationships on the other hand corresponding to the perceptual judgements.

Our approach towards Peirce's perception theory and, later, phenomenology is similar to J. Petitot's approach towards Husserl's phenomenology and is also directed at the constitution of the objectivities. J. Petitot [16] utilizes fibred spaces with special properties with which one can describe the transformation of sets of perceptible qualities (for instance, the colours) belonging to an extensive "external" space into a intensive "internal" fibre. This mathematization translates what is a priori synthetic into axiomatic and is leading up a conception "object oriented" of the objectivities. It is interesting to recall this Peirce's text, directly written in French in an "Introduction a un traité de logique" ([15]) :

"Chaque qualité à chaque présentation a son degré d'intensité. Aussi ces qualités se présentent en assemblages, en faisceaux qui se distinguent par leurs différents lieux à chaque instant. Un tel faisceau est ce que nous appelons un objet aperçu ou un percept".

2. Perception, relational structures and objects of the world

We are now obliged to recall a lot of definitions and algebraic notions, mostly taken from Adamek's book [1] in which the study of categories of relational structures is developed and from [11]. These definitions are also presented in [11] in the context of semantic networks.

Definition 1. A *relational structure of type n* is a pair (X, α) where X is a set and α is an n-adic relation on X, that is to say a subset of the Cartesian product X^n.

Definition 2. More generally, a *relational structure of type* $\{n_i\}_{i \in I}$ where each n_i is a positive integer, is a pair $(X, \{\alpha_i\}_{i \in I})$ where X is a set and $\{\alpha_i\}_{i \in I}$ a family of n_i-adic relations. The type $\{n_i\}$ is the arity-size of all participating relations in the "family". The subscript i allows for several different arity-sizes (each n-adic relation is like an n-ended directed hyperarc in a hypergraph).

Definition 3. A relational structure (X, α) of type $\{n_i\}_{i \in I}$ is *connected* if for all pairs of elements x and $x' \in X$ there exist a subset of the family $\{\alpha_i\}$

called $(\alpha_1, \alpha_2, \ldots, \alpha_k)$ and elements $x_1, x_2, \ldots, x_{k-1}$ of X such that x and x_1 belong to an n_1-tuple of α_1; x_1 and x_2 belong to an n_2-tuple of $\alpha_2, \ldots, x_{k-1}$ and x' to an n_k-tuple of α_k. (This generalizes the connectivity of a graph to a directed hypergraph.)

These definitions constitute the mathematical form of a percept. The family considered must be relative to an object. Nevertheless, the different percepts of the same object must have some relations in order to say that a set of percepts is relative to a single object. With the aim of formalizing these relations, we need two new definitions. First, we formalize the general relations between relational structures.

Definition 4. Let (X, α) and (Y, β) be two relational structures of the same type n. A function Γ of X into Y is said to be **compatible** if $(x_1, x_2, \ldots, x_n) \in \alpha$ implies that $(\Gamma(x_1), \Gamma(x_2), \ldots, \Gamma(x_n)) \in \beta$ (i.e., membership of a node in a relation hyperarc is preserved).

Now we begin to use Category Theory considering a functor F of the category "Set" of sets within itself, and we define a relational structure of type F as a pair (X, α) where X is a set and $\alpha \subseteq F(X)$; if (Y, β) is another relational structure of type F, the function Γ of X into Y is F-compatible if $F[\Gamma(\alpha)] \subseteq \beta$. The category of these relational structures with these morphisms will be called "relational category $\mathbf{S}(F)$". Then the relational category of type n is $\mathbf{S}(Q_n)$ where Q_n is the functor defined by $F(X) = X^n$ and $F(\Gamma) = \Gamma^n$. If $\coprod_{i \in I} Q_{n_i}$ is the coproduct of the functors $Q_{n_i}(i \in I)$ we obtain the relational category $\mathbf{S}(\coprod_{i \in I} Q_{n_i})$ for which the objects are defined in Definition 3 and the morphisms in Definition 4. For instance, in $\mathbf{S}(Q_2 + Q_3)$, a relational structure on a set X is a set $\alpha \subseteq X \times X + X \times X \times X$ consisting of a dyadic relation $\alpha_2 = \alpha \cap X \times X$ and a triadic relation $\alpha_3 = \alpha \cap X \times X \times X$; given the two relational structures of type $Q_2 + Q_3$, the compatible maps $\Gamma : (X, \alpha) \to (Y, \beta)$ are precisely those which preserve the dyadic relations as well as the triadic ones, i.e., $(x_0, x_1) \in \alpha_2$ implies $(\Gamma(x_0), \Gamma(x_1)) \in \beta_2$ and $(x_0, x_1, x_2) \in \alpha_3$ implies $(\Gamma(x_0), \Gamma(x_1), \Gamma(x_2)) \in \beta_3$.

The category $\mathbf{S}(\coprod i \in IQ_{n_i})$ is the exclusive framework of our formalization : it contains, in fact, with a suitable set I of indices, all mathematical forms of all possible perceptual judgements of all subjects and also all possible relations that these forms maintain between themselves.

Let us consider the surmised reality which lies behind multiple (possibly different) perceptions of a possible object, event or situation. This requires again two definitions:

Definition 5. A *source* in $\mathbf{S}(F)$ on a set X is a family $(Y_i, \beta_i, \Gamma_i)_{i \in I}$ where the (Y_i, β_i) are objects of $\mathbf{S}(F)$ and the $\Gamma_i : X \to Y_i$ are maps ; we usually denote sources as follows $\{X \to (Y_i, \beta_i)\}_{i \in I}$.

Definition 6. An *initial structure* of a source is a structure (X, α) on X such that :

(i) $\Gamma_i : (X, \alpha) \to (Y_i, \beta_i)$ is a morphism of $\mathbf{S}(F)$,

(ii) for each object (T, δ) and each function $h : T \to X$ such that $\Gamma_i.h : (T, \delta) \to (Y_i, \beta_i)$ is a morphism for each i, then $h : (T, \delta) \to (X, \alpha)$ is also a morphism.

A first condition for the possibility of an object "behind the appearances" is expressed by the existence of the set X of qualities of feelings, without a priori relations between them, the maps Γ_i between this set X and every set underlying every relational structure associated to a perception. In other words, it is necessary for the building-up of an object of the world that different perceptions may be put together by the fact that they have a possible common origin in the exterior world, a source of stimuli as cause of the qualities of feelings produced into every subject.

The second condition is that this common origin must be provided with a relational structure which is connected with every "appearance" by a morphism of the mathematical structure. It is a very natural condition because the consensus reality on the objects of the world have necessarily the same mathematical form that the one of the perception, the only form which are in the experiences of every subject.

Definition 5 expresses the first condition and Definition 6 the second. In the latter we have an universal property which demand an explanation. In fact, this property expresses that another possible objet (T, δ), also "behind the appearances", which is connected with the set X by a function (that is to say a correspondence between qualities of feelings) on the one hand and with each percept by a correspondence between relational structures on the other hand is automatically connected with (X, α). In other words, all form of an object like (T, δ) is – in a way – behind the form of the object (X, α) or (X, α) is the nearest object behind the appearances.

Fortunately, the category $\mathbf{S}(F)$ posesses a very interesting property noted by Adamek [1] :

Proposition 1. *The relational category $\mathbf{S}(F)$ is initially complete, that is to say every source possesses a single initial structure.*

In fact, $\alpha = \cap [F(\Gamma_i)]^{-1}(\beta_i) = \{x \in F(X) \mid F(\Gamma_i)(x) \in \beta_i \text{ for } i \in I\}$ is the required initial structure.

Proposition 1 ensures us of the possibility of building-up a single relational structure based only on the mathematical form of a class of perceptions which shall eventually be related to a single object as real cause of the class. The building-up of a social object, the object of a community, remains to be done.

This is very easy, since for every subject "i" we have an initial structure (X, α_i). Then, the (X, α_i), i running over all individuals of a community, form a new source of $\mathbf{S}(F)$ with the hypothesis according to which the qualities of feelings X are the same for all individuals of the community and the Γ_i of the Definition 5 are inclusion maps. By Proposition 1 this source possesses an initial structure (X, α^*) that is the mathematical form of the structure associated to an object by a community (note that this structure can be obtained considering at beginning the source of all relational structures of all perceptions of all members of the community). In other words, (X, α^*) is the "common knowledge" of the community about an object or the common connected relational structure of it. Clearly it is posible that some members of a community have incomplete class of perceptions (children, handicaped persons, mads,...) or are making other class or are dissociating some classes having in a way, special and minority conceptions of the world.

(X, α^*) corresponds also to the Peircean notion of "skeleton-set" [CP 7-426] and can be interpreted also as Husserlian notion of "eidos". That is the reason why we call this universal initial structure an "eidetic structure".

The following text extracted from MS 612 shows how these results are close to Peirce's conception (Peirce was on a ship on the way to Sicily on December the 22nd, 1870) :

"For it was only by such signs as our having been steaming due east or a little north of that since we had pass Taenarium that I knew we must by that time have got about to where Etna would be visible in the west, and so that that that obtuse isosceles triangle I saw must be Etna, which without such signs I should not have known. Nevertheless, it remains true that I was directly aware of **some** object, and equally that that object of which I was directly aware was Etna; and that would have been true if I had been quite ignorant of geography. In that sense I was directly aware of Etna, that is, of what really was Etna".

Thus, a obtuse isosceles triangle could be an eidetic structure of the Etna.

3. Eidetic structures, mental objects and inner world

Our fundamental hypotesis consists precisely in interpreting the eidetic structure obtained in the previous section in a phenomenological sense. Before we note that our results implies that in all relational structure associated to a perception of an object there is the eidetic structure, or a part of it, of this object. Then it will suffice to consider that an object is "present to the mind" if and only if this mind "forms" its eidetic structure. Indeed, when this structure is entirely included in a perception we automatically and immediatly obtains its "presence to the mind". When only a part of the structure is included there is a completion process based on a series of inferences which constitute an inquiry (with, of course, possibility of errors). This inquiry consists in finding, in the field of the previous experiences already categorized by classes having their associated eidetic structure, the class in which the new perception can take place without changing the initial structure (i.e. the eidetic structure of the object) of the new source thus obtained. This inquiry is, of course guided by the context hic et nunc of the perception.

This hypothesis is also considerably substantiated by neurophysical considerations. Indeed the "mental object" is identified by J. P. Changeux [4] with the physical state created by the electrical and chemical activity of large "*assemblies*" of neurons, mathematically described by a graph, discrete, close and autonomous. Now, each neuron is formally equivalent to n-adic relations between the other neurons belonging to the assembly with which it is linked. Therefore, it seems right to consider that this assembly is, formally, a connected relational structure.

The qualities of feelings are conveyed by the nervous system to the brain in which they are assembled in "bundles" by the neurons where they constitute relational structures materialized by the neuronal connexions which are stimulated. In addition we must suppose that the brain retains the memory of anterior experiences and functions as a system able to build the initial structure of the sources materialized. In other words, the brain should be a sort of machine to extract eidetic structures which are supposed to be "analogons" of the objects of the world. We shall see that, in the social communication by signs, the subjects have to check that the personal initial structure related to the same class of experiences are the same as the ones built by the others individuals or correct them otherwise.

The morphisms between eidetic structures are naturally interpreted as relations between world objects. Finally this modelization consists in substituting for the exterior world, considered as a "vague" category with objects and relations between these objects, the precise category $\mathbf{S}(\coprod_{i \in I} Q_{n_i})$ containing all the analogons of this objects and relations in mental objects (extracted of assemblies of neurons materializing the perceptions) form. We can describe this correspondence between objects of the world and mental objects with the aid of a "metaphorical functor" supported by the mechanism of the perception (including the brain) of the exterior world itself. This functor is created, so to speak, from the very fact of the perception of the objects and their relations. The interior world is filled with relational structures corresponding to world objects and linked by morphisms corresponding to existential or socialized and conceptual relations between this objects.

Nevertheless, the objects of the world are, most of the time, present to the mind simultaneously with other objects, if only through their own constituent parts with which they are related. In other words the objects participate in what Peirce calls a "phaneron" (synonymous for him with "phenomenon"). The phaneron is "the collective total of all that is in any way or in any sense present to the mind, quite regardless of whether it corresponds to any real thing or not" [CP 1-284].

According to the previous hypothesis, it follows that a phaneron can be produced by the perception of a set of related objects of the exterior world, or internally constituted by the mind which associates their eidetic structures already memorized, or by a combination of both. These eidetic structures are combined by means of their possible morphisms. (Changeux speaks of "associative properties of mental objects".) Again using Category Theory, we will build the formal framework for dealing with the phaneron (phenomenology), that is to say the structure of all that can be present to the mind.

Before that, we will establish a reduction theorem and give a few definitions (in keeping with the philosophical speculations and the formal intuitions of C. S. Peirce) which permit us to describe more easily the phaneron and the relations between phanerons.

Definition 7. Let (X, α) be a relational structure of type n on base-set X and (X, β) a relational structure of type m on the same base-set; we define the *relative product* of (X, α) by (X, β), and we call $(X, \alpha * \beta)$ the relational structure of type $n + m - 2$ defined by the following subset of the Cartesian-product set of X^{n+m-2}: $\alpha * \beta = \{(x_1, x_2, \ldots, x_{n-1}, y_2, \ldots, y_m)\}$ such that there exist $u \in X$ such that $(x_1, x_2, \ldots, x_{n-1}, u) \in \alpha$ and $(u, y_2, \ldots, y_m \in \beta)$.

Definition 8. A relational structure (X, α) is *relatively decomposable* on a set $K = \{(X, \alpha_i)\}_{i \in I}$ of relational structures if (X, α) is the relative product of a set of relational structures of K.

Definition 9. A relational structure (X, α) of type n is *relatively reducible* on X if and only if (X, α) is relatively decomposable on a set $K = \{(X, \alpha_i)\}_{i \in I}$ of relational structures on S of type smaller than n. If a relational structure is not relatively reducible on X it is *relatively irreducible* on X.

It is easy to establish that every relational structure of a type equal to 3 or smaller than 3 is relatively irreducible within any domain.

Theorem 1. *Let (X, α) be a relational structure of type $n > 3$ and α_0 a set of the same cardinality as α; we consider $X_0 = X \cup \alpha_0$ and the relational structure (X_0, α) to be of type n defined on X_0 by the n-tuples of α. Then (X_0, α) is relatively reducible on a set of relational structures of type 3.*

This theorem called also "reduction thesis", has been proved differently in terms of extensional logic by H. G. Herzberger [7], in terms of intentional logic by R. W. Burch [3] and directly in [12], seems to be in opposition to a well known result of W. V. O. Quine according to which every n-adic predicate can be reduced to a combination of dyadic predicates. This discussion has no place in this work, but we note simply that it is, in our opinion, a difference of viewpoint as to the importance accorded to the notion of "teridentity". The interest of a reduction thesis lies not only in the result and its consequences but also in the mechanism of proof based on the addition to every n-tuple of α of a new element which corresponds to the "quality of feeling" of the n-tuple itself. This element can be interpreted as the partial determination of the mind which precisely constitutes this n-uple in a greater entity in the perceptual judgement. This establishes a correspondence between the "external" relation structure (built by the community) and the "internal" structure in which all adicities (arities) have been increased by 1. This correspondence is defined as follows:

$$(x_1, \ldots, x_n) \longrightarrow (x_1, \ldots, x_n, (x_1, \ldots, x_n))$$

Moreover, this interpretation allows us to conceive the external structure as a cause of the internal structure in a dialectic process (see [11]). Then, eidetic structures can be interpreted as causal structures assigned to external objects the forms of which are imposed by the specific mechanisms of the perception. This remark also justifies the removal of the division between an external category, the former becoming a subcategory of the latter. Therefore, we can consider that the external category contains objects without physical materiality.

Now, the reduction theorem allows us to describe every relational structure on X of type n by means of the relative product of relational structures of type 1, 2 or 3, called elementary relational structures. We call "monads" the elements of relational structures of type 1 (1-tuples) ; we call "dyads" the ones of type 2 (2-tuples) and "triads" the ones of type 3 (3-tuples). Each monad corresponds to a simple "quality of feeling," each dyad to an existent individual or a fact, and each triad to a "concept, law or something expressible by universal proposition". This is the empirical decomposition of the phaneron into indecomposable elements often described by Peirce.

If (X, α) is an eidetic structure of an object of type $\{n_i\}_{i \in I}$, then by introducing enough new individuals like α_0 for every $n_i > 3$ such that $X \cup \{\text{new individuals}\} = X_0$, we can consider that every object of the world is represented in our model by a relational structure of $S(Q_1 + Q_2 + Q_3)$ that is to say a relational structure of type $\{1, 2, 3\}$. But, considering that the perceptual judgement which assembles n qualities of feeling of an n-tuple assembles a fortiori all the k-tuples ($n < k$) obtained erasing $n - k$ of these qualities of feeling, we define a special relational structure of type $\{1, 2, 3\}$ as follows:

Definition 10. A relational structure (X, α) of type 1, 2, 3 on the set X with $\alpha_1 = \alpha \cap X$, $\alpha_2 = \alpha \cap X \times X$, $\alpha_3 = \alpha \cap X \times X \times X$ is a *phenomenological structure* of type $\{1, 2, 3\}$ if the following conditions are fulfilled:

(i) if $(x_1, x_2, x_3) \in \alpha_3$, then $(x_1, x_2) \in \alpha_2$, $(x_1, x_3) \in \alpha_2$, $(x_2, x_3) \in \alpha_2$

(ii) if $(x_1, x_2) \in \alpha_2$, then $x_1 \in \alpha_1$ and $x_2 \in \alpha_1$.

By combination of (i) and (ii) we have:

(ii) if $(x_1, x_2, x_3) \in \alpha_3$, then $x_1 \in \alpha_1$, $x_2 \in \alpha_1$, and $x_3 \in \alpha_1$.

Proposition 2. *The relations $R_{3,2}$ defined by the above condition (i) between α_3 and α_2, $R_{2,1}$ defined by (ii) between α_2 and α_1, $R_{3,1}$ defined by (iii) between α_3 and α_1 define a category called $\alpha_3 \rightarrow \alpha_2 \rightarrow \alpha_1$ of which objects are the α_3, α_2, and α_1 and the morphisms $R_{3,2}$, $R_{2,1}$, $R_{3,1}$ and the identites on α_3, α_2 and α_1.*

Indeed we have $R_{3,1} = R_{2,1} \circ R_{3,2}$. Henceforth, we will represent the phenomenological structure associated to an object of the world by $(X, \alpha_3 \rightarrow \alpha_2 \rightarrow \alpha_1)$ where X is a set and $\alpha_3 \rightarrow \alpha_2 \rightarrow \alpha_1$ the category defined in Proposition 2. We recall that, if X and Y are two sets, a functional correspondence between X and Y is a relation $\Gamma \subseteq X \times Y$ such that if $x \in X$, $(x, y) \in \Gamma$, and $(x, z) \in \Gamma$ then $y = z$.

Definition 11. Let $(X, \alpha_3 \rightarrow \alpha_2 \rightarrow \alpha_1)$ and $(Y, \beta_3 \rightarrow \beta_2 \rightarrow \beta_1)$ two phenomenological structures and Γ a functional correspondence between X and Y; we consider the following sets:

$\Gamma(3, 3) = \{(\Gamma(x_1), \Gamma(x_2), \Gamma(x_3)) \in \beta_3 \text{ such that } (x_1, x_2, x_3) \in \alpha_3\}$

$\Gamma(3, 2) = \{(\Gamma(x_1), \Gamma(x_2)) \in \beta_2, (\Gamma(x_1), \Gamma(x_3)) \in \beta_2, (\Gamma(x_2), \Gamma(x_3)) \in \beta_2$
$\qquad\qquad \text{such that } (x_1, x_2, x_3) \in \alpha_3\}$

$\Gamma(3, 1) = \{(\Gamma(x_1) \in \beta_1, \Gamma(x_2) \in \beta_1, \Gamma(x_3) \in \beta_1 \text{ such that } (x_1, x_2, x_3) \in \alpha_3\}$

$\Gamma(2, 2) = \{(\Gamma(x_1), \Gamma(x_2)) \in \beta_2 \text{ such that } (x_1, x_2) \in \alpha_2\}$

$\Gamma(2, 1) = \{(\Gamma(x_1) \in \beta_1, \Gamma(x_2) \in \beta_1 \text{ such that } (x_1, x_2) \in \alpha_2\}$

$\Gamma(1, 1) = \{(\Gamma(x_1) \in \beta_1, \text{ such that } (x_1) \in \alpha_1\}.$

and the corresponding relations (called elementary morphisms)

$\Gamma_3 : \alpha_3 \rightarrow \Gamma(3, 3) \subseteq \beta_3; \Gamma'_3 : \alpha_3 \rightarrow \Gamma(3, 2) \subseteq \beta_2; \Gamma''_3 : \alpha_3 \rightarrow \Gamma(3, 1) \subseteq \beta_1.$

$\Gamma_2 : \alpha_2 \rightarrow \Gamma(2, 2) \subseteq \beta_2; \Gamma'_2 : \alpha_2 \rightarrow \Gamma(2, 1) \subseteq \beta_2,$

$\Gamma_1 : \alpha_1 \rightarrow \Gamma(1, 1) \subseteq \beta_1.$

Γ is called a *phenomenological morphism* if Γ determines a functor of the category $\alpha_3 \rightarrow \alpha_2 \rightarrow \alpha_1$ into the category $\beta_3 \rightarrow \beta_2 \rightarrow \beta_1$ by means of the relations Γ_3, Γ'_3, Γ''_3, Γ_2, Γ'_2, Γ_1.

Proposition 3. *There are exactly 10 phenomenological morphisms between two phenomenological structures; these phenomenological morphisms are ordered in a structure of lattices by the natural transformations of functors.*

Indeed it will suffice to write the 10 functors and to note the pairs of these functors for which a natural transformation is defined.

Proposition 4. *The set of the phenomenological structures provided with the phenomenological morphisms is a category (called the Phenomenological Category of the Objects* $\mathbf{PH}_0$.

Indeed the composition of phenomenological morphisms is defined by the composition of the functional correspondences combined with the composition of the functors.

The interpretation of these definitions and results are as follows : the phenomenological structures represent the objects of the world (present to the mind), whereas the phenomenological morphisms represent the relations between these objects, that is to say the *modes of being*. There are six fundamental classes of modes of being : Γ_3, Γ'_3, and Γ''_3 corresponding respectively to Authentic Thirdness, Degenerate Thirdness at the first degree, Degenerate Thirdness at the second degree, Γ_2 and Γ'_2 corresponding respectively to Authentic Secondness and degenerate Secondness, Γ_1 corresponding to Firstness.

These modes of being correspond with the so-called "cenopythagorean categories" of Peirce and their degenerated forms (see [8]). Moreover these results agree perfectly with the results of R. W. Burch [3]. Moreover, if $\Gamma(i,j)$ is not empty, then $\Gamma(i',j')$ with $i' \leq i$ and $j' \leq j$ is not empty ; therefore the presence in a phaneron of a mode of being corresponding to $\Gamma(i,j)$ implies the presence of a mode of being corresponding to $\Gamma(i',j')$. In fact, the modes of being are organized in a lattice of six elements and this framework permit us to develop a complete formalization and various extensions of the Peircean semiotic [11].

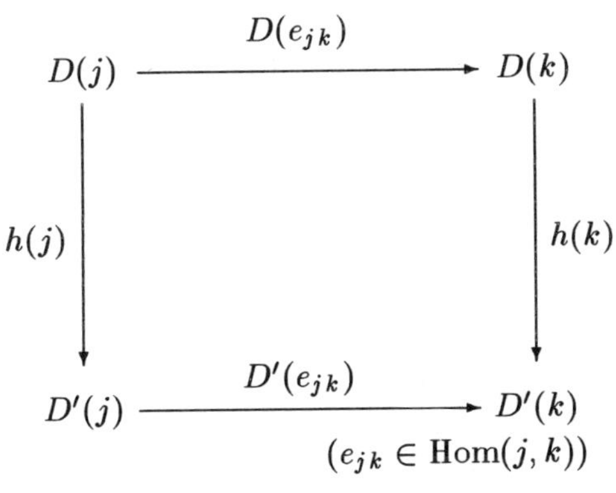

Fig. 1

Now we have something corresponding to a phaneron considered as a collective totality of objects present to the mind with relations between these objects. In our model, the phaneron will be represented by a "diagram" in the phenomenological category of objects $\mathbf{PH_0}$.

Definition 12. Let J be a poset considered as a category; we call *category of phanerons of type J* the category $\mathbf{PH}_j$ of which objects are diagrams of scheme J on $\mathbf{PH_0}$, that is to say covariant functors $D : J \to \mathbf{PH_0}$, and the morphisms are natural transformations of functors.

Remember that a natural transformation of functors $h : D \to D'$ is a family of morphisms $(h(j) : D(j) \to D'(j))_{j \in J}$ such that, for each morphism e_{jk} of J, we have the commutative diagram in figure 1.

We have moved up another level. For a suitable poset J, we can obtain all possible forms of configurations of objects which can be present to any mind, that is to say all abstract forms of phanerons. These forms are determined *a priori* by the forms of the perception, present perceptions or previously memorized perceptions.

Now, we are able to approach the phenomenology of *representation* in formal terms. In a representation one collective totality stands for another, that is one phenomenon is *substituted* for another. Therefore, in our model a diagram is substituted for another. The complex relations that these two totalities can have in the exterior world are clearly represented by the corresponding connections of diagrams. *A representation theory* is consequently possible using the categories of phanerons $\mathbf{PH}_J$. When we reduce to a representation of an object we have a sign theory.

4. Representation contexts, signs and semiotics

We continue towards the aim of build-up a general algebraic representation theory generalizing the notion of context and of lattice concepts such as they are defined by R. Wille [18], [19], as follow:

A context is a triple (G, M, I) where G is a set of objects, M is a set of attributes, and I is a binary relation between G and M indicating by gIm that the object g has the attribute m. There is a natural *Galois connection* between G and M (which we indicate with "prime" marks) defined by $A' = \{m \in M \mid g\,I\,m$ for all $g \in A\}$ for $A \subseteq G$, and $B' = \{g \in G \mid g\,I\,m$ for all $m \in B\}$ for $B \subseteq M$. A concept of the context (G, M, I) is a pair (A, B) with $A \subseteq G$, $B \subseteq M$, $A' = B$, and $B' = A$. The set $L(G, M, I)$ of the concepts of (G, M, I) is partially ordered by the definition $(A_1, B_1) \leq (A_2, B_2)$ if and only if $A_1 \subseteq A_2$ (or $B_1 \supseteq B_2$). $(L(G, M, I), \leq)$ is a complete lattice called the *lattice-concept* of (G, M, I). From our standpoint that will mean considering each attribute as *representing* all objects to which it is related.

Definition 13. Let J and K be two posets and $\mathbf{PH}_J$ and $\mathbf{PH}_K$ the corresponding categories of phanerons. $\mathbf{PH}_J$ and $\mathbf{PH}_K$ are said to be *connected* if, for at least $D \in \mathbf{PH}_J$ there exists at least $D' \in \mathbf{PH}_K$ such that, if θ is a phenomenological morphism between two objects $(X, \alpha_3 \to \alpha_2 \to \alpha_1)$ and $(Y, \beta_3 \to \beta_2 \to \beta_1)$ of D then there exists a phenomenological morphism θ' between two objects $(X', \alpha'_3 \to \alpha'_2 \to \alpha'_1)$ of D' and two phenomenological morphisms ϕ and ϕ' such that we have the commutative diagram in figure 2.

The morphism ϕ and ϕ' are called connections between $\mathbf{PH}_J$ and $\mathbf{PH}_K$ and the set Σ_{JK} of these connections is called the "connecting-set" between $\mathbf{PH}_J$ and $\mathbf{PH}_K$

$$(X, \alpha_3 \longrightarrow \alpha_2 \longrightarrow \alpha_1) \quad \xrightarrow{\ \phi\ } \quad (X', \alpha'_3 \longrightarrow \alpha'_2 \longrightarrow \alpha'_1)$$

$$\theta \Big\downarrow \qquad\qquad\qquad\qquad \Big\downarrow \theta'$$

$$(Y, \beta_3 \longrightarrow \beta_2 \longrightarrow \beta_1) \quad \xrightarrow{\ \phi'\ } \quad (Y', \beta'_3 \longrightarrow \beta'_2 \longrightarrow \beta'_1)$$

Fig. 2

Definition 14. The triple $(\mathbf{PH}_J, \mathbf{PH}_K, \Sigma_{JK})$ where $\mathbf{PH}_J$ and $\mathbf{PH}_K$ are categories of phanerons and Σ_{JK} a connecting set between them is called a *representation-context*. We call it a representation-context because this notion captures the substitution of a part of a phaneron of any type by a part of a phaneron of another type.

If $\mathbf{PH}_J$ and $\mathbf{PH}_K$ are categories of phanerons of which all the objects are diagrams reduced to one element, then the connecting set is a binary relation between two sets which are named respectively *objects* and *attributes* by Wille and our *representation-context* is in accordance with his definition of a *context*.

The notion of representation-context seems interesting as a theoretical framework for various formalizations. For instance, if $\mathbf{PH}_K$ is a part of a language in which objects are names and morphisms are predicates we can to talk about a "linguistic context of representation"; if $\mathbf{P_K}$ is a set of dots and lines with rules of combination we can to talk about a "graphic context"; likewise for "pictorial context", "musical context", etc.

Definition 15. If $(\mathbf{PH}_J, \mathbf{PH}_K, \Sigma_{JK})$ is a representation-context and if $D \in \mathbf{PH}_J$, every $D' \in \mathbf{PH}_K$ such that there exists a connection of Σ_{JK} connecting D and D' is a *sign* of D in this representation-context. (This definition agrees with Peirce's meaning of a "sign".)

Now for all sets A of objects of $\mathbf{PH}_J$, we define the subset A' of objects of $\mathbf{PH}_K$ which are signs of all objects of A and, for all subsets B of $\mathbf{PH}_K$ we define the subsets B' of all objects of $\mathbf{PH}_J$ of which the objects of B are signs. The maps $A \to A'$ and $B \to B'$ form a Galois connection between the power sets of $\mathbf{PH}_J$ and $\mathbf{PH}_K$.

Definition 16. All pairs (A, B), $A \subseteq \mathbf{PH}_J$, $B \subseteq \mathbf{PH}_K$ such that $A = B'$ and $B = A'$ are called *semiotics* of the representation-context.

Thus a concept in Wille's sense is a semiotic in which every attribute is a sign of a set of objects and the *intention* of a concept is the set of attributes related to the concept. Similarly every objects is signified by a set of attributes, and the *extension* is the set of objects related to the concept. By analogy we say that A is the *extension* of the semiotic (A, B) and B its *intention*.

Definition 17. Let (A_1, B_1) and (A_2, B_2) be two semiotics of the same representation-context; we define an order of relationship for the set of semiotics of this representation-context by:

$$(A_1, B_1) \leq (A_2, B_2) \text{ if and only if } A_1 \subseteq A_2 \text{ and } B_1 \supseteq B_2.$$

The set $\mathbf{S}(\mathbf{PH}_J, \mathbf{PH}_K, \Sigma_{JK})$ of the semiotics of the representation-context $(\mathbf{PH}_J, \mathbf{PH}_K, \Sigma_{JK})$ is partially ordered by this relation $\leq$, and we will say that the semiotic (A_1, B_1) is better than the semiotic (A_2, B_2) because it represents more objects using less signs.

The notion of the representation-context can be adapted in order to respond to particular situations. The most interesting cases seem to be when the ordered set $\mathcal{S}(\mathbf{PH}_J, \mathbf{PH}_K, \Sigma_{JK})$ is a lattice or better, when it is a complete lattice with a top, because in this latter case there exists a universal semiotic which represents everything.

Therefore we can associate with every category of phanerons the categories of phanerons obtained by decomposing it and then assembling according to their category the decomposition of their diagrams and their morphisms as previously indicated. This being done for the $\mathbf{PH}_J$ and $\mathbf{PH}_K$ (since they are simply examples of diagrams) of a representation-context we now decompose the morphisms of Σ_{JK}: we will finally obtain in a natural way a "foliation" of the original representation-context into a poset of *elementary representation-contexts*. These latter are of six types (arities) according to the previous results. This property is naturally transmitted to the "semiotics" of the elementary representation-contexts.

Thus, the questions of the determination, categorization and the description of these semiotics come down to the study of the same questions in the cases of elementary representation-contexts which are of one of the six following types:

$$((X, \alpha_3), (Y, \beta_3), \Sigma_{3;3})); \quad ((X, \alpha_3), (Y, \beta_2), \Sigma_{3;2})); \quad ((X, \alpha_3), (Y, \beta_1), \Sigma_{3;1}));$$
$$((X, \alpha_2), (Y, \beta_2), \Sigma_{2;2})); \quad ((X, \alpha_2), (Y, \beta_1), \Sigma_{2;1})); \quad ((X, \alpha_1), (Y, \beta_1), \Sigma_{1;1}));$$

where the index numbers of the letters α and β indicate the type (arity) of the relational structures and those of the letter Σ the types of elementary morphisms.

These elementary representation-contexts are naturally ordered so as to form a lattice. This order corresponds to the hierarchy of the "cenopythagorean categories". We obtain the lattice represented in figure 3. (The numbers between brackets are abbreviations used to name the relation classes). Moreover, we have similar lattices with the semiotics of every *elementary* representation-context.

This lattice show the different possible species of "representation-context" depending on the fundamental categories (1, 2 or 3) of the entities on either side of our (Galois) "representation-relations". R. Wille's lattice-concepts are of type [2,1] because they consist of sets of dyads (objects) described using monad attributes. There are five other representation possibilities, depending on the "arity" of the entities. (X, α) can be the designated and (Y, β) the designata, and Σ is the representation-relation itself.

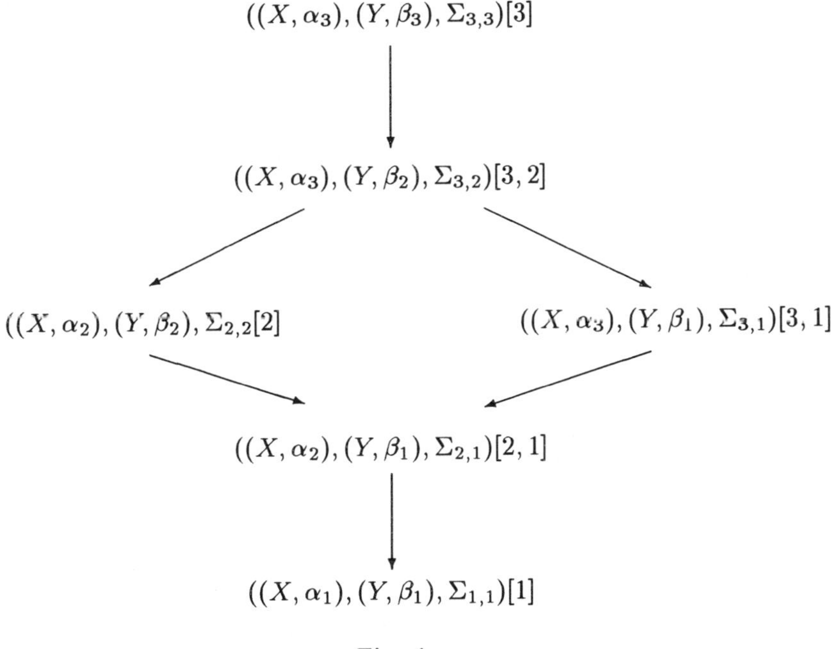

$$((X, \alpha_3), (Y, \beta_3), \Sigma_{3,3})[3]$$

$$((X, \alpha_3), (Y, \beta_2), \Sigma_{3,2})[3, 2]$$

$$((X, \alpha_2), (Y, \beta_2), \Sigma_{2,2})[2] \qquad ((X, \alpha_3), (Y, \beta_1), \Sigma_{3,1})[3, 1]$$

$$((X, \alpha_2), (Y, \beta_1), \Sigma_{2,1})[2, 1]$$

$$((X, \alpha_1), (Y, \beta_1), \Sigma_{1,1})[1]$$

Fig. 1

The connections Σ by which the structures of the inner world represents the supposed structures of the exterior world are necessarily of a sociological type. We consider it as social institutions appealing to the dialecticized concept of institution as described in [11]. The representation-contexts are determined and connected by means of social processes and agreements which governs all inter-individual communications. This latter only actualizes the social consent about representation of things by other things. But we can create, with the condition of respecting the hierarchy of representation-contexts new connections and new categories of phanerons which will or will not be incorporated in our culture. We can also continue to generalize by means of the notion of the "fusion" of individual contexts proposed by Wille [18], to the fusion of representation-contexts.

The notion of semiotics (Definition 16) can be particularized to the phanerons constituted by a single object and we obtain the classical theory of signs as formalized in [11]. Then the connections Σ correspond to the central Peircean notion of "interpretant" and the inferential process mentioned before corresponds to the other important Peircean notion of "semiosis", formalizing at the same time one of its definitions of the sign according to "a sign is a medium for the communication or extension of a Form (or feature)". Our method consists in describing the "journey" of the eidetic structure associated to the object represented, partially incorporated in the representing sign and rebuilt by the mind into this initial form. Next the phenomenological distinctions lead to the Peircean taxonomies of signs which are ordered by lattice structures of the same type that the representation-contexts.

Moreover, still using elementary Category-Theoretic notions of product and coproduct of a diagram we have built a metodology for analysis and synthesis of complex signs. It is clear that our formalization aims a diagrammatization of the thought similar to the one intended by Peirce in his Existential Graphs. Therefore its algebraic character could facilitate the connection between semiotics and Artificial Intelligence. Recall what Peirce suggests :

"This capacity of revealing unexpected truth is precisely that where in the utility of algebraical formulae consists..."

References

1. J. Adàmek, *Theory of Mathematical Structures*, D. Reidel Publising Company, Dordreckt, Holland, 1983.

2. J. Brunning, Genuine triads and teridentity, to appear.

3. R. Burch, *A Peircean Reduction Thesis and the Foundations of Topological Logic*, Texas Tech University Press, Texas, 1991.

4. J. P. Changeux, *L'homme neuronal*, Fayard, Paris, 1983.

5. R. Ceterchi, Categories in the study of communication, processes and meaning generation, to appear.

6. I. Gorun, Prosodie et syntaxe dans la poésie populaire; une application de l'Algèbre Homologique, *Sémiotique formelle du folklore* (S. Marcus, ed.), Klincksieck, Paris, 1978.

7. H. G. Herzberger, Peirce's Remarkable Theorem, *Pragmatism and Purpose*, University of Toronto Press, 1981, 49 – 58

8. K. L. Ketner, Most lucid and interesting paper, an introduction to ceno-pythagoreanism, *International Philosophical Quaterly*, XXVI(4), (1986), 375 – 392.

9. S. Marcus, *Sémiotique formelle du folklore*, Klincksieck, Paris, 1978.

10. C. Marty, R. Marty, *99 réponses sur la sémiotique*, Centre Régional de Documentation pédagogique, Montpellier (France), 1992.

11. R. Marty, *L'algèbre des signes*, John Benjamins, Amsterdam-Philadelphia, 1990.

12. R. Marty, Foliated semantic networks : concepts, facts and qualities, in *Semantic Networks* (F. Lehmann, ed.), Pergamon Press, Oxford, 1992, 679 – 696.

13. C. S. Peirce, *Collected Papers* (CP) vol. I à VI, ed. by Ch. Hartshorne and P. Weiss, Cambridge, MA : Harward University Press (1931-39) ; vol. VII and VIII ed. by A. W. Burks. Cambridge, DA : Harvard University Press, 1958.

14. C. S. Peirce, *The New Elements of Mathematics*, vol. 4, C. Eisele ed., Mouton, The Hague, 1976.

15. C S. Peirce, *Introduction à un traité de logique*, G. Deledalle ed., *Kodikas/Code*, 8, 1/2 (1985).

16. J. Petitot, Phénoménologie naturalisée et morphodynamique : la fonction cognitive du synthétique a priori, *Intellectica 1993*, 2, 17 (1993), 79 – 126.

17. R. Wille, Restructuring lattice Theory : an approach based on hierarchy of concepts, *Ordered sets* (I. Rival, ed.), D. Reidel Publishing Company, Dordrecht, Holland, 1982, 445 – 470.

18. R. Wille, Sur la fusion des contextes individuels, *Mathématiques et Sciences Humaines*, 85 (1984), 57 – 71.

19. R. Wille, Concept lattices and conceptual knowledge systems, in *Semantic Networks* (F. Lehmann, ed.), 1992, 493 – 516.

Marcus Contextual Grammars
with Shuffled Contexts[1]

Alexandru MATEESCU

Faculty of Mathematics, University of Bucharest

Str. Academiei 14, 70109 Bucureşti, Romania

Abstract. We introduce a new type of Marcus contextual grammars. Instead of considering a context as a pair of words, in our approach a context is just a word. Moreover, the context is shuffled with words from the language defining in this way new words from the language. We investigate several properties of the class of the languages obtained in this way starting from finite sets of words. These languages can be related with the theory of concurrent processes.

1. Introduction

Marcus grammars contextual grammars were introduced in [5]. The reader is referred to the monograph [6] for basic notions and results in this area. Recently, new studies are dedicated to this subject, see [7], [8] and [9].

Let V be an alphabet, i.e., a finite and nonempty set. V^* is the free monoid generated by V with the identity denoted by λ. The free semigroup generated by V is $V^+ = V^* - \{\lambda\}$. The families of regular, linear, context-free, context-sensitive and reursively enumerable languages are denoted by REG, LIN, CF, CS and RE, respectively.

The *shuffle* operation between words, denoted ⧢, is defined recursively by:

$$(au ⧢ bv) = a(u ⧢ bv) \cup b(au ⧢ v),$$

and

$$(u ⧢ \lambda) = (\lambda ⧢ u) = \{u\},$$

where $u, v \in V^*$ and $a, b \in V$.

The shuffle operation is extended in a natural way to languages. Note that the ordered system

$$\mathcal{S} = (\mathcal{P}(V^*), \cup, \emptyset, ⧢, \{\lambda\})$$

[1]Research supported by the Academy of Finland, Project 11281

is a commutative semiring, see [4].

The reader is referred to [10] for all unexplained notions of formal languages we use in the sequel.

Definition 1. A *simple Marcus contextual grammar* is an ordered system $G = (V, B, C)$, where V is *the alphabet* of G, B is a finite subset of V^*, called *the base* of G and C is a finite subset of pairs of words over V, i.e., $C \subset V^* \times V^*$, C finite, called the set of *contexts* of G.

Definition 2. Let $G = (V, B, C)$ be a simple contextual grammar. The *languge generated* by G, denoted $L(G)$, is the smallest language L over V such that:

(i) $B \subseteq L$.

(ii) if $x \in L$ and $(u, v) \in C$, then $uxv \in L$.

It is easy to observe that:

$$L(G) = B \cup \{u_n \dots u_1 x v_1 \dots v_n \mid n \geq 1, x \in B, (u_i, v_i) \in C, 1 \leq i \leq n\}.$$

The class of all Marcus simple contextual languages is denoted by $\mathcal{M}$.

Remark 3. If L is a simple contextual language, then $L \in LIN$, i.e., $\mathcal{M} \subset LIN$. Note that, if $G = (V, B, C)$ is a simple contextual grammar, then one can define an equivalent Chomsky linear grammar $G' = (\{X\}, V, X, P)$, where X is a new symbol and the set P of productions is defined as follows:

$$P = \{X \to \alpha \mid \alpha \in B\} \cup \{X \to uXv \mid (u, v) \in C\}.$$

Note that $\mathcal{M}$ is a strict subclass of LIN and, moreover, the classes $\mathcal{M}$ and REG are incomparable, see [6].

Comment. A simple contextual grammar generates a language starting from a finite set of strings (the base) and iteratively adjoining to it contexts, i.e., pairs of strings from C, at the ends of the current string. In other classes of contextual grammars, such as the *internal contextual grammars*, [6], the contexts are adjoined in the middle of the current string. The idea of *(simple) shuffled Marcus grammars* is similar except that the contexts are not only added at the ends or in the middle of the current string (like brackets) but the contexts are *shuffled* with the current string. Hence, in this case, a context is not necessarily to be a pair of words, i.e., a context is just a word that is shuffled with the current string.

Definition 4. A *(simple) shuffled contextual grammar* is an ordered system $G = (V, B, C)$, where V is *the alphabet* of G, B is a finite subset of V^*, called *the base* of G and C is a finite set of words over V, i.e., $C \subset V^*$, C finite, called the set of *(shuffled) contexts* of G.

Definition 5. Let $G = (V, B, C)$ be a shuffled contextual grammar. The *language generated* by G, denoted $L(G)$, is the smallest language L over V such that:

(i) $B \subseteq L$,

(ii) if $x \in L$ and $u \in C$, then $x \amalg u \subseteq L$.

The class of all shuffled contextual languages is denoted by $\mathcal{SM}$.

Examples

1. If F is a finite set, then $F \in \mathcal{SM}$. To show this, it is enough to define a shuffled contextual grammar with $B = F$ and $C = \{\lambda\}$.

2. If $B = \emptyset$, then we obtain that $\emptyset \in \mathcal{SM}$.

3. Let $G = (V, B, C)$ be a shuffled contextual grammar with $V = \{a, b\}$, $B = \{\lambda\}$ and $C = \{ab\}$. The language generated is D_1, the well-known language of Dyck over $V = \{a, b\}$.

4. Let $G = (V, B, C)$ be a shuffled contextual grammar with $V = \{a, b\}$, $B = \{\lambda\}$ and $C = \{ab, ba\}$. The language generated is:

$$L(G) = \{w \in \{a, b\}^* \mid N_a(w) = N_b(w)\},$$

where $N_x(w)$ denotes the number of occurrences of the symbol x in the word w.

2. General Properties

This section is devoted to the study of some general properties of shuffled contextual grammars.

Notation. Let V be an alphabet and let L be a language over V. We use the folowing notations:

$$L^{(0)} = \{\lambda\},$$
$$L^{(k+1)} = L^{(k)} \amalg L, \text{ for any } k \geq 0,$$
$$L^{\amalg} = \bigcup_{k \geq 0} L^{(k)}$$

Comment. Note that $(\mathcal{P}(V^*), \amalg, \{\lambda\})$ is a commutative monoid and, if L is a language over V, then $L^{\amalg}$ is the submonoid generated by L in the above monoid.

Theorem 6. *Let $L \subseteq V^*$ be a language. The following assertions are equivalent:*

(i) There exists a shuffled contextual grammar $G = (V, B, C)$, such that:

$$L = L(G).$$

(ii) There exist $E, F \subseteq V^*$, E, F finite sets, such that L is the minimal solution of the equation:

$$X = E \shuffle X \cup F,$$

where the equation is considered over the semiring $\mathcal{S}$.

(iii) There exist J, K finite sets, $J, K \subseteq V^*$, such that:

$$L = J \shuffle K^{\shuffle}.$$

Proof. $(i) \Rightarrow (ii)$ Define $E = C$ and $F = B$.
$(ii) \Rightarrow (iii)$ Define $J = F$ and $K = E$.
$(iii) \Rightarrow (i)$ Define $B = J$ and $C = K$. $\qquad\qquad\square$

Corollary 7. *If $G = (V, B, C)$ is a shuffled contextual grammar with $B = \{\lambda\}$, then $L(G) = L(G) \shuffle L(G)$.*

Proof. It follows from Theorem 6, (iii), that $L(G) = C^{\shuffle}$ and observe that $C^{\shuffle} \shuffle C^{\shuffle} = C^{\shuffle}$. $\qquad\qquad\square$

Definition 8. Let $w \in V^*$ be a word. We denote

$$scattsub(w) = \{u \mid \text{ there exist } v, v \in V^*, \text{ such that } w \in u \shuffle v\}.$$

Lemma 9. *If $L \in \mathcal{SM}$, then there exists $n, n \geq 1$, such that for any $w \in L$, if $\mid w \mid \geq n$, then there exists $u \in scattsub(w)$ such that, for any $v \in L$, $v \shuffle u \subseteq L$.*

Proof. Let $G = (V, B, C)$ be a shuffled contextual grammar such that $L = L(G)$. Define:

$$n = max\{\mid \alpha \mid \mid \alpha \in B\} + 1.$$

If $w \in L$ with $\mid w \mid \geq n$, then there exists $u \in C \cap scattsub(w)$ and $w' \in scattsub(w)$ such that $w \in u \shuffle w'$. Because $u \in C$, for every $v \in L$ it follows that $v \shuffle u \subseteq L$. $\qquad\qquad\square$

Lemma 10. *Let $L \subseteq V^*$ be a language in $\mathcal{SM}$ and*

$$V_0 = \{a \in V \mid \text{ for all } n \geq 1 \text{ there is } x \in L \text{ such that } \mid x \mid_a > n\}.$$

Then $V_0^* \subseteq Sub(L)$.

Proof. Let $G = (V, B, C)$ be a shuffled contextual grammar such that $L = L(G)$. For each $a \in V_0$ there is $u \in C$ with

$$u = u_1 a u_2, u_1, u_2 \in V^*.$$

Then, for $z \in V_0, z = a_1 a_2 \ldots a_r$ take $u_{1,1} a_1 u_{1,2} a_2 \ldots u_{r,1} a_r u_{r,2} \in C$ and an arbitrary $w \in B$. Clearly,

$$w u_{1,1} u_{2,1} \ldots u_{r,1} a_1 a_2 \ldots a_r u_{1,2} u_{2,2} \ldots u_{r,2} \in L(G),$$

hence $z \in Sub(L)$. $\square$

Comment. We recall that an *anti-AFL* is a family of languages that is not closed at any of the following six operations: union, catenation, Kleene star closure, intersection with regular languages, morphic images and morphic inverse images.

The previous Lemma 9 and Lemma 10 can be used for proving all the relations of the type $L \notin \mathcal{SM}$ in the following result.

Theorem 11. *The family $\mathcal{SM}$ is an anti-AFL.*

Proof. $\mathcal{SM}$ is not closed under union: Note that the languages a^*, b^* are in $\mathcal{SM}$ but, $a^* \cup b^*$ is not in $\mathcal{SM}$.

$\mathcal{SM}$ is not closed under catenation: Observe that the languages a^*, b^* are in $\mathcal{SM}$ but, $a^* b^*$ is not in $\mathcal{SM}$.

$\mathcal{SM}$ is not closed under intersection with regular languages: Note that the language $\{a, b\}^*$, is in $\mathcal{SM}$, $a^* b^*$ is regular but, $\{a, b\}^* \cap a^* b^*$ is not in $\mathcal{SM}$.

$\mathcal{SM}$ is not closed under Kleene closure, $(*)$: Observe that the language $\{ab\}$ is in $\mathcal{SM}$ but $\{ab\}^*$ is not in $\mathcal{SM}$.

$\mathcal{SM}$ is not closed under morphic images: Define the morphism h, $h : \{a\}^* \rightarrow \{a, b\}^*$, $h(a) = ab$, and note that the language a^* is in $\mathcal{SM}$, but, $h(a^*) = (ab)^*$ is not in $\mathcal{SM}$.

$\mathcal{SM}$ is not closed under inverse morphic images: Define the morphism h, $h : \{a, b\}^* \rightarrow \{a, b\}^*$, $h(a) = aa, h(b) = b$ and let D_1 be the Dyck language over the alphabet $\{a, b\}$. It is easy to notice that the language $h^{-1}(D_1)$ is not in $\mathcal{SM}$. $\square$

Theorem 12. *The family $\mathcal{SM}$ is a strict subfamily of CS.*

Proof. It is easy to observe that any language L, $L \in \mathcal{SM}$, can be recognized by a Turing machine of complexity $NSPACE(n)$. (see also Theorem 22, for the complexity of the membership problem for languages in $\mathcal{SM}$). The inclusion is strict, because the language $L = a^* b^*$ is in CS but not in $\mathcal{SM}$. $\square$

Theorem 13. *The family $\mathcal{SM}$ is incomparable with any family F such that $REG \subseteq F \subseteq CF$.*

Proof. The language a^*b^* is in REG but not in $\mathcal{SM}$, the language $(abc)^{\amalg}$ is in $\mathcal{SM}$ but not in CF.   □

Definition 14. Let n be an integer, $n \geq 2$. An *n-contextual Marcus grammar* is a triple $G = (V, B, C)$ where V is an alphabet, B is a finite subset of V^* and C is a finite set of $(n-1)$-dimensional contexts, i.e., C is a finite set of vectors of the form $(u_1, u_2, \ldots, u_{n-1})$, $u_i \in V^*, 1 \leq i \leq n-1$. Let x, y be words over V. The relation of derivation, denoted $\Rightarrow_G$, is defined as:

$$x \Rightarrow_G y \text{ if and only if } x = x_1 x_2 \ldots x_n, x_i \in V^*, 1 \leq i \leq n,$$

$$\text{and } y = x_1 u_1 x_2 u_2 \ldots x_{n-1} u_{n-1} x_n, \text{ for some } (u_1, u_2, \ldots, u_{n-1}) \in C.$$

The language generated by G is:

$$L(G) = \{x \in V^* \mid \text{ there exists } y \in B \text{ such that } y \Rightarrow_G^* x\}.$$

Theorem 15. *Let L be a language, $L \in \mathcal{SM}$. There exists an integer n such that, L is an $n-$contextual language.*

Proof. Let $G = (V, B, C)$ be a shuffled contextual grammar and define

$$n = max\{|u| \mid u \in C\}.$$

Let $w \in C$ be a context. Define:

$$K_w = \{(w_1, w_2, \ldots, w_n) \mid w_i \in V^*, 1 \leq i \leq n, w_1 w_2 \ldots w_n = w\}.$$

Note that one or more components of a vector in K_w can be λ. Define the n-contextual grammar $G' = (V, B, C')$, where:

$$C' = \bigcup_{w \in C} K_w.$$

It is easy to prove that $L(G) = L(G')$.   □

Theorem 16. *The converse of Theorem 15 is not true.*

Proof. Take the 2-contextual grammar

$$G = (\{a, b\}, \{\lambda\}, \{(aa, bb), (bb, aa)\}).$$

Assume that $L(G) = L(G')$ for some shuffled contextual grammar $G' = (\{a, b\}, B, C)$ Note that $\lambda \in L(G)$ and thus $\lambda \in B$. Consider the string $a^{2n} b^{2n}, n \geq 1$. All of them are in $L(G)$, hence they must be generated by G', too. The only contexts to be used in producing such strings must be of the form $a^{2i}b^{2i}$ (a context $a^r b^s, r \neq s, or\, r \neq 2i$, shuffled with $\lambda \in B$ leads to a parazitic string).

Take such a context $a^{2i}b^{2i}, i \geq 1$. Similarly, there is $b^{2j}a^{2j} \in C, j \geq 1$, for producing the strings $b^{2m}a^{2m} \in L(G)$. Then, starting from $\lambda \in B$ and using $a^{2i}b^{2i}$ for j times we can obtain $a^{2ij}b^{2ij}$. Continuing the derivation by using in an appropriate way i times the context $b^{2j}a^{2j}$ we can obtain the string $(ab)^{4ij}$. This string is not in $L(G)$, a contradiction. $\qquad\square$

Theorem 17. *Let V be an arbitrary alphabet and let L be an arbitrary language over V. The language L', $L' = L \shuffle V^*$, is in $\mathcal{SM}$.*

Proof. By Higman result, see [2], for any language L there is a finite subset F, $F \subseteq L$, with the property that $L \subseteq F \shuffle V^*$. It follows that:

$$F \subseteq L \subseteq F \shuffle V^*.$$

Note that the shuffle operation is monotone in both arguments and, moreover, $V^* \shuffle V^* = V^*$. From the above inclusions, we deduce that:

$$F \shuffle V^* \subseteq L \shuffle V^* \subseteq F \shuffle V^*.$$

Therefore, $L \shuffle V^* = F \shuffle V^*$ and note that $V^* = V^{\shuffle}$. Hence, we obtain that $L \shuffle V^* = F \shuffle V^{\shuffle}$ with F finite. By Theorem 6, (iii), it follows that $L \shuffle V^* \in \mathcal{SM}$. $\qquad\square$

Example. Let $(p_n)_{n \geq 1}$ be the sequence of all prime numbers, i.e., $p_1 = 2, p_2 = 3, p_3 = 5, \ldots$, and consider the language L,

$$L = \{a^n b^{p_n} \mid n \geq 1\}$$

over the alphabet $V = \{a, b\}$.

It is easy to observe that the language L', $L' = L \shuffle V^*$, is generated by the shuffled contextual grammar $G = (V, B, C)$, where $B = \{ab^2\}$ and $C = \{\lambda, a, b\}$.

Notation. Let V be an alphabet. The family of all $\mathcal{SM}$ languages over V is denoted by $\mathcal{SM}(V)$.

Theorem 18.

(i) *The family $\mathcal{SM}$ is closed under shuffle operation, i.e., if $L_1, L_2 \in \mathcal{SM}$, then $L_1 \shuffle L_2 \in \mathcal{SM}$.*

(ii) *If $L \in \mathcal{SM}$ and if $\lambda \in L$, then $L^{\shuffle} \in \mathcal{SM}$.*

(iii) *$(\mathcal{SM}(V), \shuffle, \{\lambda\})$ is a submonoid of the monoid $(\mathcal{P}(V^*), \shuffle, \{\lambda\})$*

Proof.

(i) Let L_i be in $\mathcal{SM}$, $i = 1, 2$. By Theorem 6 (iii), it follows that $L_i = B_i \shuffle C_i^{\shuffle}$, for some finite languages B_i, C_i, $i = 1, 2$. Note that:

$$L_1 \shuffle L_2 = B_1 \shuffle C_1^{\shuffle} \shuffle B_2 \shuffle C_2^{\shuffle} =$$

$$= B_1 \shuffle B_2 \shuffle C_1^{\shuffle} \shuffle C_2^{\shuffle} = B_1 \shuffle B_2 \shuffle (C_1 \cup C_2)^{\shuffle}.$$

Hence, again by Theorem 6 (iii), it follows that $L_1 \shuffle L_2 \in \mathcal{SM}$.

(ii) Assume that $L = B \shuffle C^{\shuffle}$, for some finite languages B, C. Note that from $\lambda \in L$ it follows that $\lambda \in B$. Hence,

$$L^{\shuffle} = (B \shuffle C^{\shuffle})^{\shuffle} = (B \cup C)^{\shuffle}.$$

Therefore, $L^{\shuffle} \in \mathcal{SM}$.

(iii) Obviously. $\qquad\qquad\square$

Theorem 19.

(i) *The family $\mathcal{SM}$ is not closed under intersection.*

(ii) *The family $\mathcal{SM}$ is not closed under complement.*

Proof.

(i) Consider the languages: $L_1 = \{a^2, b^2\}^{\shuffle}$ and $L_2 = \{ab\}^{\shuffle}$. Observe that the language $L_1 \cap L_2$ contains words of the form: $a^{2n}b^{2n}$, for any n, $n \geq 0$. Using Lemma 9, it follows that $L_1 \cap L_2$ is not in $\mathcal{SM}$.

(ii) Let V be the alphabet $\{a, b\}$ and consider the language $L = (ab)^{\shuffle}$. Again, using Lemma 9, one can show that $V^* - L$ is not in $\mathcal{SM}$. $\qquad\square$

Remark 20. Let V be an alphabet and $u, v \in V^*$. The relation $<$ defined as:

$$u < v \text{ if and only if } u \in scattsub(v),$$

is an order relation on V^*.

Notation. Let L be a language over V. We denote by $\overline{L}$ the language:

$$\overline{L} = \{v \mid \text{ there exists } u \in L \text{ such that } u < v\}.$$

Theorem 21. *Let V be an alphabet and let L be an arbitrary language over V. The language $\overline{L}$ is in $\mathcal{SM}$.*

Proof. Let F be the set of all minimal elements of L. By Haines Theorem, see [1], F is a finite language. Observe that:

$$\overline{L} = F \shuffle V^* = F \shuffle V^{\shuffle}.$$

Hence, by Theorem 6 (iii), it follows that $\overline{L} \in \mathcal{SM}$. $\qquad\square$

Theorem 22. *The membership problem for languages in $\mathcal{SM}$ is an NP-complete problem.*

Proof. By a result of Jantzen, [3], it follows that the problem to decide whether or not $v \in u^{\amalg}$ for arbitrary words u, v over an alphabet V with $card(V) \geq 2$ is NP-complete. Using this result, it is not difficult to prove our theorem. Let $G = (V, B, C)$ be a shuffled contextual grammar and let w be a word over V with $| w | = n$. Select nondeterministicaly a scattered subword of w and verify if this subword is in B. Note that this operation needs a polynomial amount of time. If the answer is yes, then repeat the following step until the remaining word w is λ. Select nondeterministicaly a scattered subword v of the remaining word w, i.e. from the word obtained from w after the previous scattered subword was removed, choose nondeterministicaly a context u, and apply the algorithm of Jantzen, [3], to decide the problem $v \in u^{\amalg}$. Note that this step requires a polynomial time, too. Therefore, the membership problem for languages in $\mathcal{SM}$ is an NP-complete problem. $\quad\square$

3. Conclusions

The contextual grammars with shuffled contexts are a natural extension of the (simple) contextual grammars. There are many problems to be studied concerning this new type of grammars. We point out only two important aspects. One is to consider a similar generative strategy for other sorts of Marcus grammars, see [6].

A second important direction of research is to relate Marcus contextual grammars with shuffled contexts with the theory of concurrency. One can consider that contexts are processes that are concurrently performed with a fixed set of processes, i.e., with the set B of some basic processes. Therefore, the specific problems from the theory of concurrent processes can be studied in this new framework.

4. References

1. L. H. Haines, On free monoids partially ordered by embedding, *Journal of Combinatorial Theory*, 6, (1969), 94 – 98.

2. G. H. Higman, Ordering by divisibility in abstract algebras, *Proc. London Math. Soc.*, 3, (1952), 326 – 336.

3. M. Jantzen, Extending regular expression with iterated shuffle, *Theoretical Computer Science*, 38 (1985), 223 – 247.

4. W. Kuich, A. Salomaa, *Semirings, Automata, Languages*, Springer-Verlag, Berlin, Heidelberg, New York, Tokyo, 1986.

5. S. Marcus, Contextual grammars, *Rev. Roum. Math. Pures et Appl.*, 14, 10 (1969), 1525 – 1534.

6. Gh. Păun, *Contextual Grammars*, Romanian Academy Publ. House, Bucharest, 1982. (in Romanian).

7. Gh. Păun, G. Rozenberg, A. Salomaa, Contextual Grammars: Erasing, determinism, one-sided contexts, *Fundamenta Informaticae*, to appear.

8. Gh. Păun, G. Rozenberg, A. Salomaa, Contextual Grammars: Parallelism, and blocking of derivation, in *Developments in Language Theory* (G. Rozenberg, A. Salomaa, eds.), World Sci. Publ., Singapore, 1994, 370 – 388.

9. Gh. Păun, G. Rozenberg, A. Salomaa, Marcus Contextual Grammars: Modularity and leftmost derivation, in this volume, 375 – 392,

10. A. Salomaa, *Formal Languages*, Academic Press, New York, London, 1973.

Time-Varying Grammars and Referenced Automata

Codruţ MATEI

Faculty of Informatics, "Al. I. Cuza" University of Iaşi
6600 Iaşi, Romania

Abstract. We show that referenced automata and type-3 time-varying grammars have the same power. Then some relationships between families of languages generated by time-varying grammars under primitive recursive or recursive timing function are obtained.

1. Preliminaries

For the classical notions of formal languages and automata theory the reader is referred to [2] and [3]; we present only the basic notations and terminology used in the following sections.

A Chomsky grammar will be denoted by a 4-uple $G = (V_N, V_T, S, P)$ with V_N the nonterminal alphabet, V_T the terminal alphabet, $S \in V_N$ the axiom and P the set of rules. The rules of the grammars of type 3 will be considered right-linear, that is of one of the next forms:

$$A \to aB, A, B \in V_N, a \in V_T,$$
$$A \to a, A \in V_N, a \in V_T,$$

possibly also $S \to \lambda$, providing S does not appear in the right hand side of another rule.

The rules of the grammars of type 1 will be considered monotone (for each rule $u \to v$ we have $|u| \le |v|$).

A *time-varying grammar* ([3]), TVG for short, is a pair (G, φ) where $G = (V_N, V_T, S, P)$ is a Chomsky grammar and φ is a function from $\mathbf{N}^*$ (the positive natural numbers set) into $\mathcal{P}(P)$ (the powerset of P); $\varphi(n)$ represents the rules which are permitted to be applied in the n'th step of a derivation in (G, φ).

The language generated by the grammar (G, φ) is defined by

$$L(G, \varphi) = \{w \in V_T^* \mid (S, 1) \Longrightarrow^* (w, n), n \in \mathbf{N}^*\}.$$

We see that the function φ is arbitrary and not necessarily efectively computable. In [3] it is proved that each arbitrary language can be generated by a TVG of type 3.

Let Σ and Γ be finite sets of symbols. A *reference* tape (*reference function*) over Σ is an infinite sequence $R = \gamma_1\gamma_2\ldots$ where γ_i belongs to Γ (a function $R : \mathbf{N}^* \longrightarrow \Gamma$, respectively).

A *deterministic referenced automaton* ([1]) over Σ and Γ is a 5-uple

$$A = (Q, \delta, q_1, F, R),$$

where

    (1) Q is a finite set of states,
    (2) δ is a function from $Q \times \Sigma \times \Gamma$ into Q (the transition function),
    (3) $q_1 \in Q$ is the initial state,
    (4) $F \subseteq Q$ is the set of final states,
    (5) R is a reference tape over Γ.

A *nondeterministic referenced automaton* over Σ and Γ is defined as a deterministic one considering a set of initial states and taking the transition function as $\delta : Q \times \Sigma \times \Gamma \longrightarrow \mathcal{P}(Q)$.

We define $\delta_0 : Q \times \Sigma^* \longrightarrow Q$ for the deterministic case ($\delta_0 : \mathcal{P}(Q) \times \Sigma^* \longrightarrow \mathcal{P}(Q)$ for the nondeterministic case, respectively) inductively for $q \in Q$ ($Q' \subseteq Q$, respectively) by

$$\delta_0(q, \lambda) = q,$$
$$\delta_0(q, a_1 \ldots a_n a_{n+1}) = \delta(\delta_0(q, a_1 \ldots a_n), a_{n+1}, \gamma_{n+1}) \text{ for } n \geq 0$$

($\delta_0(Q', \lambda) = Q'$ and $\delta_0(Q', a_1 \ldots a_n a_{n+1}) = \delta(\delta_0(Q', a_1 \ldots a_n), a_{n+1}, \gamma_{n+1})$ for $n \geq 0$, respectively).

If A is deterministic, then the language accepted by it, denoted by $S_0(A)$, is defined by

$$S_0(A) = \{w \in \Sigma^* \mid \delta_0(q_1, w) \in F\}$$

and if A is nondeterministic, the language accepted is defined by

$$S_0(A) = \{w \in \Sigma^* \mid \delta_0(Q_1, w) \cap F \neq \emptyset\}.$$

A set $S \subseteq \Sigma^*$ is called *metaregular* if there is a deterministic referenced automaton A such that $S = S_0(A)$.

It is known that the referenced automata, deterministic or nondeterministic, are equivalent and the set $\{a^n b^n \mid n \geq 1\}$ is not a metaregular set ([1]).

2. The generative power

In this section we present an equivalent definition for the TVG. We show that, the grammars of type 3 with a primitive recursive (recursive, respectively) timing function have the same power as the referenced automata with a primitive recursive (recursive, respectively) reference function (we recall that any recursive function is total).

We establish then some relations between the classes of languages generated by the grammars of type 0, 1, 2, 3 and the grammars with primitive recursive and recursive timing function.

For a Chomsky grammar $G = (V_N, V_T, S, P)$ we can define a timing method as follows: we associate to each rule an applicability interval (n_1, n_2) where $n_1 \in \mathbf{N}^*, n_2 \in \overline{\mathbf{N}} = \mathbf{N} \cup \infty$ (where $n < \infty$, for all $n \in \mathbf{N}$) and $n_1 \leq n_2$. The respective rule is permitted to be applied only in the interval of time (n_1, n_2). Such a method does not modify the generative power.

Indeed, let $\gamma = (G, t)$ be such a grammar where $G = (V_N, V_T, S, P)$ and t is the function which associate to each rule r an applicability interval $t(r)$ as above. If for any $r \in P$ we have $t(r) = (n_1, n_2)$ with $n_2 \in \mathbf{N}$, then the language generated by γ is finite, because each derivation will be shorter than

$$\max\{n_r'' \mid r \in P, t(r) = (n_r', n_r'')\}.$$

Otherwise, considering $r_1, \ldots, r_h$ all productions of the grammar G $(h \geq 1)$, we can suppose without loss of the generality, that the first k rules $(0 \leq k \leq h)$ have the applicability interval infinite and the next have the applicability interval finite. Consequently, we have:

$$t(r_i) = (n_i, \infty), \text{ for all } 1 \leq i \leq k,$$
$$t(r_j) = (n_j', n_j''), \text{ for all } k + 1 \leq j \leq h.$$

Let $m = \max\{n_1, \ldots, n_k, n_{k+1}'', \ldots, n_h''\}$, $D_i, 1 \leq i \leq s$, be the set of all derivations of length m in γ, and $w_1, \ldots, w_p, p \leq s$, be all final sentential forms of the derivations $D_1, \ldots, D_s$. Considering now the grammar $G' = (V_N \cup \{S'\}, V_T, S', P')$ (where S' is a new symbol which does not belong to V_N) with $P' = \{S' \rightarrow w_i \mid 1 \leq i \leq p\} \cup \{r_1, \ldots, r_k\}$, we observe that G' is of the same type as G and $L(G') = L(\gamma)$.

The same situation appears if we associate to any rule a finite number of pairwise disjoint applicability intervals.

Definition 2.1. A *time-varying grammar* of type $i, i \in \{0, 1, 2, 3\}$, is a pair $\gamma = (G, \mathcal{P})$ where:

- $G = (V_N, V_T, S, P)$ is a Chomsky grammar of type i,

- $\mathcal{P} = \{P_r \mid r \in P\}$ is a set of predicates (each rule has associated a predicate $P_r : \mathbf{N}^* \longrightarrow \{0, 1\}$).

Intuitively, $P_r(i) = 1$ means that the rule r is permitted to be applied at the step i.

Definition 2.2. Let $\gamma = (G, \mathcal{P})$ be a time-varying grammar.
(1) The relation $\Longrightarrow_\gamma \subseteq (V_G^* \times \mathbf{N}^*)^2$ given by:

$$(\alpha A\beta, k) \Longrightarrow_\gamma (\alpha w\beta, k+1) \text{ if } r = A \to w \in P \text{ and } P_r(k) = 1$$

is called the yielding relation in γ.
(2) The language generated by γ is defined by:

$$L(\gamma) = \{w \in V_T^* \mid (S, 1) \Longrightarrow_\gamma^* (w, n), n \in \mathbf{N}^*\},$$

where by $\Longrightarrow_\gamma^*$ we denote the reflexive and transitive closure of the relation $\Longrightarrow_\gamma$.

The notation $\Longrightarrow_\gamma$ will be simplified to $\Longrightarrow$ whenever γ is understood from the context.

It is natural to impose restrictions to the predicates which are associated to a time-varying grammar. The most natural restriction seems to be that which requires all predicates to be primitive recursive or recursive.

We denote by $\mathcal{L}_{i,pr}$ (respectively $\mathcal{L}_{i,rec}$) the class of languages generated by time-varying grammars of type i with a primitive recursive (respectively recursive) timing function.

The next relations follows directly from the definition :

$$(R_1) \qquad \mathcal{L}_i \subseteq \mathcal{L}_{i,pr} \subseteq \mathcal{L}_{i,rec}, \ i \in \{0, 1, 2, 3\},$$
$$(R_2) \qquad \mathcal{L}_{3,pr} \subseteq \mathcal{L}_{2,pr} \subseteq \mathcal{L}_{1,pr} \subseteq \mathcal{L}_{0,pr},$$
$$(R_3) \qquad \mathcal{L}_{3,rec} \subseteq \mathcal{L}_{2,rec} \subseteq \mathcal{L}_{1,rec} \subseteq \mathcal{L}_{0,rec}.$$

We prove that some of these inclusions are strict and some of them are satisfied by equality. We establish first a result concerning the relationship between time-varying grammars of type 3 and the referenced automata.

Theorem 2.1. *If $L \in \mathcal{L}_{3,pr}$ ($L \in \mathcal{L}_{3,rec}$, respectively) then there is an nondeterministic referenced automaton which recognizes L and whose reference function is primitive recursive (recursive, respectively) and, conversely, if L is the language accepted by a deterministic referenced automaton whose reference function is primitive recursive (recursive, respectively) then $L \in \mathcal{L}_{3,pr}$ ($\mathcal{L}_{3,rec}$, respectively).*

Proof. We treat in detail the primitive recursive case, the other being similar to this one.

Let $L \in \mathcal{L}_{3,pr}$ and $\gamma = (G, \mathcal{P})$ be a time-varying grammar of type 3 which generates L. We consider $G = (V_N, V_T, S, P)$ being right-linear.

We construct the nondeterministic referenced automaton $M = (Q, \delta, \{q_S\}, F, R)$ over Σ and Γ as follows:

$$\Sigma = V_T,$$

$$\Gamma = \{(b_1, \ldots, b_k) \mid b_i \in \{0,1\}, i \in \{1, \ldots, k\}, \text{ where } k = card(P)$$
$$(\text{each rule } r_i \text{ has associated an element } b_i \in \{0,1\})$$

$$Q = \{q_A \mid A \in V_N\} \cup \{q_f\} \quad (f \notin V_N \cup V_T)$$

$$F = \begin{cases} \{q_f\} \cup \{q_S\}, & \text{if } S \to \lambda \in P \text{ and } P_{S \to \lambda}(1) = 1, \\ \{q_f\}, & \text{otherwise.} \end{cases}$$

$$\delta : Q \times \Sigma \times \Gamma \longrightarrow \mathcal{P}(Q) \text{ is given by}$$

$$\delta(q_A, a, (b_1, \ldots, b_k)) = \{q_B \mid r_i : A \to aB \in P \text{ and} b_i = 1\} \cup$$
$$\cup \{q_f \mid r_i : A \to a \in P \text{ and } b_i = 1\},$$

$$\delta \text{ is } \emptyset \text{ in all the others cases.}$$

– the reference function R is given by:

$$R(n) = \begin{pmatrix} P_{r_1}(n) \\ \ldots \\ P_{r_k}(n) \end{pmatrix}, n \in \mathbf{N}^*.$$

Obviously, for a primitive recursive timing the reference function is primitive recursive. We prove that $S_0(M) = L$.

Let w be in $S_0(M)$; then $\delta_0(q_S, w) \cap F \neq \emptyset$.

If $w = \lambda$, then $q_S \in F$ which implies $S \to \lambda \in P$ and $P_{S \to \lambda}(1) = 1$; we have obtained $\lambda \in L(G, \mathcal{P}) = L$.

Let now $w = a_1 \ldots a_n$ and $\delta_0(q_S, w) \cap F = \{q_f\}$; it follows that we have $A_1, \ldots, A_{n-1} \in V_N$ such that:

$$q_{A_1} \in \delta(q_S, a_1, R(1)),$$

$$\cdots \cdots \cdots$$

$$q_{A_{n-1}} \in \delta(q_{A_{n-2}}, a_{n-1}, R(n-1)),$$
$$q_f \in \delta(q_{A_{n-1}}, a_n, R(n)).$$

We have the following derivation in γ:

$$(*) \qquad S \Longrightarrow a_1 A_1 \Longrightarrow \ldots \Longrightarrow a_1 \ldots a_{n-1} A_{n-1} \Longrightarrow a_1 \ldots a_n = w.$$

Hence $w \in L(\gamma) = L$ and thus we have obtained that $S_0(M) \subseteq L$.

Conversely, let w be in $L(\gamma)$. If $w = \lambda$, then $\delta_0(q_S, w) = \{q_S\}$ and $q_S \in F$, else we have a derivation of type $(*)$ in γ. We obtain $\delta_0(q_S, w) \cap F = \{q_f\} \neq \emptyset$, and hence $w \in S_0(M)$. The equality $S_0(M) = L$ is completely proved.

Conversely, let $M = (Q, \delta, q_1, F, R)$ be a deterministic referenced automaton over Σ and Γ. We consider two cases.

Case 1: $\lambda \notin S_0(M)$. We construct $G = (V_N, V_T, S, P)$ where

$$
\begin{aligned}
V_N &= \{A_q \mid q \in Q\}, \\
S &= A_{q_1}, \\
V_T &= \Sigma, \\
P &= \{A_q \to aA_{q'} \mid \text{there is } g \in \Gamma \text{ such that } \delta(q, a, g) = q'\} \cup \\
&\quad \cup \{A_q \to a \mid \text{there are } q' \in F, g \in \gamma \text{ such that } \delta(q, a, g) = q'\},
\end{aligned}
$$

and we take $\mathcal{P}$ containing the predicates

$$
\begin{aligned}
P_{A_q \to aA_{q'}}(n) &= 1 \text{ iff } \delta(q, a, R(n)) = q', \\
P_{A_q \to a}(n) &= 1 \text{ iff } \delta(q, a, R(n)) = q' \text{ for some } q' \text{ in } F.
\end{aligned}
$$

R being primitive recursive, it follows that the predicates from $\mathcal{P}$ will be primitive recursive too. Let w be in $L(G, \mathcal{P})$. We take $w = a_{i_1} \ldots a_{i_n}$ and we have the next derivation in $(G, \mathcal{P})$:

$$
(A_{q_1}, 1) \Longrightarrow (a_{i_1} A_{q_{i_1}}, 2) \Longrightarrow \ldots \Longrightarrow (a_{i_1} \ldots a_{i_{n-1}} A_{q_{i_{n-1}}}, n) \Longrightarrow (w, n+1).
$$

From the definition of $(G, \mathcal{P})$, it follows that $\delta_0(q_1, w) \in F$, so the considered derivation simulates a computation in the automaton. Hence $w \in S_0(M)$.

The converse inclusion is similar.

Case 2: $\lambda \in S_0(M)$, that is $q_1 \in F$. We equivalently modify the automaton M as follows. We add a new element to Q, $\bar{q}_1 \notin Q$. For all occurrences of q_1 as argument of δ we construct the rule obtained by replacing q_1 with $\bar{q}_1$. We modify all transition rules with q_1 in the right hand side by replacing q_1 with $\bar{q}_1$. We obtain a deterministic referenced automaton which is equivalent with M, and the proof follows as in the first case.

This modification is necessary because in the definition of the type-3 grammars we require that if $S \to \lambda \in P$ then S does not appear in the right hand side of another production. $\qquad\square$

Theorem 1 allows us to transfer certain results from referenced automata to time-varying grammars.

Lemma 2.1. $\{a^{n^2} \mid n \geq 1\} \in \mathcal{L}_{3,pr}$.

Proof. This language is generated by the time-varying grammar of type 3 with primitive recursive timing $\gamma = (G, \mathcal{P})$, where

$$
\begin{aligned}
G &= (\{A\}, \{a\}, A, \{A \to aA, A \to a\}), \\
\mathcal{P} &= \{P_{A \to aA}, P_{A \to a}\} \text{ with}
\end{aligned}
$$

$$P_{A \to aA}(n) = 1 \text{ for all } n \in \mathbf{N}^*,$$

$$P_{A \to a}(n) = \begin{cases} 1, & \text{if there is } k \in \mathbf{N}^* \text{ such that } n = k^2, \\ 0, & \text{otherwise} \end{cases} .$$

$\square$

Corollary 2.1. *We have the strict inclusions $\mathcal{L}_3 \subset \mathcal{L}_{3,pr}$ and $\mathcal{L}_2 \subset \mathcal{L}_{2,pr}$.*

Proof. It follows from Lemma 2.1. and from the fact that $\{a^{n^2} \mid n \geq 1\} \notin \mathcal{L}_2$. $\square$

Corollary 2.2. *The family $\mathcal{L}_2$ is incomparable both with the family $\mathcal{L}_{3,pr}$ and with the family $\mathcal{L}_{3,rec}$.*

Proof. It is known that $L = \{a^{n^2} \mid n \geq 1\} \notin \mathcal{L}_2$ and from Lemma 2.1 we obtain that $L \in \mathcal{L}_{3,pr}$. From Theorem 2.1 it follows that $\mathcal{L}_{3,pr}$ is included in the family of metaregular sets and consequently $L' = \{a^n b^n \mid n \geq 1\} \notin \mathcal{L}_{3,pr}$ ([1]). Since $L' \in \mathcal{L}_2$, it follows that $\mathcal{L}_2$ and $\mathcal{L}_{3,pr}$ are incomparable. Similarly for $\mathcal{L}_2$ and $\mathcal{L}_{3,rec}$. $\square$

Corollary 2.3. *We have the strict inclusions $\mathcal{L}_{3,pr} \subset \mathcal{L}_{2,pr}$ and $\mathcal{L}_{3,rec} \subset \mathcal{L}_{2,rec}$.*

Proof. It follows from the definitions and Corollary 2.2. $\square$

Proposition 2.1. $\mathcal{L}_0 = \mathcal{L}_{0,pr} = \mathcal{L}_{0,rec}$.

Proof. We show that $\mathcal{L}_{0,rec} \subseteq \mathcal{L}_0$. For this it is sufficient to prove that membership problem for $\mathcal{L}_{0,rec}$ is semi-decidable. Let $\gamma = (G, \varphi)$ be a type-0 time-varying grammar with a recursive timing. Consider w an arbitrary word over the grammar vocabulary. The algoritm will generate in lexicographicaly order the derivations from G and for each derivation which halts with w will test whether or not this derivation satisfies the conditions required by the function φ, as long as it does not find a such derivation. Since φ is recursive, the algoritm will halt with the answer "$w \in L(\gamma)$" if $w \in L(\gamma)$ and it never halts otherwise. $\square$

Proposition 2.2. $\mathcal{L}_{1,rec} \subseteq \mathcal{L}_{rec}$.

Proof. We give an algoritm which solves the membership problem for $\mathcal{L}_{1,rec}$. Let $\gamma = (G, \varphi)$ be a type-1 time-varying grammar with recursive timing and let w be an arbitrary word over the grammar vocabulary. The algoritm will list all derivations of w in G (G being monotone, there is a finite number of such derivations) and for each derivation the algorithm will effectively test whether or not it satisfies the condition required by the function φ as long as it does not find such a derivation. $\square$

3. Final remarks

The results from Section 2 can be summarized as in the diagram from figure 3.1. In this diagram, a double arrow represents a strict inclusion, a simple arrow indicates an inclusion which we do not know whether or not it is strict, and a line shows an incomparability.

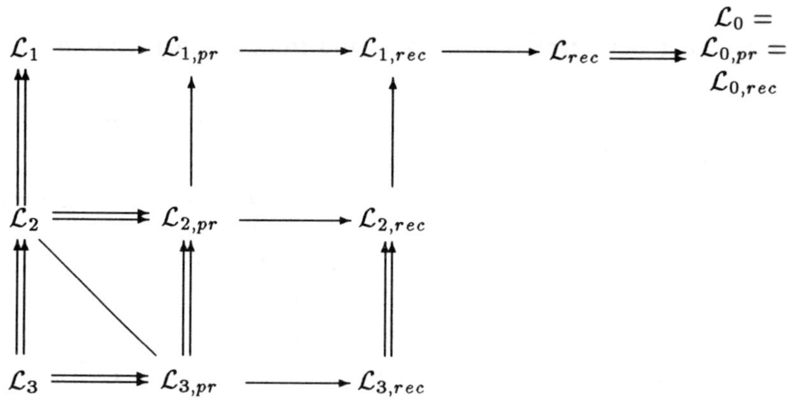

Fig. 3.1.

As it is seen, many problems on the generative power of these grammars (concerning the inclusions which were not established to be strict or not) remain open. Concerning the inclusions $\mathcal{L}_{3,pr} \subseteq \mathcal{L}_{3,rec}$ we believe that the following holds true:

Conjecture. *Let $f : \mathbf{N} \longrightarrow \mathbf{N}$ be a function which is recursive but not primitive recursive. Then $L = \{a^{f(n)} \mid n \geq 0\} \notin \mathcal{L}_{3,pr}$.*

References

1. R. M. Baer, E. H. Spanier, Referenced automata and metaregular families, *Journal of Computer and System Sciences*, 3, 4 (1969), 423 – 446.

2. J. Dassow, Gh. Păun, *Regulated Rewriting in Formal Language Theory*, Springer-Verlag, Berlin, Heidelberg, 1989.

3. A. Salomaa, *Formal Languages*, Academic Press, New York, London, 1973.

Matrix Grammars versus
Parallel Communicating Grammar Systems

Valeria MIHALACHE

Faculty of Mathematics, University of Bucharest

Str. Academiei 14, 70109 Bucureşti, Romania

Abstract. The paper compares the generative power of matrix grammars and that of some parallel communicating grammar systems. It is proved that each matrix language (generated without appearance checking) can be generated by a (non-centralized and returning) parallel communicating grammar system. Then one introduces the notion of leftmost derivation for parallel communicating grammar systems and the notion of appearance checking for rules and symbols synchronization parallel communicating grammar systems. Simulation of simple matrix grammars and of matrix grammars with appearance checking by these new classes of parallel communicating grammar systems is obtained.

1. Introduction

The study of grammar systems has been imposed by the necessity of having a formal model for the current trends in artificial intelligence, in cognitive psychology and in other related fields, where we have more and more to deal with complex tasks distributed among a set of "processors", which are working in a well defined way. Most of the results known about grammar systems can be found in [2].

There are two main classes of grammar systems, namely systems whose components work sequentially, in turn, in every moment one being active [1], and systems whose components work simultaneously, in a synchronized manner [7]. The later ones, called *parallel communicating grammar systems* (PC grammar systems, for short), are grammar systems in which each component has its own sentential form. A synchronization of components is assumed, namely by means of an universally clock and by constraining all the components to do an elementary rewriting in each time unit. The cooperation between the components is accomplished by communication, which is done by request.

The subject of the present paper are the PC grammar systems whose components are context-free grammars. More exactly, we compare the generative power of such grammar systems and that of matrix grammars.

It is known that the family of languages generated by PC grammar systems with context-free rules is intermediate between the family of context-free languages and that of context-sensitive languages. This is true also for the family of languages generated by (λ-free) matrix grammars. So an attempt to compare context-free PC grammar systems with matrix grammars is natural.

We find that the PC grammar systems are at least as powerful as the matrix grammars (without knowing whether they are strictly more powerful). Besides its own interest, this relation entails the fact that the PC grammar systems are at least as powerful as the cooperating distributed grammar systems of [1] (see also [2]) working in the $= k, \geq k$ modes (these systems generate matrix languages).

2. Preliminary definitions

We refer to [8] for general notions of formal language theory and to [2] for grammar systems. We specify here only a few notations.

For an alphabet V, V^* denotes the free monoid generated by V; the empty string is denoted by λ, $|x|$ is the length of x and $|x|_U$ is the number of occurrences of symbols of U in a string x. The classes of regular, linear, context-free, context-sensitive and arbitrary Chomsky grammars are denoted by REG, LIN, CF, CS, RE, respectively; the corresponding families of languages are denoted by $\mathcal{L}(X)$, $X \in \{REG, LIN, CF, CS, RE\}$.

For a set P of context-free rules we denote $dom(P) = \{A \mid A \rightarrow x \in P\}$.

Definition 1. Let $n \geq 1$ be a natural number. A *parallel communicating grammar system* of degree n is an $n + 3$-tuple

$$\Gamma = (N, K, T, G_1, \ldots, G_n),$$

where N is a nonterminal alphabet, T is a terminal alphabet, $K = \{Q_1, Q_2, \ldots, Q_n\}$ (these sets are mutually disjoint) and

$$G_i = (N \cup K, T, P_i, S_i), 1 \leq i \leq n,$$

are usual Chomsky grammars. Denote $V_\Gamma = N \cup K \cup T$.

The grammars $G_i, 1 \leq i \leq n$, are called the *components* of the system, and the elements of K are called *query symbols*; their indices, $1, \ldots, n$, point to the components $G_1, \ldots, G_n$, respectively.

The convention we consider throughout this paper is to denote the start symbol and the production set of a component of a system with the same indices as the grammar component is denoted. This convention holds for query symbols, too, so we do not need to specify in detail the set of query symbols for a given system.

Definition 2. Given a PC grammar system $\Gamma = (N, K, T, G_1, \ldots, G_n)$ as above, for two n-tuples $(x_1, x_2, \ldots, x_n), (y_1, y_2, \ldots, y_n), x_i, y_i \in V_\Gamma^*, 1 \leq i \leq n$, we write $(x_1, \ldots, x_n) \Longrightarrow (y_1, \ldots, y_n)$ if one of the next two cases holds:

(i) $|x_i|_K = 0, 1 \leq i \leq n$, and for each $i, 1 \leq i \leq n$, we have $x_i \Longrightarrow y_i$ in the grammar G_i, or $x_i = y_i \in T^*$;

(ii) there is $i, 1 \leq i \leq n$, such that $|x_i|_K > 0$; then for each such i, we write $x_i = z_1 Q_{i_1} z_2 Q_{i_2} \ldots z_t Q_{i_t} z_{t+1}, t \geq 1$, for $z_j \in V_\Gamma^*, |z_j|_K = 0, 1 \leq j \leq t + 1$; if $|x_{i_j}|_K = 0, 1 \leq j \leq t$, then $y_i = z_1 x_{i_1} z_2 x_{i_2} \ldots z_t x_{i_t} z_{t+1}$ [and $y_{i_j} = S_{i_j}, 1 \leq j \leq t$]; when, for some $j, 1 \leq j \leq t, |x_{i_j}|_K \neq 0$, then $y_i = x_i$; for all $i, 1 \leq i \leq n$, for which y_i is not specified above, we have $y_i = x_i$.

Point (i) defines *rewriting steps*, point (ii) defines *communication steps*. In a communication operation, when the communicated string x_j replaces the query symbol Q_j, we say that Q_j is satisfied. The communication has priority over the effective rewriting. If some query symbols are not satisfied at a given communication step, then they will have to be satisfied at a next one. No rewriting is possible when at least a query symbol is present.

The work of a PC grammar system is blocked in two cases: (1) when a component x_i of the current n-tuple $(x_1, \ldots, x_n)$ (sometimes we shall call it *configuration*) is not terminal with respect to G_i, but no rule of G_i can be applied to x_i, and (2) when a *circular query* appears, that is G_{i_1} introduces Q_{i_2}, G_{i_2} introduces Q_{i_3}, and so on until some $G_{i_{k-1}}$ which introduces Q_{i_k} and G_{i_k} introduces Q_{i_1} (because only strings without query symbols can be communicated, no communication can be done).

Definition 3. The *language generated by a PC grammar system* Γ as above is

$$L(\Gamma) = \{x \in T^* \mid (S_1, S_2, \ldots, S_n) \stackrel{*}{\Longrightarrow} (x, \alpha_2, \ldots, \alpha_n), \alpha_i \in V_\Gamma^*, 2 \leq i \leq n\}.$$

Definition 4. If in Definition 1 only the grammar G_1 is allowed to introduce query symbols, then we say that Γ is a *centralized* PC grammar system; in contrast, the unrestricted case is called *non-centralized*.

A PC grammar system is said to be *returning* (to axiom) if, after communicating, each component returns to axiom. A PC grammar system is *non-returning* if in point (ii) of Definition 2, the words written in brackets,

$$[\text{and } y_{i_j} = S_{i_j}, 1 \leq j \leq t],$$

are erased. A PC grammar system is said to be regular, linear, context-free, λ-free, etc., when the rules of its components are of these types.

For $n \geq 1$ and $X \in \{REG, LIN, CF\}$, we shall denote by

$$NCPC_n X, \ NPC_n X, \ CPC_n X, \ PC_n X,$$

the class of λ-free non-returning centralized, non-returning non-centralized, returning centralized, and returning non-centralized, respectively, grammar systems of degree at most n, with components of type X. The corresponding families of languages are denoted by $\mathcal{L}(Y_n X)$, $Y \in \{PC, CPC, NPC, NCPC\}$, $X \in \{REG, LIN, CF\}$. When an arbitrary number of components is considered, we shall use $*$ instead of n. When λ-rules are allowed, we replace X by X^λ.

A *matrix grammar* is a construct $G = (N, T, S, M, F)$, where N is a nonterminal alphabet, T is a terminal alphabet, S is the axiom, M is a finite set of sequences (called *matrices*) $(A_1 \to x_1, \ldots, A_n \to x_n)$ of context-free rules over $N \cup T$ and F is a set of occurrences of rules in the matrices of M. In a derivation step, all the rules of a matrix must be used, in order, possibily excepting the rules whose occurrences appear in F, which can be skiped if they cannot be effectively used. The reader can find details about matrix grammars in [3]. The family of languages generated by matrix grammar with λ-free context-free rules is denoted by $\mathcal{L}(MAT_{ac})$. When λ-rules are allowed, we write $\mathcal{L}(MAT_{ac}^\lambda)$. When the set F is empty (hence all rules must be effectively applied – we say that the grammar is *without appearance checking*) the corresponding families are denoted by $\mathcal{L}(MAT), \mathcal{L}(MAT^\lambda)$, respectively.

The following relations are known

$$\mathcal{L}(CF) \subset \mathcal{L}(MAT) \subset \mathcal{L}(MAT_{ac}) \subset \mathcal{L}(CS) \subset \mathcal{L}(MAT_{ac}^\lambda) = \mathcal{L}(RE),$$

without knowing the relation between $\mathcal{L}(CS)$ and $\mathcal{L}(MAT^\lambda)$.

3. The power of PC grammar systems

Proofs for the following relations can be found in [2].

$$\mathcal{L}(CF) \subset \mathcal{L}(CPC_* CF) \subseteq \mathcal{L}(PC_* CF) \subseteq \mathcal{L}(CS);$$
$$\mathcal{L}(CF) \subset \mathcal{L}(NCPC_* CF) \subseteq \mathcal{L}(NPC_* CF) \subseteq \mathcal{L}(CS).$$

Moreover, in [5] it is proved that $\mathcal{L}(NCPC_* CF) \subseteq \mathcal{L}(PC_* CF)$.

So it is appropriate to compare the generative capacity of context-free grammar systems with the power of matrix grammars. Somewhat surprising, we find

Theorem 1. $\mathcal{L}(MAT) \subseteq \mathcal{L}(PC_* CF), \mathcal{L}(MAT^\lambda) \subseteq \mathcal{L}(PC_* CF^\lambda)$.

Proof. Let $G = (N, T, S, M)$ be a matrix grammar with context-free rules (and without appearance checking). Assume first that G is λ-free.

It is known [3] that for each (λ-free) matrix grammar there is an equivalent matrix grammar, of the same type, in the 2-normal form, that is with

$$N = \{S\} \cup N_1 \cup N_2, \quad N_1 \bigcap N_2 = \emptyset, \quad S \notin N_1 \cup N_2,$$

and each matrix of M has one of the following forms:

(i) $(S \to AX), \quad A \in N_1, \; X \in N_2,$

(ii) $(A \to \alpha, X \to Y), \quad A \in N_1, \; \alpha \in (N_1 \cup T)^+, \; X, Y \in N_2,$

(iii) $(A \to \alpha, X \to a), \quad A \in N_1, \; \alpha \in (N_1 \cup T)^+, \; X \in N_2, a \in T,$

(iv) $(S \to x), \quad x \in T^*.$

Let $P_1(M)$ be the set of matrices of type (i), let $P_2(M)$ be the set of matrices of types (ii), (iii) and let r be the cardinality of $P_2(M)$. A matrix of $P_2(M)$ will be written in the following as

$$m_k : (A_k \to \alpha_k, B_k \to C_k), \; 1 \le k \le r.$$

We construct the PC grammar system

$$\Gamma = (N', K, T, G_s, G_{1,1}, G_{2,1}, G_{1,2}, G_{2,2}, \ldots, G_{1,r}, G_{2,r}, G_{a1}, G_{a2})$$

as follows:

$$N' = N \cup \{S', W, V, Z, L_1, L_2, L_3\} \cup \{S_s, S_{a1}, S_{a2}\} \cup \{S_{1k}, S_{2k} \mid k = 1, \ldots, n\}$$

($S', W, V, Z, L_1, L_2, L_3$ are new symbols) and the components contain the following sets of productions:

$$
\begin{aligned}
P_s \;=\; & \{S_s \to x \mid (S \to x) \in M, x \in T^*\} \cup \\
& \cup \{S_s \to S', S' \to Q_{2k} \mid k = 1, \ldots, r\} \cup \\
& \cup \{S_s \to AB \mid (S \to AB) \in P_1(M)\} \cup \\
& \cup \{X \to X \mid X \in N_2\}, \\
P_{1k} \;=\; & \{S_{1k} \to W, W \to Q_s\} \cup \\
& \cup \{A_k \to \alpha_k \mid m_k : (A_k \to \alpha_k, B_k \to C_k)\} \cup \\
& \cup \{X \to Z \mid X \in N_1 \cup N_2\} \cup \\
& \cup \{V \to Q_{1k}\}, \quad \text{for each } k = 1, 2, \ldots, r, \\
P_{2k} \;=\; & \{S_{2k} \to V, V \to Q_{1k}\} \cup \\
& \cup \{B_k \to C_k \mid m_k : (A_k \to \alpha_k, B_k \to C_k)\} \cup \\
& \cup \{X \to Z \mid X \in N_1 \cup N_2\}, \text{ for each } k = 1, \ldots, r, \\
P_{a1} \;=\; & \{S_{a1} \to Q_{21}Q_{22} \ldots Q_{2r}\} \cup \{V \to V\}, \\
P_{a2} \;=\; & \{S_{a2} \to L_1, \; L_1 \to L_2, \; L_2 \to L_3, \; L_3 \to L_1 Q_{21} Q_{22} \ldots Q_{2r}\}.
\end{aligned}
$$

We shall prove that $L(G) = L(\Gamma)$. Let us observe that a derivation in G, different of one-step derivations $S \Longrightarrow x$, $x \in T^*$, and using a matrix of type (iv) in M, consists of two main stages: an initial step, when a matrix of $P_1(M)$ is used, and a stage when matrices of $P_2(M)$ are used.

The grammar system defined above works as follows:

It first simulates the initial step, by applying in G_s a production $S_s \to AB$. In that time, grammar G_{a1} asks for communication from each G_{2k}, $k = 1, \ldots, r$, to hinder them to query G_{1k} at this stage, and to lead to that kind of configuration that has to be found any time when the grammar system has to start simulating the application of a matrix in G. This is the only moment when the auxiliary grammar G_{a1} actually does something useful, afterwards it will only apply the rule $V \to V$.

The application of a matrix m_k : $(A_k \to \alpha_k, B_k \to C_k)$ is simulated as follows:

Each grammar G_{1k}, receives the current sentential form, let it be β, from G_s, and changes it into a β'_k, by applying the corresponding rule $A_k \to \alpha_k$ of m_k, or a rule $X \to Z$. Then each G_{2k} asks for the corresponding β'_k from G_{1k}, and derives it either with $B_k \to C_k$, or with a rule $X \to Z$, if it is possible. Thus β''_k is obtained.

Then G_s asks for the sentential form from a G_{2k}, and one of the following cases occur:

- either β''_k is obtained from β_k using the matrix m_k, that is G_{1k} has applied $A_k \to \alpha_k$, and G_{2k} has applied $B_k \to C_k$; then, if β''_k is a terminal string, the derivation can stop here;

- or one of G_{1k}, G_{2k} has used a rule $X \to Z$, which means that β''_k contains a symbol Z; the derivation has to continue in that case, but we will not get a terminal word from this β''_k, because Z will never be rewritten.

If the derivation will continue after that step, then again each G_{1k} asks for communication from G_s, and so on.

If a G_{2k} cannot use the rule $B_k \to C_k$, nor a rule $X \to Z$ on β'_k, then the derivation will be blocked, and that is what we really want, because it means that G_s has asked for communication from a grammar G_{2j} in which a rule $B_j \to a$, $a \in T$, has been used for a β'_k that still contains symbols of N_1.

Let us observe that each couple (G_{1k}, G_{2k}), $k = 1, \ldots, r$, tries at the same time to apply the corresponding matrix m_k to the sentential form which was last sent by G_s. But after that, G_s asks a single G_{2j} for communication, and that is what we really need, because, at a step of derivation in G, a single matrix m_j is used. This gives rise to another problem, which is that all grammars G_{2k}, $k = 1, \ldots, r$, have to be "restarted" when G_s receives the sentential form from one of them, in order to prepare them to get another sentential form to derive on. That is why the auxiliary grammar G_{a2} was introduced for, with its production $L_3 \rightarrow L_1 Q_{21} Q_{22} \ldots Q_{2r}$.

With these remarks, let us observe that in representing derivations in the system, it is enough to show out only 3 couples (G_{1k}, G_{2k}) of grammars:

- (G_{1k_1}, G_{2k_1}), which will use in the derivation both rules of $m_{k_1} : (A_{k_1} \rightarrow \alpha_{k_1}, B_{k_1} \rightarrow C_{k_1})$;

- (G_{1k_2}, G_{2k_2}), for the case when a rule $X \rightarrow Z$ is used in G_{1k_2};

- (G_{1k_3}, G_{2k_3}), for the case when a rule $X \rightarrow Z$ is used in G_{2k_3}.

The starting configuration is:

$$(S_s, \ldots, S_{1k_1}, S_{2k_1}, \ldots, S_{1k_2}, S_{2k_2}, \ldots, S_{1k_3}, S_{2k_3}, \ldots, S_{a1}, S_{a2}) \quad (*)$$

If one tries to use production $S_s \rightarrow S'$ in G_s at this stage, what follows is:

$$
\begin{aligned}
(*) \quad &\Longrightarrow (S', \ldots, W, V, \ldots, W, V, \ldots, W, V, \ldots, Q_{21} Q_{22} \ldots Q_{2r}, L_1) \\
&\Longrightarrow (S', \ldots, W, S_{2k_1}, \ldots, W, S_{2k_2}, \ldots, W, S_{2k_3}, \ldots, VV \ldots V, L_2) \\
&\Longrightarrow (Q_{2k}, \ldots, Q_s, V, \ldots, Q_s, V, \ldots, Q_s, V, \ldots, VV \ldots V, L_2) \\
&\Longrightarrow (V, \ldots, Q_s, V, \ldots, Q_s, V, \ldots, Q_s, V, \ldots, Q_s, S_{2k}, \ldots, VV \ldots V, L_2),
\end{aligned}
$$

where the last Q_s is for the sentential form of G_{1k}, and S_{2k} is for G_{2k} (the couple (G_{1k}, G_{2k}) is that from which G_s has asked for communication). The next configuration we obtain is:

$$
\begin{aligned}
(S_s, \ldots, V, V, \ldots, V, V, \ldots, V, V, \ldots, V, S_{2k}, \ldots, VV \ldots V, L_2) &\Longrightarrow \\
\Longrightarrow (\alpha, \ldots, Q_{1k_1}, Q_{1k_1}, \ldots, Q_{1k_2}, Q_{1k_2}, \ldots, Q_{1k_3}, Q_{1k_3}, \ldots, Q_{1k}, & \\
V, \ldots, VV \ldots V, L_3) &
\end{aligned}
$$

and the derivation is blocked by the circular queries in $G_{1i}, i = 1, \ldots, r$.

Hence a terminal derivation in Γ has to start using a rule $S_s \rightarrow AB$, which means:

$$
\begin{aligned}
(*) \quad &\Longrightarrow (AB, \ldots, W, V, \ldots, W, V, \ldots, W, V, \ldots, Q_{21} Q_{22} \ldots Q_{2r}, L_1) \\
&\Longrightarrow (AB, \ldots, W, S_{2k_1}, \ldots W, S_{2k_2}, \ldots W, S_{2k_3}, \ldots, VV \ldots V, L_1).
\end{aligned}
$$

Let us denote $\theta_1 = VV \ldots V$. Starting from a configuration

$$(\alpha, \ldots, W, S_{2k_1}, \ldots, W, S_{2k_2}, \ldots, W, S_{2k_3}, \ldots, \theta_1, L_1 \theta_2) \quad (1),$$

with $\alpha \neq S'$, then if α is a terminal word, the derivation stops here; if α contains no symbol of N_2, then the derivation is blocked; otherwise, let us assume that there is a $k, 1 \leq k \leq r$, such that α contains both A_k, and B_k, and let k_1 be that k in our representation, that is $\alpha = \beta A_{k_1} \gamma B_{k_1}$. (If there is no such k, then we have only the situations represented by the couples (G_{1k_2}, G_{2k_2}) and (G_{1k_3}, G_{2k_3}), hence for the proof of this case, all we have to do is to disregard the sentential forms of G_{1k_1} and G_{2k_1} in the following configurations.) Then

$$(1) \quad \Longrightarrow (\alpha, \ldots, Q_s, V, \ldots, Q_s, V, \ldots, Q_s, V, \ldots, \theta_1, L_2\theta_2)$$
$$\Longrightarrow (S_s, \ldots, \beta A_{k_1} \gamma B_{k_1}, V, \ldots, \alpha, V, \ldots, \alpha, V, \ldots, \theta_1, L_2\theta_2) \quad (2)$$

Now we have two possibilities:

(i) to apply in G_s the rule $S_s \to S'$. Then

$$(2) \quad \Longrightarrow (S', \ldots, \beta \alpha_{k_1} \gamma B_{k_1}, Q_{1k_1}, \ldots, \beta' Z \gamma',$$
$$Q_{1k_2}, \ldots, \alpha', Q_{1k_3}, \ldots, \theta_1, L_3\theta_2) \quad (3),$$

where α has derived in $\beta' Z \gamma'$ by using a rule $X \to Z$, and in α' by using either $A_{k_3} \to \alpha_{k_3}$, or a rule $X \to Z$ of G_{1k_3}. Then

$$(3) \quad \Longrightarrow (S', \ldots, S_{1k_1}, \beta \alpha_{k_1} \gamma B_{k_1}, \ldots, S_{1k_2}, \beta' Z \gamma', \ldots, S_{1k_3}, \alpha', \ldots, \theta_1, L_3\theta_2)$$
$$\Longrightarrow (Q_{2i}, \ldots, W, \beta \alpha_{k_1} \gamma C_{k_1}, \ldots, W, \beta'' Z \gamma'', \ldots, W, \delta Z \delta', \ldots, \theta_1,$$
$$L_1 Q_{21} Q_{22} \ldots Q_{2r} \theta_2) \Longrightarrow$$
$$\Longrightarrow (w, \ldots, W, S_{2k_1}, \ldots, W, S_{2k_2}, \ldots W, S_{2k_3}, \ldots, \theta_1, L_1\theta_3)$$

which is a configuration similar to (1).

If the couple of grammars (G_{1i}, G_{2i}) from which last component G_s has queried last time has used both productions of m_i in the derivation (hence just as (G_{1k_1}, G_{2k_1}) has done, then w is α derived by matrix m_i; otherwise, which is the case that (G_{1k_2}, G_{2k_2}) and (G_{1k_3}, G_{2k_3}) has dealt with, w contains a symbol Z, and hence it will not lead to a terminal string.

(ii) to apply a rule $S_s \to AB$. Then

$$(2) \quad \Longrightarrow (AB, \ldots, \beta \alpha_{k_1} \gamma B_{k_1}, Q_{1k_1}, \ldots, \beta' Z \gamma', Q_{1k_2}, \ldots, \alpha', Q_{1k_3}, \ldots, \theta_1, L_3\theta_2)$$
$$\Longrightarrow (AB, \ldots, S_{1k_1}, \beta \alpha_{k_1} \gamma B_{k_1}, \ldots, S_{1k_2}, \beta' Z \gamma', \ldots, S_{1k_3}, \alpha', \ldots, \theta_1, L_3\theta_2)$$
$$\Longrightarrow (AB, \ldots, W, \beta \alpha_{k_1} \gamma C_{k_1}, \ldots, W, \beta'' Z \gamma'', \ldots, W, \delta Z \delta', \ldots, \theta_1,$$
$$L_1 Q_{21} Q_{22} \ldots Q_{2r} \theta_2) \Longrightarrow$$
$$\Longrightarrow (AB, \ldots, W, S_{2k_1}, \ldots, W, S_{2k_2}, \ldots, W, S_{2k_3}, \ldots, \theta_1, L_1\theta_2'),$$

which is the same (θ_2' does not matter) with the configuration we obtain when at the initial step we use production $S_s \to AB$.

Remark that if in configuration (1) the string α contains no $X \in N_2$, then the derivation will be blocked, because this situation is a consequence of the case when G_s has asked for communication from a grammar G_{2k} where a production $X \rightarrow a, a \in T$, had been used, but the string resulted is not a terminal one.

Hence $L(G) = L(\Gamma)$ and $\mathcal{L}(MAT) \subseteq \mathcal{L}(PC_*CF)$.

If G contains λ-rules, then the matrices of type (iii) in the normal form used at the beginning of the proof will be of the form $(A \rightarrow \alpha, X \rightarrow \lambda)$, $A \in N_1$, $\alpha \in (N_1 \cup T)^*$, $X \in N_2$. The rest of the proof remains the same, hence we also have $\mathcal{L}(MAT^\lambda) \subseteq \mathcal{L}(PC_*CF^\lambda)$. $\square$

Remark 1. If the conjecture in [3] that $L = \{xcx \mid x \in D_1\} \in \mathcal{L}(CS) - \mathcal{L}(MAT)$ is true, where D_1 is the Dyck language, then $\mathcal{L}(MAT) \subset \mathcal{L}(CPC_2 CF)$, strict inclusion.

Indeed, let us consider the system

$$\begin{aligned}
\Gamma &= (\{S_1, S_2\}, K, \{a, b\}, G_1, G_2), \\
P_1 &= \{S_1 \rightarrow S_1, S_1 \rightarrow Q_2 c Q_2, S_1 \rightarrow c\}, \\
P_2 &= \{S_2 \rightarrow S_2 S_2, S_2 \rightarrow a S_2 b, S_2 \rightarrow ab\}.
\end{aligned}$$

It is easy to see that $L(\Gamma) = \{xcx \mid x \in D_1\}$.

Definition 5. [5] Let $\Gamma = (N, K, T, G_1, G_2, \ldots, G_n)$ be a PC grammar system. We say that Γ is *with multiple queries* if there is a grammar of Γ with a production $A \rightarrow \alpha Q_i \beta Q_i \gamma$, $\quad \alpha, \beta, \gamma \in (N \cup K \cup T)^*, i \in \{1, \ldots, n\}$. Otherwise, we say that Γ is *without multiple queries*.

Definition 6. Let $\Gamma = (N, K, T, G_1, G_2, \ldots, G_n)$ be a PC grammar system and let us consider a derivation in that system. For $i \in \{1, \ldots, n\}$, we call *distance between queries from G_i* in that derivation the maximum of the numbers of steps performed in the derivation between:

- the starting point of the derivation and the first query from G_i;

- two consecutive queries from G_i;

- the last query from G_i and the ending point of the derivation.

Theorem 2. *Let $\Gamma = (N, K, T, G_1, \ldots, G_n), n \leq 1$, be a centralized PC grammar system with context-free components, without multiple queries and without λ- productions, for which there exists $k \geq 1$ such that for each $w \in L(\Gamma)$ there is a derivation of w in which the distance between queries from any $G_i, i = 2, \ldots, n$, is smaller than or equal to k. Then $L(\Gamma) \in \mathcal{L}(MAT_{ac})$.*

Proof. A derivation in the system Γ can be simulated by a matrix grammar as follows:

First, one performs a number of derivation steps using rules of P_1. When a rule $A \to \alpha_1 Q_i \alpha_2$ is to be used (which corresponds to a query from G_i in the system), we can use the production $A \to \alpha_1 S_i \alpha_2$ instead, and then we perform with rules of P_i as many derivation steps as we have performed with rules of P_1 since the last query from G_i (or since the beginning of the derivation to the first query from G_i, if that is the case). After that, the sentential form is derived again using rules of P_1, and so on.

Hence the number of derivation steps performed with rules of P_1 between two consecutive usages of P_i, until the first usage of P_i and from the last usage of P_i until the end of the derivation has to be counted for each $i = 2, \ldots, n$. But we know that this number is limited by k, for each $i = 2, \ldots n$. So, we will introduce in the sentential form the string $Y_2^k Y_3^k \ldots Y_n^k$.

Any time when we use a production of P_1, we will change a symbol Y_i into a symbol X_i, for each $i = 2, \ldots, n$, so that, when we start to use a P_i, we know that we have to apply as many productions as X_i-s are in the current sentential form. And when the derivation is performed using rules of P_i, at each step a X_i has to be changed into the corresponding Y_i. Hence by introducing symbols X_i, we know how many steps a derivation that started to use rules of P_i has to continue this way, namely until there is no more X_i in the sentential form.

To handle the situations in which G_1 is querying more grammars at a step, hence when a rule $A \to \alpha_1 Q_{i_1} \alpha_2 Q_{i_2} \ldots \alpha_l Q_{i_l} \alpha_{l+1}, l \geq 2$, is used, let us observe that we can replace this rule by the rules

$$A \to \alpha_1 Q_{i_1} B_1, \; B_1 \to \alpha_2 Q_{i_2} B_2, \ldots$$
$$\ldots, \; B_{l-2} \to \alpha_{l-1} Q_{i_{l-1}} B_{l-1}, \; B_{l-1} \to \alpha_l Q_{i_l} \alpha_{l+1},$$

where $B_1, B_2, \ldots, B_{l-1}$ are new symbols.

That is possible because G_1 is context-free and it has no multiple queries. But we have to take care that only the first rule, $A \to \alpha_1 Q_{i_1} B_1$, has to be counted when modifying nonterminals Y into nonterminals X.

It may happen that in the grammar system a component G_i cannot perform as many derivation steps as G_1 does, because, after a number of steps, the sentential form of G_i is a terminal string. In the equivalent matrix grammar, this problem will be solved using the "appearance checking" technique.

Another problem is that in the matrix grammar, when the sentential form is $x_1 S_i x_2$ and we have to use rules of P_i to derive the symbol S_i (which corresponds to a query from G_i, when the sentential form of G_1 is $x_1 Q_i x_2$), we have to be sure that the rules of P_i do not modify x_1 and x_2, but the occurrence of S_i only. That is why, before leaving a derivation using rules of P_1, we have to modify all nonterminals in $x_1 x_2$ (this modification will be $A \to A'$, for all $A \in N$).

With these observations, let us denote

$$R_1 = \{A \to \alpha, A' \to \alpha \mid A \to \alpha \in P_1, |\alpha|_K = 0\}$$
$$R_2 = \{A \to \alpha_1 S''_{i_1} B_1, A' \to \alpha_1 S''_{i_1} B_1, B_1 \to \alpha_2 S''_{i_2} B_2, \ldots$$
$$\ldots, B_{l-2} \to \alpha_{l-1} S''_{i_{l-1}} B_{l-1}, B_{l-1} \to \alpha_l S''_{i_l} \alpha_{l+1} \mid$$
$$A \to \alpha_1 Q_{i_1} \alpha_2 Q_{i_2} \ldots \alpha_l Q_{i_l} \alpha_{l+1} \in P_1, l \geq 1,$$
$$B_1, B_2, \ldots, B_{l-1} \text{ are new symbols and } |\alpha_j|_K = 0, j = 1, \ldots, l+1\}.$$

Let $N_1 = \{D_1, D_2, \ldots, D_t\}$ be the set of all new nonterminals introduced in R_2, let $dom(P_i) = \{A_{i1}, A_{i2}, \ldots, A_{ik_i}\}$, for $1 \leq i \leq n$, and let $P'_1 = R_1 \cup R_2$.
Finally, let F be the set consisting of all occurrences of productions

$$A_{ij} \to Z, \quad i = 1, \ldots, n, j = 1, \ldots, k_i,$$
$$A'_{ij} \to Z, \quad i = 1, \ldots, n, j = 1, \ldots, k_i,$$
$$X_i \to Z, \quad i = 2, \ldots, n,$$
$$D_i \to Z, \quad i = 1, \ldots, t,$$

in the following matrices:

$$(S' \to S_1 Y_2^k Y_3^k \ldots Y_n^k [1])$$

The nonterminals $[i], i = 1, \ldots, n$, are used to identify the component in which the current step is simulating a derivation.

To simulate a derivation in G_1, we will consider matrices:

$$(B \to \alpha, Y_2 \to X_2, Y_3 \to X_3, \ldots, Y_n \to X_n, [1] \to [1]), \quad \text{for all } B \to \alpha \in R_1$$

The changes required on the nonterminals of N before starting to apply productions of a set $P_i, i = 2, \ldots, n$ are performed using matrices:

$$(A \to A', [1] \to [1]), \quad \text{for all } A \in N.$$

To simulate a query from a $G_i, 2 \leq i \leq n,$, we will use

$$(A_{11} \to Z, A_{12} \to Z, \ldots, A_{1k_1} \to Z, A_{21} \to Z, A_{22} \to Z, \ldots$$
$$\ldots, A_{2k_2} \to Z, \ldots, A_{n1} \to Z, A_{n2} \to Z, \ldots, A_{nk_n} \to Z, B \to \beta',$$
$$Y_2 \to X_2, Y_3 \to X_3, \ldots, Y_n \to X_n, [1] \to [i]),$$
$$\text{for all } B \to \beta \in R_2, B \notin N_1, \beta \text{ contains } S''_i, \text{ and}$$
$$(A_{11} \to Z, \ldots, A_{1k_1} \to Z, A_{21} \to Z, \ldots$$
$$\ldots, A_{2k_2} \to Z, \ldots, A_{n1} \to Z, \ldots, A_{nk_n} \to Z, B \to \beta', [1] \to [i]),$$
$$\text{for all } B \to \beta \in R_2, B \in N_1, \beta \text{ contains } S''_i,$$

where β' is β in which all symbols $A \in N$ have been replaced by the corresponding A'.

Hence before starting to apply rules of a P_i, we have to verify, in the appearance checking mode, that there is no symbol of N in the current sentential form (if such a symbol appears, then the derivation is blocked, by introducing Z).

For $i = 2, \ldots, n$, let us denote

$$P_i' = P_i \cup \{S_i'' \to \alpha \mid S_i \to \alpha \in P_i\}.$$

To simulate the derivations in $G_i, i = 2, \ldots, n$, we will consider

$$(r, X_i \to Y_i, [i] \to [i]), \text{ for all } r \in P_i'.$$

When all the symbols X_i have been replaced by Y_i (which means that we have performed as many derivation steps with rules of P_i as we had to), the control of the derivation is given to the rules of P_1' :

$$(X_i \to Z, [i] \to [1]).$$

If we can no more perform derivation steps using rules of P_i', but we still have to do such steps (which means that in the system, G_1 is modifying its sentential form, while G_i cannot do it anymore with its sentential form, because it is a terminal string, and G_i is just waiting to be queried by G_1), it follows that the symbols X_i have to be rewritten. This will be done, in the appearance checking mode, verifying first that, indeed, the sentential form of G_i is a terminal string (with respect to Γ).

$$(A_{11} \to Z, A_{12} \to Z, \ldots, A_{1k_1} \to Z, A_{21} \to Z, \ldots, A_{2k_2} \to Z, \ldots$$
$$\ldots, A_{n1} \to Z, \ldots, A_{nk_n} \to Z, X_i \to Y_i, [i] \to [i]).$$

When no more derivations can be performed using productions of P_1', we have to check that none of the grammar components imposes restrictions on the length of derivations. This means that we have to verify that each of the grammars $G_2, \ldots, G_n$ can perform as many derivation steps as symbols X_i are in their sentential forms, respectively. For, we will use matrices:

$$(A_{11} \to Z, \ldots, A_{1k_1} \to Z, \ldots, A_{n1} \to Z, \ldots, A_{nk_n} \to Z, A'_{11} \to Z, \ldots$$
$$\ldots, A'_{1k_1} \to Z, \ldots, A'_{n1} \to Z, \ldots, A'_{nk_n} \to Z, D_1 \to Z, \ldots$$
$$\ldots, D_t \to Z, [1] \to [0]),$$
$$(X_i \to S_i X_i, [0] \to (i)),$$
$$(X_i \to c, A \to \alpha, (i) \to (i)), A \to \alpha \in P_i.$$

After we have checked that a grammar G_i can perform as many derivation steps as it was needed, before starting to check the same thing for another grammar G_j, we have to change all nonterminals in c, for G_j not derive some of them. This will be done in the presence of (i) using the matrices:

$$(X_i \to Z, A \to c, (i) \to (i)), \ A \in N',$$
$$(X_i \to Z, A_{11} \to Z, \ldots, A_{1k_1} \to Z, \ldots, A_{n1} \to Z, \ldots, A_{nk_n} \to Z, (i) \to [0]).$$

Finally, we have to change all nonterminals Y_i and $[0]$ into terminals. In this aim we use the matrices:

$$(Y_i \to c, [0] \to [0]), \ i = 2, \ldots, n,$$
$$([0] \to c).$$

Let $G = (N', T \cup \{c\}, S', M, F)$, be the matrix grammar with appearance checking, where

$$\begin{aligned} N' \ &= \ N \cup N_1 \cup \{A' \mid A \in N\} \cup \\ &\cup \{[i] \mid i = 0, 1, \ldots, n\} \cup \{(i) \mid i = 2, \ldots, n\} \cup \\ &\cup \{S_i'' \mid i = 2, \ldots, n\} \cup \{X_i, Y_i \mid i = 2, \ldots, n\}, \end{aligned}$$

and M, F are defined as above.

Thus for a string $w \in L(\Gamma)$, a string $w' = wc^m \in L(G)$ is constructed and, conversely, each string $w' \in L(G)$ is of the form wc^m for some $w \in L(\Gamma)$. We have $m \le k(n-1)(p-1) + 1$, where $p = \max\{|\alpha| \mid A \to \alpha \in P_i, i = 2, \ldots, n\}$.

Hence if we erase at most $k(n-1)(p-1) + 1$ symbols from any word of $L(G)$, we will get a word of $L(\Gamma)$. But $\mathbf{L}(MAT_{ac})$ is closed under restricted homomorphisms, hence $L(\Gamma) \in \mathcal{L}(MAT_{ac})$. $\qquad \square$

Theorem 3. *There exist grammar systems, with the same restrictions as in Theorem 2, which generate non-context-free languages.*

Proof. Let us consider

$$\Gamma = (\{S_1, S_2, S_3, A, B\}, K, \{a, b, c\}, G_1, G_2, G_3),$$

where

$$\begin{aligned} P_1 &= \{S_1 \to AB, A \to Q_2, B \to Q_3\}, \\ P_2 &= \{S_2 \to S_2', S_2' \to aAb, S_2' \to ab\}, \\ P_3 &= \{S_3 \to S_3', S_3' \to S_3'', S_3'' \to cB, S_3' \to cB, S_3' \to c\}. \end{aligned}$$

Starting from (S_1, S_2, S_3), we can derive

$$(AB, S_2', S_3') \qquad (1)$$

and then we have the following possibilities:

(a) If we use in G_1 the production $B \rightarrow Q_3$, then we distinguish the situations:

- $(1) \Longrightarrow (AQ_3, aAb, \alpha) \Longrightarrow (A\alpha, aAb, S_3)$, where $\alpha \in \{S_3'', cB, c\}$.

  At this point the derivation is blocked, because we have no production to derive the sentential form of G_2.

- $(1) \Longrightarrow (AQ_3, ab, S_3'') \Longrightarrow (AS_3'', ab, S_3)$.

  This configuration will not lead to a terminal string, because we cannot eliminate S_3'' from the sentential form of G_1.

-
$$(1) \Longrightarrow (AQ_3, ab, cB) \Longrightarrow (AcB, ab, S_3) \quad (2)$$

  We have two possibilities:

    - To apply in G_1 the production $B \rightarrow Q_3$.
      Then
      $$(2) \Longrightarrow (AcQ_3, ab, S_3') \Longrightarrow (AcS_3', ab, S_3),$$
      and the derivation is blocked because S_3' cannot be rewritten in G_1.
    - To apply in G_1 the production $A \rightarrow Q_2$.
      Then
      $$(2) \Longrightarrow (Q_2cB, ab, S_3') \Longrightarrow (abcB, S_2, S_3') \quad (3)$$
      The only successful derivation starting from (3) is when $S_3' \rightarrow c$ is used in G_3, and that lead to the terminal string abc^2.

- $(1) \Longrightarrow (AQ_3, ab, c) \Longrightarrow (Ac, ab, S_3) \Longrightarrow (Q_2c, ab, S_3') \Longrightarrow (abc, S_2, S_3')$.

  Hence in case (a) the only terminal strings that we have obtained are abc and abc^2.

(b) If we apply to configuration (1) the production $A \rightarrow Q_2$ in G_1, then we have the situations:

- $(1) \Longrightarrow (Q_2B, ab, c) \Longrightarrow (abB, S_2, c) \Longrightarrow (abQ_3, S_2', c) \Longrightarrow (abc, S_2', S_3)$

  and hence we have again obtained the terminal string abc.

- $(1) \Longrightarrow (Q_2B, \alpha, cB) \Longrightarrow (\alpha B, S_2, cB)$, where $\alpha \in \{ab, aAb\}$. The derivation is blocked because B cannot be rewritten in G_3.

- $(1) \Longrightarrow (Q_2B, ab, S_3'') \Longrightarrow (abB, S_2, S_3'') \Longrightarrow (abQ_3, S_2', cB) \Longrightarrow (abcB, S_2', S_3) \Longrightarrow (abcQ_3, \alpha, S_3') \Longrightarrow (abcS_3', \alpha, S_3)$, where $\alpha \in \{aAb, ab\}$. The derivation is blocked because we cannot rewrite S_3' in G_1

- $(1) \Longrightarrow (Q_2 B, aAb, c) \Longrightarrow (aAbB, S_2, c)$ (3)

  We have again two possibilities:

  - To apply in G_1 the production $A \to Q_2$.
    Then $(3) \Longrightarrow (aQ_2bB, S_2', c) \Longrightarrow (aS_2'bB, S_2, c)$. The symbol S_2' of the sentential form of G_1 cannot be rewritten, hence this is not a successful derivation.

  - To apply in G_1 the production $B \to Q_3$.
    Then $(3) \Longrightarrow (aAbQ_3, S_2', c) \Longrightarrow (aAbc, S_2', S_3) \Longrightarrow (aQ_2bc, \alpha, S_3')$ $\Longrightarrow (a\alpha bc, S_2, S_3')$, where $\alpha \in \{aAb, ab\}$. If $\alpha = ab$, then we have obtained the terminal string $a^2 b^2 c$. If $\alpha = aAb$, then the derivation will be blocked at the next step.

- $(1) \Longrightarrow (Q_2 B, aAb, S_3'') \Longrightarrow (aAbB, S_2, S_3'')$ (4)

  If we now apply the rule $A \to Q_2$ in G_1, then in the sentential form of G_1 would be introduced S_2', which cannot be eliminated. Hence the only successful derivation from that point is

$$(4) \Longrightarrow (aAbQ_3, S_2', cB) \Longrightarrow (aAbcB, S_2', S_3).$$

Starting from a configuration

$$(a^n Ab^n c^n B, S_2', S_3) \qquad (5),$$

where $n \geq 1$, we have the following possibilities:

- (case 1) $(5) \Longrightarrow (a^n Ab^n c^n Q_3, \alpha, S_3') \Longrightarrow (a^n Ab^n c^n S_3', \alpha, S_3)$,

  where $\alpha \in \{aAb, ab\}$. S_3' cannot be rewritten in G_1, hence the derivation is blocked.

- (case 2) $(5) \Longrightarrow (a^n Q_2 b^n c^n B, ab, S_3') \Longrightarrow (a^{n+1} b^{n+1} c^n B, S_2, S_3')$ (6)

  The possibilities for continuation from (6) are:

  - $(6) \Longrightarrow (a^{n+1} b^{n+1} c^n Q_3, S_2', S_3'') \Longrightarrow (a^{n+1} b^{n+1} c^n S_3'', S_2', S_3)$

  This is not a successful way, because S_3'' cannot be rewritten by G_1.

  - $(6) \Longrightarrow (a^{n+1} b^{n+1} c^n Q_3, S_2', c) \Longrightarrow (a^{n+1} b^{n+1} c^{n+1}, S_2', S_3)$

  We have got the terminal string $a^{n+1} b^{n+1} c^{n+1}$.

  - $(6) \Longrightarrow (a^{n+1} b^{n+1} c^n Q_3, S_2', cB) \Longrightarrow (a^{n+1} b^{n+1} c^{n+1} B, S_2', S_3) \Longrightarrow$
    $(a^{n+1} b^{n+1} c^{n+1} Q_3, \alpha, S_3') \Longrightarrow (a^{n+1} b^{n+1} c^{n+1} S_3', \alpha, S_3)$,

  where $\alpha \in \{ab, aAb\}$. The derivation is blocked, because of S_3'.

- (case 3) $(5) \Longrightarrow (a^n Q_2 b^n c^n B, aAb, S_3') \Longrightarrow (a^{n+1} Ab^{n+1} c^n B, S_2, S_3')$ (7)

  The possibilities we have now are the following:

$$(7) \Longrightarrow (a^{n+1} Q_2 b^{n+1} c^n B, S_2', \alpha),$$

where $\alpha \in \{S_3'', cB, c\}$. But that derivation will be blocked at a next step, because of S_2' that will be introduced in the sentential form of G_1.

$$(7) \Longrightarrow (a^{n+1} Ab^{n+1} c^n Q_3, S_2', S_3'')$$

This is also an unsuccessful derivation, because of S_3'' that will be introduced in the sentential form of G_1.

$$(7) \Longrightarrow (a^{n+1} Ab^{n+1} c^n Q_3, S_2', cB) \Longrightarrow (a^{n+1} Ab^{n+1} c^{n+1} B, S_2', S_3),$$

which is a configuration similar to (5), and hence the derivation will be reiterated.

$$(7) \Longrightarrow (a^{n+1} Ab^{n+1} c^n Q_3, S_2', c) \Longrightarrow (a^{n+1} Ab^{n+1} c^{n+1}, S_2', S_3)   (8)$$

From (8), we can derive either

$$(8) \Longrightarrow (a^{n+1} Q_2 b^{n+1} c^{n+1}, ab, S_3') \Longrightarrow (a^{n+2} b^{n+2} c^{n+1}, S_2, \alpha),$$

where $\alpha \in \{S_3'', cB, c\}$ (we have obtained the string $a^{n+2} b^{n+2} c^{n+1}$), or

$$(8) \Longrightarrow (a^{n+1} Q_2 b^{n+1} c^{n+1}, aAb, S_3') \Longrightarrow (a^{n+2} Ab^{n+2} c^{n+1}, S_2, \alpha),$$

where α is as above. But the derivation will be blocked either at this stage, if α is cB, or at the next step, when G_1 will ask for communication from G_2, and will receive S_2'.

From the above explanations it follows

$$L(\Gamma) = \{a^n b^n c^n \mid n \geq 1\} \cup \{a^{n+1} b^{n+1} c^n \mid n \geq 1\} \cup \{abc^2\},$$

which is not a context-free language. Obviously, all successful derivations in Γ satisfy the constraints of Theorem 2 (the component G_1 asks for communications after two steps at the beginning of a derivation and at every step after that).

Definition 7. Let $\Gamma = (N, K, T, G_1, G_2, \ldots, G_n)$ be a PC grammar system as in Definition 1. A *leftmost derivation* in Γ is a derivation as in Definition 2 where at point (i) we replace "$x_i \Longrightarrow y_i$ in the grammar G_i" by "$x_i \Longrightarrow y_i$ in the grammar G_i in the leftmost manner" (each component of the system has to derive the leftmost nonterminal it can derive in its sentential form).

The language generated by Γ in the leftmost mode of derivation will be denoted by $L_{left}(\Gamma)$ and if Γ is a PC grammar system of type X, the corresponding family of languages will be denoted by $\mathcal{L}_{left}(X)$.

Theorem 4.

(i) $\mathcal{L}(X) = \mathcal{L}_{left}(Y_1 X)$,
for $Y \in \{PC, CPC, NPC, NCPC\}$, $X \in \{REG, LIN, CF\}$;

(ii) $\mathcal{L}_{left}(Y_n X) \subseteq \mathcal{L}_{left}(Y_{n+1} X), n \geq 1$, X, Y *as above* ;

(iii) $\mathcal{L}_{left}(CPC_n X) \subseteq \mathcal{L}_{left}(PC_n X), \mathcal{L}_{left}(NCPC_n X) \subseteq \mathcal{L}_{left}(NPC_n X)$,
$n \geq 1$, X *as above;*

(iv) $\mathcal{L}_{left}(Y_n X) = \mathcal{L}(Y_n, X)$, *for* $X \in \{REG, LIN\}$, Y *as above.*

Proof. Directly from definitions. $\qquad\qquad\qquad\qquad\qquad\qquad\qquad\square$

Definition 8. A *simple matrix grammar* [4] of degree $n \geq 1$ is a construct

$$G = (V_1, \ldots, V_n, T, S, M),$$

where $V_1, \ldots, V_n$ are mutually disjoint nonterminal alphabets, T is a terminal alphabet, S is a symbol not in $V_G \cup T$, where $V_G = \cup_{i=1}^n V_i$, and M is a finite set of matrices of the forms

$(a) \qquad (S \rightarrow w_1 w_2 \ldots w_n)$, $w_i \in (V_i \cup T)^*, 1 \leq i \leq n$,

such that $|w_i|_{V_i} = |w_j|_{V_j}$ for all $1 \leq i, j \leq n, i \neq j$:

$(b) \qquad (A_1 \rightarrow w_1, \ldots, A_n \rightarrow w_n)$, $A_i \in V_i, w_i \in (V_i \cup T)^*, 1 \leq i \leq n$,

such that $|w_i|_{V_i} = |w_j|_{v_j}$ for all $1 \leq i, j \leq n, i \neq j$.

For $x, y \in (V_G \cup T)^*$ we write $x \Longrightarrow y$ iff either $x = S, (S \rightarrow y) \in M$, or $x = x_1' A_1 x_1'' x_2' A_2 x_2'' \ldots x_n' A_n x_n''$, $y = x_1' w_1 x_1'' x_2' w_2 x_2'' \ldots x_n' w_n x_n''$, for $(A_1 \rightarrow w_1, \ldots, A_n \rightarrow w_n) \in M$, $x_i' \in T^*, x_i'' \in (V_i \cup T)^*$, $1 \leq i \leq n$ (the derivation is leftmost on "components"). We denote by $\mathcal{L}(SM)$ the family of languages generated by simple matrix grammars as above (with λ-free rules). When λ-rules are allowed, we write $\mathcal{L}(SM^\lambda)$. It is known [4], [3] that $\mathcal{L}(CF) \subset \mathcal{L}(SM) \subset \mathcal{L}(CS)$.

Theorem 5. $\mathcal{L}(SM) \subset \mathcal{L}_{left}(PC_* CF), \mathcal{L}(SM^\lambda) \subseteq \mathcal{L}_{left}(PC_* CF^\lambda)$.

Proof. Let $G = (V_1, \ldots, V_n, V_T, S, M)$ be a simple matrix grammar as above. We denote by M_1 the set of matrices of types (a) of M, and by M_2 the set of matrices of types (b). Let r be the cardinality of M_2. A matrix $m_j \in M_2$ will be written in the form

$$m_j : (A_1^j \rightarrow z_1^j, A_2^j \rightarrow z_2^j, \ldots, A_n^j \rightarrow z_n^j), \; j = 1, \ldots, r$$

The idea of the proof of this theorem is similar to that of Theorem 1. For each matrix m_j of M_2, we will consider n grammars $G_{1j}, \ldots, G_{nj}$, one for each production of the matrix, and we will take care to synchronize the derivation such that a given sentential form will be modified by rules of m_j (which are productions of the components of the system), one by one, in the desired order.

Let $\Gamma = (N, K, V_T, G_s, G_{11}, G_{21}, \ldots, G_{n1}, \ldots, G_{1r}, G_{2r}, \ldots, G_{nr}, G_{a2}, \ldots, G_{an}, G_a)$ be the PC grammar system whose components have the following sets of productions, respectively:

$$
\begin{aligned}
P_s &= \{S_s \to B_1, B_1 \to B_2, \ldots, B_{n-2} \to B_{n-1}, B_{n-1} \to Q_{nj} | j = 1, \ldots, r\} \cup \\
&\quad \cup \{A \to A \mid A \in V_i, i = 1, \ldots, n\} \cup \\
&\quad \cup \{S_s \to \alpha \mid (S \to \alpha) \in M_1\}, \\
P_{1j} &= \{S_{1j} \to D_{11}, D_{11} \to D_{12}, \ldots, D_{1,n-2} \to D_{1,n-1}, D_{1,n-1} \to Q_s\} \cup \\
&\quad \cup \{A_1^j \to z_1^j\} \cup \{X_1 \to Z \mid X_1 \in V_1 - \{A_1^j\}\}, \text{ for } j = 1, \ldots, r, \\
P_{kj} &= \{S_{kj} \to D_{k1}, D_{k1} \to D_{k2}, \ldots, D_{k,n-2} \to D_{k,n-1}, D_{k,n-1} \to Q_{k-1,j}\} \cup \\
&\quad \cup \{A_k^j \to z_k^j\} \cup \{X_k \to Z \mid X_k \in V_k - \{A_k^j\}\}, \\
&\qquad \text{for } j = 1, 2, \ldots, r, \ k = 2, \ldots, n, \\
P_{a2} &= \{S_{a2} \to Q_{21}Q_{22}\ldots Q_{2r}\} \cup \{D_{21} \to D_{21}\}, \\
P_{ak} &= \{S_{ak} \to F_1, F_1 \to F_2, \ldots, F_{k-3} \to F_{k-2}, F_{k-2} \to Q_{k1}Q_{k2}\ldots Q_{kr}\} \cup \\
&\quad \cup \{D_{k,k-1} \to D_{k,k-1}\}, \text{ for } k = 3, 4, \ldots, n, \\
P_a &= \{S_a \to H_1, H_1 \to H_2, \ldots, H_{n-2} \to H_{n-1}, H_{n-1} \to T_1, \\
&\qquad T_1 \to T_2, \ldots, T_{n-1} \to T_n, T_n \to H_{n-1}Q_{n1}Q_{n2}\ldots Q_{nr}\},
\end{aligned}
$$

where $B_i, H_i, i = 1, \ldots, n - 1, D_{lj}, l = 1, \ldots, n, j = 1, \ldots, n - 1, F_t, t = 1, \ldots, k - 2, k = 3, \ldots, n, T_u, u = 1, \ldots, n$, and the start symbols of the components of Γ are new symbols, and N is the union of all sets $V_i, 1 \leq i \leq n$ with the set of the above enumerated new symbols.

Each grammar $G_{kj}, k = 1, \ldots, n, j = 1, \ldots, r$, must derive the leftmost nonterminal it can expand in its sentential form. When the sentential form of G_{k1}, let it be α, is not one of the nonterminals D which we have introduced for synchronization reasons, this means that if α contains no symbol of V_k, then the derivation is blocked. But if α contains at least a symbol of V_k, then the leftmost such symbol will be either derived with the k-th rule of m_j, if it is A_k^j, or it will be rewritten into a Z, otherwise. A successful derivation is one in which G_s asks for communication from a grammar G_{nj}, where j is such that all grammars $G_{kj}, k = 1, \ldots, n$, have used for derivation the corresponding productions of m_j. Otherwise, in the sentential form of G_s symbols Z will be introduced, and they cannot be rewritten.

The starting configuration is:

$$
\begin{aligned}
(S_s, &S_{11}, S_{21}, \ldots, S_{n1}, \ldots, S_{1j}, S_{2j}, \ldots, S_{nj}, \ldots, S_{1r}, S_{2r}, \ldots, S_{nr}, \\
&S_{a2}, S_{a3}, \ldots, S_{an}, S_a).
\end{aligned}
$$

Because of the similarity of the definitions of the production sets $P_{kj}, k = 1, \ldots, n$, for $j = 1, \ldots, r$, respectively, and because of the derivations in G_a, to show out a derivation in Γ, it is sufficient to represent only an n-tuple of grammars $(G_{1j}, \ldots, G_{nj})$, where $j \in \{1, \ldots, r\}$, together with the start grammar, G_s and with the auxiliary grammars $G_{a2}, \ldots, G_{an}, G_a$. Also, for the sake of simplicity, in a sentential form where a rule $X \to Q_{i1}Q_{i2} \ldots Q_{in}$ has just been used, we will represent only the symbol Q_{ij}.

Hence in our representation, the starting configuration is:

$$(S_s, \ldots, S_{1j}, S_{2j}, \ldots, S_{kj}, \ldots, S_{nj}, \ldots, S_{a2}, \ldots, S_{ak}, \ldots, S_{an}, S_a) \quad (1)$$

and we have the following derivations:

$$
\begin{aligned}
(1) \quad &\Longrightarrow (w_1, \ldots, D_{11}, D_{21}, \ldots, D_{k1}, \ldots, D_{n1}, \ldots, Q_{2j}, \ldots, F_1, \ldots, F_1, H_1) \\
&\Longrightarrow (w_1, \ldots, D_{11}, S_{2j}, \ldots, D_{k1}, \ldots, D_{n1}, \ldots, a_2, \ldots, F_1, \ldots, F_1, H_1) \\
&\Longrightarrow (w_2, \ldots, D_{12}, D_{21}, \ldots, D_{k2}, \ldots, D_{n2}, \ldots, a_2, \ldots, F_2, \ldots, F_2, H_2)
\end{aligned}
$$

and, after $k - 1$ derivation steps, where we count only the rewriting steps, not the steps when we perform communications, we have

$$
\begin{aligned}
\ldots \Longrightarrow &(w_{k-1}, \ldots, D_{1,k-1}, D_{2,k-2}, \ldots, D_{k,k-1}, \ldots, D_{n,k-1}, \ldots, a_2, \ldots, \\
&Q_{kj}, \ldots, F_{k-1}, H_{k-1}) \Longrightarrow \\
\Longrightarrow &(w_{k-1}, \ldots, D_{1,k-1}, D_{2,k-2}, \ldots, S_{kj}, \ldots, D_{n,k-1}, \ldots, a_2, \ldots, a_k, \ldots, \\
&F_{k-1}, H_{k-1}) \Longrightarrow \ldots
\end{aligned}
$$

and, after $n - 1$ steps since the beginning of the derivation,

$$
\begin{aligned}
\ldots \Longrightarrow &(w_{n-1}, \ldots, D_{1,n-1}, D_{2,n-2}, \ldots, D_{k,n-k}, \ldots, D_{n,n-1}, \ldots, \\
&a_2, \ldots, a_k, \ldots, Q_{nj}, H_{n-1}) \Longrightarrow \\
\Longrightarrow &(w_{n-1}, \ldots, D_{1,n-1}, D_{2,n-2}, \ldots, D_{k,n-k}, \ldots, S_{nj}, \ldots, \\
&a_2, \ldots, a_k, \ldots, a_n, H_{n-1}) \Longrightarrow \\
\Longrightarrow &(w_n, \ldots, Q_s, D_{2,n-1}, \ldots, D_{k,n-k+1}, \ldots, D_{n1}, \ldots, \\
&a_2, \ldots, a_k, \ldots, a_n, T_1) \quad\quad (2),
\end{aligned}
$$

where $a_i = D^r_{i,i-1}, i = 2, \ldots, n$.

There are two possibilities:

- If in configuration (1) we have used the production $S_s \to B_1$ to derive in G_s, then for each $i = 1, \ldots, n - 1, w_i = B_i$, and $w_n = Q_{nj}$, and

$$(2) \quad \Longrightarrow (D_{n1}, \ldots, Q_s, D_{2,n-1}, \ldots, D_{k,n-k+1}, \ldots, S_{nj}, \ldots,$$

$$a_2, \ldots, a_k, \ldots, a_n, T_1) \Longrightarrow$$
$$\Longrightarrow (S_s, \ldots, D_{n1}, D_{2,n-1}, \ldots, D_{k,n-k+1}, \ldots, S_{nj}, \ldots,$$
$$a_2, \ldots, a_k, \ldots, a_n, T_1).$$

The derivation is blocked at this point, because G_{1j} has no production for D_{n1}.

- If in configuration (1) we have used the production $S_s \to \alpha$, to derive in G_s, where $(S \to \alpha) \in M_1$, then for each $i = 1, \ldots, n, w_i = \alpha$, and we have the following derivation:

$$(2) \quad \Longrightarrow \quad (S_s, \ldots, \alpha, D_{2,n-1}, \ldots, D_{k,n-k+1}, \ldots, D_{n1}, \ldots,$$
$$a_2, \ldots, a_k, \ldots, a_n, T_1).$$

Because $a_i, i = 2, \ldots, n$ will not be modified anymore, from now on we will not represent them in a configuration.

Starting from a configuration

$$(S_s, \ldots, w_0, D_{2,n-1}, \ldots, D_{k,n-k+1}, \ldots, D_{n1}, \ldots, T_1\theta_1) \quad (3),$$

(we have represented, in order, the sentential forms for $G_s, G_{1j}, G_{2j}, G_{kj}, G_{nj}$ and G_a, respectively) where $\theta_1 \in (N \cup T)^*$ and w_0 contains symbols in $V_i, i = 1, n$, we can derive

$$(3) \quad \Longrightarrow (x_1, \ldots, w_1, Q_{1j}, \ldots, D_{k,n-k+2}, \ldots, D_{n2}, \ldots, T_2\theta_1)$$
$$\Longrightarrow (x_1, \ldots, S_{1j}, w_1, \ldots, D_{k,n-k+2}, \ldots, D_{n2}, \ldots, T_2\theta_1)$$
$$\Longrightarrow (x_2, \ldots, D_{11}, w_2, \ldots, D_{k,n-k+3}, \ldots, D_{n3}, \ldots, T_3\theta_1)$$
$$\Longrightarrow (x_2, \ldots, D_{11}, S_{2j}, \ldots, D_{k,n-k+3}, \ldots, D_{n3}, \ldots, T_3\theta_1)$$

and, after k-1 derivation steps,

$$\Longrightarrow (x_{k-1}, \ldots, D_{1,k-2}, D_{2,k-3}, \ldots, Q_{k-1,j}, \ldots, D_{nk}, \ldots, T_k\theta_1)$$
$$\Longrightarrow (x_{k-1}, \ldots, D_{1,k-2}, D_{2,k-3}, \ldots, w_{k-1}, \ldots, D_{nk}, \ldots, T_k\theta_1)$$
$$\Longrightarrow (x_k, \ldots, D_{1,k-1}, D_{2,k-2}, \ldots, w_k, \ldots, D_{n,k+1}, \ldots, T_{k+1}\theta_1)$$
$$\ldots \Longrightarrow (x_{n-1}, \ldots, D_{1,n-2}, D_{2,n-3}, \ldots, D_{k,n-k-1}, \ldots, Q_{n-1,j}, \ldots, T_n\theta_1)$$
$$\Longrightarrow (x_{n-1}, \ldots, D_{1,n-2}, D_{2,n-3}, \ldots, D_{k,n-k-1}, \ldots, w_{n-1}, \ldots, T_n\theta_1)$$
$$\Longrightarrow (x_n, \ldots, D_{1,n-1}, D_{2,n-2}, \ldots, D_{k,n-k}, \ldots, w_n, \ldots,$$
$$H_{n-1}Q_{n1}Q_{n2}\ldots Q_{nr}\theta_1) \quad (4),$$

where for $i = 1, \ldots, n, w_i$ is just w_{i-1} derived using a production of P_{ij}.

Note that if in the above sequence of derivations one of the grammars $G_{ij}, i = 1, \ldots, n$, cannot derive the sentential form it has received in a communication process, the derivation will be blocked. Hence we are not interested in that case, which means that we can assume, without loss of generality, that each $w_i, i = 0, \ldots, n-1$, contains at least a symbol of V_i. Because a production with a symbol of V_i as its left side generates only symbols in $(V_i \cup T)^*$, it must be the case that w_0 contains symbols from each $V_i, i = 1, \ldots, n$.

If the leftmost symbols of each of $V_i, i = 1, \ldots, n$, in w_0 are the left sides of productions of matrix m_j, respectively, then w_n is just w_0 derived using the matrix m_j in the matrix grammar G. Otherwise, w_n contains at least a symbol Z.

At that point, we distinguish two cases:

(a) If in configuration (3) we have applied the production $S_s \to B_1$, then for each $i = 1, \ldots, n - 1, x_i = B_i$ and $x_n = Q_{nj}$, and

$$(4) \implies (w_n, \ldots, D_{1,n-1}, D_{2,n-2}, \ldots, D_{k,n-k}, \ldots, S_{nj}, \ldots, H_{n-1}\theta_2) \quad (5)$$

If w_n is a terminal string, then the derivation can stop here.

Note that when G_s is asking for communication from a G_{nj}, grammar G_a is asking for communication from all $G_{nk}, k = 1, \ldots, r$, to prepare them to continue the derivation in the same manner.

If G_s has asked for the sentential form of a G_{nj} that has introduced symbols Z in transformations of w_0 (which corresponds to the case when matrix m_j is not applicable to w_0), then from w_n we will not get a terminal string, because Z cannot be rewritten. If G_s has asked for the sentential form of a G_{nj} that had changed w_0 according to matrix m_j, then the derivation will continue as follows:

$$(5) \quad \implies (w_n, \ldots, Q_s, D_{2,n-1}, \ldots, D_{k,n-k+1}, \ldots, D_{n1}, \ldots, T_1\theta_2)$$
$$\implies (S_s, \ldots, w_n, D_{2,n-1}, \ldots, D_{k,n-k+1}, \ldots, D_{n1}, \ldots, T_1\theta_2),$$

which is a configuration similar to (3), hence the derivation will continue from now on in the same manner.

(b) If in (3) we have used the production $S_s \to \alpha$ to derive in G_s, where $(S_s \to \alpha) \in M_1$, then for each $i, i = 1, \ldots, n, x_i = \alpha$, and

$$(4) \quad \implies (\alpha, \ldots, D_{1,n-1}, D_{2,n-2}, \ldots, D_{k,n-k}, \ldots, S_{nj}, \ldots, H_{n-1}\theta_2)$$
$$\implies (\alpha, \ldots, Q_s, D_{2,n-1}, \ldots, D_{k,n-k+1}, \ldots, D_{n1}, \ldots, T_1\theta_2)$$
$$\implies (S_s, \ldots, \alpha, D_{2,n-1}, \ldots, D_{k,n-k+1}, \ldots, D_{n1}, \ldots, T_1\theta_2),$$

which is a configuration similar to (3). From now on the derivation will continue as if at the first step we have used this production $S_s \to \alpha$. From the above explanations it follows $L(\Gamma) = L(G)$. Moreover, note that the construction we have considered does not introduce λ-productions.

The proof is the same in the case of using λ-rules.

To prove that the inclusion is strict, we give an example which can be also found in [2]. Let

$$
\begin{aligned}
\Gamma \;=\; & (\{S_1, S_2\}, K, \{a, b\}, G_1, G_2), \\
& P_1 = \{S_1 \to S_1, S_1 \to Q_2 Q_2 Q_2, S_1 \to Q_2 Q_2 Q_2 S_1\}, \\
& P_2 = \{S_2 \to a S_2, S_2 \to b\}.
\end{aligned}
$$

We have

$$
L(\Gamma) = \{a^n b a^n b a^n b \mid n \geq 0\}^+,
$$

a language which is not in the family $\mathcal{L}(SM^\lambda)$. $\qquad\square$

4. Rules and symbols synchronization

We will deal now with different types of synchronization, namely using n-tuples of rules and of nonterminals as synchronization devices as introduced in [6]. We consider in addition the existence of an appearance checking set which controls the derivation, in the same manner as in the derivation with respect to a matrix grammar.

Definition 9. A *PC grammar system with rules synchronization with appearance checking* is a construct

$$
\Gamma = (N, K, T, G_1, \ldots, G_n, M, F),
$$

where $(N, K, T, G_1, \ldots, G_n)$ is a usual PC grammar system of degree n, M is a subset of $(P_1 \cup \{\#\}) \times (P_2 \cup \{\#\}) \times \ldots \times (P_n \cup \{\#\})$ (an element of M is called a *vector*), and F is a set of occurrences of rules in the vectors of M.

A derivation in such a system is defined by adding, in the usual manner, the *appearance checking* control to the definition of a derivation in PC grammar systems with rules synchronization. That is, at a rewriting step $(x_1, \ldots, x_n) \Longrightarrow (y_1, \ldots, y_n)$ in Γ, an element $m = (r_1, \ldots, r_n)$ of M is used in the appearance checking mode, i. e. $x_i = y_i, x_i \in T^*$, if $r_i = \#$, and if $r_i \in P_i$, either $x_i \Longrightarrow y_i$ by the rule r_i, and r_i is applicable to x_i, or $x_i = y_i, r_i$ is not applicable to x_i, and this occurrence of r_i in the vector m is in F. The communication is performed as usual.

The family of languages generated by rules synchronization PC grammar systems with appearance checking associated to a usual family $\mathcal{L}(Y_n X)$ is denoted by $\mathcal{L}(RY_n X_{ac})$.

Theorem 6.

(i) $\mathcal{L}(RCPC_*X_{ac}) \subseteq \mathcal{L}(RPC_*X_{ac}), \mathcal{L}(RNCPC_*X_{ac}) \subseteq \mathcal{L}(RNPC_*X_{ac})$;

(ii) $\mathcal{L}(RY_*X) \subseteq \mathcal{L}(RY_*X_{ac})$, *for arbitrary X.*

Proof. Both points (i) and (ii) follow directly form definition.   □
As an immediate consequence of the definition and of Theorem 1, we have

$$\mathcal{L}(MAT) \subseteq \mathcal{L}(RPC_*CF_{ac}).$$

Moreover, we have

Theorem 7. $\mathcal{L}(MAT_{ac}) \subseteq \mathcal{L}(RPC_*CF_{ac})$.

Proof. The proof is based on the same ideas as in Theorem 1. So, let $G = (V_N, V_T, S, M, F)$ be a matrix grammar with appearance checking, in the 2-normal form.

Let Γ be the same PC grammar system as in the proof of Theorem 1 , which means that the sets of rules $P_s, P_{1k}, P_{2k}, P_{a1}, P_{a2}, k = 1, \ldots, r$ are entirely the same. Let

$$
\begin{aligned}
M' \;=\; & \{(S_s \to AX, S_{1k} \to W, S_{2k} \to V, S_{a1} \to Q_{21} \ldots Q_{2r}, S_{a2} \to L_1) \mid \\
& (S \to AX) \in M, k = 1, \ldots, r\} \cup \\
& \cup\{(X \to X, W \to Q_s, S_{2k} \to V, V \to V, L_1 \to L_2) \mid \\
& \quad X \in V_N^2, k = 1, \ldots, r\} \cup \\
& \cup\{(S_s \to T, A_k \to \alpha_k, V \to Q_{1k}, V \to V, L_1 \to L_2) \mid \\
& m_k : (A_k \to \alpha_k, B_k \to C_k)k = 1, \ldots, r\} \cup \\
& \cup\{(T \to Q_{2k}, S_{1k} \to W, B_k \to C_k, V \to V, L_3 \to L_1 Q_{21} \ldots Q_{2r}) \mid \\
& m_k : (A_k \to \alpha_k, B_k \to C_k), k = 1, \ldots, r\} \cup \\
& \cup\{(S_s \to T, X \to Z, V \to Q_{1k}, V \to V, L_2 \to L_3) \mid \\
& X \in V_N^1 \cup V_N^2, k = 1, \ldots, r\} \cup \\
& \cup\{(T \to Q_{2k}, S_{1k} \to W, X \to Z, V \to V, L_3 \to L_1 Q_{21} \ldots Q_{2r}) \mid \\
& X \in V_N^1 \cup V_N^2, k = 1, \ldots, r\}
\end{aligned}
$$

and let F' be the set of those occurrences of rules $A_k \to \alpha_k$ in the preceding matrices that correspond to occurrences of rules of F.

With the same observations as in the proof of Theorem 1, we have $L(G) = L(\Gamma)$, where Γ' is the system obtained by adding M' and F' to Γ.   □

Corollary. $\mathcal{L}(RPC_*CF_{ac}^\lambda) = \mathcal{L}(RE)$.

Proof. It follows from the above theorem and from the known equality $\mathcal{L}(MAT_{ac}^\lambda) = \mathcal{L}(RE)$.   □

Let us extend the definition of a PC grammar system with symbols synchronization, [6], to take into account the appearance checking mode, in the natural way.

Definition 10. A *PC grammar system with symbols synchronization with appearance checking* is a construct

$$\Gamma = (N, K, T, G_1, \ldots, G_n, M, F)$$

where $(N, K, T, G_1, \ldots, G_n)$ is a usual PC grammar system of degree n, M is a subset of $(N \cup \{\#\}) \times \ldots \times (N \cup \{\#\})$, and F is a set of occurrences of nonterminals in the vectors of M.

At a rewriting step $(x_1, \ldots, x_n) \Longrightarrow (y_1, \ldots, y_n)$ in Γ, an element $m = (A_1, \ldots, A_n)$ of M is used in the appearance checking mode, that is $x_i = y_i, x_i \in T^*$, if $A_i = \#$, and if $A_i \in N$, either $x_i \Longrightarrow y_i$ by a rule $A_i \to w$, or $x_i = y_i$, no rule $A_i \to w$ is applicable to x_i, and this occurrence of A_i in m is in F. The communication is performed as usual.

Denote the family of languages generated by such systems, with context-free components, by $\mathcal{L}(SY_nCF_{ac}), Y \in \{PC, CPC, NPC, NCPC\}$.

Theorem 8. $\mathcal{L}(SY_nCF_{ac}) = \mathcal{L}(RY_nCF_{ac}), n \geq 1$, *for all* $Y \in \{PC, CPC, NPC, NCPC\}$.

Proof. (i) Let $(\Gamma = (N, K, T, G_1, \ldots, G_n, M, F)$ be a symbols synchronized grammar system with appearance checking. Construct the sets

$$C(X_i) = \begin{cases} \{r \mid r \in P_i, r = X_i \to \alpha\}, & \text{for } X_i \neq \# \\ \{\#\}, & \text{for } X_i = \# \end{cases}$$

for $X_i \in N \cup \{\#\}$, and let

$$\Gamma' = (N, K, T, G_1, \ldots, G_n, M', F'),$$

with

$$M' = \bigcup_{(X_1, \ldots, X_n) \in M} (C(X_1) \times C(X_2) \times \ldots \times C(X_n)),$$

and F' be the set of all occurrences of productions of $C(X_i)$ in M', which correspond to the occurrences of X_i in F.

Then $L(\Gamma) = L(\Gamma')$, hence $\mathcal{L}(SY_nCF_{ac}) \subseteq \mathcal{L}(RY_nCF_{ac})$.

(ii) For the reverse inclusion, consider a rules synchronized PC grammar system

$$\Gamma = (N, K, T, G_1, \ldots, G_n, M, F).$$

We will replace each vector

$$m = (A_1 \to x_1, \ldots, A_n \to x_n)$$

in M by the vector m' obtained by replacing in m each rule $A_i \to x_i$ on positions not equal to $\#$, by $(A_i, m) \to x_i$.

Also, we will consider the vectors $m'' = (r_1, \ldots, r_n)$, where $r_i = A_i \to (A_i, m)$, when the i-th position in m is not $\#$, and $r_i = \#$, otherwise. Denote by M' the set of all these vectors and introduce all the new symbols (A_i, m) in N and the new rules in the corresponding sets P_i.

Replace each rule $A_i \to x_i$ in F by the corresponding occurrence of $(A_i, m) \to x_i$ in m' and by the occurrence of $A_i \to (A_i, m)$ in m'', thus resulting a set F'.

For

$$\Gamma' = (N', K, T, G'_1, \ldots G'_n, M', F'),$$

it is easy to see that $L(\Gamma) = L(\Gamma')$.

Denote by F'' the set of occurrences of nonterminals in the left sides of rules of F' and let $M'' = \{(X_1, \ldots, X_n) \mid$ there is a vector $(r_1, \ldots, r_n) \in M'$ with $r_i = X_i \to x_i$, when $r_i \neq \#$, and $X_i = \#$, for $r_i = \# \}$.

Consider $\Gamma'' = (N', K, T, (P'_1, S_1), \ldots, (P'_n, S_n), M'', F'')$.

It is easy to see that $L(\Gamma'') = L(\Gamma')$, which implies $\mathcal{L}(RY_n CF_{ac}) \subseteq \mathcal{L}(SY_n CF_{ac})$. $\qquad \square$

Hence the rules and the symbols synchronization grammar systems are equally powerful for all types of PC grammar systems, even in the appearance checking case. (This corresponds to the equivalence of the two synchronization devices, proved in [6] for the case without appearance checking.)

Corollary. $\mathcal{L}(SPC_* CF^\lambda_{ac}) = \mathcal{L}(RE)$.

Proof. It follows from the above theorem and from Theorem 7. $\qquad \square$

5. Conclusions

We have investigated connections between PC grammar systems and matrix grammars. The properties outlined in this paper help us to localize more exactly the languages generated by PC grammar systems, between the context-free and context-sensitive languages. Moreover, from these properties and from the relations known between matrix grammars and cooperating distributed grammar systems, which can be found in [1], [2], connections between PC grammars systems and certain classes of cooperating distributed grammars systems follow.

Also, the relations outlined in Section 4 show us not only that even for rules and symbols synchronized PC grammar systems one can consider an appearance checking control of derivation, but also that in that case we obtain results similar to those known for matrix grammars and N-matrix grammars with appearance checking (see [3]), to which these PC grammar systems are similar in spirit.

References

1. E. Csuhaj-Varju, J. Dassow, On cooperating distributed grammar systems, *J. Inf. Processing and Cybern. EIK*, 26 (1990), 49 – 63.

2. E. Csuhaj-Varju, J. Dassow, J. Kelemen, Gh. Păun, *Grammar Systems*, Gordon and Breach, London, 1994.

3. J. Dassow, Gh. Păun, *Regulated Rewriting in Formal Language Theory*, Springer-Verlag, Berlin, Heidelberg, 1989.

4. O. Ibarra, Simple matrix languages, *Inform. Control*, 17 (1970), 359 – 394.

5. V. Mihalache, On parallel communicating grammar systems with context-free components, in *Mathematical Linguistics and Related Topics* (Gh. Păun, ed.), The Publ. House of the Romanian Academy of Sciences, Bucureşti, 1994.

6. Gh. Păun, On the synchronization in parallel communicating grammar systems, *Acta Informatica*, 30 (1993), 351 – 367.

7. Gh. Păun, L. Sântean, Parallel communicating grammar systems, *Ann. Univ. Buc., Ser. Matem.-Inform.*, 38 (1989), 55 – 63.

8. A. Salomaa, *Formal Languages*, Academic Press, New York, London, 1973.

Contextual Grammars:
The Strategy of Minimal Competence

Victor MITRANA

Faculty of Mathematics, University of Bucharest

Str. Academiei 14, 70109 Bucureşti, Romania

Abstract. We consider contextual grammars with a parallel derivation similar with the t-mode of derivation considered in [8]. The current string is splitted into substrings, in a maximal mode, and the contexts are adjoined to these substrings in a parallel manner. The generative capacity, some decision problems about such grammars and the degree of parallelism are investigated.

0. Introduction

The contextual grammars have been introduced in [3] as a generative mechanism that is not using auxiliary symbols, based on acceptance of a context by a word. Motivations can be found in [2], [4]. A contextual grammar produces a language by starting from a given finite set of strings and adding, iteratively, pairs of strings (called contexts) to the strings already obtained.

There were considered many ways to adjoin the contexts: in the interior of the string, only at its end, with the contexts selected by a mapping. On the other hand, the contexts can be added sequentially or in parallel [8]. A survey can be found in [5] and also, with recent developments in [6].

The present paper is devoted to the study of the families of languages generated by contextual grammars with choice (the selection of contexts is done in a regular way: the set of strings which accept the same context is a language of a given type) in a derivation mode called *the strategy of minimal competence* (the name of this derivation mode was suggested us by a similar derivation mode in grammar systems). The whole current string is splitted into subwords in such a way that some subwords appear in the selection sets of the grammar (and contexts are adjoined to them) and the other subwords contain no subword in these sets (the maximal number of adjoinings is done, for a given splitting of the current string). First, one investigates the generative capacity and some decision problems. Then, a complexity measure, namely *the degree of parallelism* is defined and studied.

We start with some basic definitions. If V is a finite alphabet we denote by V^* the free monoid generated by V under catenation. For a word $x \in V^*$ we write $lg(x)$ for the length of x. Denote by λ the empty word; $lg(\lambda) = 0$ and $V^+ = V^* - \{\lambda\}$. The set of subwords of a string x is denoted by $Sub(x)$.

Denote by $FIN, REG, CF, CS, REC, RE$ the family of finite, regular, context-free, context sensitive, recursive and recursively enumerable languages, respectively.

Let F be a family of languages over an alphabet V. A contextual grammar of degree n, with F choice, is a construct

$$G = (V, B, (R_1, C_1), \ldots, (R_n, C_n))$$

where

B is a finite subset of V^*,
R_i are languages in $F, 1 \leq i \leq n,,$
C_i are finite subsets of $V^* \times V^*$ of contexts,$1 \leq i \leq n,.$

For a grammar G and two strings $x, y \in V^*$ we define the following derivation and we call it the strategy of minimal competence:

$$x \Longrightarrow^{mc} y \quad \text{iff} \quad x = x_1 z_1 x_2 z_2 \ldots x_m z_m x_{m+1},$$
$$y = x_1 u_1 z_1 v_1 x_2 \ldots x_m u_m z_m v_m x_{m+1},$$
$$z_j \in R_{i_j}, (u_j, v_j) \in C_{i_j}, i_j \in \{1, 2, \ldots, n\}, 1 \leq j \leq m,$$
$$x_t \in V^*, Sub(x_t) \cap \bigcup_{k=1}^{n} R_k = \emptyset, 1 \leq t \leq m+1.$$

The language generated by G with the strategy of minimal competence is:

$$L_{mc}(G) = B \cup \{y \in V^* \mid x \Longrightarrow^{mc} y_1 \Longrightarrow^{mc} \cdots \Longrightarrow^{mc} y_p = y, x \in B, p \geq 1\}.$$

The family of languages generated by contextual grammars of degree at most n, with F choice, using the strategy of minimal competence, is denoted by $C_n(F, mc)$. Furthermore, $C(F, mc) = lim_{n \to \infty} C_n(F, mc)$. When no restriction is put on the family F we write $F = ARB$.

When for each (R_i, C_i) as above, $card(C_i) = 1$ we say that G is a *deterministic grammar*. We denote by $DC_n(F, mc), DC(F, mc), n \geq 1$, the families of languages generated by deterministic contextual grammars corresponding to $C_n(F, mc), C(F, mc)$, respectively.

Let us consider some examples: For

$$G_1 = (\{a\}, \{a\}, (\{a\}, \{(\lambda, a)\}))$$

we obtain $L_{mc}(G_1) = \{a^{2^n} \mid n \geq 0\}$. Indeed, only derivations of the following form are possible in G_1:

$$a \Longrightarrow^{mc} aa \Longrightarrow^{mc} a^4 \Longrightarrow^{mc} a^8 \Longrightarrow^{mc} a^{16} \Longrightarrow \cdots$$

Consequently, $\{a^{2^n} \mid n \geq 0\} \in C_1(FIN, mc)$. Consider also

$$
\begin{aligned}
G_2 &= (\{a, b, c\}, \{abc, a^2b^2c^2\}, (R_1, C_1), (R_2, C_2)) \\
&\quad R_1 = \{a^2b\}, C_1 = \{(a, b)\}; \\
&\quad R_2 = \{bc^2\}, C_2 = \{(\lambda, c)\}.
\end{aligned}
$$

We obtain $L_{mc}(G_2) = \{a^n b^n c^n \mid n \geq 1\}$ (every string $a^n b^n c^n, n \geq 2$, can be decomposed in an unique way as $a^{n-2}a^2bb^{n-2}bc^2c^{n-2}$). Therefore, $\{a^n b^n c^n \mid n \geq 1\} \in C_2(FIN, mc)$.

Note that both these grammars are deterministic and have finite choice. However, the languages generated by them are non-context-free, the first one is even a one-letter non-context-free language.

1. The power of the strategy of minimal competence

It is obvious that $C_n(F, mc) \subseteq C_{n+1}(F, mc)$ and $DC_n(F, mc) \subseteq DC_{n+1}(F, mc)$ for any family of languages F and any $n \geq 1$. A natural problem is to see for which values of F these hierarchies are infinite ?

Theorem 1. *For any family F including the family of finite languages the fellowing inclusions are proper:*

$$
\begin{aligned}
C_n(F, mc) &\subset C_{n+1}(F, mc), \quad n \geq 1, \\
DC_n(F, mc) &\subset DC_{n+1}(F, mc), \quad n \geq 1.
\end{aligned}
$$

Proof. Let $k \geq 1$ and take $L_k = \{a_1^{2^n} a_2^{2^n} \ldots a_k^{2^n} \mid n \geq 0\}$. We shall prove that

$$
L_k \in DC_k(F, mc) - C_{k-1}(F, mc)
$$

Consider

$$
G' = (\{a_1, a_2, \ldots, a_k\}, \{a_1 a_2 \ldots a_k\}, (\{a_1\}, \{(\lambda, a_1)\}), \ldots, (\{a_k\}, \{(\lambda, a_k)\})).
$$

Clearly, $L_{mc}(G') = L_k$, hence $L_k \in DC_k(F, mc)$. Take now an arbitrary grammar $G = ((\{a_1, \ldots a_k\}, B, (R_1, C_1), \ldots, (R_p, C_p))$ such that $L_{mc}((G) = L_k$.

Assume that for some $i, 1 \leq i \leq k$, the sets $R_1, \ldots, R_p$ do not contain strings $a_i^t, t \geq 1$. There is a derivation

$$
a_1^{2^m} a_2^{2^m} \ldots a_k^{2^m} \Longrightarrow^{mc} a_1^{2^s} a_2^{2^s} \ldots a_k^{2^s}, s \geq 1
$$

with arbitrarly large m. The substring $a_i^{2^m}$ has been derived only using a decomposition

$$
a_{i-1}^{2^m} a_i^{2^m} a_{i+1}^{2^m} = x_1 a_{i-1}^{r_1} a_i^{r_2} a_i^{2^m - r_2 - r_3} a_i^{r_3} a_{i+1}^{r_4} x_2
$$

such that $a_{i-1}^{r_1} a_i^{r_2} \in R_{j_1}, a_i^{r_3} a_{i+1}^{r_4} \in R_{j_2}$ for some $j_1, j_2 \in \{1, 2 \ldots, p\}$. Then we obtain a string of the form $x_1' u_1 a_{i-1}^{r_1} a_i^{r_2} v_1 a_i^{2^m - r_2 - r_3} u_2 a_i^{r_3} a_{i+1}^{r_4} v_2 x_2'$, for $(u_1, v_1) \in C_{j_1}, (u_2, v_2) \in C_{j_2}$, hence with $r_2 + lg(v_1) + 2^m - r_2 - r_3 + lg(u_2) + r_3 = 2^m + lg(v_1 u_2)$ occurrences of a_i. Because $lg(v_1 u_2)$ is bounded (the sets C_{j_1}, C_{j_2} are finite) and m is arbitrarily large, we can obtain a string with $2^m + lg(v_1 u_2) < 2^{m+1}$ occurrences of a_i. This contradicts the form of strings in L_k; hence for each i we must have strings $a_i^{t_i}, t_i \geq 1$, in the sets $R_j, j = 1, 2 \ldots, p$.

Assume now that for R_j containing $a_i^t, t \geq 1$, the set C_j contains a context (u, v) such that a_l appears in uv, for some $l \neq i$. From a string $a_1^{2^m} a_2^{2^m} \ldots a_k^{2^m}$ with $2^m > t$ we can produce, by rewriting the substring $a_i^{2^m}$, a string containing $u a_i^t v u a_i^t v$. If $l < i$ then we have $u a_i^t v u a_i^t v = y_1 a_i y_2 a_l y_3$, for appropiate y_1, y_2, y_3, if $l > i$ then we have $u a_i^t v u a_i^t v = y_1 a_l y_2 a_i y_3$, in both cases parasitic strings. Consequently, if some R_j contains a string a_i^t, then C_i contains only contexts (u, v) with $u, v \in a_i^*$. Because for every $i = 1, 2 \ldots, k$ we need strings $a_i^{t_i}$ in sets R_j, it follows that at least k such sets are necessary, hence we must have $p \geq k$, L_k cannot be in $C_{k-1}(F, mc)$. The type of languages $R_j, 1 \leq j \leq p$, plays no role in this argument, hence $L_k \notin C_{k-1}(ARB, mc)$. $\square$

In [7] five derivation relations in a contextual grammar with F choice were considered. The last of them, the so-called t-mode of derivation is closely related to our strategy of derivation. We recall its definition. For a contextual grammar $G = (V, B, (R_1, C_1), \ldots, (R_n, C_n))$ one defines the relation

$$\begin{aligned}
x \Longrightarrow^t y \text{ iff } x &= z_1 z_2 \ldots z_m, \\
y &= u_1 z_1 v_1 \ldots u_m z_m v_m, \\
z_j &\in R_{i_j}, (u_j, v_j) \in C_{i_j}, i_j \in \{1, 2, \ldots, n\}, 1 \leq j \leq m.
\end{aligned}$$

The language generated by G in this way is

$$L_t(G) = B \cup \{y \in V^* \mid x \Longrightarrow^t y_1 \Longrightarrow^t \cdots \Longrightarrow^t y_p = y, x \in B, p \geq 1\}.$$

Denote by $C_n(F, t)$ the family of all languages generated by contextual grammars of degree at most n, with F choice, in the t-mode of derivation.

Theorem 2. *The following relations hold for all $n \geq 1, F \in \{REG, CS, RE, ARB\}$*

$$C_n(F, t) \subseteq C_{n+1}(F, mc).$$

Moreover

$$C_n(FIN, t) \subseteq C_{n+1}(REG, mc),$$

$$C_n(CF, t) \subseteq C_{n+1}(CS, mc).$$

Proof. Let L be a language in $C_n(F,t)$ generated by a contextual grammar $G = (V, B, (R_1, C_1), \ldots, (R_n, C_n)), R_i \in F, 1 \le i \le n$. If $\bigcup_{i=1}^{n} R_i = V^*$ then $L = L_{mc}(G)$. If $\bigcup_{i=1}^{n} R_i \ne V^*$, then construct $G' = (V, B, (R_1, C_1), \ldots, (R_n, C_n), (R_{n+1}, C_{n+1}))$ with $R_{n+1} = V^* - \bigcup_{i=1}^{n} R_i, C_{n+1} = \emptyset$. Clearly, $L = L_{mc}(G')$. For F closed under union and difference, $R_{n+1} \in F$. This is the case for $F \in \{REG, CS, RE, ARB\}$, but not for FIN and CF. $\square$

In a similar way as in the case of Theorem 1 we can prove

Theorem 3.
$$C_n(F,t) \subset C_{n+1}(F,t),$$
$$DC_n(F,t) \subset DC_{n+1}(F,t),$$

for any $n \ge 1$ and any family of languages F including the family of finite languages.

Theorem 4. *The family of internal contextual languages [7] is strictly included in $C(F, mc)$.*

Proof. For an internal contextual grammar with F choice $G = (V, B, (R_1, C_1), \ldots, (R_n, C_n))$ construct $G' = (V, B, (R_1, C_1'), \ldots, (R_n, C_n')), C_i' = C_i \cup \{(\lambda, \lambda)\}$.

The inclusion $L(G) = L_{mc}(G')$ is obvious. Conversely, if $x \Longrightarrow^m cy$ in G', $x = x_1 z_1 x_2 \ldots x_m z_m x_{m+1}, y = x_1 u_1 z_1 v_1 x_2 \ldots x_m u_m z_m v_m x_{m+1}$, then the following derivation is possible in G:

$$x_1 z_1 x_2 z_2 x_3 \ldots x_m z_m x_{m+1} \Longrightarrow^{mc} x_1 u_1 z_1 v_1 x_2 z_2 x_2 \ldots x_m z_m x_{m+1} \Longrightarrow^{mc}$$
$$\Longrightarrow^{mc} x_1 u_1 z_1 v_1 x_2 u_2 z_2 v_2 x_3 \ldots x_m z_m x_{m+1} \Longrightarrow^{mc}$$
$$\ldots \Longrightarrow^{mc} x_1 u_1 z_1 v_1 x_2 u_2 z_2 v_2 x_3 \ldots x_m u_m z_m v_m x_{m+1}.$$

Consequently, $L_{mc}(G')) \subseteq L_i(G)$ and we have the inclusion $C(F, int) \subseteq C(F, mc)$

The inclusion is proper because $C_1(FIN, mc)$ contains one-letter non-regular languages, but every one-letter internal contextual language is regular [5]. $\square$

Corollary. $REG \subset C(REG, mc)$.

Proof. In [10] it is proved that $REG \subseteq C(REG, int)$. Combine it with the previous theorem. $\square$

Theorem 5.

1. Every context-free language L can be represented as $L = h(L' \cap R)$, where h is a morphism, L' is a language in $C(FIN, mc)$ and R is a regular language.

2. Every recursively enumerable language L can be represented as $L = h(L' \cap R)$, where h is a morphism, L' is a language in $C(CS, mc)$ and R is a regular language.

Proof. The following contextual grammar with finite choice generates Dyck language of degree n, hence the first assertion holds from the known Chomsky-Schutzenberger representation of context-free languages:

$$G = (\{a_1, a_2, \ldots, a_n\} \cup \{b_1, b_2, \ldots, b_n\}, \{\lambda\},$$
$$(\{\lambda\}, \{(a_i, b_i) \mid 1 \le i \le n\} \cup \{(\lambda, \lambda)\})).$$

Now, let L be a recursively enumerable language; we have $L = h(L_1)$ where $L_1 \subseteq V^*$ is a context sensitive language.

Construct a contextual grammar with context sensitive choice as follows:

$$G = (V \cup \{c, d\}, \{c\}, (R_1, C_1), (R_2, C_2), (R_3, C_3))$$

where

$$R_1 = \{d\}L_1\{d\} \cup \{c\}, C_1 = \{(\lambda, a) \mid a \in V\},$$
$$R_2 = L_1, C_2 = \{(d, d)\} \cup \{(\lambda, a) \mid a \in V\},$$
$$R_3 = \{d\}, C_3 = \emptyset.$$

Obviously, $L_{mc}(G) = \{c\}V^* \cup \{c\}V^*\{d\}L_1\{d\}V^* \cup M$, where all strings in M contain more than two occurrences of the symbol d. If $R = \{cd\}V^*\{d\}$ and g is a morphism which erases the symbols c, d and does not modify the other letters of V then $L_1 = g(L_{mc}(G) \cap R)$. Because the composition of two morphisms is a morphism we conclude that $L = f(L_{mc}(G) \cap R)$, therefore the second assertion is also valid. $\square$

Conjecture. Every linear language is the homomorphic image of a language in $C(FIN, mc)$.

Theorem 6.   *There are linear languages which are not in the family $C(ARB, mc)$.*

Proof. Take the linear language

$$L = a^+ \cup b^+ \cup \{a^n b^n \mid n \ge 1\}.$$

Assume that $L_{mc} = L(G)$ for some $G = (\{a, b\}, B, (R_1, C_1), \ldots, (R_n, C_n))$ with arbitrary $R_i, 1 \le i \le n$.

If a context (a^{i_1}, a^{i_2}) appears in a set $C_j, 1 \leq j \leq n$, then we can replace it by $(\lambda, a^{i_1+i_2})$ and the generated language remains the same. Similarly for contexts of the form (b^{j_1}, b^{j_2}). Thus, without loss of generality we may assume that all contexts in the sets $C_j, 1 \leq j \leq n$, containing occurrences of a only or occurrences of b only are of the form $(\lambda, a^t), (\lambda, b^k), t, k \geq 1$.

As $a^+ \subset L$ and $b^+ \subset L$, there exist R_i, R_j such that $a^k \in R_i, b^r \in R_j$, $k, r \geq 1$.

We have the derivation

$$a^{kr} b^{kr} \implies a^{r(k+t)} b^{k(r+s)}$$

therefore, we must have $rt = ks$.

Assume that C_i contains also another context (λ, a^q). We conclude again that $rq = ks$, therefore $q = t$. In conclusion, C_i contains only one context of the form $(\lambda, a^t), t \geq 1$. The same argument is valid also for C_j and the context $(\lambda, b^s), s \geq 1$.

Suppose now that R_i contains a word a^p different from a^k. As $ps = rt$ it follows that $p = k$; we conclude that a^k is the only string of this form which belongs to R_i. Again, the same is true also for the string b^r and R_j.

Consider now all pairs (string, context) involving only occurrences of the symbol a and related by the pairs (R_i, C_i) in G, namely $(a^{k_q}, (\lambda, a^{t_q})), q = 1, 2, \ldots, m$ and similarly for the symbol b, consider all the pairs of the form $(b^{r_u}, (\lambda, b^{s_u})), u = 1, 2, \ldots, p$. Assume also that $k_1 < k_2 < \ldots < k_m$ and $r_1 < r_2 < \ldots < r_p$. By induction we shall prove that $m = p$ and $k_q = r_q, t_q = s_q$, for all $q = 1, 2, \ldots, m$.

If $k_1 < r_1$ then

$$a^{k_1} b^{k_1} \implies^{mc} a^{k_1+t_1} b^{k_1}$$

and $a^{k_1+t_1} b^{k_1}$ is not in L, contradiction. Hence $k_1 = r_1$ which implies $t_1 = s_1$.

Assume that $k_1 = r_1, k_2 = r_2, \ldots, k_q = r_q$ and $t_1 = s_1, t_2 = s_2, \ldots, t_q = s_q$. Suppose $k_{q+1} < r_{q+1}$ and consider the derivation

$$a^{k_1+\cdots+k_{q+1}} b^{k_1+\cdots+k_{q+1}} \implies^{mc}$$
$$\implies^{mc} a^{k_1+\cdots+k_{q+1}+t_1+t_2+\cdots+t_{q+1}} b^{k_1+\cdots+k_{q+1}+s_1+s_2+\cdots+s_q}.$$

By the induction assumption, $t_i = s_i, 1 \leq i \leq q$, hence the obtained string is not in L, again a contradiction. Therefore, $k_{q+1} = r_{q+1}$, which implies $t_{q+1} = s_{q+1}$. The induction argument is complete, hence $m = p$ and $k_q = r_q, t_q = s_q, q = 1, 2, \ldots, m$. If $k_q = k_1 \cdot c_q + d_q$ for some $c_q \geq 1, 0 \leq d_q < k_1$, then

$$a^{k_q} b^{k_q} \implies^{mc} a^{c_q(k_1+t_1)+d_q} b^{k_q+t_q}$$

which implies $c_q(k_1 + t_1) + d_q = k_1.c_q + d_q + t_q$, therefore $t_q = c_q t_1$. But $k_q.s_1 = t_q.r_1$ which leads to $d_q = 0$.

In conclusion, $k_q = c_q \cdot k_1, t_q = c_q \cdot t_1, q = 2, 3, \ldots, m$. In this case, the effect of all pairs $(a^{k_q}, (\lambda, a^{t_q}))$ can be simulated by the pair $(a^{k_1}, (\lambda, a^{t_1}))$. Therefore, we may assume that (R_i, C_i) is the only pair involving only occurrences of the symbol a. Now it is clear that G cannot produce all the strings $a^n, n \geq 1$ (and $b^n, n \geq 1$, too), a contradiction to the fact $a^+ \subset L$. The equality $L = L(G, mc)$ is impossible.

Note that the family of languages to which $R_1, R_2, \ldots, R_n$ belong plays no role in our proof. $\qquad\square$

Corollary. *The families $C(F, mc)$, for any F including FIN, are not closed under union, catenation and λ-free morphisms.*

Proof. The languages $L_1 = a^+ \cup b^+$ and $L_2 = \{a^n b^n \mid n \geq 1\}$ are in $C(FIN, mc)$, but $L_1 \cup L_2$ is not in $C(ARB, mc)$.

The language $L_2 \cup \{\lambda\}$ is also in $C(FIN, mc)$ but $(L_2 \cup \{\lambda\})L_1 = a^+ \cup b^+ \cup \{a^n b^n a^m, a^n b^n b^m \mid n, m \geq 1\}$ is not in $C(ARB, mc)$ (a similar argument as in the previous theorem).

The language $L = c^+ \cup d^+ \cup L_2$ can be generated by the contextual grammar

$$
\begin{aligned}
G \;=\; & (\{a, b, c, d\}, \{ab, c, d\}, (R_1, c_1), (R_2, C_2), (R_3, C_3)), \\
& R_1 = \{c\}, C_1 = \{(\lambda, \lambda), (\lambda, c)\}, \\
& R_2 = \{d\}, C_2 = \{(\lambda, \lambda), (\lambda, d)\}, \\
& R_3 = \{ab\}, C_3 = \{(a, b)\}.
\end{aligned}
$$

With the morphism h defined by $h(a) = h(c) = a, h(b) = h(d) = b$ we obtain $h(L) = a^+ \cup b^+ \cup \{a^n b^n \mid n \geq 1\}$, hence $h(L) \notin C(ARB, mc)$. $\qquad\square$

2. Decision problems

Theorem 7.

1. The emptiness problem is decidable for $C(F, mc)$, for any family of languages F.

2. The finiteness and the membership problem are decidable for $C(F, mc)$ if F is a family of languages included in REC.

Proof. For a contextual grammar with F choice $G = (V, B, (R_1, C_1), \ldots, (R_n, C_n))$, $L(G, mc) = \emptyset$ if and only if $B = \emptyset$ so the first assertion is immediate.

As for every derivation $x \Longrightarrow^{mc} y$, the strings in R_i appearing in x are still present in y, the derivation can continue. Therefore, $L_{mc}(G)$ is infinite if and only if $Sub(B) \cap \bigcup_{i=1}^{n} R_i \neq \emptyset$, where the union contains only the sets R_i such that $C_i \neq \{(\lambda, \lambda)\}$ and $Sub(B) = \bigcup_{x \in B} Sub(x)$.

As $Sub(B)$ is a finite set and a finite union of recursive languages is a recursive language, the finitness problem is decidable.

For a string w and a positive integer k define

$$D(w, k) = \{x \mid lg(x) \leq k, w \Longrightarrow^{mc} x\},$$

extend it to

$$D(A, k) = \bigcup_{w \in A} D(w, k),$$

and

$$D^0(A, k) = \{x \in A \mid lg(x) \leq k\},$$
$$D^{i+1}(A, k) = D(D^i(A, k), k), i \geq 1.$$

($D^i(A, k)$ is the set of all strings of length at most k which can be generated by G starting from strings in A and using at most i derivation steps $\Longrightarrow^{mc}$).

For a word $z \in V^+$ we have

$$z \in L_{mc}(G) \text{ iff } z \in \bigcup_{i=0}^{lg(z)} D^i(B, lg(z)).$$

At every step $\Longrightarrow^{mc}$ the length of the string is increased, excepting derivations using only contexts (λ, λ); skipping such derivations, for every $z \in L_{mc}(G)$ there is a derivation of length at most $lg(z)$.

As R_i are recursive sets, $D^i(B, lg(z))$ can be effectively computed, hence one can decide whether $z \in L_{mc}(G)$ or not. $\square$

Let $x = (x_1, x_2, \ldots, x_n)$ and $y = (y_1, y_2, \ldots, y_n)$ be two n-tuples of nonempty words over $\{a, b\}$.

Lemma 1. *The languages*

$$L(x) = \{ba^{i_k} \ldots ba^{i_1} c x_{i_1} \ldots x_{i_k} \mid k \geq 1, 1 \leq i_j \leq n\},$$

$$L(y) = \{ba^{i_k} \ldots ba^{i_1} c y_{i_1} \ldots y_{i_k} \mid k \geq 1, 1 \leq i_j \leq n\}$$

are in $C(FIN, mc)$.

Proof. The following contextual grammar generates $L(x)$

$$G = (\{a, b, c\}, \{ba^i c x_i \mid 1 \leq i \leq n\}, (\{c\}, \{(ba^i, x_i) \mid 1 \leq i \leq n\}))$$

hence $L(x)$ is in $C(FIN, mc)$. Similarly, $L(y) \in C(FIN, mc)$. $\square$

Theorem 8. *The following problems are undecidable for L_1, L_2 in $C(F, mc)$, F including the family FIN:*

1. $L_1 \cap L_2 = \emptyset$?
2. *Is $L_1 \cap L_2$ finite ?*
3. $L_1 \cap L_2 \in REG$?

Proof. Combine Post Correspondence Problem with Lemma 1.   □

Let G be a contextual grammar. Define

$$H_0(G, mc) = B,$$
$$H_{i+1}(G, mc) = \{y \in V^* \mid x \Longrightarrow^{mc} y, x \in H_i(G, mc)\}.$$

It is clear that $L_{mc}(G) = \bigcup_{k \geq 0} H_k(G, mc)$.

The *sequence equivalence problem* for contextual grammars with F choice and the mc-mode of derivation consists of deciding for an arbitrary pair (G_1, G_2) of contextual grammars, whether or not $H_i(G_1, mc) = H_i(G_2, mc)$. The language equivalence problem asks whether or not $L_{mc}(G_1) = L_{mc}(G_2)$.

Theorem 9. *For any family of languages including FIN, if the language equivalence problem is decidable for grammars with F choice, then the sequence equivalence problem is decidable for such grammars.*

Proof. Given a pair (G_1, G_2) of contextual grammars with F choice

$$G_1 = (V, B_1, (R_1^1, C_1^1), \ldots, (R_n^1, C_n^1)),$$
$$G_2 = (V, B_2, (R_1^2, C_1^2), \ldots, (R_m^2, C_m^2)),$$

construct two new contextual grammars with F choice

$$G_1' = (V \cup \{c, d\}, \{d\}B_1, (R_1^1, C_1^1), \ldots, (R_n^1, C_n^1), (\{d\}, \{(c, \lambda)\})),$$
$$G_2' = (V \cup \{c, d\}, \{d\}B_2, (R_1^2, C_1^2), \ldots, (R_m^2, C_m^2), (\{d\}, \{(c, \lambda)\})),$$

where c and d are two new letters.

Clearly,

$$H_k(G_i', mc) = \{c^k d\}H_k(G_i, mc), i = 1, 2, k = 0, 1, \ldots$$

and thus $L_{mc}(G_1') = L_{mc}(G_2')$ iff $H_k(G_1', mc) = H_k(G_2', mc)$ which is equivalent to $H_k(G_1, mc) = H_k(G_2, mc), k = 0, 1, \ldots$ □

Open problems

1. Can the language equivalence problem be reduced to the sequence equivalence problem?

2. Which of these problems is decidable for a given family F ?

3. The degree of parallelism

If $x \in L_{mc}(G)$ then we have either $x \in B$ or x can be obtained from a finite number of words in $L_{mc}(G)$ by a derivation step.

A natural dynamic measure of the syntactical complexity for a word x is the smallest number of subwords in which a string in $L_{mc}(G)$ has to be splitted in order to obtain x. This number will be called *the degree of parallelism* associated to x.

Formally, for a contextual grammar $G = (V, B, (R_1, C_1), \ldots, (R_n, C_n))$ and $x \in L_{mc}(G)$ we define the degree of parallelism as follows:

$$pd_G(x) = min\{k \mid \text{there exists } y \in L_{mc}(G)$$
$$\text{such that } y \Longrightarrow^{mc} x \text{ by adjoining } k \text{ contexts}\},$$

$$pd(G) = sup\{pd_G(x) \mid x \in L_{mc}(G)\},$$

$$pd(L) = inf\{pd(G) \mid L = L_{mc}(G)\}.$$

Lemma 2. *If $pd(L) = k$ then exist two constants $p, q > 0$ such that for each $z \in L, lg(z) > p$, the following conditions hold:*

$$(i) \qquad z = z_1 u_1 x_1 v_1 z_2 u_2 x_2 v_2 \ldots z_t u_t x_t v_t z_{t+1}, \textit{ for some } 1 \le t \le k,$$

$$(ii) \qquad z_1 x_1 z_2 x_2 \ldots z_t x_t z_{t+1} \in L,$$

$$(iii) \qquad 0 \le lg(u_i v_i) \le q, 1 \le i \le t,$$

$$(iv) \qquad lg(u_1 v_1 u_2 v_2 \ldots u_t v_t) > 0.$$

Proof. Let $G = (V, B, (R_1, C_1), \ldots, (R_n, C_n))$ be a contextual grammar with $L_{mc}(G) = L$ and $pd(G) = k$. Take

$$p = max\{lg(x) \mid x \in B\},$$
$$q = max\{lg(uv) \mid (u, v) \in C_i, 1 \le i \le n\}.$$

If $z \in L, lg(x) > p$, then there exits $y \in L$ such that $y \Longrightarrow^{mc} z$ by adjoining at most k contexts. Suppose that $y = z_1 x_1 z_2 x_2 \ldots z_t x_t z_{t+1}, t \le k$, and $z = z_1 u_1 x_1 v_1 z_2 u_2 x_2 v_2 \ldots z_t u_t x_t v_t z_{t+1}, x_j \in R_{i_j}, (u_j, v_j) \in C_{i_j}, 1 \le j \le t, 1 \le i_j \le n$. Obviously, we have $(u_j, v_j) \ne (\lambda, \lambda)$ for some $1 \le j \le t$.

Thus, all conditions of our lemma are fulfilled. $\qquad\qquad\square$

Theorem 10.

1. For any nonnegative integer n exists a language L in $C(F, mc), FIN \subseteq F$, such that $pd(L) = n$.

2. There exists a language $L \in C(F, mc), FIN \subseteq F$, such that $pd(L) = \infty$. (In other words the measure pd is connected.)

Proof. For the first assertion let us consider the language $L = \{a_1^k a_2^k \ldots a_{2n-1}^k\, a_{2n}^k \mid k \geq 1\}$. From Lemma 2 we cannot have $pd(L) < n$. On the other hand, the following contextual grammar with finite choice generates L:

$$
\begin{aligned}
G &= (V, B, (R_1, C_1), \ldots, (R_n, C_n)), \\
V &= \{a_1, a_2, \ldots, a_{2n}\}, \\
B &= \{a_1 a_2 \ldots a_{2n}\}, \\
R_i &= \{a_{2i-1} a_{2i}\},\, C_i = \{(a_{2i-1}, a_{2i})\}, i = 1, 2, \ldots, n.
\end{aligned}
$$

As one can easily see, $pd(G) = n$, therefore $pd(L) = n$.

Now, consider $L = a^{2^n} \mid n \geq 1 \in C(FIN, mc)$. Assume that $pd(L) = k$, for some k. Take $a^{2^n} \in L$ with $2^n > p$ and $2^{n-1} > kq$, where p and q are the constants associated to L as in Lemma 2. From the condition (ii) of Lemma 2 we obtain that $a^r \in L$, for some r such that $2^{n-1} < r < 2^n$, contradiction. In conclusion, $pd(L) = \infty$. $\qquad\square$

Theorem 11. *The measure pd is not computable for contextual grammars with F choice, F including the family of linear languages.*

Proof. Let $x = (x_1, x_2, \ldots, x_n)$ and $y = (y_1, y_2, \ldots, y_n)$ be two n-tuples of nonempty words over $\{a, b\}$. The language $L(y)$ is a linear one. If

$$
G = (\{a, b, c, d\}, \{c\}, (\{c\}, \{(ba^i, x_i) \mid 1 \leq i \leq n\}), (L(y) \cup \{d\}, \{(\lambda, d)\})),
$$

then $pd(G)$ is finite if and only if $pd(G) = 1$, hence if and only if the Post's Correspondence Problem has no solution for x, y which is undecidable. Therefore, $pd(G)$ is not computable for the above G.

Note that G has linear choice. $\qquad\square$

Corollary. *The measure pd is not computable for the family $C(F, mc)$, F including the family of linear languages.*

Open problems

1. What is the status of this measure for contextual grammars with finite or regular choice ?

2. Is it true that for every contextual grammar G with a finite degree of parallelism, the language $L_{mc}(G)$ is semilinear ?

References

1. S. Istrail, Contextual grammars with regulated selection, *Stud. Cerc. Matem.*, 30, 3 (1978), 287 – 294.

2. S. Marcus, *Algebraic Linguistics. Analytical Models*, Academic Press, New York, 1967.

3. S. Marcus, Contextual grammars, *Rev. Roum. Math. Pures Appl.*, 14, 10 (1969), 1525 – 1534.

4. S. Marcus, Deux types nouveaux de grammaires generatives, *Cah. Ling. Th. Appl.*, 6 (1969), 69 – 74.

5. Gh. Păun, *Contextual Grammars*, The Publ. House of the Romanian Academy of Sciences, Bucureşti, 1982 (in Romanian).

6. Gh. Păun, Marcus contextual grammars. After 25 years. *Bull. EATCS*, 52 (February 1994), 263 – 273.

7. Gh. Păun, X. M. Nguyen, On the inner contextual grammar, *Rev. Roum. Math. Pures Appl.*, 25, 4 (1980), 641 – 651.

8. Gh. Păun, G. Rozenberg, A. Salomaa, Contextual grammars: parallelism and blocking of derivations, *Fund. Inform.*, to appear.

9. A. Salomaa, *Formal Languages*, Academic Press, New York, London, 1973.

10. S. Vicolov, Two theorems about Marcus contextual languages, *Bull. Math. Soc. Sci. Math. Roumanie*, 35, 1-2 (1991), 167 – 170.

Computing Natural Language Presuppositions:
A Partial Information Logic Based Approach

M. Areshi NAIT ABDALLAH

Department of Computer Science, The University of Western Ontario
London, Ontario, N6A 5B7 Canada

Abstract. Natural language presuppositions are approached from
the point of view of partial information logic. Partial information
logic was specifically designed for the needs of reasoning in partially
described contexts, and formalizes Popper and Lakatos' dichotomy
between hard knowledge and soft knowledge. This dichotomy is at
the basis of the formal mathematical definition of presuppositions
given in this paper. This definition induces a simple algorithm for
generating, in a uniform way, the appropriate natural language presuppositions of compound sentences, as well as the corresponding
existential presuppositions. We thus reduces the problem of generating natural language presuppositions to the simpler problem of
translating natural language statements into ionic logic.

1. Introduction

The problem of generating natural language presuppositions has been discussed by many authors from the natural language literature (e.g. [2], [4], [17])
who have presented various pragmatic approaches.

We present here a new approach that is based on the formal semantics of
partial information logic [10]. The algorithm we suggest for generating the
presuppositions of a given natural language statement is obtained as a by-
product of the general method for constructing models of a given set of ionic
formulae. The method uses Beth tableaux [14]. We show that, for a large class
of natural language statements, our method yields the appropriate results.

The paper is organized as follows. The general problem of generating
presuppositions for natural language statements is outlined in Section 2. In
Section 3 we give an overview of the framework of partial information logic.
Section 4 presents our formal definition of the presuppositions of a given set
of ionic formulae. Computing these presuppositions requires using the tableau
method introduced in Section 3. Various examples are discussed to illustrate
our approach. Section 5.1 shows how to compute the presuppositions of complex natural language sentences of the form *"Possibly A"* as well as disjunctive

and conditional sentences. In other words our method solves the projection problem (see e.g. [2], [17]) for these constructions. Section 5.2 shows that our method also computes the correct existential presuppositions for some classes of natural language statements. Section 6 points out some open problems.

2. Presuppositions and partial information logic

Consider the following example:

1. Mozart died in misery.

2. Mozart did not die in misery.

To be able to assign truth values to either 1 or 2 presupposes that there is some individual that is identical with the object named by the string "Mozart." In other words, *"the name 'Mozart' has a denotation"* is a presupposition. According to Frege [1], the truth of the presupposition is a necessary condition for either 1 or 2 to make an assertion, i.e. say something that has a truth value. In other words, *the satisfaction of a presupposition is a precondition for a sentence to have a truth value.*

Consider now the following example.

1. The present king of France is bald.

2. The present king of France is not bald.

From either sentence one intuitively infers that there is a present king of France (this is an existential presupposition). Following Russell's theory of definite descriptions [13], the first-order logic translation of the the first sentence is given by:

$$\exists x.((KFx \wedge \forall y(KFy \rightarrow x = y)) \wedge Bx)$$

Russell analyzes a sentence with a referring expression as a conjunction that contains the presupposition. Thus Frege's distinction between assertion and presupposition has disappeared in Russell's theory.

Strawson's [16] analysis goes back to Frege's. For him, presupposition is a purely logical phenomenon. The truth of the presuppositions of a sentence is a condition for the possibility of making an assertion by means of that sentence. The following definition is introduced [15]:

> *A statement S presupposes a statement φ if and only if the truth of φ is a necessary condition for the truth or falsity of S.*

The authors in the natural language literature (e.g. [4], [18]) sharply distinguish between presuppositions and entailments. Entailments are logical consequences of the statement under consideration: they must be true in every model of the statement. Presuppositions constitute defeasible information, whereas entailments are never defeasible. Thus, from the point of view of ionic logic [10] (see below), entailments correspond to *hard information* in the sense of Popper and Lakatos [6], [11], whereas presuppositions constitute *soft information*. We claim that this dichotomy between hard and soft knowledge is what is missing from Russell's analysis.

For example, from statement *"My cousin is not a bachelor"* one may pull the soft conclusion that "my cousin is a male and an adult." Such a soft conclusion is a presupposition. Upon receiving the incoming hard information *"My cousin is a five year-old boy,"* the new logical theory does not collapse into inconsistency, but, rather, the soft conclusion "my cousin is an adult" is withdrawn in view of contradicting evidence.

2.1. Defining a formal notion of presupposition in partial information logic

The Strawsonian approach is used here. The natural language statements will be translated into ionic logic. The information conveyed by a sentence S will be represented by some set Φ of ionic formulae. Each of the concepts called upon in Strawson's definition is formalized in the framework of ionic logic. These concepts are (i) the notion of truth to be used and (ii) the choice of models where the truth of S is to be evaluated.

The *notion of truth to be used* is of paramount importance. From the point of view of ionic logic, presuppositions are *soft, defeasible* information. Consider for example, the following statement:

My cousin is not a bachelor.

It has as a presupposition that my cousin is a male adult. This "intuitive" understanding of the utterance will correspond to a certain class C of partial models of the world, where my cousin is a male and an adult. Assume now that the above natural language statement is made more precise by adding that

He is only five years old.

Then the presupposition that *"my cousin is an adult"* must be withdrawn: the soft information *"my cousin is an adult"* must give way to the hard information that *"he is five years old,"* since five years-old people are not adults. From the model-theoretic point of view, adding the new information does not lead to any inconsistency. Such an inconsistency would be the case if one were to force the models in C above to satisfy the fact that my cousin is a non-adult. Instead, C is replaced by a new class C'. This means that:

- Neither C nor C' exhaust the set of *all* models of the initial utterance "*My cousin is a bachelor.*" Classes C and C' only include those models that are trying to make the best possible use of the partial information available. (These "preferred" models are called "minimal" in the terminology of this paper.)

- To formalize the dichotomy between defeasible inferences and hard, non-defeasible, ones, one must use the ionic logic dichotomy between soft truth and hard truth [8].

Making the *class of models to be considered* more precise requires clarifying the mathematical foundations of our approach.

3. Mathematical foundations

The *logic of partial information* (or *ionic logic*) developed in [7], [8], [9], [10] is essentially classical logic augmented with contexts. The purpose of this logic is to allow one to do reasoning with partial information as well as with tentative information. The basic difference with classical logic is that one now has gaps in the information being made available to the reasoner. A rigorous exposition can be found in [10]. We shall limit ourselves here to giving some intuition and motivations for the concepts and definitions used in this paper.

3.1. Propositional partial information ionic logic

Propositional partial information ionic logic is defined as follows. We extend the alphabet of partial propositional logic, and consider an infinite enumerable set P of propositional variables together with the single higher-order binary operator (we call *partial information ionic operator*), $\star(\ .\ ,\ .\ )$ and the usual set of connectives. In essence, the set of formulae of *propositional partial information ionic logic* (partial information ionic formulae) is the smallest set such that:

1. Each propositional variable or logical constant is a formula.

2. The set of formulae is closed under the propositional logic connectives.

3. The set of ionic formulae is closed under the ionic operator: for every formulae φ_1 and φ_2, the expression $\star(\varphi_1, \varphi_2)$ is a formula, called *partial information ion*.

Ion $\star(\varphi, \varphi)$ will be abbreviated as $[\varphi]$.

3.1.1. Hard knowledge, soft knowledge and justification knowledge

The intent of ionic operator $\star$ is to express statements of the form "*if φ_1 is good enough, i.e. is an acceptable justification, then φ_2 is somewhat true.*" This corresponds to ion $\star(\varphi_1, \varphi_2)$.

By definition, φ_1 *is an acceptable justification* means that φ_1 belongs to the current justification knowledge[1] $Th(+\star)(i)$, and φ_2 is somewhat true means that φ_2 belongs to the current soft knowledge.

In ionic logic, one is concerned with how the world should look according to the partial description (information) provided by the ionic formulae at hand. Ions are taken as "gap-filling" devices that attempt to fill-in some of the missing information one would like to have about the world. The *soft* added information is there to complete the *hard* information already supplied by the classical logic formulae already available, but should not be confused with it. As an example, one does not attach the same credibility to the statement of Pythagoras's theorem as to the statements of the weather forecast service. Pythagoras's theorem is hard information, whereas the weather forecast statements are soft information. The soft information is only there because some *justifications* have been deemed to be acceptable, although this might change, depending on incoming new information. This leads us to introducing the notion of an *ionic interpretation* as a 3-component object (i_0, J, i_1), where i_0 and i_1 are partial propositional interpretations that respectively represent the *hard knowledge* and the *soft knowledge*, and J is the set of "expectations" (interpretations that are expected values of the world) representing the *justification knowledge*. Ionic interpretations are partially ordered via the information ordering $\sqsubseteq$. This separation of knowledge into three components (hard, soft and justification knowledge) generalizes and refines Popper and Lakatos' [6], [11] dichotomy between hard knowledge and soft knowledge.

In partial information logic, definitions of two notions of truth are required: truth $\models$ and *potential truth* (i.e. non-falsehood) $|\!\models$. There is also a dichotomy between *(plain) truth* and *soft truth,* depending on whether, in the evaluation of the truth of a formula, one calls upon the *soft* knowledge part i_1 of the ionic interpretation (i_0, J, i_1).

To sum up, in essence, the semantic status of a formula φ under some given ionic interpretation i may be any one of the following:

1. true (respectively false), denoted by $\models \varphi$ (respectively $|\!\models \varphi$). This corresponds to the usual notion of truth. This is called *hard knowledge.*

2. true in a soft sense (respectively false in a soft sense), denoted by $\models_{soft} \varphi$ (respectively $|\!\models_{soft} \varphi$). This akin to the previous case, but now these

---

[1] The definition of $Th(+\star)(i)$ is discussed later in this section.

values are defeasible ("soft"). This is called *soft knowledge* and expresses our set of conjectures as to what is the case in the real world.

3. acceptable (respectively unacceptable), denoted by $+\star\varphi$ (respectively $-\star\varphi$). This corresponds to the expectations one has about the world, i.e. which justifications one is ready to accept (respectively reject). This is called *justification knowledge* and expresses our set of "prejudices" as to what is the case in the real world.

Given an interpretation i, one defines as in classical logic the theory $Th(\models)(i)$ of i, i.e. the class of formulae satisfied by i:

$$Th(\models)(i) = \{\varphi : i \models \varphi\}.$$

This notion is generalized in partial information logic by allowing potential satisfaction $\|\!\models$ as well as satisfaction $\models$, and also weaker varieties of truth such as acceptability as a justification, and weaker varieties of falsehood such as unacceptability as a justification. This leads to sets such as:

$$Th(\models_{soft})(i) = \{\varphi : i \text{ satisfies } \varphi \text{ in a soft sense}\}.$$

Since every formula that is true is also true in a soft sense, the difference set $Th(\models_{soft})(i) \setminus Th(\models)(i)$ constitutes the amount of intrinsically (positive, i.e. true) *soft* knowledge that is conveyed by ionic interpretation i. As discussed below, this fact will be at the basis of our approach to the formalization of natural language presuppositions.

One also has from the point of view of justifications:

$$Th(+\star)(i) = \{\varphi : i \text{ accepts justification } \varphi\},$$
$$Th(-\star)(i) = \{\varphi : i \text{ rejects justification } \varphi\},$$

3.1.2. The preferred models and how to compute them

The *justification ordering* between two ionic interpretations i and i' is defined by saying that $i \leq_{\star p} i'$ if and only if i accepts more justifications than i', and i refuses less justifications than i'. The $\leq_{\star p}$-minimal models of some set Φ of ionic formulae are in some sense the "maximally optimistic" ones, since they accept a maximum amount, and reject a minimum amount, of justifications. Thus they make an "optimal" (or "maximum") use of the default information that is provided by the ions.

An ionic interpretation m is a $\sqsubseteq$-*minimal model* of a set of ionic formulae Φ if and only if $m \models \Phi$ and $\forall m'$ such that $m' \sqsubseteq m$ and $m' \models \Phi$ one has $m = m'$. Recall that $\sqsubseteq$ is the information ordering.

An ionic interpretation m is a *minimal model* of a set of ionic formulae Φ if and only if m is a $\sqsubseteq$-*minimal model* of Φ and m is $\leq_{\star p}$-minimal among all models of Φ. For the purpose of this paper, the *preferred models* will be the minimal models.

The tool used here for reasoning with partial information ionic formulae are Beth tableaux. These tableaux extend the ones for classical propositional logic [14]. The generalization is essentially obtained by adding the tableau rules for the ions. The rule in figure 1 is the counterpart of the semantic definition of truth of ions given earlier.

$$\frac{\models \star(\varphi_1, \varphi_2)}{\begin{array}{cc} +\star\varphi_1 & -\star\varphi_1 \\ \models_{soft} \varphi_2 & \end{array}}$$

Fig. 1: Beth tableau for plain truth of partial information ions

Ion $\star(\varphi_1, \varphi_2)$ is true if its justification φ_1 is rejected (i.e. $-\star\varphi_1$) or if its justification is accepted (i.e. $+\star\varphi_1$) and its conclusion φ_2 is true in a soft sense (i.e. $\models_{soft} \varphi_2$).

Open branches of Beth tableaux yield *patterns* $< \alpha, \Phi^\varepsilon, \beta >$, where α represents the kernel knowledge, β represents the belt knowledge, and Φ^ε represents the justification knowledge. To obtain models for the theory one started from, one must find some ionic interpretations $i = (i_0, J, i_1)$ such that, roughly speaking, i_0 satisfies α, i_0 put together with i_1 satisfy β, and $\Phi^\varepsilon \subseteq Th(+\star)(i) \cup Th(-\star)(i)$. Actually, since the interpretations considered here are all partial, more than one interpretation may satisfy a given pattern. i.e. may provide a model of the initial set of formulae. The pattern being fixed, the set of all interpretations satisfying this pattern constitute a *model scheme*.

In this paper, we use the following indented linear representation for Beth trees. Nodes in the tree will be represented by lines of text. Each node occupies a single line. Multiple signed formulae belonging to the same node will be separated by commas. When a line is too long, we split it and mark the splitting point by the symbol &. Depth in the tree will be represented by indentation. If two lines have the same indentation, this means that they represent nodes with the same depth. A given line will be indented with respect to a previous line if and only if the node it represents is a descendant of the node represented by the previous line. If a tree has a left and a right subtree, then the set of lines corresponding to the left subtree will be above the set of lines corresponding to the right subtree.

3.2. First-order partial information ionic logic and the computation of existence presuppositions

First-order partial information ionic logic is a generalization of both classical first-order logic with equality and propositional ionic logic. Information gaps are now present in the definitions of the meaning of variables, constants, function and relation symbols. The presence of an equality predicate in the logic modifies in depth the structure of the logic. This is because the equality predicate allows the *existence* of an object to be represented, e.g.:

$$\exists x \,.\, x = a$$

means that object a exists ("There exists some object that is identical to the value named by a.") This is an application of Quine's thesis [12]: *"To be is to be the value of a bound variable."* The partialness of our logic means that not every object exists. The ionic nature of our logic implies that one has two notions of existence: existence in the sense of hard knowledge, and existence in the sense of soft knowledge.

The (hard knowledge) existence of object d is represented by $\models (d = d)$. The semantic treatment of the equality predicate $=$ along the lines of truth *versus* potential truth already discussed earlier, leads to the introduction of a new kind of objects, *fictions,* which are some kind of potential objects, satisfying $|\models (d = d)$. In the example

Achilles likes Briseis. Achilles and Briseis don't exist.

both Achilles and Briseis are fictions. Fictions are not "absence of information", they are a different kind of information, i.e. *potential objects.*

The remarkable feature is that the equality predicate separates between actual objects, but does not separate between fictions, i.e. from the point of view of the equality relation, fictions are indistinguishable from each other, and from the undefined. This is some kind of nominalistic view of being an actual object. This is reminiscent of the undistinguishability of Turing machines by means of another Turing machine, and also of the non-computability of the equality relation in the semantics of programming languages.

Since one can only assert the existence of actual objects (the statement *"Snow White exists"* is meaningless as far as reality is concerned), existential quantification ranges over actual objects only. On the other hand, universal quantification ranges over actual objects and fictions. In the example *"Birds fly. The phoenix is a bird."* we still infer that *"The phoenix flies"* even though we know that *"The phoenix is a fiction."* Hence, one has two kinds of quantifications: actual quantification $\forall^a$ and $\exists^a$ (over actual objects), and "potential" quantification $\forall^p$ and $\exists^p$ (over actual objects and fictions.) Thus the logical treatment of quantification (definition of truth, tableaux, etc.) is duplicated along two lines: actual and potential quantification. From an axiomatic point of view, the partialness of the logic forces one to make the *existential presuppositions* (in the sense of Hintikka [5]) about the objects one is reasoning about, *explicit* in the reasoning process. To express the soft knowledge that there is some actual object whose name is d, one uses *existential ion* $\star(\exists^a u(u = d), \exists^a u(u = d))$. In partial information logic, every object is a potential object, and a central issue in the reasoning process is: how does one make some of these potential objects into soft, i.e. conjectural, actual objects by accepting some suitable justification. (An analogy in the field of physics is as follows: under which suitable theoretical and experimential justifications would gravitons (some class of potential objects) exist as conjectural, actual objects belonging to the real world.)

4. A semantic definition of presuppositions

In the framework of partial information logic, to accommodate the definition of presuppositions given by Strawson [15], one must call upon the fundamental principle of the statics of logic systems [10] (Chap. 10): this principle says that one is not interested in all the models, but only in the *minimal* ones. These are the *preferred* models. Following this fundamental principle, we interpret "being a necessary condition for the truth or falsity of $\mathcal{S}$" as "being true in a soft sense in every preferred, i.e. minimal, model of $\mathcal{S}$." Adopting such a view has two advantages:

1. Strawson's requirement of "being a necessary condition for the truth or falsity of $\mathcal{S}$" is met.

2. The defeasibility of presuppositions is ensured by the "softness" of the information. Soft information may be cancelled by any contradicting hard information that may be received later on.

Since the *class of models to be considered* is obtained via the application of the universal principle of the statics of logic systems, interpretations i get restricted to minimal models (maximally optimistic ones). This restriction is, to some extent, a formal counterpart of the linguistic notion of Grice's *cooperation principle* [3]. Grice's cooperation principle includes the following requirements:

- Make your contribution as informative as possible.
- Do not make your contribution more informative than is required.
- Be brief.

The issue of which preorder to take in order to evaluate the minimality is settled empirically, and the solution adopted below corresponds to the *justification ordering*.

Intuitively, the presuppositions of a given utterance will be defined as the intrinsically soft information that is contained in all "maximally optimistic" models of the utterance.

Definition: Let Φ be a set of ionic formulae. Let φ some formula. We say that φ is a *presupposition* of Φ provided that φ bel ongs to the difference set $(\Phi) \setminus H(\Phi)$ where:

- $S(\Phi) = \cap \{ Th(\models_{soft})(m) : m$ minimal model of $\Phi \}$ is the set of statements that are true in a soft sense in all minimal models of Φ, where minimality of models means minimal in both the information ordering and the justification ordering.

- $H(\Phi) = \cap \{ Th(\models)(m) : m \models \Phi \}$ is the set of statements that are true in all models of Φ.

One can see that $H(\Phi)$ is the set of all logical consequences of Φ (the entailments of Φ). Also, $S(\Phi)$ is the set of all (optimistic) soft logical consequences of Φ. Intuitively, set $S(\Phi)$ represents the soft information that is conveyed by a "maximally optimistic" interpretation of Φ (interpretation is meant here in an informal sense). On the other hand, set $H(\Phi)$ represents the hard information that is carried by Φ. Thus the presuppositions are exactly the difference $S(\Phi) \setminus H(\Phi)$ between what is soft and what is hard. Another way to put it is to say that the presuppositions are all the "optimistic" soft logical consequences of Φ that are not entailments.

The above definition is now applied to the derivation of natural language presuppositions as follows. One first translates the given natural language statements into ionic logic. This yields a set of ionic formulae Φ. One then uses the above definition to compute the presuppositions of Φ.

We show in this paper various classes of natural language statements for which the presuppositions thus computed coincide with the intuitively derived natural language presuppositions. Since the formal computation of presuppositions is purely algorithmic, the difficulty of generating natural language presuppositions for these classes is thus reduced to that of correctly translating natural language statements into partial information ionic logic. Any natural language statement that is correctly translatable into ionic logic falls under the scope of our method.

Example: Let S be the statement *"My cousin is not a bachelor."* One intuitively derives the presuppositions that my cousin is both an adult and a male. We now show that these are obtained by means of the above definition. The set Φ of ionic formulae corresponding to this sentence is given by:

$$\neg bachelor$$
$$bachelor \leftrightarrow male \wedge adult \wedge \neg married$$
$$\neg bachelor \rightarrow [male]$$
$$\neg bachelor \rightarrow [adult]$$

This yields the tableau in figure 2.

$\models \neg bachelor, \models bachelor \leftrightarrow adult \wedge male \wedge \neg married, \models \neg bachelor \rightarrow \&$
$\qquad \&[male], \models \neg bachelor \rightarrow [adult]$
$\quad |\not\models bachelor, \quad \models [male], \quad \models [adult], \quad |\not\models (male \wedge adult \wedge \neg married)$
$\qquad -\star male$
$\qquad\qquad -\star adult$
$\qquad\qquad\quad |\not\models male$
$\qquad\qquad\quad |\not\models adult$
$\qquad\qquad\quad \models married$
$\qquad\qquad +\star adult \quad , \quad \models_{soft} adult$
$\qquad\qquad\quad |\not\models (male \wedge \neg married)$
$\qquad\qquad\qquad |\not\models male$
$\qquad\qquad\qquad \models married$
$\qquad +\star male \quad , \quad \models_{soft} male$
$\qquad\qquad -\star adult$
$\qquad\qquad\quad |\not\models (adult \wedge \neg married)$
$\qquad\qquad\qquad |\not\models adult$
$\qquad\qquad\qquad \models married$
$\qquad\qquad +\star adult \quad , \quad \models_{soft} adult$
$\qquad\qquad\quad |\not\models \neg married$
$\qquad\qquad\qquad \models married$

Fig. 2: My cousin in not a bachelor

Whence the following eight patterns.

$|\not\models bachelor, \; |\not\models adult, \; -\star adult, \; -\star male$
$|\not\models bachelor, \; |\not\models male, \; -\star adult, \; -\star male$
$|\not\models bachelor, \; \models married, \; -\star adult, \; -\star male$
$|\not\models bachelor, \; |\not\models male, \; +\star adult, \; -\star male, \; \models_{soft} adult$
$|\not\models bachelor, \; \models married, \; +\star adult, \; -\star male, \; \models_{soft} adult$
$|\not\models bachelor, \; |\not\models adult, \; -\star adult, \; +\star male, \; \models_{soft} male$
$|\not\models bachelor, \; \models married, \; -\star adult, \; +\star male, \; \models_{soft} male$
$|\not\models bachelor, \; \models married, \; +\star adult, \; +\star male, \; \models_{soft} adult, \models_{soft} male$

The last pattern listed above yields the unique minimal model m_8. Thus $S(\Phi) = Th(\models_{soft})(m_8)$, and $adult, male \in S(\Phi)$. Also $adult, male \notin H(\Phi)$, since, e.g. $m_1 \not\models male$ and $m_1 \not\models adult$, where m_1 is the $\sqsubseteq$-minimal model yielded by the first pattern. Whence $male$ and $adult$, i.e. the properties "*My cousin is male*" and "*My cousin is adult,*" are presuppositions of Φ.

Example: Consider utterance S given by "*Mary stopped beating the rug.*" Intuitively, there are no presuppositions that can be derived. The corresponding set of ionic formulae Φ is:

$$(\forall xy.stop(x,y) \to \exists t.(t \leq t_0) \land do(x,y,t)) \ , \ \ stop(mary, beat\_rug)$$

where *beat_rug* denotes the action of beating the rug. This yields the tableau in figure 3.

$$\models \forall xy.stop(x,y) \to \exists t.(t \leq t_0) \land do(x,y,t) \ , \ \ \models stop(mary, beat\_rug)$$
$$\models stop(mary, beat\_rug) \to \exists t.(t \leq t_0) \land do(mary, beat\_rug, t)$$
$$\models \exists t.(t \leq t_0) \land do(mary, beat\_rug, t)$$

Fig. 3: Mary stopped beating the rug

Clearly, for this example, since no soft information appears in the tableau,

$$\cap\{Th(\models_{soft})(m) : \ m \text{ minimal model of } \Phi\} = \cap\{Th(\models)(m) : \ m \models \Phi\}$$

i.e. $S(\Phi) = H(\Phi)$. Therefore, there are no presuppositions.

Example: Consider utterance *"Mary did not stop beating the rug."* Intuitively, one derives the presupposition that *"Mary was beating the rug."* The corresponding set of ionic formulae Φ is:

$$\forall xy.stop(x,y) \to \exists t.(t \leq t_0) \land do(x,y,t)$$
$$\forall xy.\neg stop(x,y) \to [\exists t.(t \leq t_0) \land do(x,y,t)]$$
$$\neg stop(mary, a)$$

where a denotes the action of beating the rug. We get the tableau in figure 4.

$$\models \forall xy.stop(x,y) \to \exists t.(t \leq t_0) \land do(x,y,t) \ , \ \ \forall xy.\neg stop(x,y) \to \&$$
$$\&[\exists t.(t \leq t_0) \land do(x,y,t)], \ \ |\not\models stop(mary, a)$$
$$\models \neg stop(mary, a) \to [\exists t.(t \leq t_0) \land do(mary, a, t)]$$
$$\models stop(mary, a) \text{ closed}$$
$$\models [\exists t.(t \leq t_0) \land do(mary, a, t)]$$
$$-\star \exists t.(t \leq t_0) \land do(mary, a, t)$$
$$+\star \exists t.(t \leq t_0) \land do(mary, a, t), \models_{soft} \exists t.(t \leq t_0) \land do(mary, a, t)$$
$$\models_{soft} (\theta \leq t_0) \land do(mary, a, \theta)$$
$$\text{for some new constant } \theta \text{ such that } \models_{soft} (\theta = \theta)$$

Fig. 4: Mary did not stop beating the rug

There is a unique model scheme that is minimal for the justification ordering. It is given by

"hard part"	$\not\models stop(mary, a)$
"justification part"	$+\star \exists t.(t \le t_0) \wedge do(mary, a, t)$
"soft part"	$\models_{soft} (\theta \le t_0), \models_{soft} do(mary, a, \theta)$
"soft objects"	$\models_{soft} (\theta = \theta)$

Clearly, formula $\exists t.(t \le t_0) \wedge do(mary, a, t)$ is true in a soft sense in that model scheme, and is a presupposition of Φ. The soft actual object θ here is some time θ at which Mary has been beating the rug.

Example: Consider the utterance: *"John regrets that Mary came to the party."* Intuitively, one derives no presupposition. The set Φ of ionic formulae corresponding to the utterance is:[2]

$$regret(john, come(mary, party)) \quad , \quad \forall xyz.regret(x, come(y, z)) \rightarrow come(y, z)$$

To simplify things, we assume that the predicates are correctly typed, so as to avoid the construction of meaningless formulae such as $come(party, mary)$. By simply examining the syntax of Φ, since Φ contains no partial information ion, constructing its $\sqsubseteq$-minimal models will generate no soft information. Hence Φ has no presupposition.

Example. Consider the utterance: *"John does not regret that Mary came to the party."* The intuitively derived presupposition is that *"Mary came to the party."* The set of ionic formulae corresponding to this utterance is:

$$\neg regret(john, come(mary, party))$$
$$\forall xyz.regret(x, come(y, z)) \rightarrow come(y, z)$$
$$\forall xyz.\neg regret(x, come(y, z)) \rightarrow [come(y, z)]$$

This yields the tableau in figure 5.

$$\models \neg regret(john, come(mary, party)) \quad , \quad \models \forall xyz.regret(x, come(y, z)) \ \&$$
$$\& \rightarrow come(y, z) \ldots \quad , \quad \models \forall xyz.\neg regret(x, come(y, z)) \&$$
$$\& \rightarrow [come(y, z)]$$
$$\models \neg regret(john, come(mary, party)) \rightarrow [come(mary, party)]$$
$$\models regret(john, come(mary, party)) \text{ closed}$$
$$\models [come(mary, party)]$$
$$-\star come(mary, party)$$
$$+\star come(mary, party), \models_{soft} come(mary, party)$$

Fig. 5: John does not regret that Mary came to the party

The computation yields a unique model scheme that is minimal for the justification ordering. This scheme is as follows.

---

[2]Strictly speaking, this example and some of the following ones require second-order logic. But the ionic framework described earlier easily extends to second-order logic.

"hard part"	$\not\Vdash regret(john, come(mary, party))$
"justification part"	$+\star come(mary, party)$
"soft part"	$\models_{soft} come(mary, party)$

One easily sees that $come(mary, party)$ is a presupposition.

5. Computing presuppositions of complex sentences

The previous section has illustrated the computation of presuppositions for simple sentences. We now examine some more complex linguistic structures. Many authors (see e.g. [17], [4]) have proposed various algorithms and rules for determining the presuppositions of complex sentences. These algorithms were based on pragmatic considerations.

As explained earlier, in our approach, we suggest to use of the model construction of partial information logic, together with the principle of the statics of logic systems. We show that this method is adequate for several classical cases, and that it also easily handles some instances of the problem of existential presuppositions.

The "propositional logic" part of the model construction of ionic logic takes care of the projection problem, whereas the "quantification logic" part handles the existential presupposition problem.

5.1. Presuppositions of propositional logic structures: the projection problem

The projection problem ([17], [4]) is that of constructing the presuppositions of complex sentences using the presuppositions of their subcomponents.

In all of the following problem examples, the existence of the objects referred to is taken for granted. We only consider the propositional structure of the sentences.

5.1.1. Possibly

We first consider statements of the form *"Possibly A."* Consider the following utterance: *"Possibly John regrets that Mary came to the party."* Intuitively, one derives the presupposition *"Mary came to the party."* The corresponding set of ionic formulae Φ is:

$$\star(regret(john, come(mary, party)), regret(john, come(mary, party)))$$
$$\star(\neg regret(john, come(mary, party)), \neg regret(john, come(mary, party)))$$
$$\forall xyz.regret(x, come(y, z)) \rightarrow come(y, z)$$
$$\forall xyz.\neg regret(x, come(y, z)) \rightarrow [come(y, z)]$$

In set Φ, "Possibly A" is translated here by means of the two ions $[A]$ and $[\neg A]$. The corresponding tableau construction yields the following patterns:

"justification part"	$+\star regret(john, come(mary, party))$, $-\star \neg regret(john, come(mary, party))$
"soft part"	$\models softregret(john, come(mary, party))$, $\models softcome(mary, party)$

and

"justification part"	$-\star regret(john, come(mary, party))$, $+\star \neg regret(john, come(mary, party))$, $+\star come(mary, party)$
"soft part"	$\not\models softregret(john, come(mary, party))$, $\models softcome(mary, party)$

Since signed formula $\models softcome(mary, party)$ belongs to both patterns, one sees that $come(mary, party)$ is a presupposition.

5.1.2. Disjunction

We next consider disjunctive statements of the form *"A or B."*

Example: Consider utterance: *"My cousin is a bachelor or a spinster."* Intuitively, one derives no presuppositions.

Let us use the following abbreviations: b = "my cousin is a bachelor," s = "my cousin is a spinster," m = "my cousin is male," f = "my cousin is female," a = "my cousin is adult" and r = "my cousin is married."

This yields the following set of formulae Φ:

$$b \lor s \; , \;\; b \leftrightarrow m \land a \land \neg r \; , \;\; \neg b \to \star(m, m) \; , \;\; \neg b \to \star(a, a) \; ,$$
$$s \leftrightarrow f \land a \land \neg r \; , \;\; \neg s \to \star(f, f) \; , \;\; \neg s \to \star(a, a) \; , \;\; f \leftrightarrow \neg m$$

The coresponding tableau yields two symmetrical patterns, one of which is characterized by:

$$\models b, \; \models m, \; \models a, \; \not\models r, \; \not\models f, \; \not\models s, \; -\star f, \; +\star a, \models softa$$

In the model scheme corresponding to this pattern, my cousin is a male adult (hard knowledge). The other pattern is obtained from this one by exchanging b and s, as well as m and f. One easily sees that $S(\Phi) = H(\Phi)$ for the above set Φ. Hence, there are no presuppositions.

Example: Consider utterance: *"Mary stopped beating the rug or John stopped beating the egg."* This example somewhat generalizes the previous one, and is formalized by means of the following set of ionic formulae. The following abbreviations are used: s = "Mary stopped beating the rug," s' = "John stopped beating the egg," p = "Mary was beating the rug" and p' = "John was beating the egg."

$$s \to p, \; \neg s \to \star(p, p), \; s' \to p', \; \neg s \to \star(p', p'), \; s \vee s'$$

This yields the tableau in figure 6.

$$\models s \to p, \; \models \neg s \to \star(p, p), \; \models s' \to p', \; \models \neg s' \to \star(p', p'), \; \models s \vee s'$$

$$\models s$$

$$\| \not\models s \text{ closed}$$

$$\models p$$

$$\| \not\models s'$$

$$\models p'$$

$$\models \star(p', p')$$

$$-\star p'$$

$$+\star p' \; , \quad \models softp'$$

$$\models s'$$

et cetera ...

Fig. 6: Mary stopped beating the rug or John stopped beating the egg.

Whence the following patterns:

$$\models s, \models p, \| \not\models s', -\star p'$$
$$\models s, \models p, \| \not\models s', +\star p', \models softp'$$
$$\models s, \models p, \models p'$$
$$\models s', \models p', \| \not\models s, -\star p$$
$$\models s', \models p', \| \not\models s, +\star p, \models softp$$
$$\models s', \models p', \models p$$

Whence the following minimal model schemes:

$$\models s, \models p, \| \not\models s', +\star p', \models softp'$$
$$\models s', \models p', \| \not\models s, +\star p, \models softp$$

In both of them $p \wedge p'$ is true in a soft sense. Formula $p \wedge p'$ is not true in the models corresponding to patterns:

$$\models s, \models p, \| \not\models s', -\star p'$$

and

$$\models s', \models p', \| \not\models s, -\star p$$

Whence formula $p \wedge p'$ is a presupposition of Φ. But, according to our definition, neither p nor p' is a presupposition or an entailment. This example is interesting, because it shows that the set of presuppositions of a given sentence is not necessarily closed under modus ponens.

5.1.3. Conditional

In this section, we consider conditional structures of the form "If A then B."

Example: Consider the following utterance: *"If Mary came to the party, then John regrets that she did."* Intuitively, no presuppositions are derived.

The corresponding set of ionic formulae is as follows:

$$come(mary, party) \rightarrow regret(john, come(mary, party))$$
$$\forall xyz.regret(x, come(y, z)) \rightarrow come(y, z)$$
$$\forall xyz.\neg regret(x, come(y, z)) \rightarrow [come(y, z)]$$

This yields the tableau in figure 7.

$\models come(mary, party) \rightarrow regret(john, come(mary, party)), \&$
$\quad \& \models \forall xyz.regret(x, come(y, z)) \rightarrow come(y, z)$
$\ldots\ , \models \forall xyz.\neg regret(x, come(y, z)) \rightarrow [come(y, z)]$
$\quad |\not\models come(mary, party)$
$\quad\quad |\not\models regret(john, come(mary, party))$
$\quad\quad\quad \models [come(mary, party)]$
$\quad\quad\quad\quad -\star come(mary, party)$
$\quad\quad\quad\quad +\star come(mary, party), \models softcome(mary, party)$ closed
$\quad \models regret(john, come(mary, party))$
$\quad\quad \models come(mary, party)$

Fig. 7: If Mary came to the party, then John regrets that she did.

One sees that no intrinsically soft information is generated in any resulting model. Whence $H(\Phi) = S(\Phi)$, and there are no presuppositions.

Example: Consider the following utterance: *"If Mary came to the party, then John regrets that Sue came to the party."* Intuitively, presupposition *"Sue came to the party"* is derived.

The corresponding set of ionic formulae is as follows:

$$come(mary, party) \rightarrow regret(john, come(sue, party))$$
$$\forall xyz.regret(x, come(y, z)) \rightarrow come(y, z)$$
$$\forall xyz.\neg regret(x, come(y, z)) \rightarrow [come(y, z)]$$

This yields the tableau in figure 8.

$\models come(mary, party) \rightarrow regret(john, come(sue, party)), \&$
$\quad \& \models \forall xyz.regret(x, come(y, z)) \rightarrow come(y, z)$

$$\ldots \ , \ \models \forall xyz. \neg regret(x, come(y, z)) \rightarrow [come(y, z)]$$
$$\| \not\models come(mary, party)$$
$$\| \not\models regret(john, come(mary, party))$$
$$\models \neg regret(john, come(sue, party)) \rightarrow [come(sue, party)]$$
$$\models regret(john, come(sue, party))$$
$$\models come(sue, party)$$
$$\models [come(sue, party)]$$
$$-\star come(sue, party)$$
$$+\star come(sue, party), \models softcome(sue, party)$$
$$\models regret(john, come(sue, party))$$
$$\models come(sue, party)$$
$$\models \neg regret(john, come(mary, party)) \rightarrow [come(mary, party)]$$
$$\models regret(john, come(mary, party))$$
$$\models come(mary, party)$$
$$\models [come(mary, party)]$$
$$-\star come(mary, party)$$
$$+\star come(mary, party), \models softcome(mary, party)$$

Fig. 8: If Mary came to the party, then John regrets that Sue came to the party.

The following six patterns are then obtained.

$$\| \not\models come(mary, party), \| \not\models regret(john, come(mary, party)),$$
$$\models regret(john, come(sue, party)), \models come(sue, party)$$
$$\| \not\models come(mary, party), \| \not\models regret(john, come(mary, party)),$$
$$-\star come(sue, party)$$
$$\| \not\models come(mary, party), \| \not\models regret(john, come(mary, party)),$$
$$+\star come(sue, party), \models softcome(sue, party)$$
$$\models regret(john, come(sue, party)), \models come(sue, party),$$
$$\models regret(john, come(mary, party), \models come(mary, party),$$
$$\models regret(john, come(sue, party)), \models come(sue, party),$$
$$-\star come(mary, party)$$
$$\models regret(john, come(sue, party)), \models come(sue, party),$$
$$+\star come(mary, party), \models softcome(mary, party)$$

The third pattern yields a minimal model. In that model, $come(sue, party)$ holds in a soft sense. The last pattern also yields a minimal model, where $come(sue, party)$ holds in a hard sense (hence in a soft sense). These are the only minimal models. Hence $come(sue, party) \in S(\Phi)$. On the other hand, $come(sue, party)$ is not true in any model corresponding the second pattern. Hence $come(sue, party) \notin H(\Phi)$. Hence $come(sue, party)$ is a presupposition of the given Φ.

Example: Consider the following statement S: *"If John regrets that Mary* *came to the party, then Mary came to the party.*" Intuitively, no presuppositions are derived.

The corresponding set of ionic formulae is as follows:

$$come(mary, party) \rightarrow regret(john, come(mary, party))$$
$$\forall xyz.regret(x, come(y, z)) \rightarrow come(y, z)$$
$$\forall xyz.\neg regret(x, come(y, z)) \rightarrow [come(y, z)]$$

This yields the tableau in figure 9.

$$\models regret(john, come(mary, party)) \rightarrow come(mary, party)$$
$$\dots\ ,\ \models \forall xyz.regret(x, come(y, z)) \rightarrow come(y, z), \&$$
$$\&\models \forall xyz.\neg regret(x, come(y, z)) \rightarrow [come(y, z)]$$
$$\not\models regret(john, come(mary, party))$$
$$\models [come(mary, party)]$$
$$-\star come(mary, party)$$
$$+\star come(mary, party),\ \models softcome(mary, party)$$
$$\models come(mary, party)$$

Fig. 9: If John regrets that Mary came to the party,
then Mary came to the party.

The following three patterns are then obtained:

$$\not\models regret(john, come(mary, party)), -\star come(mary, party)$$
$$\not\models regret(john, come(mary, party)), +\star come(mary, party),$$
$$\models softcome(mary, party)$$
$$\models come(mary, party)$$

The second pattern yields a minimal model, which is the unique minimal model. In that model, $come(mary, party)$ holds in a soft sense. Hence $come(mary, party) \in S(\Phi)$. Statement $come(mary, party)$ is not true in any model corresponding the first pattern. Hence $come(mary, party) \notin H(\Phi)$. Hence $come(mary, party)$ is a presupposition of the given set of formulae Φ. But intuitively, no presupposition should be derived.

Therefore, from a practical point of view, this result is unsatisfactory. This unsatisfactory result comes from a bad translation of statement S into ionic logic. More precisely, it comes from the use of the material implication $\rightarrow$ for translating the natural language implication "*If ...then ....*" Using $\rightarrow$ interprets S as "*If it is not false that John regrets that Mary came to the party, then Mary came to the party.*" Using the alternative, more accurate, translation [10]:

$$\models \neg \sim regret(john, come(mary, party)) \rightarrow \neg \sim come(mary, party)$$

which means "$\models regret(john, come(mary, party))$ implies $\models come(mary, party)$," gives a formalization that yields no presupposition. This example shows the importance of a correct translation of natural language statement S into ionic logic.

5.2. Computing presuppositions of quantification logic structures: the existential presupposition problem

In this section, we show how our method is used to compute presuppositions of existence. It is shown that the appropriate presuppositions of existence *"There is some object x such that p(x)"* are computed, on the condition that such an x is presupposed to be an actual object. This restriction is due to the fact that in ionic logic every object is a potential object, and presuppositions are disjoint from entailments. Thus existential presuppositions express the existence of actual objects.

Consider the following utterance:

> *The king has a son.*

The corresponding presupposition is that "there is a king." Recall that to express the soft knowledge that "there is some actual object whose name is d," one uses ion $\star(\exists^a u(u = d), \exists^a u(u = d))$. Let us assume that the king's son is an actual object. The utterance is then expressed in ionic logic as follows:

$$\exists^p x.(king(x) \wedge \exists^a y.son(y, x)) \ , \ \ \forall^p z. \star (\exists^a u(u = z), \exists^a u(u = z))$$

The first formula states that *"There is some potential object that is a king and has a son."* The second formula says that, by default, every potential object is some actual object. The resulting Beth tableau is given in figure 10.

$$\models \exists^p x.(king(x) \wedge \exists^a y.son(y, x)) \ , \ \ \models \forall^p z. \star (\exists^a u(u = z), \exists^a u(u = z))$$
$$\models (king(d) \wedge \exists^a y.son(y, d))$$
$$\models king(d) \ , \ \ \models son(e, d) \ , \ \ \models (e = e)$$
$$\models \star (\exists^a u(u = d), \exists^a u(u = d))$$
$$+\star \exists^a u(u = d) \ , \ \ \models soft(u_0 = d) \ , \ \ \models soft(u_0 = u_0)$$
$$-\star \exists^a u(u = d)$$

Fig. 10: The king has a son.

One obtains one single minimal model scheme, which is as follows:

"hard part"	$\models (e = e), \models king(d), \models son(e, d)$
"justification part"	$+\star \exists^a u.(u = d)$
"soft part"	$\models softking(u_0)$
"soft objects"	$\models soft(d = d)$

One has that hard actual object e is the son of king d, and soft actual object d is a king. Formula $\exists^a x.king(x)$ is a presupposition.

Example: Consider the following utterance: *"The king's son is bald."* Intuitively, one derives the presupposition "the king has a son." The formalization of this sentence yields the following set Φ of ionic formulae:

$$\exists^p x.(bald(x) \wedge \exists^p y.son(x, y) \wedge king(y)) \quad , \quad \forall^p z. \star (\exists^a u(u = z), \exists^a u(u = z))$$

The resulting tableau is given in figure 11.

$$\models \exists^p x.(bald(x) \wedge \exists^p y.son(x, y) \wedge king(y)), \models \forall^p z. \star (\exists^a u(u = z), \exists^a u(u = z))$$
$$\models (bald(d) \wedge \exists^p y.son(d, y) \wedge king(y))$$
$$\models bald(d), \models king(e), \models son(d, e)$$
$$\models \star (\exists^a u(u = d), \exists^a u(u = d))$$
$$+\star\exists^a u(u = d), \models soft(u_0 = d), \models soft(u_0 = u_0)$$
$$\models \star (\exists^a u(u = e), \exists^a u(u = e))$$
$$+\star\exists^a u(u = e), \models soft(u_1 = e), \models soft(u_1 = u_1)$$
$$-\star\exists^a u(u = e)$$
$$-\star\exists^a u(u = d)$$
$$\models \star (\exists^a u(u = e), \exists^a u(u = e))$$
$$+\star\exists^a u(u = e), \models soft(u_1 = e), \models soft(u_1 = u_1)$$
$$-\star\exists^a u(u = e)$$

Fig. 11: The king's son is bald.

This tableau yields a unique minimal model scheme. In the corresponding set $S(\Phi)$, the king d is a soft actual object, since $\models soft(d = d)$, whereas his son e is a hard actual objects, because $\models (e = e)$. One has the hard information that the son is bald. The soft part of the scheme says that there is a king. In other words, formula $\exists^a x.king(x)$ is a presupposition. One easily checks that formula

$$\exists^a x.king(x) \wedge \exists^a y.son(y, x)$$

is true in a *soft sense* in the unique minimal model scheme of Φ. The formula says that *"There is some actual object that is a king and has a son"* (i.e. the king has a son). This formula is obviously not true in that scheme. Observe that formula

$$\exists^p x.king(x) \wedge \exists^a y.son(y, x)$$

saying that *"There is some potential object that is a king and has a son."* is not a presupposition, but a logical consequence, i.e. an entailment. Therefore, it is a presupposition of Φ. More generally, since the king is a soft actual object, the rules of partial information logic force any true statement involving the king as an actual object to be a soft statement.

Example: Consider utterance: *"If the king has a son, then the king's son is bald."* Intuitively, one derives the presupposition that "there is a king." Such an utterance corresponds to a conditional statement. The formalization of this sentence yields set of ionic formulae:

$$\exists^P x.king(x) \wedge \exists^P y.son(y,x) \rightarrow bald(y) \ , \ \ \forall^P z. \star (\exists^a u(u=z), \exists^a u(u=z))$$

The resulting tableau is given in figure 12.

$$\models \exists^P x.king(x) \wedge \exists^P y.son(y,x) \rightarrow bald(y), \models \forall^P z. \star (\exists^a u(u=z), \exists^a u(u=z))$$
$$\models king(d) \wedge \exists^P y.son(y,d) \rightarrow bald(y)$$
$$\models king(d), \models \exists^P y.son(y,d) \rightarrow bald(y)$$
$$\models son(e,d) \rightarrow bald(e)$$
$$\not\models son(e,d)$$
$$\models \star (\exists^a u(u=d), \exists^a u(u=d)), \models \star (\exists^a u(u=e), \exists^a u(u=e))$$
$$+\star\exists^a u(u=d), \models soft(u_0=d), \models soft(u_0=u_0),$$
$$\ldots + \star\exists^a u(u=e), \models soft(u_1=e), \models soft(u_1=u_1)$$
$$\models bald(e), \models son(e,d)$$
$$\models \star (\exists^a u(u=d), \exists^a u(u=d)), \models \star (\exists^a u(u=e), \exists^a u(u=e))$$
$$+\star\exists^a u(u=d), \models soft(u_0=d), \models soft(u_0=u_0),$$
$$\ldots + \star\exists^a u(u=e), \models soft(u_1=e), \models soft(u_1=u_1)$$

Fig 12: If the king has a son, the king's son is bald.

One obtains two minimal model schemes. In both of them, d corresponds to the king and is a hard potential object, as well as a soft actual object. Only in the second model scheme is the statement $\exists^a y.son(y,x) \wedge king(x)$ true in a soft sense, where x is interpreted as d (the king). In both model schemes $\exists^a x.king(x)$ is true in a soft sense, because in both of them d is a soft actual object. Therefore, one obtains as a presupposition that *"There is a king."* (i.e., there is some actual object that is a king).

Some examples of the same type are as follows:

1. *"John talked to his brother."* which is expressed as

$$\exists^P x.john(x) \wedge \exists^P y.brother(y,x) \wedge talked(x,y)$$

2. *"John realized that he had lost."* which is expressed as

$$\exists^P x.john(x) \wedge \exists^P y.brother(y,x) \wedge talked(x,y)$$

6. Open problems

In the previous sections, we have established the existence of a useful link between the logic of partial information and the problem of generating natural language presuppositions, and we also have given a simple algorithm for solving this problem. We have shown that in several important cases our algorithm yields in a straightforward manner the appropriate answer. The treatment we have given here is, however, far from complete, and there are many open problems and questions deserving further investigation. As an example, the intuitive meaning of "presupposition" should be clarified in order to get a better grasp of results such as the one computed for the *"Mary stopped beating the rug or John stopped beating the egg"* example. There are also some presupposition problems that seem to be, from a purely logical point of view, more difficult. This difficulty has to do with the translation of natural language statements into ionic logic. The examples we now give of such situations all address linguistic structures that are more complex than the ones discussed above.

Example: (Embedded conjunction) Consider the following utterance: *"I dreamed that I was German and that I regretted it."* Here no presuppositions are derived.[3] In our analysis of the utterance, we assume that

$$dream(x) \rightarrow \star(\neg x, \neg x)$$
$$regret(x, u) \rightarrow u$$
$$\neg regret(x, u) \rightarrow \star(u, u)$$

Whence the tableau in figure 13.

$$\models dream(german(i) \wedge regret(i, german(i))), \models \forall xy.dream(x, y) \rightarrow \star(\neg y, \neg y),$$
$$\ldots \models \forall xy.regret(x, y) \rightarrow y \ , \quad \models \forall xy.\neg regret(x, y) \rightarrow \star(y, y)$$
$$\models [\neg german(i) \vee \neg regret(i, german(i))]$$
$$-\star \neg german(i) \vee \neg regret(i, german(i))$$
$$+\star \neg german(i) \vee \neg regret(i, german(i)), \&$$
$$\& \models soft \neg german(i) \vee \neg regret(i, german(i))$$
$$\not\Vdash softgerman(i)$$
$$\not\Vdash softregret(i, german(i))$$
$$\models soft \star (german(i), german(i))$$
$$-\star german(i)$$
$$+\star german(i) \ , \quad \models softgerman(i)$$

Fig. 13: Embedded conjunction

---

[3] One may compare this statement with the following ones:

- I dreamed that I regretted I was German. (presuppostion: I a German.)

- I dreamed that I was German. (presupposition: I am not German.)

This tableau yields patterns:

$$-\star\neg(german(i) \wedge regret(i, german(i)))$$
$$+\star\neg(german(i) \wedge regret(i, german(i))),$$
$$\|\not\models softgerman(i)$$
$$+\star\neg(german(i) \wedge regret(i, german(i))),$$
$$\|\not\models softregret(i, german(i)), -\star german(i)$$
$$+\star\neg(german(i) \wedge regret(i, german(i))),$$
$$\|\not\models softregret(i, german(i)), +\star german(i), \models softgerman(i)$$

This yields the presupposition that *"I am German."* This conclusion is obviously incorrect. A possible explanation for this incorrect answer seems to be the fact that the logical conjunction $\wedge$ is symmetrical and parallel: $\wedge$ yields true as soon as one of its conjuncts is true. For example, our translation of the natural language utterance assumes that the following two sentences are equivalent:

- I dreamed that I was German and that I regretted it.

- I dreamed that (I regretted I was German) and that (I was German).

There seems to be a "sequential" character to the natural language conjunction *and* appearing in the first sentence *"I dreamed that I was German and that I regretted it."* Indeed, one first commits to the dream that one is German, and then inside that dream one regrets being German. (Thus, logical connective $\wedge$ is a bad translation of the natural language connective *and.*) A translation that is more in line with this sequentiality is needed.

Example: (Temporal structures) An example is given by: *John is cooking. He wil stop (cooking) when tomorrow's football game starts.*

Example: (Metalanguage-level structures) An example is given by: *If I later realize that I have not told you the truth, I will tell you.*

7. Conclusion

The results presented above seem promising. They provide a firm mathematical foundation for investigating natural language presuppositions and their generation. The application of partial information logic for providing a comprehensive compuational treatment of natural language presuppositions warrants further investigation. As we have seen, one of the difficulties is one of formalizing into the language of ionic logic the given natural language statements.

Any natural language statement that is correctly translatable into the language of ionic logic falls under the scope of our method.

References

1. G. Frege, Über Sinn and Bedeutung, *Zeitschrift für Philosophie und philosophische Kritik*, 100 (1892), 25 – 50.

2. G. J. M. Gazdar, *Pragmatics: Implicatures, Presupposition and Logical form*, Academic Press, 1979.

3. H. P. Grice, Utter's meaning and intention, *Philosophical Review*, 78 (1969), 147 – 177.

4. I. Heim, Presupposition projection, in *Presupposition, Lexical Meaning and Discourse Processes, Workshop of the Esprit WG 3315, U. Of Nijmegen*, December 1990.

5. K. J. J. Hintikka, Existential presuppositions and existential commitments, *J. Philosophy*, 56 (1959), 125 – 137.

6. I. Lakatos, Falsification and the methodology of scientific research programmes, in *Problems in the Philosophy of Science* (Lakatos, Musgrave, eds.), North Holland, Amsterdam, 1970, 91 – 196.

7. M. A. Nait Abdallah, An extended framework for default reasoning, in *Fundamentals of Computation Theory* (F. Gecseg, ed.), *LNCS* 380, Springer-Verlag, 1989, 339 – 348.

8. M.A. Nait Abdallah, Kernel knowledge versus belt knowledge in default reasoning: a logical approach, in *Advances in Computing and Information* (F. Dehne, F. Fiala, W. Koczkodaj, eds.), *LNCS* 497, Springer-Verlag, 1991, 675 – 686.

9. M. A. Nait Abdallah, Syntax and semantics of a monotonic framework for non-monotonic reasoning, in *Mathematical Foundations of Computer Science* (A. Tarlecki, ed.), *LNCS* 520, Springer-Verlag, 1991, 357 – 366.

10. M. A. Nait Abdallah, *The Logic of Partial Information*, Springer-Verlag, Berlin, 1994.

11. K. R. Popper, *The Logic of Scientific Discovery*, Hutchinson, London, 1959.

12. W. V. O. Quine, On what there is, *Review of Metaphysics*, 2 (1948), 21 – 38.

13. B. Russell, On denoting, *Mind*, 14 (1905), 479 – 493.

14. R. Smullyan, *First-Order Logic*, Springer-Verlag, Berlin, 1968.

15. P. Strawson, *Introduction to Logical Theory*, Methuen, London, 1952.

16. P. Strawson, On referring, *Mind*, 59 (1950), 320 – 344.

17. R. A. Van der Sandt, *Context and Presupposition*, Croom Helm, 1988.

18. R. A. Van der Sandt, Presupposition and discourse structure, in *Semantic and Contextual Expression* (J. Van Benthem, R. Bartsch, P. Van Emde Boas, eds.), Foris Publications, Dordrecht, Holland, 1989, 267 – 294.

Reducts versus Reducing Operators

Miroslav NOVOTNÝ

Department of Computer Science, Masaryk University
Burešova 20, 602 00 Brno, Czech Republic

Abstract. For the set of all pure generalized grammars over a finite set a dependence space is defined and the theory of such spaces is elaborated. The existence of a pure grammar that generates the same language as the given pure generalized grammar is equivalent to the existence of a reduct with particular properties corresponding to an element of the dependence space. The theory of dependence spaces is inspired by the theory of dependence spaces corresponding to information systems.

1. Introduction

In this paper, we transfer the methods developed for information systems to systems of pure generalized grammars. The central concept enabling to solve several important problems concerning information systems is the concept of dependence space. Any information system has its dependence space and the problems concerning an information system may be regarded as problems concerning the corresponding dependence space. The most important problem including almost all others is the problem of finding a reduct of an element of the dependence space.

We demonstrate that the system of all pure generalized grammars over a finite set has also a dependence space. To this aim, we must generalize the concept of dependence space introduced for information systems. The theory of these spaces includes some theorems concerning reducts of an element of the space that can be interpreted as theorems concerning existence of a pure grammar generating the same language as a given pure generalized grammar.

2. Pure grammars

The study of natural languages led to investigation of syntactic configurations. Various authors introduced different types of syntactic configurations for formal languages and described their properties (cf. [11]). Professor Solomon Marcus and his collaborators contributed to this trend by several outstanding papers (cf. [3]).

Syntactic configurations may be considered to be an instrument for construction of a pure generalized grammar to a given language (cf. [2]). We describe briefly this situation.

Let V be a finite nonempty set, V^* the set of all strings over V, i.e., the set of all finite sequences of elements in V. For any $x \in V^*$, we denote by $|x|$ the length of the string x; if $a \in V$, then $|x|_a$ is the number of occurrences of a in x. If $u \in V^*$, $v \in V^*$, then the operation of catenation provides the string $uv \in V^*$. A set L with the property $L \subseteq V^*$ is called a *language over* V.

Let V be a finite nonempty set, $S \subseteq V^*$, $R \subseteq V^* \times V^*$. Then the ordered triple $G = < V, S, R >$ is said to be a *pure generalized grammar* (cf. [4], Definition 2.6). The strings in S are called *initial*, the elements of R are said to be *productions*. If $s \in V^*$, $t \in V^*$, then we put $s \Rightarrow t$ (R) if there exist $u \in V^*$, $v \in V^*$, $(y, x) \in R$ such that $s = uyv$, $uxv = t$. Furthermore, we put $s \Rightarrow^* t$ (R) if there exist an integer $n \geq 0$ and some strings $s_0, s_1, \ldots, s_n$ in V^* such that $s = s_0$, $s_{i-1} \Rightarrow s_i$ (R) for any i with $1 \leq i \leq n$ and $s_n = t$. Finally, we put $\mathbf{L}(G) = \{w \in V^*;$ there exists $s \in S$ with $s \Rightarrow^* w$ $(R)\}$. Then $\mathbf{L}(G)$ is said to be the *language generated by* G. For any $w \in \mathbf{L}(< V, S, R >)$ we denote by $\|w\|_R^S$ the least integer $N \geq 0$ such that there exist $s \in S$ and a finite set $R' \subseteq R$ with the properties $s \Rightarrow^* w$ (R'), $\max\{|y|, |x|\} \leq N$ for any $(y, x) \in R'$.

Lemma 1. *Let V be a finite nonempty set, $S_1 \subseteq S_2 \subseteq V^*$, $R_1 \subseteq R_2 \subseteq V^* \times V^*$. Then $\mathbf{L}(< V, S_1, R_1 >) \subseteq \mathbf{L}(< V, S_2, R_2 >)$.*

Proof. See [4], Lemma 2.3, 2.7. □

The following question is natural. If L is a language over V, is it possible to construct a pure generalized grammar G such that $\mathbf{L}(G) = L$? Many authors used various types of syntactic configurations for this construction. We characterize the most important definitions of configurations.

Suppose that L is a language over V. Let us have $(y, x) \in V^* \times V^*$. Then x is called a *configuration with the resultant* y if for any $u \in V^*$, $v \in V^*$, the condition $uyv \in L$ implies that $uxv \in L$; many authors add a further condition imposed on the string $uxv \in L$ in order to provide $uyv \in L$. The form of this condition characterizes various types of configurations. These details will not play any role in what follows and, therefore, are omitted. The common kernel of all these definitions is the *domination relation* that is defined as follows.

Let L be a language over V. Put

$$\mathbf{d}(V, L) = \{(y, x) \in V^* \times V^* \quad ; \quad \text{for any } u \in V^*, v \in V^* \text{ the condition}$$
$$uyv \in L \text{ implies that } uxv \in L\}.$$

It is easy to prove

Lemma 2. *Let L be a language over V. Then $\mathbf{L}(< V, L, \mathbf{d}(V, L) >) = L$.*

Proof. Cf. [4], Corollary 5.3. □

Thus, our question is answered in a simple way. We may obtain more information on the pure generalized grammar generating a given language L.

Lemma 3. *Let L be a language over V and $< V, S, R >$ a pure generalized grammar generating L. Then $S \subseteq L$ and $R \subseteq \mathbf{d}(V, L)$.*

Proof. See [4], Lemma 5.4. □

A pure generalized grammar $< V, S, R >$ is said to be a *pure grammar* if the sets S, R are finite. While a pure generalized grammar G exists to any language L in such a way that $\mathbf{L}(G) = L$, a pure grammar with a similar property need not exist. Thus, we have

Problem 1. Let L be a language over V. Does there exist a pure grammar $G =< V, S, R >$ generating L ?

Regarding Lemma 3, Problem 1 may be reformulated as follows.

Problem 2. Let L be a language over V. Do there exist finite sets S, R such that $S \subseteq L$, $R \subseteq \mathbf{d}(V, L)$ and that $< V, S, R >$ generates L ?

The rest of the paper will be devoted to the study of this problem using the results on dependence spaces inspired by information systems.

3. Information systems

In what follows, we denote by $\mathbf{B}(M)$ the system of all subsets of M for any set M. If K is an equivalence on M, then elements in M/K will be called K-blocks.

Let U, A, V be finite nonempty sets and f a mapping of the set $U \times A$ into V. Then the ordered quadruple $S = (U, A, V, f)$ is said to be an information system (cf. [7], [8], [10]). Elements in U are called objects, elements in A are interpreted to be attributes, elements in V are said to be values of attributes. If $(u, a) \in U \times A$ and $f(u, a) = v$, then the attribute a is said to have the value v for the object u.

Let $S = (U, A, V, f)$ be an information system and $X \in \mathbf{B}(A)$. We put $\mathbf{IND}_S(X) = \{(u_1, u_2) \in U \times U; \ f(u_1, a) = f(u_2, a) \text{ for any } a \in X\}$. Clearly, $\mathbf{IND}_S(X)$ is an equivalence on the set U. The set X can be regarded as a test and $\mathbf{IND}_S(X)$ as the result of the test X: Any block of $\mathbf{IND}_S(X)$ consists of all objects that are indiscernible by means of the attributes of X. Furthermore, we put $\mathbf{K}_S = \{(X, Y) \in \mathbf{B}(A) \times \mathbf{B}(A); \ \mathbf{IND}_S(X) = \mathbf{IND}_S(Y)\}$.

Lemma 4. *Let $S = (U, A, V, f)$ be an information system. Then $\mathbf{K}_S$ is a congruence on the semilattice $(\mathbf{B}(A), \cup)$ where $\cup$ denotes the operation of union.*

Proof. See [7]. □

In [7], [8], [10], the ordered pair $(A, \mathbf{K}_S)$ is called the dependence space of the information system S; this is an abbreviation for the ordered triple $(\mathbf{B}(A), \subseteq, \mathbf{K}_S)$ where $\mathbf{B}(A)$ is a set, $\subseteq$ its ordering, and $\mathbf{K}_S$ an equivalence on $\mathbf{B}(A)$.

Let $S = (U, A, V, f)$ be an information system, $X \in \mathbf{B}(A)$ a set. A set $X' \in \mathbf{B}(A)$ is said to be a $\mathbf{K}_S$-reduct of X if X' is minimal with respect to inclusion among all sets $Z \in \mathbf{B}(A)$ such that $Z \subseteq X$ and $(Z, X) \in \mathbf{K}_S$. Hence, X' is minimal among all sets $Z \subseteq X$ with $\mathbf{IND}_S(Z) = \mathbf{IND}_S(X)$. Thus, a $\mathbf{K}_S$-reduct of the test X is a minimal subtest of X that has the same result as X.

The ideas of this section will motivate our investigations in what follows.

4. Dependence spaces

Let B be a nonempty set, $\leq$ an ordering on B such that $(B, \leq)$ is a complete lattice (see, e.g., [1], [12]). An equivalence K on B is said to be a *generalized congruence* on $(B, \leq)$ if any K-block has a greatest element with respect to the ordering $\leq$. Then the ordered triple $(B, \leq, K)$ is said to be a *dependence space*.

This is a generalization of the concept defined in [6], [7], [8]. In these papers, the role of B is played by the set $\mathbf{B}(A)$ of all subsets of a finite nonempty set A, the ordering $\leq$ coincides with the inclusion $\subseteq$, and K is a congruence on the semilattice $(\mathbf{B}(A), \cup)$. A dependence space is denoted by (A, K) in the above mentioned papers which is an abbreviation of $(\mathbf{B}(A), \subseteq, K)$.

Example 1. Suppose $A = \{a, b, c\}$. Then $\mathbf{B}(A) = \{\emptyset, \{a\}, \{b\}, \{c\}, \{a, b\}, \{a, c\}, \{b, c\}, A\}$. Let K have the following blocks: $\{\emptyset, \{a\}\}$, $\{\{b\}, \{a, b\}\}$, $\{\{c\}, \{a, c\}\}$, $\{\{b, c\}, \{a, b, c\}\}$. Then $(\mathbf{B}(A), \subseteq, K)$ is a dependence space. Cf. figure 1.

Let $(B, \leq)$ be a complete lattice, C a mapping of B into itself such that the following conditions are satisfied.
- $x \leq C(x)$ for any $x \in B$.
- $C(x) = C(C(x))$ for any $x \in B$.

Then C is said to be a *generalized closure operator* on $(B, \leq)$ which will be abbreviated as *gc-operator*.

Let $(B, \leq, K)$ be a dependence space. For any $x \in B$ we denote by $\mathbf{C}(K)(x)$ the greatest element of the K-block that contains x. Hence, $\mathbf{C}(K)$ is a mapping of B into itself.

Theorem 1. *Let $(B, \leq, K)$ be a dependence space. Then $\mathbf{C}(K)$ is a gc-operator.*

Proof. By definition, $\mathbf{C}(K)(x)$ is the greatest element of the K-block containing x which implies that $x \leq \mathbf{C}(K)(x)$ for any $x \in B$. Similarly,

$\mathbf{C}(K)(\mathbf{C}(K)(x))$ is the greatest element of the K-block containing $\mathbf{C}(K)(x)$, i.e., of the K-block containing x. Thus, if $x \in B$, then $\mathbf{C}(K)(\mathbf{C}(K)(x)) = \mathbf{C}(K)(x)$. $\qquad\square$

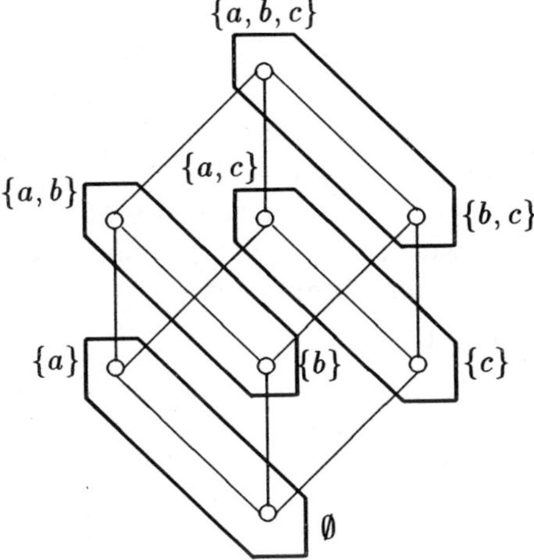

Fig. 1

Example 2. If considering the dependence space of Example 1, we obtain $\mathbf{C}(K)(\emptyset) = \{a\} = \mathbf{C}(K)(\{a\})$, $\mathbf{C}(K)(\{b\}) = \{a, b\} = \mathbf{C}(K)(\{a, b\})$, $\mathbf{C}(K)(\{c\}) = \{a, c\} = \mathbf{C}(K)(\{a, c\})$, $\mathbf{C}(K)(\{b, c\}) = \{a, b, c\} = \mathbf{C}(K)(\{a, b, c\})$.

We have seen that a generalized congruence on a complete lattice defines a *gc*-operator. On the other hand, a *gc*-operator on a complete lattice defines a generalized congruence and, hence, a dependence space.

Let $(B, \leq)$ be a complete lattice, C a *gc*-operator on $(B, \leq)$. We put $\mathbf{K}(C) = \{(x, x') \in B \times B;\ C(x) = C(x')\}$. Clearly, $\mathbf{K}(C)$ is an equivalence on B.

Theorem 2. *Let $(B, \leq)$ be a complete lattice, C a gc-operator on $(B, \leq)$. Then $\mathbf{K}(C)$ is a generalized congruence on $(B, \leq)$ and $(B, \leq, \mathbf{K}(C))$ is a dependence space.*

Proof. If $x \in B$ is arbitrary, then $C(C(x)) = C(x)$ which implies that $(x, C(x)) \in \mathbf{K}(C)$. Hence, x, $C(x)$ are in the same $\mathbf{K}(C)$-block. If x, y are in the same $\mathbf{K}(C)$-block, then $y \leq C(y) = C(x)$ which implies that $C(x)$ is the greatest element of the $\mathbf{K}(C)$-block containing x. $\qquad\square$

Example 3. If extending Example 2, we obtain that $\mathbf{K}(\mathbf{C}(K))$ has the following blocks: $\{\emptyset, \{a\}\}$, $\{\{b\}, \{a, b\}\}$, $\{\{c\}, \{a, c\}\}$, $\{\{b, c\}, \{a, b, c\}\}$. Thus, $\mathbf{K}(\mathbf{C}(K)) = K$. This is no accidental result as it follows from the next theorem.

Theorem 3. *Let $(B, \leq, K)$ be a dependence space. Then $\mathbf{K}(\mathbf{C}(K)) = K$.*

Proof. Let $x \in B$, $x' \in B$ be arbitrary. Then $(x, x') \in K$ is equivalent to $\mathbf{C}(K)(x) = \mathbf{C}(K)(x')$ by definition of the operator $\mathbf{C}$; the last condition means $(x, x') \in \mathbf{K}(\mathbf{C}(K))$ by definition of the operator $\mathbf{K}$.   □

Theorem 4. *Let $(B, \leq)$ be a complete lattice, C a gc-operator on $(B, \leq)$. Then $\mathbf{C}(\mathbf{K}(C)) = C$.*

Proof. If C is a gc-operator and $x \in B$ is arbitrary, then $\mathbf{C}(\mathbf{K}(C))(x)$ is the greatest element $y \in B$ with $(y, x) \in \mathbf{K}(C)$. If $(y, x) \in \mathbf{K}(C)$, then $y \leq C(y) = C(x)$. Since $C(C(x)) = C(x)$, we have $(C(x), x) \in \mathbf{K}(C)$ and, hence, $C(x)$ is the greatest element $y \in B$ with $(y, x) \in \mathbf{K}(C)$. Thus $\mathbf{C}(\mathbf{K}(C))(x) = C(x)$ for any $x \in B$ which is the assertion of our theorem.   □

Let $(B, \leq)$ be a complete lattice.

A generalized congruence K on $(B, \leq)$ is said to be *convex* if any K-block is convex with respect to the ordering $\leq$, i.e., if $C \in B/K$, x, y, $z \in B, x \leq y \leq z$, $x \in C$, $z \in C$ imply $y \in C$.

A gc-operator C on $(B, \leq)$ is called *convex* if for any $x \in B$, $y \in B$ the condition $x \leq y \leq C(x)$ implies that $C(y) = C(x)$.

A dependence space $(B, \leq, K)$ with a convex generalized congruence K is said to be *convex*.

Example 4. If considering the dependence space $(\mathbf{B}(A), \subseteq, K)$ of Example 1, then K is a convex generalized congruence and, therefore, the dependence space $(\mathbf{B}(A), \subseteq, K)$ is convex.

Example 5. The gc-operator $\mathbf{C}(K)$ of Example 2 is convex.

The convexity of a gc-operator can be expressed in a simpler way.

Lemma 4. *Let $(B, \leq)$ be a complete lattice, C a mapping of B into itself such that $x \leq C(x)$ for any $x \in B$. Suppose that $x \leq y \leq C(x)$ implies $C(y) = C(x)$ for any $x \in B$ and any $y \in B$. Then $C(x) = C(C(x))$ for any $x \in B$.*

Proof. Since $x \leq C(x) \leq C(x)$ holds for any $x \in B$, we have $C(C(x)) = C(x)$.   □

Corollary 1. *Let $(B, \leq)$ be a complete lattice, C a mapping of B into itself. Then the following assertions (i), (ii) are equivalent.*
    (i) *C is a convex gc-operator.*
    (ii) *C satisfies the following conditions:*
        (a) *$x \leq C(x)$ for any $x \in B$.*
        (b) *$x \leq y \leq C(x)$ implies that $C(y) = C(x)$ for any $x \in B$ and $y \in B$.*

Proof. Clearly, *(i)* implies *(ii)*. On the other hand, *(ii)* implies *(i)* by Lemma 4.   □

The convexity is preserved by the operators $\mathbf{C}$ and $\mathbf{K}$ as it follows from the following theorems.

Theorem 5. *Let $(B, \leq, K)$ be a dependence space. Then the following assertions are equivalent.*

(i) *The generalized congruence K is convex.*

(ii) *The gc-operator $\mathbf{C}(K)$ is convex.*

Proof. Let *(i)* hold and suppose that $x \in B$, $y \in B$ are arbitrary elements such that $x \leq y \leq \mathbf{C}(K)(x)$. Since $(x, \mathbf{C}(K)(x)) \in K$ by definition of $\mathbf{C}(K)(x)$, then $(x, y) \in K$ which implies that $\mathbf{C}(K)(x) = \mathbf{C}(K)(y)$. Thus, $\mathbf{C}(K)$ is convex and *(ii)* holds.

Let *(ii)* hold and suppose that x, y, z are in B and that $x \leq y \leq z, (x, z) \in K$. Thus, $x \leq y \leq z \leq \mathbf{C}(K)(z) = \mathbf{C}(K)(x)$ which implies that $\mathbf{C}(K)(y) = \mathbf{C}(K)(x)$. Hence, $(x, y) \in K$. Thus, K is convex and *(i)* holds. $\qquad\square$

Theorem 6. *Let $(B, \leq)$ be a complete lattice and C a gc-operator on $(B, \leq)$. Then the following assertions are equivalent.*

(i) *The gc-operator C is convex.*

(ii) *The generalized congruence $\mathbf{K}(C)$ is convex.*

Proof. By Theorem 5, $\mathbf{K}(C)$ is a convex generalized congruence if and only if $\mathbf{C}(\mathbf{K}(C))$ is a convex gc-operator. By Theorem 4, $\mathbf{C}(\mathbf{K}(C)) = C$ holds which implies the assertion. $\qquad\square$

5. Reducts

Let $(B, \leq, K)$ be a dependence space, $x \in B$ an element. An element $x' \in B$ is said to be a *K-reduct* of x if the following conditions are satisfied.

(i) $x' \leq x$.

(ii) $(x', x) \in K$.

(iii) If $y \in B$ and $y < x'$, then $(y, x) \notin K$.

This means that x' is minimal among all elements $z \in B$ such that $(z, x) \in K$, $z \leq x$.

Example 6. Let $(\mathbf{B}(A), \subseteq, K)$ be the dependence space of Example 1. Then $\{c\}$ is a K-reduct of $\{a, c\}$.

Example 7. Let A be an infinite set. We define the equivalence K on $\mathbf{B}(A)$ as follows. $K = \{(X, X) \in \mathbf{B}(A) \times \mathbf{B}(A); \ X \text{ is finite}\} \cup \{(X, Y) \in \mathbf{B}(A) \times \mathbf{B}(A); \ X, \ Y \text{ are infinite}\}$. Then a K-block is of the form $\{X\}$ if $X \in \mathbf{B}(A)$ is finite; furthermore, the set of all infinite subsets of A is a K-block. Clearly, any K-block has a greatest element which implies that $(\mathbf{B}(A), \subseteq, K)$ is a dependence space. The set A has no reduct because there exists no minimal infinite subset of A.

Thus, if $(B, \leq, K)$ is a dependence space, there may exist elements in B that have no K-reducts. We are interested in conditions sufficient for the existence of K-reducts.

For the reader's convenience, we recall some concepts of the theory of ordered sets needed in what follows. Let $(B, \leq)$ be an ordered set. A subset C of B is said to be a *chain* if for any elements $x \in C$, $y \in C$ either $x \leq y$ or $y \leq x$ holds. If a chain C has a least and a greatest element, they are said to be the *end-points* of C. An element $y \in B$ is said to *cover* the element $x \in B$ if $x < y$ and if $t \in B$, $x \leq t \leq y$ imply either $x = t$ or $t = y$.

Let $(B, \leq, K)$ be a dependence space, $x \in B$ an element. Then x is said to be *K-accessible* if there exists an integer $n(x) \geq 1$ such that for any chain C in $(B, \leq)$ whose greatest element is x the set $\{z \in C;\ (z, x) \in K\}$ has at most $n(x)$ elements.

Example 8. We continue Example 7. Let X be an infinite subset of A, C an infinite chain of infinite subsets of X; such a chain always exists. It follows that X is not K-accessible.

As consequences of the definition we obtain

Corollary 2. *Let $(B, \leq, K)$ be a dependence space, $x \in B$ a K-accessible element. If $y \in B$ is such that $y \leq x$, $(y, x) \in K$, then y is K-accessible.*   □

Corollary 3. *Let $(B, \leq, K)$ be a dependence space, $x \in B$ a K-accessible element, $y \in B$ such an element that $y \leq x$, $(y, x) \in K$. Then any chain in $(B, \leq)$ with end-points x, y consisting of elements $z \in B$ such that $(z, x) \in K$ has at most $n(x)$ elements.*   □

Corollary 4. *Let $(B, \leq, K)$ be a convex dependence space, $x \in B$ a K-accessible element. Then for any $y \in B$ with $y \leq x$, $(y, x) \in K$ there exists an integer $m(y) \geq 0$ and elements $t_0, t_1, \ldots, t_{m(y)}$ in B such that $t_0 = x$, $t_{m(y)} = y$, t_i covers t_{i+1} for any i with $0 \leq i < m(y)$, and $(t_i, x) \in K$ for any i with $0 \leq i \leq m(y)$.*

Indeed, the convexity of K implies that $(t, x) \in K$ for any $t \in B$ with $y \leq t \leq x$. The assertion follows by Corollary 3.   □

Theorem 7. *Let $(B, \leq, K)$ be a dependence space, $x \in B$ an element. Then the following assertions are equivalent.*
   (i) *There exists a K-accessible element $y \in B$ such that $y \leq x$, $(y, x) \in K$.*
   (ii) *The element x has a K-reduct.*

Proof. If *(i)* holds, we take the set $M = \{z \in B;\ z \leq y,\ (z, y) \in K\}$. If $z \in M$ is arbitrary, then any chain in M has at most $n(y)$ elements by Corollary 3 which implies that the set of minimal elements in M is nonempty. If x' is a minimal element of this set, we have $x' \leq y$, $(x', y) \in K$ which implies that $x' \leq x$, $(x', x) \in K$. The minimality of x' implies that x' is a K-reduct of x. Thus, *(ii)* holds.

If *(ii)* holds, there exists a K-reduct x' of x. By definition, we obtain $x' \leq x$, $(x', x) \in K$. If C is a chain in $(B, \leq)$ with the greatest element x', then x' is the only element z in C with $(z, x) \in K$. Thus, $n(x') = 1$ and x' is K-accessible. Hence *(i)* holds. $\qquad\square$

Theorem 7 enables to construct K-reducts in a convex dependence space. We now present such a construction. Some of its steps require comments and explanations which are put into square brackets [ ] that are inserted into the description of the construction.

Construction of K-reducts

Let $(B, \leq, K)$ be a convex dependence space, $x \in B$ a K-accessible element. We put $t_0 = x$.

Suppose that $i \geq 0$ is an integer and that t_i has been constructed in such a way that $t_i \leq x$, $(t_i, x) \in K$.

If $(t, x) \notin K$ for any $t \in B$ with $t < t_i$, we put $t_{i+1} = t_i$.

If there exists some $t \in B$ such that $t < t_i$ and $(t, x) \in K$, then [by Corollary 2 the element t_i is K-accessible and by Corollary 4] there exists $z \in B$ such that t_i covers z and $(z, t_i) \in K$ [this implies that $(z, x) \in K$]. We choose such an element z and put $t_{i+1} = z$.

[The K-accessibility of x implies the existence of an index $i \geq 0$ such that $t_{i+1} = t_i$.]

We take the least index $i \geq 0$ such that $t_{i+1} = t_i$. The sequence $(t_0, \ldots, t_i)$ will be said to be a *reducing sequence starting in* x, the element t_i will be referred to as an *element constructed by means of a reducing sequence starting in* x.

[There may exist several reducing sequences starting in x and, therefore, several elements constructed by means of these sequences.]

We denote by $\mathbf{R}(x)$ the set of all elements constructed by means of all reducing sequences starting in x.

Theorem 8. *Let $(B, \leq, K)$ be a convex dependence space, $x \in B$ a K-accessible element. Then $\mathbf{R}(x)$ is the set of all K-reducts of the element x.*

Proof. Let us have $x' \in \mathbf{R}(x)$. If $(t_0, \ldots, t_i)$ is the reducing sequence starting in x that constructs x', then $x' = t_i$ and $(x, t_j) \in K$ for any j with $0 \leq j \leq i$. By definition, $x' = t_i$ is minimal among all elements $t \in B$ with the properties $t \leq x$, $(t, x) \in K$. Thus, x' is a K-reduct of x.

If x' is a K-reduct of x, then $t < x'$ implies that $(t, x) \notin K$. By Corollary 4, there are elements $t_0, t_1, \ldots, t_m$ such that $t_0 = x$, $t_m = x'$, t_i covers t_{i+1} for any i with $0 \leq i < m$ and $(t_i, x) \in K$ for any i with $0 \leq i \leq m$. Thus, $(t_0, \ldots, t_m)$ is a reducing sequence starting in x and we obtain $x' \in \mathbf{R}(x)$. $\qquad\square$

Example 9. If considering the dependence space $(\mathbf{B}(A), \subseteq, K)$ of Example 6, then $\{c\}$ is a K-reduct of $\{a, c\}$ and $\{c\} \in \mathbf{R}(\{a, c\})$.

Let $(B, \leq, K)$ be a dependence space, $x \in B$ an element. This element is said to be *strongly K-accessible* if there exists an integer $p(x) \geq 1$ such that any chain in $(B, \leq)$ whose greatest element is x has at most $p(x)$ elements.

Corollary 5. *Let $(B, \leq, K)$ be a dependence space. Then any strongly K-accessible element in B is K-accessible.*

Corollary 6. *Let $(B, \leq, K)$ be a dependence space, x a strongly K-accessible element in B. If $y \in B$ is such that $y \leq x$, then y is strongly K-accessible.*

Example 10. An arbitrary element $X \in \mathbf{B}(A)$ of the dependence space $(\mathbf{B}(A), \subseteq, K)$ in Example 9 is strongly K-accessible.

6. Dependence

Let $(B, \leq, K)$ be a dependence space, $x \in B$, $y \in B$ elements. The element y is said to be *dependent on x in* $(B, \leq, K)$, which is symbolized by $x \to y$ $(B, \leq, K)$, if $\mathbf{C}(K)(y) \leq \mathbf{C}(K)(x)$.

Example 11. Consider the dependence space $(\mathbf{B}(A), \subseteq, K)$ of Example 1. Then $\mathbf{C}(K)(\{a, b\}) = \{a, b\} \subseteq \{a, b, c\} = \mathbf{C}(K)(\{b, c\})$ which implies that $\{b, c\} \to \{a, b\}$ $(\mathbf{B}(A), \subseteq, K)$.

Let $(B, \leq, K)$ be a dependence space, $y \in B$ an element. For any $x \in B$, $x' \in B$, we put $(x, x') \in \mathbf{D}(K, y)$ if and only if one of the following conditions (i), (ii) is satisfied.

    (i) $\mathbf{C}(K)(y) \leq \mathbf{C}(K)(x)$, $\mathbf{C}(K)(y) \leq \mathbf{C}(K)(x')$.
    (ii) $\mathbf{C}(K)(y) \not\leq \mathbf{C}(K)(x) = \mathbf{C}(K)(x')$.

Theorem 9. *Let $(B, \leq, K)$ be a dependence space, $y \in B$ an element. Then $(B, \leq, \mathbf{D}(K, y))$ is a dependence space.*

Proof. Clearly, $\mathbf{D}(K, y)$ is an equivalence on the set B.

Let $x \in B$ be arbitrary. We denote by e the greatest element in $(B, \leq)$.

If $\mathbf{C}(K)(y) \leq \mathbf{C}(K)(x)$, then $\mathbf{C}(K)(y) \leq e = \mathbf{C}(K)(e)$ and, hence, $(x, e) \in \mathbf{D}(K, y)$. Clearly, e is the greatest element of the $\mathbf{D}(K, y)$-block containing x.

Suppose that $\mathbf{C}(K)(y) \not\leq \mathbf{C}(K)(x)$. If $(x', x) \in \mathbf{D}(K, y)$, then $\mathbf{C}(K)(y) \not\leq \mathbf{C}(K)(x) = \mathbf{C}(K)(x')$. Furtheromore, $x' \leq \mathbf{C}(K)(x') = \mathbf{C}(K)(x)$ and $\mathbf{C}(K)(y) \not\leq \mathbf{C}(K)(x) = \mathbf{C}(K)(\mathbf{C}(K)(x))$ which implies that $(\mathbf{C}(K)(x), x) \in \mathbf{D}(K, y)$. It follows that $\mathbf{C}(K)(x)$ is the greatest element of the $\mathbf{D}(K, y)$-block containing x.

We have proved that any $\mathbf{D}(K, y)$-block has a greatest element which means that $\mathbf{D}(K, y)$ is a generalized congruence and, therefore, $(B, \leq, \mathbf{D}(K, y))$ is a dependence space. $\qquad\square$

Example 12. Let $(\mathbf{B}(A), \subseteq, K)$ be the dependence space of Example 11. Put $y = \{a, b\}$. Then $\mathbf{D}(K, y)$ has the following blocks: $\{\emptyset, \{a\}\}$, $\{\{c\}, \{a, c\}\}$, $\{\{b\}, \{a, b\}, \{b, c\}, \{a, b, c\}\}$.

Theorem 10. *Let $(B, \leq, K)$ be a dependence space, $x \in B$, $y \in B$ elements such that $x \to y\,(B, \leq, K)$. Then for any element $x' \in B$ the following assertions are equivalent.*

(i) *x' is minimal among all elements $z \in B$ with the properties $z \leq x$, $z \to y\,(B, \leq, K)$.*

(ii) *x' is a $\mathbf{D}(K, y)$-reduct of x.*

Proof. By hypothesis, the condition $\mathbf{C}(K)(y) \leq \mathbf{C}(K)(x)$ holds.

We prove that for any $z \in B$ with $z \leq x$ the conditions $z \to y\,(B, \leq, K)$ and $(z, x) \in \mathbf{D}(K, y)$ are equivalent.

Indeed, $z \to y\,(B, \leq, K)$ means that $\mathbf{C}(K)(y) \leq \mathbf{C}(K)(z)$ which is equivalent to $(z, x) \in \mathbf{D}(K, y)$ by definition of $\mathbf{D}(K, y)$. As an immediate consequence, we obtain the assertion of our theorem. $\qquad\square$

Example 13. We continue our Example 12. Clearly, $\{b\}$ is a $\mathbf{D}(K, \{a, b\})$-reduct of $\{b, c\}$. Hence, $\{b\}$ is a minimal subset X' of $\{b, c\}$ satisfying $X' \to \{a, b\}\,(\mathbf{B}(A), \subseteq, K)$.

7. Systems of pure generalized grammars

The theory elaborated in Sections 4, 5, 6 will be applied to a concrete dependence space. We now give its definition.

Let V be a finite nonempty set. As we have recalled in Section 2, a pure generalized grammar is an ordered triple $< V, S, R >$ where $S \subseteq V^*$ and $R \subseteq V^* \times V^*$. Since the set V will be fixed in what follows, a pure generalized grammar is an ordered pair (S, R) where $S \in \mathbf{B}(V^*)$ and $R \in \mathbf{B}(V^* \times V^*)$. Thus, pure generalized grammars form the set $\mathbf{Z}$ of all such ordered pairs, i.e., $\mathbf{Z} = \mathbf{B}(V^*) \times \mathbf{B}(V^* \times V^*)$. If $(S, R) \in \mathbf{Z}$, $(S', R') \in \mathbf{Z}$, we put $(S, R) \leq (S', R')$ if and only if $S \subseteq S'$, $R \subseteq R'$. Hence, $(\mathbf{Z}, \leq)$ is an ordered set that coincides with the cardinal product of ordered sets $(\mathbf{B}(V^*), \subseteq)$ and $(\mathbf{B}(V^* \times V^*), \subseteq)$. Since these sets are complete lattices, $(\mathbf{Z}, \leq)$ is a complete lattice as well.

Remark 1. For the reader's convenience we recall some basic information about cardinal products. If $(A_1, \leq_1)$, $(A_2, \leq_2)$ are ordered sets, then their cardinal product is the set $A_1 \times A_2$ provided with the relation $\leq$ that is defined as follows: If $(a_1, a_2) \in A_1 \times A_2$, $(b_1, b_2) \in A_1 \times A_2$, then $(a_1, a_2) \leq (b_1, b_2)$ holds if and only if $a_1 \leq_1 b_1$, $a_2 \leq_2 b_2$. It is easy to see that $\leq$ is an ordering on $A_1 \times A_2$. Many properties of the ordered sets $(A_1, \leq_1)$, $(A_2, \leq_2)$ are transferred to their cardinal products, e.g., the property of being a lattice or a complete lattice. Particularly, the following will be useful in our considerations. If $c_1 <_1$ $c_2 <_1 \ldots <_1 c_p$ where $c_1, \ldots, c_p$ are in A_1 and if $d_1 <_2 d_2 <_2 \ldots <_2 d_q$ where $d_1, \ldots, d_q$ are in A_2, then $(c_1, d_1) < (c_2, d_1) < \ldots < (c_p, d_1) < (c_p, d_2) < \ldots < (c_p, d_q)$, i.e., a chain with $p + q - 1$ elements may be constructed in $(A_1 \times A_2, \leq)$ if a chain with p elements is given in $(A_1, \leq_1)$ and a chain with q elements is given in $(A_2, \leq_2)$.

Let $(S, R) \in \mathbf{Z}$, $(S', R') \in \mathbf{Z}$ be given. We put $(S, R) \equiv (S', R')$ if $\mathbf{L}(< V, S, R >) = \mathbf{L}(< V, S', R' >)$. Clearly, $\equiv$ is an equivalence on the set $\mathbf{Z}$.

Since the set V is fixed, we shall write $\mathbf{d}(L)$ for $\mathbf{d}(V, L)$ if $L \subseteq V^*$. Similarly, we write $\mathbf{L}(S, R)$ for $\mathbf{L}(< V, S, R >)$ where $(S, R) \in \mathbf{Z}$.

Theorem 11. *The equivalence $\equiv$ is a convex generalized congruence on the complete lattice $(\mathbf{Z}, \leq)$ and $\mathbf{C}(\equiv)(S, R) = (\mathbf{L}(S, R), \mathbf{d}(\mathbf{L}(S, R)))$ holds.*

Proof. Let $(S, R) \in \mathbf{Z}$ be arbitrary, put $S_0 = \mathbf{L}(S, R)$, $R_0 = \mathbf{d}(S_0)$. By Lemma 2, we have $\mathbf{L}(S_0, R_0) = \mathbf{L}(S_0, \mathbf{d}(S_0)) = S_0 = \mathbf{L}(S, R)$ and, hence, $(S, R) \equiv (S_0, R_0)$. If $(S', R') \in \mathbf{Z}$ is such that $(S', R') \equiv (S, R)$, then $\mathbf{L}(S', R') = \mathbf{L}(S, R) = S_0$ which implies that $S' \subseteq S_0$, $R' \subseteq \mathbf{d}(S_0) = R_0$ by Lemma 3. It follows that $(\mathbf{L}(S, R), \mathbf{d}(\mathbf{L}(S, R))) = (S_0, R_0)$ is the greatest element of the $\equiv$-block containing (S, R). Thus, $\equiv$ is a generalized congruence on $(\mathbf{Z}, \leq)$.

Let us have (S_1, R_1), (S_2, R_2), (S_3, R_3) in $\mathbf{Z}$ such that $(S_1, R_1) \leq (S_2, R_2) \leq (S_3, R_3)$, $(S_1, R_1) \equiv (S_3, R_3)$. Then $\mathbf{L}(S_1, R_1) = \mathbf{L}(S_3, R_3)$, $\mathbf{L}(S_1, R_1) \subseteq \mathbf{L}(S_2, R_2) \subseteq \mathbf{L}(S_3, R_3)$ by Lemma 1 which implies that $\mathbf{L}(S_2, R_2) = \mathbf{L}(S_1, R_1)$. Hence, $\equiv$ is convex. $\square$

Corollary 8. $(\mathbf{Z}, \leq, \equiv)$ *is a convex dependence space.*

Theorem 12. *Let (S, R) be an element in $\mathbf{Z}$. Then the following assertions are equivalent.*

 (i) (S, R) is strongly $\equiv$-accessible.
 (ii) The sets S, R are finite.

Proof. By Remark 1, any chain in $(\mathbf{B}(V^*), \subseteq)$ with p elements and any chain in $(\mathbf{B}(V^* \times V^*), \subseteq)$ with q elements define a chain with $p+q-1$ elements in the cardinal product of these ordered sets, i.e., in $(\mathbf{Z}, \leq)$.

Let *(i)* hold. Thus, if any chain in $(\mathbf{Z}, \leq)$ with the greatest element (S, R) has at most m elements, then any chain in $(\mathbf{B}(V^*), \subseteq)$ with the greatest element S has at most m elements which means that S has at most m elements; similarly, R has at most m elements. Hence *(ii)* holds.

On the other hand, if S has p elements and R has q elements, then any chain in $\mathbf{B}(V^*)$ with the greatest element S has at most $p+1$ elements and any chain in $\mathbf{B}(V^* \times V^*)$ with the greatest element R has at most $q + 1$ elements and, therefore, any chain in $(\mathbf{Z}, \leq)$ with the greatest element (S, R) has at most $p + q + 1$ elements. Thus, *(ii)* implies *(i)*. $\square$

Let (S, R) be a pure generalized grammar. We put

$$\mathbf{b}(S, R) = \{s \in S;\ t \Rightarrow^* s\ (R)\ \text{implies}\ |t| \geq |s|\},$$

$$\mathbf{z}(S, R) = \{(y, x) \in R;\ \text{there exists}\ z \in \mathbf{L}(S, R)\ \text{with}\ \max\{|y|, |x|\} \leq ||z||_R^S\}.$$

In the terminology of [4], the mappings $\mathbf{b}$, $\mathbf{z}$ define the so called reducing operators on $\mathbf{Z}$: For any $(S, R) \in \mathbf{Z}$, we put

$$\beta(S, R) = (\mathbf{b}(S, R), R),\ \ \zeta(S, R) = (S, \mathbf{z}(S, R)),$$

$$\delta(S, R) = \zeta(\beta(S, R)) = \zeta(\mathbf{b}(S, R), R) = (\mathbf{b}(S, R), \mathbf{z}(\mathbf{b}(S, R), R)).$$

A reducing operator assigns a pure generalized grammar to any pure generalized grammar in such a way that both generate the same language and the assigned pure generalized grammar is less or equal to the given one.

Particularly, we obtain

Theorem 13. *If $(S, R) \in \mathbf{Z}$ is arbitrary, then $\delta(S, R) \equiv (S, R)$, $\delta(S, R) \leq (S, R)$.*

Proof. See Theorem 3.17 of [4]. $\qquad\qquad\square$

Theorem 14. *Let us have $(S, R) \in \mathbf{Z}$. Then the following assertions are equivalent.*

(i) There exist finite sets $S' \in \mathbf{B}(V^*)$ and $R' \in \mathbf{B}(V^* \times V^*)$ such that $(S', R') \leq (S, R)$, $(S', R') \equiv (S, R)$.

(ii) $\delta(S, R)$ is a pure grammar.

Proof. See Theorem 4.7 of [4]. $\qquad\qquad\square$

Theorem 15. *Let (S, R) be in $\mathbf{Z}$. Then the following assertions are equivalent.*

(i) $\delta(S, R)$ is strongly $\equiv$-accessible.

(ii) (S, R) has a $\equiv$-reduct (S', R') where S', R' are finite sets.

Proof. If *(i)* holds, then $\delta(S, R)$ has a strongly $\equiv$-accessible $\equiv$-reduct (S', R') by Corollary 5, Theorem 7, and Corollary 6. By Theorem 13, this $\equiv$-reduct is also a $\equiv$-reduct of (S, R) and, by Theorem 12, the sets S', R' are finite. Thus, *(ii)* holds.

If *(ii)* holds, we have $(S', R') \leq (S, R)$, $(S', R') \equiv (S, R)$. By Theorem 14, we obtain that $\delta(S, R)$ is a pure grammar which means that the sets $\mathbf{b}(S, R)$, $\mathbf{z}(\mathbf{b}(S, R), R)$ are finite. Thus, $\delta(S, R)$ is strongly $\equiv$-accessible by Theorem 12. Hence *(i)* holds. $\qquad\qquad\square$

Example 14. Let us have $V = \{a, b\}$, $S = \{a^m b a^m;\ m \geq 0\}$, $R = \{(b, a^m b a^m);\ m \geq 1\}$. Clearly, $\mathbf{L}(S, R) = S$, $\mathbf{d}(S) = \{(a^p b a^q, a^r b a^s); p \geq 0,\ q \geq 0,\ r \geq 0,\ s \geq 0,\ p - r = q - s\} \cup \{(x, x);\ x \in V^*\} \cup \{(y, x) \in$

$V^* \times V^*$; $|y|_b \geq 2\}$, $\mathbf{b}(S, R) = \{b\}$. Since $b \Rightarrow^* w$ $(\{(b, aba)\})$, we obtain $\|w\|_R^{\mathbf{b}(S,R)} \leq 3$ for any $w \in S$. Thus $\mathbf{z}(\mathbf{b}(S, R), R) = \{(b, aba)\}$. Hence $\delta(S, R) = (\mathbf{b}(S, R), \mathbf{z}(\mathbf{b}(S, R), R))$ is a pure grammar which implies that (S, R) has a $\equiv$-reduct (S', R') with finite sets S', R', by Theorems 12 and 15. Using Construction, we state that $\delta(S, R)$ is a $\equiv$-reduct of (S, R).

Remark 2. According to these results, we may give solution of Problem 2. The existence of finite sets S, R such that $S \subseteq L$, $R \subseteq \mathbf{d}(L)$, and that (S, R) generates L is equivalent to the condition that $\delta(L, \mathbf{d}(L))$ is a pure grammar; this is equivalent to the strong $\equiv$-accessibility of $\delta(L, \mathbf{d}(L))$ which means that there exists a $\equiv$-reduct (S', R') of $(L, \mathbf{d}(L))$ such that the sets S', R' are finite.

We now interpret the notion of dependence in the space $(\mathbf{Z}, \leq, \equiv)$.

Theorem 16. *If $(S, R) \in \mathbf{Z}$, $(S', R') \in \mathbf{Z}$, then the following assertions are equivalent.*

(i) $(S, R) \to (S', R')$ $(\mathbf{Z}, \leq, \equiv)$.

(ii) $\mathbf{L}(S', R') \subseteq \mathbf{L}(S, R)$, $\mathbf{d}(\mathbf{L}(S', R')) \subseteq \mathbf{d}(\mathbf{L}(S, R))$.

This is a consequence of the definition of dependence and of Theorem 11.

By Theorem 16, the condition $(S, R) \to (S', R')$ $(\mathbf{Z}, \leq, \equiv)$ has a natural meaning. Any pure generalized grammar (S, R) defines a pure generalized grammar $(\mathbf{L}(S, R), \mathbf{d}(\mathbf{L}(S, R)))$ that is greatest among all pure generalized grammars generating the same language as (S, R). Clearly, (S, R) produces $(\mathbf{L}(S, R), \mathbf{d}(\mathbf{L}(S, R)))$ in a natural way. Condition $(S, R) \to (S', R')$ $(\mathbf{Z}, \leq, \equiv)$ means that this greatest pure generalized grammar produced by (S, R) is greater or as great as the pure generalized grammar produced by (S', R'), i.e., $(\mathbf{L}(S', R'), \mathbf{d}(\mathbf{L}(S', R')))$ can be obtained from $(\mathbf{L}(S, R), \mathbf{d}(\mathbf{L}(S, R)))$ by cancelling some initial strings and some productions. In this sense, (S, R) is "better" than (S', R'). Thus also the following problem is natural.

Problem 3. Let us have $(S, R) \in \mathbf{Z}$, $(T, P) \in \mathbf{Z}$ with the property $(S, R) \to (T, P)$ $(\mathbf{Z}, \leq, \equiv)$. Find a minimal element $(S', R') \in \mathbf{Z}$ such that $(S', R') \leq (S, R)$, $(S', R') \to (T, P)$ $(\mathbf{Z}, \leq, \equiv)$.

Hence, we look for a minimal element that is less or equal to (S, R) and better or as good as (T, P).

By Theorem 10, $(S', R') \in \mathbf{Z}$ is a solution of Problem 3 if and only if it is a $\mathbf{D}(\equiv, (T, P))$-reduct of (S, R). The question whether $((S, R), (S', R')) \in \mathbf{D}(\equiv, (T, P))$ holds or not can be answered by means of the following.

Theorem 17. *Let us have $(S, R) \in \mathbf{Z}$, $(T, P) \in \mathbf{Z}$ such that $(S, R) \to (T, P)$ $(\mathbf{Z}, \leq, \equiv)$. Then $((S, R), (S', R')) \in \mathbf{D}(\equiv, (T, P))$ holds if and only if $\mathbf{C}(\equiv)(T, P) \leq \mathbf{C}(\equiv)(S', R')$.*

Proof. Condition $(S, R) \to (T, P)$ $(\mathbf{Z}, \leq, \equiv)$ means $\mathbf{C}(\equiv)(T, P) \leq \mathbf{C}(\equiv)(S, R)$. By definition of $\mathbf{D}(\equiv, (T, P))$ condition $((S, R), (S', R')) \in \mathbf{D}(\equiv, (T, P))$ is equivalent to $\mathbf{C}(\equiv)(T, P) \leq \mathbf{C}(\equiv)(S', R')$. $\qquad\square$

Example 15. Put $V = \{a, b\}$, $S = \{b\}$, $R = \{(a^m ba^n, a^p ba^q); m \geq 0,\ n \geq 0,\ p \geq 0,\ q \geq 0\}$, $T = \{a^m ba^m;\ m \geq 0\}$, $P = \{(b, aba)\}$. Then $\mathbf{L}(S, R) = \{a^m ba^n;\ m \geq 0,\ n \geq 0\}$, $\mathbf{d}(\mathbf{L}(S, R)) = \{(x, x);\ x \in V^*\} \cup \{(y, x) \in V^* \times V^*;\ |y|_b \geq 2\} \cup \{(a^m, a^n);\ m \geq 0,\ n \geq 0\} \cup \{(a^m ba^n, a^p ba^q); m \geq 0,\ n \geq 0,\ p \geq 0,\ q \geq 0\}$, $\mathbf{L}(T, P) = \{a^m ba^m;\ m \geq 0\}$, $\mathbf{d}(\mathbf{L}(T, P)) = \{(x, x);\ x \in V^*\} \cup \{(y, x) \in V^* \times V^*;\ |y|_b \geq 2\} \cup \{(a^m ba^n, a^p ba^q); m \geq 0,\ n \geq 0,\ p \geq 0,\ q \geq 0,\ m - p = n - q\}$.

Clearly, $\mathbf{L}(T, P) \subseteq \mathbf{L}(S, R)$, $\mathbf{d}(\mathbf{L}(T, P)) \subseteq \mathbf{d}(\mathbf{L}(S, R))$ which means that $\mathbf{C}(\equiv)(T, P) \leq \mathbf{C}(\equiv)(S, R)$ by Theorem 11. Hence $(S, R) \to (T, P)(\mathbf{Z}, \leq, \equiv)$ holds. Put $S' = \{b\}$, $R' = \{(b, aba)\}$. Then $(S', R') \leq (S, R)$ and $\mathbf{L}(S', R') = \mathbf{L}(T, P)$, $\mathbf{d}(\mathbf{L}(S', R')) = \mathbf{d}(\mathbf{L}(T, P))$. Hence, $\mathbf{C}(\equiv)(T, P) = \mathbf{C}(\equiv)(S', R')$. By Theorem 17 we have $((S, R), (S', R')) \in \mathbf{D}(\equiv)(T, P)$. If $(S'', R'') \leq (S', R')$, $(S'', R'') \neq (S', R')$, then either S'' or R'' is empty which implies that $\mathbf{L}(S'', R'')$ is finite. Hence, $\mathbf{L}(T, P) \subseteq \mathbf{L}(S'', R'')$ does not hold while $\mathbf{L}(T, P) \subseteq \mathbf{L}(S, R)$ holds. By Theorem 11, $\mathbf{C}(\equiv)(T, P) \leq \mathbf{C}(\equiv)(S'', R'')$ does not hold and, thus, $((S, R), (S'', R'')) \notin \mathbf{D}(\equiv)(T, P)$ by Theorem 17. It follows that (S', R') is a $\mathbf{D}(\equiv, (T, P))$-reduct of (S, R).

8. Concluding remarks

The above mentioned results concerning pure generalized grammars are destined to demonstrate applications of dependence spaces. Theory of formal languages offers further applications: Instead of arbitrary sets $R \subseteq V^* \times V^*$ of productions, we may study, e.g., sets of productions $(y, x) \in V^* \times V^*$ where either $1 \leq |y| < |x|$ or $1 = |y| < |x|$ or $1 = |y| \leq |x|$. Pure grammars with such productions appear in [9], [5] where the grammatical inference problem is solved. This offers dependence spaces consisting of ordered pairs (S, R) where elements in R satisfy one of the above mentioned conditions.

This approach regards a language L as the pure generalized grammar $(L, \mathbf{f}(L))$ where $\mathbf{f}(L)$ equals either $\mathbf{d}(L)$ or a subset of $\mathbf{d}(L)$ formed of productions satisfying one of the above mentioned conditions. Thus, a construction assigning a pure generalized grammar to any language may be considered to be a mapping of the corresponding dependence space into itself. The author is of opinion that this point of view could be useful when solving, e.g., the grammatical inference problem.

References

1. G. Birkhoff, *Lattice Theory*, Third edition, American Math. Society, Providence, 1984.

2. A. V. Gladkij, Konfiguracionnye charakteristiki jazykov (The configurational characteristics of languages), *Problemy Kibernetiki*, 10 (1963), 251 – 260.

3. S. Marcus, *Algebraic Linguistics; Analytical Models*, Academic Press, New York, 1966.

4. M. Novotný, On some operators reducing generalized grammars, *Information and Control*, 26 (1974), 225 – 235.

5. M. Novotný, *S algebrou od jazyka ke gramatice a zpět (With algebra from language to grammar and back)*, Academia, Praha, 1988.

6. M. Novotný, Dependence spaces of information systems, To appear.

7. M. Novotný, Z. Pawlak, Algebraic theory of independence in information systems, *Fundamenta Informaticae*, 14 (1991), 454 – 476.

8. M. Novotný, Z. Pawlak, On a problem concerning dependence spaces, *Fundamenta Informaticae*, 16 (1992), 275 – 287.

9. J. Ostravský, Effective constructions of grammars for languages of two particular classes, *Fundamenta Informaticae*, 8 (1985), 235 – 252.

10. Z. Pawlak, *Rough Sets. Theoretical Aspects of Reasoning about Data*, Kluwer, Dordrecht, Boston, London, 1991.

11. M. Semeniuk-Polkowska, The theory of configurations in algebraic linguistics, *Intern. J. Computer Math.*, 14 (1983), 239 – 257.

12. G. Szász, *Introduction to Lattice Theory*, Academic Press, Budapest, 1963.

Marcus Contextual Grammars: Modularity and Leftmost Derivation[1]

Gheorghe PĂUN

Institute of Mathematics of the Romanian Academy of Sciences
PO Box 1-764, 70700 Bucureşti, Romania

Grzegorz ROZENBERG

University of Leiden, Department of Computer Science
Niels Bohrweg 1, 2333 CA Leiden, The Netherlands
and
Department of Computer Science, University of Colorado at Boulder
Boulder, CO 80309, USA

Arto SALOMAA

Academy of Finland and University of Turku
Department of Mathematics, 20500 Turku, Finland

Abstract. We consider special kinds of contextual grammars which are similar to the cooperating grammar systems: one gives several languages having associated sets of contexts (such a pair is a *module* of the grammar); a context can be adjoined only to strings in the corresponding language. Derivations consisting of a given number of such steps, of at least a given number, or at most a given number, and maximal derivations in the components of a grammar are investigated (from the generative capacity point of view), both for external and for internal modular contextual grammars. Finally, the leftmost derivation in an internal modular grammar is considered. Some open problems are formulated, too.

1. Introduction

The contextual grammars have been introduced in [6], as an intrinsic generative mechanism (that is not using auxiliary symbols) based on the phenomenon of acceptance of a context by a word (a string of words) or of a word (a string of words) by a context [5]. Roughly speaking, a contextual grammar produces a language by starting from a finite set of strings and adding, iteratively, contexts (pairs of strings) to the strings already obtained; the added

[1]Research supported by the Basic Research ASMICS II Working Group, the Alexander von Humboldt Foundation and the Academy of Finland, grant 11281

contexts depend in some specified way on the current string to which they are adjoined, and they can be adjoined either in the interior of the string or only at its ends. (More precise definitions are given in the next section.) Motivations can be found also in [7]. As it was pointed out in [14], such mechanisms are intimately related with many fundamental notions in formal language theory, such as recurrent symbols in Chomsky grammars and in Lindenmayer systems, operations of deletion and insertion [3], etc., or with elaborated notions, such as the cooperating grammar systems [1], [2], [8]. In this broad perspective, many topics not considered so far for contextual grammars were investigated in [14], [15]: determinism, erasing, parallel derivation and so on.

The present paper continues this line of research, by examining two more new topics, namely modularity and leftmost derivation. In a modular grammar, as in the case of cooperating grammar systems, several components are considered (pairs language–set of contexts); the derivation is defined in the style of grammar systems: every component can became active in any moment, but it must became inactive only when certain precise conditions are fulfilled (when no more step can be performed in that component, or when the number of steps already made equals a given constant, is smaller than or greater than a given constant, etc). The language generated by the grammar is obtained by such a collaboration of its components.

The derivations mentioned have a surprisingly different influence on the generative capacity of external and on the capacity of internal contextual grammars, compared with the power of grammars with the usual mode of derivation (corresponding to the mode "one step in each component, iteratively").

As in the preceding two papers, [14], [15], too, some problems remain open here; in general, the contextual grammars raise many interesting combinatorial questions, which we believe will require significant efforts. (See, for instance, the problem of finding *aholographic* languages, in Section 5.)

2. Contextual grammars with choice

Because in this paper we shall work only with external and with internal contextual grammars with choice, we shall present only their definitions; the reader is referred to [10], [12], [14], [15] for other classes. Moreover, we shall not explicitly mention the specification "with choice", [14], because this is the only case we consider.

An *external contextual grammar* is a quadruple $G = (V, B, C, \varphi)$, where V is a finite non-empty alphabet, B is a finite language over V, $C \subseteq V^* \times V^*$ is a finite set of *contexts* over V (V^* is the free monoid generated by V; its identity is denoted by λ and $V^* - \{\lambda\} = V^+$), and $\varphi : V^* \longrightarrow 2^C$ is the *selection mapping*.

The language generated by G, denoted $L_{ex}(G)$, is the smallest set $L \subseteq V^*$ which includes B and has the following property: if $x \in L$, and $(u, v) \in \varphi(x)$, then $uxv \in L$.

(The context (u, v) is added to x to obtain uxv, if and only if it is selected by the mapping φ.)

An *internal contextual grammar* is a quadruple $G = (V, B, C, \varphi)$ as above, with the language generated by G, denoted $L_{in}(G)$, defined as the smallest subset L of V^* which includes B and has the following property: if $x \in L$, and $(u, v) \in \varphi(x_2)$ for some decomposition $x = x_1 x_2 x_3, x_1, x_2, x_3 \in V^*$, then $x_1 u x_2 v x_3 \in L$.

(The context (u, v) is added to x in interior, selected by the subword around which the context is adjoined.)

The language generated by a contextual grammar can be defined also using a derivation relation; for instance, when $G = (V, B, C, \varphi)$ is an internal contextual grammar (the modification for the external case is obvious), for $x, y \in V^*$ we can define

$$x \Longrightarrow_{in} y \text{ iff } x = x_1 x_2 x_3, y = x_1 u x_2 v x_3, \text{for } x_1, x_2, x_3 \in V^*, (u, v) \in \varphi(x_2).$$

Then

$$L_{in}(G) = \{w \in V^* \mid z \Longrightarrow_{in}^* w, z \in B\}.$$

When the mapping φ is defined by $\varphi(x) = C, x \in V^*$, then the grammar is said to be without choice; we shall not consider such grammars here.

The external contextual grammars (with and without choice), have been defined in [6], the internal contextual grammars (with and without choice), are introduced in [13].

Here are two examples; in general, when giving a contextual grammar, we specify only the definition of φ on strings x for which $\varphi(x) \neq \emptyset$ and it is assumed that for all non-specified strings x we have $\varphi(x) = \emptyset$.

Consider the external contextual grammar

$$G_M = (\{a, b\}, \{b\}, \{(\lambda, a), (\lambda, b)\}, \varphi),$$
$$\varphi(ba^i) = \begin{cases} \{(\lambda, a), (\lambda, b)\}, & i \in M, \\ \{(\lambda, a)\}, & \text{otherwise,} \end{cases}$$

where M is an arbitrary subset of $\mathbf{N}$. We obtain

$$L_{ex}(G_M) = \{ba^n \mid n \geq 0\} \cup \{ba^n b \mid n \in M\}.$$

For the internal contextual grammar

$$G = (\{a, b, c\}, \{babccab\}, \{(\lambda, a), (a, a), (b, b), (c, c)\}, \varphi),$$
$$\varphi(ab^n cca) = \{(a, a)\}, \ n \geq 1,$$
$$\varphi(bcca^n b) = \{(b, b)\}, \ n \geq 1,$$
$$\varphi(ba^n b^m c) = \{(\lambda, a)\}, \ n, m \geq 1,$$
$$\varphi(a^n b^n caca^m b^m) = \{(c, c)\}, \ n, m \geq 1,$$

we have

$$
\begin{aligned}
L_{in}(G) = \ & \{ba^n b^m cca^n b^m \mid n, m \geq 1\} \cup \\
& \cup \{ba^n b^m ca^p ca^n b^m \mid n, m, p \geq 1\} \cup \\
& \cup \{bc^i a^n b^n caca^n b^n c^i \mid i, n \geq 1\}.
\end{aligned}
$$

Note that $L_{ex}(G_M)$ is of a complexity comparable with the complexity of M (for instance, it is non-recursively enumerable if M is not recursively enumerable), and that $L_{in}(G)$ is not context-free.

We shall denote by EC, IC the families of languages generated by external and by internal contextual grammars (E stands for *external*, I for *internal* and C stands for *choice*), respectively. We also denote by REG, LIN, CF, CS, RE the families of regular, linear, context-free, context-sensitive and recursively enumerable languages in the Chomsky hierarchy; by FIN we denote the family of finite languages and ARB is the family of arbitrary languages.

We do not recall here results concerning the generative power of the contextual grammars mentioned above; the reader can find details in [10] , [12].

In grammars without any restriction on the mapping φ, this mapping can define the generated language in the same way as the membership mapping of the language does (see the first example above). In general, the infinitary definition of φ is unpleasant. Various restrictions have been considered (see references in [10], [12]), the most natural being either to define the mapping φ only on a finite subset of V^* (hence to take $\varphi(x) = \emptyset$ for other strings) or to define it uniformly on regular subsets of V^* [4], namely to consider the following equivalence relation for strings $x, y \in V^*$,

$$
x \equiv_\varphi y \text{ iff } \varphi(x) = \varphi(y),
$$

and to impose the condition that all its equivalence classes are regular languages. In such a case, the grammar is said to be *with regular choice* and it can be given as a construct

$$
G = (V, B, C, (R_1, D_1), \ldots, (R_n, D_n)),
$$

$n \geq 1$, where $R_i \in REG, D_i \subseteq C, 1 \leq i \leq n$, such that $R_i \cap R_j = \emptyset, D_i \neq D_j$, for $i \neq j$, with the meaning that D_i is the set of contexts which can be adjoined to strings in $R_i, 1 \leq i \leq n$ (that is, in terms of the selection mapping, $\varphi(x) = D_i$ for all $x \in R_i$).

In general, if the languages $R_i, 1 \leq i \leq n$, considered above (hence the languages $\varphi^{-1}(D) = \{x \in V^* \mid \varphi(x) = D\}$, for all $D \subseteq C$) belong to a given family F of languages, then we say that the grammar is *with F choice*. The corresponding families of languages generated by external and by internal contextual grammars are denoted by $EC(F), IC(F)$, respectively (hence $EC =$

$EC(ARB), IC = IC(ARB))$. (The previous example of an internal contextual grammar had context-free choice.)

As it has been shown in [11], the family $IC(FIN)$ contains non-context-free languages, whereas in [18] it is proved that $REG \subset IC(REG)$. Moreover, $EC(REG) \subset LIN$ (Theorem 1 in [14]).

3. Modular contextual grammars

A *modular contextual grammar* of degree $n, n \geq 1$ (with F choice, F a family of languages) is a construct

$$G = (V, B, (R_1, C_1), (R_2, C_2), \ldots, (R_n, C_n)),$$

where V is an alphabet, B is a finite language over V, R_i are languages over V (in the family F) and C_i are finite sets of contexts over V. (The pairs (R_i, C_i) are called *modules* or *components* of the grammar.)

This is exactly a contextual grammar with F choice as defined at the end of the preceding section (we do not take $R_1, \ldots, R_n$ a partition of V^*, but this can be obtained by replacing the sets R_i with all their possible intersections and differences). However, the way of generating a language is now different, namely it is based on derivation modes similar to those usual for grammar systems. For $x, y \in V^*, 1 \leq i \leq n$, we define

$$x \Longrightarrow_{i,ex} y \quad \text{iff} \quad x \in R_i, y = uxv, (u, v) \in C_i,$$
$$x \Longrightarrow_{i,in} y \quad \text{iff} \quad x = x_1 x_2 x_3, x_2 \in R_i, y = x_1 u x_2 v x_3, (u, v) \in C_i.$$

Then, for $g \in \{ex, in\}$ and $k \geq 1$, we define

$$x \Longrightarrow_{i,g}^{=k} y \quad \text{iff} \quad x \Longrightarrow_{i,g} x_1 \Longrightarrow_{i,g} \cdots \Longrightarrow_{i,g} x_k = y,$$
$$x \Longrightarrow_{i,g}^{\leq k} y \quad \text{iff} \quad x \Longrightarrow_{i,g}^{=k'} y, \text{ for some } k' \leq k,$$
$$x \Longrightarrow_{i,g}^{\geq k} y \quad \text{iff} \quad x \Longrightarrow_{i,g}^{=k'} y, \text{ for some } k' \geq k,$$
$$x \Longrightarrow_{i,g}^{*} y \quad \text{iff} \quad x \Longrightarrow_{i,g}^{=k'} y, \text{ for some } k' \geq 1,$$
$$x \Longrightarrow_{i,g}^{t} y \quad \text{iff} \quad x \Longrightarrow_{i,g}^{*} y \text{ and there is no } z \in V^* \text{ such that } y \Longrightarrow_{i,g} z.$$

The language generated by a grammar G in the derivation mode $f \in \{*, t\} \cup \{\leq k, = k, \geq k \mid k \geq 1\}$ and the style $g \in \{ex, in\}$ is defined by

$$L_{g,f}(G) = B \cup \{w \in V^* \mid z \Longrightarrow_{i_1,g}^{f} z_1 \Longrightarrow_{i_2,g}^{f} \cdots \Longrightarrow_{i_m,g}^{f} z_m = w,$$
$$z \in B, m \geq 1, 1 \leq i_j \leq n, 1 \leq j \leq m\}.$$

The families of languages generated in this way by grammars of degree at most n and with F choice, F a family of languages, are denoted by $M_n EC_F(f)$, $M_n IC_F(f)$, respectively; when n can be unbounded, we replace it by ∞.

Here is an **example** of an external modular contextual grammar (with regular choice):

$$G = (\{a, b, c\}, \{aca\}, (R_1, C_1), (R_2, C_2)),$$
$$R_1 = a^+ca^+, \ C_1 = \{(a, a), (b, b)\},$$
$$R_2 = b^+a^+ca^+b^+, \ C_2 = \{(b, b)\}.$$

We obtain

$$L_{ex,*}(G) = L_{ex,\leq k}(G) = L_{ex,\geq 1}(G) = L_{ex,=1}(G) =$$
$$= \{b^m a^n ca^n b^m \mid n \geq 1, m \geq 0\},$$
$$L_{ex,=k}(G) = \{a^{sk+1} ca^{sk+1} \mid s \geq 0\} \cup$$
$$\cup \{b^{rk+1} a^{sk} ca^{sk} b^{rk+1} \mid s \geq 1, r \geq 0\}, k \geq 2,$$
$$L_{ex,\geq k}(G) = \{a^n ca^n \mid n \geq k+1\} \cup$$
$$\cup \{b^m a^n ca^n b^m \mid n \geq k, m \geq k+1\}, k \geq 2,$$
$$L_{ex,t}(G) = \{ba^n ca^n b \mid n \geq 1\}.$$

Indeed, for all modes different from t, the derivation must start in the first module, (R_1, C_1), and can end either here or in the second module. For t, the derivation must consist of maximal derivations in the used modules, but the derivation never ends in (R_2, C_2), hence the only accepted strings are those generated in the t mode by the first module.

4. The power of external modular grammars

The necessary condition in Lemma 1, whose proof can be found in [10], will be useful when comparing families EC and $M_n EC_F(f)$. For $L \subseteq V^*$ define

$$Min_0(L) = \{x \in L \mid \text{there is no } y \in L \text{ such that } x = uyv, uv \neq \lambda\},$$
$$Min_i(L) = Min_{i-1}(L) \cup Min_0(L - Min_{i-1}(L)), \text{ for } i \geq 1.$$

Lemma 1. *If $L \in EC$, then every set $Min_i(L), i \geq 0$, is finite.*

The next relations follow directly from definitions.

Lemma 2. $M_n EC_F(f) \subseteq M_n EC_{F'}(f), \ n \geq 1,$ *for all f and $F \subseteq F'$.*
$M_n EC_F(f) \subseteq M_{n+1} EC_F(f),$ *for all $n \geq 1$, and all f, F.*

Theorem 1. $M_\infty EC_{FIN}(f) = FIN,$ *for all f.*

Proof. If $G = (V, B, (R_1, C_1), \ldots, (R_n, C_n)), R_i \in FIN, 1 \leq i \leq n$, then $L_{ex,f}(G) \subseteq B \cup \{uxv \mid (u, v) \in C_i, x \in R_i, 1 \leq i \leq n\}$, which is a finite language.

Conversely, every $L \subseteq V^*, L \in FIN$, is generated by $G = (V, L, (\{x\}, \{(\lambda, \lambda)\}))$, for some $x \in V^*, |x| > \max\{|z| \mid z \in L\}$. □

Theorem 2. *For all $f \neq t$ we have $EC = M_\infty EC_{ARB}(f)$. If F is a family closed under intersection, complement and under right and left derivatives, then $EC(F) = M_\infty EC_F(f)$.*

Proof. For a grammar $G = (V, B, C, \varphi)$ we can construct the modular grammar $G' = (V, B, (R_1, C_1), \ldots, (R_n, C_n))$, with $R_i = \varphi^{-1}(D_i), C_i = D_i \cup \{(\lambda, \lambda)\}$, for $D_i \subseteq C$, and we obtain $L_{ex}(G) = L_{ex,g}(G')$ for all values of g different from t, including $g \in \{= k, \geq k \mid k \geq 1\}$ (we use the context (λ, λ) for completing $= k$ or $\geq k$, $k \geq 1$, derivations in G' corresponding to derivations in G), hence $EC \subseteq M_\infty EC_{ARB}(f)$ for all f as in the theorem. Note that when G is with F choice, then the sets R_i are languages in F.

Conversely, for a modular grammar $G = (V, B, (R_1, C_1), \ldots, (R_n, C_n))$ we construct the usual contextual grammar $G' = (V, B, C, \cup_{i=1}^n C_i, \varphi)$, with

$$\varphi(x) = \{(u, v) \mid (u, v) \in C_i, x \in R_i, 1 \leq i \leq n\}, x \in V^*.$$

Clearly, $L_{ex,f}(G) = L_{ex}(G')$ for $f \in \{*, = 1, \geq 1\} \cup \{\leq k \mid k \geq 1\}$. On the other hand, one can see that

$$x \equiv_\varphi y \text{ iff } \{i \mid x \in R_i, 1 \leq i \leq n\} = \{i \mid y \in R_i, 1 \leq i \leq n\}.$$

Hence the equivalence classes with respect to φ are obtained as intersections and complements of sets R_i; therefore if $R_i, 1 \leq i \leq n$, are in a family F with the properties specified in the theorem, then also G' is a grammar with F choice.

In order to complete the proof, we have to consider also the cases $= k$, $\geq k$, for $k \geq 2$. For a modular grammar $G = (V, B, (R_1, C_1), \ldots, (R_n, C_n))$ with $R_i \in F, 1 \leq i \leq n$, we construct the grammar, also modular, $G' = (V, B, (R_1', C_1'), \ldots, (R_m', C_m'))$, $m = (card(C_1))^k + (card(C_n))^k$, where

$$C_s' = \{(u_k \ldots u_2 u_1, v_1 v_2 \ldots v_k)\}, \ (u_j, v_j) \in C_i, 1 \leq j \leq k,$$

for values of s corresponding to $i, 1 \leq i \leq n$ (namely, $\sum_{j=1}^{i-1}(card(C_j))^k < s \leq \sum_{j=1}^{i}(card(C_j))^k$), and the associated R_s' defined by

$$R_s' = R_i \cap \partial_{u_1}^l(\partial_{v_1}^r(R_i)) \cap \partial_{u_2 u_1}^l(\partial_{v_1 v_2}^r(R_i)) \cap \ldots \cap \partial_{u_{k-1} \ldots u_1}^l(\partial_{v_1 \ldots v_{k-1}}^r(R_i)).$$

($\partial_z^l, \partial_z^r$ denote the left and the right derivatives with respect to z.) We obviously have $L_{ex,=k}(G) = L_{ex,=1}(G')$. Moreover, R_s' are in the family F if R_i are in F and F has the properties mentioned in the theorem. Consequently, $M_\infty EC_F(= k) \subseteq M_\infty EC_F(= 1)$. The latter family, in turn, is included into $EC(F)$ as we have seen above.

For the $\geq k$ mode of derivation we proceed as for the $= k$ mode, namely we construct the modular grammar G' considering all sets

$$C_s' = \{(u_p \ldots u_2 u_1, v_1 v_2 \ldots v_p)\}, \ (u_j, v_j) \in C_i, 1 \leq j \leq p,$$

for all p, $k \le p \le 2k - 1$. (Every derivation in the $\ge k$ mode, say, using $rk + q$ contexts, $r \ge 1$, $0 \le q < k$, can be decomposed into $r - 1$ derivations in the $= k$ mode and one more derivation in the $= (k+q)$ mode; clearly, $k \le k+q < 2k$.) The languages R_s' are defined according to the considered contexts. $\qquad\square$

Consequently, for all the derivation modes other than t, the modularity does not change the generative power of external contextual grammars. The situation is different for the t mode.

Theorem 3. $M_2 EC_{REG}(t) - EC \ne \emptyset$; $EC \subset M_\infty EC_{ARB}(t)$.

Proof. The language $L_{ex,t}(G) = \{ba^n ca^n b \mid n \ge 1\}$ considered in Section 3 is not in the family EC, due to the condition in Lemma 1: $Min_0(L_{ex,t}(G)) = L_{ex,t}(G)$. It is therefore sufficient to prove the inclusion $EC \subseteq M_\infty EC_{ARB}(t)$.

To this aim, take a contextual grammar $G = (V, B, C, \varphi)$ and, for every $x \in L_{ex}(G)$, denote

$$d(x) = \min\{m \mid w \Longrightarrow_{ex} x_1 \Longrightarrow_{ex} x_2 \Longrightarrow_{ex} \ldots \Longrightarrow_{ex} x_m = x, w \in B\}.$$

(The length of the shortest derivation of x in G.) Then define

$$D_{even} = \{x \in L_{ex}(G) \mid d(x) = 2j,\ j \ge 0\},$$
$$D_{odd} = \{x \in L_{ex}(G) \mid d(x) = 2j + 1,\ j \ge 0\}.$$

This is clearly a partition of the language $L_{ex}(G)$ (if there are several derivations to a string x, we consider a derivation of minimal length and this length is unique). Construct the contextual grammar $G' = (V, B, C, \varphi')$ with

$$\varphi'(x) = \begin{cases} \varphi(x) - \{(u, v) \mid uxv \in D_{odd}\}, & x \in D_{odd}, \\ \varphi(x) - \{(u, v) \mid uxv \in D_{even}\}, & x \in D_{even}, \\ \emptyset, & \text{otherwise.} \end{cases}$$

We have $L_{ex}(G) = L_{ex}(G')$: the shortest derivation in G leading to a string x remains possible in G', hence $L_{ex}(G) \subseteq L_{ex}(G')$; the converse inclusion is obvious, because φ' allows the adjoining of contexts which are allowed also by φ. Every derivation in G' is of the form $z_0 \Longrightarrow_{ex} z_1 \Longrightarrow_{ex} z_2 \Longrightarrow_{ex} \ldots$ with $z_0 \in B$, $z_{2j+1} \in D_{odd}$, $z_{2j} \in D_{even}$, $j \ge 0$.

Consider now all the subsets $C_1, \ldots, C_n$ of C such that $\varphi'^{-1}(C_i) \ne \emptyset$, and define the modular grammars

$$G'' = (V, B, (R_1, C_1), \ldots, (R_n, C_n)),$$
$$R_i = \varphi'^{-1}(C_i), 1 \le i \le n,$$
$$G''' = (V, B, (R_1', C_1), (R_1'', C_1), \ldots, (R_n', C_n), (R_n'', C_n)),$$
$$R_i' = R_i \cap D_{even},\ 1 \le i \le n,$$
$$R_i'' = R_i \cap D_{odd}, 1 \le i \le n.$$

We have $L_{ex}(G') = L_{ex,=1}(G'')$ (the sets R_i are another mode to present the selection made by the mapping φ') and $L_{ex,=1}(G'') = L_{ex,t}(G''')$: if $x \in R_i'$ (or $x \in R_i''$) and $(u, v) \in C_i$, then $uxc \notin R_i'$ (respectively, $uxv \notin R_i''$), hence we cannot use the same component (R_i', C_i) or (R_i'', C_i) in two consecutive steps. This concludes the proof. $\square$

Remark 1. The power of modular grammars with the t derivation mode and arbitrary choice is very large. For instance, given an arbitrary language $L \subseteq V^*$ and a symbol c not in V, the language $L\{c\}$ is in $M_1 EC_{ARB}(t)$, because it is generated by the grammar $G = (V \cup \{c\}, \{\lambda\}, ((V \cup \{c\})^* - L\{c\}, \{(\lambda, a) \mid a \in V\} \cup \{(\lambda, c)\}))$. (Starting from the empty string, one constructs all strings in $V^*\{c\}$ (and other strings), but the derivation can stop only in the moment of producing strings in $L\{c\}$, the only strings which accept no context.

The relation $EC(REG) \subset LIN$ was proved in [14]. The same inclusion is true for modular grammars with regular selection, and the proof is based on the same idea as the proof in [14]. However, the strictness of this inclusion remains an **open problem**.

Theorem 4. $M_\infty EC_{REG}(t) \subseteq LIN$.

Proof. Let $G = (V, B, (R_1, C_1), \ldots, (R_n, C_n))$ be a modular contextual grammar with $R_i \in REG, 1 \leq i \leq n$. Consider the deterministic finite automata $A_i = (K_i, V, s_{0,i}, \delta_i, F_i), A_i' = (K_i', V, s_{0,i}', \delta_i', F_i')$ such that $L(A_i) = R_i, L(A_i') = V^* - R_i, 1 \leq i \leq n$. Without loss of the generality we may assume that all sets $K_1, K_1', \ldots, K_n, K_n'$ are pairwise disjoint. We construct the linear grammar $G' = (N, V, S, P)$, with

$$N = \{S\} \cup \{[M, j] \mid M \subseteq \bigcup_{i=1}^{n} (K_i^2 \cup K_i'^2), 1 \leq j \leq n\},$$

and P containing the following rules:

(1) $S \to u[\{(s_{0,j}, s_f), (s, s')\}, j]v$, where

- $(u, v) \in C_j$, for some $1 \leq j \leq n$;

- $s_f \in F_j$, $s, s' \in K_j'$;

- $s = \delta_j'(s_{0,j}', u), \delta_j'(s', v) \in F_j'$.

(We ensure both that the context (u, v) is added correctly, to a string in R_j, and that after adding this context the derivation cannot continue in the component (R_j, C_j), because the obtained string is in the complement of R_j.)

(2) $[M, j] \to u[M', j]v$, where

- $[M, j] \in N, 1 \leq j \leq n, (u, v) \in C_j$;

- if $(s, s') \in M, s, s' \in K_i$ (or $s, s' \in K_i'$) for some $1 \le i \le n$, then M' contains a pair $(q, q'), q, q' \in K_i$ (respectively, $q, q' \in K_i'$), such that $q = \delta_i(s, u), s' = \delta_i(q', v)$ $(q = \delta_i'(s, u), s' = \delta_i'(q', v))$;

- besides the pairs (q, q') defined above, we add to M' a pair $(s_{0,j}, s_f), s_f \in F_j$, providing it is not already in M'.

(We simulate the correct adjoining of the context (u, v) by adding the new pair $(s_{0,j}, s_f)$ to M, and we continue at the same time the work of all automata A_i, A_i' having pairs of states in the current set M; this is done in two directions, beginning from the initial states and going forward, and beginning from final states and going backward. The second component of nonterminals, the integer j, ensures the fact that we do not change the components of G without checking whether the derivation is carried out in the t mode, that is it is maximal in the used component.)

$\qquad$ (3) $[M, j] \to u[M', k]v$, where

- $[M, j] \in N, 1 \le j \le n, 1 \le k \le n, k \ne j$;

- $(u, v) \in C_k$;

- if $(s, s') \in M, s, s' \in K_i$ (or $s, s' \in K_i'$) for some $1 \le i \le n$, then M' contains a pair $(q, q'), q, q' \in K_i$ (respectively, $q, q' \in K_i'$), such that $q = \delta_i(s, u), s' = \delta_i(q', v)$ $(q = \delta_i'(s, u), s' = \delta_i'(q', v))$;

- besides the pairs (q, q') defined above, we add to M' also the pairs $(s_{0,k}, s_f)$, for some $s_f \in F_k$, and $(s, s'), s, s' \in K_k'$, such that $s = \delta_k'(s_{0,k}, u), \delta_k'(s', v) \in F_k'$, providing that these pairs are not already in M'.

(The transition from the component (R_k, C_k) to the component (R_j, C_j) is carried out only after adjoining a context which leads from a string in R_k to a string not in R_k.)

$\qquad$ (4) $[M, j] \to x$, where

- $x \in B, [M, j] \in N, 1 \le j \le n$;

- for all $(s, s') \in M, s, s' \in K_i$ (respectively, $s, s' \in K_i'$), $1 \le i \le n$, we have $s' = \delta_i(s, x)$ $(s' = \delta_i'(s, x))$.

(The pairs of states are matched on a string in B, hence all pairs of states introduced when adding contexts are linked by correct derivations in automata A_i, A_i' associated to the components of the grammar G simulated by G'.)

$\qquad$ (5) $S \to x, \ x \in B$.

From the above explanations it is easy to see that $L_{ex,t}(G) = L(G')$ (the derivations in G are reproduced in G' in a reversed form, starting with the last added context and ending with a string in B), therefore we have $M_\infty EC_{REG}(t) \subseteq LIN$. $\qquad\qquad\square$

We do not known whether the above inclusion is proper and we have no conjecture about this either because of, for instance, the next result, which shows that the power of modular grammars with regular choice is in some sense comparable with that of linear grammars. Moreover, "complex" linear languages can be generated by regular modular grammars (with only one component !). For instance, for $k \geq 2$, consider the language

$$L_k = \{a_k a_{k-1}^{i_{k-1}} a_{k-2}^{i_{k-2}} \ldots a_1^{i_1} a_0 a_1^{i_1} \ldots a_{k-2}^{i_{k-2}} a_{k-1}^{i_{k-1}} a_k \mid i_j \geq 1, 1 \leq j \leq k-1\}.$$

The grammar $G = (V, B, (R_1, C_1))$ with

$$\begin{aligned}
V &= \{a_0, a_1, \ldots, a_k\}, \\
B &= \{a_0\}, \\
R_1 &= V^* - a_k a_{k-1}^+ a_{k-2}^+ \ldots a_1^+ a_0 a_1^+ \ldots a_{k-2}^+ a_{k-1}^+ a_k, \\
C_1 &= \{(a_i, a_i) \mid 1 \leq i \leq k\},
\end{aligned}$$

generates L_k: starting from a_0, one adds contexts from C_1 to all strings in V^* excepting those in L_k, hence the only way to stop the derivation is to reach a string in L_k.

Theorem 5. *Every linear language is the morphic image of a language in* $M_1 EC_{REG}(t)$.

Proof. Let $L \subseteq V^*$ be a linear language, generated by the linear grammar $G = (N, V, S, P)$. We construct the right-linear grammar

$$\begin{aligned}
G' = \ &(N, V \cup \{[A] \mid A \in N\}, S, P'), \\
&P' = \{A \to [A]uB \mid A \to uBv \in P, u, v \in V^*, B \in N\} \cup \\
&\quad \cup \{A \to [A]x \mid A \to x \in P, x \in V^*\}.
\end{aligned}$$

(Only the "left-hand part" of strings in L is generated, together with new terminals associated to the nonterminals of G used in these derivations.)

We construct now the modular grammar $G'' = (V', B, (R_1, C_1))$, with

$$\begin{aligned}
V' &= V \cup \{[A] \mid A \in N\} \cup \{c\}, \\
B &= \{[A]xc \mid A \to x \in P, x \in V^*\}, \\
R_1 &= V'^*\{c\}V'^* - \{c\}L(G')\{c\}V^*\{c\}, \\
C_1 &= \{([A]u, v) \mid A \to uBv \in P, u, v \in V^*, B \in N\} \cup \{(c, c)\}.
\end{aligned}$$

With the morphism $h : V'^* \longrightarrow V^*$ defined by $h(c) = h([A]) = \lambda, A \in N$, $h(a) = a, a \in V$, we obtain the equality $L = h(L_{ex,t}(G''))$. Indeed, the contexts in C_1 can be added to any string in $(V' - \{c\})^*\{c\}(V' - \{c\})^*$, and they corresponds to pairs of strings introduced by the rules in P. Therefore we can generate all strings $[A_1]u_1[A_2]u_2 \ldots [A_s]u_s[A_{s+1}]xcv_s \ldots v_2v_1$ corresponding to a string $u_1u_2 \ldots u_s x v_s \ldots v_2v_1$ in $L(G)$, as well as strings which do not correspond to correct derivations in G. The only possibility to have a t derivation in G'' is to produce a string in $\{c\}R_1\{c\}$, to which no context can be adjoined. This implies that both the correct pairing of strings u, v associated to rules in P and the correct sequence of them are ensured (by the contexts and by the regular language R_1, respectively). Erasing the symbols not in V, we obtain the strings in L. Observe that, in fact, the morphism h is simply the projection of V' onto V. $\qquad\square$

On the other hand, we have

Theorem 6. $M_2EC_{LIN}(f) - CF \neq \emptyset$, *for all f.*

Proof. Take the grammar

$$G = (\{a, b, c\}, \{c\}, (R_1, C_1), (R_2, C_2)),$$
$$R_1 = \{a, b\}^*\{c\}\{a, b\}^*, \quad C_1 = \{(\lambda, \lambda), (a, a), (b, b), (\lambda, c)\},$$
$$R_2 = \{a^p b^q cb^n a^n c \mid n, p, q \geq 1\}, \quad C_2 = \{(\lambda, \lambda), (c, \lambda)\}.$$

The derivations must begin in the first component and continue until using the context (λ, c). After that, (R_1, C_1) cannot be used, but (R_2, C_2) can continue, but with only one effective step, adding one more occurrence of c, providing that the contexts $(a, a), (b, b)$ have been used the same number of times, first (b, b) and then (a, a). Due to the presence of the context (λ, λ), derivations of any length can be performed in each component. Consequently, we obtain

$$L_{ex,f}(G) = \{xc\, Mi(x) \mid x \in \{a, b\}^*\} \cup \{xc\, Mi(x)c \mid x \in \{a, b\}^*\} \cup$$
$$\cup\{ca^n b^n cb^n a^n c \mid n \geq 1\},$$

for all $f \neq t$, and

$$L_{ex,t}(G) = \{xc\, Mi(x)c \mid x \in \{a, b\}^*\} \cup \{ca^n b^n cb^n a^n c \mid n \geq 1\},$$

where $Mi(x)$ is the mirror image of x. Obviously, these languages are not context-free. $\qquad\square$

5. The power of the internal modular grammars

Two of the five derivation modes considered above have a surprisingly different influence on (modular) internal contextual grammars, compared to the case of external grammars: the t mode decreases the generative capacity, whereas the $= k$ mode increases the power of internal grammars.

Theorem 7. $M_\infty IC_{ARB}(t) \subseteq FIN \subseteq M_1 IC_F(t)$, *for any F containing singleton languages.*

Proof. If $G = (V, B, (R_1, C_1), \ldots, (R_n, C_n))$ is an internal modular grammar with arbitrary languages $R_i, 1 \le i \le n$, and $x \Longrightarrow_{in,j} y, 1 \le j \le n$, then $y = x_1 u x_2 v x_3$, for $x = x_1 x_2 x_3, (u, v) \in C_j, x_2 \in R_j$, therefore $y \Longrightarrow_{in,j} x_1 u u x_2 v v x_3$, which implies that no derivation can be finished in the t mode. In conclusion, $L_{in,t}(G) = B \in FIN$.

Moreover, for every $L \in FIN$ we have $L = L_{in,t}(G)$, where $G = (V, L, (x, \{(\lambda, \lambda)\}))$, for $x \in V^*, |x| > \max\{|z| \mid z \in L\}$. $\qquad\square$

Theorem 8. $M_\infty IC_{ARB}(f) = IC, \ f \in \{*, = 1, \ge 1\} \cup \{\le k \mid k \ge 1\}$.

Proof. Obvious (see also the proof of Theorem 2). $\qquad\square$

Theorem 9. $IC \subseteq M_\infty IC_{ARB}(f), \ f \in \{= k, \ge k \mid k \ge 2\}$; *for $n \ge 4$, $k \ge 3$, $M_n IC_{REG}(= k) - IC \ne \emptyset$.*

Proof. The inclusions $IC \subseteq M_\infty IC_{ARB}(f), f$ as in the theorem, can be proved as in the proof of Theorem 2 (starting from an internal contextual grammar G, construct a modular contextual grammar G' such that $L_{in}(G) = L_{in,=1}(G')$, then add to each component of G' the context (λ, λ), thus obtaining a grammar G'' for which $L_{in,=k}(G'') = L_{in,\ge k}(G'') = L_{in,=1}(G')$).

Consider now the the modular grammar

$$G = (V, \{\lambda\}, (R_1, C_1), (R_2, C_2), (R_3, C_3), (R_4, C_4)),$$
$$V = \{a_i \mid 1 \le i \le 8\},$$
$$R_i = V^*, \ C_i = \{(a_{2i-1}, a_{2i})\}, \ i = 1, 2, 3, 4.$$

We obtain

$$\begin{aligned}
L_{in,=k}(G) = \{x \in V^* \mid \ &|x|_{a_1} = |x|_{a_2} = r_1 k, r_1 \ge 0, \\
&|x|_{a_3} = |x|_{a_4} = r_2 k, r_2 \ge 0, \\
&|x|_{a_5} = |x|_{a_6} = r_3 k, r_3 \ge 0, \\
&|x|_{a_7} = |x|_{a_8} = r_4 k, r_4 \ge 0\},
\end{aligned}$$

Assume that there is an internal contextual grammar $G' = (V, B, C, \varphi)$ which generates this language, and consider the strings

$$w_r = a_8^{8rk}(a_1 a_3^2)^{rk}(a_4 a_5^2)^{2rk}(a_6 a_7^2)^{4rk} a_2^{rk},$$

for $r \ge 1$. We have

$$\begin{aligned}
|w_r|_{a_1} = |w_r|_{a_2} = rk, \ |w_r|_{a_3} = |w_r|_{a_4} = 2rk, \\
|w_r|_{a_5} = |w_r|_{a_6} = 4rk, \ |w_r|_{a_7} = |w_r|_{a_8} = 8rk,
\end{aligned}$$

hence w_r is in the above language, for all $r \geq 1$. Therefore $w_r \in L_{in}(G')$. Take a value for r large enough so that $w_r \notin B$. It follows that there is a derivation $x \Longrightarrow x_1 \Longrightarrow x_2 \Longrightarrow \ldots \Longrightarrow x_m = w_r$ in the grammar $G', m \geq 1$. The context (λ, λ), if present in C, can be ignored; consider the last nonempty context adjoined in the previous derivation: $w_r = z_1 u z_2 v z_3, uv \neq \lambda$. As $z_1 z_2 z_3 \in L$, if $|uv|_{a_i} > 0$ for some $1 \leq i \leq 8$, then $|uv|_{a_i} = sk, s \geq 1$, moreover, there is another symbol, a_j, for which we have the same relation, because the symbols are introduced in pairs with the same number of occurrences. It follows that there are $a_i, a_{i+1}, i \in \{1, 3, 5, 7\}$, such that $|uv|_{a_i} = |uv|_{a_{i+1}} = sk, s \geq 1$. For each such pair a_i, a_{i+1} of symbols, there is one symbol which appears in w_r in blocks of length one; in order to remove at least three occurrences of it by removing two substrings of w_r, we have to remove at least two consecutive occurrences, hence also the intermediate symbol. This intermediate symbol has a pair symbol which must be removed, too, and again at least three occurrences of it. And so on, until taking into consideration all symbols. (Even if we start with the pair a_7, a_8, because the distance between the block of a_8 symbols and the pairs of occurrences of a_7 is arbitrarily large, we have to remove at least two blocks of a_7, which contain between them occurrences of a_6; the latter is paired with a_5, which is intercalated with a_4, and so on.) However, we cannot have occurrences of all symbols in two subwords of w_r of bounded length (the bound being $\max\{|uv| \mid (u, v) \in C\}$), a contradiction. The language L cannot be generated by an internal contextual grammar. $\qquad\square$

The case of the derivation mode $\geq k$ and the question whether $M_n IC_{REG}(= k)$ with $n \leq 4$ and/or $k = 2$ contains languages not in IC remain **open**.

Remark 2. The above proof suggests a general combinatorial problem, related also with the previous open problems. Namely, consider a *predicate* $P : V^* \longrightarrow \{0, 1\}$ defined on strings over a given alphabet V. Denote by $Sub(L)$ the set of proper non-empty substrings of strings in L and say that a language $L \subseteq V^*$ is *P-holographic* if $P(x) = 1$ for all $x \in L$ and $P(x) = 1$ for all $x \in Sub(L)$, too. Example: take P the predicate "is square-free".

Consider the dual of the P-holographicness: a language L is called *P-aholographic* if $P(x) = 1$ for all $x \in L$ and $P(x) = 0$ for all $x \in Sub(L)$. (The property P holds for all strings in L but for no proper non-empty substring of a string in L.) For some predicates, it is easy to find aholographic languages: take $P(x) =$ "x is of the form $a^n b^n c^n, n \geq 1$". For other predicates, the question does not seem to be trivial. Consider, for instance, the property

$$P_k(x) = 1 \text{ iff for each } a \in V, \text{ there is } r \geq 1 \text{ such that } |x|_a = rk.$$

Are there infinite P_k-aholographic languages ? For which k, for which (minimal) cardinality of V ?

In the previous proof appears a sort of bi-aholographic language: $P(x) = 1$ for $x \in L$ and $P(uv) = 0$ for $u, v \in Sub(L) \cup \{\lambda\}, uv \neq \lambda$.

6. The leftmost derivation

In an internal modular grammar $G = (V, B, (R_1, C_1), \ldots, (R_n, C_n))$ as in the preceding sections we can define also another type of derivation, namely the leftmost one:

$$x \Longrightarrow_{left} y \quad \text{iff} \quad x = x_1 x_2 x_3, x_1, x_2, x_3 \in V^*, y = x_1 u x_2 v x_3,$$
$$(u, v) \in C_i, x_2 \in R_i, \text{for some } 1 \leq i \leq n,$$
$$\text{and there is no decomposition } x = x_1' x_2' x_3', \text{ with}$$
$$|x_1'| < |x_1|, \text{ and } x_2' \in R_j, \text{ for some } 1 \leq j \leq n.$$

(One adjoins a context on the leftmost possible place, taking into consideration all possible decompositions of the current string and all components of the grammar.)

The language generated in this way is denoted $L_{left}(G)$ and the family of such languages generated by grammars with at most n components and with the choice restricted to a family F is denoted by $M_n IC_F(left)$.

Here is an **example**:

$$G = (\{a, b, c, d\}, \{cd\}, (\{cd\}, \{(c, d), (a, b)\}), (\{c^2 d^2\}, \{(c, d)\})).$$

Starting from cd, we work in the first component until using the context (c, d): $cd \Longrightarrow^* a^i cdb^i \Longrightarrow a^i ccddb^i, i \geq 0$. From now on the first component cannot be used, because the decomposition $(a^i)(ccdd)(b^i)$ forces the derivation to the second component: $a^i ccddb^i \Longrightarrow^* a^i c^j d^j b^i, j \geq 2$. Therefore,

$$L_{left}(G) = \{a^n c^m d^m b^n \mid n \geq 0, m \geq 1\}.$$

This is a linear non-regular language. In fact, we have,

Theorem 10. $M_1 IC_{FIN}(left) - REG \neq \emptyset, M_2 IC_{REG}(left) - CF \neq \emptyset.$

Proof. For $G_1 = (\{a, b\}, \{b\}, (\{b\}, \{(a, a)\}))$ we have $L_{left}(G_1) = \{a^n ba^n \mid n \geq 0\}$, which is linear non-regular. Observe that the condition of derivations being leftmost is not even needed here.

Consider also the grammar

$$G_2 = (\{a, b\}, \{aba\}, (a^+ ba, \{(a, a)\}), (a^+ b, \{(b, b)\})).$$

Starting from aba we can use both components. If we use the first one, then we get $a^2 ba^2$. In general, to a string $a^n ba^n$ we can use both the components; the first one adds one more pair of symbols a, hence we obtain a string of the same form. If we use the second component, then we obtain $ba^n bba^n$ and from now on the first component cannot be applied. Consequently, we have

$$L_{left}(G_2) = \{b^m a^n b^{m+1} a^n \mid n \geq 1, m \geq 0\},$$

a language which is not context-free. $\qquad\qquad\qquad\qquad\qquad\qquad\qquad\Box$

Theorem 11. *The families $M_n IC_F(left)$, for any $n \geq 2$, and for any family F containing the regular languages, are incomparable with each of LIN, CF, IC.*

Proof. We have seen that $M_2 IC_{REG}(left)$ contains non-context-free languages. It contains also languages not in the family IC. Such a language is

$$L = \{bba^m, \ a^{n+1}ba^nba^{m+1} \mid n, m \geq 0\},$$

which can be generated in the leftmost manner by the modular grammar

$$G = (\{a, b\}, \{bb\}, (\{bb\}, \{(\lambda, a), (a, a)\}), (\{ab\}, \{(a, a)\})).$$

Indeed, starting from bb only the first component can be used. Assume we add m times the context $(\lambda, a), m \geq 0$, and then we use the context (a, a). We obtain the string $abba^{m+1}$. From now on the first component cannot be used, because the second one can be applied on a position to the left. Therefore we add $n \geq 0$ contexts (a, a) and we get $a^{n+1}ba^nba^{m+1}$, exactly the mentioned language. (Note that the grammar G has finite choice, hence $L \in M_2 IC_{FIN}(left)$.)

The language L is not in IC: in order to increase the number of a occurrences in the first two substrings of a, we need a context (a^r, a^r) accepted by some string $a^g ba^h, g, h \geq 0$, and such a context can be used also for increasing the number of a around the second occurrence of b, thus obtaining strings of the form $a^n ba^m ba^p$ with $m > n$, a contradiction.

On the other hand, the language

$$L = \{a^m ba^n ca^n \mid n, m \geq 1\},$$

is clearly linear and can be generated by the internal contextual grammar $G = (\{a, b, c\}, \{abaca\}, \{(a, a), (a, \lambda)\}, \varphi)$, with $\varphi(b) = \{(a, \lambda)\}, \varphi(c) = \{(a, a)\}$. However, this language is not in $M_\infty IC_{ARB}(left)$.

Assume that $L = L_{left}(G')$ for some $G' = (V, B, (R_1, C_1), \ldots, (R_n, C_n))$. For increasing the number of a occurrences around c we need a context (a^r, a^r), $r \geq 1$, in some C_i such that $a^g ca^h \in R_i, g, h \geq 0$. In order to increase the number of a occurrences in the front of b we need a context $(a^r, a^q), r + q \geq 1$, in some C_j with R_j containing a string $a^s, s \geq 0$, or a context $(a^r, v), r \geq 1$, in some C_j with R_j containing a string $a^s bz, s \geq 0$. Consider such strings in

R_j with the smallest s. To every string of the form $a^p ba^l ca^l, l \geq 1, p \geq s$, respectively $a^p bzy, p \geq s$, only the contexts in C_j can be added, therefore the generated language will contain strings $a^n ba^m ca^m$ with arbitrarily large m only for $n < s$. In conclusion, $L \neq L_{left}(G')$, which concludes the proof. $\square$

Conjecture: $M_\infty IC_{FIN}(left) \subseteq CF$.

Remark 3. The family $M_\infty IC_{FIN}(left)$ is not closed under concatenation (take $L_1 = a^+, L_2 = \{ba^n ba^n \mid n \geq 1\}$), union (the same L_1 and $L_2' = \{a^n ba^n \mid n \geq 1\}$; the contexts used for producing strings a^m with arbitrarily large m can be used for producing strings $a^s ba^n, s > n$, starting from $a^n ba^n$), Kleene + (for $L = \{ba^n ca^n b \mid n \geq 1\} \cup \{a\}$, which is in $M_\infty IC_{FIN}(left)$, L^+ must contain all the strings $a^m ba^n ca^n b$, and this is impossible), and morphisms (the language $L = \{a^n ba^n \mid n \geq 1\} \cup \{c\}$ is in $M_\infty IC_{FIN}(left)$, but $h(L)$, for $h(a) = a, h(b) = b, h(c) = a$, not).

We do not know whether this family is closed under inverse morphisms and intersection with regular sets. These questions are related to the **open** problem whether or not every regular language is in $M_\infty IC_{FIN}(left)$.

Remark 4. The previous leftmost derivation can be called *global*, because it is defined with respect to all components of the grammar. We can also define a *local* relation of this type: first we non-deterministically choose a component of the grammar and then we add a context to the current string in the leftmost position with respect to the chosen component. This variant remains to be investigated (a result like Theorem 10 is true also for this case, but Theorem 11 not).

Note added in proof. In the paper "On the generative capacity of certain classes of contextual grammars", by A. Exrenfeucht, L. Ilie, Gh. Păun, G. Rozenberg, A. Salomaa, to appear in *Mathematical Linguistics and Related Topics* (Gh. Păun, ed.), The Publ. House of the Romanian Academy of Sciences, Bucureşti, 1994, it is proved that $LIN - M_\infty EC_{REG}(t) \neq \emptyset$, thus solving the open problem formulated before Theorem 4 above, and that $M_1 IC_{FIN}(left) - LIN \neq \emptyset$, a strenghtening of the first relation in Theorem 10. Some problems left open in [14] are also solved in the above mentioned paper.

References

1. E. Csuhaj-Varju, J. Dassow, On cooperating distributed grammar systems, *J. Inform. Process. Cybern., EIK*, 26 (1990), 49 - 63.

2. E. Csuhaj-Varju, J. Dassow, J. Kelemen, Gh. Păun, *Grammar systems*, Gordon and Breach, London, 1994.

3. L. Kari, *On Insertion and Deletion in Formal Languages*, PhD Thesis, University of Turku, 1991.

4. S. Istrail, Contextual grammars with regulated selection, *Stud. Cerc. Matem.*, 30, 3 (1978), 287 - 294.

5. S. Marcus, *Algebraic Linguistics. Analytical Models*, Academic Press, New York, 1967.

6. S. Marcus, Contextual grammars, *Rev. Roum. Math. Pures Appl.*, 14, 10 (1969), 1525 - 1534.

7. S. Marcus, Deux types nouveaux de grammaires génératives, *Cah. Ling. Th. Appl.* 6 (1969), 69 - 74.

8. R. Meersman, G. Rozenberg, Cooperating grammar systems, *Proc. MFCS '78 Symp.*, *LNCS* 64, Springer-Verlag, 1978, 364 - 374.

9. X. M. Nguyen, *On Some Generalizations of Contextual Grammars*, PhD Thesis, University of Bucharest, 1981.

10. Gh. Păun, *Contextual grammars*, The Publ. House of the Romanian Academy of Sciences, Bucureşti, 1982 (in Romanian).

11. Gh. Păun, On some open problems about Marcus contextual languages, *Intern. J. Computer Math.*, 17, 1 (1985), 9 - 23.

12. Gh. Păun, Marcus contextual grammars. After 25 years, *Bulletin EATCS*, 52 (February 1994), 263 - 273.

13. Gh. Păun, X. M. Nguyen, On the inner contextual grammars, *Rev. Roum. Math. Pures Appl.*, 25, 4 (1980), 641 - 651.

14. Gh. Păun, G. Rozenberg, A. Salomaa, Contextual grammars: erasing, determinism, one-side contexts, in *Developments in Language Theory* (G. Rozenberg, A. Salomaa, eds.), World Sci. Publ., Singapore, 1994, 370 - 388.

15. Gh. Păun, G. Rozenberg, A. Salomaa, Contextual grammars: parallelism and blocking of derivations, *Fundamenta Inform.*, to appear.

16. G. Rozenberg, A. Salomaa, *The Mathematical Theory of L Systems*, Academic Press, New York, 1980.

17. A. Salomaa, *Formal Languages*, Academic Press, New York, 1973.

18. S. Vicolov, Two theorems about Marcus contextual languages, *Bull. Math. Soc. Sci. Math. Roumanie*, 35, 1 - 2 (1991), 167 - 170.

On Rough Mereological Constructibility: Anaphorically Constructible Many–Object Events

Lech T. POLKOWSKI

Institute of Mathematics, Warsaw University of Technology
Pl. Politechniki 1, 00-650 Warsaw, Poland

Maria SEMENIUK-POLKOWSKA

Chair of Formal Linguistics, Warsaw University
Browarna 8/10, 00-950 Warsaw, Poland

Abstract. We apply ideas of rough mereology – a newly proposed extension of the Lesniewski mereology – to obtain a language for discussing and expressing properties of many-object events based on a given text with respect to their constructibility from anaphora resolutions of this text. We explore some approaches to constructibility of complex objects from their parts in case when complex objects are collections of syntactically possible substitutions approximated by anaphora resolutions: substitutions which are also possible semantically. We introduce a new type of upper rough mereological approximation to represent collections of anaphora resolutions as constructible sets.

1. Introduction

Uncertainty of knowledge may arise from the partiality of knowledge, vagueness of terms used for the description of a phenomenon, indiscernibility of objects caused by granularity of knowledge, interference of various local structures etc. Among mathematical tools proposed to study various forms of uncertain knowledge one may mention fuzzy set theory of Zadeh [23], rough set theory of Pawlak [10], [11], and mathematical morphology [8], [21].

Uncertainty of knowledge in natural and formal languages has been studied by Marcus et.al [4] as ambiguity. Some of the ideas expressed there were applied by the authors in [14], [15] to propose an approach to the problem of anaphora resolution of a text. This approach has been based on the conviction borne out by experience that anaphoric resolution of a text is in most cases ambiguous i.e. one has as a rule more than one plausible anaphoric reading of

"

the text; this point of view is more general than the point of view adopted by some researchers in Artificial Intelligence (cf. [2]) that the aim of the anaphora resolution algorithm is to produce a unique anaphora resolution. Uncertainty caused by partial character of knowledge about objects is responsible for the ambiguous character of anaphora resolution. Any object x is represented by some information $Inf(x)$ and we are in fact given only equivalence classes $INF(x)$ of objects, equivalent objects having the same properties of acting as anaphors for a given antecedent.

Representing objects by their information vectors is a basic assumption of rough set theory of Pawlak [10], [11]. As a consequence of this assumption, one can discuss degree in which an object is an element of a collection of objects. This degree is measured by a rough membership function [18]. It seems however that a more natural approach is to consider a function on collections of objects measuring the degree in which one collection is included in another. Such a function called rough inclusion has been introduced in [19]. By means of such a function one is able to introduce on a given collection of objects a family of relations of being a part in degree $\alpha \in [0, 1]$. Among these relations is the relation of being a "full" part which provides a model for mereology, an alternative set theory proposed by St. Lesniewski [3] as means to resolve the Russell antinomy in Cantorian set theory. One can therefore regard the hierarchy introduced by a rough inclusion as an extension of mereology called rough mereology [19].

One of main features of mereology is that it collapses the set-theoretical hierarchy of an element, a set, a power set etc. regarding collections of objects as objects. It offers therefore a semantics for higher-level language for reasoning about complex structures in terms of their parts when it is sufficient to deal only with objects and relations among them of being a part in some degree. Specifications of objects are implemented in a lower-level language based usually on standard set theory. As shown in [19], one is able to introduce into rough mereology approximations of objects by objects of a specified class. These approximations generalize lower, respectively, upper approximations of rough set theory as well as openings, respectively, closings, of mathematical morphology.

A study of various notions of constructibility in terms of rough mereological approximations is an intricate problem and we offer here some propositions for a possible approach to this problem illustrated by examples taken from the model of anaphora resolution of a text [14] – [17].

We introduce a notion of a many-object event based on a text, which can be regarded as a list of some syntactically possible substitutions for corresponding antecedents in the text and we regard it as a complex object. We define constructibility of an object in some ways which extend the notion of an exact set from rough set theory. We obtain then various classes of constructible objects, among them class of objects for which constructibility means that they are sets in rough mereological sense of anaphora resolutions.

2. Distributional-algebraic approach to anaphora

Anaphora means a pointing-back device of language by means of which a certain string (an anaphor) refers to an object referred earlier to by another string (an antecedent).

The problem of anaphora resolution is to match properly anaphors to antecedents. Our approach to anaphora is based on a distributional-algebraic approach in Mathematical Linguistics [4], [5], [6]. We recall here briefly basic notions relevant to this approach.

A *language* is a triple (V, P, L) where

- V is a finite set called *vocabulary*,

- L is a non-empty subset of V^*, where V^* is the set of all finite sequences over V,

- P is a partition of V called a *paradigmatic partition*.

The symbol xy will denote the concatenation of strings $x, y \in V^*$, and a string $x \in V^*$ will be called a *substring* of a string $y \in V^*$ in case $y = uxv$ for some $u, v \in V^*$.

A *context* is an ordered pair of strings in V^*; we will say that a context (u, v) *accepts* a string $x \in V^*$ in case $uxv \in L$ and then the context (u, v) will be called an occurrence of x in y.

We will say that a string $x \in V^*$ *dominates* a string $y \in V^*$ if any context (u, v) accepting x accepts y. For subsets $A, B \subseteq V^*$, we will say that A *dominates* B if x dominates y for each $x \in A$ and each $y \in B$. We will write $x \to y$ (respectively, $A \to B$) in case x dominates y (respectively, A dominates B).

Strings x, y are in the reciprocal domination relation $\leftrightarrow$ in case $x \to y$ and $y \to x$; the relation $\leftrightarrow$ is an equivalence relation and its classes are called *distributional classes*. The symbol $dc(x)$ will denote the distributional class containing x.

A subset $A \subseteq V^*$ is *initial* if $x \to A$ implies $x \in A$ for each $x \in V^*$. An initial set of the form $dc(x)$ generates the set

$$C(x) = \{y \in V^* : dc(x) \to y\}$$

called the *elementary* grammatical category generated by x ($gc(x)$, for short).

Following Marcus [4], we introduce in $gc(x)$ the notion of *rank*. We will call a sequence $(x_1, x_2, \ldots, x_n) \subseteq gc(x)$ a *path* if $x_i \to x_{i+1}$ for $i = 1, 2, \ldots, n$ but $non(x_{i+1} \to x_i)$ for $i = 1, 2, \ldots, n$. For $y \in gc(x)$, $rank(y) = m$ if m is the greatest natural number k such that there exists a path $(x_1, x_2, \ldots, x_k) \subseteq gc(x)$ with $x_1 = x$ and $x_k = y$; otherwise, $rank(y) = \infty$.

The paradigmatic partition P extends from V to the partition P^* on V^* defined by $P^*(v_1 v_2 \ldots v_n) = P(v_1)P(v_2) \ldots P(v_n)$.

For a context (u, v), we let

$$acc(u, v) = \{z \in V^* : (u, v) \text{ accepts } z\}$$

and

$$Pacc(u, v) = \{z \in V^* : \exists z' \in P^*(z), z' \in acc(u, v)\}.$$

For a $gc(x)$, we let

$$gc(x)|y = \{z \in gc(x) : y \to z\}$$

and

$$gc(x)||y = \{z \in gc(x) : y \to z \text{ and } non(z \to y)\}.$$

A *text* T over V will be any finite sequence $(x_1|x_2|\ldots|\ldots|x_k)$ where $x_i \in L$ for $i = 1, 2, \ldots, k$. The symbol $<$ will denote the natural precedence order of occurrences in T. An occurrence of $y \in V^*$ in T will be denoted by $y = (y, (u, v), i)$ where $x_i = uyv$. The symbol T^{occ} will denote all occurrences in the text T of strings from $gc(x)||x$.

For $y = (y, (u, v), i)$, we let

$$acc(y) = \{z \in V^* : z \in acc(u, v)\}$$

and

$$Pacc(y) = \{z \in V^* : z \in Pacc(u, v)\}.$$

A formalization of the anaphoric relation anaphor-antecedent based on the notion of rank in a grammatical category due to Marcus [4] has been proposed in [14] in the form of an anaphoric pair. We restrict ourselves for the simplicity sake to the case of $gc(x)$ for some initial x. We will say that a pair (y, z) of occurrences $y = (y, (u, v), i)$ and $z = (z, (w, t), j)$ in T is an *x-anaphoric pair* if

(i) $y < z$,

(ii) $y \in Pacc(z)$,

(iii) $\exists y', z' \in gc(x).y' \in P^*(y) \wedge z' \in P^*(z) \wedge y' \in gc(x)||z'$.

Postulates (i) - (iii) mean that z refers to an object denoted earlier by y on a higher level of reference than y (by (iii), $rank(y'') > rank(z'')$).

Anaphoric pairs provide a starting point for an algorithm to define anaphora resolutions of a text T which we will present in Section 5, below.

3. Rough set preliminaries

Information systems [9] are used for representing knowledge. Rough sets [10], [11] have been introduced as a tool to deal with uncertain knowledge in cases where uncertainty has been caused by indiscernibility of objects due to partial knowledge about them.

Knowledge is understood in rough set theory as the ability to classify objects by means of certain patterns usually represented as functions on objects.

An *information system* is a pair $A = (U, A)$ where

- U is a non-empty finite set of objects called *the universe,*

- A is a non-empty finite set of *attributes*, each attribute $a \in A$ being a mapping $a : U \to V_a$ of the universe U into a set V_a, the value set of a.

Objects in U are interpreted as cases, states, processes, patients etc. and attributes are interpreted as features, variables, conditions etc. Collections of objects are called *concepts.*

For a non-empty set $B \subseteq A$ of attributes, the *B-information function Inf_B* is defined on U as

$$Inf_B(x) = \{(a, a(x)) : a \in B\}.$$

The partial character of knowledge represented by B is reflected by the B-indiscernibility relation $IND(B)$ defined as:

$$IND(B) = \{(x, y) : Inf_B(x) = Inf_B(y)\}.$$

We denote by $INF_B(x)$ the equivalence class of $IND(B)$ which contains x. Objects x, y with $INF_B(x) = INF_B(y)$ are indiscernible by means of classification patterns represented by attributes from B and sets of the form $INF_B(x)$ represent granules of knowledge from which knowledge represented by B is built. As a rule, due to the granularity of knowledge, concepts cannot be described precisely but approximately only.

For a concept $X \subseteq U$, its *B-approximations* are defined as follows:))

$$L_B X = \cup\{INF_B(x) : INF_B(x) \subseteq X\},$$
$$U_B X = \cup\{INF_B(x) : INF_B(x) \cap X \neq \emptyset\}.$$

The set $L_B X$ is the *B-lower approximation* of X and the set $U_B X$ is the *B-upper approximation* of X.

A concept X is said to be *B-exact* in case $L_B X = U_B X$; otherwise X is *B-rough*. The set $BN_B X = U_B X - L_B X$ called *the boundary region* of X is the measure of the inaccuracy of description of X in terms of clasifying patterns from B. Objects in $L_B X$ are classified with certainty into X while objects in $U_B X$ are classified as being in X possibly only.

It has been noticed [13] that approximations L_B, U_B are formally analogous to approximations of objects provided by mathematical morphology [8], [21] viz. to, respectively, *B-opening* and *B-closing* by a structuring element B.

Any object x is represented by its class $INF_B(x)$; one can discuss *the degree of membership* of x in a concept X. It has been introduced in [18] in the form of the rough membership function m_X defined on U by the formula

$$\mu_X(x) = \frac{card(X \cap INF_B(x))}{card(INF_B(x))}.$$

Functions of this type serve as one of the main tools to define an appropriate family of approximation functions for analytical filtration of decision tables [22].

Functions of the type of μ_X can be perceived as measuring the degree to which one set is included in another rather than the degree of membership of an element in a set. This point of view has been adopted in [19]. Basic properties of $\mu = \mu_X$ extended to the power set 2^U seem to be the following [19]:

(A) $m(X, Y) \in [0, 1]$,

(B) $m(X, X) = 1$,

(C) $m(X, Y) = 1$ implies $(\mu(Z, Y) \geq \mu(Z, X))$,

(D) $\exists Z. \forall Y. [\mu(Z, Y) = 1 \wedge (\mu(Y, Z) < 1 \Rightarrow \mu(Y, Z) = 0)]$,

(E) for any pair X, Y the condition
$\forall Z \neq \emptyset. (\mu(Z, Y) = 1 \Rightarrow \exists T \neq \emptyset. \mu(T, Z) = 1 = \mu(T, X))$
implies $\mu(Y, X) = 1$,

(F) for each collection $U \subseteq 2^U$ of concepts there exits X such that

   (i) $\forall Z \neq \emptyset. [\mu(Z, X) = 1 \Rightarrow \exists W \neq \emptyset. (\mu(W, Z) = 1 = \mu(W, X) \wedge W \in U)]$,

   (ii) $\forall Z \in U. \mu(Z, X) = 1$,

   (iii) $\forall Y. \mu(X, Y) < 1 \Rightarrow non(Y$ satisfies (i)–(ii) when substituted for X).

Condition (C) expresses monotonicity of μ, (D) means the existence of a null element, (E) means inference about being a part from sub-parts and (F) is a completeness condition.

Any function $\mu(X, Y)$ satisfying (A) – (F) on a collection of objects is called *rough inclusion* [19].

A *decision system* is an information system $A = (U, A \cup \{d\})$, where $d \notin A$ is called a *decision attribute*; the decision attribute represents the classification pattern of an expert, a diagnostician, an operator etc. We denote by

$Inf_d, INF_d, IND(d)$ the constructs defined as above with $B = \{d\}$. Sets of the form $INF_d(x)$ are called *decision classes* of A.

One of main problems concerning a decision system is that of *generating decision rules*. We follow here a presentation of main ideas given in [20]. An *atomic formula* over $B \subseteq A \cup \{d\}$ is an expression of the form $a = v$ where $a \in B$ and $v \in V_a$. The set $F(B, V)$ of formulas over B and V is the smallest set containing all atomic formulas and closed under propositional connectives $\vee, \wedge$. For $\tau \in F(B, V)$, we denote by τ_A the meaning of τ defined inductively by $(a = v)_A = \{x \in U : a(x) = v\}$, $(\tau \wedge \tau')_A = \tau_A \cap \tau'_A$, and $(\tau \vee \tau')_A = \tau_A \cup \tau'_A$. The set $F(A, V)$ is called the *set of conditional formulas* of A and is denoted by $C(A, V)$.

A *decision rule* of A is any formula of the form

$$(*) \qquad \tau \Rightarrow d = v$$

where τ is a conditional formula of A and $v \in V_d$. A rule $(*)$ is true in A in case $\tau_A \subseteq (d = v)_A$. The fact that $(*)$ is a true rule is denoted $\tau \Rightarrow_A (d = v)_A$.

Let us add that some ideas concerning a more general approach to indiscernibility in terms of tolerance rough sets have been recently put forth by Marcus [7].

4. Rough mereology

Rough mereology formulated in [19] is an extension of the Lesniewski mereology [3]. Various applications of mereology have been investigated in natural language processing [1], production theory [12] etc.

The basic notion of mereology is that of being a part. The mereological theory of sets and classes collapses the hierarchy of an element, a set, a power set etc. of Cantorian set theory, regarding collections of objects as objects. These features of mereology make it a very suitable tool in applications dealing with cases where we do not have a direct access to objects but are given their records in the form of information vectors, images, signals etc. In this case as a rule it is only possible to discuss parts of objects and not their elements.

Rough mereology is based on a rough inclusion μ satisfying postulates (A) – (F) of Section 3 on a collection of objects described in the lower level language of ordinary set theory. As shown in [19], one can use μ to introduce a hierarchy of relations of being a part in degree, including the relation of being a (full) part; in this way the Lesniewski mereology is contained within rough mereology.

The basic relations of rough mereology are the following [19].

The relation π of being a part is defined via

$$X \pi Y \text{ iff } \mu(X, Y) = 1 \wedge \mu(Y, X) < 1.$$

The relation ι of being an ingredient is defined via

$$X\iota Y \text{ iff } \mu(X,Y) = 1.$$

They satisfy axioms A1, A2 of mereology (cf. [3]; par. 1, 2).

Objects are identified by means of the π-congruence $=_\mu$ defined via $X =_\mu Y$ iff $\mu(X,Y) = 1 = \mu(Y,X)$.

The notions of a set and of a class are introduced in the following way [19]. Let m be a property of objects; we denote by N the null object provided by (D) and abbreviate 'X has property m' to 'X object m'. Then

- an object X is a set of objects m, X set m in short, when
$\forall Z \neq \emptyset.[Z\iota X \Rightarrow \exists T, W.(T \neq \emptyset \wedge T\iota Z \wedge T\iota W \wedge W\iota X \wedge W$ object $m)]$,

- an object X is a class of objects m, X class m in short, when

  (i) X set m,

  (ii) $\mu(Y,X) = 1$ for each Y object m,

  (iii) $\mu(X,Y) < 1$ implies $non(Y$ satisfies (i), (ii) when substituted for X.

The relation ϵ of being exterior to each other is defined as follows [19]:

$$X\epsilon Y \text{ iff } non(\exists Z \neq \emptyset.Z\iota X \wedge Z\iota Y).$$

Rough mereological approximations $L_m X$ and $U_m X$ are introduced in [19] following the idea of rough approximations in rough set theory and morfological approximations of opening and closing. Their definitions are :

$L_m X = \text{class}(T : T \text{ object } m \wedge T\iota X)$,
$U_m X = \text{class}(T : \forall Z \neq \emptyset \ [Z\iota T \Rightarrow (\forall W.W \text{ object } m \wedge Z\iota W \Rightarrow non(W \in X))])$.

The approximation $L_m X$ is called the *m-lower approximation* of X and the approximation $U_m X$ is said to be the *m-upper approximation* of X.

5. Multi-anaphora resolution of a text

We will continue with a $gc(x)$ and $T = (w_1|w_2|\ldots|w_k)$ as in Section 2. Anaphoric pairs introduced in Section 2 provide a fragmentation of T into paradigmatic sequences of anaphors (p.s.a's for short) as follows. A sequence $(x_1, x_2, \ldots, x_m)$ is a p.s.a if:

(i) $x_1 < x_2 \ldots < x_m$,

(ii) $\exists y \in gc(x)||x.\exists y = (y, (u, V), i).y < x_1$,

(iii) $non(\exists \in gc(x)||x.\exists z = (z, (w, t), j).\exists i.x_i < z < x_{i+1})$,

(iv) $(x_1, x_2, \ldots, x_m)$ is a maximal sequence that satisfies (i) – (iii).

The meaning of (i) – (iv) is that we group together in a p.s.a. those antecedents which are not separated by a potential anaphor.

In [15], [16], [17] a model has been presented of anaphora resolution based on syntactic and semantic considerations carried out in the frame of distributional-algebraic models. Here we will retain basic ideas of this approach, in particular the idea of the construction of the multi-anaphora resolution – a family of anaphora resolutions. We will however base our syntactic and semantic factors on inference from an information system. We will present here a conceptual scheme for such construction.

We will consider the case of a $gc(x)$. We assume that strings from V are represented as objects in a one-one way and that these objects form a universe U. We assume that an information system $A = (U, A_1 \cup A_2)$ where $A_1 \cap A_2 = \emptyset$ is given; we let $A_1 = (U, A_1)$. Informally, the information system A_1 provides us with necessary syntactic knowledge while the information system A is a source of semantic knowledge as well i.e. our algorithm for finding anaphora resolutions is based on inferences from A.

We will be concerned with x-anaphora hence we will first write the text T down in a convenient form to represent occurrences of paradigmatic forms of x. We will adopt the following notation for T:

$$(u_1^1[x_1^1, t_1^1] \ldots u_{k_1}1^1[x_{k_1}^1, t_{k_1}^1]u_{k_1+1}^1 | \ldots | u_1^k[x_1^k, t_1^k] \ldots u_{k_k}^k[x_{k_k}^k, t_{k_k}^k]u_{k_k+1}^k)$$

where x_i^j denotes an occurrence of a string from $P^*(x)$ and $t_i^j \in C(A_1, V)$. The meaning $t_i^j{}_{A_1}$ is the collection of strings from $gc(x)||x$ that can be substituted for x_i^j preserving syntactic correctness of the sentence w_i. We denote by $O(x)$ the sequence $(x_1^1, \ldots, x_{k_k}^k)$. We will write t_x for t_i^j in case $x = x_i^j$.

We will now present an algorithm for building the multi-anaphora resolution of T. For $x = x_i^j$, we denote by $C(x)$ the set of occurrences from T^{occ} which precede x i.e.

$$y \in C(x) \text{ iff } y \in T^{occ} \text{ and } y < x.$$

We will assume that a sequence $(v_1^1, \ldots, v_{k_1}^1, v_1^2, \ldots, v_{k_2}^2, \ldots, v_{k_k}^k)$ is constructed of formulas from $C(A, V)$ with $v_i^j \Rightarrow_A t_i^j$. The meaning $v_i^j{}_A$ is the collection of objects that can be substituted for x_i^j after all preceding x_u^v's have been correctly substituted with the result that the obtained text is semantically correct. The symbol v_x will denote v_i^j when $x = x_i^j$. We will write the set $\{x_i^j : j < k, i < k_j\}$ down in the form $O(x) = \{x_i : i < t\}$ preserving the order of occurrences.

The algorithm (AT) is as follows.

(AT0) Let x_0 be the first element of $O(x)$ and $C(x_0) = \{y_0, y_1, y_2, \ldots, y_p\}$ For $j \leq p$, we denote by g_j' the function on $\{x_0\}$ defined by $g_{j'}(x_0) = y_j$. Then we let $g_j = g_{j'}$ when $y_j \in v_{1\,A}^1$ and $g_j = \emptyset$ otherwise. Let $g_0, g_1, \ldots, g_r$ be the functions defined in this way.

(AT1) Assume that we have defined inductively up to $x = x_i^j$ functions, say, $g_0, g_1, \ldots, g_q$ assigning to each $x' < x, x' \in O(x)$ the string $g(x') \in C(x') \cap v_{x'A}$. We extend each of these functions over x, if possible, by considering $C(x) = \{z_0, z_1, \ldots, z_l\}$ and defining the function g_{ij} as follows : $g_{ij} = g_i \cup \{(x, z_j)\}$ when $z_j \in y_{x\,A}$ and $g_{ij} = g_i$ otherwise. This produces a set of functions providing syntactically and semantically correct substitutions (i.e. anaphors) up to the level of x including x.

(AT2) The set G of functions obtained as in (AT1) for $x = x_k^k$ is the multi-anaphora resolution of the text T. Elements of G are called anaphora resolutions of the text T.

6. Many-object events

It seems natural to regard the text T as a propositional function allowing for different substitutions of plausible anaphors for antecedents and being therefore a scheme of an "abstract" event with many possible realizations. It is our purpose in this section to formalize the notion of a many-object event as such realization.

For each $x_i \in O(x)$, we consider finite sets of the form

$$A_{x_i} = \{(z, \mu_z) : z \text{ is an object}, \ \mu_z \in C(A, V) \text{ and } \mu_z \Rightarrow_A \tau_{x_i}\}.$$

In particular, any anaphora resolution $(A_{x_i} : x_i \in O(x))$ where A_{x_i} is a singleton (z, m_z) with $\mu_z \Rightarrow_A y_{x_i}$ is of this form for each i.

Suppose a sequence $(A_{x_i} : i < t)$ satisfies the above condition for A_{x_i} for each $i < t$ and the following conditions hold:

(a) for $j < t$, if there exists $i < j$ with $\mu_z \Rightarrow_A \tau_{x_j}$ for each $(z, m_z) \in A_{x_i}$, then $A_{x_j} = A_{x_i}$ for the first i with this property,

(b) for $i < j, A_{x_i} \cap A_{x_j} = \emptyset$ in case there exists $z \in A_{x_i}$ with $non(\mu_z \Rightarrow_A t_{x_j})$ and then $non(\mu_z \Rightarrow_A \tau_{x_j})$ for each $z \in A_{x_i}$.

Let the sequence $(B_{x_i} : i < t)$ be defined by the condition $B_{x_i} = \cup \{A_{x_j} : j < i\}$. We will call the sequence $(B_{x_i} : i < t)$ a many-object event based on the text T. We will denote many-object events in general with letters E, F, G, and small letters $e, f, g, \ldots$ will be reserved for many-object events being anaphora resolutions written down in the format of a many-object event.

We will admit the empty many-object event o defined by $o = (\emptyset : i < t)$ and we will require that any many-object event $E = (E_{x_i} : i < t)$ distinct from o satisfies the condition that $E_{x_i} \neq \emptyset$ for $i < t$.

We should now define the function $\mu(E, F)$ indicating for any pair E, F of many-object events the degree of inclusion of E into F.

We will let:

(i) $\mu(o, E) = 1$ for each E.

(ii) for $E \neq \emptyset$: $\mu(E, F) = k/t$ where k is the greatest $j < t$ satisfying the condition:
   (a) $E_{x_i} \subseteq F_{x_i}$ for $i < j$.

We have to make sure that μ is a rough inclusion i.e. it fulfills (A) - (F) of Section 3.

(A) and (B) are obviously satisfied.

For (C): let $\mu(E, F) = 1$. Consider any G and assume that $\mu(G, E) = j/t$. This means that up to the level j all sets G_{x_i} are subsets of the corresponding sets E_{x_i}; hence G_{x_i} is a subset of F_{x_i} for $i \leq j$ i.e. $\mu(G, F) \geq j/t$ and so $\mu(G, F) \geq m(G, E)$.

For (D): the object o satisfies $\mu(o, E) = 1$ for any E and $\mu(E, o) = 0$ for any $E \neq \emptyset$.

For (E): consider non-null E, F. Assume that for any non-null G with $\mu(G, E) = 1$ there exists non-null H with $\mu(H, G) = 1 = \mu(H, F)$. It follows that for any anaphora resolution e with $\mu(e, E) = 1$ we have $\mu(e, F) = 1$ as well. Similarly, one can observe that given any non-null G such that $\mu(G, E) = 1$ and there is no non-null G' with $G' \neq G$ and $\mu(G', G) = 1$, we have $\mu(G, F) = 1$. But this implies that $E_{x_i} \subseteq F_{x_i}$ for $i \leq t$ i.e. $\mu(E, F) = 1$.

For (F): suppose a collection m of many-object events given. Let $F_{x_i} = \cup\{E_{x_i} : E \text{object} m\}$ for $i \leq t$. The many-object event $F = (F_{x_i} : i \leq t)$ satisfies clearly $\mu(E, F) = 1$ for each E object m. Thus (F)(ii) holds. The condition F(i) holds obviously, too. To check (F)(iii), consider G with $\mu(F, G) < 1$. Then clearly, $\mu(E, G) < 1$ for some E object m.

We have therefore defined a rough inclusion μ. By results presented in Section 4, the relations π, ι of being, respectively, a part or an ingredient, and notions of a set m and a class m are defined by means of μ.

7. Constructibility

We will propose a few schemes for defining the notion of constructibility as a rough mereological counterpart of the notion of an exact set in rough set theory. We will see that various notions of constructibility lead to various types of constructible objects.

We will exploit first the m-lower approximation L_m and the m-upper approximation U_m defined in Section 4.

The two notions of constructibility based on L_m and U_m are the following. Objects m-constructible in degree 1 will be called *m-constructible*.

(Con1)

An object X is m-constructible in degree α if $\mu(L_m X, U_m X) = \alpha$.

(Con2)

An object X is m-constructible in degree α if $\mu(L_m X, L_m U_m X) = \alpha$.

One may observe that (Con1)-m-constructibility and (Con2)-m-constructibility amount to exactness in the rough set interpretation of μ as the rough membership function and m as the property of being a set of the form $INF(x)$.

We now introduce the property m satisfied by a many-object event E if and only if E is an anaphora resolution.

Let now E be a many-object event. Concerning the approximations of E, we have

$$L_m E =_\mu class(e : \mu(e, E) = 1 \text{ and } e \text{ object } m).$$

Therefore the object $L_m E$ represents all anaphora resolutions which are ingredients of E.

To define the approximation $U_m X$ we introduce the property n satisfied by E if and only if E has no ingredient being an anaphora resolution i.e. E object $n \Leftrightarrow \forall e.\, non(e\iota E)$. Then we will say that an object E has the property p if and only if either E is an ingredient of X or E object n. Then we have $U_m X = class\ p$.

It follows that each many-object event E is (Con2)-m-constructible and: in case there exists a minimal non-null many-object event E not being an anaphora resolution, no many-object event $E \neq N$ is (Con1)-constructible, otherwise each many-object event E is (Con1)-m-constructible.

In the light of the above results, it seems desirable to work out a notion of the m-upper approximation which would lead to a natural result that a many-object event E is constructible if and only if E is of the form set m i.e. an object representing a collection of anaphora resolutions.

The following is a definition of a new kind of rough mereological approximation.

For an object X, we let

$$U_m^* X \;=\; class(T : (\exists Z.T\iota Z \;\wedge\; Z \text{ object } m) \wedge \forall W \neq N.[W\iota T$$
$$\Rightarrow \forall U.(W\iota U \wedge U \text{ object } m) \Rightarrow non(W \in X)])$$

We will regard $U_m^* X$ as a new upper approximation with properties similar to those of $U_m X$ (cf. [19]) save extensivity (i.e. $X\iota U_m X$) only. We observe that this new approximation also extends rough set approximations under standard interpretation of μ, m.

We introduce a new notion of constructibility.

An object X is m-constructible in degree α if $L_m X = U_m^* X$ and $\mu(L_m X, X) = \alpha$.

We have therefore the result announced above: an object X is (Con3)-m-constructible if and only if X set m. It follows that a many-object event E is (Con3)-m-constructible iff it represents a collection of anaphora resolutions. This seems to be the most natural and important of the three constructibility notions invoked in this note.

References

1. M. Aurnague, L. Vieu, Toward a formal representation of space in language: A commonsense reasoning approach, *IJCAI '93 Workshop on Spatial and Temporal Reasoning*, 1993.

2. M. Brady, R. C. Berwick (eds.), *Computational Models of Discourse*, MIT Press, Cambridge MA, 1983.

3. S. Lesniewski, *Foundations of the General Theory of Sets* (in Polish), Moscow, 1916; eng. transl. in: S. J. Surma, J. T. Srzednicki, D. I. Barnett, V. F. Rickey (eds.), Stanislaw Lesniewski, *Collected Works*, Kluwer - Polish Scientific Publishers, Dordrecht, Warsaw, 1992.

4. S. Marcus et.al., *Contextual Ambiguities in Natural & Artificial Languages*, vol. 1, *Communication and Cognition*, Ghent, 1981.

5. S. Marcus, *Algebraic Linguistics; Analytical Models*, Academic Press, New York, London, 1967.

6. S. Marcus, *Introduction Mathematique a la Linguistique Structurale*, Dunod, Paris, 1967.

7. S. Marcus, Tolerance rough sets, Cech topologies, learning processes, *Bull. Acad. Polon. Sci.*, to appear.

8. G. Matheron, *Random Sets and Integral Geometry*, Wiley, New York, 1975.

9. Z. Pawlak, *Information Systems – Theoretical Foundations*, Polish Scientific Publishers, Warsaw, 1981 (in Polish).

10. Z. Pawlak, Rough sets, *International Journal of Information and Computer Science*, 11 (1982), 344 – 356.

11. Z. Pawlak, *Rough Sets: Theoretical Aspects of Reasoning about Data*, Kluwer, Dordrecht, 1991.

406   L. T. Polkowski and M. Semeniuk-Polkowska

12. Z. Pawlak, *Mathematical Aspects of Production Organization*, Economics Publishing House, Warsaw, 1969 (in Polish).

13. L. T. Polkowski, Mathematical morphology of rough sets, *Bull. Acad. Polon. Sci.*, to appear.

14. L. T. Polkowski, M. Semeniuk-Polkowska, A formal model of anaphora resolution – a case of inference, *Proc. OUIC'86*, Ohio Univ., Athens, Ohio, October 1986.

15. L. T. Polkowski, M. Semeniuk-Polkowska, An analytic model of anaphora resolution in Algebraic Linguistics, *International Journal of Computer Mathematics*, 23 (1988), 251 – 263.

16. L. T. Polkowski, M. Semeniuk-Polkowska, A semantics for anaphora resolution in Algebraic Linguistics, *International Journal of Computer Mathematics*, 32 (1990), 137 – 147.

17. L. T. Polkowski, M. Semeniuk-Polkowska, A model of anaphora resolution based on distributional-algebraic approach in analytical models theory of Algebraic Linguistics, in *Current Issues in Mathematical Linguistics* (C. Martin-Vide, ed.), Elsevier-North-Holland, 1994, 29 – 37.

18. Z. Pawlak, A. Skowron, Rough membership functions, in *Advances in the Dempster-Shafer Theory of Evidence* (M. Federizzi, J. Kacprzyk, R. R. Yager, eds.), Wiley, New York, 1994, 251 – 271.

19. L. T. Polkowski, A. Skowron, *Rough mereology*, to appear.

20. A. Skowron, Extracting laws from decision tables: a rough set approach, *Proc. Intern. Workshop on Rough Sets and Knowledge Discovery RSKD '93*, Banff, 1993, 101 – 104.

21. J. Serra, *Image Analysis and Mathematical Morphology*, Academic Press, New York, London, 1982.

22. A. Skowron, L. T. Polkowski, Analytical Morphology: mathematical morphology of decision tables, *ICS Res. Report 41/93*, Institute of Computer Sci., Warsaw Univ. Technology, Warsaw, 1993.

23. L. Zadeh, Fuzzy sets, *Information and Control*, 8 (1965), 338 – 353.

Acyclic Structure Grammars
and Reducing Operators

Rudolf RICHTER
Department of Computer Science, Masaryk University
Burešova 20, 602 00 Brno, Czech Republic

Abstract. Grammars generating finite acyclic structures (finite labelled symbol sets with acyclic relations) are presented in this paper. Acyclic structures can be regarded as acyclic node-labelled directed graphs, too. The theory of reducing operators is applied to pure generalized structure grammars as a basic tool for effective constructions of pure structure grammars.

1. Introduction

This paper includes an attempt to generate finite acyclic structures by means of grammars. Grammars that generate strings are well-known (cf. [8], [11]), there are monographs concerning tree grammars (cf., e.g. [2]). Graph grammars, web grammars, plex grammars and shape grammars have been studied in the literature (cf. [1], [3], [4], [6]). Our structure grammars are situated between tree grammars and graph grammars, they include tree grammars as special cases and they are similar to them by a simple use of productions.

Our investigations are motivated by various problems of Artificial Intelligence, particularly by Syntactic Pattern Recognition. Our structures are finite labelled symbol sets with acyclic relations. They can be regarded as acyclic node-labelled directed graphs, too. Thus, the acyclic structures describe finite hierarchies which may lead to various applications.

This paper is devoted to basic concepts of our theory. We define the acyclic structure over a finite alphabet, the production (or rewriting rule), the language of acyclic structures and the pure generalized structure grammar. Similarly to [5] or [9], the theory of reducing operators (cf.[7]) is applied to pure generalized structure grammars.

2. Acyclic structures

The basic notion of our investigations is that one of an acyclic structure over a finite nonempty set. The acyclic structure is defined to be a finite labelled symbol set with an acyclic relation. The acyclic structure (briefly a structure) can be regarded as a partially ordered set, too, the ordering is introduced as the reflexive transitive closure of the acyclic relation. From another point of view, the structure is an acyclic directed graph, i.e. node-labeled digraph without cycles.

There are some differences between our approach and Schneider's 1-diagrams [12], [13]. Our approach has two main advantages:

- the application of a production rule is simpler – the acyclicity of a relation on a derived structure is preserved without introduction of additional conditions on the form of production,

- the projection of structures into strings is pure – without additional conditions on the use of productions ([13]).

First, let us review the basic notions used in our paper to prevent ambiguity. Let X and Y be sets. The set $r \subseteq X \times Y$ is called a *(binary) relation from X to Y*. If $X = Y$, the relation r is called a *relation on X*. The relation $r^{-1} = \{(a, b) \in Y \times X; (b, a) \in r\} \subseteq Y \times X$ is an *inverse of r*. If r is a relation from X to Y and q is a relation from Y to Z, the relation $p = \{(a, b) \in X \times Z;$ there exists $c \in Y$ such that $(a, c) \in r$ and $(c, b) \in q\} \subseteq X \times Z$ is called a *composition* or a *relative product of r and q*. We denote the compositions of relations by $p = r \cdot q$.

If r is a relation on a finite set X, the set X with the relation r can be regarded as a *directed graph* (X, r). The elements of X and r are called the *nodes* and the *edges of digraph* (X, r), respectively.

Let M be a set and t relation on M. The relation t is called an *acyclic relation on M*, if for any $n \geq 2$ the following condition holds. If $m_1, \ldots, m_n \in M$ and $m_1 t m_2, \ldots, m_{n-1} t m_n$, then $m_1 \neq m_n$. (The condition $m_1 t m_2, \ldots, m_{n-1} t m_n$ will be written in the form $m_1 t m_2 t \ldots t m_n$ in what follows.) It is easy to see that any subset of an acyclic relation on M is an acyclic relation on M, too. Let us denote the identity relation on M by id_M. Clearly, $t \cap id_M = \emptyset$, if t is an acyclic relation on M.

Let (M, t) be a set with an acyclic relation t, p and q belong to M. Suppose that $n \geq 0$, $p = m_0$, $q = m_n$ a $m_0 t m_1, \ldots, m_{n-1} t m_n$. The sequence $(m_i)_0^n$ is said to be a $t-path$ *from p to q in M* and n is called the *length of the path*.

Let (M, t) be a set with an acyclic relation t. A subset $M' \subseteq M$ is called a *convex subset of M with respect to t*, if for any pair $p, q \in M'$ and an arbitrary $t-$path $(m_i)_0^n$ from p to q in M, m_i belongs to M' for any $i = 0, \ldots, n$. In other words, $(m_i)_0^n$ is a $t \mid M'-$path from p to q in M' ($t \mid M'$ denotes t restricted to M', i.e. $t \mid M' = t \cap (M' \times M')$).

If (K, s) and (L, t) are sets with acyclic relations s and t, a mapping $f\ K \longrightarrow L$ is said to be an *isomorphism of (K, s) into (L, t)* whenever the two following conditions hold.

(i) f is a bijection of K into L,

(ii) $(a, b) \in s$ iff $(f(a), f(b)) \in t$.

Let us define our basic notion – the acyclic structure over V – as follows. Let (M, t) be a finite nonempty set with an acyclic relation t, V a finite nonempty set called the *alphabet*. Let o be a mapping of M into V called the *labelling function*. The triple $m = (M, t, o)$ is said to be an *acyclic structure over an alphabet V* (or, briefly, a *structure over V*). The set of all structures over V will be denoted by $STR(V)$. The number $|m| = card\, M$ (the number of elements of set M) is called the *norm of the structure m*.

Since the carrier of the above defined structure has no special signification, it appears suitable to work with the whole classes of isomorphic structures. Formally, we define a relation $\equiv$ on the set $STR(V)$ as follows. Let $k = (K, s, o)$ and $l = (L, t, p)$ be structures over V. We put $k \equiv l$ iff the following two conditions hold:

(i) there is an isomorphism f of (K, s) into (L, t),

(ii) $o = p \cdot f$, where $p \cdot f$ denotes the composition of mappings p and f.

It is easy to see that the relation $\equiv$ is an equivalence relation on $STR(V)$. Consequently, the structures k and l can be called equivalent structures, if $k \equiv l$. So in what follows, a structure k is understood as the whole class of $STR(V)/\equiv$ containing k. This generalization of the notion of a structure allows to select a structure with suitable properties among all equivalent structures.

A structure $m' = (M', t', o')$ over V is called a *substructure of a structure* $m = (M, t, o)$ over V, $m' \subseteq m$, if the following conditions hold:

$\quad$ (i) $\quad M' \subseteq M$,

$\quad$ (ii) $\quad t' = t \cap (M' \times M')$,

$\quad$ (iii) $\quad o' = o \mid M'$ (o restricted to M').

(In the sense of preceding considerations, it is sufficient if there exists some equivalent structure to the structure m' such that above described three conditions hold.) A substructure m' is said to be a *convex substructure of m*, if M' is a convex subset of M with respect to the relation t. The set of all convex substructures of m is denoted by $CONV(m)$.

Any substructure m' of the structure m generates some restricted relation of the relation t:

$$INP(m, m') - t \cap (M - M') \times M' \subseteq M \times M',$$
$$OUT(m, m') = t \cap M' \times (M - M') \subseteq M' \times M.$$

The relation $INP(m, m')$ defines the entering edges, the relation $OUT(m, m')$ the leaving ones of the substructure m'.

Now, we define further important notions in our investigations, the rewriting rule (production) and the derivation from a structure. In addition, we must prove that the derived object is a structure in our sense.

Let $x, y \in STR(V)$, $x = (X, t_x, o_x)$, $y = (Y, t_y, o_y)$ and $Y \cap X = \emptyset$. Let $r_i \subseteq Y \times X$ and $r_o \subseteq X \times Y$ be relations. The quadruple $p = (y, x, r_i, r_o)$ is said to be a *production* (or a *rewriting rule*) *over* V. The set of all productions over V is denoted by $PR(V)$. The number $|p| = |(y, x, r_i, r_o)| = max\{|x|, |y|\}$ is called the *norm of the production* p.

Let $g = (G, t_g, o_g)$, $x = (X, t_x, o_x)$, $y = (Y, t_y, o_y)$ be structures over an alphabet V, $r_i \subseteq Y \times X$ and $r_o \subseteq X \times Y$, $p = (y, x, r_i, r_o) \in PR(V)$. Furthermore, let $G \cap X = \emptyset$ and $y \in CONV(g)$. A triple $h = (H, t_h, o_h)$ is defined as follows.

(i) $H = (G - Y) \cup X$,

(ii) o_h is a mapping of H into V:

$$o_h(a) = \begin{cases} o_g(a), & \text{if } a \in G - Y, \\ o_x(a), & \text{if } a \in X, \end{cases}$$

(iii) t_h is a relation on H defined in the following way.

$$t_h = [t_g \cap (G - Y) \times (G - Y)] \cup t_x \cup INP(g, y) \cdot r_i \cup r_o \cdot OUT(g, y),$$

The triple h is said to be a *triple directly derived from the structure g by the production p* and this fact is denoted by $g \Longrightarrow h$ ($\{p\}$). The set of all triples directly derivable from the structure g by the production $p = (y, x, r_i, r_o)$ is denoted by $DER(g, y, x, r_i, r_o)$ or, briefly, $DER(g, p)$. Thus, $DER(g, p) = \{h \in STR(V); g \Longrightarrow h \ (\{p\})\}$. We put $DER(g, p) = \emptyset$ if $y \notin CONV(g)$.

Lemma 2.1. *Let $h = (H, t_h, o_h)$ be a triple directly derived from a structure g by a production (y, x, r_i, r_o). If $p, q \in X \subseteq H$ and if there is a t_h-path $(m_i)_0^n$ from p to q in H, then $m_i \in X$ for any $i = 0, \ldots, n$.*

Proof. Clearly, if $n < 2$, then the assertion holds. Assume that $n \geq 2$ and let there be $k, l \in \{1, \ldots, n - 1\}$ such that $k \leq l$, $m_{k-1} \in X$, $m_{l+1} \in X$ and $m_k, \ldots, m_l \in G - Y$. The definition of t_h implies $m_k t_g \ldots t_g m_l$. Moreover, $(m_{k-1}, m_k) \in t_h$ implies $(m_{k-1}, m_k) \in r_o \cdot OUT(g, y)$ and $(m_l, m_{l+1}) \in t_h$ implies $(m_l, m_{l+1}) \in INP(g, y) \cdot r_i$. Thus, there exists $y_1, y_2 \in Y$ such that $(m_{k-1}, y_1) \in r_o$, $(y_1, m_k) \in OUT(g, y)$ and $(y_2, m_{l+1}) \in r_i$, $(m_l, y_2) \in INP(g, y)$. Since $INP(g, y) \subseteq t_g$ and $OUT(g, y) \subseteq t_g$, there exists the t_g-path from y_1 to y_2 in G: $y_1 t_g m_k t_g \ldots t_g m_l t_g y_2$. The assumption $y \in CONV(g)$ implies $m_k, \ldots m_l \in Y$, which is a contradiction. $\square$

Theorem 2.2. *A triple $h = (H, t_h, o_h)$ directly derived from the structure g by the production (y, x, r_i, r_o) is a structure.*

Proof. It is sufficient to prove that t_h is an acyclic relation on H. Let $n \geq 1$ and $m_1, \ldots, m_n \in H$. Furthermore, suppose that $m_1 t_h m_2 t_h \ldots t_h m_n$.

If $m_i \in G - Y$ for any $i = 1, \ldots, n$, then we can replace the relation t_h by the relation t_g and the acyclicity of t_g implies $m_1 \neq m_n$.

Similarly, if $m_i \in X$ for any $i = 1, \ldots, n$, then the acyclicity of t_x implies $m_1 \neq m_n$.

Suppose that $n \geq 2$. Let $m_{i_0} \in G - Y$, $m_{j_0} \in X$, $i_0, j_0 \in \{1, \ldots, n\}$. To prove $m_1 \neq m_n$, assume the contrary: let $m_1 = m_n$. It follows from the existence of the t_h−path $m_1 t_h \ldots t_h m_n$ that there exists a t_h−path $m_{j_0} t_h \ldots t_h m_{i_0} t_h \ldots t_h m_{j_0}$. Lemma 2.1. implies $m_{i_0} \in X$, which is a contradiction. $\square$

As a consequence of Theorem 2.2. and of the definitions, we obtain the following.

Corollary 2.3. *Let* $h = (H, t_h, o_h)$ *be a structure directly derived from the structure* g *by the production* (y, x, r_i, r_o). *Then*

(i) $x \in CONV(h)$,

(ii) $INP(h, x) = INP(g, y) \cdot r_i$,

(ii) $OUT(h, x) = r_o \cdot OUT(g, y)$.

3. Structure languages and structure grammars

Now, we define some concepts on structures similar to those which are defined on strings.

Let V be a finite set, $L \subseteq STR(V)$. The pair (V, L) is said to be a *structure language over* V. Let V be a finite alphabet, $R \subseteq PR(V)$.

Structure t is said to be *directly derived from structure* s *in a set of productions* R iff there is a production $p \in R$ such that $t \in DER(s, p)$. The fact that t is directly derived from s in R is denoted by $s \Longrightarrow t$ (R). Furthermore, we define the *weak norm* $|(s, t)|_R$ *of the pair* (s, t) as follows. $|(s, t)|_R = min\{|p|;\ p \in R$ and $s \Longrightarrow t$ $(\{p\})\}$.

Let $s, t \in STR(V)$, $s_0, \ldots, s_k \in STR(V)$, $k \geq 0$. Furthermore, let $s = s_0$, $t = s_k$ and $s_{i-1} \Longrightarrow s_i$ (R) for any $i = 1, \ldots, k$. The sequence of structures $(s_i)_0^k$ is said to be an s−*derivation of the structure* t *in* R and k is called the *lenght of the* s−*derivation*. We put $\|(s_i)_0^k\|_R = 0$ if $k = 0$ and $\|(s_i)_0^k\|_R = max\{|(s_{i-1}, s_i)|_R; i - 1, \ldots, k\}$ if $k > 0$. The number $\|(s_i)_0^k\|_R$ is called the *norm of* s−*derivation of* t *in* R.

Let $s, t \in STR(V)$. *Structure* t *is derived from structure* s *in* R iff there is an s−derivation of the structure t in R. Furthermore, the *norm* $\|(s, t)\|_R$ *of the pair* (s, t) is defined to be the minimum of norms in R of all derivations of t in R: $\|(s, t)\|_R = min\{\|(s_i)_0^k\|_R;\ (s_i)_0^k$ is an s−derivation of t in $R\}$. The fact that t is derived from s in R is denoted by $s \Longrightarrow^* t$ (R).

Algebraically, $\Longrightarrow^*$ is the reflexive transitive closure of the relation $\Longrightarrow$.

These definitions complete the tools sufficient for the definition of pure structure grammars. Let V be a finite alphabet, $S \subseteq STR(V)$ and $R \subseteq PR(V)$. The ordered triple $\langle V, S, R \rangle$ is said to be a *pure generalized structure grammar over* V. The class of all pure generalized structure grammars is denoted by $\mathcal{Z}$. A pure generalized structure grammar $\langle V, S, R \rangle$ is said to be a *pure structure grammar* iff the sets S and R are finite. The class of all structure grammars is denoted by $\mathcal{G}$.

For $G \in \mathcal{Z}$, we put $L(G) = \{t \in STR(V);$ there is $s \in S$ such that $s \Longrightarrow^* t\ (R)\}$. The structure language $(V, L(G))$ is called the *structure language generated by the generalized structure grammar* G. Let $z \in L(G)$. The *norm* $|z|_G$ *of the structure* z *with respect to the grammar* G is defined to be $|z|_G = min\{|(s, t)|_R; s \in S$ and $s \Longrightarrow^* z\ (R)\}$.

4. Operators reducing pure generalized structure grammars

The theory of reducing operators on pure generalized grammars (of strings) is presented in [7]. This theory is a basic tool in the development of effective constructions of pure grammars (cf. [9], [10]). The theory of reducing operators was applied to other objects similar to grammars (cf. [5]). Since we are only interested in pure structure grammars, we will omit the attribute pure in this part of our paper.

Lemma 4.1 *Let V be a finite alphabet.*

(i) *Let $s, t \in STR(V)$, $R \subseteq PR(V)$, $s \Longrightarrow^* t\ (R)$, $\mathbf{N} = \{0, 1, \ldots\}$. Then $|(s, t)|_R = min\{i \in \mathbf{N};$ there exists $R' \subseteq R$ such that $|p| \leq i$ for any $p \in R'$ and $s \Longrightarrow^* t\ (R')\}$.*

(ii) *Let $s, t, z \in STR(V)$, $R \subseteq PR(V)$, $s \Longrightarrow^* t\ (R)$, $t \Longrightarrow^* z\ (R)$. Then $s \Longrightarrow^* z\ (R)$, and $|(s, z)|_R \leq max\{|(s, t)|_R, |(t, z)|_R\}$.*

(iii) *Let $s, t \in STR(V)$, $R_1 \subseteq R_2 \subseteq PR(V)$, $s \Longrightarrow^* t\ (R_1)$. Then $s \Longrightarrow^* t\ (R_2)$ and $|(s, t)|_{R_2} \leq |(s, t)|_{R_1}$.*

(iv) *Let $R \subseteq PR(V)$ be a finite set. Then there is a number $N \geq 0$ such that $|(s, t)|_R \leq N$ for any $s, t \in STR(V)$ with the property $s \Longrightarrow^* t\ (R)$.*

(v) *Let $G_1 = \langle V, S_1, R \rangle$, $G_2 = \langle V, S_2, R \rangle$ be generalized structure grammars. Furthermore, let $S_1 \subseteq S_2$. Then $L(G_1) \subseteq L(G_2)$ and the condition $|z|_{G_2} \leq |z|_{G_1}$ holds for any $z \in L(G_1)$.*

(vi) *Let $G = \langle V, S, R \rangle$ be a generalized structure grammar and let R be a finite set. Then there is a number $N \geq 0$ such that $|z|_G \leq N$ for any $z \in L(G)$.*

Proof. Assertions (i) and (v) are immediate consequences of the definitions. Assertions (ii), (iii) and (iv) are consequences of assertion (i) and assertion (iv) implies assertion (vi). $\qquad\square$

Now, we define some relations on the class of all generalized structure grammars $\mathcal{Z}$.

Let $G_1, G_2 \in \mathcal{Z}$, $G_1 = \langle V_1, S_1, R_1 \rangle$, $G_2 = \langle V_2, S_2, R_2 \rangle$. We put $G_1 \equiv G_2$ iff $V_1 = V_2$ and $L(G_1) = L(G_2)$. Furthermore, we put $G_1 \leq G_2$ iff $V_1 = V_2$, $S_1 \subseteq S_2$ and $R_1 \subseteq R_2$.

Clearly, the relation $\equiv$ is an equivalence relation on $\mathcal{Z}$ and the relation $\leq$ is an ordering on $\mathcal{Z}$.

Let $\alpha \; : \; \mathcal{Z} \longrightarrow \mathcal{Z}$ be a mapping such that $\alpha G \equiv G$ and $\alpha G \leq G$. The mapping α is called a *reducing operator on $\mathcal{Z}$*. The class of all reducing operators on $\mathcal{Z}$ is denoted by Δ.

Let us have $G \in \mathcal{Z}$, $\alpha \in \Delta$. We say that G is *well reducible by means of α* if $\alpha G \in \mathcal{G}$. We say that $G \in \mathcal{Z}$ is *well reducible* if there is $\alpha \in \Delta$ such that G is well reducible by means of α.

Clearly, $G \in \mathcal{Z}$ is well reducible iff there is a structure grammar $G' \in \mathcal{G}$ such that $G' \equiv G$ and $G' \leq G$.

Now, we are interested in special reducing operators. Let $G = \langle V, S, R \rangle \in \mathcal{Z}$. We put $\beta G = \langle V, B(G), R \rangle$, where $B(G) = \{s \in S;$ the condition $t \in S,\ t \Longrightarrow^* s\ (R)$ imply $|t| \geq |s|\}$,
$\zeta G = \langle V, S, Z(G) \rangle$, where $Z(G) = \{p \in R;$ there is $z \in L(G)$ such that $|p| \leq |z|_G\}$.

We prove that operators β and ζ are reducing operators on $\mathcal{Z}$.

Lemma 4.2. *Let $G = \langle V, S, R \rangle$ be a generalized structure grammar. Then*

(i) $\beta G \leq G$.

(ii) $\zeta G \leq G$.

(iii) For any $s \in S$, the condition $s \notin B(G)$ is satisfied iff there is $t \in B(G)$ such that $t \Longrightarrow^* s\ (R)$ and $|t| < |s|$.

(iv) Put

$$q = \begin{cases} \min\{|s|; t \in S\}, & \text{if } S \neq \emptyset, \\ 0, & \text{if } S = \emptyset, \end{cases}$$

$$S' = \{s \in S; |s| = q\}.$$

Then $S' \subseteq B(G)$.

Proof. Assertions (i), (ii) and (iii) are immediate consequences of definitions and assertion (iv) is a consequence of assertion (iii).   □

Lemma 4.3. *Let* $G = \langle V, S, R \rangle \in \mathcal{Z}$. *Then*

(i) $L(G) = L(\beta G)$,

(ii) $B(G) = (B(B(G))$ *and* $\beta(\beta G) = \beta G$.

Proof. Assertion (ii) is a consequence of definition. The condition $B(G) \subseteq S$ implies $L(\beta G) \subseteq L(G)$. To prove the inverse inclusion, we assume that $z \in L(G)$. We denote $m = min\{|s|; s \in S \text{ and } s \Longrightarrow^* z \ (R)\}$. Let $s_0 \in S$ be such that $|s_0| = m$ and $s_0 \Longrightarrow^* z \ (R)$. The assertion 4.2. (iii) implies $s_0 \in B(G)$ and $z \in L(\beta G)$. Thus, the condition $L(G) \subseteq L(\beta G)$ holds.   □

Lemma 4.4. *Let* $G = \langle V, S, R \rangle \in \mathcal{Z}$, $z \in L(G)$, $s \in S$ *and let* $(s_i)_0^k$ *be an* s-*derivation of* z *in* R *such that* $|(s_i)_0^k|_R = |(s, z)|_R = |z|_G$. *Then* $(s_i)_0^k$ *is an* s-*derivation of* z *in* $Z(G)$ *and* $|(s_i)_0^k|_{Z(G)} \leq |(s_i)_0^k|_R$.

Proof. Clearly, both assertions hold if $k = 0$. Now, let $k > 0$. Then $|(s_{i-1}, s_i)|_R \leq |(s_i)_0^k|_R = |z|_G$ for any $i = 1, \ldots, k$. Thus, there exists a production $p_i \in R$ such that $s_{i-1} \Longrightarrow s_i \ (\{p_i\})$ and $|p_i| = |(s_{i-1}, s_i)|_R \leq |z|_G$ for any $i = 1, \ldots, k$. The last conclusion implies $p_i \in Z(G)$ for any $i = 1, \ldots, k$ and $(s_i)_0^k$ is an s-derivation of z in $Z(G)$. Furthermore, $|(s_i)_0^k|_{Z(G)} = max\{|(s_{i-1}, s_i)|_{Z(G)}; i = 1, \ldots, k\} \leq max\{|(p_i)|; i = 1, \ldots, k\} = |(s_i)_0^k|_R$.   □

Lemma 4.5. *Let* $G = \langle V, S, R \rangle$ *be a generalized structure grammar. Then*

(i) $L(G) = L(\zeta G)$,

(ii) $Z(G) = Z(Z(G))$ *and* $\zeta(\zeta G)) = \zeta G$.

(iii) $|z|_G = |z|_{\zeta G}$ *for any* $z \in L(G)$.

Proof. (a) The condition $Z(G) \subseteq R$ implies $L(\zeta G) \subseteq L(G)$. Lemma 4.4. entails $L(G) \subseteq L(\zeta G)$ and assertion (i) holds.

(b) Assertion (iii) is an immediate consequence of 4.4. and of 4.1. (iii).

(c) Clearly, $Z(Z(G)) \subseteq Z(G)$. If $p \in Z(G)$, then there is $z \in L(G) = L(\zeta G)$ such that $|p| \leq |z|_G = |z|_{\zeta G}$. Thus, $p \in Z(Z(G))$, $Z(G) \subseteq Z(Z(G))$ and assertion (ii) holds.   □

Assertions 4.2. (i) and (ii), 4.3. (i) and 4.5. (i) imply that the operators β and ζ are reducing operators. We prove stronger assertions in the next part.

Lemma 4.6.

(i) *Let* $G_1 = \langle V, S_1, R \rangle$, $G_2 = \langle V, S_2, R \rangle$ *be generalized structure grammars,*
   $S_1 \subseteq S_2$ *and* $L(G_1) = L(G_2)$. *Then* $Z(G_2) \subseteq Z(G_1)$.

(ii) Let $G_1 = \langle V, S, R_1 \rangle$, $G_2 = \langle V, S, R_2 \rangle$ be generalized structure grammars, $R_1 \subseteq R_2$. Then $B(G_2) \subseteq B(G_1)$.

Proof. The assertion (i) is a consequence of the definitions and Lemma 4.1. (v), the assertion (ii) is an immediate consequence of the definitions. □

Lemma 4.7. *Let $G = \langle V, S, R \rangle$ be a generalized structure grammar. Then*

(i) $\beta(\zeta(\beta G)) = \zeta(\beta G)$,

(ii) $\zeta(\beta(\zeta G)) = \beta(\zeta G))$.

Proof. Let us denote

$$G_1 = \beta G = \langle V, B(G), R \rangle, \quad G_2 = \zeta(\beta G) = \langle V, B(G), Z(G_1) \rangle,$$

$$G_3 = \zeta G = \langle V, S, Z(G) \rangle, \quad G_4 = \beta(\zeta G) = \langle V, B(G_3), Z(G) \rangle.$$

Lemma 4.3. (ii) implies $B(G) = B(B(G)) = B(G_1)$. Since $Z(G_1) \subseteq R$, we obtain $B(G_1) \subseteq B(G_2)$ by Lemma 4.6. (ii). Directly by the definition, the condition $B(G_2) \subseteq B(G)$ holds. Thus, $B(G) = B(G_2)$, $\beta G_2 = G_2$ and assertion (i) holds.
Similarly, Lemma 4.5. (ii) implies $Z(G) = Z(Z(G)) = Z(G_3)$. Furthermore, $L(G_3) = L(G_4)$ holds by Lemma 4.3. (i). Lemma 4.6. (i) implies $Z(G_3) \subseteq Z(G_4)$. Consequently, $Z(G) = Z(G_4)$ and $\zeta G_4 = G_4$. Thus, the assertion (ii) holds. □

We have proved the following equalities: $\beta \zeta \beta = \zeta \beta$, $\zeta \beta \zeta = \beta \zeta$, $\beta \beta = \beta$, $\zeta \zeta = \zeta$. Let us denote by Γ the monoid of all transformations of the class $\mathscr{Z}$ generated by the set $\{\beta, \zeta\}$ provided by the binary operation of composition. It can be shown (cf. [7]) that Γ contains exactly five elements, $\Gamma = \{id_{\mathscr{Z}}, \beta, \zeta, \gamma, \delta\}$, where $\gamma = \beta \zeta$ and $\delta = \zeta \beta$.
The operator $\delta = \zeta \beta$ has an important property ([7]).

Theorem 4.8. *The generalized structure grammar $G = \langle V, S, R \rangle \in \mathscr{Z}$ is well reducible iff it is well reducible by means of δ.*

Proof. (1) If the generalized grammar G is well reducible, then there is a structure grammar $G' \in \mathscr{G}$ such that $G' \equiv G$ and $G' \leq G$. We denote $G' = \langle V, S', R' \rangle$ where S' and R' are finite sets.
(2) We put $N = 0$ if $S' = \emptyset$ and $N = max\{|s|; s \in S'\}$ if $S' \neq \emptyset$. If $z \in S$, $|z| > N$, then $z \in L(G) = L(G')$ and there is $s \in S'$ such that $s \Longrightarrow^* z \ (R')$. The conditions $|s| \leq N < |z|$, $s \in S$, $s \Longrightarrow^* z \ (R)$ hold because $S' \subseteq S$ and $R' \subseteq R$. Thus, $z \notin B(G)$. Consequently, $z \in B(G)$ implies $|z| \leq N$ and the set $B(G)$ is finite. Let us denote $G_1 = \beta G = \langle V, B(G), R \rangle$.

(3) By Lemma 4.1. (vi), there is a number $M \geq 0$ such that $|z|_{G'} \leq M$ for any $z \in L(G')$. We put $P = 0$ if $S' = \emptyset$ and $P = max\{|t|_{G_1}; t \in S'\}$ if $S' \neq \emptyset$. Furthermore, we put $Q = max\{M, P\}$.

(4) If $z \in L(G) = L(G')$, then there is $t \in S'$ such that $t \Longrightarrow^* z$ (R') and $|(t, z)|_{R'} = |z|_{G'} \leq M$. Lemma 4.1. (iii) implies $t \Longrightarrow^* z$ (R) and $|(t, z)|_R \leq |(t, z)|_{R'} \leq M'$. Since $t \in S' \subseteq S \subseteq L(G)$, there is $s \in B(G)$ such that $s \Longrightarrow^* t$ (R) and $|(s, t)|_R = |t|_{G_1} \leq P$. Consequently, $s \Longrightarrow^* z$ (R) and $|(s, z)|_R \leq max\{|(s, t)|_R, |(t, z)|_R\} \leq max\{M, P\} = Q$ by Lemma 4.1. (ii). Since $s \in B(G)$, the condition $|z|_{G_1} \leq |(s, z)|_R \leq Q$ holds.

(5) If $p \in Z(G_1)$, then there is $z \in L(G_1) = L(\beta G)$ such that $|p| \leq |z|_{G_1}$. Since $L(\beta G) = L(G)$, the condition $|z|_{G_1} \leq Q$ holds. Consequently, $|p| \leq Q$ and $Z(G_1)$ is a finite set.

We have proved that $\delta G \in \mathcal{G}$. On the other hand, if a generalized structure grammar is well reducible by means of δ, then obviously it is well reducible. $\qquad\qquad\qquad\qquad\qquad\qquad\qquad\qquad\qquad\qquad\qquad\qquad\qquad\qquad\square$

Example. If (M, t, o) is a structure, o is a set of ordered pairs $(v, o(v))$; we shall write $v \mapsto o(v)$ for $(v, o(v))$ for the sake of brevity. According to the convention we may replace any structure by an isomorphic one. Thus, in what follows the elements v_0, v_1, w_0, w_1, w_2 appearing in structures x_i, y_i of productions p_i, $(i = 1, 2, 3, 4)$ may be replaced by suitable elements when applying these productions.

Let $s_0 = (\{v_0\}, \emptyset, \{v_0 \mapsto b\})$, $s_k = (\{v_0, v_1, \ldots, v_k\}, t_{s_k}, o_{s_k})$, $k = 1, 2, \ldots$ be structures, where $t_{s_k} = \{(v_i, v_0); i = 1, \ldots, k\}$ and $o_{s_k}(v_0) = b$, $o_{s_k}(v_i) = a$ for any $i = 1, \ldots, k$.

Let $G = \langle\{a, b\}, S, R\rangle$ be a pure generalized structure grammar, where

$$S = \{s_0, s_1, s_3, \ldots, s_{2k+1}, \ldots\}, k = 0, 1, \ldots, R = \{p_1, p_2, p_3, p_4\},$$

$$p_1 = (y_1, x_1, r_{i_1}, r_{o_1}),$$

$$y_1 = (\{v_0\}, \emptyset, \{v_0 \mapsto b\}),$$

$$x_1 = (\{w_0, w_1\}, \{(w_1, w_0)\}, \{w_0 \mapsto b, w_1 \mapsto a\}),$$

$$r_{i_1} = \{(v_0, w_0)\},$$

$$r_{o_1} = \{(w_0, v_0)\} = r_{i_1}^{-1},$$

$$p_2 = (y_2, x_2, r_{i_2}, r_{o_2}),$$

$$y_2 = (\{v_0\}, \emptyset, \{v_0 \mapsto b\}),$$

$$x_2 = (\{w_0, w_1, w_2\}, \{(w_1, w_0), (w_2, w_0)\}, \{w_0 \mapsto b, w_1 \mapsto a, w_2 \mapsto a\}),$$

$$r_{i_2} = \{(v_0, w_0)\},$$

$$r_{o_2} = \{(w_0, v_0)\} = r_{i_2}^{-1},$$

$$p_3 = (y_3, x_3, r_{i_3}, r_{o_3}),$$

$$y_3 = (\{v_0, v_1\}, \emptyset, \{v_0 \mapsto a, v_1 \mapsto a\}),$$

$$x_3 = (\{w_0, w_1\}, \{(w_1, w_0)\}, \{w_0 \mapsto a, \ w_1 \mapsto a\}),$$
$$r_{i_3} = \{(v_0, w_0), (v_1, w_1)\},$$
$$r_{o_3} = \{(w_0, v_0)\},$$
$$p_4 = (y_4, x_4, r_{i_4}, r_{o_4}), y_4 = (\{v_0, v_1\}, \emptyset, \{v_0 \mapsto a, \ v_1 \mapsto a\}),$$
$$x_4 = (\{w_0, w_1\}, \{(w_1, w_0)\}, \{w_0 \mapsto a, \ w_1 \mapsto a\}),$$
$$r_{i_4} = \{(v_0, w_0), (v_1, w_1)\}, r_{o_4} = \{(w_0, v_0), (w_1, v_1)\}.$$

Let $Q \subseteq STR(\{a, b\})$ be a set of structures with the greatest element satisfying the following conditions. The greatest element of any structure is labelled by b and the other elements are labeled by a's. (An element $w \in Z$ of structure (Z, t, o) is said to be the greatest element if there is a t-path in Z from an arbitrary element $w' \in Z$ to w.)
Then the following equalities hold.

1. $L(G) = Q$,

2. $|s_k| = k + 1$ for any $k = 0, 1, \ldots,$

3. $|p_1| = |p_3| = |p_4| = 2, |p_2| = 3,$

4. $B(G) = \{s_0\}$,

5. $\beta G = \langle \{a, b\}, B(G), R \rangle,$

6. $Z(\beta G) = \{p_1, p_3, p_4\},$

7. $\delta G = \zeta(\beta G) = \langle \{a, b\}, \{s_0\}, \{p_1, p_3, p_4\} \rangle$ and G is well reducible.

5. Conclusions

There are some problems about structure grammars to be solved. First, let (y, x, r_i, r_o) and (y, x, q_i, q_o) be productions of the structure grammar G. Does there exist a relationship between the pairs (r_i, r_o) and (q_i, q_o) to derive always the same structures from an arbitrary structure $s \in L(G)$? In other words, under which conditions $DER(s, y, x, r_i, r_o) = DER(s, y, x, q_i, q_o)$ holds for any $s \in L(G)$?

Second, structure grammars (generative devices that generate structure languages) are described in our paper. In some cases, the concept dual to generative structure grammars can be an interesting problem. Structure language $L_A(G)$ recognized by analytic structure grammar $G = \langle V, S, R \rangle$ is defined as a set of structures over V from which any structure $s \in S$ can be derived in R. More precisely, $L_A(G) = \{t \in STR(V); \text{ there is } s \in S \text{ such that } t \Longrightarrow^* s\,(R)\}$. Let G be an arbitrary (generative) structure grammar. The question then is whether exist an (analytic) structure grammar G' to recognize the same language $L(G)$, i.e. $L_A(G') = L(G)$?

References

1. K. S. Fu, L. B. Taylor, Grammatical Inference: Introduction and Survey, *IEEE Trans. on Systems, Man and Cyb.*, 5 (1975), 95 – 111.

2. F. Gécseg, M. Steinby, *Tree Automata*, Akademiai Kiadó, Budapest, 1984.

3. J. Gips, *Shape Grammars and Their Uses*, Birhäuser, Basel, 1975.

4. R. C. Gonzalez, M. G. Thomason, *Syntactic Pattern Recognition*, Addison Wesley, Reading Mass., 1978.

5. M. Kudlek, M. Novotný, On a reducing operator for combinatorial systems, *Information and Control*, 37 (1978), 197 – 206.

6. M. Nagl, A tutorial and bibliographical survey on graph grammars, *Lect. Notes in Comp. Science* 73, Springer-Verlag, Berlin, (1979), 70 – 126.

7. M. Novotný, On some operators reducing generalized grammars, *Information and Control*, 26 (1974), 225 – 235.

8. M. Novotný, *S algebrou od jazyka ke gramatice a zpět*, Academia, Praha, 1988.

9. J. Ostravský, Effective constructions of grammars for languages of two particular classes, *Fundamenta Informaticae*, 8 (1985), 235 – 252.

10. Gh. Păun, M. Novotný, On some parameters occurring in certain effective constructions of grammars, *Fundamenta Informaticae*, 1 (1987), 69 – 80.

11. A. Salomaa, *Formal Languages*, Academic Press, New York, 1973.

12. H. J. Schneider, *Chomsky-like Systems for Partially Ordered Symbol Sets*, Techn. Rep. 2/2/71, Informationverarbeitung II, TU Berlin, 1971.

13. H. J. Schneider, A necessary and sufficient condition for Chomsky productions over partially ordered symbol sets, *Lect. Notes Econom. Math. Syst.* 78 (1973), Springer-Verlag, Berlin, 90 – 98.

Redundant Retreat Free Words[1]

Patrice SÉÉBOLD
LAMIFA, Université de Picardie
33, rue Saint Leu, F-80039 Amiens Cedex 01, France

Karine SLOWINSKI
LIFL, CNRS - UA 369, Université de Lille 1
F-59655 Villeneuve d'Ascq Cedex, France

Abstract. A *picture word* is a word over the four letter alphabet $\Pi = \{r, l, u, d\}$. We show that the operator *r-red*, which deletes redundant retreats in words, associates with any picture word a unique irreducible word.

1. Introduction

A picture word is a word over the four letter alphabet $\Pi = \{r, l, u, d\}$. With any picture word, we associate a connected picture as follows: each letter induces a unit line drawn in one of the four directions (right, left, up and down). Maurer, Rozenberg, Welzl [4] and Hinz [2] introduced two reduction operators to delete retreats (i.e. ways back in the picture) in picture words. To connect the present work with those of Maurer at al and Hinz, we will use here the notations introduced by these authors.

The first operator, *red*, deletes all retreats and was shown to associate with any word a *unique* irreducible word [4] (see Theorem 1 below). However, these deletions do not preserve pictures.

The second operator, *r-red*, deletes redundant retreats and preserves pictures. We prove (Theorem 2) that it also associates with any picture word a *unique* irreducible word. This result greatly improves that of Pécuchet [5] who proved something similar but in a very restricted context (see Section 4).

2. Preliminaries

We assume the reader to be familiar with the basic formal language theory [1], [6] and we just remind him of several notations.

Let A be a finite set called *alphabet*. The elements of A are *letters* and A^* is the set of finite strings (*words*) over A, ε denotes the *empty word*. For $w \in A^*$, $|w|$ denotes its length (i.e. its number of letters; for example, $|\varepsilon| = 0$).

---

[1]Partially supported by PRC "Mathématiques et Informatique" and by ESPRIT BRA working group 6317 - ASMICS 2.

A word $w' \in A^*$ is a *factor* (*left factor, right factor* resp.) of the word $w \in A^*$ if there exist $w_1, w_2 \in A^*$ ($w_1 = \varepsilon$, $w_2 = \varepsilon$ resp.) such that $w = w_1 w' w_2$. $F(w)$ ($LF(w)$, $RF(w)$ resp.) denotes the set of factors (left factors, right factors resp.) of w.

Let G be a grid of the plane and $\Pi = \{r, l, u, d\}$ a four letter alphabet. With each letter from Π, we associate a unit line in G as follows:

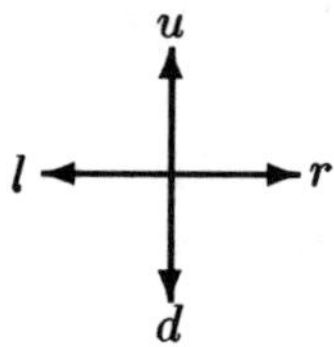

(r induces a unit line to the *right*, l induces a unit line to the *left*, u induces a unit line to the *up*, d induces a unit line to the *down*.)

A *picture word* is a word over Π. With any picture word w, we associate a connected *picture dpic(w)* in the following way: we start from the origin of the grid and we read the word letter by letter drawing simultaneously the unit lines defined above. The picture $dpic(w)$ is characterized by the set of described segments $S(w)$ and the ending point of the tracing $e(w)$.

Remark. If a segment is described several times by a picture word w, we draw it several times but the picture $dpic(w)$ contains only one occurrence of this segment.

Example. $w = rulr$

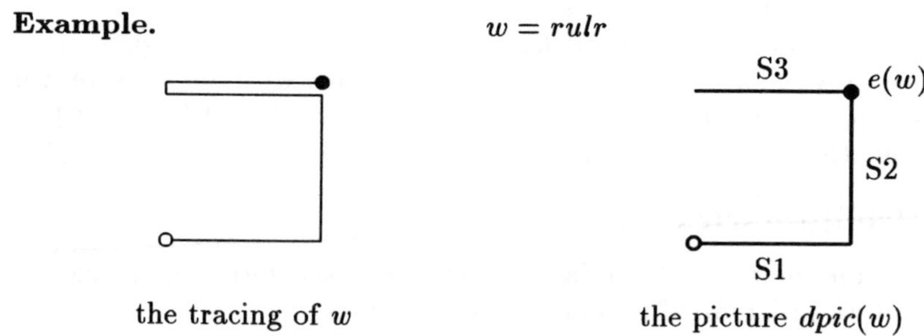

the tracing of w   the picture dpic(w)

o denotes the starting point and ● the ending point.

The *inverse* of a word w, denoted by $inv(w)$ or in short $\bar{w}$, is defined inductively by: $inv(\varepsilon) = \varepsilon$

$$inv(r) = l; \, inv(l) = r; \, inv(u) = d; \, inv(d) = u$$
$$inv(w'x) = inv(x)inv(w') \text{ where } w' \in \Pi^* \text{ and } x \in \Pi.$$

Remark. Starting from $e(w)$, the tracing of $\bar{w}$ corresponds to the tracing of w in the opposite way.

3. Results

The operators defined in this section allow us to reduce a word w by deleting some passages on its segments.

The operator *red* was introduced by Maurer & all [4]. It deletes two consecutive letters from a word w which induce a "go and back" drawing. A *retreat* is a word from $R = \{rl, lr, ud, du\}$. The *retreat deletion image* of a word w, denoted by $red(w)$, is defined inductively as the smallest set with $w \in red(w)$ and if $v_1 x v_2 \in red(w)$ then $v_1 v_2 \in red(w)$ where $v_1, v_2 \in \Pi^*$ and $x \in R$.

Remark. The set $red(w)$ is the set of all the words obtained from w by deleting the retreats. We note that the operator *red* does not preserve the picture $dpic(w)$: the ending point is preserved but some segments can disappear. This reduction is used when one is only interested in the final point independently of the way followed to reach it (for instance, to simulate a move with pen-up).

Example. $\qquad\qquad w = rlruldurd$

The elements of $red(w)$ are:

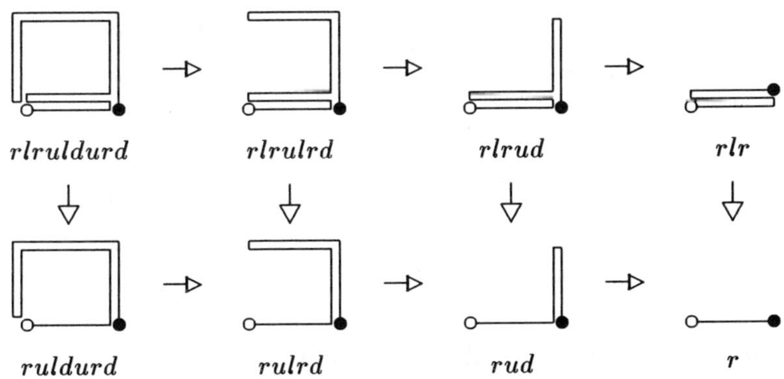

The associated pictures are:

A word $w \in \Pi^*$ is a *retreat-free word* if $F(w) \cap R = \vee$. Note that a retreat-free word is irreducible for the operator *red*.

Theorem 1. ([4]) *For all $w \in \Pi^*$ the set red(w) contains exactly one retreat-free word.*

Indeed independently of the order in which reductions are made, the irreducible word is unique. But this result would be more interesting if the operator *red* could preserve the pictures. So Hinz defined the following operator *r-red* [2].

A *redundant retreat* is a word from $RR = \{z\bar{z}z / z \in \Pi^+\}$. The *redundant retreat deletion image* of a word w, denoted by $r\text{-}red(w)$, is defined inductively as the smallest set with $w \in r\text{-}red(w)$ and if $v_1 z\bar{z}z v_2 \in r\text{-}red(w)$ then $v_1 z v_2 \in r\text{-}red(w)$ where $v_1, v_2 \in \Pi^*$ and $z \in \Pi^+$.

Remark. Contrary to the previous operator, *r-red* eliminates from a word w only letters corresponding to redundant passages on segments. So all the segments of the picture $dpic(w)$ are preserved along the reductions.

Example. $w = rlruldurd$

The elements of $r\text{-}red(w)$ are:

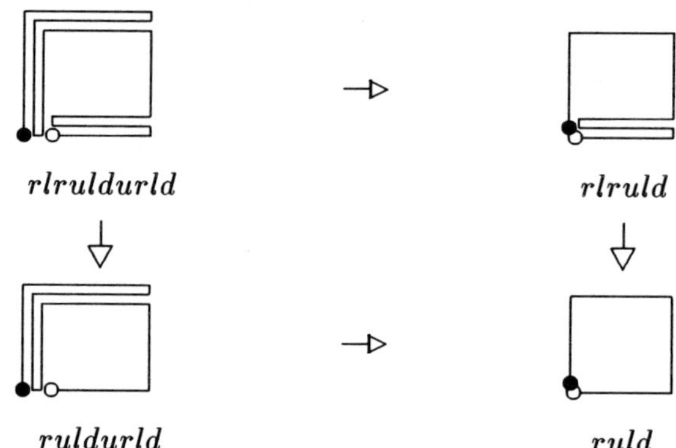

rlruldurld   *rlruld*

ruldurld   *ruld*

The picture associated with all the words of $r\text{-}red(w)$ is:

A word $w \in \Pi^*$ is a *redundant retreat-free word* if $F(w) \cap RR = \vee$. Note that a redundant retreat-free word is irreducible for the operator *r-red*.

In what follows we will show that, as for the operator *red*, the set $r\text{-}red(w)$ contains a unique irreducible word.

Theorem 2. *For all $w \in \Pi^*$ the set r-red(w) contains exactly one redundant retreat-free word.*

4. Pécuchet's result

Theorem 2 is very similar to a result of J. P. Pécuchet [5] and seems to be a direct consequence of his survey. However this idea is wrong and we give now some arguments in this way.

Let A be an alphabet. We set $\bar{A} = \{\bar{a}/a \in A\}$ verifying $A \cap \bar{A} = \vee$. For any word $w \in (A \cup \bar{A})^*$, $inv(w)$ or in short $\bar{w}$ is defined inductively by

$$inv(\varepsilon) = \varepsilon, \ \forall a \in A, \ inv(a) = \bar{a}, \ \forall \bar{a} \in \bar{A}, \ inv(\bar{a}) = a \text{ and}$$
$$inv(w'x) = inv(x)inv(w') \text{ where } w' \in (A \cup \bar{A})^* \text{ and } x \in (A \cup \bar{A}).$$

Let $\sigma(w)$ be the smallest set with $w \in \sigma(w)$ and if $v_1 z\bar{z}zv_2 \in \sigma(w)$ then $v_1 z v_2 \in \sigma(w)$ where $v_1, v_2 \in (A \cup \bar{A})^*$ and $z \in A^+ \cup \bar{A}^+$. According to Lemma 4.1 in [5], for any word $w \in (A \cup \bar{A})^*$ there exists a unique word $\rho(w)$ such that $\rho(w) \in \sigma(w)$ and $\rho(w)$ contains no factor $z\bar{z}z$ with $z \in A^+ \cup \bar{A}^+$.

If we try to apply this lemma to our problem, two cases are possible:

- either we choose for A a two letter alphabet: for instance, we set $A = \{r, u\}$ with $\bar{r} = l$ and $\bar{u} = d$. Then for every word w over Π there exists a unique word $\rho(w)$ in $\sigma(w)$ such that $\rho(w)$ contains no factor $z\bar{z}z$ with $z \in A^+ \cup \bar{A}^+$. But since z is only composed of letters of A or only composed of letters of $\bar{A}$, a word as $r\bar{u}\bar{r}ur\bar{u}$ cannot be anymore reduced by the operator σ (but can be reduced by the operator r-red).

- or we choose for A a four letter alphabet: for instance, we set $A = \Pi$. We define a morphism ϕ such that $\phi(r) = \phi(\bar{l}) = r$ and so on (for any word $w \in A^*$, $\phi^{-1}(w)$ is the set containing $2^{|w|}$ words over $(A \cup \bar{A})^*$). For each word w' in $\phi^{-1}(w)$, there exists a unique irreducible word $\phi(\rho(w'))$ according to the operator σ, but the irreducible words are not the same for all words in $\phi^{-1}(w)$.

Thus Pécuchet's result cannot be applied to prove Theorem 2. Indeed the proof of Pécuchet's lemma uses the fact that the factors z and $\bar{z}$ are defined over separate alphabets. This restriction strongly decreases the number of overlaps between two possible reductions of a word.

5. Proof of Theorem 2

Let S be the rewriting system defined as $S = \{z\bar{z}z \rightarrow z/z \in \Pi^+\}$ (for details about definitions and properties of rewriting systems see, for instance, [3]).

A rewriting system is *confluent* if it is both a *terminating reduction system* (no infinite derivation) and a *locally confluent* one (any two elements with a common ancestor have a common descendant). So, to prove Theorem 2 is equivalent to show that S is confluent (indeed, in this case any word of Π^* has a unique normal form by S).

The system S is obviously a terminating reduction system: the length of the derived word strictly decreases at each step.

We will now show that the system S is locally confluent.

Let $w \in \Pi^*$ and suppose that w contains at least two redundant retreats. We set w_1 the word obtained from w by deleting one of the redundant retreats and w_2 by deleting another one. We have to prove that, in all cases, there exists a word $m \in \Pi^*$ which can be derived independently from w_1 and w_2 (that is to say that we have to find a word $m \in r\text{-}red(w_1) \cap r\text{-}red(w_2)$). One can easily understand that finding such a word depends on the overlap of the deleted redundant retreats. So we have to study many cases. Without loss of generality, we can assume that the two redundant retreats denoted by $x\bar{x}x$ and $z\bar{z}z$ with $x,z \in \Pi^+$ verify $|x| \geq |z|$. We set $w = u_1 x\bar{x}x u_2 = v_1 z\bar{z}z v_2$ with $u_1,u_2,v_1,v_2 \in \Pi^*$, $w_1 = u_1 x u_2 \in r\text{-}red(w)$, $w_2 = v_1 z v_2 \in r\text{-}red(w)$ and we are going to show that, in every case of overlap, there exists a word $m \in r\text{-}red(w_1) \cap r\text{-}red(w_2)$).

First we give, without proof, a simple lemma used in some of the different cases:

Lemma 1. *Let* $v, v_1, z \in \Pi^*$.

1. If $v_1 \in LF(v)$ *then* $v \in r\text{-}red(v_1 \bar{v}_1 v)$ *and* $\bar{v} \in r\text{-}red(\bar{v} v_1 \bar{v}_1)$

2. If $v \in LF[(z\bar{z})^*]$ *then* $z\bar{z} \in r\text{-}red(z\bar{z} v \bar{v})$ *and* $z\bar{z} \in r\text{-}red(v\bar{v} z\bar{z})$

3. If $v = \bar{v}$ *then there exists* $v' \in \Pi^*$ *such that* $v'\bar{v}' = v$

5.1. Notations

In what follows,

- we have $x_1, x_2, z_1, z_2, z_3, z_4, z_5, z_6 \in \Pi^*$ with $x = x_1 x_2$, $z = z_1 z_2 = z_3 z_4 = z_5 z_6$.

- $w \xrightarrow{i} w'$ denotes that applying part 1 of Lemma 1 to the underlined factor of w, we can deduce that $w' \in r\text{-}red(w)$.

5.2. The different cases

- If the two redundant retreats are disjointed, i.e. $w = u_1 x\bar{x}xyz\bar{z}z v_2$ with $y \in \Pi^*$ (similarly for the case $w = v_1 z\bar{z}zyx\bar{x}x u_2$), we obviously have $m = u_1 xyz v_2 \in r\text{-}red(w_1) \cap r\text{-}red(w_2)$.

- If the shorter redundant retreat $z\bar{z}z$ is a factor of x (or $\bar{x}$), i.e. $w = u_1 x_1 z'\bar{z}'z'x_2\ \bar{x}_2\ \bar{z}'z'\bar{z}'\bar{x}_1 x_1 z'\bar{z}'z'x_2 u_2$ with $z' = z$ or $z' = \bar{z}$, we obviously have $m = u_1 x_1 z' x_2 u_2 \in r\text{-}red(w_1) \cap r\text{-}red(w_2)$.

- In the other cases, we consider the two following groups of overlaps:

  a) the redundant retreat $z\bar{z}z$ is a factor of the redundant retreat $x\bar{x}x$

  b) the redundant retreat $z\bar{z}z$ is not a factor of the redundant retreat $x\bar{x}x$

$$\textbf{a)}\ \ z\bar{z}z \in F(x\bar{x}x)$$

In this case, we will show a stronger property: there exists a way to reduce w_1 in w_2 (that is to say we can choose $m = w_1$).

In the following cases, we suppose that the factor $z\bar{z}z$ is in the left part of the factor $x\bar{x}x$. The proof would be exactly the same for the symetrical cases.

Case a.1) $z\bar{z} \in F(x)$ or $\bar{z}z \in F(\bar{x})$

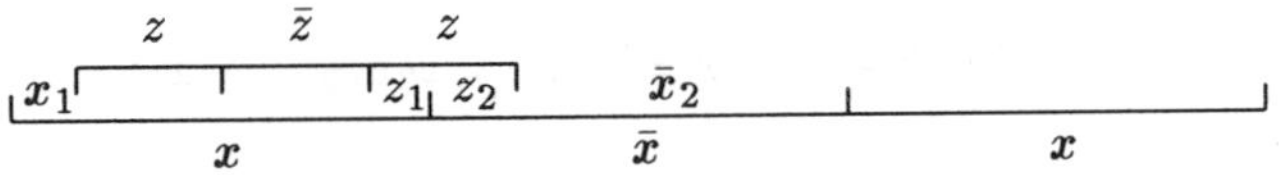

In this case $x = x_1 z\bar{z}z_1 = x_2\bar{z}_2$

We have $w = u_1 x\bar{x}x u_2 = u_1 x_1 z\bar{z}z_1 \bar{x}x u_2$.

We also have $w_2 = u_1 x_1 z_1 \bar{x}x u_2 = u_1 x_1 z_1 \bar{z}_1 z\bar{z}\bar{x}_1 x u_2$.

We deduce: $w_2 = u_1 x_1 \underline{z_1 \bar{z}_1} z\bar{z}\bar{x}_1 x u_2 \overset{1}{\to} u_1 x_1 \underline{z\bar{z}\bar{x}_1} x u_2 \overset{1}{\to} u_1 x u_2 = w_1.$

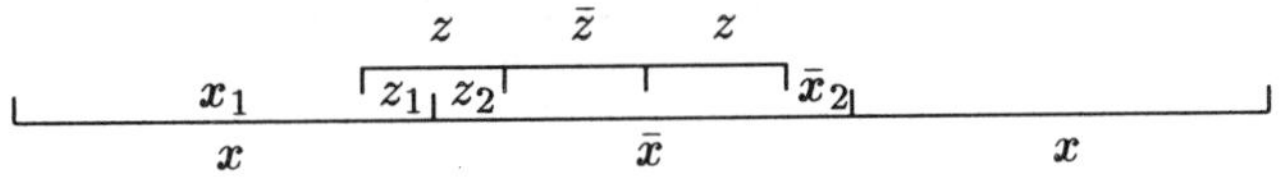

In this case $x = x_1 z_1 = x_2\bar{z}z\bar{z}_2$

We have $w = u_1 x\bar{x}x u_2 = u_1 x z_2 \bar{z}z\bar{x}_2 x u_2$.

We also have $w_2 = u_1 x z_2 \bar{x}_2 x u_2 = u_1 x z_2 \bar{z}z\bar{z}_2 z_2 \bar{x}_2 x u_2$.

We deduce: $w_2 = u_1 x z_2 \bar{z}z\underline{\bar{z}_2 z_2}\bar{x}_2 x u_2 \overset{1}{\to} u_1 x_2 \bar{z}z\bar{x}_2 x u_2 \overset{1}{\to} u_1 x u_2 = w_1.$

Case a.2) $z\bar{z}z \in F(x\bar{x})$ (except case a.1)

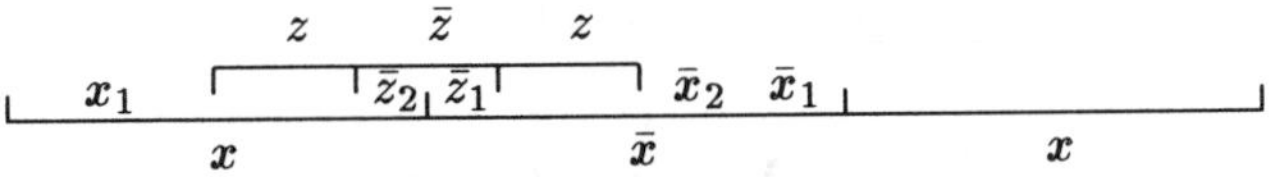

In this case $x = x_1 z \bar{z}_2 = x_1 x_2 \bar{z} z_1$

Assume $|z_1| \leq |z_2|$ (the other case is similar). We can set $\bar{z}_2 = \bar{c} z_1, c \in \Pi^*$. Since $x_1 z \bar{z}_2 = x_1 x_2 \bar{z} z_1$ and $\bar{z}_2 = \bar{c} z_1$, we have $z\bar{c} = x_2 \bar{z}$, thus $|c| = |x_2|$. Knowing that $|c| \leq |z_2| \leq |z|$, we have $x_2 \in LF(z)$ and $c \in LF(z)$. So, $x_2 = c$. Moreover, $x_2 \in LF(z) \Rightarrow x_2 \in LF(z_1 z_2) \Rightarrow x_2 \in LF(z_1 \bar{z}_1 x_2) \Rightarrow x_2 \in LF[(z_1 \bar{z}_1)^*]$.

We have $w = u_1 x \bar{x} x u_2 = u_1 x_1 z \bar{z}_2 \bar{z}_1 z \bar{x}_2 \bar{x}_1 x u_2$.

We also have $w_2 = u_1 x_1 z \bar{x}_2 \bar{x}_1 x u_2 = u_1 x_1 z_1 \bar{z}_1 x_2 \bar{x}_2 \bar{x}_1 x u_2$.

We deduce: $w_2 = u_1 x_1 \underline{z_1 \bar{z}_1 x_2 \bar{x}_2} \bar{x}_1 x u_2 \xrightarrow{2} u_1 \underline{x_1 z_1 \bar{z}_1 \bar{x}_1} x u_2 \xrightarrow{1} u_1 x u_2 = w_1$.

Case a.3) $z\bar{z}z \in F(x\bar{x}x)$ (except cases a.1 and a.2)

Two overlaps are possible:

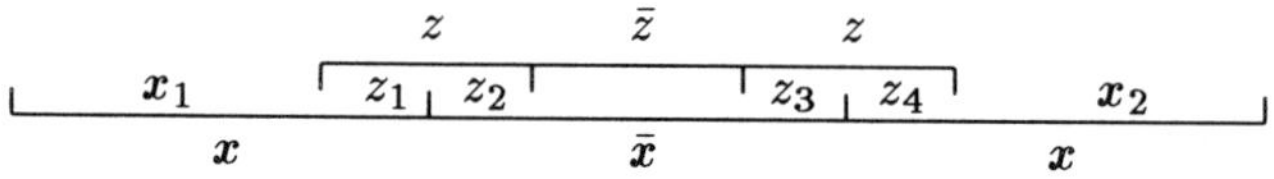

In this case $x = x_1 z_1 = \bar{z}_3 z \bar{z}_2 = z_4 x_2$

We have $w = u_1 x \bar{x} x u_2 = u_1 x z_2 \bar{z} z_3 z_4 x_2 u_2$.

We also have $w_2 = u_1 x z_2 x_2 u_2 = u_1 \bar{z}_3 z \bar{z}_2 z_2 x_2 u_2$.

We deduce: $w_2 = u_1 \bar{z}_3 z \underline{\bar{z}_2 z_2} x_2 u_2 \xrightarrow{1} u_1 \bar{z}_3 z x_2 u_2 = u_1 \bar{z}_3 z z_3 z_4 x_2 u_2 = u_1 \underline{\bar{z}_3 z_3} x u_2 \xrightarrow{1} u_1 x u_2 = w_1$.

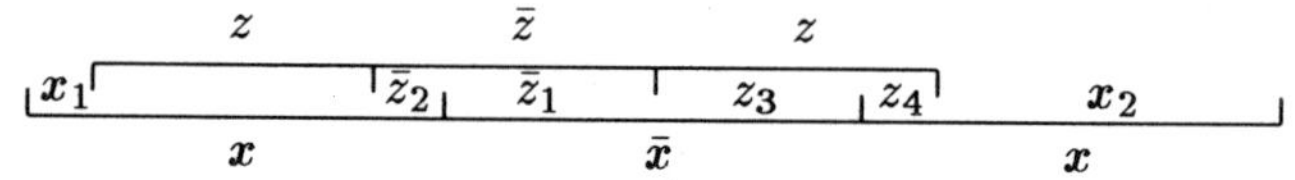

In this case $x = x_1 z \bar{z}_2 = \bar{z}_3 z_1 = z_4 x_2$

We have $x = x_1 z_1 z_2 \bar{z}_2 = \bar{z}_3 z_1$: so $|\bar{z}_3| \geq |x_1|$ and we can set $\bar{z}_3 = x_1 d, d \in \Pi^*$. Since $x = x_1 z \bar{z}_2 = x_1 z_3 z_4 \bar{z}_2 = x_1 d \bar{x}_1 z_4 \bar{z}_2$ and $x = \bar{z}_3 z_1 = x_1 d z_1$, we have $d = \bar{d}$ and applying part 3 of Lemma 1, we deduce that there exists $d' \in \Pi^*$ such that $d = d' \bar{d}'$ (note that $x_1 d' \in LF(x)$).

We have $w = u_1 x \bar{x} x u_2 = u_1 x_1 z \bar{z}_2 \bar{z}_1 z_3 x u_2$.

We also have $w_2 = u_1 x_1 z_3 x u_2 = u_1 x_1 d' \bar{d}' \bar{x}_1 x u_2$.

We deduce: $w_2 = u_1 \underline{x_1 d' \bar{d}' \bar{x}_1} x u_2 \xrightarrow{1} u_1 x u_2 = w_1$.

b) $z\bar{z}z \notin F(x\bar{x}x)$

We suppose, in this part, that the factor $z\bar{z}z$ overlaps the right part of $x\bar{x}x$. The proof would be exactly the same for the symetrical cases.

So in what follows, the overlapping factor denoted by ovf verifies $ovf \in RF(x\bar{x}x) \cap LF(z\bar{z}z)$.

For each possible overlap, we will find a word $m \in r\text{-}red(w_1) \cap r\text{-}red(w_2)$.

Case b.1) $|ovf| < |x|$

Three overlaps are possible:

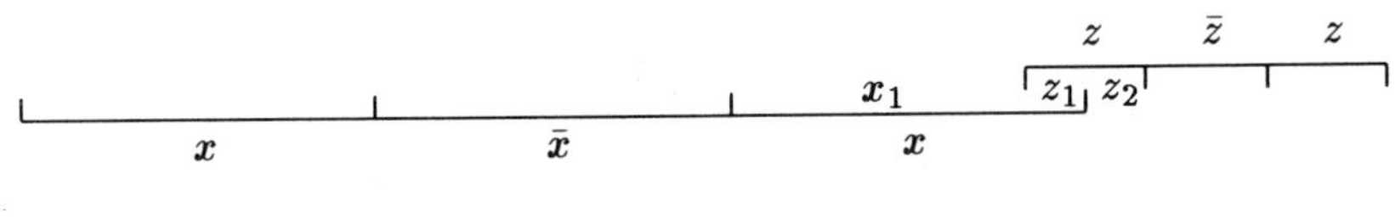

(1) In this case $x = x_1 z_1$

(2) In this case $x = x_1 z \bar{z}_2$

(3) In this case $x = x_1 z \bar{z} z_1$

We have $w = u_1 x \bar{x} x u_2 = v_1 z \bar{z} z v_2 = u_1 x \bar{x} x_1 z \bar{z} z v_2$ and we obviously obtain $w_1 = u_1 x_1 z \bar{z} z v_2$ and $w_2 = u_1 x \bar{x} x_1 z v_2$. Let $m = u_1 x_1 z v_2$.

Clearly, we have $w_1 = u_1 x_1 z \underline{\bar{z} z} v_2 \xrightarrow{1} u_1 x_1 z v_2 = m$.

So, $m \in r\text{-}red(w_1)$.

To show that $m \in r\text{-}red(w_2)$, we need to distinguish the 3 cases of overlap.

(1) We have $w_2 = u_1 x \bar{x} x_1 z v_2 = u_1 x \bar{x} x_1 z_1 z_2 v_2 = u_1 x \bar{x} x z_2 v_2$.

We deduce: $w_2 = u_1 \underline{x \bar{x} x} z_2 v_2 \xrightarrow{1} u_1 x z_2 v_2 = u_1 x_1 z_1 z_2 v_2 = u_1 x_1 z v_2 = m$.

(2) We have $w_2 = u_1 x \bar{x} x_1 z v_2 = u_1 x_1 z \bar{z}_2 z_2 \bar{z} \bar{x}_1 x_1 z v_2$.

We deduce: $w_2 = u_1 x_1 z \underline{\bar{z}_2 z_2} \bar{z} \bar{x}_1 x_1 z v_2 \xrightarrow{1} u_1 x_1 z \underline{\bar{z} \bar{x}_1} x_1 z v_2 \xrightarrow{1} u_1 x_1 z v_2 = m$.

(3) We have $w_2 = u_1 x \bar{x} x_1 z v_2 = u_1 x_1 z \bar{z} z_1 \bar{z}_1 z \bar{z} \bar{x}_1 x_1 z v_2$.

We deduce: $w_2 = u_1 x_1 z \bar{z} z_1 \underline{\bar{z}_1 z} \bar{z} \bar{x}_1 x_1 z v_2 \xrightarrow{1} u_1 x_1 z \underline{\bar{z} z} \bar{z} \bar{x}_1 x_1 z v_2 \xrightarrow{1}$

$$u_1 \underline{x_1 z \bar{z} \bar{x}_1 x_1 z} v_2 \xrightarrow{1} u_1 x_1 z v_2 = m.$$

So, $m \in r\text{-}red(w_2)$.

Case b.2) $|x| \leq |ovf| \leq 2|x|$

Three overlaps are possible:

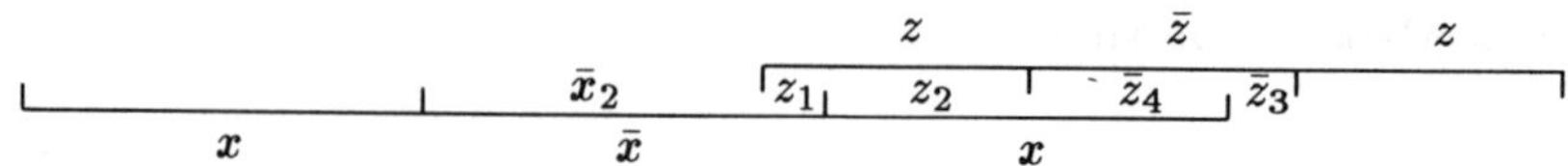

(1) In this case $x = \bar{z}_1 x_2 = z_2 \bar{z}_4$

(2) In this case $x = \bar{z}_1 x_2 = z_2 \bar{z} z_3$

(3) In this case $x = z_2 \bar{z} x_2 = \bar{z}_1 z_3$

We have $w = u_1 x \bar{x} x u_2 = v_1 z \bar{z} z v_2 = u_1 x \bar{x}_2 z \bar{z} z v_2$.

For cases (1) and (2), we obtain $w = u_1 x \bar{x}_2 z \bar{z} z v_2 = u_1 x \bar{x}_2 z_1 z_2 \bar{z} z v_2 = u_1 x \bar{x} z_2 \bar{z} z v_2$. Thus, we deduce $w_1 = u_1 z_2 \bar{z} z v_2$ and $w_2 = u_1 x \bar{x} z_2 v_2$.

(1) Let $m = u_1 z_2 \bar{z}_2 z_2 v_2$. To prove that $m \in r\text{-}red(w_1) \cap r\text{-}red(w_2)$, we will show that $\bar{z}_4 \in LF[(\bar{z}_2 z_2)^*]$ and $\bar{z}_1 \in LF[(z_2 \bar{z}_2)^*]$.

If $|z_4| > |z_2|$, we can set $\bar{z}_4 = \bar{z}_2 \bar{c}$ with $c \in \Pi^*$. Since $z_1 z_2 = z_3 z_4$ and $\bar{z}_4 = \bar{z}_2 \bar{c}$, we obtain $z_1 = z_3 c$. Since $\bar{z}_1 x_2 = z_2 \bar{z}_4$, $z_1 = z_3 c$ and $\bar{z}_4 = \bar{z}_2 \bar{c}$, we have $\bar{c} \bar{z}_3 x_2 = z_2 \bar{z}_2 \bar{c}$. So, we deduce: $\bar{c} \in LF(z_2 \bar{z}_2 \bar{c}) \Rightarrow \bar{c} \in LF[(z_2 \bar{z}_2)^*] \Rightarrow \bar{z}_4 \in LF[(\bar{z}_2 z_2)^*]$.

If $|z_4| \leq |z_2|$, we obviously have $\bar{z}_4 \in LF(\bar{z}_2)$. Hence, we deduce $x = z_2 \bar{z}_4 \in LF[(z_2 \bar{z}_2)^*]$ and since $\bar{z}_1 \in LF(x)$, we have $\bar{z}_1 \in LF[(z_2 \bar{z}_2)^*]$.

We have $w_1 = u_1 z_2 \bar{z} z v_2 = u_1 z_2 \bar{z}_2 \underline{\bar{z}_1 z_1} z_2 v_2 \xrightarrow{2} u_1 z_2 \bar{z}_2 z_2 v_2 = m$ and $w_2 = u_1 x \bar{x} z_2 v_2 = u_1 z_2 \underline{\bar{z}_4 z_4} \bar{z}_2 z_2 v_2 \xrightarrow{2} u_1 z_2 \bar{z}_2 z_2 v_2 = m$.

So $m \in r\text{-}red(w_1) \cap r\text{-}red(w_2)$.

(2) Let $m = w_1 = u_1 z_2 \bar{z} z v_2$. We only have to prove that $m \in r\text{-}red(w_2)$.

We have $w_2 = u_1 x \bar{x} z_2 v_2 = u_1 z_2 \bar{z} z_3 \bar{z}_3 z \bar{z}_2 z_2 v_2 \xrightarrow{1} u_1 z_2 \bar{z} z \bar{z}_2 z_2 v_2 \xrightarrow{1} u_1 z_2 \bar{z} z v_2 = m$.

So $m = w_1 \in r\text{-}red(w_2)$.

For case (3), we obtain $w = u_1 x \bar{x}_2 z \bar{z} z v_2 = u_1 x \bar{x}_2 z \bar{z}_2 \bar{z}_1 z v_2 = u_1 x \bar{x} \bar{z}_1 z v_2$. Thus, we deduce $w_1 = u_1 \bar{z}_1 z v_2$ and $w_2 = u_1 x \bar{x}_2 z v_2$.

(3) Let $m = w_1 = u_1 \bar{z}_1 z v_2$. We only have to prove that $m \in r\text{-}red(w_2)$.

Since $z_2 \bar{z} x_2 = \bar{z}_1 z_3$ and $|z_1| \leq |z_2 z|$, we can set $z_3 = c x_2$ with $c \in \Pi^*$. We obtain: $z_2 \bar{z} x_2 = \bar{z}_1 c x_2 \Rightarrow z_2 \bar{z}_4 \bar{z}_3 x_2 = \bar{z}_1 c x_2 \Rightarrow z_2 \bar{z}_4 \bar{x}_2 \bar{c} = \bar{z}_1 c$. Hence we have $c = \bar{c}$ and applying part 3 of Lemma 1, we deduce that there exists $c' \in \Pi^*$ such that $c = c' \bar{c}'$ (note that $\bar{x}_2 c' \in LF(\bar{x})$).

We have $w_2 = u_1 x \bar{x}_2 z v_2 = u_1 x \bar{x}_2 z_3 z_4 v_2 = u_1 x \bar{x}_2 c' \bar{c}' x_2 z_4 v_2 \xrightarrow{1} u_1 x z_4 v_2$ and $u_1 x z_4 v_2 = u_1 \bar{z}_1 z_3 z_4 v_2 = u_1 \bar{z}_1 z v_2 = m$.

So $m = w_1 \in r\text{-}red(w_2)$.

Case b.3) $|ovf| > 2|x|$

	z		$\bar{z}$		z	
x_1	z_1	z_2	$\bar{z}_4$	$\bar{z}_3$	z_5	z_6
x		$\bar{x}$		x		

In this case $x = x_1 z_1 = z_4 \bar{z}_2 = \bar{z}_3 z_5$

We have $w = u_1 x \bar{x} x u_2 = v_1 z \bar{z} z v_2 = v_1 x \bar{x} x z_6 v_2 = u_1 x_1 z \bar{z} z v_2$ and we obviously obtain $w_1 = u_1 x z_6 v_2$ and $w_2 = u_1 x_1 z v_2$.

Let $m = u_1 z_4 v_2$.

If $|z_3| > |z_4|$, we can set $\bar{z}_3 = z_4 c$ with $c \in \Pi^*$. Since $z_4 \bar{z}_2 = \bar{z}_3 z_5$ and $\bar{z}_3 = z_4 c$, we obtain $\bar{z}_2 = c z_5$. Since $z_1 z_2 = z_3 z_4$, $\bar{z}_2 = c z_5$ and $\bar{z}_3 = z_4 c$, we have $z_1 \bar{z}_5 \bar{c} = \bar{c} \bar{z}_4 z_4$. So, we deduce: $z_1 \bar{z}_5 \bar{c} = \bar{c} \bar{z}_4 z_4 \Rightarrow c z_5 \bar{z}_1 = \bar{z}_4 z_4 c \Rightarrow c \in LF(\bar{z}_4 z_4 c) \Rightarrow c \in LF[(\bar{z}_4 z_4)^*] \Rightarrow \bar{z}_3 \in LF[(z_4 \bar{z}_4)^*]$.

If $|z_3| \leq |z_4|$, we obviously have $\bar{z}_3 \in LF(z_4)$. Hence, we deduce $\bar{z} = \bar{z}_4 \bar{z}_3 \in LF[(\bar{z}_4 z_4)^*]$ and since $\bar{z}_2 \in LF(\bar{z})$, we have $\bar{z}_2 \in LF[(\bar{z}_4 z_4)^*]$.

We have $w_1 = u_1 x z_6 v_2 = u_1 \bar{z}_3 z_5 z_6 v_2 = u_1 \bar{z}_3 z_3 z_4 v_2$.

Therefore if $|z_3| \leq |z_4|$ then $w_1 = u_1 \bar{z}_3 z_3 z_4 v_2 \xrightarrow{1} u_1 z_4 v_2 = m$, else $w_1 = u_1 \bar{z}_3 z_3 z_4 v_2 = u_1 z_4 c \bar{c} \bar{z}_4 z_4 v_2 \xrightarrow{2} u_1 z_4 \bar{z}_4 z_4 v_2 \xrightarrow{1} u_1 z_4 v_2 = m$.

So $m \in r\text{-}red(w_1)$.

We have $w_2 = u_1 x_1 z v_2 = u_1 x_1 z_1 z_2 v_2 = u_1 z_4 \bar{z}_2 z_2 v_2$.

If $|z_2| \leq |z_4|$ then $\bar{z}_2 \in LF(\bar{z}_4)$ and we obtain $w_2 = u_1 z_4 \bar{z}_2 z_2 v_2 \xrightarrow{1} u_1 z_4 v_2 = m$, else we can set $\bar{z}_2 = \bar{z}_4 d$ with $d \in LF[(z_4 \bar{z}_4)^*]$ and we obtain $w_2 =$

$$u_1 z_4 \bar{z}_2 z_2 v_2 = u_1 \underline{z_4 \bar{z}_4 d \bar{d}} z_4 v_2 \xrightarrow{2} u_1 \underline{z_4 \bar{z}_4 z_4} v_2 \xrightarrow{1} u_1 z_4 v_2 = m.$$

So $m \in r\text{-}red(w_2)$.

This completes the proof of Theorem 2. $\qquad\qquad\qquad\qquad\qquad\qquad\square$

6. Conclusion

In this paper, we have studied the operator *r-red* which deletes redundant retreats in picture words. In particular, we have shown that it associates with any word a unique irreducible word. However, it must be remarked that such an irreducible word is not necessarily minimal (with respect to the length of the words) [7]. For instance, the word *rruldurdr* is irreducible for *r-red* but there exists a strictly shorter word *rurdlrr* describing the same picture.

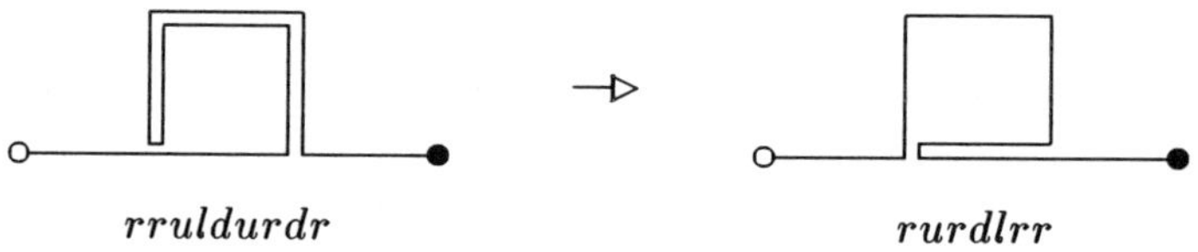

rruldurdr $\qquad\qquad\qquad\qquad\qquad\qquad\qquad$ *rurdlrr*

References

1. M. Harrison, *Introduction to Formal Language Theory*, Addison-Wesley, Reading, Massachusetts, 1978.

2. F. Hinz, Classes of picture Languages that cannot be distinguished in the chain code concept and deletion of redundant retreats, *Lecture Notes in Computer Science* 349 (1989), 132 – 143.

3. M. Jantzen, *Confluent String Rewriting*, EATCS Monographs on Theoretical Computer Science, vol. 14, Springer-Verlag, 1988.

4. H. A. Maurer, G. Rozenberg, E. Welzl, Using string languages to describe picture languages, *Information and Control*, 54 (1982), 155 – 185.

5. J.-P. Pécuchet Automates boustrophédons, semi-groupe de Birget et monoïde inversif libre, *RAIRO Theoretical Informatics*, 19 (1985), 71 – 100.

6. A. Salomaa, *Formal Languages*, Academic Press, New York, London, 1973.

7. P. Séébold, K. Slowinski, Minimising picture words, in *IMYCS'90*, *Lecture Notes in Computer Science* 464 (1990), 234 – 243.

On Conditional Grammars and Conditional Petri Nets

Ferucio-Laurenţiu ŢIPLEA
Faculty of Informatics, ”Al. I. Cuza” University of Iaşi
6600 Iaşi, Romania

Abstract. The conditional Petri nets have been introduced in [12] as a new type of controlled Petri nets, by modifying the classical transition rule. The aim of this paper is twofold. First, we continue the study both of the conditional grammars and of the conditional Petri nets, and second we survey the results obtained until now concerning this subject. The newly obtained results are in connection with decision problems, the computational power, comparisons between families of languages, homomorphic characterizations, and closure properties. Among these a constructive proof of the inclusion of the family of labelled Petri net languages into the family of context-sensitive languages is given.

1. Introduction

A Petri net is a very useful tool for the modelling and the analysis of concurrent systems. But there exist important examples of concurrent systems which cannot be satisfactorily modelled by Petri nets (i.e. reader-writer systems). This fact has led to the necessity of the modification of the definition of Petri nets. One way is to impose some restrictions on the transition rule ([2], [3], [13], [15], [16]).

In [12] a new restriction on the transition rule has been introduced and the Petri nets obtained in this way have been called *conditional Petri nets* (CPTN, for short). In a CPTN γ to each transition t we associate a language L_t. Then w is a transition sequence of γ if it is a transition sequence in the classical way and additionally, w_1 is in L_t for any decomposition $w = w_1 t w_2$. In other words, the transition t is conditioned by the transition sequence previously applied. Moreover, in [12] some results on the computational power of these nets have been obtained.

In this paper we continue the study of CPTN in the following directions : decision problems (Section 3), the computational power and comparisons with other families of languages (Section 4), and homomorphic characterizations and closure properties (Section 5). New results on conditional grammars ([4], [12]) are also derived. In Section 2 we present the basic definitions, notations and preliminary results which will be used in the next sections. A list of open problems will be given in Section 6.

Among the newly proved results, known results will be also included. Thus the paper will be self-contained and the results on CPTN will follow in a natural order.

2. Preliminaries

The aim of this section is to specify the basic terminology, notations and results concerning languages, grammars, Petri nets, and counter machines in order to give the reader the necessary prerequisites for the understanding of this paper. For unexplained notions the reader is referred to [10].

The set of integers (non-negative integers, positive integers, respectively) is denoted by $\mathbf{Z}$ ($\mathbf{N}, \mathbf{N}^+$, respectively).

2.1. Languages and grammars

For an alphabet V, V^* denotes the free monoid generated by V under the operation of concatenation and λ denotes the unity of V^*. Given a word $w \in V^*$, $|w|$ denotes the length of w, and for a subset V' of V we denote the number of occurrences of symbols of V' in w by $\#(V', w)$. If $V' = \{a\}$, then we simply write $\#(a, w)$.

For a language L we denote by $alph(L)$ the smallest alphabet V such that $L \subseteq V^*$. If L_1, L_2 are languages and w is a word, then $\partial_w^l(L_1), \partial_w^r(L_1), L_1/L_2$ and $L_1 \uplus L_2$ denote the *left derivative, right derivative, right quotient* and *shuffle product*, respectively.

A Chomsky grammar is denoted $G = (V_N, V_T, X_0, P)$, where V_N is the nonterminal alphabet, V_T is the terminal alphabet, $X_0 \in V_N$ is the axiom, and P is the set of production rules. Further we set $V_G = V_N \cup V_T$. The direct derivation relation is denoted by $\Longrightarrow$ and the reflexive transitive closure of $\Longrightarrow$ is denoted by $\Longrightarrow^*$. The language generated by a grammar G is denoted by $L(G)$. As usual in formal language theory, we shall refer the phrase structure, monotone, context-free and regular grammars as grammars of type 0, 1, 2, 3, respectively (in monotone and regular grammars we also allow the λ-rule $X_0 \to \lambda$ providing X_0 does not appear in the right-hand member of any rule). The corresponding families of languages are denoted by $\mathcal{L}_i, i = 0, 1, 2, 3$, respectively; $\mathcal{L}_{rec}$ denotes the family of recursive languages.

The *Dyck language* D_n over $V_n = \{a_1, a_1', \ldots, a_n, a_n'\}$, $n \geq 1$, is the language generated by the context-free grammar $(\{X_0\}, V_n, X_0, \{X_0 \to X_0 X_0, X_0 \to \lambda, X_0 \to a_1 X_0 a_1', \ldots, X_0 \to a_n X_0 a_n'\})$.

A result with many applications in the sequel is the following: Let $G =$

(V_N, V_T, X_0, P) be a type-0 grammar. For a derivation

$$D \; : \; X_0 = w_0 \Longrightarrow w_1 \Longrightarrow \ldots \Longrightarrow w_n = w \in V_T^*,$$

we set

$$WS(D) = \max\{|w_i| \mid 0 \le i \le n\}.$$

Then let

$$WS(w, G) = \min\{WS(D) \mid D \text{ is a derivation of } w \text{ in the grammar } G\}.$$

($WS(w, G)$ is called the *workspace* needed to produce w in the grammar G.)
If there is a constant k such that for all $w \in L(G) - \{\lambda\}$ we have $WS(w, G) \le k|w|$, then we say that G has *bounded workspace*.

Theorem 2.1.1. [10] *If G is a type-0 grammar with bounded workspace, then $L(G)$ is a type-1 language.*

An *$\mathcal{L}$-conditional grammar of type i*, where $\mathcal{L}$ is an arbitrary family of languages and $0 \le i \le 3$, is a pair (G, ρ), where G is a type-i grammar $G = (V_N, V_T, X_0, P)$ and ρ is a mapping from P into $\mathcal{P}(V_G^*) \cap \mathcal{L}$. If (G, ρ) is an $\mathcal{L}$-conditional type-i grammar, we define the relation $\Longrightarrow_{(G,\rho)}$ by $x \Longrightarrow_{(G,\rho)} y$ iff $x = w_1 u w_2, y = w_1 v w_2, u \to v \in P$ and $x \in \rho(u \to v)$. If (G, ρ) can be seen from context, we write only $\Longrightarrow$. The language generated by (G, ρ) is defined by $L(G, \rho) = \{w \in V_T^* \mid X_0 \Longrightarrow^* w\}$.

We denote by $\mathcal{C}(\mathcal{L}_i, \mathcal{L})$ the family of languages generated by $\mathcal{L}$-conditional type-i grammars, where $\mathcal{L}$ is an arbitrary family of languages and $0 \le i \le 3$. For further information on conditional grammars the reader is referred to [4], [7], [8], [10], [12], [14].

2.2. Petri nets

A (finite) *Petri net* (with infinite capacities), abbreviated PTN, is a 4-tuple $\Sigma = (S, T; F, W)$, where S and T are two finite non-empty sets (of *places* and *transitions*, respectively), $S \cap T = \emptyset$, $F \subseteq (S \times T) \cup (T \times S)$ is the *flow relation* and $W : (S \times T) \cup (T \times S) \longrightarrow \mathbf{N}$ is the *weight function* of Σ verifying $W(x, y) = 0$ iff $(x, y) \notin F$. A *marking* of a PTN Σ is a function $M : S \longrightarrow \mathbf{N}$; it will be sometimes identified with a vector $M \in \mathbf{N}^{card(S)}$. The operations and relations on vectors are componentwise defined. The set of all markings of Σ will be denoted by $\mathbf{N}^S$. A *marked* PTN, abbreviated mPTN, is a pair $\gamma = (\Sigma, M_0)$, where Σ is a PTN and M_0, the *initial marking* of γ, is a marking of Σ. An mPTN *with final markings*, abbreviated mPTNf, is a 3-tuple $\gamma = (\Sigma, M_0, \mathcal{M})$, where the first two components form an mPTN and $\mathcal{M}$, the *set of final markings* of γ, is a finite set of markings of Σ. A *labelled* mPTN (mPTNf, respectively), abbreviated lmPTN (lmPTNf), is a 3-tuple (4-tuple) $\gamma = (\Sigma, M_0, l)$ ($\gamma = (\Sigma, M_0, \mathcal{M}, l)$, respectively), where the first two (three) components form an mPTN (mPTNf) and l, the *labelling function* of γ, assigns to each transition a letter. A λ-*labelled* mPTN (mPTNf, respectively), abbreviated l^λmPTN (l^λmPTNf), is defined as an lmPTN (lmPTNf) with the difference that the labelling function, called now λ-*labelling function* of γ, assigns to each transition either a letter or the empty word λ.

In the sequel we shall often use the term "net" whenever we shall refer to a PTN (mPTN, mPTNf, lmPTN, lmPTNf, l^λmPTN, l^λmPTNf, respectively). Moreover, the components of a net γ will be always considered as above.

Pictorially, a net γ will be represented by a graph. Then the places are denoted by circles, the transitions are denoted by boxes; the flow relation is represented by arcs. The arc $f \in F$ is labelled by $W(f)$ whenever $W(f) > 1$. The initial marking M_0 is presented by putting $M_0(s)$ tokens into the circle representing the place s. The labelling function is denoted by placing letters into the boxes representing transitions and the final markings are explicitly listed.

Let γ be a net, $t \in T$ and $w \in T^*$. We define the functions $t^-, t^+, \Delta w$ from S to $\mathbf{Z}$ by $t^-(s) = W(s,t)$, $t^+(s) = W(t,s)$, and $\Delta w(s) = 0$ if $w = \lambda$ and

$$\Delta w(s) = \sum_{i=1}^{n}(t_i^+ - t_i^-) \text{ if } w = t_1 \ldots t_n, n \geq 1, \text{ for any } s \in S.$$ The behaviour of the net γ is given by the so-called *transition rule*, which consist of:

(i) the *enabling rule*: a transition t is enabled at a marking M (in γ), abbreviated $M[t >_\gamma$, iff $t^- \leq M$;

(ii) the *computing rule*: if $M[t >_\gamma$ then t may *occur* yielding a new marking M', abbreviated $M[t >_\gamma M'$, defined by $M' = M + \Delta t$.

In fact, for any transition t of γ we have defined a binary relation on $\mathbf{N}^S$, denoted by $[t >_\gamma$ and given by:

$$M[t >_\gamma M' \text{ iff } t^- \leq M \text{ and } M' = M + \Delta t.$$

If $t_1, \ldots t_n, n \geq 1$, are transitions of γ, then the classical product of the relations $[t_1 >_\gamma, \ldots, [t_n >_\gamma$ will be denoted by $[t_1 \ldots t_n >_\gamma$; i.e. $[t_1 \ldots t_n >_\gamma = [t_1 >_\gamma \circ \ldots \circ [t_n >_\gamma$. Moreover, we consider the relation $[\lambda >_\gamma$ given by $[\lambda >_\gamma = \{(M, M) \mid M \in \mathbf{N}^S\}$.

Let γ be a marked Petri net and M_0 its initial marking. The word $w \in T^*$ is called a *transition sequence* of γ if there exists a marking M of γ such that $M_0[w >_\gamma M$. Moreover, the marking M is called *reachable* in γ. The set of all reachable markings of γ is denoted by $[M_0 > \gamma$.

In the sequel, the notation "$[\cdot >_\gamma$" will be simplified to "$[\cdot >$" whenever γ is undestood from the context.

The nets can be considered as generators of languages. Let γ_1 be an mPTN, γ_2 either an lmPTN or an l^λmPTN, γ_3 an mPTNf, and γ_4 either an lmPTNf or an l^λmPTNf. The language generated by these nets are defined as follows:

$$P(\gamma_1) = \{w \mid w \in T^*, (\exists M \in \mathbf{N}^S \; : \; M_0[w >_{\gamma_1} M)\},$$
$$P(\gamma_2) = \{l(w) \mid w \in T^*, (\exists M \in \mathbf{N}^S \; : \; M_0[w >_{\gamma_2} M)\},$$
$$L(\gamma_3) = \{w \mid w \in T^*, (\exists M \in \mathcal{M} \; : \; M_0[w >_{\gamma_3} M)\},$$
$$L(\gamma_4) = \{l(w) \mid w \in T^*, (\exists M \in \mathcal{M} \; : \; M_0[w >_{\gamma_4} M)\}.$$

The language generated by mPTN (lmPTN, l^λmPTN, respectively) are called *free P-type languages* (*P-type languages, arbitrary P-type languages* and the family of these languages is denoted by $\mathbf{P}^f$ ($\mathbf{P}, \mathbf{P}^\lambda$, respectively). For Petri nets with final markings, the terminology is as above, by changing "P" into "L". These languages are usually referred to as *Petri net languages* or *Petri languages*.

The following theorem summarize the relationships between the Chomsky languages and Petri net languages.

Theorem 2.2.1. [6] *The relationships in the diagram in figure 2.2.1 hold ($\longrightarrow$ indicates a strict inclusion and $\longmapsto$ an incomparability; the unrelated families are not necessarily incomparable).*

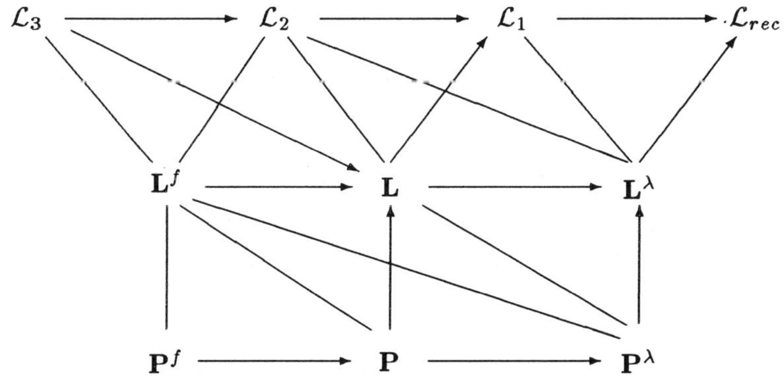

Fig. 2.2.1

We recall now a basic result from [11] concerning the language generated by mPTNf which have only one place.

Theorem 2.2.2. [11] *Let $\gamma = (\Sigma, M_0, \mathcal{M})$ be an mPTNf such that Σ has only one place, s. Then there exists a λ-free homomorphism $h : T \longrightarrow \{a, b\}^*$,* *a and b being new symbols, such that*

$$L(\gamma) = h^{-1}(\partial_x^r(D_1(a,b)/\{b^{M_1(s)},\ldots,b^{M_n(s)}\})),$$

where $x = a^{M_0(s)}, \mathcal{M} = \{M_1,\ldots,M_n\}, n \geq 1$, and $D_1(a,b)$ is the Dyck language over $\{a,b\}$.

The conditional Petri nets have been introduced in [12]. We recall the basic definitions.

Let $\mathcal{L}$ be an arbitrary family of languages. An $\mathcal{L}$-*conditional* PTN, abbreviated $\mathcal{L}$-CPTN, is a pair $\gamma = (\Sigma, \varphi)$ where Σ is a PTN and φ, the $\mathcal{L}$-*conditioning function* of γ, is a function from T into $\mathcal{P}(T^*) \cap \mathcal{L}$. A marked $\mathcal{L}$-CPTN (*marked $\mathcal{L}$-CPTN with final markings, labelled marked $\mathcal{L}$-CPTN, labelled marked $\mathcal{L}$-CPTN with final markings, λ-labelled marked $\mathcal{L}$-CPTN, λ-labelled marked $\mathcal{L}$-CPTN with final markings,* respectively), abbreviated m$\mathcal{L}$-CPTN (m$\mathcal{L}$-CPTNf, lm$\mathcal{L}$-CPTN, lm$\mathcal{L}$-CPTNf, l^λm$\mathcal{L}$-CPTN, l^λm$\mathcal{L}$-CPTNf, respectively), is defined as an mPTN (mPTNf, lmPTN, lmPTNf, l^λmPTN, l^λmPTNf, respectively), by changing "Σ" into "Σ, φ". For example, $\gamma = (\Sigma, \varphi, M_0, \mathcal{M}, l)$ denotes either an lm$\mathcal{L}$-CPTNf or an l^λm$\mathcal{L}$-CPTNf.

In the sequel whenever we shall refer to a conditional net we implicitly assume that its components are defined as above. Pictorially a conditional net will be represented as a classical net. Moreover, the function φ will be separately listed.

The behaviour of a conditional net γ is given by the *c-transition rule* which consist of:

(i) the *c-enabling rule*: let M be a marking of γ and $u \in T^*$; the transition t is enabled at (M, u) (in γ), abbreviated $(M, u)[t >_{\gamma,c}$, iff $t^- \leq M$ and $u \in \varphi(t)$;

(ii) the *c-computing rule*: if $(M, u)[t >_{\gamma,c}$, then t may *occur* yielding a pair (M', v), abbreviated $(M, u)[t >_{\gamma,c} (M', v)$, defined by $M' = M + \Delta t$ and $v = ut$.

Let us observe that the c-enabling rule is obtained by restricting the enabling rule; the c-computing rule is the same as the computing rule. Again, for any transition t of γ we have defined a binary relation on $(\mathbf{N}^S \times T^*)$, denoted by $[t >_{\gamma,c}$ and given by

$$(M, u)[t >_{\gamma,c} (M', v) \text{ iff } v = ut, u \in \varphi(t) \text{ and } M[t >_\Sigma M'.$$

The classical product of the relations $[t_1 >_{\gamma,c}, \ldots, [t_n >_{\gamma,c}$ will be denoted by $[t_1 \ldots t_n >_{\gamma,c}$ ($t_1, \ldots, t_n$ being transitions of γ and $n \geq 1$); i.e. $[t_1 \ldots t_n >_{\gamma,c} = [t_1 >_{\gamma,c} \circ \ldots \circ [t_n >_{\gamma,c}$. We also consider the relation $[\lambda >_{\gamma,c} = \{((M, u), (M, u)) \mid M \in \mathbf{N}^S, u \in T^*\}$.

Let γ be a marked conditional net and M_0 its initial marking. The word $w \in T^*$ is called a *transition c-sequence* of γ if there exists a marking M of γ such that $(M_0, \lambda)[w >_{\gamma,c} (M, w)$. Moreover, the marking M is called *c-reachable* in γ. The set of all reachable markings of γ is denoted by $[M_0 >_{\gamma,c}$.

The notation $"[\cdot >_{\gamma,c}"$ will be simplified to $"[\cdot >_c"$ whenever γ is understood from the context.

The conditional nets can be considered as generators of languages in the same way as the classical nets, by changing $"[\cdot >"$ into $"[\cdot >_c"$. For example, if $\gamma = (\Sigma, \varphi, M_0, \mathcal{M}, l)$ is an l^λmPTNf, then the language generated by γ is

$$L(\gamma) = \{l(w) \mid w \in T^*, (\exists M \in \mathcal{M} \; : \; (M_0, \lambda)[w >_c (M, w))\}.$$

Thus, $\mathcal{C}(\mathbf{X}^f, \mathcal{L})$, $(\mathcal{C}(\mathbf{X}, \mathcal{L}), \mathcal{C}(\mathbf{X}^\lambda, \mathcal{L})$, respectively) will denote the family of free X-type $\mathcal{L}$-conditional Petri net languages (X-type $\mathcal{L}$-conditional Petri net languages, arbitrary X-type $\mathcal{L}$-conditional Petri net languages, respectively), for any $X \in \{P, L\}$. Further information on conditional nets can be found in [12].

2.3. Counter machines

For counter machines we use the same (unusual) definition as in [2], [3], [5], [6]. A *deterministic k-counter machine*, $k \geq 1$, is a 5-tuple $A = (Q, q_0, q_f, C, I)$, where

(i) Q is a finite set of *states*,

(ii) $q_0 \in Q$ is the *initial state*,

(iii) $q_f \in Q$ is the *final state*,

(iv) $C = \{c_1, \ldots, c_k\}$ is a set of k *counters* each of which can contain an arbitrary non-negative integer,

(v) I is a finite set of *instructions* which can have the following forms:

- *increment instruction*: in the state q_1 increment the counter $c_i, 1 \leq i \leq k$, and goto q_3 (such an instruction is abbreviated by $I(q_1, i, q_2)$);
- *test instruction*: in the state q_1 test the counter $c_i, 1 \leq i \leq k$. If the content of c_i equals zero then goto q_2. Otherwise decrement c_i and goto q_3 (such an instruction is abbreviated by $I(q_1, i, q_2, q_3)$).

For each $q \in Q - \{q_f\}$ there is exactly one instruction; for q_f we have no instruction.

The instruction labelled by q_0 is also called the *start instruction* of A.

The configurations of the machine A are given by (q, x) where q is the actual state and $x : C \longrightarrow \mathbf{N}$ denotes the actual contents of the counters. The changes of the configurations are defined by performing the corresponding increment and test instruction. First the start-instruction is executed. Then the flow of control is determined by the "goto" contained in each instruction. The machine A *halts* if it reaches the state q_f. It is not decidable whether a deterministic counter machine halts, i.e. whether a configuration containing q_f is reachable from the initial configuration (q_0, x_0), where $x_0(c) = 0$ for any counter c.

A *non-deterministic counter machine* is defined as a deterministic one additionally having choice-instructions. These have the form:

- *choice-instruction*: in state q_1 goto q_2 or to q_3 (such an instruction is abbreviated by $I(q_1, q_2, q_3)$).

3. Decision problems

According to the c-transition rule, the reachability problem for conditional Petri nets is the problem whether or not a given marking is c-reachable. The coverability, boundedness, and liveness problems for conditional Petri nets are similarly defined ([9]).

In this section we show that the decision problems mentioned above are all undecidable for $\mathcal{L}$-conditional Petri nets, where $\mathcal{L}$ is a family of languages with certain properties. It is also shown that any recursively enumerable language is a member of the family of arbitrary L-type $\mathcal{L}$-conditional Petri nets. Both results will be obtained following a classical way: the simulation of the counter machines.

Theorem 3.1. *Let $\mathcal{L}$ be a family of languages with the properties:*

(i) it contains the Dyck language D_1;

(ii) it is closed under inverse morphisms and the letter-disjoint shuffle product (i.e. shuffle product on letter-disjoint languages).

Then

(1) the reachability, coverability, boundedness and liveness problems are all undecidable for the class of the $\mathcal{L}$-conditional Petri nets;

(2) $\mathcal{L}_0 \subseteq \mathcal{C}(\mathbf{L}^\lambda, \mathcal{L})$.

Proof. (1) We show that the $\mathcal{L}$-conditional Petri nets, where $\mathcal{L}$ is a family of languages as in the statement of the theorem, can simulate the deterministic counter machines with the counters initially 0, and the undecidability results are consequences of the undecidability of the halting problem for these machines.

Let $A = (Q, q_0, q_f, C, I)$ be a deterministic k-counter machine, $k \geq 1$. We construct an $\mathcal{L}$-conditional net as follows. We associate a place s_z with each $z \in Q \cup C$. With each increment-instruction $I(q_1, i, q_2), 1 \leq i \leq k$, we associate a transition t. It will be connected to places as in figure 3.1. With each test-instruction $I(q_1, i, q_2, q_3), 1 \leq i \leq k$, we associate two transitions t' and t''. They will be connected to places as in figure 3.2.

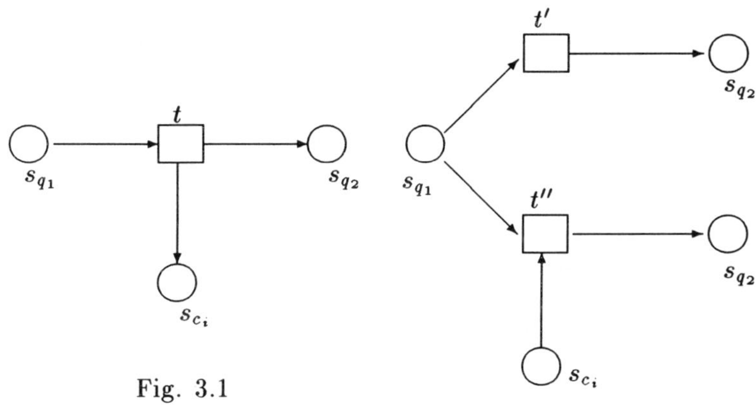

Fig. 3.1

Fig. 3.2

The does not contain other places and transitions. Let $\Sigma = (S, T; F, W)$ be the net just described and let M_0 be the marking given by $M_0(s_{q_0}) = 1$ and $M_0(s) = 0$ for any $s \neq s_{q_0}$. The essential point is how to construct the function $\varphi : T \longrightarrow \mathcal{P}(T^*) \cap \mathcal{L}$. The following notations are useful.

Let T_i^1 be the set of all transitions connected to the place s_{c_i} and let $T_i^2 = T - T_i^1, 1 \leq i \leq k$. Let Σ_i be the subnet of Σ generated by the place s_{c_i} as in [11], $M_0^i = (0)$ and $\mathcal{M}_i = \{(0)\}$. Let L_i be the language generated by the mPTNf $\gamma_i = (\Sigma_i, M_0^i, \mathcal{M}_i)$. We remark that for any $w \in L_i$ we have $\Delta w(s_{c_i}) = 0, 1 \leq i \leq k$.

From Theorem 2.2.2 it follows that there exists a λ-free homomorphism h_i such that $L_i = h_i^{-1}(D_1(a, b))$. Now, if t is a transition associated with an increment-instruction then we set $\varphi(t) = T^*$. If t' and t'' are two transitions associated with a test-instruction $I(q_1, i, q_2, q_3)$, we set $\varphi(t'') = T^*$ and $\varphi(t') = (T_i^2)^* \amalg L_i, 1 \leq i \leq k$. From our construction we have $\{w \in T^* \mid M_0[w >_\Sigma$ and $\Delta w(s_{c_i}) = 0\} \subseteq \varphi(t')$, where t' is as above and $1 \leq i \leq k$.

It is easy to see that $\gamma = (\Sigma, \varphi, M_0)$ is an $\mathcal{L}$-CPTN, and a transition t' as in figure 3.2 may be only applied after transition sequences $w \in T^*$ with $\Delta w(s_{c_i}) = 0$; i.e. only if the transition t'' is not possible. Following the same line as in [2], [3] we have: the deterministic counter machine A halts

(a) iff the place s_{q_f} can be marked by one token in γ;

(b) iff the marking M given by $M(s_{q_f}) = 1$ and $M(s) = 0$ for any $s \neq s_{q_f}$, is reachable and coverable in the net γ_1 in figure 3.3;

(c) iff the place s^* is bounded in the net γ_2 in figure 3.4;

(d) iff the transition t^* is live in the net γ_3 in figure 3.5.

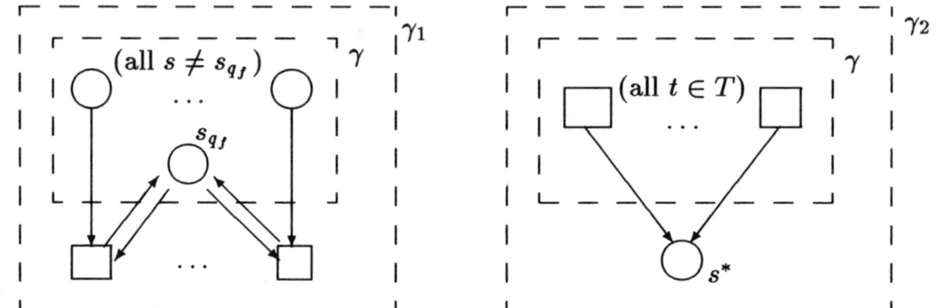

Fig.3.3   Fig. 3.4

Fig. 3.5

(2)   Using the additional choice construction in figure 3.6, and setting $\varphi(t') = \varphi(t'') = T^*$, the $\mathcal{L}$-conditional Petri nets can simulate non-deterministic counter machines, too.

Then with the help of the final markings and homomorphism $h : T \longrightarrow V \cup \{\lambda\}$ we can generate arbitrary recursively enumerable sets $L \subseteq V^*$ as hommomorphic images $h(L')$ of the free L-type conditional Petri net language L' of m$\mathcal{L}$-CPTNf ([5]). We thus obtain $\mathcal{L}_0 \subseteq \mathcal{C}(\mathbf{L}^\lambda, \mathcal{L})$. $\square$

Corollary 3.1. *Let* $\mathcal{L} \in \{\mathbf{L}^f, \mathbf{L}, \mathbf{L}^\lambda, \mathcal{L}_2, \mathcal{L}_1, \mathcal{L}_{rec}, \mathcal{L}_0\}$. *Then we have*

*(1) the reachability, coverability, boundedness, and liveness problems are
all undecidable for the class of $\mathcal{L}$-conditional Petri nets;*

(2) $\mathcal{L}_0 \subseteq \mathcal{C}(\mathbf{L}^\lambda, \mathcal{L})$.

Proof. Each family $\mathcal{L}$ as above has the properties (i) and (ii) in Theorem
3.1. $\qquad\square$

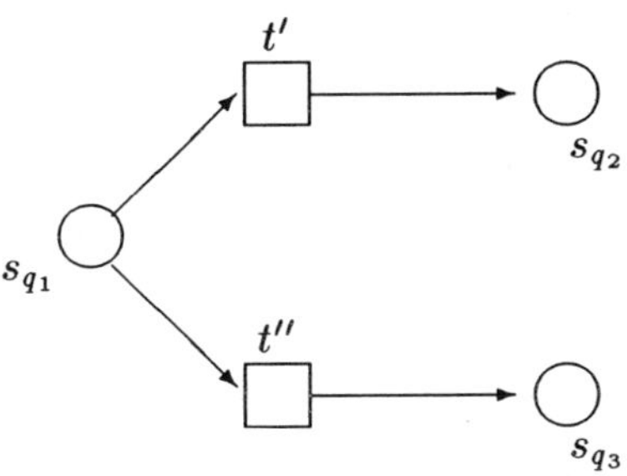

Fig. 3.6

4. The generative power

In this section we continue to investigate the generative power of the conditional grammars and the conditional Petri nets. We also establish some new
relationships between families of the conditional Petri net languages and the
families of Chomsky, Petri and conditional languages.

Proposition 4.1. *If $\mathcal{L} \in \{\mathcal{L}_3, \mathcal{L}_2, \mathcal{L}_1, \mathcal{L}_0\} \cup \{\mathbf{X}^f, \mathbf{X}, \mathbf{X}^\lambda \mid X \in \{P, L\}\}$ and
$\mathcal{L}'$ is a family of languages which contains the language V^* for any alphabet
V, then $\mathcal{L} \subseteq \mathcal{C}(\mathcal{L}, \mathcal{L}')$.*

Proof. Given a grammar G (a Petri net γ, respectively), we construct an
$\mathcal{L}'$-conditional grammar (G, ρ) (an $\mathcal{L}'$-conditional Petri net) mapping to each
rule of G (transition of γ) the language V_G^* (T^*, respectively). $\qquad\square$

Proposition 4.2. *If $\mathcal{L} \in \{\mathcal{L}_3, \mathcal{L}_2, \mathcal{L}_1, \mathcal{L}_0\} \cup \{\mathbf{X}^f, \mathbf{X}, \mathbf{X}^\lambda \mid X \in \{P, L\}\}$
and $\mathcal{L}', \mathcal{L}''$ are two arbitrary families of languages such that $\mathcal{L}' \subseteq \mathcal{L}''$, then
$\mathcal{C}(\mathcal{L}, \mathcal{L}') \subseteq \mathcal{C}(\mathcal{L}, \mathcal{L}'')$.*

Proof. Directly from definitions. $\qquad\square$

Theorem 4.1.

(1) $\mathcal{C}(\mathcal{L}_0, \mathbf{X}^f) = \mathcal{C}(\mathcal{L}_0, \mathbf{X}) = \mathcal{C}(\mathcal{L}_0, \mathbf{X}^\lambda) = \mathcal{C}(\mathcal{L}_0, \mathcal{L}_{rec}) = \mathcal{L}_0,$
   for any $X \in \{P, L\}$.

(2) $\mathcal{C}(\mathcal{L}_1, \mathbf{X}^f) = \mathcal{C}(\mathcal{L}_1, \mathbf{X}) = \mathcal{L}_1$, *for any* $X \in \{P, L\}$.

(3) $\mathcal{C}(\mathcal{L}_2, \mathbf{L}) = \mathcal{C}(\mathcal{L}_2, \mathbf{L}^\lambda) = \mathcal{C}(\mathcal{L}_2, \mathcal{L}_{rec}) = \mathcal{L}_0.$

(4) $\mathcal{C}(\mathbf{L}^\lambda, \mathcal{L}_0) = \mathcal{C}(\mathbf{L}^\lambda, \mathcal{L}_{rec}) = \mathcal{C}(\mathbf{L}^\lambda, \mathcal{L}_1) = \mathcal{C}(\mathbf{L}^\lambda, \mathcal{L}_2) = \mathcal{C}(\mathbf{L}^\lambda, \mathbf{L}^f) = \mathcal{C}(\mathbf{L}^\lambda, \mathbf{L}) = \mathcal{C}(\mathbf{L}^\lambda, \mathbf{L}^\lambda) = \mathcal{L}_0$.

Proof. Using Propositions 4.1 and 4.2, Corollary 3.1, and the equalities $\mathcal{L}_0 = \mathcal{C}(\mathcal{L}_0, \mathcal{L}_0) = \mathcal{C}(\mathcal{L}_2, \mathcal{L}_3) = \mathcal{C}(\mathcal{L}_2, \mathcal{L}_0)$ and $\mathcal{L}_1 = \mathcal{C}(\mathcal{L}_1, \mathcal{L}_1)$, which can be found either in [8] or in [7] and [10], we obtain:

1. $\mathcal{L}_0 \subseteq \mathcal{C}(\mathcal{L}_0, \mathbf{X}^f) \subseteq \mathcal{C}(\mathcal{L}_0, \mathbf{X}) \subseteq \mathcal{C}(\mathcal{L}_0, \mathbf{X}^\lambda) \subseteq \mathcal{C}(\mathcal{L}_0, \mathcal{L}_{rec}) \subseteq \mathcal{C}(\mathcal{L}_0, \mathcal{L}_0) = \mathcal{L}_0$, for any $X \in \{P, L\}$.

2. $\mathcal{L}_1 \subseteq \mathcal{C}(\mathcal{L}_1, \mathbf{X}^f) \subseteq \mathcal{C}(\mathcal{L}_1, \mathbf{X}) \subseteq \mathcal{C}(\mathcal{L}_1, \mathcal{L}_1) = \mathcal{L}_1$, for any $X \in \{P, L\}$.

3. $\mathcal{L}_0 = \mathcal{C}(\mathcal{L}_2, \mathcal{L}_3) \subseteq \mathcal{C}(\mathcal{L}_2, \mathbf{L}) \subseteq \mathcal{C}(\mathcal{L}_2, \mathbf{L}^\lambda) \subseteq \mathcal{C}(\mathcal{L}_2, \mathcal{L}_{rec}) = \mathcal{L}_0$.

4. $\mathcal{L}_0 \subseteq \mathcal{C}(\mathbf{L}^\lambda, \mathcal{L}) \subseteq \mathcal{C}(\mathbf{L}^\lambda, \mathcal{L}_0) \subseteq \mathcal{L}_0$, for any $\mathcal{L} \in \{\mathcal{L}_{rec}, \mathcal{L}_1, \mathcal{L}_2, \mathbf{L}^f, \mathbf{L}, \mathbf{L}^\lambda\}$ (the last inclusion was obtained in [12]).

$\square$

Proposition 4.3. *If* $\mathcal{L} \in \{\mathcal{L}_3, \mathcal{L}_2, \mathcal{L}_1, \mathcal{L}_{rec}, \mathcal{L}_0\} \cup \{\mathbf{L}^f, \mathbf{L}, \mathbf{L}^\lambda\}$, *then* $\mathcal{L} \subseteq \mathcal{C}(\mathcal{L}_3, \mathcal{L})$.

Proof. The case when $\mathcal{L}$ is a family in Chomsky hierarchy was solved in [7]. Using the same construction and the fact that any family of L-type Petri net languages is closed under right derivative and concatenation with distinct symbols, the proposition holds for the other case, too. $\square$

Proposition 4.4. *If* $\mathcal{L}$ *is an arbitrary family of languages and* $\mathcal{L}', \mathcal{L}'' \in \{\mathcal{L}_3, \mathcal{L}_2, \mathcal{L}_1, \mathcal{L}_0\} \cup \{\mathbf{X}^f, \mathbf{X}, \mathbf{X}^\lambda \mid X \in \{P, L\}\}$ *such that*

(i) $\mathcal{L}' \subseteq \mathcal{L}''$,

(ii) $(\mathcal{L}', \mathcal{L}'') \neq (\mathcal{L}_2, \mathcal{L}_1)$,

(iii) $\mathcal{L}', \mathcal{L}''$ *are either both Chomsky or both Petri of the same type,*

then $\mathcal{C}(\mathcal{L}', \mathcal{L}) \subseteq \mathcal{C}(\mathcal{L}'', \mathcal{L})$.

Proof. Directly from definitions. $\square$

Proposition 4.5. *If* $\mathcal{L} \in \{\mathcal{L}_3, \mathcal{L}_2, \mathcal{L}_1, \mathcal{L}_{rec}, \mathcal{L}_0\} \cup \{\mathbf{L}^f, \mathbf{L}, \mathbf{L}^\lambda\}$, *then* $\mathcal{C}(\mathcal{L}_3, \mathcal{L}) \subseteq \mathcal{C}(\mathbf{L}, \mathcal{L})$.

Proof. Let $L \in \mathcal{C}(\mathcal{L}_3, \mathcal{L})$, $\mathcal{L}$ being as in the statement of the proposition. There exists an $\mathcal{L}$-conditional type-3 grammar (G, ρ) such that $L = L(G, \rho)$. Let $G = (V_N, V_T, X_0, P)$. We construct an $\mathcal{L}$-conditional Petri net $\gamma = (\Sigma, \varphi, M_0, \mathcal{M}, l)$ as follows:

$$S = \{s_A \mid A \in V_N\},$$
$$T = \{t_r \mid r : A \to aB \in P, \text{ or } r : A \to a \in P\},$$

$$F = \{(s_A, t_r) \mid r : A \to aB \in P \text{ or } r : A \to a \in P\} \cup$$
$$\cup\{(t_r, s_B) \mid r : A \to aB \in P\},$$
$$W(x, y) = 1 \text{ for any } (x, y) \in F,$$
$$M_0(s_{X_0}) = 1 \text{ and } M_0(s) = 0 \text{ for any } s \neq s_{X_0},$$
$$\mathcal{M} = \{(0, \ldots, 0), M_0\} \text{ if } X_0 \to \lambda \in P \text{ and } X_0 \in \rho(X_0 \to \lambda),$$
$$\text{and } \mathcal{M} = \{(0, \ldots, 0)\}, \text{ otherwise,}$$
$$l(t_r) = a \text{ for any rule } r : A \to aB \in P \text{ or } r : A \to a \in P,$$
$$\varphi(t_r) = l^{-1}(\partial_A^r(\rho(r) \cap V_T^*)) \text{ for any rule } r : A \to aB \in P$$
$$\text{or } r : A \to a \in P.$$

The family $\mathcal{L}$ being closed under right derivatives, inverse homomorphisms and intersection by V_T^*, it follows that γ is in $\text{lm}\mathcal{L}$-CPTNf (for the case $\mathcal{L} = \mathbf{L}^f$ the proof of Lemma 2.5 [12] can be consulted). The equality $L(G, \rho) = L(\gamma)$ can be easily verified. $\qquad\square$

Theorem 4.2.

(1) $\mathcal{L} \subseteq \mathcal{C}(\mathbf{L}, \mathcal{L})$, *for any* $\mathcal{L} \in \{\mathcal{L}_3, \mathcal{L}_2, \mathcal{L}_1, \mathcal{L}_{rec}, \mathcal{L}_0\} \cup \{\mathbf{L}^f, \mathbf{L}, \mathbf{L}^\lambda\}$.

(2) $\mathcal{C}(\mathbf{L}, \mathcal{L}_0) = \mathcal{L}_0$.

(3) $\mathcal{C}(\mathcal{L}_3, \mathcal{L}_{rec}) = \mathcal{C}(\mathbf{L}, \mathcal{L}_{rec}) = \mathcal{C}(\mathcal{L}_1, \mathcal{L}_{rec}) = \mathcal{L}_{rec}$.

Proof. (1) follows from Propositions 4.3 and 4.5.

(2) $\mathcal{L}_0 \subseteq \mathcal{C}(\mathbf{L}\mathcal{L}_0) \subseteq \mathcal{C}(\mathbf{L}^\lambda, \mathcal{L}_0) = \mathcal{L}_0$.

(3) $\mathcal{L}_{rec} \subseteq \mathcal{C}(\mathcal{L}_3, \mathcal{L}_{rec}) \subseteq \mathcal{C}(\mathbf{L}, \mathcal{L}_{rec})$ and $\mathcal{L}_{rec} \subseteq \mathcal{C}(\mathcal{L}_3, \mathcal{L}_{rec}) \subseteq \mathcal{C}(\mathcal{L}_1, \mathcal{L}_{rec})$. Let us prove that $\mathcal{C}(\mathbf{L}, \mathcal{L}_{rec}) \cup \mathcal{C}(\mathcal{L}_1, \mathcal{L}_{rec}) \subseteq \mathcal{L}_{rec}$. In order to show that $\mathcal{C}(\mathbf{L}, \mathcal{L}_{rec}) \subseteq \mathcal{L}_{rec}$ we shall show that for any $\text{lm}\mathcal{L}_{rec}$-CPTNf γ there exists an algorithm $A(\gamma)$ such that for any word w, $A(\gamma)$ starting with the input w halts either with the output "Yes" if $w \in L(\gamma)$ or with the output "No" if $w \notin L(\gamma)$.

Let $\gamma = (\Sigma, \varphi, M_0, \mathcal{M}, l)$ be an $\text{lm}\mathcal{L}_{rec}$-CPTNf and w a word. The algorithm $A(\gamma)$ works as follows. Those words $u \in T^*$ with $l(u) = w$ are computed. These words can be computed by analysing the word w and the function l; there exists a finite number of such words. If there is no such a word, then $A(\gamma)$ halts with the output "No". Otherwise, let $u_1, \ldots, u_n$ be all words such that $l(u_i) = w$, $1 \leq i \leq n$. For any i and any decomposition $u_i = u_i' t u_i''$ we can effectively decide whether w is in $L(\gamma)$ or not. Hence $\mathcal{C}(\mathbf{L}, \mathcal{L}_{rec}) \subseteq \mathcal{L}_{rec}$. The proof for $\mathcal{C}(\mathcal{L}_1, \mathcal{L}_{rec}) \subseteq \mathcal{L}_{rec}$ is omitted; the monotonicity of the rules is used. $\qquad\square$

Proposition 4.6. *If* $\mathcal{L} \in \{\mathcal{L}_3, \mathcal{L}_2, \mathcal{L}_1, \mathcal{L}_{rec}, \mathcal{L}_0\} \cup \{\mathbf{X}^f, \mathbf{X}, \mathbf{X}^\lambda \mid X \in \{P, L\}\}$, *then* $\mathcal{C}(\mathbf{P}^\lambda, \mathcal{L}) \subseteq \mathcal{C}(\mathbf{L}^\lambda, \mathcal{L})$.

Proof. Let $\gamma = (\Sigma, \varphi, M_0, l)$ be an $1^\lambda m\mathcal{L}$-CPTN. We consider two new places s_1, s_2 not in S, a new transition t_1 and a set of new transitions $T_{new} = \{t_s \mid s \in S\}$. Let $\gamma' = (\Sigma', \varphi', M_0', \mathcal{M}', l')$ be given by:

$$S' = S \cup \{s_1, s_2\},$$

$$T' = T \cup \{t_1\} \cup T_{new},$$

$$F' = F \cup \{(t, s_1), (s_1, t)) \mid t \in T\} \cup \{(s_1, t_1), (t_1, s_1)\} \cup$$
$$\cup \{(t, s_2), (s_2, t) \mid t \in T_{new}\} \cup \{(s, t_s) \mid s \in S\},$$

$$W'(x, y) = W(x, y) \text{ for any } (x, y) \in F \text{ and } W'(x, y) = 1$$
$$\text{for any } (x, y) \in F' - F,$$

$$M_0'(x) = M_0(x) \text{ for any } x \in S, \, M_0(s_1) = 1 \text{ and } M_0(s_2) = 0,$$

$$\mathcal{M}' = \{(\underbrace{0, \ldots, 0}_{S}, \underbrace{0}_{s_1}, \underbrace{1}_{s_2})\},$$

$$l'(x) = l(x) \text{ if } x \in T \text{ and } l'(x) = \lambda \text{ otherwise,}$$

$$\varphi'(x) = \varphi(x) \text{ for any } x \in T, \, \varphi'(t_1) = T^*,$$

$$\text{and } \varphi'(x) = (T \cup \{t_1\} \cup T_{new})^* \text{ for any } x \in T_{new}.$$

Pictorially, the net Σ' is represented in figure 4.1.

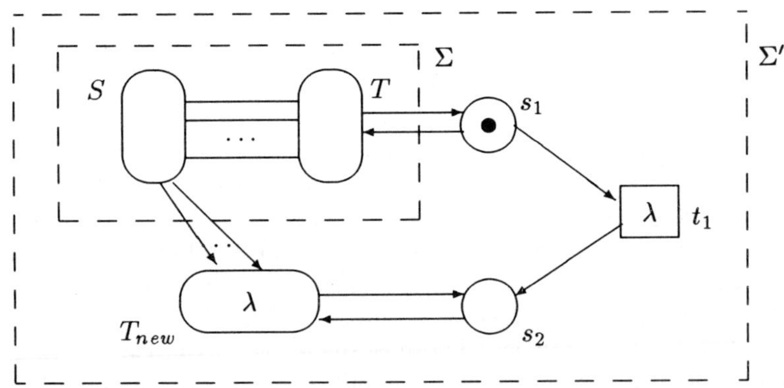

Fig. 4.1

The idea is the following: after any transition sequence $w \in T^*$ of γ, the transition t_1 can occur. Then the transitions $t \in T$ are blocked (by s_1) and the transitions $t \in T_{new}$ are now free. They reset the places $s \in S$ producing the final marking $(0, \ldots, 0, 0, 1)$. The labelling erases only the transitions from $T_{new} \cup \{t_1\}$. It is easy to see that γ' is an $1^\lambda m\mathcal{L}$-CPTNf and $L(\gamma') = P(\gamma)$. $\square$

We shall prove now a basic result, namely $\mathcal{C}(\mathbf{L}, \mathcal{L}_1) = \mathcal{L}_1$. We begin with a technical lemma.

Lemma 4.1. *For any lmPTNf γ a 0-type grammar with bounded workspace G can be effectively constructed such that $L(\gamma) = L(G)$.*

Proof. Let $\gamma = (\Sigma, M_0, \mathcal{M}, l)$ be an lmPTNf, $\Sigma = (S, T; F, W)$, $S = \{s_1, \ldots, s_m\}$, $T = \{t_1, \ldots, t_n\}$ and $\mathcal{M} = \{M_1, \ldots, M_k\}$, where $m, n, k \geq 1$.

We construct the grammar $G = (V_N, V_T, X_0, P)$ by

(i) $V_N = \{A_1, \ldots, A_m\} \cup \{B_1, \ldots, B_n\} \cup \{X_0, \$, \&\}$,

(ii) $V_T = \{l(t_i) \mid 1 \leq i \leq n\}$,

(iii) For any marking M of γ we set

$$seq(M) = \{w \in \{A_1, \ldots, A_m\}^* \mid \text{for any } 1 \leq i \leq m, \#(A_i, w) = M(s_i)\}.$$

The set $seq(M)$ is finite and any $w \in seq(M)$ is used to simulate the marking M. For any transition t_i of γ we set

$$
\begin{aligned}
seq(pre(t_i)) &= \{w \in \{A_1, \ldots, A_m\}^* \mid \text{for any } j \in \{1, \ldots, m\}, \\
&\quad \#(A_j, w) = W(s_j, t_i)\}, \\
seq(post(t_i)) &= \{w \in \{A_1, \ldots, A_m\}^* \mid \text{for any } j \in \{1, \ldots, m\}, \\
&\quad \#(A_j, w) = W(t_i, s_j)\}.
\end{aligned}
$$

Now, the set P consists of the following rules:

1. $r_0 : X_0 \to \$\alpha_0\&$, where $\alpha_0 \in seq(M_0)$ is an arbitrary but fixed sequence,

2. $r_{ij} : A_i A_j \to A_j A_i$, for all $i, j \in \{1, \ldots, m\}$ and $i \neq j$ (distinct symbols A_i and A_j can commute),

3. $r_i : \$\alpha \to B_i\$\beta$ for each $1 \leq i \leq n$, where $\alpha \in seq(pre(t_i))$ and $\beta \in seq(post(t_i))$ are two arbitrary but fixed sequences (the rule r_i simulates the occurring of the transition t_i);

4. $r'_i : B_i \to l(t_i)$ for any $1 \leq i \leq n$,

5. $r''_i : \$\alpha_i\& \to \lambda$ for any $1 \leq i \leq k$, where $\alpha_i \in seq(M_i)$ is an arbitrary but fixed sequence.

G is a type-0 grammar and we have (it is easy to verify) $L(\gamma) = L(G)$. To complete the proof we need only to verify that G has bounded workspace. Let $w \in L(G)$ and $w \neq \lambda$. There exists $v \in T^+$ and $j \in \{1, \ldots, k\}$ such that $M_0[v > M_j$ and $l(v) = w$. Moreover $|v| = |w|$. Let $h : T \to \{B_1, \ldots, B_n\}$ be given by $h(t_i) = B_i$ for any i. The following is a derivation (of w) in G:

$$D : X_0 \Longrightarrow \$\alpha_0\& \Longrightarrow^+ h(v)\$\alpha\& \Longrightarrow^* h(v)\$\alpha_j\& \Longrightarrow h(v) \Longrightarrow^+ w.$$

Let $n_0 = |\alpha_0|$ $(= \sum_{j=1}^{m} M(s_j))$ and $n_1 = \max_{1 \leq i \leq n} \{\sum_{j=1}^{m} \Delta t_i(s_j)\}$. We have

$$WS(w, G) = (n_0 + 2) + (n_1 + 1)|v| \leq (n_0 + n_1 + 3)|v| = (n_0 + n_1 + 3)|w|.$$

Choosing $N = n_0 + n_1 + 3$ we deduce that for any $w \in L(G) - \{\lambda\}$ we have $WS(w, G) \leq N|w|$. Hence G has bounded workspace. $\square$

One can easily see that we have obtained a direct proof of the strict inclusion $\mathbf{L} \subset \mathcal{L}_1$.

Corollary 4.1. $\mathbf{L} \subset \mathcal{L}_1$.

Proof. The inclusion follows from Lemma 4.1 and Theorem 2.1.1. The inclusion is strict because the family $\mathcal{L}_1$ is closed under Kleene star but $\mathbf{L}$ is not closed. $\square$

We are now in position to prove

Theorem 4.3. $\mathcal{C}(\mathbf{L}, \mathcal{L}_1) = \mathcal{L}_1$.

Proof. The inclusion $\mathcal{L}_1 \subseteq \mathcal{C}(\mathbf{L}, \mathcal{L}_1)$ follows from Theorem 4.2(1). Let $L \in \mathcal{C}(\mathbf{L}, \mathcal{L}_1)$. There exists an lm$\mathcal{L}_1$-CPTNf $\gamma = (\Sigma, \varphi, M_0, \mathcal{M}, l)$ such that $L = L(\gamma)$. Let $\Sigma = (S, T; F, W)$ be, with $S = \{s_1, \ldots, s_m\}$, $T = \{t_1, \ldots, t_n\}$ and $\mathcal{M} = \{M_1, \ldots, M_k\}$, where $m, n, k \geq 1$. The proof will be now developed in two stages:

(I) We construct an $\mathcal{L}_1$-conditional type-0 grammar (G, ρ) such that $L = L(G, \rho)$ and G has bounded workspace;

(II) Starting from (G, ρ) we construct a type-0 grammar G' such that $L(G, \rho) = L(G')$ and G' has bounded workspace.

Stage I. Starting from $\gamma' = (\Sigma, M_0, \mathcal{M}, l)$ we construct a type-0 grammar with bounded workspace, G, as in the proof of Lemma 4.1. Moreover, $L(G) = L(\gamma')$. Now with each rule r of G we associate a context-sensitive language (by a function ρ) in the following manner:

1. $r_0 : X_0 \rightarrow \$\alpha_0\&$, with $\alpha_0 \in seq(M_0)$. We set $\rho(r_0) = \{X_0\}$.

2. $r_{ij} : A_i A_j \rightarrow A_j A_i$, for any $i, j \in \{1, \ldots, m\}$ and $i \neq j$. We set $\rho(r_{ij}) = V_G^*$.

3. $r_i : \$\alpha \rightarrow B_i\$\beta$ for any $i \in \{1, \ldots, n\}$, where $\alpha \in seq(pre(t_i))$ and $\beta \in seq(post(t_i))$. We set $\rho(r_i) = h(\varphi(t_i))\{\$\}\{A_1, \ldots, A_m\}^*\{\&\}$, h being as in the proof of Lemma 4.1.

4. $r_i' : B_i \rightarrow l(t_i)$, for any $i \in \{1, \ldots, n\}$. We set $\rho(r_i') = \{B_1, \ldots, B_n\}^*$.

5. $r_i'' : \$\alpha_i\& \rightarrow \lambda$ for any $i \in \{1, \ldots, k\}$, where $\alpha_i \in seq(M_i)$. We set $\rho(r_i'') = V_G^*$.

Clearly, for any rule r of G, $\rho(r) \in \mathcal{L}_1 \cap V_G^*$ and hence (G, ρ) is an $\mathcal{L}_1$-conditional type-0 grammar. It is not hard to verify that $L(\gamma) = L(G, \rho)$.

Stage II. Let $G, \rho)$ be the conditional grammar constructed in Stage I. The construction which follows is similar to the one used in [7] where it is shown that $\mathcal{C}(\mathcal{L}_1, \mathcal{L}_1) = \mathcal{L}_1$. Let p be the number of rules of G. We can write $P = \{r_1, \ldots, r_p\}$. There exist the monotone grammars $G_1, \ldots, G_p$ such that $\rho(r_i) = L(G_i)$, $1 \le i \le p$. Let $G_i = (V_N^i, V_T^i = V_G, X_0^i, P^i)$, $1 \le i \le p$. Let $G' = (V_N', V_T', X_0', P')$ be the grammar given by:

$$
V_N' = (V_N \cup V_T) \times (V_G \cup \bigcup_{i=1}^{p} V_N^i \cup \{@\}) \cup
$$
$$
\cup \{X_0', \#, X, Y, Z\} \cup \{Y_i, \Delta_i, \Delta_i' \mid 1 \le i \le p\},
$$
$$
V_T' = V_T,
$$

and P' consists of the following rules:

1. $X_0' \to \# X(X_0, @)\#$ (the derivation begins with the introduction of the marker $\#$ and the nonterminals X and $(X_0, @)$);

2. $X(z, @) \to Y_i(z, X_0^i)$ for any $z \in V_G$ and $1 \le i \le p$ (on the second component of the symbols of the current string, the nonterminal Y_i determine a derivation with respect to the grammar G_i);

3. $Y_i(z, y) \to (z, y)Y_i$,
   $(z, y)Y_i \to Y_i(z, y)$, for any $z \in V_G, y \in V_{G_i}$ and $1 \le i \le p$ (Y_i can freely circulate from left to right and vice versa);

4. $(z, y)(z', @) \to (z, @)(z', y)$,
   $(z, @)(z', y) \to (z, y)(z', @)$, for any $z, z' \in V_G, y \in V_{G_i}, 1 \le i \le p$ (on the second component, @ can freely circulate from left to right and vice versa);

5. $Y_i(z_1, y_1) \ldots (z_u, y_u)(z_{u+1}, @) \ldots (z_v, @) \to Y_i(z_1, y_1') \ldots (z_v, y_v')$, for any $y_1 \ldots y_u \to y_1' \ldots y_v' \in P_i$ ($v \ge u$), $1 \le i \le p$ (a rule of G_i is simulated on the second component);

6. $\#Y_i \to \#\Delta_i$ for any $1 \le i \le p$ (we prepare the verification of the strings from the first and second components);

7. $\Delta_i(z, z) \to (z, @)\Delta_i$ for any $z \in V_G$ and $1 \le i \le p$ (pairwise verification);

8. $\Delta_i\# \to \Delta_i'\#$ for any $1 \le i \le p$ (the verification shows the coincidence of the strings);

9. $(z, @)\Delta_i' \rightarrow \Delta_i'(z, @)$ for any $z \in V_G$ and $1 \leq i \leq p$ (Δ_i' can circulate from right to left);

10. $\Delta_i'(z_1, @) \ldots (z_u, @) \rightarrow Y(z_1', @) \ldots (z_v', @)$ for any $r_i : z_1 \ldots z_u \rightarrow z_1' \ldots z_v' \in P$ ($z_1' \ldots z_v' \neq \lambda$) and $1 \leq i \leq p$;
    $\Delta_i'(z_1, @) \ldots (z_u, @) \rightarrow Y$ for $r_i : z_1 \ldots z_u \rightarrow \lambda \in P, 1 \leq i \leq p$ (on the first component the derivation continues with a rule of G);

11. $(z, @)Y \rightarrow Y(z, @)$ for any $z \in V_G$;
    $\#Y \rightarrow \#X$;

12. $\#X \rightarrow Z, Z(a, @) \rightarrow a$ for any $a \in V_T$,
    $Z\# \rightarrow \lambda$.

The reader can verify that G' has bounded workspace (G' being a type-0 grammar, too) and $L(G, \rho) = L(G')$. Hence we obtain that $L(G') \in \mathcal{L}_1$ and so $L \in \mathcal{L}_1$. $\qquad\square$

We recall a basic result from [12].

Lemma 4.2. *Let* $\mathcal{L} \in \{\mathcal{L}_3, \mathcal{L}_2, \mathcal{L}_1, \mathcal{L}_{rec}, \mathcal{L}_0\} \cup \{\mathbf{X}^f, \mathbf{X}, \mathbf{X}^\lambda \mid X \in \{P, L\}\}$, L *a language not contained in* $\mathcal{L}$ *and* $c \notin alph(L)$. *The language* $L' = L\{c\} \cup (alph(L))^*$ *is not a member of the family* $C(\mathbf{L}^f, \mathcal{L})$.

Proof. Contained in the proof of Lemma 2.5 [12]. $\qquad\square$

Theorem 4.4. *Let* $\mathcal{L}, \mathcal{L}' \in \{\mathcal{L}_3, \mathcal{L}_2, \mathcal{L}_1, \mathcal{L}_{rec}, \mathcal{L}_0\} \cup \{\mathbf{X}^f, \mathbf{X}, \mathbf{X}^\lambda \mid X \in \{P, L\}\}$.

1. *If* $\mathcal{L} \subset \mathcal{L}'$, *then* $C(\mathbf{L}^f, \mathcal{L}) \subset C(\mathbf{L}^f, \mathcal{L}')$.

2. *If* $\mathcal{L}$ *and* $\mathcal{L}'$ *are incomparable, then* $C(\mathbf{L}^f, \mathcal{L})$ *and* $C(\mathbf{L}^f, \mathcal{L}')$ *are incomparable, too.*

3. *If* $\mathbf{L}^f - \mathcal{L} \neq \emptyset$ *and* $\mathcal{L} - \mathcal{L}' \neq \emptyset$, *then* $\mathcal{L}$ *and* $C(\mathbf{L}^f, \mathcal{L}')$ *are incomparable.*

Proof. (1) See Lemma 2.5 [12]. (2) follows from Lemma 4.2 (applied twice) and using the construction given in the proof of Lemma 2.5 [12]. For (3), the inclusion $\mathbf{L}^f \subseteq C(\mathbf{L}^f, \mathcal{L})$, Lemma 4.2, and the closure properties of the family $\mathcal{L}$ are used. $\qquad\square$

Theorem 4.5. *The relationships in the diagram in figure 4.2 hold; the question mark indicates an inclusion which is not known to be proper.*

Proof. All incomparabilities (with the exception of those between the families $\mathcal{L}_i$ and $\mathbf{L}^f, \mathbf{L}, \mathbf{L}^\lambda$ which are known) follow directly from Theorem 4.4. The strict inclusion $\mathbf{L}^f \subset C(\mathbf{L}^f, \mathbf{L}^f)$ follows from Proposition 2.6(6) [12] and from the fact that the language $a^* + b^*$ is not in the family $\mathbf{L}^f$

([13]) but it is in $\mathcal{C}(\mathbf{L}^f, \mathbf{L}^f)$ (Example 2.4 [12]). The inclusions $\mathcal{C}(\mathbf{L}^f, \mathcal{L}_1) \subseteq \mathcal{L}_1$, $\mathcal{C}(\mathbf{L}^f, \mathcal{L}_{rec}) \subseteq \mathcal{L}_{rec}$ and $\mathcal{C}(\mathbf{L}^f, \mathcal{L}_0) \subseteq \mathcal{L}_0$ can be obtained as follows: $\mathcal{C}(\mathbf{L}^f, \mathcal{L}_1) \subseteq \mathcal{C}(\mathbf{L}, \mathcal{L}_1) = \mathcal{L}_1$, $\mathcal{C}(\mathbf{L}^f, \mathcal{L}_{rec}) \subseteq \mathcal{C}(\mathbf{L}, \mathcal{L}_{rec}) = \mathcal{L}_{rec}$, $\mathcal{C}(\mathbf{L}^f, \mathcal{L}_0) \subseteq \mathcal{C}(\mathbf{L}, \mathcal{L}_0) = \mathcal{L}_0$. $\square$

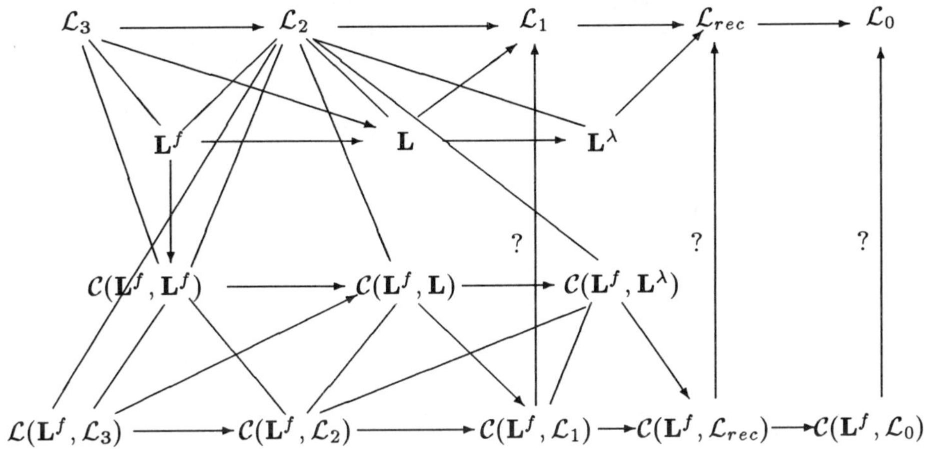

Fig. 4.2

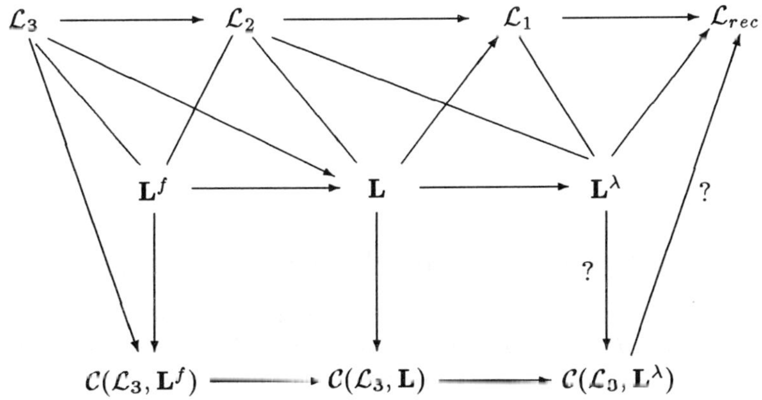

Fig. 4.3

Theorem 4.6. *The relationships in the diagram in figure 4.3 hold.*

Proof. The strict inclusions $\mathcal{L}_3 \subset \mathcal{C}(\mathcal{L}_3, \mathbf{L}^f)$ and $\mathbf{L}^f \subset \mathcal{C}(\mathcal{L}_3, \mathbf{L}^f)$ follow from the fact that $\mathcal{L}_3 \cup \mathbf{L}^f \subseteq \mathcal{C}(\mathcal{L}_3, \mathbf{L}^f)$ and $\mathcal{L}_3$ is incomparable with $\mathbf{L}^f$. $\square$

Theorem 4.7. *The relationships in the diagram in figure 4.4 hold.*

The results obtained until now on the generative power of the conditional grammars and the conditional Petri nets are summarized in the diagram in figure 4.5. (An entry in this matrix gives the power of the $\mathcal{L}$-conditional grammar or Petri net specified in the first column; the family $\mathcal{L}$ is specified in the first line). Known results from [7] and [12] have been supplementary added. (Some families $\mathcal{C}(\mathcal{L}_i, \mathcal{L}_j)$ have been written in figures 4.4 and 4.5 as $\mathcal{C}(i, j)$, for saving space.)

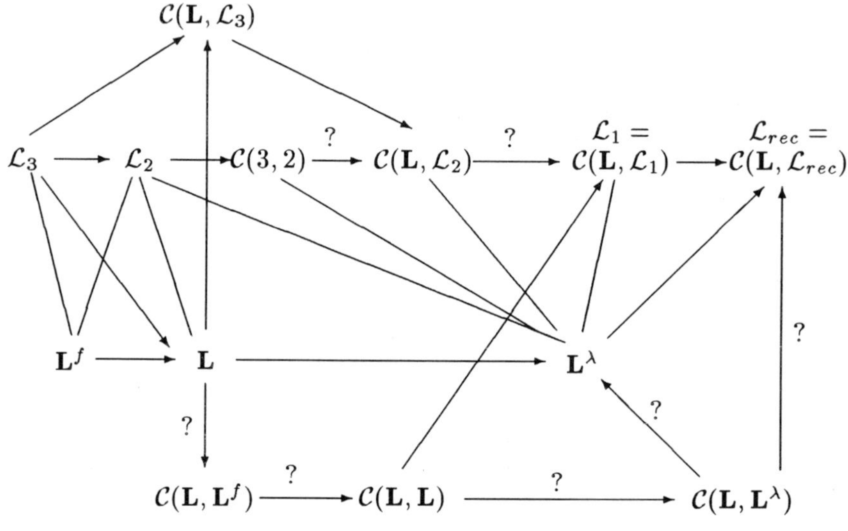

Fig. 4.4

5. Characterizations and closure properties

In the previous section we have seen that if $\mathcal{L} \in \{\mathcal{L}_0, \mathcal{L}_{rec}, \mathcal{L}_1, \mathcal{L}_2, \mathcal{L}_3\} \cup \{\mathbf{L}^f, \mathbf{L}, \mathbf{L}^\lambda\}$, then $\mathcal{L} \subseteq \mathcal{C}(\mathbf{L}, \mathcal{L})$ (Theorem 4.2(1)). This result does not hold if we change the family $\mathbf{L}$ by $\mathbf{L}^f$. However we can prove:

Theorem 5.1. *Let $\mathcal{L}$ be a family of languages such that the language V^* is a member of $\mathcal{L}$ for any alphabet V. Then, for any $L \in \mathcal{L}$ and any symbol $c \notin alph(L)$ we have $L\{c\} \in \mathcal{C}(\mathbf{L}^f, \mathcal{L})$.*

Proof. Let $\mathcal{L}$ be as in the statement of the theorem, $L \in \mathcal{L}$ and c a new symbol. Let $alph(L) = \{a_1, \ldots, a_n\}, n \geq 1$. We construct an m$\mathcal{L}$-CPTNf $\gamma = (\Sigma, \varphi, M_0, \mathcal{M})$ as follows: Σ is the net in figure 5.1, $M_0 = (0)$, $\mathcal{M} = \{(0)\}$

and φ is given by $\varphi(x) = (alph(L))^*$ if $x \in alph(L)$ and $\varphi(x) = L$ if $x = c$.
We have $L(\gamma) = L\{c\}$. $\qquad\qquad\square$

	$\mathcal{L}_0$	$\mathcal{L}_{rec}$	$\mathcal{L}_1$	$\mathcal{L}_2$	$\mathcal{L}_3$	$\mathbf{L}^f$	$\mathbf{L}$	$\mathbf{L}^\lambda$
type-0 grammar	$\mathcal{L}_0$	$\mathcal{L}_0$	$\mathcal{L}_0$	$\mathcal{L}_0$	$\mathcal{L}_0$	$\mathcal{L}_0$	$\mathcal{L}_0$	$\mathcal{L}_0$
type-1 grammar	$\mathcal{L}_1$	$\mathcal{L}_{rec}$	$\mathcal{L}_1$	$\mathcal{L}_1$	$\mathcal{L}_1$	$\mathcal{L}_1$	$\mathcal{L}_1$	$\mathcal{C}(1,\mathbf{L}^\lambda)$
type-2 grammar	$\mathcal{L}_0$	$\mathcal{L}_0$	$\mathcal{L}_0$	$\mathcal{L}_0$	$\mathcal{L}_0$	$\mathcal{C}(2,\mathbf{L}^f)$	$\mathcal{L}_0$	$\mathcal{L}_0$
type-3 grammar	$\mathcal{L}_0$	$\mathcal{L}_{rec}$	$\mathcal{L}_1$	$\mathcal{C}(3,2)$	$\mathcal{L}_3$	Figure 4.3		
mPTNf	Figure 4.2							
lmPTNf	$\mathcal{L}_3$	$\mathcal{L}_{rec}$	$\mathcal{L}_1$	Figure 4.4				
l^λmPTNf	$\mathcal{L}_0$	$\mathcal{L}_0$	$\mathcal{L}_0$	$\mathcal{L}_0$	$\mathcal{C}(\mathbf{L}^\lambda,3)$	$\mathcal{L}_0$	$\mathcal{L}_0$	$\mathcal{L}_0$

Fig. 4.5

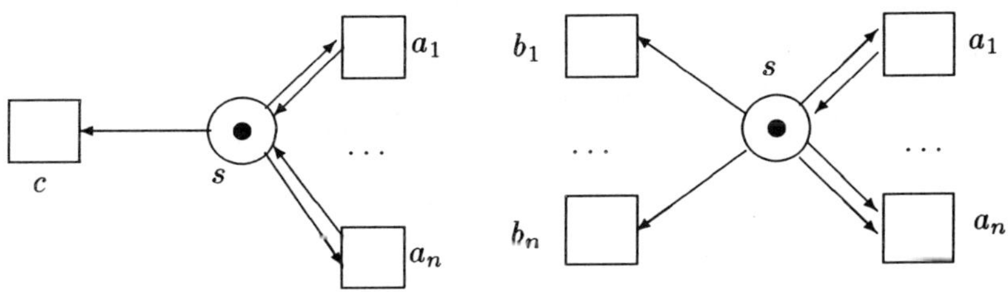

Fig. 5.1   Fig. 5.2

Corollary 5.1. *Let $\mathcal{L}$ be a family of languages as in the statement of Theorem 5.1. Then, for any $L \in \mathcal{L}$ there exists $L' \in \mathcal{C}(\mathbf{L}^f, \mathcal{L})$ and a symbol $c \notin alph(L)$ such that $L = \partial_c^r(L')$.*

Proof. If c is a symbol not in $alph(L)$, then the language $L\{c\}$ is in $\mathcal{C}(\mathbf{L}^f, \mathcal{L})$. We set $L' = L\{c\}$ and we have $L = \partial_c^r(L')$. $\square$

Corollary 5.2. *Let $\mathcal{L}$ be a family of languages as in statement of Theorem 5.1. Then, for any $L \in \mathcal{L}$ there exists $L' \in \mathcal{C}(\mathbf{L}^f, \mathcal{L})$ and a homomorhism h such that $l = h(L')$.*

Proof. We choose L' as above and the homomorphisms h defined by $h(a) = a$ for any $a \in alph(L)$ and $h(c) = \lambda$. Clearly, $L = h(L')$. $\square$

The homomorphism h given in the proof of Corollary 5.2 is an erasing one. If we additionally suppose that $\mathcal{L}$ is closed under right derivatives then we can choose h to be a coding.

Theorem 5.2. *Let $\mathcal{L}$ be a family of languages which is closed under right derivatives and which contains the language V^* for any alphabet V. Then, for any one-to-one mapping $f : alph(L) \longrightarrow A$, where A and $alph(L)$ are disjoint sets, we have*

$$\bigcup_{a \in alph(L)} \partial_a^r(L)\{f(a)\} \in \mathcal{C}(\mathbf{L}^f, \mathcal{L}).$$

Proof. Let $\mathcal{L}$ be as above, $L \in \mathcal{L}$ and f an one-to-one mapping from $alph(L)$ into A, where $A \cap alph(L) = \emptyset$. Let $alph(L) = \{a_1, \ldots, a_n\}$, $A = \{b_1, \ldots, b_n\}$, $n \geq 1$, and $f(a_i) = b_i$ for any $1 \leq i \leq n$. We construct an $m\mathcal{L}$-CPTNf $\gamma = (\Sigma, \varphi, M_0, \mathcal{M})$ as follows: Σ is the net in figure 5.2, $M_0 = (1)$, $\mathcal{M} = \{(0)\}$ and φ is given by $\varphi(x) = (alph(L))^*$ for any $x \in alph(L)$ and $\varphi(b_i) = \partial_{a_i}^r(L)$ for any $1 \leq i \leq n$.

It is not hard to verify that $L(\gamma) = \cup_{i=1}^n \partial_{a_i}^r(L)\{b_i\}$. $\square$

Corollary 5.3. *Let $\mathcal{L}$ be a family of languages as in Theorem 5.2. Then, for any $L \in \mathcal{L}$ there exist a language $L' \in \mathcal{C}(\mathbf{L}^f, \mathcal{L})$ and an one-to-one mapping $f : alph(L) \to A$, where A and $alph(L)$ are disjoint sets, such that*

$$L = \bigcup_{b \in A} \partial_b^r(L')\{f^{-1}(b)\}.$$

Proof. If $f : alph(L) \to A$ is an one-to-one mapping, where A and $alph(L)$ are disjoint sets, then $\displaystyle\bigcup_{a \in alph(L)} \partial_a^r(L)\{f(a)\}$ is in $\mathcal{C}(\mathbf{L}^f, \mathcal{L})$. We set

$$L' = \bigcup_{a \in alph(L)} \partial_a^r(L)\{f(a)\}$$

and we have the relation in the statement of the corollary. $\qquad\square$

Corollary 5.4. *Let $\mathcal{L}$ be a family of languages as in Theorem 5.2. Then, for any $L \in \mathcal{L}$ there exist a language $L' \in \mathcal{C}(\mathbf{L}^f, \mathcal{L})$ and a coding h such that $L = h(L')$.*

Proof. We choose L' as in the proof of Corollary 5.3, and the homomorphism h is given by $h(x) = x$ for any $x \in alph(L)$ and $h(x) = a$ for any $x = f(a)$, $a \in alph(L)$. This h is a coding and we have $L = h(L')$. $\qquad\square$

We conclude this section by a non-closure property of the families $\mathcal{C}(\mathbf{L}^f, \mathcal{L}_3)$ and $\mathcal{C}(\mathbf{L}^f, \mathcal{L}_2)$.

Proposition 5.1. *The families $\mathcal{C}(\mathbf{L}^f, \mathcal{L}_3)$ and $\mathcal{C}(\mathbf{L}^f, \mathcal{L}_2)$ are not closed under union.*

Proof. Since $\mathbf{L}^f$ is incomparable with the families $\mathcal{L}_3$ and $\mathcal{L}_2$, there exists a language L such that $L \in \mathbf{L}^f - \mathcal{L}_2$. Let c be a symbol not in $alph(L)$. It is easy to see that both $L\{c\}$ and $(alph(L))^*$ are in $\mathbf{L}^f$. If $\mathcal{C}(\mathbf{L}^f, \mathcal{L}_2)$ would be closed under union, then $L\{c\} \cup (alph(L))^*$ will be a member of this family: this contradicts Lemma 4.2. $\qquad\square$

6. Conclusions and open problems

Many problems concerning conditional grammars and nets remain open. Many of them could be solved if we could prove that the language $Rev = \{ww^T \mid w \in \{a, b\}^*\}$ is not a member of the family $\mathcal{C}(\mathbf{L}, \mathbf{L}^\lambda)$ (w^T denotes the reversal of w).

Conjecture 6.1. $Rev \notin \mathcal{C}(\mathbf{L}, \mathbf{L}^\lambda)$.

Should this conjecture be positively solved, then

1. $\mathcal{C}(\mathcal{L}_3, \mathbf{L}^\lambda) \subset \mathcal{L}_{rec}$ (because $\mathcal{C}(\mathcal{L}_3, \mathbf{L}^\lambda) \subseteq \mathcal{L}_{rec}$ and $Rev \in \mathcal{L}_{rec} - \mathcal{C}(\mathcal{L}_3, \mathbf{L}^\lambda)$);

2. $\mathcal{C}(\mathcal{L}_3, \mathbf{L}) \subset \mathcal{L}_1$ (as above);

3. The families $\mathcal{C}(\mathcal{L}_3, \mathbf{L}^\lambda), \mathcal{C}(\mathcal{L}_3, \mathbf{L})$ and $\mathcal{C}(\mathcal{L}_3, \mathbf{L}^\lambda)$ are incomparable with $\mathcal{L}_2$ ($Rev \in \mathcal{L}_2$ but $\{a^n db^n ec^n \mid n \geq 1\}$ is not in $\mathcal{L}_2$; this language is in $\mathcal{C}(\mathcal{L}_3, \mathbf{L}^f)$);

4. The families $\mathcal{C}(\mathbf{L}, \mathbf{L}^f), \mathcal{C}(\mathbf{L}, \mathbf{L}^\lambda)$ are all incomparable with the family $\mathcal{L}_2$ (as above);

5. $\mathcal{C}(\mathbf{L}, \mathbf{L}) \subset \mathcal{L}_1$;

6. The families $\mathcal{C}(\mathbf{L}, \mathbf{L}^\lambda)$ and $\mathcal{L}_1$ are incomparable ($Rev \in \mathcal{L}_1 - \mathcal{C}(\mathbf{L}, \mathbf{L}^\lambda)$ and $\mathbf{L}^\lambda \subseteq \mathcal{C}(\mathbf{L}, \mathbf{L}^\lambda)$ and the families $\mathbf{L}^\lambda$ and $\mathcal{L}_1$ are incomparable);

7. The families $C(\mathbf{L}, \mathcal{L}_3)$ and $\mathcal{L}_2$ are incomparable ($Rev \in \mathcal{L}_2 - C(\mathbf{L}, \mathcal{L}_3)$ and $\{a^n db^n ec^n \mid n \geq 1\} \in C(\mathbf{L}, \mathcal{L}_3) - \mathcal{L}_2$);

8. $C(\mathbf{L}, \mathbf{L}^\lambda) \subset \mathcal{L}_{rec}$ (from (6)).

Conjecture 6.2. The families $C(\mathcal{L}_3, \mathbf{L})$ and $\mathbf{L}^\lambda$ are incomparable. Positively solving this conjecture we can obtain

$$C(\mathcal{L}_3, \mathbf{L}) \subset C(\mathcal{L}_3, \mathbf{L}^\lambda) \text{ and } \mathbf{L}^\lambda \subset C(\mathcal{L}_3, \mathbf{L}^\lambda).$$

Conjecture 6.3. The families $C(\mathcal{L}_3, \mathbf{L}^f)$ and $\mathbf{L}$ are incomparable. Positively solving this conjecture we have:

$$C(\mathcal{L}_3, \mathbf{L}) \text{ and } \mathbf{L} \subset C(\mathcal{L}_3, \mathbf{L}).$$

Conjecture 6.4. The families $C(\mathbf{L}, \mathbf{L})$ and $\mathbf{L}^\lambda$ are incomparable. Positively solving this conjecture we obtain

$$C(\mathbf{L}, \mathbf{L}) \subset C(\mathbf{L}, \mathbf{L}^\lambda) \text{ and } \mathbf{L}^\lambda \subset C(\mathbf{L}, \mathbf{L}^\lambda).$$

References

1. E. Best, C. Fernandez, *Notations and Terminology on Petri Net Theory*, Arbeitspapiere der GMD 195, 1987.

2. H. D. Burkhard, Ordered firing in Petri nets, *EIK*, 17, 2/3, (1981), 71 – 86.

3. H. D. Burkhard, *What Gives Petri Nets More Computational Power*, Preprint 45, Sektion Mathematik, Humboldt-Universitat zu Berlin, 1982.

4. J. Fris, Grammars with partial ordering of rules, *Information and Control*, 12 (1968), 415 – 425.

5. M. Hack, *Petri Net Languages*, CSG Memo 124, Project MAC, M. I. T. Press, 1975.

6. M. Jantzen, Language Theory of Petri Nets, *LNCS 254*, 1986, 397 – 413.

7. Gh. Păun, On the generative capacity of conditional grammars, *Information and Control*, 43 (1979), 178 – 186.

8. Gh. Păun, *Recent Results and Problems in Formal Language Theory*, Ed. Ştiinţifică şi Enciclopedică, Bucureşti, 1984 (in Romanian).

9. W. Reisig, Place/transition systems, *LNCS 254*, 1986, 117 – 142.

10. A. Salomaa, *Formal Languages*, Academic Press, New York, London, 1973.

11. P. Starke, Free Petri nets languages, *LNCS 64*, 1978, 506 – 515.

12. F. L. Ţiplea, T. Jucan, C. Masalagiu, Conditional Petri net languages, *J. Inf. Process. Cybern. EIK*, 27, 1 (1991), 55 – 66.

13. F. L. Ţiplea, Selective Petri net languages, *Int. J. of Comput. Math.*, 43, 1+2 (1991).

14. F. Urbanek, A note on conditional grammars, *Rev. Roumaine Math. Pures et Appl.*, 28, 4 (1983), 341 – 342.

15. T. Ushio, On controllability of controlled Petri nets, *Control-Theory and Advanced Technology*, 5, 3 (1989), 265 – 275.

16. R. Valk, Self-modifying nets, a natural extension of Petri nets, *LNCS 62*, 1978, 464 – 476.

Applied Semirings: Some Examples Related to Fuzzy Theory and Languages

Dragoş VAIDA

Duke University, Department of Mathematics, USA [1]

Abstract. The note is devoted to examples and related properties concerning the algebraic basis of Fuzzy Theory and the use of formal languages. One presents the algebraic structure based on semirings and the order structure related. The essential examples are 0.3 – 0.5. One emphasizes the role of po-algebraic structures. Different properties of partial hemirings are given.

0.1. The monograph of J. S. Golan devoted to the theory of *semirings* and their applications [12] gives many interesting examples of these applications in Theoretical Computer Science and in Fuzzy Theory. The present note adds some more examples related to (A) *the algebraic basis* of Fuzzy Theory [3], [4], [6], [7], [9], [11], [22], [27], [29], [35], [36] and to (B) Linguistic variables and *formal languages* [14], [30], [32], [33].

In the context of (A) some remarks are inserted on topics which need some clarification [26]. Related to (B) the (partial) *order* defined by *subwords* is considered [16]. Because of (A) *partial functions* and *partial hemirings* are studied [12], [20].

The semirings terminology and fundamentals are from [12] (see also the monograph of W. Kuich and A. Salomaa [15] and [20] for partial semirings and convergence). The fundamentals of Fuzzy Theory are all based on the papers of L. A. Zadeh [30]. The other sources are [12], [15] and [16] for formal languages, [14] for syntactic pattern recognition and [9] and [20] for some results included in this note. New examples and properties appear in connection with the rough sets investigated in [18], [19]. Tolerance relations and iterations of a tolerance operator replacing equivalence from the theory of Z. Pawlak by a similarity, resp. degree of membership, are introduced in [18], [19].

0.2. In this note partial hemirings/semirings are considered for modeling the following three basic examples.

0.3. Example. Let $(E \longrightarrow [0,1], \leq, \vee, \wedge, c, 0, 1)$ be the structure where one has: E – an universe of discourse (a *crisp* set); $[0,1]$ – the real interval;

---

[1]On leave from: University of Bucharest (Romania), Faculty of Mathematics

$\leq$ – the (partial) order defined by $f \leq g$ iff $f(x) \leq g(x)$ for all x in E; $\vee$ – the maximum (of two functions componentwise); $\wedge$ – the minimum; c – the complement with respect to 1; 0 – the function identically 0; 1 – the function identically 1.

One has a bound distributive non-complemented lattice satisfying De Morgan's Laws [31]. It is a po (partially-ordered)-semiring with the following properties: additively idempotent; positive; simple; sum/difference ordered.

0.4. Example. Let $(\mathcal{P}(A^*), \cup, \circ, \emptyset, \{\lambda\}, \leq)$ be the basic structure for languages, where A is a finite non-void alphabet, A^* the set of finite words over A, $\mathcal{P}(A^*)$ is the family of languages over A, the operation $\circ$ is a multiplicative operation associative and distributive over $\cup$ providing the necessary structure of a semiring, $\emptyset$ is the void set/language, $\{\lambda\}$ is the language consisting in the void word and having the role of the identity element with respect to multiplication and where $\leq$ is the order defined by the set inclusion [12], [13], [15], [21].

One can see that we have an upper complete semilattice-ordered semiring with first/least element $\emptyset$ and last/greatest element A^*.

0.5. Example. Let $(PFN(D, D), \sigma, \circ, 0, \leq)$ be the basic structure introduced by E. G. Manes and M. A. Arbib [20] for the algebraic approaches to semantics, where $PFN(D, D)$ is the family of partial function from D (data set) to D $f : D \xrightarrow{0} D$, σ an operation of summation with no arity partially defined for *summable* families of functions, i.e., families of functions with *disjoint* domains, by

$$\sigma(f_i : i \in I)(x) ::= \text{ if } x \in dom(f_i) \text{ then } f_i(x) \text{ else undefined}, \qquad (1)$$

$\circ$ is the functional composition, 0 is the function with $dom(0)$ void, and where $f \leq g$ iff g is an extension of f.

This example is a *po-partially additive hemiring* and it constitutes the motivation for introducing *partial hemirings*. The system $(PFN(D, D), \sigma)$ has been introduced as a *partially additive monoid* [20].

0.6. The operation of finding the inverse – relevant in classical Algebra – appears in the context of many applications as less natural. Fuzzy Theory and Languages Theory and applications make explicit interesting order structures not yet systematically covered (see [5] for a general theory of po-sets).

I.1. The basic idea in the construction of L. A. Zadeh [30], [31] was to built up a *morphism* between two bound distributive lattices:

$$F : (\mathcal{P}(E), \cup, \wedge, ', \emptyset, E) \longrightarrow (E \longrightarrow [0, 1], \vee, \wedge, c, 0, 1), \qquad (2)$$

where one has: $\mathcal{P}(E)$ is the family of the subsets of E; $\cup$ - the set-union; $\wedge$ - dually, the intersection; $'$ - the set-complement. For this morphism, the domain is a Boolean Algebra of sets.

I.2. In the classical construction of Fuzzy Subsets Theory [23], [31], the introduction of the membership function was motivated by the eventual absence of defined criteria or by the intervention of some ambiguity. Different possible extensions have been foreseen: (i) replacing the real interval [0,1] by a suitable *partially ordered set*; (ii) considering *partial functions*. The note examines both topics.

I.3. Several extensions have been proposed as solutions for (i). For example, for Fuzzy Logic H. Rasiowa considers complete *pseudo-boolean algebra* of sets ([20], p. 11-12) and related lattice-theoretic concepts. A very natural framework could be found in the theory of semirings. A main point linking Fuzzy Theory with semirings consists in the applications of the *bounded distributive lattices*: if R is a commutative, idempotent, simple semiring then $(R, +, \cdot)$ is a bounded distributive lattice with the first element 0 and the last element 1 ([12], p. 7); similarly, $(R, \vee, \wedge)$ is a bounded distributive lattice iff it is a commutative idempotent semiring and for all a, b in R (idem),

$$a \wedge (a \vee b) = a = a \vee (a \wedge b). \qquad (3)$$

The semiring $E \longrightarrow [0, 1]$ of all fuzzy subsets of E is a *frame*, i.e., a *complete lattice* in which *meets distribute* over arbitrary *joins*. The semiring $([0, 1], \vee, W)$, where W is a triangular norm is fundamental in Fuzzy Theory and pattern recognition [12], p. 13, [3], while $(\mathbf{R} \cup \{-\infty\}, \vee, +)$ ($\mathbf{R}$ – real numbers) is an additivelly idempotent commutative semiring in modelling the behaviour of industrial processes.

In order to verify De Morgan's Laws and the distributivity in [28], p. 33-34, one uses total order and the proof is done by enumerating all possible cases [31].

I.4. Remark. For many proofs in Fuzzy Theory it is *sufficient* to use *partial* order and the computation rules valid for *l-groups / lo-groups (lattice-ordered groups* (even non-commutative) of the following form (and dual) [2], [9], [10], [20], [24]:

$$x + (a \vee b) + y = (x + a + y) \vee (x + b + y), \qquad (4)$$
$$-(a \vee b) = -a \wedge -b. \qquad (5)$$

It follows

$$1 - (a \vee b) = (1 - a) \vee (1 - b), \qquad (6)$$

which is the equality (11) from [28], p. 33. The distributivity considered in (12) ([28], p. 34) and necessary for obtaining a semiring is a consequence of the above (4), (5) [2], [10], namely,

$$a \vee b = a - (a \wedge b) + b \qquad (7)$$

with applications in valuation theory.

I.5. Example. The following examples illustrate the (implicit) use of *po-algebraic structure* in Fuzzy Theory: (i) The lattice operation $\wedge/\vee$ is the strongest t-norm/weakest t-conorm; The norm/conorm is continuous and not Archimedean; (ii) Any Archimedean t-conorm T provides an example of a po-algebraic structure because $([0,1], T)$ is a po-commutative semigroup with unit 0; (iii) For any t-conorm, one has a residual, in the sense of po-semigroups (similar for t-norms); (iv) The conjugate of a t-norm is defined using a particular case of the given computation rules; (v) The distributivity of the first type of integral (Sugeno) with respect to $\vee$ has a similar nature.

I.6. The previous computation rules (4) and (5) could be applied for obtaining an extension of Theorem 6 quoted in [9] (with a slight correction of the proof).

Proposition. [9] *If R is a fuzzy relation valuated in the interval $[0, 1]$ of a conditionally complete l-group and if R is transitive, then the (negation) relation*

$$R'(x, y) = 1 - R(x, y) \qquad (8)$$

satisfies the ultrametric inequality and the triangular inequality.

Proof. One has

$$R(x, y) \wedge R(y, z) = 1 - (R'(x, y) \vee R'(y, z)) \qquad (9)$$

hence

$$R(x, z) = 1 - R'(x, z) \geq \vee((1 - (R'(x, y) \vee R'(y, z))) \ : \ \text{all } y) \qquad (10)$$

from which one concludes

$$R'(x, z) \leq \wedge((R'(x, y) \vee R'(y, z)) \ : \ \text{all } y). \qquad (11)$$

$$\square$$

I.7. Proposition. *If G is a commutative l-group then for a given u in G and for all a, b in G positive, the set*

$$\{x \in G \mid x \leq u \text{ and } x * a \leq b\}, \qquad (12)$$

where $*$ is the bold intersection of [6], has a last element

$$l = u \wedge (u - a + b). \qquad (13)$$

Moreover, if $a, b \leq u$, then $0 \leq l$.

Proof. (j) If $x * a \leq b$ then $x \leq l$. Indeed, one has $x * a = 0 \vee (a + x - u) \leq b$ and therefore $a + x - u \leq b$ as $0 \leq b$. This gives by commutativity $x \leq u - a + b$. But $x \leq u$ so that $x \leq l$.

(jj) One has $l * a \leq b$. Indeed, by definition, $l * a = 0v(a + l - u)$. But we have

$$a + l - u = a + (u \wedge (u - a + b)) - u = a + (0 \wedge (-a + b)) = a \wedge b. \qquad (14)$$

Therefore,

$$l * a = 0 \vee (a \wedge b) = (0 \vee a) \wedge (0 \vee b) = a \wedge b \leq b \qquad (15)$$

because the lattice of a l-group is distributive. If now $a, b \leq u$ then $0 \leq u - a$ and thus $\leq u - a + b$. $\qquad \square$

The interpretation of l as a *residual* in lattice theory is obvious.

I.8. Using po-algebraic structures one can extend a proposition concerning the entropy of a fuzzy set (see quoted Proposition 1 in [9]). Let us consider a finite set I and a l-group G. One introduces a functional H, $H : (I \longrightarrow G) \longrightarrow G$ for $f : I \longrightarrow G$ defined as the (finite) sum in G

$$H(f) = F(f)(x_1) + \ldots + F(f)(x_n), \qquad (16)$$

where $n = card(I)$ and $F : (I \longrightarrow G) \longrightarrow (I \longrightarrow G)$ is defined such as to verify the valuation identity

$$F(f \vee g) + F(f \wedge g) = F(f) + F(g). \qquad (17)$$

I.9. Proposition. $H(f)$ *is a valuation on the commutative l-group G.*

Proof. From the Definition (16), $H(f \vee g)$ is the sum of the terms $F(f \vee g)(x_i)$ and dually for $H(f \wedge g)$. One has to use (17) to obtain the result without being necessary to assume that $f(x)$ and $g(x)$ are comparable values. $\qquad \square$

I.10. One obtains the envisaged extension by taking

$$F(f)(x) = -Kf(x)ln(x). \qquad (18)$$

By taking

$$d(f) = H(f) + H(f') \quad \text{and} \quad f'(x) = 1 - f(x), \qquad (19)$$

one verifies De Morgan's Laws. A similar extension could be obtained by showing that $d(f)$ is a valuation on a commutative l-group.

I.11. In conclusion, the theory of po-algebraic structures appears as a natural framework for Fuzzy Theory when an order structure is concerned. Computation rules with lattice-ordered groups are identified as a convenient source for different extensions. The structure of a semiring is automatically obtained for the order structure provided by a lattice-ordered group. It is expected that others similar extensions could be obtained.

II.1. Some more limited issues remain still open in Fuzzy Theory and further re-thinking of the fundamentals seem necessary for the following topics: (i) the difficulty of not being meaningful to speak about a specific *element* as belonging to a fuzzy subset; (ii) the absence of a concept of a *finite fuzzy subset* (finite in the conventional sense); (iii) the absence of a concept of a function for domain and range fuzzy subsets [23] – [27].

II.2. For (ii) the solution given in [30], p. 449, based on σ-count requires to have

$$\sigma\text{-}count(A) = f_A(a_1) + \ldots + f_A(a_n), \qquad (20)$$

with the additional convention: the sum may be *rounded* to the nearest integer; the terms whose grade of membership fall below a specified threshold be *excluded*. Consequently, (a) cardinals are not preserved via bijections and (b) the sum (20) might have no sense because by definition f_A is defined on E (and not on a subset of the universe of discourse).

II.3. For (iii) the solution given in [30], p. 611, is the following. If

$$A = b_1/a_1 = \ldots + b_n/a_n, \qquad (21)$$

where A is a finite fuzzy subset of E expressed as above in which a_i are elements and b_i the corresponding degree of membership, i.e., $b_i = f_A(a_i)$, then the image via F of A would be

$$F(A) = b_1/F(a_1) + \ldots + b_n/F(a_n), \qquad (22)$$

i.e., one takes the images of the elements from the domain via F but one preserves the degree of membership, in spite of the fact that we have a new universe of discourse, the range.

III.1. The motivation to associate Formal Languages to Fuzzy Theory comes among others from the following sources: the concept of *linguistic variable* introduced by L. A. Zadeh for its applications to approximate reasoning [30], p. 219 – 327; the applications related to fuzzy geometry, visual languages and *syntactic pattern recognition* in which it is natural to consider fuzzy subsets [12], [14], [29]; the development for theoretical reasons of *fuzzy languages*, automata and semantics [12]. For example in [30], p. 290 – 291, one considers equations with languages without introducing po-semirings [30], p. 201 – 277, as a framework for dealing with fixed points of affine maps associated to the production rules of context-free grammars.

III.2. The solution would be to consider the structure $(\mathcal{P}(A^*), \cup, \circ, \emptyset, , \leq)$. One could proceed to solving equations when it is proved that the multiplicative operation is isotone with respect to inclusion (of sets) and in this case one has a greatest fixed point. If one can prove that this operation is omega-continuous, one obtains the least fixed point.

III.3. Formal Languages theoretical background [11] – [13], [17], [21], may be used for an economic-oriented model specification new with respect to tools – po-partially additive semirings – and to the nature of the problem – (complex) processes of decisional or industrial type featuring *concurrency* of *parallel* activities to some extent similar to *growth* problems. The modeling would be mainly based on the following: (i) a *process* is described as a finite sequence of elementary/basic/atomic operations, i.e., by a *word* over the alphabet constituted by these operations; (ii) *concatenation* describes functional composition of operations and processes; (iii) *summing* up in a *po-partially additive semiring* [20] would describe the *semantics* of the family of different possible processes, i.e., the *sum* will be the expression representing all possible *executions*; (iv) a *shuffle*-type operation would be used to describe *interleaving*, i.e., parallel execution of several processes; (v) the *order structure* introduced would be that based on *subwords* [16], chapter 6 – for describing the relation process – subprocess or on set-inclusion $\subseteq$ for comparing languages, i.e., sets of processes.

In the following, attention is foccussed on subwords order structure. The division ordering is that of [16], p. 105 – 106, used as a source.

III.4. Division is a partial ordering of A^*, which is compatible with the shufle and partial shuffle [16], [21].

It has been noted that A^*, equipped with the division ordering, is neither an inf- nor a sup- semilattice [16], p. 106, (see Figure 6. 1 from [16]).

In the following, the *order* structure is that provided by *division*.

III.5. Remark. Any *interval* $[u, v]$ is finite. Indeed, if w is in the interval then $|u| \leq |w| \leq |v|$. If $|v| = |u| + 1$ then the interval is *prime* and if $|u| = |v|$ then the interval contains only $u = v$.

III.6. Let A be a subset of a poset P and let $U(A)$, dually $L(A)$, be the subset of P consisting in all (common) upper bounds, dually lower bounds, for A. The following concept has to play an important role [9] (see [20] for further references).

III.7. Definition. A multilattice ML is a poset with the following property, and with its dual, for any a, b in ML:

(ML) If there is M such that M is in $U(a, b)$, then there is also M' in ML such that

(ML1) M' is in $L(M)$ and in $U(a, b)$, and

(ML2) M' is minimal with previous properties (ML1) (i.e., if M'' is in $U(a, b)$ and in $L(M')$, then $M'' = M'$).

III.8.   In order to get a fuzzy multilattice, it is now sufficient to use the definitions for $U(A)/L(A)$ from [28] or from an alternative definition provided for a *foset* (fuzzy poset).

III.9. Proposition. $(A^*, \cdot, \{\}, |)$ *with the division ordering* $|$ *is a directed multilattice-ordered monoid with first/least element* λ *such that multiunion and multisection are both non-void and finite.*

Proof. Division is compatible with the product/concatenation of A^* ([16], Proposition 6. 1. 1).

The set A^* is directed. Indeed, by convention one makes the empty/void word λ subword of any word. For any two words u and v in A^* there exists a word w in A^* such that both u and v divide w ([16], Theorem 6. 2. 11).

If now $u, v | w' | w$, then $|u|, |v| \leq |w'| \leq |w|$ and one applies Remark III. 5 showing that there is a finite number of words w' such as the given conditions are satisfied. $\square$

III.10. In [16], p. 108, it is shown that $u|v$ iff there exists a word w such that v belongs to $u \amalg w$ where $\amalg$ is the shuffle (product).

III.11. Definition. ([16], p. 109) A language $L \subseteq A^*$ is called a *shuffle ideal* iff $L = L \amalg A^*$. A shuffle ideal is *principal* iff it is generated by *one* word. The shuffle ideal L is the shuffle ideal *generated* by L.

III.12.   Definition. ([16], p. 107) For a poset $(E, \leq)$ an *ideal* (with respect to the order structure $\leq$) is a subset X of E such that if x is in X and $y \geq x$ then y is in X. The *ideal generated* by X is the *smallest* ideal of E containing X, and is equal to the set of elements of E greater than at least one element of X.

III.13. Because for any $u, v \in A^*, u|v$ iff v belongs to $u \amalg A^*$, the shuffle ideals are exactly the ideals of the ordered set A^* ([16], p. 108 – 109).

III.14. Theorem. ([16], Theorem 6. 1. 2) (Higman) *Any subset of words over a finite alphabet that are not comparable pairwise for the division ordering is finite.*

III.15. Theorem. ([16], Proposition 6.1.3) *The following conditions on a poset E are equivalent:*

(j) *The ideals of E are finitely generated;*

(jj) *The ascending chain condition holds for the ideals of E;*

(jjj) *There exist in E neither an infinite strictly descending sequence nor an infinite set of pairwise incomparable elements;*

(jv) *For every nonempty subset X of E, min X is nonempty and finite.*

III.16. Proposition. ([16], p. 109) *Any shuffle ideal is finitely generated. The Boolean Algebra generated by the principal shuffle ideals is equal to the Boolean Algebra generated by the shuffle ideals.*

III.17. The applications to parallel processing due to A. Mateescu are presented in [21], the algebraic framework being provided by J. S. Golan [13]. One relates formal languages with new families of upper complete semilattice-ordered semirings with first element. Closure properties are obtained. A theory of systems of equations is sketched.

The properties of the semirings involved and of the order structures will be given in a future paper together with more details on this application (see [17]).

IV.1. It is natural (even necessary, in accordance with the background of the theory) to consider in Fuzzy Theory *partial functions*. These might appear in evaluations with incomplete data or in fuzzy databases with unspecified entries. In the model provided by E. G. Manes and M. A. Arbib and presented in a more formalized way with proofs in [20] one considers: (i) *summing* up functions iff the domains are *disjoint*: (ii) the order relation $f \leq \cdot\; g$ with $\leq \cdot$ = ldf = less defined.

This would provide a *po-partially additive semiring*. Consequently, the study of *partial functions* would contribute with two new ideas: (i) the possibility to have *addition* as a *partial* operation; an alternative order structure for functions.

IV.2. Definition. A *partial hemiring* $(R, +, \cdot, 0)$ is a nonempty set R on which operations of addition and multiplication have been defined such that the following conditions are satisfied:

(1) $(R, +, 0)$ is a commutative *partial monoid*, in the sense that the operation $+$ is partial, the existence of a member of the axioms for commutativity or associativity implying the existence of the other and their equality, 0 being the identity element;

(2) $(R, \cdot)$ is a semigroup;

(3) Multiplication distributes over addition from either side provided that this addition is possible (terms are summable);

(4) $0r = 0 = r0$, for all r in R.

A *partially additive hemiring* is the structure $(R, sigm, \cdot, 0)$ such that $(R, sigm, 0)$ is a partially additive monoid, in the sense of [20], verifying (2), (3) for all summable family of terms and (4).

The existence of 0 is a consequence. The corresponding terminology for semirings is introduced in the usual way (see [12], p. 1). Partial semirings were introduced for modelling the algebraic approach of program semantics [20].

IV.3. Definition. A *po-partial hemiring* (partially-ordered partial hemiring) is a partial hemiring such that $(R, \leq)$ is a po-set and for all r, r' and r'' in R with $r' \leq r''$ the following conditions are satisfied:

(1) if $r + r''$ exists in R then $r + r'$ exists in R and one has $r + r' \leq r + r''$;

(2) if $r \geq 0$ then $rr' \leq rr''$ and $r'r \leq r''r$.

IV.4. The following propositions are extensions of the corresponding propositions from J. S. Golan [12]. The proof is given when there is a new element to consider due to the fact that the addition is partial. One should note [1] for an algebraic and order structure of the semigroup of partial functions (in a further version of this note).

IV.5. Proposition. ([12], Proposition (18.14)) *If a is an element of a partially-ordered partial hemiring R satisfying $a \leq b$ for all b in R then a is in $I(R)$ (the set of additively idempotent elements of R).*

Proof. If $a \leq 0$ then $a + c$ exists for any $c \in R$. $\qquad\square$

IV.6. Proposition. ([12], Proposition (18.15)) *Positive partially-ordered hemirings are zerosumfree.*

IV.7. Proposition. ([12], Proposition (18.16)) *If R is a positive partially-ordered Gel'fand partial semiring then for each a, b in R there exist units u, v in $U(R)$ such that $ab \leq au$ and $ab \leq vb$.*

IV.8. Proposition. ([12], Proposition (18.17)) *If $a_1, \ldots, a_n$ are elements of a positive simple partial semiring R and if $1 \leq h < i \leq n$ are indices such that $a_h a_i = 0$ then $a_1 \ldots a_n = 0$.*

Proof. Because R is positive $1 \geq 0$. Because $1 + r$ exists for any $r \in R$ by definition, one has $1 = 1 + r \geq r \geq 0$ showing that $R = [0, 1]$.

Let $b = a_1 \ldots a_h$ and let $c = a_{h+1} \ldots a_i$. One has $0 \leq b \leq a_h$ and $0 \leq c \leq a_i$. This implies $bc = 0$.

IV.9. Proposition. ([12], Proposition (18.18)) *If R is an (additively) idempotent partial hemiring then R is partially-ordered by the relation $a \leq b$ iff $a + b = b$. Under this relation, R is positive and R is a join multilattice with $a \vee b = a + b$. Moreover, if R is a partial semiring and if a, b are in $U(R)$ then $a \geq b$ iff $1/a \leq 1/b$.*

Proof. If $a \leq b$ and $b \leq c$ then $a+b = b$ and $b+c = c$. One has $(a+b)+c = c$ as the sum $b+c$ exists and is c. By associativity one has that $a+(b+c)$ exists and is c. Therefore, R is a poset.

If $r' \leq r''$ then $r' + r'' = r''$. If $r + r''$ exists then $r + r'$ exists and thus we have a po-partial semiring.

The existence of c with $a, b \leq c$ is equivalent with the existence of the sum $a + b$. Indeed, if $a + b$ exists then we take $c = a + b$. If $a, b \leq c$ then $a + c = c$ and $b + c = c$. Because R is idempotent, $a + b$ exists and $a + b \leq c$ showing that in this case $a + b$ is the least upper bound. $\qquad\square$

IV.10. Proposition. ([12], Proposition (18.24)) *Every zerosumfree division partial semiring is difference ordered.*

Proof. For a and b in R, $a \leq b$ iff there exists c in R such that $a + c = b$. Clearly, this is an order compatible with the partial semiring structure. One has to prove that if $a \leq b \leq a$ then $a = b$.

Notation. In a partial hemiring, let $a \tilde{<} b$ iff there is c such that $b = a + c$.

The following lemma is used.

IV.11. Lemma. *Let R be a partial semiring with the following properties: R is zerosumfree; If $1 = 1 + a$ and a is not 0 then $1/a$ exists; If $a \tilde{<} b$ and $b \tilde{<} a$ with a, b different from zero then $1/a$ and $1/b$ exist. Under these conditions, R is difference ordered by $\tilde{<}$.*

Proof. If $a \tilde{<} b$ then $b = a + c$ and if $b \tilde{<} a$ then $a = b + d$. If $a = 0$ then $b + d = 0$ and therefore $b = 0$ and similarly for $b = 0$. Suppose a and b are not zero and thus $a' = 1/a$ and $b' = 1/b$ exist. One has $a'b = 1 + a'c$ and $1 = a'b + a'd$ or $a'b = 1 + h$ and $1 = a'b + k$. Since $c + d$ exists it follows that $h + k$ exists. If $h + k = 0$ then $c = d = 0$. As $1 = (1 + h) + k$ it follows that $h + k$ exists and $1 + h + k = 1$. Because $h + k$ is not zero, $l = 1/(h + k)$ exists and

$$1 = l(h + k) = lk + lh = lk + (1 + h + k)lh = lk + lh + h = 1 + h = a'b. \qquad (23)$$

$$\square$$

IV.12. Proposition. ([12], Proposition (18.28)) *If R is an additively idempotent partially-ordered partial semiring satisfying $0 < 1$ then $S = \{r \in R \mid 0 \leq r \leq 1\}$ is a partial subsemiring of R.*

IV.13. Proposition. ([12], Proposition (18.30)) *The following conditions on a partial hemiring are equivalent:*

(1) R is difference ordered;

(2) If a, b, c are elements of R satisfying $a = a + b + c$ then $u = u + b$.

Proof. If (2) holds one defines $a \tilde{<} b$ iff $b = a + c$. If a and b are such that $b = a + c$ and $a = b + d$ then $a = a + c + d$ and therefore $a = a + c$ proving that $a = b$. $\qquad\square$

IV.14. Proposition. ([12], Corollary (18.31)) *If R is a nonzero difference-ordered partial hemiring then $Z(R)$ is a strong ideal of R.*

IV.15. Proposition. ([12], Proposition 9 (18.32)) *An ideal I of a difference-ordered partial hemiring R is strong iff $a \leq b$ and b in I imply that a is in I.*

IV.16. Proposition. ([12], Proposition (18.34)) *If R is a difference-ordered Gel'fand partial semiring and $d \geq c$, c in $U(R)$, then d is in $U(R)$.*

IV.17. Remark. ([15], p. 87, 5.4) If $(R, \leq')$ is a partially-ordered positive idempotent partial hemiring then $a \leq' b$ iff $a+b = b$. If $a \leq' b$ then $a+b$ exists because $b + b$ exists and $a + b \leq' b$. But $b \leq' a + b$. If $a + b = b$ then $b \geq' a$.

IV.18. We consider partially-ordered positive partial hemirings with the following ortogonality property: (O) for a, b in R such that $a+b$ exist if $c \leq a, b$ then $c = 0$. If R is such a hemiring then $a \tilde{<} b$ previously considered is an order. Let $a \tilde{<} b$ and $b \tilde{<} a$, i.e., $b = a + a'$ and $a = b + b'$. One has $a = a + c$ with $c = a' + b'$. We have $c \tilde{<} a$ and $c \tilde{<} c$. Since $a + c$ exists, because of (O) $c = 0$.

IV.19. Proposition. ([20], p. 203 – 204, 4.5, 4.6) *If R is a partially additive semiring then the set of sequences possesing lim is a set of convergent sequences in the sense of [15], p. 11, for which the condition (D2)(i) is the following condition:*

$\quad$ *(D2)(i) If two sequences are summable then their sum is in D.* $\qquad$ (24)

IV.20. Definition. ([20], Definition 4.7, [15], p. 11) Let D be a set of convergent sequences in a semiring R. A *mapping lim* $: D \longrightarrow P(R)$ satisfying the following conditions (lim1) - (lim3):

- (lim1) $\quad$ 1 is in $lim(e)$;

- (lim2)(i) $\quad$ If a and b are in D and if $a+b$ exists then $lim(a) + lim(b)$ is included in $lim(a + b)$;

- $\quad$ (ii) $\quad$ If a is in D and r is in R then $r\, lim(a)$ is included in $lim(ra)$ and $(lim(a))r$ is included in $lim(ar)$;

- (lim3) $\quad$ If a is in D and r in R then $lim(a)$ is included in $lim(a_n)$

is called a *limit function* (on D).

IV.21. Proposition. ([20], p. 204, 4.8) *The mapping lim is a limit function.*

References

1. M. Anderson, Partially ordered semigroups with an abundance of principal idempotents, in *Ordered Algebraic Structures* (W. B. Powell, C. Tsinakis, eds.), M. Dekker, New York, 1985, *Lecture Notes in Pure and Applied Mathematics*, vol. 99.

2. A. Bigard, K. Keimel, S. Wolfenstein, *Groupes et Anneaux Reticules*, Springer-Verlag, Berlin, Heidelberg, 1977, *Lecture Notes in Mathematics*, vol. 608 (A. Dold, B. Eckmann, eds.).

3. D. Butnariu, E. P. Klement, *Triangular Norm-Based Measures and Games with Fuzzy Coalitions*, Kluwer, Dordrecht, 1993.

4. R. A. Cuninghame-Green, Minimax algebra and applications, *Fuzzy Sets and Systems*, 41 (1991), 251 – 267.

5. B. A. Davey, H. A. Priestley, *Introduction to Lattices and Order*, Cambridge University Press, Cambridge, 1990.

6. D. Dubois, H. Prade, *Fuzzy Sets and Systems: Theory and Applications*, Academic Press, New York, 1980.

7. D. Dubois, H. Prade, *Possibility Theory: An Approach to Computerized Processing of Uncertainty*, Plenum, New York, 1988.

8. M. Fedrizzi, J. Kacprzyk, J. L. Verdegay, A survey of fuzzy optimization and mathematical programming, in *Interactive Fuzzy Optimization* (M. Fedrizi, J. Kacprzuk, M. Roubens, eds.), Springer-Verlag, Berlin, Heidelberg, 1991, 15 – 28.

9. M. Fedrizzi, D. Vaida, Po-algebraic structures in Fuzzy Theory and parallel decisions processes, *Proceedings CIFT'94*, University of Trento (Italy), June 1-3, 1994.

10. A. M. W. Glass, W. C. Holland, Eds., *Lattice-Ordered Groups – Advances and Techniques*, Kluwer, Dordrecht, 1989.

11. J. A. Goguen Jr., Concept representation in natural and artificial languages: Axioms, extensions and applications for fuzzy sets, in *Fuzzy Reasoning and its Applications* (E. H. Mamdani, R. R. Gaines, eds.), Academic Press, London, New York, 1981, 67 – 115.

12. J. S. Golan, *The Theory of Semirings with Applications in Mathematics and Theoretical Computer Science*, Longman Scientific & Technical, Harlow Essex, 1992, *Pitman Monographs and Surveys in Pure and Applied Mathematics 54*.

13. J. S. Golan, Semirings of formal series over hypermonoids: Some interesting cases, *Preprint*, Preliminary version, 1993.

14. R. C. Gonzalez, M. G. Thomason, *Syntactic Pattern Recognition – An Introduction*, Addison-Wesley Publ. Comp., Reading Mass., 1978.

15. W. Kuich, A. Salomaa, *Semirings, Automata, Languages*, Springer-Verlag, Berlin, 1986, *EATCS Monographs on Theoretical Computer Science*, vol. 5.

16. M. Lothaire, *Combinatorics of Words*, Addison-Wesley Publ. Comp., Reading Mass., 1983.

17. Z. Manna, A. Pnueli, *The Temporal Logic of Reactive and Concurrent Systems. Specification*, Springer-Verlag, New York, 1992.

18. S. Marcus, Tolerance rough sets, Cech topologies, learning processes, *ICS Research Report* 51 (1993), Institute of Computer Science, Warsaw Univ. of Technology, to appear in *Bulletin of the Polish Academy of Science, Mathematics*.

19. S. Marcus, Imprecission, between uniformity and variety: the conjugate pairs, *ICS Research Report* 52 (1993), Institute of Computer Science, Warsaw Univ. of Technology, to appear in *The World of Signs* (J. J. Jadacki, W. Strawinski, eds.), The Publ. House of the Academy of Science, Warsaw, 1994.

20. A. Mateescu, D. Vaida, *Discrete Mathematical Structures. Applications*, Romanian Academy Publ. House, 1989 (in Romanian).

21. A. Mateescu, D. Vaida, Towards a unified theory of sequential, parallel and semi-parallel processes, *Preprint*, University of Turku and Duke University, 1993 (In cooperation with J. S. Golan, see [13]).

22. H. Rasiowa, *Toward fuzzy logic*, in [35], p. 5 – 25.

23. A. Rosenfeld, Fuzzy mathematics: Some basic concepts, in [29], p. 1 – 8.

24. F. A. Smith, A structure theory for a class of lattice ordered semirings, *Fund. Math.*, 59 (1966), 49 – 64.

25. D. E. Tamir, Cao Zhi-Qiang, A. Kandel, J. L. Mott, An axiomatic approach to fuzzy set theory, *Information Sciences*, 52 (1990), 75 – 83.

26. H. Toth, From fuzzy-set theory to fuzzy-set theory: some critical remarks on existing concepts, *Fuzzy Sets and Systems*, 23 (1987), 219 – 237.

27. H. Toth, Categorial properties of f-set theory, *Fuzzy Sets and Systems*, 33 (1989), 99 – 109.

28. P. Venugoplan, Fuzzy ordered sets, *Fuzzy Sets and Systems*, 46 (1992), 221 – 226.

29. P. P. Wang, Ed., *Advances in Fuzzy Theory and Technology* (Vol. 1), Bookwrights Press, Durham N. C., 1993.

30. R. R. Yager, S. Ovchinnicov, R. M. Tong, H. T. Nguyen, Eds., *Fuzzy Sets and Applications: Selected Papers by L. A. Zadeh* (A Wiley - Interscience Publication), John Wiley & Sons, New York, 1987.

31. L. A. Zadeh, Fuzzy sets, *Information and Control*, 8 (1965), 338 – 353, and in [30], p. 29 – 44.

32. L. A. Zadeh, The concept of a linguistic variable and its applications to approximate reasoning, Parts 1 and 2, *Information Sciences*, 8 (1975), 199 – 249; 301 – 357, and in [30], p. 219 – 327.

33. L. A. Zadeh, A computational approach to fuzzy quantifiers in natural language, *Comp. and Maths. with Appls.*, 9 (1983), 149 - -184, and in [30], p. 569 – 613.

34. L. A. Zadeh, Syllogistic reasoning in fuzzy logic and its application to usuality and reasoning with dispositions, *IEEE Trans. Systems, Man, and Cybernetics*, SMC-15 (1985), 754 – 763, and in [30], p. 443 – 466.

35. L. A. Zadeh, J. Kacprzyk, Eds., *Fuzzy Logic for the Management of Uncertainty*, John Wiley & Sons, New York, 1992.

36. H.-J. Zimmermann, Ed., *EUFIT'93 - First European Congress on Fuzzy and Intelligent Technologies*, Aachen, Germany, September 7-10, 1993 Proceedings, vol. 1-3, Augustinus Buchhandlung, Aachen, 1993.

Grammars, Grammar Systems,
and GSM Mappings with Valences

Sorina VICOLOV–DUMITRESCU

Faculty of Mathematics, University of Bucharest

Str. Academiei 14, 70109 Bucureşti, Romania

Abstract. In this paper we study a series of questions about valence variants of Chomsky grammars, of grammar systems and of gsm mappings. Namely, the closure properties of the families of languages generated by valence grammars and valence grammar systems are investigated, an open problem about the valence gsm's is solved and some results about synchronized multihead valence gsm's are proved.

1. Introduction

The necessity of increasing the power of Chomsky grammars and of gsm mappings has motivated the introduction of new features to them. One possibility is to consider valences assigned to rewriting rules, another one is to consider grammar systems, with the components cooperating in generating a common language; valences can be assigned also to rules in grammar systems.

For a grammar or a gsm where each rule has a valence – an element of a given group T – the valence of a derivation is the composition of the valences of all used rules with respect to the operation of the group T.

Imposing the condition that a generated string must have the valence of its derivation equal to the identity of the group T, the valence grammars and valence gsm's were defined in [7], [6], respectively. If T is the group of the integer (positive rational) numbers $\mathbf{Z}$ ($\mathbf{Q}_+$), the valences are called *additive* (*multiplicative*, respectively). The main results about additive and multiplicative valence grammars are provided in [3]. In [5] and [9] the case of valences in $\mathbf{Z}^n$ (the group of the n-tuples of integers) are investigated.

In [6] the synchronized multihead valence gsm's were introduced, by considering a finite number of reading-rewriting heads working in parallel, on consecutive segments of the input string, assigning a valence to each rule and imposing the condition for the work to be synchronized (all heads have to terminate the translation at the same moment).

The idea of the cooperating distributed grammar systems with registers may be considered a generalization of the concept of valence grammars. The cooperation distributed grammar systems were introduced in [1] and their basic idea can be explained as follows: more grammars are working, in turn, one at each moment, on a common sentential form; the process continues until a terminal string is obtained. In [4] the cooperating distributed grammar systems with registers were defined, by adding one or two registers to the system. A derivation step consists of an application of a rule to the sentential form and a change of the registers by values (valences) associated to the applied rule. The start and stop condition for the work of a grammar of the system is the emptiness of the register or of a fixed register, emptiness meaning that the register contains the identity with respect to the operation used in the change of the registers.

Here we continue the study of the valence variants of generative mechanisms mentioned above. In Section 2 we investigate the closure properties of the families of languages generated by valence grammars (with context-free and regular rules) with valences in $\mathbf{Z}^n, n \geq 1$ (we prove that all these families are full semi-AFL's). Section 3 contains the study of the closure properties of the families of languages generated by the cooperating distributed grammar systems with registers (we show that for the right-linear case these families are full AFL's and for the context-free case they are full semi-AFL's). In Section 4 we solve an open problem formulated in [6] about the valence gsm mappings. Namely, we establish that the hierarchies obtained by iterating additive valence gsm mappings on regular or context-free languages are infinite. Section 5 contains several results about the synchronized multihead valence gsm's, especially concerning the comparison of their power and the power of the valence gsm's. The composition of synchronized multihead valence gsm's is also investigated. In each of these sections we give first the necessary definitions and then the obtained results.

For the basic definitions in formal language theory we refer the reader to [8]; [2] can be used for details concerning grammar systems. Our conventions are as follows. For a finite alphabet V, V^* (V^+) denotes the free monoid (semigroup, respectively) generated by V under the operation of concatenation; λ denotes the null element ($V^+ = V^* - \{\lambda\}$). The elements of V^* are called strings or words. The length of a string $x \in V^*$ is denoted $|x|$. For a letter $b \in V$ and a string $x \in V^*$, $|x|_b$ denotes the number of the occurrences of b in x. $\mathcal{L}_i, i = 0, 1, 2, 3$, are the families of languages in Chomsky hierarchy and $\mathcal{M}$ is the family of matrix languages generated by grammars with arbitrary context-free rules and without appearance checking.

In what follows two languages will be considered equal if they differ only by the null string λ.

2. Closure properties (I)

Here we prove some closure properties of the families of languages generated by the valence grammars of type 2 and 3 with valences in $\mathbf{Z}^n$ ($\mathbf{Z}^n$ is the set of the n-tuples of integers), which are similar to those of the families of additive valence languages, investigated in [7]. Finally we conclude that these families are full semi-AFL′s.

Definition 2.1. A *valence grammar* is a system $G = (V_N, V_T, S, P, v)$, where $G' = (V_N, V_T, S, P)$ is a usual Chomsky grammar and $v : P \longrightarrow T$ is a mapping, $(T, \circ, e)$ being a given group (″$\circ$″ is the operation of this group and e is its identity).

For a derivation

$$D : S \Longrightarrow^{r_1} w_1 \Longrightarrow^{r_2} w_2 \Longrightarrow^{r_3} \ldots \Longrightarrow^{r_n} w_n$$

in G' we define

$$v(D) = v(r_1) \circ v(r_2) \circ \ldots \circ v(r_n).$$

The language generated by G is

$$L(G) = \{x \in V_T^* \mid D : S \Longrightarrow^* x \text{ in } G' \text{ and } v(D) = e\}.$$

If $(T, \circ, e) = (\mathbf{Z}, +, 0)$ $((T, \circ, e) = (\mathbf{Q}_+, \cdot, 1)$, respectively), then G is called an additive (multiplicative) valence grammar.

We denote by $\mathcal{V}_i^a$ ($\mathcal{V}_i^m$, respectively) the family of languages generated by additive (multiplicative) valence grammars of type $i, i = 0, 1, 2, 3$. (Note that the grammars are allowed to contain λ-rules.)

The following results are proved in [7]:

$$\text{(1)} \qquad \mathcal{L}_0 = \mathcal{V}_0^a = \mathcal{V}_0^m, \ \mathcal{L}_1 \subseteq \mathcal{V}_1^a \subseteq \mathcal{V}_1^m,$$
$$\text{(2)} \qquad \mathcal{L}_i \subset \mathcal{V}_i^a \subset \mathcal{V}_i^m \subset \mathcal{M}, i = 2, 3, \text{ strict inclusions.}$$

Denote by $\mathcal{V}_i^a(n)$ the family of languages generated by valence grammars of type i with $(T, \circ, e) = (\mathbf{Z}^n, +, (0, \ldots, 0))$, for $n \geq 1$, $i = 2, 3$. Then, for $i = 2, 3$ we obtain a hierarchy which lies in between $\mathcal{V}_i^a$ and $\mathcal{V}_i^m$, since $\mathcal{V}_i^a = \mathcal{V}_i^a(1)$, $\mathcal{V}_i^a(n) \subseteq \mathcal{V}_i^a(n+1)$, for $n \geq 1$, and $\bigcup_{n \geq 1} \mathcal{V}_i^a(n) = \mathcal{V}_i^m$ [5]. Moreover, in [9] it is shown that this hierarchy is infinite (the inclusions $\mathcal{V}_i^a(n) \subset \mathcal{V}_i^a(n+1), n \geq 1$, $i = 2, 3$, are proper).

Lemma 2.2. *For $n \geq 1$, the families $\mathcal{V}_3^a(n)$ are closed under union, mirror image, intersection with regular languages, substitution by regular languages, concatenation with regular languages, but they are not closed under concatenation, Kleene +, intersection, substitution and complement.*

Proof. For $n = 1$ these assertions are known from [7]. The proof for the positive closure properties of $\mathcal{V}_3^a$ also holds for $\mathcal{V}_3^a(n), n \geq 2$, replacing the valences in $\mathbf{Z}$ with valences in $\mathbf{Z}^n$.

Consider now the languages $L_n = \{a^m b^m \mid m \geq 1\}^n, n \geq 1$. We have $L_n \in \mathcal{V}_3^a(n)$ [9] and $L_1 \in \mathcal{V}_3^a(n)$ (since $\mathcal{V}_3^a(1) \subseteq \mathcal{V}_3^a(n)$). But $L_1 L_n \notin \mathcal{V}_3^a(n)$ [9] and $L_1^* \notin \mathcal{V}_3^a(n)$ (since $L_1^* \notin \mathcal{V}_3^m$ [7] and $\mathcal{V}_3^a(n) \subset \mathcal{V}_3^m$). We conclude that $\mathcal{V}_3^a(n)$ are not closed under concatenation and Kleene closure.

Let $M = L_1\{c\}\{a,b\}^*, N = \{a,b\}^*\{c\}L_n$. Since the families $\mathcal{V}_3^a(n)$ are closed under concatenation by regular languages, we have $M, N \in \mathcal{V}_3^a(n)$. Obviously, $M \cap N = L_1\{c\}L_n$. As $\mathcal{V}_3^a(n)$ are closed under homomorphisms, and $L_1 L_n \notin \mathcal{V}_3^a(n)$, it follows that $M \cap N \notin \mathcal{V}_3^a(n)$. Thus we obtain the nonclosure under intersection.

The nonclosure under substitution follows from $\{ab\} \in \mathcal{V}_3^a(n)$ and $L_1 L_n \notin \mathcal{V}_3^a(n)$.

As the families $\mathcal{V}_3^a(n)$ are closed under union and they are not closed under intersection, it follows that they are not closed under complement.   □

Lemma 2.3. *For $n \geq 1$, the families $\mathcal{V}_2^a(n)$ are closed under union, mirror image, intersection with regular languages, substitution by context-free languages and concatenation with context-free languages, but they are not closed under concatenation, Kleene $+$, intersection, substitution and complement.*

Proof. For $n = 1$ the assertions were proved in [7] ($\mathcal{V}_2^a(1) = \mathcal{V}_2^a$). The proof of the positive closure properties of $\mathcal{V}_2^a$ also holds for $\mathcal{V}_2^a(n), n \geq 2$, replacing the valences in $\mathbf{Z}$ by valences in $\mathbf{Z}^n$. The proof of the nonclosure properties can be done in a way similar to that followed for the regular case, considering the languages $L_n = \{a^m b^m c^m \mid m \geq 1\}^n$, for $n \geq 1$, and using the facts that $L_1^* \notin \mathcal{V}_2^m$ [7], $L_n \in \mathcal{V}_2^a(n)$, $L_1 L_n \notin \mathcal{V}_2^a(n)$ [9].   □

Theorem 2.4. *The families $\mathcal{V}_i^a(n)$ are full semi-AFL's, for $i = 2, 3$ and $n \geq 1$.*

Proof. From Lemmas 2.2 and 2.3 it follows that these families are closed under intersection with regular languages, union with regular languages, substitution with regular λ-free languages and restricted homomorphisms, which implies the closure under inverse homomorphisms. Also the closure under arbitrary homomorphisms follows from the closure under substitution by regular or context-free languages. Using again the lemmas above we conclude that the families $\mathcal{V}_i^a(n)$, $i = 2, 3$ and $n \geq 1$, are full semi-AFL's.   □

3. Closure properties (II)

Here we investigate the closure properties of the families of languages generated by the cooperating distributed grammar systems with registers. We show that some of these families are full AFL's, other families are full semi-AFL's.

Definition 3.1. A *cooperating distributed grammar system* (CD grammar system, for short), Γ is a $(3 + r)$-tuple

$$\Gamma = (V_N, V_T, P_1, P_2, \ldots, P_r, S),$$

where V_N and V_T are disjoint finite non-empty sets, $S \in V_N$, and for $1 \leq i \leq r$, P_i is a finte subset of rewriting rules over $V_N \cup V_T$ (hence subsetes of $V_N \times (V_N \cup V_T)^*$).

Let $V_\Gamma = V_N \cup V_T$. The sets $P_1, \ldots, P_r$ are called the components of Γ.

Definition 3.2. Let Γ be a CD grammar system as in Definition 3.1, $x, y \in V_\Gamma^*$ and $P \in \{P_1, \ldots, P_r\}$. Then we write

$$x \Longrightarrow_P^* y \quad \text{iff} \quad x = y \text{ or there are } k \geq 1, x_1, x_2, \ldots, x_{k-1} \in V_\Gamma^*,$$
$$\text{and the rules } p_1, p_2, \ldots, p_k \in P \text{ such that}$$
$$x \Longrightarrow_{p_1} x_1 \Longrightarrow_{p_2} x_2 \Longrightarrow_{p_3} \cdots \Longrightarrow_{p_{k-1}} x_{k-1} \Longrightarrow_{p_k} y.$$

Definition 3.3. (i) A CD grammar system *with an additive register* is a construct

$$\Gamma = (V_N, V_T, P_1, \ldots, P_r, v_1, \ldots, v_r, S),$$

where $V_N, V_T, P_1, \ldots, P_r, S$ are as in Definition 3.1 and, for $1 \leq i \leq r$, $v_i : P_i \longrightarrow \mathbf{Z}$ is a mapping.

(ii) Let $(x, \alpha), (y, \beta) \in V_\Gamma^* \times \mathbf{Z}, i\{\in 1, 2, \ldots, r\}, p \in P_i$. Then we write $(x, \alpha) \Longrightarrow_p (y, \beta)$ iff $x = x_1 A x_2, y = x_1 w x_2$, for $p = A \to w$ and $\beta = \alpha + v_i(p)$, where $x_1, x_2 \subset V_\Gamma^*$.

(iii) The language $L(\Gamma)$ generated by Γ is defined as

$$L(\Gamma) = \{z \in V_T^* \mid \text{ there are } x_1, \ldots, x_{n-1} \in V_\Gamma^*$$
$$\text{and components } H_1, \ldots, H_n \text{ of } \Gamma \text{ such that}$$
$$(S, 0) \Longrightarrow_{H_1}^* (x_1, 0) \Longrightarrow_{H_2}^* (x_2, 0) \Longrightarrow_{H_3}^* \cdots$$
$$\cdots \Longrightarrow_{H_{n-1}}^* (x_{n-1}, 0) \Longrightarrow_{H_n}^* (z, 0)\}.$$

(iv) A CD grammar system with a multiplicative register is a construct Γ as in (i) but, for $1 \leq i \leq r$, the mapping v_i maps P_i into $\mathbf{Q}_+$; the derivation process and the language generated are defined as in (ii) and (iii) but we have to replace the addition by multiplication and 0 by 1.

Definition 3.4. (i) A CD grammar system *with two additive registers* is a construct

$$\Gamma = (V_N, V_T, P_1, \ldots, P_r, v_1, \ldots, v_r, u_1, \ldots, u_r, S),$$

where $V_N, V_T, P_1, \ldots, P_r, S$ are defined as in Definition 3.1 and, for $1 \leq i \leq r$, $v_i : P_i \longrightarrow \mathbf{Z}$, and $u_i : P_i \longrightarrow \mathbf{Z}$ are mappings.

(ii) For $(x, \alpha, \alpha'), (y, \beta, \beta') \in V_\Gamma^* \times \mathbf{Z} \times \mathbf{Z}, p \in P_i$, for some $i \in \{1, 2, \ldots, r\}$, we write $(x, \alpha, \alpha') \Longrightarrow_p (y, \beta, \beta')$ iff $x = x_1 A x_2, y = x_1 w x_2, p = A \to w, \beta = \alpha + v_i(p)$ and $\beta' = \alpha' + u_i(p)$, where $x_1, x_2 \in V_\Gamma^*$.

(iii) The language $L(\Gamma)$ generated by Γ is defined as

$$L(\Gamma) = \{z \in V_T^* \mid \text{there are } x_1, \ldots x_{n-1} \in V_\Gamma^*,$$
$$\text{and components } H_1, \ldots, H_n \text{ such that}$$
$$(S, 0, 0) \Longrightarrow_{H_1}^* (x_1, 0, \beta_1) \models (x_1, \beta_1, 0) \Longrightarrow_{H_2}^* (x_2, 0, \beta_2)$$
$$\models (x_2, \beta_2, 0) \Longrightarrow_{H_3}^* \cdots \Longrightarrow_{H_{n-1}}^* (x_{n-1}, 0, \beta_{n-1}) \models$$
$$\models (x_{n-1}, \beta_{n-1}, 0) \Longrightarrow_{H_n}^* (z, 0, 0)\}.$$

(iv) In order to define a CD grammar system with two multiplicative registers we change the mappings v_i, u_i to mappings from P_i to $\mathbf{Q}_+$, addition to multiplication, and 0 to 1.

We note that the CD grammar systems with one register and one component are, in fact, additive or multiplicative valence grammars.

Denote by xCD_i^a (xCD_i^m, respectively), for $x \in \{1, 2\}, i \in \{2, 3\}$, the family of languages generated by the CD grammar systems with x additive (multiplicative) registers and with all components containing only rules of type i – right-linear rules for $i = 3$, i.e. rules of the form $A \to xB$ or $A \to x$, $A, B \in V_N, x \in V_T^*$, and context-free rules for $i = 2$.

The following relations were proved in [3].

$$(1) \qquad \mathcal{V}_3^\alpha \subset 1CD_3^\alpha \subset 2CD_3^\alpha, \; \alpha \in \{a, m\},$$
$$(2) \qquad \mathcal{V}_2^\alpha \subset 1CD_2^\alpha \subseteq 2CD_2^\alpha, \; \alpha \in \{a, m\},$$
$$(3) \qquad 1CD_3^a \subset 1CD_3^m,$$
$$(4) \qquad 1CD_2^a \subseteq 1CD_2^m,$$
$$(5) \qquad 2CD_i^a \subseteq 2CD_i^m, \; i = 2, 3.$$

Lemma 3.5. (i) *The families xCD_3^α, for $x \in \{1, 2\}, \alpha \in \{a, m\}$, are closed under union, concatenation, Kleene +, intersection with regular languages and substitution with regular languages.*

(ii) *The family $1CD_3^\alpha$ is not closed under intersection, substitution and complement.*

Proof. (i) It is enough to prove the assertion for the family $2CD_3^a$ only (the multiplicative case is similar to the additive one; the constructions which follow can be adapted for the family $1CD_3^a$ by suppressing the second register).

First we shall prove the closure under union and concatenation. Consider two CD grammar systems with two registers and right-linear rules: $\Gamma_i = (V_{N,i}, V_{T,i}, P_{1,i}, \ldots, P_{r_i,i}, v_{1,i}, \ldots, v_{r_i,i}, u_{1,i}, \ldots, u_{r_i,i}, S_i), i = 1, 2$. We may suppose that $V_{\Gamma_1} \cap V_{N,2} = \emptyset$ and $V_{N,1} \cap V_{\Gamma_2} = \emptyset$. We construct two new CD grammar systems with two registers and right-linear rules

$$\begin{aligned}
\Gamma \;=\;& (V_N, V_T, P_0, P_{1,1}, \ldots, P_{r_1,1}, P_{1,2}, \ldots, P_{r_2,2}, \\
& v_0, v_{1,1}, \ldots, v_{r_1,1}, v_{1,2}, \ldots, v_{r_2,2}, u_0, u_{1,1}, \ldots, u_{r_1,1}, u_{1,2}, \ldots, u_{r_2,2}, S), \\
\Gamma' \;=\;& (V_N, V_T, P_0', P_{1,1}', \ldots, P_{r_1,1}', P_{1,2}, \ldots, P_{r_2,2}, \\
& v_0', v_{1,1}', \ldots, v_{r_1,1}', v_{1,2}, \ldots, v_{r_2,2}, u_0', u_{1,1}', \ldots, u_{r_1,1}', u_{1,2}, \ldots, u_{r_2,2}, S_1),
\end{aligned}$$

where

$$\begin{aligned}
V_N \;=\;& V_{N,1} \cup V_{N,2} \cup \{S\}, \; S \notin V_{N,1} \cup V_{N,2}, \\
V_T \;=\;& V_{T,1} \cup V_{T,2}, \\
P_0 \;=\;& \{S \to S_1, S \to S_2\}, \; v_0(p) = u_0(p) = 0, \text{ for } p \in P_0, \\
P_0' \;=\;& \{S \to S_2\}, \; v_0'(S \to S_2) = u_0'(S \to S_2) = 0, \\
P_{j,1}' \;=\;& (P_{j,1} - \{A \to x \mid A \to x \in P_{j,1}, x \in V_{T,1}^*\}) \cup \\
& \cup \{A \to xS \mid A \to x \in P_{j,1}, x \in V_{T,1}^*\}, \\
& v_{j,1}'(p) = v_{j,1}(p), u_{j,1}'(p) = u_{j,1}(p), \text{ for } p \in P_{j,1} \cap P_{j,1}', \\
& v_{j,1}'(A \to xS) = v_{j,1}(A \to x), \\
& u_{j,1}'(A \to xS) = u_{j,1}(A \to x), \text{ for } A \to xS \in P_{j,1}',
\end{aligned}$$

$1 \le j \le r_1$.

Any derivation in Γ starts by applying only one rule of P_0 and both registers remain equal to zero. If we started by applying $S \to S_i, i = 1, 2$, we can continue only by using the components of Γ_i, because $V_{\Gamma_1} \cap V_{N,2} = \emptyset$ and $V_{N,1} \cap V_{\Gamma_2} = \emptyset$. It follows that $L(\Gamma) = L(\Gamma_1) \cup L(\Gamma_2)$.

For obtaining a derivation in Γ' we first apply components of the set $\{P_{1,1}', \ldots, P_{r_1,1}'\}$, then we apply the component P_0' and then components of $\{P_{1,1}, \ldots, P_{r_2,2}\}$ (because $V_{\Gamma_1} \cap V_{N,2} = \emptyset$ and $V_{N,1} \cap V_{\Gamma_2} = \emptyset$). Since the application of P_0' cannot change the registers, it follows that both registers must be empty before and after using P_0'. In conclusion, $L(\Gamma') = L(\Gamma_1)L(\Gamma_2)$.

For proving the closure under Kleene $+$, consider the CD grammar system with two registers and right-linear rules $\Gamma = (V_N, V_T, P_1, \ldots, P_r, v_1, \ldots, v_r, u_1, \ldots, u_r, S)$ and construct the system

$$\Gamma' = (V_N \cup \{T\}, V_T, P_0, P_1', \ldots, P_r', v_0, v_1', \ldots, v_r', u_0, u_1', \ldots, u_r', S),$$

with

$$\begin{aligned}
& P_0 = \{T \to S\}, \; v_0(T \to S) = u_0(T \to S) = 0, \\
& P_i' = P_i \cup \{A \to xT \mid A \to x \in P_i, x \in V_T^*\}, \\
& v_i'(p) = v_i(p), u_i'(p) = u_i(p), \text{ for } p \in P_i, \\
& v_i'(A \to xT) = v_i(A \to x), \\
& u_i'(A \to xT) = u_i(A \to x), \text{ for } A \to x \in P_i, \text{ for } 1 \le i \le r.
\end{aligned}$$

Note that before and after using the component P_0, both registers must be empty. It is easy to see that $L(\Gamma') = L(\Gamma)^+$.

For proving the closure under intersection with regular sets, consider a CD grammar system Γ as above and a right-regular grammar (that is with rules of the form $A \to aB$ or $A \to a$, A, B nonterminals, a terminal) $G = (V_N', V_T, S', P')$. Construct a CD grammar system with two registers and right-linear rules

$$\Gamma'' = (V_N'', V_T, P_1', \ldots, P_r', v_1', \ldots, v_r', u_1', \ldots, u_r', (S, S')),$$

where

$$V_N'' = V_N \times (V_N' \cup \{*\})$$

and for $1 \le i \le r$ the set P_i' contains the following rules:

1) $p = (A, B) \to x(C, D)$ if $A \to xC \in P_i, B \Longrightarrow^* xD$ is a
   derivation in $G, x \in V_T^*, A, C \in V_N, B, D \in V_N'$,
   $v_i'(p) = v_i(A \to xC), u_i'(p) = u_i(A \to xC)$,

2) $p = (A, B) \to x(C, *)$, if $A \to xC \in P_i, B \Longrightarrow^* x$ is a
   derivation in $G, A, C \in V_N, B \in V_N'$,
   $v_i'(p) = v_i(A \to xC), u_i'(p) = u_i(A \to xC)$,

3) $p = (A, B) \to x$ if $A \to x \in P_i, B \Longrightarrow^* x$ is a
   derivation in $G, x \in V_T^*, A \in V_N, B \in V_N'$,
   $v_i'(p) = v_i(A \to x), u_i'(p) = u_i(A \to x)$,

4) $p = (A, *) \to (C, *)$, if $A \to C \in P_i, A, C \in V_N$,
   $v_i'(p) = v_i(A \to C), u_i'(p) = u_i(A \to C)$,

5) $p = (A, *) \to \lambda$ if $A \to \lambda \in P_i, A \in V_N$,
   $v_i'(p) = v_i(A \to \lambda), u_i'(p) = u_i(A \to \lambda)$.

One can easily see that $L(\Gamma'') = L(\Gamma) \cap L(G)$.

For a CD grammar system Γ as above consider a substitution $s : V_T^* \longrightarrow 2^{V^*}$ such that $s(a) \in \mathcal{L}_3, a \in V_T$. For each component P_i of Γ, $1 \le i \le r$, and each rule $p = A \to xB$ or $p = A \to x$ in $P_i, x \in V_T^*, A, B \in V_N$, consider the regular grammar $G_{(p,i)} = (V_N^{(p,i)}, V_T^{(p,i)}, S^{(p,i)}, P^{(p,i)})$ such that $L(G_{(p,i)}) = s(x)$ ($s(x)$ is clearly a regular language). Suppose that $V_N \cap V_N^{(p,i)} = \emptyset$ and $V_N^{(p,i)} \cap V_N^{(p',j)} = \emptyset$ for every $i, j, 1 \le i, j \le r, i \ne j$, and $p \in P_i, p' \in P_j$. Construct the CD grammar system with two registers and right-linear rules

$$\Gamma' = (V_N', V, P_1', \ldots, P_r', v_1', \ldots, v_r', u_1', \ldots, u_r', S),$$

where

$$V_N' = V_N \cup \{A \in V_N^{(p,i)} \mid p \in P_i, 1 \le i \le r\},$$

and, for $1 \leq i \leq r$, the set P_i' contains the following rules:

1) $p' = A \to B$ if $A \to B \in P_i, A, B \in V_N$,

      $v_i'(p') = v_i(p'), u_i'(p') = u_i(p')$,

2) $p' = A \to S^{(p,i)}$ if p is a rule of $P_i, p = A \to xB$ or

      $p = A \to x, x \in V_T^+, A, B \in V_N$,

      $v_i'(p') = v_i(p), u_i'(p') = u_i(p)$,

3) $p' = A' \to yB'$ if $A' \to yB' \in P^{(p,i)}$,

      where $p \in P_i, A', B' \in V_N^{(p,i)}, y \in (V_T^{(p,i)})^*$,

      $v_i'(p') = u_i'(p') = 0$,

4) $p' = A' \to yB$ if $A' \to y \in P^{(p,i)}$, for $p \in P_i, p = A \to xB$,

      $A, B \in V_N, x \in V_T^+, A' \in V_N^{(p,i)}, y \in (V_T^{(p,i)})^*$,

      $v_i'(p') = u_i'(p') = 0$,

5) $p' = A' \to y$ if $A' \to y \in P^{(p,i)}$, for $p \in P_i, p = A \to x$,

      $A \in V_N, x \in V_T^+, A' \in V_N^{(p,i)}, y \in (V_T^{(p,i)})^*$,

      $v_i'(p') = u_i'(p') = 0$,

6) $p' = A \to \lambda$ if $A \to \lambda \in P_i, A \in V_N$,

      $v_i'(p') = v_i'(p'), u_i'(p') = u_i(p')$.

One can see that $L(\Gamma') = s(L(\Gamma))$ and we obtain in this way the closure under substitution by regular languages.

    (ii) Consider the languages

$$L_1 = \{b^n c^n \mid n \geq 1\},$$
$$L_2 = \{a^m f d^m \mid m \geq 1\},$$
$$L_3 = \{a\}^* L_1 \{d\}^*,$$
$$L_4 = \{a^m x d^m \mid m \geq 1, x \in \{b, c\}^*\}.$$

We have $L_1 \in \mathcal{V}_3^a$ [7] and $L_2 \in \mathcal{V}_3^a$ (this is easy to prove). As $\mathcal{V}_3^a \subset 1CD_3^a$, it follows that $L_1, L_2 \in 1CD_3^a$. Since $1CD_3^a$ is closed under concatenation and substitution by regular languages, L_3 and L_4 are in $1CD_3^a$, too. It is clear that $L_3 \cap L_4 = \{a^m b^n c^n d^m \mid n, m \geq 1\}$ and this language is not in $1CD_3^a$ [3].

    Consider the substitution $s : \{a, d, f\}^* \longrightarrow 2^{\{a,b,c,d\}^*}$ with $s(a) = \{a\}$, $s(d) = \{d\}, s(f) = L_1$. Obviously, $s(x) \in 1CD_3^a$, for $x \in \{a, d, f\}$. We obtain $s(L_2) = \{a^m b^n c^n d^m \mid n, m \geq 1\} \notin 1CD_3^a$.

    The nonclosure under complement follows from the closure under union and the nonclosure under intersection. $\square$

Theorem 3.6. *The families $xCD_3^\alpha, x \in \{1, 2\}, \alpha \in \{a, m\}$, are full AFL's.*

Proof. Using Lemma 3.5 and the same arguments as in the proof of Theorem 2.4 we obtain the assertion. $\square$

Lemma 3.7. *The families xCD_2^α, $x \in \{1, 2\}, \alpha \in \{a, m\}$, are closed under union, substitution by context-free languages and intersection with regular languages.*

Proof. It is enough to prove the assertion for the family $2CD_2^\alpha$ only (for the same reasons as in the proof of Lemma 3.5).

For proving the closure under union we can use the same construction as in the case of systems with right-linear rules.

For the closure under substitution with context-free languages, consider a CD grammar system with two registers and context-free rules $\Gamma = (V_N, V_T, P_1, \ldots, P_r, v_1, \ldots, v_r, u_1, \ldots, u_r, S)$, and the substitution $s : V_T^* \longrightarrow 2^{V^*}$ with $s(a) \in \mathcal{L}_2$ for each $a \in V_T$. Suppose that $V_T = \{a_1, \ldots, a_n\}$ and consider the context-free grammars $G_i = (V_{N,i}, V_{T,i}, S_i, R_i)$, $1 \le i \le n$, such that $L(G_i) = s(a_i)$, $1 \le i \le n$, and $V_N \cap V_{N,i} = \emptyset$, $V_{N,i} \cap V_{N,j} = \emptyset$ for all $i \ne j$, $1 \le i, j \le n$. We construct the CD grammar system

$$\Gamma' = (V_N', V, P_0, P_1', \ldots, P_r', v_0, v_1', \ldots, v_r', u_0, u_1', \ldots, u_r', S),$$

where

$$V_N' = V_N \cup \bigcup_{i=1}^n V_{N,i},$$

$$P_0 = \bigcup_{i=1}^n R_i, \quad v_0(p) = u_0(p) = 0, \text{ for } p \in P_0,$$

and, for $1 \le j \le r$,

$$P_j' = \{A \to h(x) \mid A \to x \in P_j, x \in (V_N \cup V_T)^*\},$$

where $h : (V_N \cup V_T)^* \to (V_N \cup \{S_i \mid 1 \le i \le n\})^*$ is the homomrphism defined by $h(X) = X, X \in V_N$, $h(a_i) = S_i, a_i \in V_T, 1 \le i \le n$, and

$$v_j'(a \to h(x)) = v_j(A \to x), u_j'(A \to h(x)) = u_j(A \to x), \ A \to x \in P_j.$$

Since the application of the component P_0 in a derivation of Γ' does not change the registers, from the definition of components of Γ' it follows that for any word z generated by Γ there is a derivation of the following form

$$(S, 0, 0) \Longrightarrow_{H_1}^* \cdots \Longrightarrow_{H_m}^* (z', 0, 0) \Longrightarrow_{P_0}^* (z, 0, 0),$$

where $H_1, \ldots, H_m \in \{P_1', \ldots, P_r'\}, z' \in \{S_i \mid 1 \le i \le n\}^*$. It follows that there is $z'' \in V_T^*$ such that $z' = h(z''), z'' \in L(\Gamma)$, and $z \in s(z'')$. For a fixed $z'' \in L(\Gamma)$, Γ' generates all strings z contained in $s(z'')$. It follows that $L(\Gamma') = s(L(\Gamma))$.

For proving the closure under intersection with regular languages the classical triple construction can be used. $\qquad\qquad\Box$

Theorem 3.8. *The families $xCD_2^\alpha, x \in \{1,2\}, \alpha \in \{a,m\}$, are full semi-AFL's.*

Proof. We use Lemma 3.7 and the same arguments as in the proof of Theorem 2.4. $\qquad\qquad\Box$

4. Valence gsm mappings

The aim of this section is to solve an open problem formulated in [6] (and then in [5]), namely we prove that for the families of languages generated by iterating n times additive valence gsm mappings on regular (context-free, respectively) languages, the parameter n induces an infinite hierarchy which lies in between $\mathcal{V}_3^a$ ($\mathcal{V}_2^a$, respectively) and $\mathcal{V}_3^m$ ($\mathcal{V}_2^m$). Moreover, this hierarchy and the hierarchy $\mathcal{V}_3^a(1) \subset \mathcal{V}_3^a(2) \subset \mathcal{V}_3^a(3) \subset \ldots \subset \mathcal{V}_3^m$ ($\mathcal{V}_2^a \subset \mathcal{V}_2^a(2) \subset \mathcal{V}_2^a(3) \subset \ldots \subset \mathcal{V}_2^m$) mentioned in Section 2 are identical.

Definition 4.1. A *valence gsm* is a system $g = (K, I, O, s_0, F, P, v)$, where $g' = (K, I, O, s_0, F, P)$ is a gsm whose moves are encoded by rewriting rules, as in [8], and with $v : P \longrightarrow T$, $(T, \circ, e)$ being a given group.

Only rewritings

$$D \ : \ s_0 a_1 a_2 \ldots a_n \Longrightarrow x_1 s_1 a_2 \ldots a_n \Longrightarrow \ldots$$
$$\Longrightarrow x_1 x_2 \ldots x_{n-1} s_{n-1} a_n \Longrightarrow x_1 x_2 \ldots x_n s_n,$$

$s_n \in F, a_i \in I, x_i \in O^*, s_i \in K, s_{i-1} a_i \to x_i s_i \in P, 1 \le i \le n$, with $v(D) = e$ are accepted as correct. ($v(D)$ is equal to $v(s_0 a_1 \to x_1 s_1) \circ v(s_1 a_2 \to x_2 s_2) \circ \ldots \circ v(s_{n-1} a_n \to x_n s_n)$.)

Denote by $\mathcal{G}_a, \mathcal{G}_m$ the class of the valence gsm mappings with $(T, \circ, e) = (\mathbf{Z}, +, 0)$, $(T, \circ, e) = (\mathbf{Q}_+, \cdot, 1)$, respectively (additive and multiplicative valence gsm, respectively). For a given family $\mathcal{L}$ of languages denote

$$\mathcal{G}_\alpha(\mathcal{L}) = \{g(L) \mid g \in \mathcal{G}_\alpha, L \in \mathcal{L}\}, \alpha \in \{a, m\}.$$

The following results are proved in [6]:

(1) $\mathcal{V}_i^\alpha = \mathcal{G}_\alpha(\mathcal{L}_i), i = 2, 3, \alpha \in \{a, m\}$.

(2) The class $\mathcal{G}_a$ is not closed under composition, but $\mathcal{G}_m$ is closed.

(3) $\mathcal{G}_a(\mathcal{L}) \subseteq \mathcal{G}_m(\mathcal{L})$, for $\mathcal{L}$ an arbitrary family of languages.

We denote $\mathcal{G}_a^0(\mathcal{L}) = \mathcal{L}$ and $\mathcal{G}_a^{n+1}(\mathcal{L}) = \mathcal{G}_a(\mathcal{G}_a^n(\mathcal{L}))$, for $n \geq 0$ and $\mathcal{L}$ an arbitrary family of languages. The inclusions $\mathcal{G}_a^n(\mathcal{L}) \subseteq \mathcal{G}_a^{n+1}(\mathcal{L}), n \geq 0$, follow immediately from the definition of additive valence gsm's.

Thus we obtain the hierarchies

$$\mathcal{G}_a(\mathcal{L}_i) \subseteq \mathcal{G}_a^2(\mathcal{L}_i) \subseteq \mathcal{G}_a^3(\mathcal{L}_i) \subseteq \ldots, \quad i = 2, 3,$$

which lie in between V_i^a and $V_i^m, i = 2, 3$, because $V_i^a = \mathcal{G}_a(\mathcal{L}_i)$ and $\mathcal{G}_a^n(\mathcal{L}_i) \subseteq \mathcal{G}_m^n(\mathcal{L}_i) = \mathcal{G}_m(\mathcal{L}_i) = V_i^m, i = 2, 3$.

In [5] it was conjectured that the inclusions $\mathcal{G}_a^n(\mathcal{L}_i) \subseteq \mathcal{G}_a^{n+1}(\mathcal{L}_i), i = 2, 3$, $n \geq 2$, are proper. (For $n = 1$ this assertion is proved in [6].) We confirm here this conjecture, proving that $V_i^a(n) = \mathcal{G}_a^n(\mathcal{L}_i)$ for $i = 2, 3, n \geq 1$ (the inclusions $V_i^a(n) \subset V_i^a(n+1), i = 2, 3, n \geq 1$, are known to be proper [9]).

Denote by $\mathcal{G}_{a,n}, n \geq 1$, the class of valence gsm's with valences in $\mathbf{Z}^n$ (i.e. $(T, \circ, e) = (\mathbf{Z}^n, +, (0, \ldots, 0)))$. For a given family of languages, $\mathcal{L}$, denote

$$\mathcal{G}_{a,n}(\mathcal{L}) = \{g(L) \mid g \in \mathcal{G}_{a,n}, L \in \mathcal{L}\}.$$

Lemma 4.2. $\mathcal{G}_{a,n}(\mathcal{L}) = \mathcal{G}_a^n(\mathcal{L})$, *for $n \geq 1$ and $\mathcal{L}$ an arbitrary family of languages.*

Proof. We shall prove the equality by induction on n.

For $n = 1$ the assertion is obvious.

Suppose that we have $\mathcal{G}_{a,n}(\mathcal{L}) = \mathcal{G}_a^n(\mathcal{L})$ for an arbitrary $n \geq 1$. We must show that $\mathcal{G}_{a,n+1}(\mathcal{L}) = \mathcal{G}_a^{n+1}(\mathcal{L})$.

Since $\mathcal{G}_a^{n+1}(\mathcal{L}) = \mathcal{G}_a(\mathcal{G}_a^n(\mathcal{L}))$ and $\mathcal{G}_a^n(\mathcal{L}) = \mathcal{G}_{a,n}(\mathcal{L})$, it is enough to prove that $\mathcal{G}_a(\mathcal{G}_{a,n}(\mathcal{L})) = \mathcal{G}_{a,n+1}(\mathcal{L})$.

($\subseteq$) Let L be a language in $\mathcal{G}_a(\mathcal{G}_{a,n}(\mathcal{L}))$. It follows that there are $L' \in \mathcal{L}, g_1 \in \mathcal{G}_{a,n}$, and $g_2 \in \mathcal{G}_a$, $g_i = (K_i, I_i, O_i, s_{0,i}, F_i, P_i, v_i), i = 1, 2$, with $v_1 : P_1 \longrightarrow \mathbf{Z}^n$, $v_2 : P_2 \longrightarrow \mathbf{Z}$, $I_2 = O_1$, such that $L = g_2(g_1(L'))$.

We shall construct a valence gsm $g, g \in \mathcal{G}_{a,n+1}$, such that $g(L') = g_2(g_1(L'))$. Consider $g = (K_1 \times K_2, I_1, O_2, (s_{0,1}, s_{0,2}), F_1 \times F_2, P, v)$ with $v : P \longrightarrow \mathbf{Z}^{n+1}$ and P containing the following rules:

1) $r = (s_1, s_2)a \to y(t_1, t_2)$, where $s_i, t_i \in K_i, i = 1, 2, a \in I_1, y \in O_2^*$, and $s_1 a \to x t_1 \in P_1, x \in O_1^+, s_2 x \Longrightarrow^* y t_2$ in g_2,

2) $r = (s_1, s_2)a \to (t_1, s_2), s_1, t_1 \in K_1, s_2 \in K_2, a \in I_1$, and $s_1 a \to t_1 \in P_1$.

For defining the mapping v we consider the group homomorphisms $h_1 : \mathbf{Z}^n \longrightarrow \mathbf{Z}^{n+1}, h_2 : \mathbf{Z} \longrightarrow \mathbf{Z}^{n+1}$, defined by $h_1(e_i) = f_i, 1 \leq i \leq n$, and $h_2(1) = f_{n+1}, e_1, \ldots, e_n$ being the generators of $\mathbf{Z}^n$ and $f_1, \ldots, f_{n+1}$ the generators of $\mathcal{Z}^{n+1}$ (1 is the generator of $\mathbf{Z}$). Then, for the rules r in the first group above we define $v(r) = h_1(v_1(s_1 a \to x t_1)) + h_2(v_2(s_2 x \Longrightarrow^* y t_2))$ and for rules r in the second group we put $v(r) = h_1(v_1(s_1 a \to t_1))$.

Clearly, $g(L') = g_2(g_1(L')) = L$, hence $\mathcal{G}_a(\mathcal{G}_{a,n}(\mathcal{L})) \subseteq \mathcal{G}_{a,n+1}(\mathcal{L})$.

($\supseteq$) Consider $L \in \mathcal{G}_{a,n+1}(\mathcal{L})$. It follows that there are $L' \in \mathcal{L}$ and $g \in \mathcal{G}_{a,n+1}$ such that $L = g(L')$. Let $g = (K, I, O, s_0, F, P, v)$ with $v : P \longrightarrow \mathbf{Z}^{n+1}$. Consider each rule $sa \to xt$ in P having a distinct label, $b = Lab(sa \to xt)$, and denote by $Lab(P)$ the set of all these labels. We construct the valence gsm $g_1 \in \mathcal{G}_{a,n}$ as follows. Let $g_1 = (K, I, O \cup Lab(P), s_0, F, P_1, v_1)$, with $v_1 : P_1 \longrightarrow \mathbf{Z}^n$,

$$P_1 = \{sa \to xbt \mid sa \to xt \in P, b = Lab(sa \to xt)\},$$

and $v_1(sa \to xbt) = h_1(v(sa \to xt))$, where $h_1 : \mathbf{Z}^{n+1} \longrightarrow \mathbf{Z}^n$ is a group homomorphism defined by $h_1(f_1) = (0, \ldots, 0)$, $h_1(f_2) = e_1, \ldots, h_1(f_{n+1}) = e_n$ (we have considered $f_1, \ldots, f_{n+1}$ the generators of $\mathbf{Z}^{n+1}$ and $e_1, \ldots, e_n$ the generators of $\mathbf{Z}^n$).

Consider also the additive valence gsm $g_2 \in \mathcal{G}_a$, $g_2 = (\{s\}, O \cup Lab(P), O, s, \{s\}, P_2, v_2)$ with $v_2 : P_2 \longrightarrow \mathbf{Z}$,

$$P_2 = \{sa \to as \mid a \in O\} \cup \{sb \to s \mid b \in Lab(P)\},$$

and $v(sa \to as) = 0$, for $a \in O$, $v_2(sb \to s) = h_2(v(s'a \to xt'))$, if $b = Lab(s'a \to xt')$, where $h_2 : \mathbf{Z}^{n+1} \longrightarrow \mathbf{Z}$ is a group homomorphism defined by $h_2(f_1) = 1, h_2(f_i) = 0$, for $2 \leq i \leq n+1$.

Clearly, $g_2(g_1(L')) = g(L') = L$, hence $\mathcal{G}_{a,n+1}(\mathcal{L}) \subseteq \mathcal{G}_a(\mathcal{G}_{a,n}(\mathcal{L}))$. $\qquad\square$

Remark 4.3. Any $g \in \mathcal{G}_{a,n}, n \geq 1$, can be simulated by a multiplicative valence gsm mapping (from the previous proof it follows that there are $g_1, g_2, \ldots, g_n \in \mathcal{G}_a$ such that $g(L) = g_1(g_2(\ldots(g_n(L))\ldots))$ for any language L; from [6] it follows that there is $g' \in \mathcal{G}_m$ such that $g'(L) = g_1(g_2(\ldots(g_n(L))\ldots))$.

Theorem 4.4. $V_i^a(n) = \mathcal{G}_a^n(\mathcal{L}_i), n \geq 1, i = 2, 3$.

Proof. According to Lemma 4.2, it is enough to prove that $V_i^a(n) = \mathcal{G}_{a,n}(\mathcal{L}_i), i = 2, 3, n \geq 1$. For $n = 1$ the equality is proved in [6]. For $n \geq 2$ we can use the same proof, replacing everywhere the valences in $\mathbf{Z}$ with valences in $\mathbf{Z}^n$. $\qquad\square$

5. Synchronized multihead valence gsm's

We continue the study of the synchronized multihead valence gsm's defined in [6]. The results established concern especially their power, the comparison between the power of these gsm mappings and the power of the valence gsm's and the composition of synchronized multihead valence gsm's.

Definition 5.1. A *synchronized valence gsm* is a sequence $g = (g_1, g_2, \ldots, g_n)$, $n \geq 1$, of additive valence gsm's $g_i = (K_i, I_i, O_i, s_{0,i}, F_i, P_i, v_i)$, with

$v_i : P_i \longrightarrow \mathbf{N}$ ($\mathbf{N}$ is the set of positive integers), $1 \le i \le n$. For $x_i \in I_i^+$, $y_i \in O_i^*, 1 \le i \le n$, we write

$$s_{0,1}x_1 s_{0,2}x_2 \ldots s_{0,n}x_n \Longrightarrow^* y_1 s_{f,1} y_2 s_{f,2} \ldots y_n s_{f,n}$$

if and only if $s_{0,i}x_i \Longrightarrow^* y_i s_{f,i}$ in g_i, $s_{f,i} \in F_i$, for all $i, 1 \le i \le n$, and, moreover,

$$v_i(s_{0,i}x_i \Longrightarrow^* y_i s_{f,i}) = v_j(s_{0,j}x_j \Longrightarrow^* y_j s_{f,j}),$$

for all $i, j, 1 \le i, j \le n$.

For a language $L \subseteq I_1^+ I_2^+ \ldots I_n^+$ we define

$$
\begin{aligned}
g(L) \;=\; & \{y \in O_1^* O_2^* \ldots O_n^* \mid \text{there are } y_i \in O_i^*, x_i \in I_i^+, s_{f,i} \in F_i, \\
& 1 \le i \le n, \text{ such that } y_1 y_2 \ldots y_n = y, x_1 x_2 \ldots x_n \in L \text{ and} \\
& s_{0,1}x_1 s_{0,2}x_2 \ldots s_{0,n}x_n \Longrightarrow^* y_1 s_{f,1} y_2 s_{f,2} \ldots y_n s_{f,n}\}.
\end{aligned}
$$

Remark 5.2. For $n = 1$ a synchronized multihead valence gsm is, in fact, a usual gsm.

Denote by $\mathcal{G}_s$ the class of arbitrary synchronized multihead valence gsm's and consider the families $\mathcal{G}_s(\mathcal{L})$, for given $\mathcal{L}$, of images of languages in $\mathcal{L}$ by gsm's in $\mathcal{G}_s$.

In [6] it is proved that $\mathcal{G}_s(\mathcal{L}_i) - \mathcal{L}_2 \ne \emptyset, i = 2, 3$, and that $\mathcal{G}_s(\mathcal{L}_2) \subseteq \mathcal{M}$. We shall prove here that $\mathcal{G}_s(\mathcal{L}_i) \subseteq \mathcal{V}_i^m, i = 2, 3$.

Lemma 5.3. $\mathcal{G}_s(\mathcal{L}) \subseteq \bigcup_{n \ge 1} \mathcal{G}_{a,n}(\mathcal{L}) = \bigcup_{n \ge 1} \mathcal{G}_a^n(\mathcal{L})$, for arbitrary $\mathcal{L}$.

Proof. Let L be a language in $\mathcal{L}$ and $g = (g_1, \ldots g_n), n \ge 2$ (the case $n = 1$ is trivial) a synchronized multihead valence gsm with $g_i = (K_i, I_i, O_i, s_{0,i}, F_i, P_i, v_i), 1 \le i \le n$. We may consider that $K_i \cap K_j = \emptyset, 1 \le i, j \le n, i \ne j$.

Case 1. For each $i, 1 \le i \le n, F_i$ consists of only one element.

Denote the unique element of F_i by $s_{f,i}$. We shall construct an additive valence gsm g' with valences in $\mathbf{Z}^n$ such that $g'(L) = g(L)$. Let

$$g' = \left(\bigcup_{i=1}^{n} K_i, \bigcup_{i=1}^{n} I_i, \bigcup_{i=1}^{n} O_i, s_{0,1}, \{s_{f,n}\}, P, v\right),$$

with $v : P \longrightarrow \mathbf{Z}^n$ with

$$P = \bigcup_{i=1}^{n} P_i \cup \{sa \to ys_{0,i+1} \mid sa \to ys_{f,i} \in P_i, 1 \le i \le n-1\},$$

$$v(sa \to ys') = (e_1 + \ldots + e_n - n \cdot e_i) \cdot v_i(sa \to ys'),$$
$$\text{for } sa \to ys' \in P_i,$$

$$v(sa \to ys_{0,i+1}) = (e_1 + \ldots + e_n - n \cdot e_i) \cdot v_i(sa \to ys_{f,i}),$$
$$\text{for } sa \to ys_{f,i} \in P_i.$$

We have considered $e_1, \ldots, e_n$ the generators of $\mathbf{Z}^n$.

A derivation $s_{0,1}x \Longrightarrow^* y s_{f,n}$ is correct in g' if and only if there are $x_i \in I_i^+, y_i \in O_i^*, 1 \leq i \leq n$, such that $x = x_1 x_2 \ldots x_n$, $y = y_1 y_2 \ldots y_n$, and $s_{0,i} \Longrightarrow^* y_i s_{f,i}$ in $g_i, 1 \leq i \leq n$, and

$$\sum_{i=1}^{n}(e_1 + \ldots + e_n - n \cdot e_i) \cdot v_i(s_{0,i}x_i \Longrightarrow^* y_i s_{f,i}) = (0, \ldots, 0). \qquad (1)$$

Denote $\alpha_i = v_i(s_{0,i}x_i \Longrightarrow^* y_i s_{f,i})$, for $1 \leq i \leq n$. Then (1) is equivalent to

$$\sum_{j=1}^{n}(\sum_{i=1}^{n} \alpha_i - n \cdot \alpha_j) \cdot e_j = (0, \ldots, 0),$$

which is equivalent to

$$\sum_{i=1}^{n} \alpha_i = n \cdot \alpha_j, \quad \text{for each } j, 1 \leq j \leq n. \qquad (2)$$

It is obvious that (2) is true if and only if $\alpha_1 = \alpha_2 = \ldots = \alpha_n$. Consequently, (1) is true if and only if $y \in g(x)$. It follows that $g(L) = g'(L)$.

Case 2. There are sets $F_i, 1 \leq i \leq n$, containing more than one element.

For $(s_1, \ldots, s_n) \in F_1 \times \ldots \times F_n$ consider the synchronized multihead valence gsm $g(s_1, \ldots, s_n) = (g_1(s_1), \ldots, g_n(s_n))$, where $g_i(s_i) = (K_i, I_i, O_i, s_{0,1}, \{s_i\}, \Gamma_i, v_i), 1 \leq i \leq n$. It is clear that

$$g(L) = \bigcup_{(s_1, \ldots, s_n) \in F_1 \times \ldots \times F_n} g(s_1, \ldots, s_n)(L).$$

It follows that we have to prove only that for $g_1', g_2' \in \mathcal{G}_{a,n}$, there is $g' \in \mathcal{G}_{a,n}$ such that $g'(L) = g_1'(L) \cup g_2'(L)$.

Consider $g_i' = (K_i', I_i', O_i', s_{0,i}', F_i', P_i', v_i'), i = 1, 2$, where $K_1' \cap K_2' = \emptyset$, and construct $g' \in \mathcal{G}_{a,n}$,

$$g' = (K', I_1' \cup I_2', O_1' \cup O_2', s_0', F', P', v'),$$

where

$$
\begin{aligned}
K' &= K_1' \cup K_2' \cup \{s_0'\}, \\
P' &= P_1 \cup P_2 \cup \{s_0'a \rightarrow xs \mid \text{ there is } i, \in \{1, 2\} \\
&\quad \text{such that } s_{0,i}'a \rightarrow xs \in P_i\}, \\
&\quad v'(p) = v_1(p), \text{ for } p \in P_1, v'(p) = v_2(p) \text{ for } p \in P_2, \\
&\quad v'(s_0'a \rightarrow xs) = v_1(s_{0,i}'a \rightarrow xs) \text{ if } s_{0,i}'a \rightarrow xs \in P_i.
\end{aligned}
$$

Obviously, we have $g'(L) = g'_1(L) \cup g'_2(L)$.

Finally, using Lemma 4.2, we obtain the desired relations.   □

Theorem 5.4. $\mathcal{G}_s(\mathcal{L}_i) \subseteq \mathcal{G}_s(\mathcal{V}_i^a(1)) \subseteq \mathcal{G}_s(\mathcal{V}_i^a(2)) \subseteq \ldots \subseteq \mathcal{G}_s(\mathcal{V}_i^m) = \mathcal{V}_i^m, i = 2, 3$.

Proof. We know that $\mathcal{L}_i \subseteq \mathcal{V}_i^a(1) \subseteq \mathcal{V}_i^a(2) \subseteq \ldots \subseteq \mathcal{V}_i^m, i = 2, 3$. It follows that $\mathcal{G}_s(\mathcal{L}_i) \subseteq \mathcal{G}_s(\mathcal{V}_i^a(1)) \subseteq \mathcal{G}_s(\mathcal{V}_i^a(2)) \subseteq \ldots \subseteq \mathcal{G}_s(\mathcal{V}_i^m), i = 2, 3$. We shall prove the equality $\mathcal{G}_s(\mathcal{V}_i^m) = \mathcal{V}_i^m, i = 2, 3$.

($\subseteq$) From the proof of Lemma 5.3 and from Remark 4.3 we conclude that any synchronized multihead valence gsm can be simulated by a multiplicative valence gsm. Since the families $\mathcal{V}_i^m, i = 2, 3$, are closed under multiplicative valence gsm mappings, it follows that $\mathcal{G}_s(\mathcal{V}_i^m) \subseteq \mathcal{V}_i^m, i = 2, 3$.

($\supseteq$) The following inclusions are obvious: $\mathcal{V}_i^m \subseteq \mathcal{G}(\mathcal{V}_i^m) \subseteq \mathcal{G}_s(\mathcal{V}_i^m)$, where $\mathcal{G}$ is the class of the usual gsm's (see Remark 5.2).   □

Definition 5.5. Let $\Gamma = (V_N, V_T, P_1, \ldots, P_r, v_1, \ldots, v_r, S)$ be a CD grammar system with an additive register and right-linear rules (see Section 3), such that $v_i(P_i) \subseteq \mathbf{N}, 1 \leq i \leq r$. We define

$$
\begin{aligned}
L_{(=)}(\Gamma) \quad = \quad &\{x \in V_T^* \mid \text{there are } x_1, \ldots, x_r \in V_T^*, A_1, \ldots, A_{r-1} \in V_N, \\
&\text{with } x_1 x_2 \ldots x_r = z, S \Longrightarrow_{P_1}^* x_1 A_1 \Longrightarrow_{P_2}^* x_1 x_2 A_2 \Longrightarrow_{P_3}^* \ldots \\
&\ldots \Longrightarrow_{P_{r-1}}^* x_1 \ldots x_{r-1} A_{r-1} \Longrightarrow_{P_r}^* x_1 \ldots x_r, \text{ and} \\
&v_1(S \Longrightarrow_{P_1}^* x_1 A_1) = v_2(A_1 \Longrightarrow_{P_2}^* x_2 A_2) = \ldots \\
&= v_r(A_{r-1} \Longrightarrow_{P_r}^* x_r)\}.
\end{aligned}
$$

Lemma 5.6. *For any $g \in \mathcal{G}_s$ and $L \in \mathcal{L}_3$, there is a CD grammar system Γ as in the previous definition such that $g(L) = L_{(=)}(\Gamma)$.*

Proof. Let $g = (g_1, \ldots, g_n)$ with $g_i = (K_i, I_i, O_i, s_{0,i}, F_i, P_i, v_i), 1 \leq i \leq n$, and let $G' = (V_N', \bigcup_{i=1}^n I_i, P', S')$ be a right-regular grammar such that $L(G') = L$. We may consider that $K_i \cap K_j = \emptyset$ for $i \neq j, 1 \leq i, j \leq n$. Construct the CD grammar system Γ

$$
\Gamma = (V_N, \bigcup_{i=1}^n O_i, P_1', \ldots, P_n', v_1', \ldots, v_n', (S', s_{0,1})),
$$

with

$$
V_N = \bigcup_{i=1}^n (V_N' \times K_i)
$$

and, for $1 \leq i \leq n, P_i'$ contains the following rules:

1) $p = (A, s) \rightarrow x(B, s')$ if $A \rightarrow aB \in P', A, B \in V_N', a \in I_i$,

$$sa \rightarrow xs' \in P_i, s, s' \in K_i, x \in O_i^*,$$
$$v_i'(p) = v_i(sa \rightarrow xs'),$$

2) $p = (A, s) \rightarrow x$ if $i = n$ and $A \rightarrow a \in P', A \in V_N', a \in I_n,$
$$sa \rightarrow xs' \in P_n, s \in K_n, s' \in F_n, x \in O_n^*,$$
$$v_n'(p) = v_n(sa \rightarrow xs'),$$

3) $p = (A, s_{f,i-1}) \rightarrow (A, s_{0,i})$, if $i \neq 1, s_{f,i-1} \in F_{i-1},$
$$v_i'(p) = 0.$$

The equality $L_{(=)}(\Gamma) = g(L)$ is easy to be proved. $\qquad\qquad\square$

Lemma 5.7. *Let $L = \{a^n b^m c^m d^n \mid n, m \geq 1\}$. Then $L \notin \mathcal{G}_s(\mathcal{L}_3)$.*

Proof. Assume the contrary. According to Lemma 5.6 there is a CD grammar system with an additive register and right-linear rules, $\Gamma = (V_N, V_T, P_1, \ldots, P_r, v_1, \ldots, v_r, S)$, $V_T = \{a, b, c, d\}$, $v_i : P_i \longrightarrow \mathbf{N}, 1 \leq i \leq n$, such that $L = L_{(=)}(\Gamma)$. Then $x \in L$ if and only if there is a derivation

$$D : S \Longrightarrow_{P_1}^* z_1 A_1 \Longrightarrow_{P_2}^* z_1 z_2 A_2 \Longrightarrow_{P_3}^* \cdots$$
$$\Longrightarrow_{P_{r-1}}^* z_1 \ldots z_{r-1} A_{r-1} \Longrightarrow_{P_r}^* z_1 \ldots z_r = z,$$

with $z_1, \ldots, z_r \in V_T^*, A_1, \ldots, A_{r-1} \in V_N$ and $v_1(D_1) = v_2(D_2) = \ldots = v_r(D_r)$. We denoted by $D_1, D_2, \ldots, D_n$, respectively, the following subderivations of D

$$S \Longrightarrow_{P_1}^* z_1 A_1, \ A_1 \Longrightarrow_{P_2}^* z_2 A_2, \ldots, A_{r-1} \Longrightarrow_{P_r}^* z_r.$$

Denote $v(D) = v_1(D_1)$. Since the components $P_1, \ldots, P_r$ may be used only in this order, for $z = a^n b^m c^m d^m$ with n or m large enough, D must have a subderivation $A \Longrightarrow_{P_{i_0}}^* wA$ with $w \in V_T^+, A \in V_N, 1 \leq i_0 \leq r$. It follows that $v_{i_0}(A \Longrightarrow_{P_{i_0}}^* wA) \neq 0$ (assuming the contrary, the iteration of the subderivation $A \Longrightarrow_{P_{i_0}}^* wA$ leads to a pumping of the word w, i.e. there are $w_1, w_2 \in V_T^*$ such that $y_k = w_1 w^k w_2$ is contained in L for all $k \geq 1$; this is a contradiction since y_k contains the letters x and y in the wrong order if x and y occur in w and since y_k has not the same number of occurrences of a and d, or b and c if only one letter occurs in w). Hence we obtain that, for m or n large enough $v(D)$ is large enough, too. Then each $D_i, 1 \leq i \leq n$, must have a subderivation $D_i' : B_i \Longrightarrow_{P_i}^* w_i B_i, w_i \in V_T^*, B_i \in V_N$, with $v_i(D_i') \neq 0$ for increasing $v_i(D_i)$ (since $v(D) = v_i(D_i), 1 \leq i \leq n$). If we suppose that m and n are large enough and, moreover, $m > n, m - n$ large enough, too, then it follows that each D_i must have a subderivation $D_i'' : C_i \Longrightarrow_{P_i}^* y_i C_i$ with $v_i(D_i'') \neq 0$ which contributes to the increasing of $v_i(D_i)$, but without contributing to the increasing of the number of occurrences of a or d in z, i.e. $y_i \in \{b, c\}^*$. Also, since n is large enough and the components $P_1, \ldots, P_r$ can be used only in this order, there is an $i_0, 1 \leq i_0 \leq r$, such that D_{i_0} has a subderivation $D_{i_0}''' : C \Longrightarrow^*_{P_{i_0}} d^k C$, $k > 0$ (then $v_{i_0}(D_{i_0}''') \neq 0$).

Denote $\alpha = v_{i_0}(D_{i_0}''') \cdot \Pi_{i \neq i_0} v_i(D_i'')$. We can obtain a new terminal derivation D' starting from D as follows: for each $i \neq i_0, 1 \leq i \leq r$, we apply D_i'' for $\dfrac{\alpha}{v_i(D_i'')}$ more times in D and we apply D_{i_0}''' for $\dfrac{\alpha}{v_{i_0}(D_{i_0}''')}$ more times in D (then $v(D') = v(D) + \alpha$). Thus we obtain a string z' contained in L, with $|z'|_a < |z'|_d$ (the application of D_i'' for $i \neq i_0$ does not change the number of the occurrences of a, whereas the application of D_{i_0}''' increases only the number of occurrences of d). This is a contradiction. Consequently, $L \notin \mathcal{G}_s(\mathcal{L}_3)$.   □

Theorem 5.8. (i) *The following inclusions are proper:* $\mathcal{G}_s(\mathcal{L}_3) \subset \mathcal{G}_s(\mathcal{V}_3^a(n))$, $n \geq 1$, $\mathcal{G}_s(\mathcal{L}_3) \subset \mathcal{V}_3^m$.

(ii) *The class $\mathcal{G}_s$ is not closed under composition.*

Proof. (i) The inclusions are known (Theorem 5.4). For proving their properness it is enough to show that $\mathcal{G}_s(\mathcal{V}_3^a(1)) - \mathcal{G}_s(\mathcal{L}_3) \neq \emptyset$. Consider $L = \{a^n b^m c^m d^n \mid n, m \geq 1\}$; then L is not in $\mathcal{G}_s(\mathcal{L}_3)$ (Lemma 5.7), but it is in $\mathcal{G}_s(\mathcal{V}_3^a)$. Indeed, let $g = (g_1, g_2)$ with

$$g_1 = (\{s_{0,1}, s_1, t_1\}, \{a\}, \{a, b\}, s_{0,1}, \{s_1\}, P_1, v_1),$$
$$g_2 = (\{s_{0,2}, s_2, t_2\}, \{d\}, \{c, d\}, s_{0,2}, \{s_2\}, P_2, v_2),$$

where

$$P_1 = \{r_1 : s_{0,1}a \to as_{0,1}, \; r_2 : s_{0,1}a \to at_1, \; r_3 : t_1 a \to bs_1, \; r_4 : s_1 a \to bs_1\},$$
$$v_1(r_1) = v_1(r_2) = 0, \; v_1(r_3) = v_1(r_4) = 1,$$
$$P_2 = \{r_5 : s_{0,2}d \to cs_{0,2}, \; r_6 : s_{0,2}d \to ct_2, \; r_7 : t_2 d \to ds_2, \; r_8 : s_2 d \to ds_2\},$$
$$v_2(r_5) = v_2(r_6) = 1, \; v_2(r_7) = v_2(r_8) = 0.$$

It is obvious that $L = g(\{a^n d^n \mid n \geq 1\})$. As $\{a^n d^n \mid n \geq 1\}$ is in $\mathcal{V}_3^a$, the proof of point (i) is complete.

(ii) Take the same L as above and the same $g \in \mathcal{G}_s$. Consider also $g' = (g_1', g_2')$ with

$$g_1' = (\{s_1\}, \{a\}, \{a\}, s_1, \{s_1\}, P_1', v_1'),$$
$$g_2' = (\{s_2\}, \{a\}, \{d\}, s_2, \{s_2\}, P_2', v_2'),$$
$$P_1' = \{r_1 : s_1 a \to as_1\}, \; v_1'(r_1) = 1,$$
$$P_2' = \{r_2 : s_2 a \to ds_2\}, \; v_2'(r_2) = 1.$$

Then we have $g'(\{a\}^*) = \{a^n d^n \mid n \geq 1\}$ and $L = g(\{a^n d^n \mid n \geq 1\})$. Hence $L \in \mathcal{G}_s(\mathcal{G}_s(\mathcal{L}_3))$, but $L \notin \mathcal{G}_s(\mathcal{L}_3)$ (Lemma 5.7). It follows that $\mathcal{G}_s$ is not closed under composition.   □

References

1. E. Csuhaj-Varju, J. Dassow, On cooperating distributed grammar systems, *J. Inform. Processing, EIK*, 26 (1990), 49 – 63.

2. E. Csuhaj-Varju, J. Dassow, J. Kelemen, Gh. Păun, *Grammar Systems*, Gordon and Breach, London, 1994.

3. J. Dassow, Gh. Păun, *Regulated Rewriting in Formal Language Theory*, Springer-Verlag, Berlin, Heidelberg, 1989.

4. J. Dassow, Gh. Păun, Cooperating distributed grammar systems with registers, *Found. Control Engineering*, 15 (1990), 19 – 38.

5. M. Gheorghe, Gh. Păun, Two (infinite ?) hierarchies of vector languages, *Bulletin EATCS*, 29 (1986), 27 – 31.

6. M. Marcus, Gh. Păun, Valence gsm-mappings, *Bull. Math. Soc. Sci. Math. Roumanie*, 31(79), 3 (1987), 219 – 229.

7. Gh. Păun, A new generative device: valence grammars, *Rev. Roum. Math. Pures Appl.*, 25 (1980), 911 – 924.

8. A. Salomaa, *Formal Languages*, Academic Press, New York, London, 1973.

9. S. Vicolov, Infinite hierarchies of valence languages, *Bulletin EATCS*, 49 (1993), 192 – 194.